The Cambridge Introduction to Biblical Hebrew

The Cambridge Introduction to Biblical Hebrew is designed for anyone studying Biblical Hebrew for the first time. It is well suited for students enrolled in introductory-level courses as well as clergy and laity engaged in self-study. The accompanying CD (suitable for Mac and PC) includes the workbook, answers, paradigms, and the interactive program TekScroll.

TekScroll greatly facilitates learning through grammar illustrations with moving graphics, interactive parsing programs, translation practice items, and a vocabulary program. The grammar illustrations demonstrate key grammatical points. The parsing programs provide feedback, hints, and corrections. Translation practice comes primarily from biblical verses. The vocabulary quizzing program includes audio of the vocabulary words.

The textbook is designed for a two-semester course covering one chapter of grammar per week (22 chapters) and then turning to select syntactical items. Each chapter begins with a Focus section, identifying key elements, and is followed by a summary, vocabulary list, and description of the learning activities on the CD. The practice translation items and workbook exercises only use vocabulary from previous chapters (with few exceptions), so that they can be used immediately in classroom instruction.

Brian L. Webster received his Ph.D. from Hebrew Union College – Jewish Institute of Religion and is currently Associate Professor of Old Testament Studies at Dallas Theological Seminary. He is the author of *The Essential Psalms Companion* (2009). Professor Webster has been published in *Bibliotheca Sacra* as well as the Discoveries in the Judaean Desert series.

The Cambridge Introduction to Biblical Hebrew

Brian L. Webster

Dallas Theological Seminary

CAMBRIDGE
UNIVERSITY PRESS

CAMBRIDGE
UNIVERSITY PRESS

University Printing House, Cambridge CB2 8BS, United Kingdom

One Liberty Plaza, 20th Floor, New York, NY 10006, USA

477 Williamstown Road, Port Melbourne, vic 3207, Australia

4843/24, 2nd Floor, Ansari Road, Daryaganj, Delhi – 110002, India

79 Anson Road, #06–04/06, Singapore 079906

Cambridge University Press is part of the University of Cambridge.

It furthers the University's mission by disseminating knowledge in the pursuit of education, learning and research at the highest international levels of excellence.

www.cambridge.org
Information on this title: www.cambridge.org/9780521712842

First published 2009
Reprinted 2016

Printed in the United States of America

A catalog record for this publication is available from the British Library.

Library of Congress Cataloging in Publication data

Webster, Brian L., 1965–
The Cambridge introduction to biblical Hebrew : with CD-ROM / Brian L. Webster.
p.   cm.
ISBN 978-0-521-88542-3 (hardback) – ISBN 978-0-521-71284-2 (paperback)
1. Hebrew language – Grammar – Textbooks.   2. Hebrew language – Grammar – Problems, exercises, etc.   3. Bible O.T. – Language, style.   I. Title.
PJ4567.3.W357   2009
492.4′82421–dc22   2008062326

ISBN 978-0-521-88542-3 hardback
ISBN 978-0-521-71284-2 paperback

Contents

Acknowledgments

I would like to thank the Hebrew Union College – Jewish Institute of Religion and their faculty for their training in Hebrew and in the languages and history of the Ancient Near East. I am grateful for the opportunity to have studied under such sensitive readers of ancient texts and models of methodology. I would like to specially thank the members of my examining committee, Drs. Alan Cooper, Samuel Greengus, and David Weisberg, for their encouragement during my studies and after.

I am particularly thankful to Isaac Jerusalmi for his influence in approaching morphology. Dr. Jerusalmi teaches the structure of Hebrew morphology with great enthusiasm and I consider his teaching a key inspiration in the planning of this project.

I am also particularly thankful to Stephen Kaufman for his influence on my understanding of Hebrew syntax. His mastery of Semitic languages, not simply of grammars and theories but of the behaviors of real texts, has been a wellspring for teaching Hebrew.

Statistical information, such as word frequency counts, is generally taken from *Accordance 6.8*, OakTree Software, Inc., 2005.

The NewJerusalem, ScriptHebrewII, and TranslitLS fonts used in this work are available from Linguist's Software Inc., www.linguistsoftware.com. My thanks to Phil Payne and staff for customizing the NewJerusalem font with a few special characters. My compliments on the fonts' appearance and ability to work in the applications required to put these materials together.

The portable document files (PDFs) on the CD were made with Adobe Acrobat, and the interactive content was done in Flash; both are programs of Adobe (see www.adobe.com).

Thanks to my students who have offered suggestions and corrections.

Thanks to Robert B. Chisholm and Bill T. Arnold for their encouragement and support.

Thanks to John Dyer for timely advice on programming the CD.

My deepest thanks for their patience and encouragement go to my wife Hope and daughters Angela, Lily, Robyn, and Starla.

Introduction

The English alphabet can be traced to the Greek alphabet, which in turn can be traced through the Phoenicians to that also used by the Hebrews. One thing the Greeks did was to start writing backwards, reversing the direction of writing to go from left to right. Hebrew is written from right to left.

The Greeks also added vowels. The Jews and their neighbors wrote only consonants. Because of the nature of Hebrew, writing only the consonants is sufficient to read it – for people who already know the language. But, as vowels are indeed helpful, the scribes later added vowel signs and other marks, solidifying the reading tradition and the text. These vowel signs were added below and sometimes above or within the consonants.

After adjusting to the different looks of the writing, we will find things more familiar. It may initially feel odd to read Hebrew, but you can do it. Considering that you have been successfully reading backwards (left to right) for years, you will do fine reading Hebrew frontward (right to left).

Besides the writing system, Hebrew spellings primarily involve the following:

    10 noun endings,

    20 verb endings and/or prefixes,

    11 main verb stem and infinitive patterns (for 7 stems),

    3 participle indicators, and

    15 or so *basic* pronominal suffix forms (depending on how you count).

In addition to those 59 basic spelling items, there are

    7 syllable principles and

    5 special consonant principles.

There are still many vocabulary words to learn and matters of syntax to master. But these 71 basic forms and principles combine and recombine to form the vast majority of all Hebrew words. The trick is in recognizing the combinations. Your overall workload is reduced if you can see it as a small number of morphological pieces responding to a couple of handfuls of syllable principles and deviant consonants.

Knowing those pieces is your passageway to reading Hebrew. And reading Hebrew opens your access to the Bible.

A Book and CD Package.

The book and accompanying CD are closely integrated. You could think of them as a CD with an accompanying book just as well as a book with a CD. The CD has the Workbook, the Workbook Answers, and Paradigms in PDF documents. In addition, it contains the interactive program TekScroll to help you learn Hebrew.

TekScroll includes several Learning Activities, including Practice Readings, Parsing Programs, a Vocabulary Program, and Grammar Illustrations. The role these play is described in more detail later in the Introduction. But the basic elements and how to interact with them are described here.

After loading, an index appears on the left side of the "book" on the screen. Click on the chapter number or its abbreviated title to get the menu of Learning Activities for that chapter. You can also go right to the vocabulary program by clicking the arrow at the bottom left of the page. After you select a chapter from the index, its menu appears on the right. The Learning Activities (abbreviated LA) that are part of TekScroll have an arrow button; the others are in the Workbook. The list of Learning Activities is repeated from the end of the chapters in the grammar.

The Cambridge Introduction to Biblical Hebrew by Webster

Index

1 Alphabet	12 Qal impf.
2 Syllables	13 Qal impf. wk.
3 Noun Forms	14 Volitives
4 Noun Roots	15 Suff. on verbs
5 Preps., Art.	16 Der. Inf. & Ptc.
6 Pron., Suff.	17 I-class impf.
7 Adjectives	18 I-class impf. wk.
8 Ptc., Inf. cs.	19 I-class impf. wk.
9 Misc. words	20 A-class impf.
10 Qal pf.	21 Derived stem pf.
11 Qal pf. wk.	22 Der. Pf. wk.
⏵Vocabulary	⏵ Quit

Chapter 10

⏵ LA1 Grammar Illustration

LA2 Practice Parsing. Focus on:

⏵ Set A: Endings (12)

⏵ Set B: Root (12)

⏵ Set C: Stem (12)

⏵ Set D: Review (15)

LA3 Parsing Exercise

⏵ LA4 Practice Readings (57)

LA5 Translation Exercise

⏵ LA6 Learn Ch 10 Vocabulary

Practice Readings.

    The Practice Readings first present a Hebrew selection, usually a Bible verse, along with its number in the set, in this case reading number 1 of 75. After trying to read it, you can click to see the translation.

    Typically, the Practice Readings only use the vocabulary from previous chapters (not the current chapter) and use the last chapter's vocabulary a minimum of three times. The   button in the lower left returns you to the chapter index.

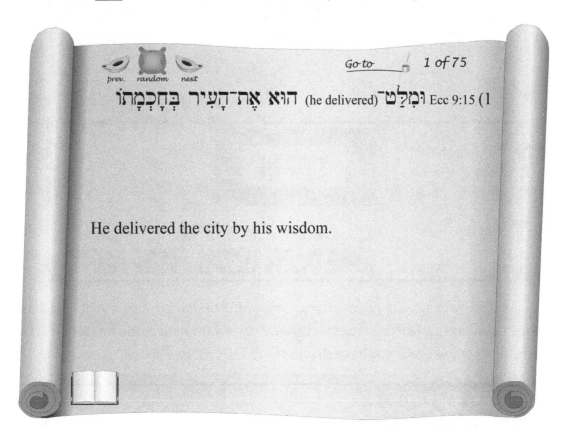

    Go to   1 of 75

וּמִלַּט־ (he delivered) הוּא אֶת־הָעִיר בְּחָכְמָתוֹ   Ecc 9:15 (1

He delivered the city by his wisdom.

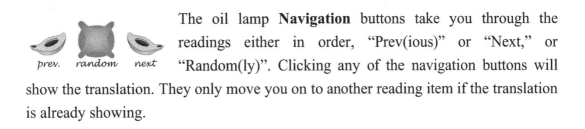

The oil lamp **Navigation** buttons take you through the readings either in order, "Prev(ious)" or "Next," or "Random(ly)". Clicking any of the navigation buttons will show the translation. They only move you on to another reading item if the translation is already showing.

Go to   To go to a particular practice reading, which is useful if you want to ask a question about one of them, type in the item number on the line after "*Go to*" and then click on the quill and inkwell to the right of the line.

Practice Reading variants.

In the later chapters, the Practice Readings are combined with the Parsing Program (see below) so that verbs are parsed from context.

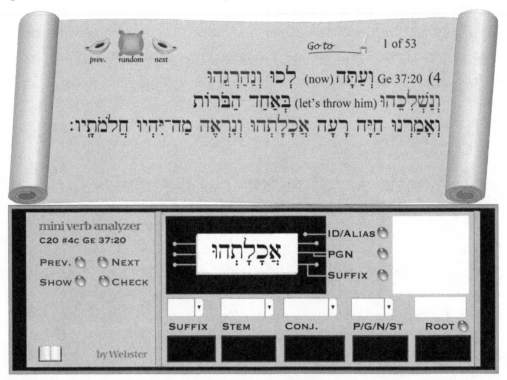

The first two chapters have readings on a different background due to different navigation concerns. Different reading lists are chosen from the menu on the left. The Navigation buttons move you through whichever list you have chosen.

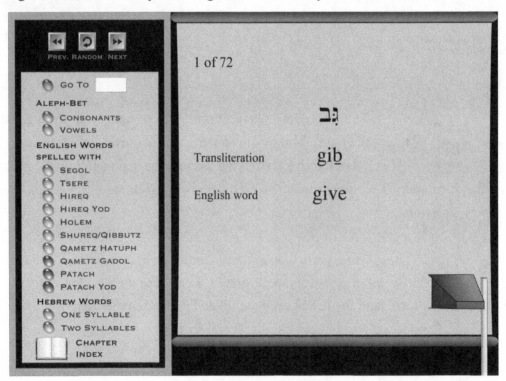

Parsing Programs.

The noun and verb parsing programs look very similar. The word to be parsed is the **Specimen** in the center. Enter your answers in the row of boxes directly below the specimen. The answer for **Root**, right center, must be typed in from the **Enter Root** keypad. (You must use appropriate final forms of the consonants. ו and ך are only used for verb roots with a ו for the second root letter.) The other answers can be chosen from the dropdown menus or they can be typed in, but must be typed exactly.

The **Show Answer** button reveals the answers in the row of black boxes directly below the answers that you entered. The **Check Answer** button will confirm the correct parts of your answer by revealing them in the bottom boxes. Incorrect answers are highlighted in red and the correct answers are kept hidden.

In the upper right are **Diagnostic Tests**, three buttons which reveal a clue (if there is one). In this example, the student has missed two items, the pronominal **suffix** and the **P/G/N/St** field. Clicking on the **suffix** button under Diagnostic Tests gave no hint because there is no suffix. Clicking on the PGN button under Diagnostic Tests did reveal a clue, comparing the pronoun נַחְנוּ to the verb ending on בָּכִינוּ.

On the left side are the Navigation buttons. The navigation buttons will first show the answer and only go to the next item if the answer is already showing. The book button ▭ in the lower left returns you to the chapter index.

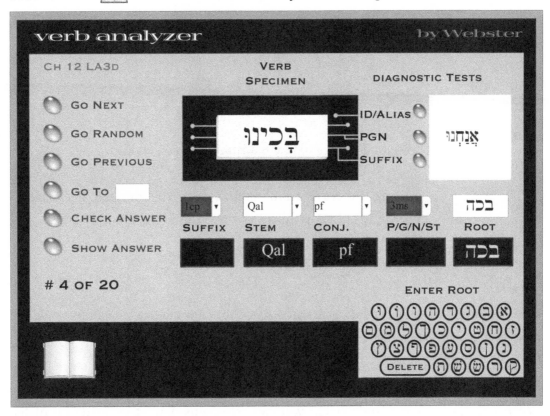

Vocabulary Program.

The vocabulary program is a great way to practice your vocabulary. First you select your desired options (see next page). Then a Hebrew word (e.g. גָּדוֹל) appears along with where it is in the "stack," in this case word 47 of 192. When you click for the answer, it displays the English glosses ("great, large"), where it is in the textbook ("Ch 1 #6"), its part of speech ("adj.") and the number of times it appears in the Bible ("527 times"). Press the 🔊 button to hear the word. (You can also select the option to play the audio when a navigation button is pressed.) The 📖 button in the lower left returns you to the chapter index.

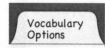

This button takes you to the **options** you can choose.

The circular **Navigation** buttons take you through the "stack," either in order, "Prev(ious)" or "Next," or "Random(ly)".

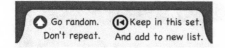

⬆ **Go random. Don't repeat.** You can also go through the stack randomly without repeating any of the words. The number of cards in the stack counts down as you go.

⏮ Pressing the **Keep in** button tells the program to keep the word in the stack (if you are using the Non-repeating random button). It also puts it in a new "stack" of cards. When you finish your current stack, you can select this new stack made up of the words you marked. A word will be in the new stack as many times as you mark it.

Setting the Vocabulary Options:

1. Select chapter lists and options. This can be done in any order.
   It is not necessary to select options, but you must select at least one chapter.
2. When finished with selections, click the arrow on the tab that says "Create list from selections."

Clicking the **Vocabulary Options** button will clear all your selections.

You can limit the list by selecting one or more **parts of speech**. "Substantives" has nouns, pronouns, and adjectives. "Other" includes prepositions, adverbs, and conjunctions.

Type in either or both **frequency** options.

The list can be **alphabetized**.

Audio of the Hebrew is always available, but click this box to automatically include audio whenever a navigation button (prev., random, next) is pressed.

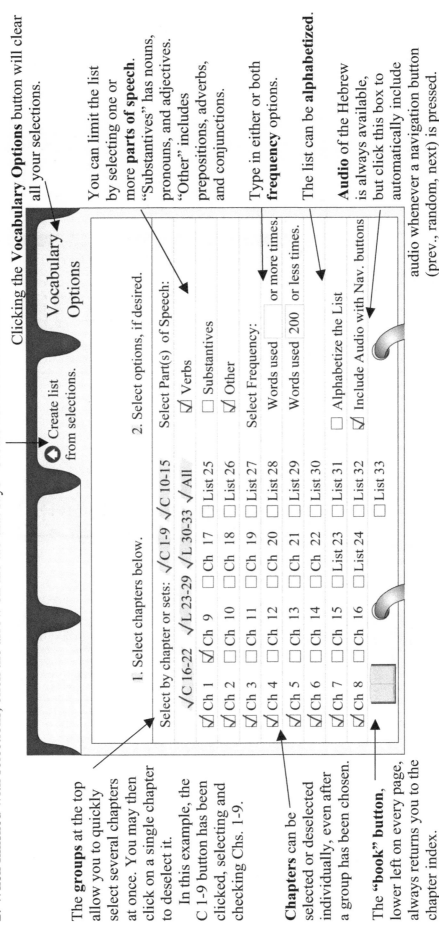

The **groups** at the top allow you to quickly select several chapters at once. You may then click on a single chapter to deselect it.
   In this example, the C 1-9 button has been clicked, selecting and checking Chs. 1-9.

Chapters can be selected or deselected individually, even after a group has been chosen.

The **"book" button**, lower left on every page, always returns you to the chapter index.

Grammar Illustrations usually appear on a whiteboard theme:

The buttons are adapted to fit the content, so they may vary. This example has forward and backward buttons in the upper left corner that take you through different segments of the illustration. As point 4 instructs, the stem names "Niphal," "Piel," "Hitpael," and "Hiphil" are also buttons. In this segment, the "Piel" button has been pressed. This causes the key part of the Piel stem from the infinitive on the right to move over and fill in the paradigm in the middle of the board. This illustration, from ch. 17:

1) starts with the paradigm on the left, the "Qal impf" (Qal imperfect *i*-class, learned in ch. 12),
2) duplicates it and changes the letters to those in the middle of the board (for the standard paradigm),
3) removes the key part that makes it Qal, then
4) takes the key part of the infinitives on the right (learned in ch. 16) and moves them to the middle to create the new paradigm.

Go buttons go through the segments of the grammar illustration. This illustration is at the end, so it only has a "back" button.

The **"book" button**, lower left, returns you to the chapter index.

As the *instructions* say, these stem names (Niphal, Piel, Hitpael, Pual) are **buttons**. And so are the arrows ● the next to them.

Here the Piel has been clicked, sending its characteristic vowel pattern from its infinitive over to complete its imperfect paradigm.

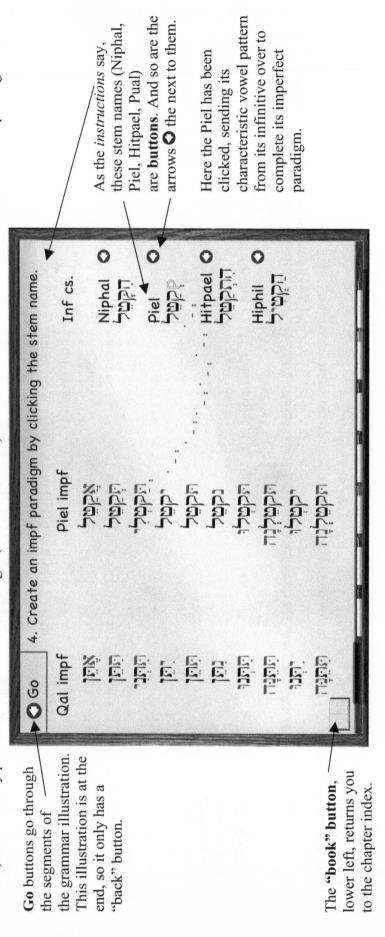

The Structure of this Grammar.

Chapters 1–22: The morphology section; Activities on the CD.

Each chapter begins with a *Focus* section, identifying the essential elements of the chapter. The main discussion explains these items. It is followed by a *Summary*, a *Vocabulary* list, and a description of the *Learning Activities* on the CD. The design is to do one chapter per week, or even two chapters every three weeks. This fits one-day-a-week classes well and allows for classes that meet more than one day per week to reserve entire class periods for practicing with the students, or for labs.

The CD contains the *Workbook, Workbook Answers*, and *Paradigms* in Adobe® PDF documents. Adobe Acrobat Reader is available as a free download from www.adobe.com. The interactive program TekScroll includes: *Grammar Illustrations* (for some chapters), *Practice* items (e.g. readings, parsings), and a *Vocabulary* program. TekScroll was made in Flash, also a product of Adobe® Macromedia®.

The *Grammar Illustrations* in TekScroll provide a visual aid for understanding select grammatical points in the main discussion of a chapter. It is useful to view them while reading through the chapters.

The *Practice* items, such as *Practice Parsing* and *Practice Readings*, provide practice before doing the exercises. They offer a low-stress environment for students to check their understanding and can be used for classroom instruction or for labs. The *Practice Readings* present Hebrew phrases or sentences with the English translation available at the click of a button. Students can read the Hebrew and then immediately verify their understanding. They provide review of previous material as well as integrating some grammar elements of the current chapter. In general, the *Practice Readings* only require knowing vocabulary from previous chapters (rather than the current chapter), so that the student who keeps up with the vocabulary requirements can go from the textbook right to the *Practice Readings*. They also provide multiple contexts for the vocabulary items (using the previous list's items a minimum of three times each). The *Practice Parsing* items allow the student to drill or practice forms. In the later chapters the *Practice Parsing* items are integrated with the *Practice Readings*.

The *Workbook Exercises* and *Workbook Answers* are available in separate PDF files. This structure asks the student to do the work based on having built up their skills while doing the *Practice Readings. Exercises* in the later chapters are not just randomly selected verses but also include progressing through passages of the Bible. Whole verses in the *Exercises* may include accent marks.

The *Vocabulary* program allows students to practice their vocabulary in a flash card style. The students can choose which chapters' vocabulary they want to review, as well as choose by part of speech (verbs, substantives, other) and by frequency. The flash cards can be played with or without audio of the Hebrew.

Chapters 23–32: The Syntax section.

Each chapter begins with a *Focus* section leading into the main discussion. Most end with a *Summary*. They do not include vocabulary lists.

This section samples items of syntax and discourse. It is too small a space to cover all of Hebrew syntax. Instead it selects some features as an introduction to syntactical issues and as a model of how to view the information in reference works on syntax. A repeating mantra is that "meaning arises from combinations" of several factors. To illustrate this, the chapters often comment on how various discourse features affect meaning. The focus is on how to think about syntax rather than trying to learn lots of lists of syntactical functions. The design is for two chapters per week, as a supplement to reading extended texts from the Hebrew Bible. Alternatively, several of these chapters may be integrated with the morphology chapters.

The students should be ready to read whatever texts a first-year Hebrew program may require (note that 2Chr 34 and Neh 8 are given with vocabulary aids in the workbook appendix). The syntax chapters can be read in any order and should provide fruitful modeling to supplement the varied goals of first-year programs and whatever passages a course requires. Consequently, the remaining vocabulary lists occur in a separate section rather than at the end of each chapter.

The Vocabulary.

The vocabulary lists include words used 50 or more times in the Hebrew Bible (approximately 650 words in 33 lists averaging 20 items each) but do not include proper nouns (cf. 328–329). During the syntax unit, professors can decide how many vocabulary lists to require of their students, but all the lists for 50+ are provided.

As much as possible, the lists consist of words from one or two semantic domains. But they may have cognates or similar-sounding terms from different domains. In the early chapters especially, the choice of vocabulary may be partly determined by the needs of the upcoming grammar topics. For example, ch. 1's vocabulary is chosen to reflect all consonant forms and vowels. Nonetheless, semantic domains are emphasized as much as possible. One opportunity afforded by this structure is to assign groups of students to present memory devices for a list to the rest of the class.

Vocabulary requirements are coordinated with both the grammar chapters and the Exercises. Many words used as examples in the grammar are introduced as vocabulary items in advance to provide a level of familiarity. Exercises primarily involve vocabulary from earlier chapters, and typically employ the words in the previous vocabulary list a minimum of three times each.

For the morphology unit, the exercises provide meanings in parentheses for words that have not yet appeared in the lists. After the morphology unit (chs. 1–22) the remaining 11 lists occur in a separate section, since chs. 23–32 may be read in any order to suit the needs of the course. The last four lists are based on frequency, having words occurring 50–60 times in the Bible or words that occur more than 50 times due only to being common in Exod 25–Num 10. The CD also contains a PDF document (CIBH Vocab Tools) with three lists arranged by frequency for the sake of programs which stipulate their vocabulary requirements by frequency.

To the Student.

As you study this book, you would do well to adopt this reading strategy. Begin each chapter by reading its *Focus* section. Then jump ahead to the *Summary* at the end of the chapter. Also scan the list of *Learning Activities* at the end. Then go back to the beginning and read through the chapter, watching any *Grammar Illustrations* from the CD as you go.

The *Focus* and *Summary* sections and *Grammar Illustrations* in TekScroll should help you see what is essential to the chapter's lesson. The *Practice* items and *Workbook Exercises* on the CD target these things. Some chapters will also have material to satisfy curiosity (e.g. why does it do that?), for future reference (that is, not necessary to memorize right away, but which you may want to refer to when doing exercises), or for advanced exposure to a coming concept. The chapter sections usually signal this. Read these portions for a basic comprehension at the moment and so you will know where to look if you want to refer to it at a later time. Pay special attention to items mentioned in the *Focus* and *Summary* sections.

To the Teacher. On connections between chapters.

This grammar presents Hebrew morphology in 22 chapters, a presentation made compact by making the most of comparisons to previously learned material, organizing related forms together, and presenting all morphemes through the common lens of syllable behavior. This part of the Introduction highlights the connections between chapters as a part of course planning and helping prepare students for coming chapters. Note that the CD *Illustrations* and *Practice Readings* can be very useful for teaching – highlight the *Focus* points and then go quickly to the examples.

Chapter one. The main goal is to learn to read the alphabet and vowels. The words in the vocabulary list contain all the letter forms, so that ready ability to read and write the vocabulary is an indicator of having learned the chapter's material.

Since it concerns the alphabet, ch. one also discusses the weak consonant behaviors. They do not need to be mastered at this point. The discussion serves as advanced exposure for when different weak consonant behaviors appear in coming chapters and collects the weak consonant behaviors in one place for later review.

As to pronunciation, variations are mentioned along with advice to follow your instructor. A 5-vowel versus 7-vowel system is not directly discussed. This seems the least complicated way to inform students of differences while allowing instructors to explain it however they want or to omit the discussion. Vowels are described as short and long. Even if "long" vowels are considered qualitatively different rather than quantitatively different, "lengthening" is a complementary term to "reducing."

Chapter two. The main goal is to learn the syllable principles by which all Hebrew morphology will be described. There are seven principles; three apply only to nouns (accented syllables) and the rest to all parts of speech. This chapter's immediate application for students is to aid in pronunciation. But more importantly, it lays the groundwork for ch. 3 and subsequent chapters on morphology. In chapter 3, the syllable principles will explain the vowel changes in nouns with their different endings and help distinguish the construct and absolute forms of nouns.

Hebrew grammars differ in classifying the syllabic status of vocal *shewa*.[1] There are probably two different questions at work. One, is there enough vocalic stuff to call it a syllable? Maybe or maybe not, depending on how one defines a syllable phonologically. This first may be debated. But we can also ask, does vocal *shewa* play the same role in the language system as (other) syllables? To this question the answer is no, they do not have equal status in this regard. (The resulting consistency of description for Hebrew morphology is anticipated in the examples in 2.11.) So pedagogically, vocal *shewa* is not treated as a syllable; the syllable principles skip over them.[2]

Take special note of the term "*shewa* in problem position"[3] (2.5.3), which describes either a vocal shewa starting a pretonic syllable (as in דְּכָ רִים) or a silent shewa closing a distant syllable (as in מִשְׁ פָּ טִים). In the position before the pretonic vowel, that consonant usually has a *shewa*, which may be vocal or silent. Since it is

---

[1] "To early Mediaeval Hebrew grammarians [vocal] shewa as in דְּרָכִים or ḥaṭef's did not have the same syllabic status as full vowels: thus the Hebrew word mentioned was segmented into דְּרָ and כִים" (Paul Joüon, *A Grammar of Biblical Hebrew*, translated and revised by T. Muraoka [Rome: Pontifical Biblical Institute, 1991] p. 96). "A consonant with vocal Šewâ never has the value of an independent syllable" (Wilhelm Gesenius, *Gesenius' Hebrew Grammar*, edited and enlarged by E. Kautsch, 2nd edition revised by E. Cowley [Oxford: Clarendon Press, 1910] p. 87). The classic grammars by Weingreen and Harris and the more recent grammar of Borneman are examples of beginning grammars which do not accord vocal *shewa* the status of a syllable. J. Weingreen, *A Practical Grammar for Classical Hebrew*, 2nd ed. (New York: Oxford University Press, 1959); R. Laird Harris, *Introductory Hebrew Grammar* (Grand Rapids: Eerdmans, 1955); Robert Bornemann, *A Grammar of Biblical Hebrew* (New York: University Press of America, 1998).

[2] It can be argued that certain vocal *shewas* represent a late reduction of a vowel. For students, this adds to the pedagogical burden. For example, the 3fs perfect is קָטְלָה. We describe this as having two syllables: טְלָה + קָ, where קָ is pretonic open long. Our main concern is explaining why the qametz is a long vowel in this position. If one teaches that *shewa* is a syllable on its own, then קָ is an unusual propretonic open long, requiring its history to be explained. This form was reduced from קָטֲלָה, having the accent on the ט. So the *qametz* under קָ is there because it was pretonic and open, making it long at that stage and then staying long. It is more straightforward to adopt the view that *shewas* are not syllables, and this is simpler for explaining the forms (all noun and verb forms) as they are preserved in the Bible. See also Joshua Blau, "the long vowel in the first syllable [of שָׁמְרוּ] is due to pretonic lengthening," *Topics in Hebrew and Semitic Linguistics* (Jerusalem, The Magnes Press, 1998), p. 17.

[3] We adopt this term from Rabbi Dr. Isaac Jerusalmi of Hebrew Union College.

an apparent problem for Hebrew to keep a vowel in this position, it is called *"shewa in problem position."* (Sudents learn later how this *shewa* may trigger changes like the contraction of מַיְ to מוֹ.) We recommend emphasizing to students that "problem position" is not a syllable, but a position that can be in different syllables and that the "*shewa* in problem position" may be either vocal or silent (Cf. 2.5.3 and 2.11).

Chapter three. The main goal is to learn the 10 noun endings and parse accordingly. The vowel changes in the nouns are triggered by the placement of the accent and explained in terms of the syllable principles in ch. 2. They allow for a unified explanation of vowel changes in words both like דָּבָר and שָׂדֶה which means fewer rules and less rote memorization (students who thrive on rote memorization can still do so). The syllable principles are also used to explain the difference between the absolute and construct forms of nouns that use the same ending for both states.

By chapter 3, all forms of the independent pronoun have appeared in vocabulary lists. These forms are used as points of comparison in ch. 6 and subsequent chapters, especially 10 and 15. It is good practice to require students to write the forms of the pronoun from memory before covering ch. 6. Chapter 6 treats pronominal suffixes on nouns and prepositions.

Chapter four. The main goals of the chapter are to reinforce the 10 noun endings, give students more exposure to the weak consonants, and begin training them to see the roots of words. Depending on the choice of dictionary for the course, specifically whether it lists nouns under their root, the chapter may warrant extra time. Otherwise the exposure to weak consonants, roots, and noun patterns may be viewed as advanced training for later chapters on weak verbs. In the latter case only a basic comprehension of weak letter behaviors needs to be achieved at this point.

The weak consonant behaviors are explained as being triggered by the syllable principles. The syllable principles apply first, then weak consonant behaviors may react. If the result looks different from the syllable principles, it is not considered an exception, but rather a clue, for example a clue to the root.[4]

Chapter five. The chapter consists mainly of vocabulary. It explains the vowel variations of the inseparable prepositions, the conjunction *vav*, and the article (whose basic forms have already occurred as vocabulary), as well as the preposition מִן and the interrogative particle הֲ. The discussion has the detail necessary for consultation when a student wants to verify forms found in real texts. But students can be advised to focus on recognition, while leaving the details about creating the forms for reference. In this chapter, the vocabulary list, one of the shortest in the book, needs to be learned before doing the *Practice Readings*.

---

[4] *Ḥolem vav*, for example, is explained (not as "unchangeably long" but) often as a contraction resulting from the syllable principles placing *vav* over silent *shewa*. The *vav* may be a root consonant (though if it is the first radical, its root will be listed in the dictionary as first *yod*).

Chapter six. The main goal is to recognize the pronominal suffixes on substantives based on already knowing the independent pronouns. The first chart, comparing the independent pronoun to the suffixes, is the essence of the chapter. The subsequent charts illustrate the specifics of how the suffixes attach to nouns of different types and to prepositions. They explain how the vowels in nouns can vary according to the syllable principles and noun pattern. Students should be directed to focus on the first chart and view the others for reference. Class can be taught by projecting the first chart on a screen and making observations with the students, then (perhaps after brief comments on the other charts) going to the *Practice Readings* and discussing the forms as they are encountered, referring to the additional paradigms as needed. Several of the *Practice Readings* have the independent pronoun and corresponding pronominal suffix in the same sentence to help reinforce the comparison between the two.

Chapter seven. The main goal is to learn to recognize and translate adjectives (in different syntactical positions), the comparative use of מִן, and the demonstratives. The demonstratives have already occurred in the vocabulary lists. The CD has a practice component that is very useful for teaching the material. It uses only a few nouns and adjectives along with the demonstratives and מִן. These are packaged into 464 statements using adjectives in attributive or predicate position. There are too many for students to feel they should complete them all, but they can be practiced randomly until the students feel confident with the material. At that point they can go to the *Practice Readings* (which also have a number of substantival adjectives) and then on to the *Exercises*.

Chapter eight. Building on ch. 7's discussion of adjective position, ch. 8 introduces the Qal participles and also the Qal infinitive construct. A few verbs have been introduced in the vocabulary by this point, including some infinitives which drop their first radical in their infinitive form, e.g. קַחַת, דַּעַת, לָכֶת and תֵּת. This makes the discussion of the weak infinitives easier, since these forms have been learned as vocabulary and can be used for comparison to others. Their lexical forms are in the vocabulary list for ch. 8.

The chapter does include the small number of weak forms that Qal participles and infinitives have. Since the students' vocabulary has had only thirteen verbs at this point and they are only responsible for participles and infinitive constructs, they are able to focus on the morphemes. Again the *Practice Readings* are helpful, as Part B of the *Practice Readings* includes 20 sentences with participles and infinitives of roots that they should know. Part A of the *Practice Readings* focuses on drilling vocabulary but also includes some participles and infinitives (with the meaning provided when they are not vocabulary words). Students can be asked to identify these as an assignment if they are not used as classroom material.

Chapter nine. The chapter consists mainly of vocabulary. The special vocabulary items in this chapter (e.g. יֵשׁ, אַיִן, הִנֵּה, אֲשֶׁר, directional ה, and numbers) have already occurred in the vocabulary lists. It gives students a break before starting on verbs and is a good opportunity for review or testing. There are two sets of *Practice Readings* and *Translation Exercises*. The second set requires having learned the vocabulary list in ch. 9. The translation exercises begin to include short paragraphs, including here Josh 3:16–4:2, 5–6, and Num 14:1–8. The extra readings provide the opportunity for extended review to solidify the material covered thus far.

Chapter ten. The main goal is to learn the Qal perfect strong verb. The endings are compared to the independent pronoun (1ˢᵗ and 2ⁿᵈ persons) and the noun (3ʳᵈ persons). The behavior of the first radical's vowel is explained by the syllable principles. The unique markers of the stems go by various terms, such as principal parts, stem characteristics, etc., in the grammars. We use "ID badge" because it identifies the stem, works with the art in the computer program, and offers a label for weak forms as "aliases." All the verb forms are taught as the root plus the affixes plus the stem ID badge (not simply as modifications of the 3ms).

The *Practice Parsing* items on the CD include several sections: verbs from past vocabulary, new verbs, and forms that are not Qal. In this last set, students label all other stems as "non-Qal." The purpose is to train them to look for the stem's ID badge, even though they only know one stem. The chapter briefly comments on the nature of *vav* plus perfect consecutive. The exercises reinforce this through footnotes that identify what certain *vav* plus perfects are consecutive to. More is added briefly in ch. 14 (volitional verbs). Chapter 31 addresses this topic in more detail, but the approach at this point, ch. 10, is primarily inductive.

The chapter also distinguishes stative and fientive verbs, and gives initial pointers on the timeframe they may have and their use in different genres. The stative or fientive distinction will be revisited several times in the verb section. The paradigm for כָּבֵד is considered as important as the paradigm for קָטַל because the כָּבֵד paradigm will be used as the point of comparison for the Piel, Hitpael, and Hiphil perfects. It is good for students to be able to write out these two paradigms.

Chapter eleven. The main goal is to learn the Qal perfect weak verb. Paradigms of the weak verb types are included. This does not mean that students need to memorize each of the paradigms. The paradigms need to be included for reference but the student should focus on finally mastering the weak consonant behaviors and how they interact with the syllable principles. The end of the chapter collects the structures of Qal perfect weak verbs in template form, using boxes as place holders and C or V to represent a consonantal or vowel ending (11.5). These are called *Alias Profiles* and are collected at the end of every chapter on weak verbs. They can be used in more than one way. They can be used for review. If the student can explain how such and such a structure resulted from a weak root, this shows that they understand the basic concept. Or students may be allowed to use the *Alias Profiles* while they parse. Instructors vary in attitude toward such tools or may have their own system, but this is provided as an available tool. When the verb forms are finished, the *Alias Profiles* will conveniently fit on two sides of one page.

Chapter twelve. The main goal is to learn the Qal imperfect and *vayyiqtol* strong verb with each class of theme vowel. The forms are presented as adding the imperfect affixes to the infinitive construct (not as built on the 3ms form). Whether or not they were formed this way historically, this is a useful memory device. The ID badge of the Qal imperfect is explained according to the syllable principles.

The paradigms for יִלְמַד and יִתֵּן are considered as important as יִקְטֹל, because the יִלְמַד and יִתֵּן paradigms will be used as points of comparison for the derived stem imperfects. Being able to write all three paradigms reduces later work. Again this chapter gives consideration to whether the verb is fientive or stative and to genre.

Chapter thirteen. The main goal is to learn to recognize Qal imperfect weak verbs. As with the Qal perfect weak verb, all the paradigms needed for consultation are included. It is especially advisable for students to read the summary before the chapter to help reinforce where they are to get to. Though much of the information confirms how minor some changes are, it is still a lot of information. Each section summarizes the main issues, which appear at the chapter's end. Then the chapter summary collects all the *Alias Profiles* (which could be used on an exam).

Chapter fourteen. This chapter covers the volitional verbs and infinitive absolute. These forms are related to the forms just studied. Students should be advised to focus on what cohortative, imperatives, and jussives do and to view the notes on weak forms as a chance to review the weak behaviors covered in ch. 13. Advancing a thread begun in ch. 10, ch. 14 points out the use of *vav* plus perfect consecutive following volitional forms. It also illustrates the use of volitional verbs in a sequence to indicate intention.

Chapter fifteen. The main goal is to recognize the pronominal suffixes on verbs based on already knowing the independent pronouns. As in ch. 6, the pronominal suffixes are again compared to the independent pronoun, and the chapter mostly boils down to the first chart. Since the principles for attaching pronominal suffixes to derived stem verbs are the same, there is not another chapter on attaching suffixes to verbs.

Chapter sixteen. The main goal is to learn the nine patterns that characterize the six derived stems, their ID badges, and their application in infinitives and participles. Students should learn to write the ID badges from memory, since all the rest of the derived stem verb forms will be presented as a combination of a paradigm that they already know plus the appropriate ID badge. Already in this chapter, learning the stem ID badges and learning the infinitives are nearly the same thing, Likewise the participles simply take the ID badge and add the noun endings at the end and a preformative at the beginning. The ID badges are described as normally involving the syllable that the first radical is in. For example, in the Hiphil, R_1 joins a prefix which has *pataḥ*, a pretonic closed short syllable; while in the Piel, R_1 has a *pataḥ* and joins a doubled R_2, also a pretonic closed short syllable. This leads to approaching parsing with the question, "What happens to R_1?" The question is asked about the syllable that the first radical is in as a means of directing students to the "ID badge" to determine the stem.

The chapter provides an overview of how word meaning is affected by the stems with fientive and stative roots, but students are advised to also rely on their dictionary, not to just infer a verb's meaning from the stem. After this point the remaining morphology chapters, 17–22, have no new morphemes and no new grammatical concepts. The derived stem morphemes are presented as combinations of information already learned. Chapters 16–18 also reduce the number of items in the vocabulary section.

The exercises for ch. 16 present infinitives and participles in two groups. This enables the chapter material to be divided into two sections if desired. In addition, the Exercises for chs. 16–22 include 2Chr 34 and Neh 8. They have a high percentage of derived stem verbs as well as content of interest. These passages appear in the appendix of the workbook. The Learning Activities for each chapter of the grammar assign a few verses of each passage, though Neh 8 starts in ch. 17. A list of vocabulary for each of these passages is provided as a "mini-dictionary" to help students with words they have not yet had in their vocabulary requirements. In the earlier verses of each of these chapters, vocabulary helps may also appear in parentheses after certain words. Since there are plenty of exercises for each chapter of the grammar, another approach would be to wait until after ch. 22 to read through these chapters. They appear in the workbook appendix to accommodate this option.

Chapter seventeen. The main goal is to learn the imperfect and preterite strong verb for the Niphal, Piel, Hitpael, and Hiphil. These paradigms all use an *i*-class theme vowel, so they are compared to the Qal imperfect of נָתַן, i.e. אֶתֵּן, etc. (ch. 12). The four ID badges learned in these stems' infinitives are substituted for the Qal ID badge. Presented as combining two sets of information that they already know, the students can quickly grasp the strong verb paradigms for these stems. Students should be able to write these paradigms by having known how to write אֶתֵּן, etc., and being directed to write in the stem's ID badge (ch. 16) around the first radical. The *Grammar Illustration* on the CD is particularly useful as part of the classroom presentation.

Chapters eighteen and nineteen. The main goal is to learn to recognize the weak imperfects, preterites, and imperatives of the Niphal, Piel, Hitpael, and Hiphil. The changes are discussed systematically in terms of when the syllable principles trigger the weak letter behaviors. Then they are gathered as templates in the *Alias Profiles* as an aid to parsing and/or review. The discussions identify some issues as minor and others as major. Thus the discussion tries to answer why even small changes occur while also directing students to where they should concentrate.

Chapter twenty. The main goal is to learn the imperfect and preterite of the Pual and Hophal. These paradigms, using an *a*-class theme vowel, are compared to the imperfect of לָמַד, i.e. אֶלְמַד, etc. (learned in ch. 12). The Pual and Hophal ID badges are substituted for the Qal ID badge. Presented as combining two sets of information that are already known, the strong verb paradigms for these stems are quickly grasped by students. Since these are not common stems and certain weak forms are more common than the strong verb, the chapter includes weak verbs and collects their *Alias Profiles* at the end. A good teaching method is to quickly review the charts or the *Grammar Illustration* on the CD, and then go straight to *Practice Parsing* items on the CD to practice identifying just the stem. The drill can simply ask the students, "Where is the *u*-vowel, with the prefix or R_1? So it is a Hophal/Pual."

Chapter twenty-one. The main goal is to learn the derived stem perfects for the strong verb. The Piel, Hitpael, and Hiphil perfects are compared to כָּבֵד (learned in ch. 10). The Niphal, Pual, and Hophal perfects are compared to קָטַל (also learned in ch. 10). The derived stem ID badges are substituted for the Qal ID badge. It is presented once again as combining two sets of information that are already known. Students can quickly grasp the strong verb paradigms for these stems.

Chapter twenty-two. The main goal is to learn to recognize weak perfects of the derived stems. The changes are discussed systematically in terms of when the syllable principles trigger the weak letter behaviors. Then they are gathered as templates in the *Alias Profiles* as an aid to parsing and/or review.

Excursus A: Sorting through forms. This section discusses forms that could be confused and clues for telling them apart. It leads up to and includes a two-page summary of the *Alias Profiles* for parsing weak verbs. The *Alias Profiles* assume that the student knows the strong verb well.

Excursus B and the Syntax Section. These sections aim to illustrate how several factors combine to create meaning. They intend to help the student have perspective on the kinds of information presented in reference works and help them ask good questions.

These chapters can be used in several ways. They may be read as a supplement to translation work, in which case they mainly make the student aware of what kinds of factors need to be considered in translation and exegetical work. They can be used as a jumping-off point for a class unit related to that chapter's topic. Also many may be integrated with the morphology chapters. This can allow a brief break in learning new forms, without necessarily making a shift in topics. The syntactical categories presented are largely taken from and refer to *A Guide to Biblical Hebrew Syntax* by Bill T. Arnold and John H. Choi (Cambridge: Cambridge University Press, 2003).

Chapter twenty-three. The main purpose of this chapter is to remind us that the Bible is great literature – in Hebrew. The chapter considers how the use of pause adds drama to storytelling. It is intended to give students a refreshing breather, reminding them that it's not all about paradigms.

Chapter twenty-four. This chapter presents some basic theoretical foundations for lexical studies and then illustrates many of the issues with the word פָּקַד. The purpose is to highlight issues in lexical studies and arm the student with questions to ask when using a dictionary, questions other than just, "What does this word mean?" It points out the difference between glosses, definitions, and the reality being referred to; notes the importance of paradigmatic relationships in the lexica; and illustrates how different items of grammar, syntax, or discourse bear on the meaning of the word פָּקַד in specific contexts. (This chapter may be done whenever dictionaries are discussed. But note that the examples include derived stem verbs.)

Chapter twenty-five. Language is more flexible than any reference work can summarize, so this chapter illustrates categories of noun syntax and pushes the discussion outside the boundaries of the syntax lists. A few construct plus genitive noun constructions are selected at the end because they do not fit neatly into the list. The rhetorical message for the student is that syntax lists are not the end all, but a guide to how to think about syntax, specifically noun relationships. (This chapter may be done with ch. 4.)

Chapter twenty-six. This chapter covers common functions of the doubling stems and points out the flexibility of the D-stems. It discusses the limits of making syntactical labels. And by discussing different meanings of the Piel of שָׁהַר, it illustrates that the meaning of a verb can depend on more than the root and stem. (This chapter may be done any time after ch. 16 or in conjunction with it.)

Chapter twenty-seven. Besides listing common syntactical functions of participles, the chapter discusses how genre and context signal the time frame in which a participle should be translated. This includes a brief overview of narrative clauses which are not verb first. (This chapter may be done any time after ch. 16 or in conjunction with it.)

Chapter twenty-eight. This chapter focuses on preterite and non-preterite clauses in narrative. The emphasis is not only on translation technique, but to think through how the action is supposed to play out in the hearer's mind. More than just labeling clauses, we want to know how the clausal structure contributes to the story. We want to learn to see and retell how the action moves, how the scenes shift, etc. (This chapter may be done in conjunction with ch. 23, but note that it refers to a section in ch. 27.)

Chapter twenty-nine. This chapter continues to look at how meaning arises from combinations. These particles were preliminarily discussed in ch. 9. The categories assigned to the particles in reference works are viewed as translation advice for when the particles occur in similar circumstances. The particles are presented as having a base meaning that interacts with the context, emphasizing how larger discourse features affect their meaning. הִנֵּה is discussed in relation to genre, who the speaker is, and who is having (or is to have) the הִנֵּה experience. (This chapter may be done along with ch. 9.)

Chapter thirty. Besides surveying common functions of the infinitive construct, this chapter discusses the infinitive absolute in various combinations: paronomastic, in pairings, individually, and with *vav*. It agrees with and argues for the perspective that the paronomastic infinitive absolute emphasizes the modality of the verb. It argues that with *vav*, the infinitive absolute is parenthetic rather than like a perfect consecutive. The chapter ends by discussing a passage with an uncommon construction and comparing this context to the more common constructions. (This chapter may be done any time after ch. 16 or in conjunction with it.)

Chapter thirty-one. This chapter adds some historical notes about the Hebrew verb to supplement the list of syntactic functions for uses of the *vav* plus perfect. It views the syntactical labels as dependent on the setting, in each case indicating succession or logical sequence. (This chapter may be done any time after ch. 14.)

Chapter thirty-two. This offers a beginning to approaching poetry. Lacking the prevalent preterite forms of narrative, students are advised to pay attention to a combination of parallelism, the fientive or stative nature of the verb, and the stem of the verb. Examples from the Psalms of Asaph illustrate the use of the verb in the same categories already learned for narrative. The chapter closes with Psalm 76 as an example. The translations commonly treat one or more verb forms in a way that is abnormal in comparison to prose. But treating the Psalm with the above considerations yields the more probable structure for the Psalm.

The Cambridge Introduction
to Biblical Hebrew

chapter one

The Signs and Sounds of Hebrew: Orthography and Pronunciation

1.1   Focus.

In this chapter you are to learn:

23 consonants, 5 of which have two forms,

15 vowels, and

3 dots: *dagesh lene, dagesh forte*, and *mappiq*.

Besides the consonants, vowels, and three dots, this chapter also contains transliteration symbols (English-looking characters for the Hebrew alphabet). They are an initial aid to learning the sounds of the Hebrew characters. The chapter also exposes you to the 5 "weak" consonant principles. They do not need to be mastered now, but you need to be aware of these groups of consonants and categories of behavior. Future chapters will apply them as their topics require.

The CD has flashcards for learning the consonants and vowels as well as phonics lists for pronouncing syllables. You may find it helpful to use these while going through the chapter. The vocabulary for this chapter uses all the consonant forms and nearly all the vowels, so it acts as practice in reading Hebrew.

1.2   The Aleph-Bet.

The letters of the Hebrew alphabet appear in the following chart.

There are no capitals, but some letters have different forms when written at the end of a word. These 5 final forms are listed to the right.

A few letters were pronounced two ways, as signaled by the presence or absence of a dot, called a *dagesh lene* (dah-géysh léy-ney, explained below). Note that a few letters with *dagesh lene* are no longer pronounced differently. (Modern Hebrew pronunciations are favored. Your instructor may prefer another system.)

See the CD for practice writing the letters. Handwritten block letters are more simplified in form than the print that appears in books. Most letters are written beginning at their upper left point and finishing with a down stroke or a stroke moving left (since Hebrew is written from right to left).

1.2.1   Hebrew Alphabet.

ʾaleph	א	ʾ	unpronounced (or guttural stop, like h in heir)
bet	בּ	b	**b** as in **b**ent
	ב	ḇ	**v** as in **v**ent
gimel	גּ	g	**g** as in **g**as
	ג	ḡ	**g** as in **g**as (formerly **g** as in **d**og)
dalet	דּ	d	**d** as in **d**ime
	ד	ḏ	**d** as in **d**ime (formerly **th** as in **th**en)
he (hey)	ה	h	**h** as in **h**at (typically silent if ending a word)
vav	ו	v	**v** as in **v**ent (formerly **w** as in **w**ay)
zayin	ז	z	**z** as in **z**ebra
ḥet	ח	ḥ	as **ch** in Lo**ch** Ness
ṭet	ט	ṭ	**t** as in **t**oy
yod (yōd)	י	y	**y** as in **y**es
kaf	כּ	k	**k** as in **k**ick
	כ ך	ḵ	as **ch** in Lo**ch** Ness
lamed	ל	l	**l** as in **l**ove
mem	מ ם	m	**m** as in **m**om
nun	נ ן	n	**n** as in **n**o
samech	ס	s	**s** as in **s**ay
ʿayin	ע	ʿ	unpronounced (or guttural stop made farther back in the throat than aleph)
pe (pey)	פּ	p	**p** as in **p**it
	פ ף	p̄	**ph** as in **ph**one or as **f** in **f**it
tsade	צ ץ	ṣ	**ts** as in ski**ts**
qof	ק	q	**k** as in **k**ick / **q** as in pla**q**ue
resh (reysh)	ר	r	**r** as in **r**un
sin	שׂ	ś	**s** as in **s**ay
shin	שׁ	š	**sh** as in **sh**ip
tav	תּ	t	**t** as in **t**oy
	ת	ṯ	**t** as in **t**oy (formerly **th** as in **th**in)

1.3 The 3 Dots. They look the same but do different things.

(a) Dagesh lene (dah-géysh léy-ney).

Dagesh lene can only occur in six letters, ב, ג, ד, כ, פ, and ת, known by the acronym *BeGaDKePhaT* letters. This is only a pronunciation issue. Without *dagesh lene* breath is moving, as in *graphite*, e.g. פ. *Dagesh lene* tells you that breath stopped, as in *crackpot*, e.g. פּ. *Dagesh lene* is like a stop sign.

(b) Dagesh forte (dah-géysh fór-tey).

Dagesh forte indicates that a letter is doubled, i.e. pronounced twice. If we used it in English, we would write *lader* for *ladder*. A few letters called gutturals, א, ה, ח, ע, and ר, will not double and so can not take *dagesh forte* (see further at 1.8.2).

(c) Mappiq (mahp-pík).

The *mappiq* can occur only in a *he* at the end of a word. Normally a *he*, ה, ending a word is not pronounced; the *mappiq* in a *he*, הּ, tells you to pronounce it (in which case it is usually a pronominal suffix; cf. ch. 6).

1.4 Consonant groupings for study.

Be careful to discern the differences between letters in these sets.

(a) With upper right corner.

ת	ח	ה	ד	ר	ך	ף
Tav	Ḥet	He	Dalet	Resh	Kaph (final)	Pe (final)

(b) With main vertical stroke.

י	ו	ז	ן	ך	נ	ג
Yod	Vav	Zayin	Nun (final)	Kaph (final)	Nun	Gimel

(c) With upper right corner and a bottom line.

ב	כ	פ	נ	ג
Bet	Kaph	Pe	Nun	Gimel

(d) Boxish.

ס	ם	ט	שׂ	שׁ
Samech	Mem (final)	Ṭet	Sin	Shin

(e) Two point tops.

צ	ע	ץ	א
Tsade	Ayin	Tsade (final)	Aleph

(f) BeGaDKePhaT letters, with and without dagesh lene.

	Bet		Gimel		Dalet		Kaph		Pe		Tav	
stop	בּ	b	גּ	g	דּ	d	כּ	k	פּ	p	תּ	t
spirant	ב	b̠ (v)	ג	ḡ	ד	ḏ	כ	k̠ (kh)	פ	p̠ (ph)	ת	ṯ

Stop means breath has stopped; *spirant* means breath is moving. Even if they are pronounced the same in modern Hebrew, they will still be transliterated differently. For example, ת is transliterated ṯ, even though now pronounced like תּ, t.

(g) Letters with final forms.

	Kaph	Mem	Nun	Pe	Tsade
beg. or middle	כ	מ	נ	פ	צ
final	ך	ם	ן	ף	ץ

(h) Letters with similar sounds.

א Aleph and   ע Ayin

ו Vav and   ב Bet (no dagesh)

ח Ḥet and   כ Kaph (no dagesh)

ק Qof and   כּ Kaph (with dagesh)

שׂ Sin and   ס Samech

ט Ṭet and   ת Tav

Speakers with an Arabic background may distinguish between ט and ת, שׂ and ס, and א and ע.

(i) Letters with similar transliteration symbols.

Dentals. ט, ת, תּ (as well as ד and דּ) are dentals, made by pressing part of the tongue against the back of the upper teeth.

ṭ   t   ṯ

ט Ṭet   תּ Tav   ת Tav

Gutturals. Gutturals are made near the back of the throat. English lacks letters corresponding to א, ח and ע.

h   ḥ   ʾ   ʿ

ה He   ח Ḥet   א Aleph   ע Ayin

Sibilants. Sibilants contain an "s" sound.

s   ś   š   ṣ

ס Samech   שׂ Sin   שׁ Shin   צ Tsade

1.5   Vowels.

Hebrew vowels come in three classes and three lengths. The three main classes are *a*-class (*ah*-class), *i*-class (*ee*-class) and *u*-class (*oo*-class). The *i*-class includes both "i" and "e"; the *u*-class includes both "u" and "o." The three vowel lengths are long, short, and slurred. Slurs include half-vowels, also called composite *shewas*.

But we should first be aware that English is odd in how it writes vowels. In English, the letter "a" makes the sounds in fat and fate; "e" those in bet or beet; "i" those in high or hit. But most languages use "i" for the sound in b**ee**t; "e" for the sound in h**ay**; and "a" for "ah," as in f**a**ther, but *not* that in fate. Hebrew vowels are treated in this more common way. In this chart, a ו or י is part of writing the vowel; they are not consonants in these cases (cf. 1.8.5). A box stands for any consonant.

Hebrew Vowel chart 1.

class	length	name	vowel	*trlit.*	pronunciation
a-class	long	qametz (gadol)	☐	ā	ah as in f**a**ther (longer than *pataḥ*)
	short	pataḥ	☐	a	ah as in f**a**ther (shorter than *qametz*)
	half	ḥaṭaph pataḥ	☐	ă	like *pataḥ*, but extra short
i-class	long	ḥireq yod	י☐	ī	ee as 2nd i in intr**i**gue (normally with *yod*)
	short	ḥireq	☐	i	i as 1st i in **i**ntrigue
	long	tsere yod or tsere	י☐ ☐	ē	e as in h**e**y (with or without *yod*)
	short	segol	☐	e	e as in g**e**t (rarely with *yod*)
	half	ḥaṭaph segol	☐	ĕ	like *segol*, but extra short
u-class	long	shureq	ו☐	ū	oo as in sh**oo**t
	long or short	qibbutz	☐	ū u	oo as in sh**oo**t (may be long or short)
	long	ḥolem vav or ḥolem	ו☐ ☐	ō	o as in v**o**te
	short	qametz ḥaṭuph	☐	o	o as in b**o**ttle (or as in v**o**te, but short)
	half	ḥaṭaph qametz	☐	ŏ	like *qameṣ ḥaṭuph*, extra short
class: all	slur	vocal shewa	☐	ə / ᵉ	very short vocalic slur
class: none	not a vowel	silent shewa = absence of vowel	☐	none	silent; marks end of a syllable within a word and rarely at the end of a word

There are variations in how people speak. In modern Hebrew *pataḥ* and *qametz* may sound alike; *tsere* may be pronounced like *segol*. Follow your instructor.

1.5.₁   Notes on vowels.

(a) ***Qametz***, long *ā*, and *qametz ḥaṭuph*, short *o*, look alike, ◌ָ. (English also uses the same vowel sign for more than one sound, e.g. the letter "o" in *lob, lobe, love*.) Most *qametzim* are long *ā*. Distinguishing the two will be explained in ch. 2.

(b) ***Qibbutz***, ◌ֻ, can be long *ū* or short *u*.

(c) ***Ḥolem***. The *ḥolem*'s dot, ◌ֹ, may blend into that of a following שׁ.

(d) ***Shewa***.

    Vocal and silent *shewa* look alike, ◌ְ. Distinguishing them is best done in the context of learning syllables (ch. 2), but see also 1.7 below.

    A composite *shewa* is a *shewa* written beside a vowel to show that its length is in between a short vowel and a slur. Composite *shewas* appear with the gutturals: א, ה, ח, and ע. (These letters can sometimes accept a silent *shewa*; but they always take a composite shewa instead of a vocal *shewa*.)

    Vocal *shewa* is a slur. Vowels may reduce to a vocalic slur, as some English dialects slur (or virtually skip) the first "o" in *potato* or "e" in *Melissa*. Not much vowel remains, less than the short vowels in *pot* and *melt*. Regardless of the original vowel class, once they are reduced the vocal *shewas* sound alike. Unlike English, which writes the same letter regardless of how much it is actually pronounced, Hebrew signals this reduction by writing a vocal *shewa*.

(e) ***Full vowels***. Long and short vowels are considered full vowels. Slurs, both vocal *shewas* and composite *shewas* are not full vowels; they are too much reduced.

1.5.₂   Changing vowel lengths.

As we learn more about the structure of Hebrew, we will find that different circumstances affect vowel length. Changes in vowel length typically occur within the same vowel class. For example, short *a* may lengthen to a long *ā* or reduce to vocal *shewa*. The next chart helps to see the vowels by class and length at the same time. After the names and sounds are learned, this will be the more useful chart.

Hebrew Vowel chart 2.

		long	short	slur (vocal *shewa*)	slur with א, ה, ח, ע (composite *shewa*)
a-class	a	◌ָ	◌ַ	◌ְ	◌ֲ
i-class	e	◌ֵ ◌ֵי	◌ֶ	◌ְ	◌ֱ
	i	◌ִי	◌ִ		
u-class	o	וֹ ◌ֹ	◌ָ	◌ְ	◌ֳ
	u	וּ ◌ֻ	◌ֻ		

1.6   Distinguishing one *dagesh* from another.

Remember what each *dagesh* does. *Dagesh forte* indicates a letter is doubled. *Dagesh lene* indicates a begadkephat letter is spoken as a stop, i.e. the sound cannot be held out as in "ph," but must have stopped as in "p," (*graphite* vs. *crackpot*). Distinguishing them is practiced in ch. 2.

***Rule 1. Dagesh forte* follows a *full* vowel *within* the word**, e.g. אֵלֶּה *'ēl/le(h)* and הַגָּדוֹל *hag/gā/dōl*. In begadkephat letters, both will be pronounced as stops.

Corollary A: *Dagesh* beginning a word is *dagesh lene*,[1] e.g. בֵּן *ben*.

***Rule 2. Dagesh lene* follows a stop.** A stop is either a consonant ending a syllable or a pause between words (if there is a pause), e.g. מִקְדָּשׁ *miq/daš*.

Corollary B: *Dagesh lene* cannot follow a vowel or vocal *shewa*; the moving breath of the vowel does not permit it. If a word ends in a vowel and the next word begins with a begadkephat letter, the begadkephat letter will not have *dagesh lene* unless there is a pause, or stoppage of breath, between the words, such as between sentences. We will learn about pauses later.

Corollary C: If *dagesh* follows *shewa*, the *shewa* must be silent and the *dagesh* must be *dagesh lene*.

Illustrations from English. In the word *ladder*, the doubled "d" is pronounced after a vowel (Rule 1). The first "d" ends a syllable and the next "d" begins a syllable. Hebrew writes one "d" and puts a dot, *dagesh forte*, in it to show it is doubled, e.g. לַדֶּר for *lad/der*, i.e. לִדְדֶר (with both *dalets* pronounced as stops with *dagesh lene*).

In the word *crackpot*, the "p" follows a consonant which ended a syllable *crack/pot* (Rule 2). Since it is not preceded by a vowel, doubling it would make no sense, e.g. *crack/ppot*. Likewise it would make no sense to begin a word with a *dagesh forte*, e.g. *ppot* (Corollary A). The moving air of a preceding vowel blows *dagesh lene* out of *begadkephat* letters, turning them into spirants. Hebrew does not say *tap*, but would say *taph* instead (Corollary B).

1.7   Distinguishing *Shewas*, initial rules of thumb:

Remember what they do. Vocal *shewa* is a reduced vowel; silent *shewa* ends a syllable (more in ch. 2). Distinguishing *shewas* need not be fully mastered in ch. 1.

(a)   Silent *shewa* is *usually* preceded by a short vowel.[2]

(b)   Vocal *shewa* is *usually* preceded by a long vowel or silent *shewa*.

(c)   Beginning a word, *shewa* is vocal, always.

(d)   If there are two *shewas* in a row, the first is silent, the second vocal (almost always).

---

[1] The rare occasions in which *dagesh forte* can begin a word are discussed in ch. 23.

[2] Silent *shewa* may also be preceded by an accented long vowel. Accents are discussed in ch. 2.

1.8   Weak Consonants: consonants with special behaviors.

Some consonants have special rules. We will deal with them more as chapter topics raise them. This list exposes you to what is coming. At this point you only need to know what the special groups are and have a basic recognition of their behaviors.

1.8.1   Begadkephat Letters: ב, ג, ד, כ, פ, ת.

Begadkephat letters can take *dagesh lene* and are then pronounced as stops.

1.8.2   Gutturals: א, ה, ח, ע and sometimes ר.

Shewa problem: Gutturals reject vocal *shewa* (and sometimes silent *shewa*), taking a composite *shewa* instead.

Dagesh problem: Gutturals and ר reject *dagesh forte*. This often results in lengthening the preceding vowel, called *compensatory lengthening*. If not, we treat it as doubled anyway and call it *semi-doubling* or *virtual doubling*.

Gutturals also prefer *a*-class vowels. Gutturals may take a preceding or following *a*-class vowel when a word pattern normally does not. Also a **furtive *patah*** may appear before a ה, ח or ע at the end of a word, even though preceded by another vowel. For example, רוּחַ is *rū^{a}h*; מִזְבֵּחַ is *miz/bē^{a}h*.

1.8.3   Quiet Letters: א and ע.

א **'Aleph.** Today *aleph* is not pronounced. When scholars, called the Masoretes, added the vowels, א was pronounced at the start of a syllable but had usually become silent (quiesced) at the end of a syllable. This quiescence means that *aleph* will not have a silent *shewa*, and a following *begadkephat* letter will not have a *dagesh lene*.

ע **'Ayin.**   ע was a full consonant in all positions for the Masoretes, so it is followed by *dagesh lene*. But since it is a silent letter today, it will "sound" like *aleph*. Pay attention to the spellings, especially as you study vocabulary.

1.8.4   *Matres lectionis*: ו, י and ה.

When ו and י are used as part of writing vowels, they are called *matres lectionis*, Latin for "mothers of reading." Scribes used ו and י, as well as ה, to indicate vowels as an aid to reading. ו and י are vowels when they have no vowel or *shewa* underneath. At the end of a word, ה is usually a *mater*, not a consonant.

ו is consistently used for *u*-class vowels, e.g. וֹ and וּ.

י is consistently used for *i*-class vowels, e.g. ֵי, ִי and rarely ַי.

ה usually indicates a preceding long *qametz*, הָ. But it can support *a*-class, *i*-class, and *u*-class vowels, e.g. הֶ , הֵ , הֹ, and הוּ. Some transliteration systems write *mater* ה with parentheses, e.g. ā(h).

With a *mater*, vowels are said to be written "fully." If a *mater* is not used where it is usually expected, it is called "defective." (As you will learn in the paradigms, some *holems* are usually written with *vav*, others without.)

1.8.5 Diphthongs or contractions.

A consonantal **ו** or **י** may become part of a vowel, typically when ending an unaccented syllable. The contraction of the vowel plus the **ו** or **י** is called a diphthong. It is transliterated differently than other long vowels, with a circumflex (*ê*) rather than a macron (*ē*). Some systems use a circumflex for all *matres*, e.g. *â* for *ā(h)*.

Unaccented **וְ** becomes **וֹ** (*aw* → *ô*).[3] The *vav* is now a *mater*.

Unaccented **יְ** becomes **י** (*ay* → *ê*). The *yod* is now a *mater*.

When you do see **יְ**, it represents a glide between the vowel and the consonant, similar to "aye" as in "aye, aye, sir."

1.8.6 The assimilation of Nun.

When **נ** ends a syllable inside of a word (*nun* over a silent *shewa*, **נְ**) it transforms into a copy of the next consonant. Then it is written as a *dagesh forte* in that letter. To a limited degree we have this pronunciation issue in English:

in + resistible = irresistible,   in + measurable = immeasurable,

tin + śā' = tiś-śā':   תִּשָּׂא = תִּשְׂשָׂא ← תִּנְ + שָׂא

As you might guess, there will be issues when the letter after *nun* is a guttural.

1.9 Summary.

Alphabet and vowels. See the charts. Learn the names, sounds, and transliteration values of each consonant and vowel.

Other symbols: *dagesh lene, dagesh forte, mappiq.*

Dagesh lene signals that *begadkephat* letters (בּגּדּכּפּתּ) are stops; it follows a consonant or a pause; it cannot follow a vowel.

Dagesh forte indicates a consonant is doubled; it follows a full vowel in a word.

Mappiq indicates that a final *he* is consonantal and to be pronounced.

For future reference: Peculiarities of certain consonants.

1. Only *begadkephat* letters can have *dagesh lene.*
2. Gutturals reject *dagesh forte.*
   Solution: Compensatory lengthening or virtual doubling.
3. Gutturals reject vocal (and sometimes silent) *shewa.*
   Solution: composite *shewa.*
4. *Aleph* quiesces at the end of a syllable.
5. *He, Yod*, and *Vav* may be *matres lectionis.*
6. *Yod* and *Vav* may be part of diphthongs or represent contractions.
7. *Nun* closing a syllable within a word may assimilate into the following consonant as a *dagesh forte.*

---

[3] Historically *vav* was pronounced "w."

At this point you need to focus on learning the consonant and vowel signs well. Review the rest of the material so that you can consult it quickly. It will become more meaningful when we start to look at the structure of syllables and words.

1.10   Vocabulary.

All the letter forms of the Hebrew alphabet and nearly all the vowels (except *ḥaṭaph segol* and *ḥaṭaph qametz*) are used in this chapter's vocabulary. Practice saying the names of the letters and vowels as you learn these words. When you have learned them, you will have learned the basic information of ch. 1.

1	מִי	**mî**	*prn.* who? (424)
2	הוּא	**hû᾿**	*prn.* he (1398)
3	הִיא	**hî᾿**	*prn.* she (491)
4	אֲנִי / אָנֹכִי	**᾿ănî**	*prn.* I (1233*)
5	אֲנַחְנוּ	**᾿ănaḥ-nû**	*prn.* we (121)
6	גָּדוֹל	**gā-ḏōl**	*adj.* great, large (527)
7	זָקֵן	**zā-qēn**	*adj.* old, elder (180)
8	עָם	**‘ām**	*n.m.* a people (1869)
9	שָׂדֶה	**śā-ḏe(h)**	*n.m.* field (329)
10	דָּבָר	**dā-ḇār**	*n.m.* word, matter, thing (1454)
11	מִדְבָּר	**miḏ-bār**	*n.m.* wilderness, pasture, steppe (269)
12	מִשְׁפָּט	**miš-pāṭ**	*n.m.* law, custom, legal claim/decision (425)
13	שַׁבָּת	**šab-bāṯ**	*n.f/m.* rest, Sabbath (111)
14	מִצְוָה	**miṣ-vā(h)**	*n.f.* commandment (184)
15	חֻקָּה	**ḥuq-qā(h)**	*n.f.* statute, enactment (104)
16	חָכְמָה	**ḥok-mā(h)**	*n.f.* wisdom (153)
17	תְּפִלָּה	**t᾽pil-lā(h)**	*n.f.* prayer (77)
18	מַלְכָּה	**mal-kā(h)**	*n.f.* queen (35)
19	מֶלֶךְ	**me-leḵ**	*n.m.* king (2530)
20	אֶרֶץ	**᾿e-reṣ**	*n.f.* land, earth, ground, territory, region (2505)
21	כֶּסֶף	**ke-sep̄**	*n.m.* silver, money (403)
22	נֶגֶד	**ne-ḡeḏ**	*prp.* in front of, opposite of (151)
23	תּוֹרָה	**tô-rā(h)**	*n.f.* instruction, law (223)

adj. = adjective	*n.f/m.* = noun (may be masculine or feminine)
n.m. = noun masculine	*prn.* = pronoun
n.f. = noun feminine	*prp.* = preposition

1.11   Learning Activities on the CD.

The CD includes interactive learning activities and the workbook in PDF form. After opening the program, click number 1 from the chapter list for these learning activities. (Clicking the book icon in the lower left corner of a learning activity returns you to its chapter menu.)

1   Writing Hebrew.

Watch the letters being drawn and practice writing them in your workbook.

2   Reading Hebrew.

This activity has several components:

      A. Consonant flashcards and vowel flashcards.

      B. Phonics lists.

      C. Practice reading one-syllable and two-syllable Hebrew words.

3   Learn ch. 1 vocabulary.

Your primary goal is to learn to read the consonants, vowels, and *dagesh*. Secondarily you should be able to name the groups of the weak consonants as found in the summary (1.9). When you can easily read the chapter's vocabulary and the Hebrew words in the Practice Reading, you have accomplished the main goal.

You can approach learning the alphabet in different ways according to your learning style. Visual learners may want to start with the consonant and vowel flashcards. Audio learners may want to first learn to recite the names of the consonants and vowels, then add their sounds, and finally practice writing them. Kinesthetic learners might best begin with writing out the letters. As you write them, repeat their names and sounds out loud. Some may want to go right to the phonics lists. Just remember that the goal is not simply to do activities – the goal is to learn to read. Here is what the learning activities involve.

1   Writing Hebrew.

Click a consonant to see how it is written. Both block print and script options are available. Remember that handwriting varies, whether in English or in Hebrew. Printing will not normally be as square as the computer draws. Follow your instructor in any variations. Practice writing in your workbook (print out the appropriate pages). It is valuable to say the letters and their sounds aloud while writing them.

2   A. Consonant and vowel flashcards.

This activity has two lists, one of the consonants and another of the vowels. After you choose a list to work on, the letters are displayed one at a time. You can click for the answer, which gives the name and transliteration of the letter. An audio option says the name of the letter. Then click again for the next letter. You can go through the lists forward, backward, or randomly. If you start here it is a good idea to have your textbook open for consultation (1.2.1 and 1.4 for consonants or 1.5 for vowels).

2   B. Phonics lists.

Practice reading Hebrew letters by reading one-syllable English words that have been written in Hebrew. They are arranged in phonics lists that share a vowel sound. When you click on the name of a vowel on the left, you get that set of English words spelled in Hebrew. The answer button shows the transliteration of the Hebrew and the English word it represents; click again for the next word. (Since English dialects differ, you may occasionally feel that an English word does not fit a particular phonics list. If this happens, write it down and ask your instructor later.) *Do as many of these as it takes to be confident of your reading.*

N.B. English does not accommodate the difference between *pataḥ* and *qametz gadol*, since they both make a similar *a* sound. Nor does English have many one-syllable words spelled with "a" that make the *a* sound of *pataḥ* and *qametz gadol*. Consequently the lists for *pataḥ* and *qametz gadol* use the same English words and some examples are a bit forced. On the other hand, there are many more English words spelled with "o" that can represent *qametz ḥaṭuph*. This could give the false impression that *qametz ḥaṭuph* is more common in Hebrew than *qametz gadol*. But in fact most of the *qametzim* that you meet in Hebrew will be *qametz gadol* with long *ā*.

2   C. Practice Reading Hebrew words.

There are two lists: one-syllable words and two-syllable words. The set of two-syllable words gives each syllable separately, then the whole word. Being able to read these easily confirms that you have met the goals of the chapter. You can also practice reading Hebrew words in the vocabulary program. The audio option allows you to hear them pronounced.

3   Read and memorize ch. 1 vocabulary.

This link takes you to the vocabulary quizzing program and loads ch. 1 vocabulary. To set options, click on the Parameters button on the top right tab, or go directly to the Parameters by clicking on the Vocabulary button on the left side of the opening page of the CD program. You can also make your own flashcards on note cards, which is a good pedagogical exercise on its own. (Flashcards are also provided on the CD as PDFs that can be printed and cut out. Note the instructions in the document called CIBH VocabCards ReadMe.pdf.) Another technique is to make short English sentences that use each word, but say the Hebrew word aloud where it belongs in the English sentence.

Remember that if you find certain letters easy to confuse, consult the lists in 1.4.

Also review the summary of weak letter groups in 1.9. Future chapters will expand on this basic overview.

chapter two

Syllables:
The Structural Girders of Hebrew

2.1   Focus.

In this chapter you are to learn:

to recognize three accent marks (◌֫, ◌֑ and ׃◌◌֖) and

the **7 syllable principles**, which requires learning

the 2-part definition of a Hebrew syllable and

the 3 characteristics of a Hebrew syllable.

The main goal of the chapter is to apply the seven syllable principles. Initially they will help you pronounce words and distinguish between *dagesh lene* and *dagesh forte*, between vocal and silent *shewa*, and between *qametz* and *qametz ḥaṭuph*. As we go on, they will help you understand word forms and vowel changes.

The principles for accented syllables apply only in the world of nouns (which includes adjectives and participles). The other principles apply to all parts of speech. Because they apply throughout the language system, they are critical to understanding how Hebrew words form and change. We will use the syllable principles immediately to explain noun forms in ch. 3, and continue to use them when explaining the verb.

A brief warning – depending on how you have been pronouncing vocal *shewas*, they may sound like syllables to you. But for the Masoretes (the scholars who added vowels to the text, 600–900 c.e.), *shewas* were not syllables. Letting Hebrew work by its own rules will simplify our understanding of its forms.

2.2   Accent marks.

We will mostly mark accented syllables by ◌֫, e.g. דָּבָ֫ר. But you should also learn two others. *Aṭnaḥ*, ◌֑ as in דָּבָ֑ר, is the major accent, or pause, in the middle of a verse. *Sof pasuq*, ׃◌◌֖ as in דָּבָ֖ר׃, always occurs on the last word of a verse, like a period (note the two 'diamonds' at the end of the word and the vertical line, where the accent is pronounced). As in English, an accented syllable is spoken with more emphasis than the other syllables. *Aṭnaḥ* and *sof pasuq* represent even heavier accents than normal, since they also involve pausing.

2.3   Biblical Hebrew Syllables: the basics.

A syllable is a distinct segment of a word with a vowel. Observe the syllable divisions in English words: ob/serve, bib/li/cal, He/brew, ba/sics. In the Hebrew preserved by the Masoretes (who added the vowel signs), Hebrew syllables **(1) begin with a consonant** and **(2) have one full vowel** (*shewa* does not count).

1)   All syllables must begin with a consonant.

These are all genuine Hebrew syllables: הֶעָ, הִתְ, מוּ, עַ, הָ, דְ.
They all begin with a consonant (and have one full vowel). A syllable may end in a consonant or a vowel, but must begin with a consonant.

These are unacceptable as Hebrew syllables: וּד, ִים, אַב, ֹון.
Yes, they can be pronounced, ūd, îm, ab, ōn, but in Hebrew they are not kosher syllables. Hebrew requires that consonants begin syllables. There is just one exception. The word for "and" is normally a consonantal וּ but in some situations it becomes vocalic וּ when it follows an extra rule (5.3.3).

2)   Each syllable must have *one and only one full* vowel.

A vocal or composite *shewa* is not enough. They are only slurs; syllables require a full vowel. (The last syllable is accented unless otherwise marked.)

So these have 2 syllables: חָ / לִי   דָ / רוֹם   מֶ / לֶךְ
But these have 1 syllable: חֲלִי   חֲלוֹם   אֱמֶת

These have 3 syllables: יִכְ / תָּ / בוּ   כָּ / בֶ / דָה
But these have 2 syllables: יִכְ / תְּבוּ   כָּ / בְדָה

From an English perspective, a vocal or composite *shewa* may feel like a syllable. *But it does not get full vocalic treatment from the Masoretes.*[1] The syllabic structures skip over them; understanding this will simplify our approach to word forms.
Each syllable must have one full vowel!

Corollaries: For every full vowel there is a syllable.
No type of *shewa* by itself is enough to make a syllable.

2.4   Three Characteristics of Hebrew syllables.

Hebrew syllables are described in relation to vowel length, whether they end with a vowel or consonant, and their relation to the accent.

2.4.₁   Long or short.

A syllable is **long or short** if its full vowel is long or short (cp. 1.5.2).

---

[1] See the reference grammars. "To early Mediaeval Hebrew grammarians [vocal] shewa as in דְּרָכִים or ḥaṭef's did not have the same syllabic status as full vowels: thus the Hebrew word mentioned was segmented into דְּרָ and כִים" (Joüon-Muraoka, p. 96). "A consonant with vocal Šewâ never has the value of an independent syllable" (Gesenius, p. 87).

2.4.₂   Open or closed.

(a) Open Syllables end in a vowel (*matres lectionis* do not count).

Open: דָ   מֶ   דְּבָ   אֲדוֹ   רָה   (the ה is a *mater*)

(b) Closed Syllables end in a consonant (which may have a silent *shewa*).

Closed: בַּר   לֶךְ   שָׁמַר   אֹכֶל

2.4.₃   Accented or position relative to the accent.

(a) Accented– the syllable with the accent, also called the tone syllable. The accented syllable has more emphasis, e.g. the second syllable of to/**má**/to.

(b) Pretonic– the syllable before the accented syllable.

(c) Distant– any syllable farther before the accent than the pretonic.
(The syllable right before the pretonic may be called propretonic.)

(d) Post-tonic– A syllable may also follow the accented syllable.

2.5   The 7 Syllable Principles.

The seven syllable principles describe Hebrew syllables in terms of the above characteristics. These principles are the language's underlying structure. Other rules will also apply, like special consonant behaviors, but syllable structure is the base.

We start at the end. Hebrew words are accented on the last syllable or the next to last. Most are accented on the last syllable, called *Milra* (*downwards*). The rest are accented on the next to last syllable, called *Millel* (*from above*).

2.5.₁   Accented syllables in the noun world (including adjectives and participles).

(a) **ACL**: **A**ccented noun syllables *prefer* to be **C**losed and **L**ong (like בָּר) or

(b) **AOS**: **A**ccented noun syllables *prefer* to be **O**pen and **S**hort (like מֶ) or

(c) **AQH**: **A**ccented noun syllables *prefer* to end with **Q**ametz-**H**e (like כָּה).

דָּבָר	דְּ/בָר is a classic *Milra* word accented on the last syllable.
	בָר is an *accented* (has the stress or tone),
	  closed (ends in a consonant),
	  long (*qametz* is long *ā*) syllable.

מֶלֶךְ	מֶ/לֶךְ is a classic *Millel* word, accented on the 2ⁿᵈ to last syllable.
	מֶ is an *accented* (has the stress or tone),
	  open (ends in a vowel),
	  short (*segol* is short) syllable.

מַלְכָּה	מַלְ/כָּה has a classic feminine noun ending, *qametz-he*. The *he* is a *mater lectionis*, so it isn't closed. It followed another rule to lose its original consonantal *tav*, which was replaced by the *he*.

Milra (final accented) words can be AOS; Millel words can be ACL.

שָׂדֶה	שָׂ is an uncommon *Milra* word ending in a *mater lectionis*.
	דֶה is an **accented** (has the stress or tone),
	open (ends in a vowel, not the *mater he*),
	short (segol is short) syllable, just like מֶ of מֶלֶךְ.
אֵלֶּה	אֵלֶּה is an uncommon type of *Millel* word.
	Its structure is אֶל/לֶה (note the *dagesh forte* in the לֹ).
	Like דָּבָר of דָּבָר, אֶל is **accented**, **closed**, and **long**.

The fine print. For nouns, these are the base principles. Additional rules, e.g. the weak consonants, may cause variations from these preferences. Variations from the syllable principles are not exceptions; as we shall see, they are clues to look for the other rules.

2.5.2   Pretonic Syllables in all parts of speech.

(a) **POL: Pretonic** syllables *prefer* to be **Open** and **Long** (like דָ) or

(b) **PCS: Pretonic** syllables *prefer* to be **Closed** and **Short** (like מִן).

דָּבָר דָּ / בָר	דָ is a *pretonic* (precedes the accented syllable בָר),
	open (ends in a vowel),
	long (qametz is long *ā*) syllable.
מִדְבָּר מִדְ / בָּר	מִדְ is a *pretonic* (precedes the accented syllable בָּר),
	closed (ends in a consonant with silent *shewa*),
	[note that the *dagesh lene* in בּ resulted from this stop]
	short (ḥireq is short) syllable.

The fine print. Variations, resulting from secondary rules, are clues to other issues.

2.5.3   SPP: *Shewa* in "Problem Position" in all parts of speech.

This is not a syllable. This is *the place* before the vowel of a pretonic syllable. Hebrew has a *problem* keeping vowels in the *position* before the pretonic syllable's full vowel. It typically has *shewa*, either a vocal *shewa* beginning the pretonic syllable or a silent *shewa* closing a distant syllable.

"Problem position" vocal *shewa* in a *pretonic* syllable.

דְּבָרִים דְּ / בָ / רִים	רִים is an *accented closed long* syllable, ACL.
	בָ is a *pretonic open long* syllable, POL.
	דְּ has **vocal *shewa* in problem position** in a *pretonic* syllable.

"Problem position" silent *shewa* in a *distant* syllable.

מִשְׁפָּטִים מִשְׁ / פָּ / טִים	טִים is an *accented closed long* syllable, ACL.
	פָּ is a *pretonic open long* syllable, POL.
	מִשְׁ, a *distant* syllable, has **silent *shewa* in problem position**.

The fine print. A vowel can be in this position if an additional rule(s) is also applied.

2.5.4   **PSV: A *shewa* in problem position is typically P̲receded by a S̲hort V̲owel.**

Before the pretonic syllable, the normal speaking pattern for Hebrew is to shorten vowels. But they cannot all become *shewas*, so whenever there would be two vocal *shewas* in a row, the first becomes a *ḥireq*. For example, two *shewas* distant from the accent would make an unpronounceable מְשְׁפָּטִים, so the two *shewas* in a row generate a *ḥireq*, מִשְׁפָּטִים. Some words prefer a particular vowel class and will get (or preserve) a different short vowel. In either case, the result is to alternate: *shewa*, short vowel, *shewa*, etc.

(a)   Two vocal *shewas* in a row create a short vowel in place of the first *shewa*. The vowel will normally be *ḥireq*. But some words prefer a particular vowel class, either for historical reasons or because guttural letters prefer *a*-class vowels.

(b)   If two *shewas* do appear in a row, the first is silent and the second vocal. This typically results because a prefix was added to the beginning of a word.

(c)   When you do see a long vowel in a distant syllable, it is a clue to something else at work in the language system, such as a weak consonant (more later).

2.6   **Summary of Masoretic Hebrew Syllables.**

Hebrew syllables begin with a consonant and have one full vowel.

A syllable is long or short if its full vowel is long or short.

Open syllables end in a vowel. Closed syllables end in a consonant (but not a *mater*).

The accent is usually on the last syllable (*Milra*) or second-to-last syllable (*Millel*).

2.6.1   **Memorize the seven syllable principles.** This is the heart of the chapter.

Accented *noun* syllables prefer to be ACL, AOS, or AQH.

     1. **ACL** = Accented Closed Long.

     2. **AOS** = Accented Open Short.

     3. **AQH** = Accented *Qametz-He*, i.e. הָ֫.

Pretonic syllables *for all parts of speech* prefer to be POL or PCS.

     4. **POL** = Pretonic Open Long.

     5. **PCS** = Pretonic Closed Short.

The main examples to know are:

AOS	ACL POL	ACL PCS	AQH PCS
מֶ֫לֶךְ	דָּ֫בָר	מִדְבָּ֫ר	מַלְכָּ֫ה

     6. **SPP** = *Shewa* in Problem Position. The *position* before the pretonic vowel prefers *shewa* rather than a vowel.

     7. **PSV** = Preceded by a Short Vowel. Distant syllables tend to precede SPP with a short vowel. (But silent *shewa* may precede vocal *shewa* if a prefix has been added to the beginning of a word.)

2.7 **Syllables and the "rules of thumb" for *shewa* (1.7).**

The syllable principles explain the rules of thumb for *shewa*.

(a) Silent *shewa* is *usually* preceded by a short vowel – because pretonic closed syllables take short vowels and, in front of pretonic syllables, *shewas* and short vowels alternate. But we will find some ACL syllables ending in silent *shewa*.

(b) Vocal *shewa* is *usually* preceded by a long vowel or silent *shewa* – because the long vowel is usually pretonic open long and because when there actually are two *shewas* in a row, the first is silent, the second vocal.

(c) If there are two *shewas* in a row, the first is silent, the second vocal – because, if there were two vocal *shewas* in a row, the first would become a short vowel.[2]

The pronunciation issues will clear up as you get used to the syllable principles.

2.8 **Decision making and the will of syllables:** Syllabifying and placing the accent.

So how do we use syllable principles to aid in reading? First, divide words into syllables so that every syllable begins with a consonant and has one full vowel. Then, if we know two of the three characteristics of a syllable, we can infer the third characteristic. These examples are from the world of nouns.

Hint 1) For comparing the syllable structure, start at the last syllable and see if it makes sense as the accented syllable.

Hint 2) always try *qametz*, $\Box$, as long *ā* first, since *qametz ḥaṭuph* is rare.

(a) נַעֲרְנָהָר and נַעַר. Where is the accent on these similar looking words?

Step 1, divide into syllables: הָר / נָ and עַר / נַ. (Only consonants begin syllables).

Step 2, compare to the syllable principles, starting at the end.

   For נָהָר, הָר is closed. First try *qametz* as long. Most words are accented on the last syllable, suggesting ACL (accented closed long), which in turn implies a very normal POL (pretonic open long) נָ, just like דָּבָר.

   For נַעַר, עַר is closed short, not an accented syllable type. The next to last syllable, נַ, is open short; AOS is an accented syllable type, like מֶלֶךְ.

(b) מִשְׁפָּט. What kind of *shewa* does שׁ have? What kind of dagesh is in פ?

Step 1, divide into syllables. Is it פָּ / מִשְׁ or שְׁפָּט / מִ?

   פ does not follow a full vowel. So it has *dagesh lene*. שׁ has silent *shewa* (1.6). It must be divided מִשְׁ / פָּט.

Step 2, compare to the syllable principles.

   פָּט would be a very normal ACL (accented closed long) and
   מִשְׁ would be PCS (pretonic closed short), like מִד / בָּר.

---

[2] When the two *shewas* end a word, the last cannot stay vocal, because a vocal *shewa* is insufficient to make a syllable, so they switch. The first becomes vocal and the last becomes silent.

(c) בְּהֵמָה.

Step 1, divide into syllables. It must be בְּ / הֵ / מָה (one vowel each).

Step 2, compare. מָה is AQH (accented *qametz-he*).

     בְּ is POL (pretonic open long) with vocal SPP (*shewa* in problem position).

(d) חָכְמָה.

This example introduces a problem. Is it חָכְ / מָה or חָ / כְמָה ?

     Both would be AQH (accented *qametz-he*).

     חָכְ / מָה would have a PCS (pretonic closed short) *qametz ḥaṭuph*.

     חָ / כְמָה would have a POL (pretonic open long) *qametz*.

And the answer is that either could be correct (cp. 2.10).

     חָכְ / מָה is a noun, "wisdom."

     חָ / כְמָה is a verb, "she is wise."

2.9   *Metheg.*

Sometimes a special symbol called a *metheg* is written to help identify an open syllable. The *metheg*, the small vertical stroke next to the first *qametz* in חָכְמָה tells you the structure is חָ / כְמָה. *Metheg* is most common with long vowels, particularly *qametz*. *Metheg* is not always used, so you cannot plan to simply rely on this mark.

2.10   **For future reference.**

חָכְ / מָה and חָ / כְמָה, both built on the root חכם, demonstrate classic verb and noun behaviors. The key is the 2nd root letter, which we will call R$_2$, in this case כ. Vocal *shewa* under R$_2$ with the accented syllable (כְמָה) is a classic verb behavior. Silent *shewa* under R$_2$ closing a pretonic syllable (חָכְ) is a classic noun behavior.

It is too early to learn all about nouns and verbs. But here is a snapshot of how nouns and verbs differ. (Ignore the length of accented syllables since they have suffixes.) The next chapters focus on nouns, so expect R$_2$ to be silent *shewa*.

These are nouns.		These are verbs.	
accented last syl.	R$_2$ has silent *shewa*; pretonic closed short	R$_2$ has vocal *shewa* accented last syllable	pretonic
לָה אָכְ		כְלָה אָ	open long
או חָטְ		טְאוּ חָ	open long
אָה טָמְ		מְאָה טָ	open long
(composite shewa doing a shewa's job)[3]		תִטַמְ מְאוּ → תִטַמְּאוּ	closed short
לָה נָחֲ		חֲלוּ נָ	open long
רו נָעֲ		עֲרוּ נָ	open long

---

[3] The structure calls for PCS but the gutturals prefer composite *shewa*. It does take a pretonic short vowel. But if it were followed by a begadkephat letter, it would not take *dagesh lene* due to the composite *shewa*. A composite *shewa* should be viewed simply as a *shewa*. In the structure of words it does the same job as a simple *shewa*, not that of a vowel.

2.11 Illustrations of the pretonic rules and SPP.

Following are short lists of words based on the root דבר, including nouns, verbs, participles, and infinitives. They are organized by whether their pretonic syllable is POL or PCS. The accented syllable can be ignored here, since the accent principles apply only in the noun world. *Take the time to recognize how each word conforms to the syllable principles.* As we study Hebrew, we will find additional rules at work, but these basic syllable structures are the foundation.

The accented syllable is marked only if it is not the last syllable. Sometimes a word does not have its own accent (more in ch. 3) and reacts as if the entire following word is the accented syllable. For these, we put "fw" (following word) in the spot for the accented syllable, and the last syllable of the example word will be pretonic, e.g.

דְּבָ רִים | דְּבָ is pretonic open long; דְּ is in problem position.

fw | דְּבָ רֵי | רֵי is pretonic open long; בָ is in problem position.

When there is a *dagesh forte*, the word is written normally to the left and with two consonants in the syllabification.

In all of these, the **pretonic** syllable is **open** and **long**.

דָּ בָר		
דְּ בָרִים		

דְּבָ רִים		vocal *shewa* in problem position
וְדָ בָר		

	fw רֵי	דְּבָ	silent *shewa* in problem position
הַדָּבָר →	הַדָ בָר	הַדְ	preceded by a short vowel
הַדִּבְרוֹת →	הַדְ בָרוֹת	הַדְ	

In all of these, the **pretonic** syllable is **closed** and **short**.

דִּבֶּר →	דִּבְ בֶּר	
	יַדְ בֶּר	
דִּבַּרְתִּי →	דִּבְ בַּרְ תִּי	
	נְדַבְ בֶּר נוּ	

	fw דִּבֶּר	vocal *shewa* in problem position
מִדְבָּר →	מִדְבְ בָר	
	בָּדְבְ לְ ךְ	(n.b. pretonic closed short *qametz ḥaṭuph*)
אֲדַבְּרָה →	אֲדַבְ בְּרָה	(composite *shewa* under guttural)
כְּדַבְּרָה →	כְּדַבְ בְּרָה	

מְדַבֵּר →	דַבְ בֵר	מְ	silent *shewa* in problem position
וַיְדַבֵּר →	יְדַבְ בֵר	וַ	preceded by a short vowel

2.12 Decision making and the will of syllables, part two.

Test your understanding of the syllable principles. Cover the answers; try them on your own, and then check your understanding. (They are from the noun world, so R$_2$ would have silent *shewa*.)

Divide these words into syllables.

Describe the syllables (ACL, AOS, AQH, POL, PCS) and *shewa* in problem position.

Explain *shewas* as silent or vocal. Explain each *dagesh* as *lene* or *forte*.

1. בַּעַל   בַּ / עַל
   בַּ is AOS (like מֶ of מֶלֶךְ). עַל is post-tonic (like לֶךְ of מֶלֶךְ).
   בַּ has *dagesh lene*; only *dagesh lene* can begin a word.

2. אֶבְיוֹן   אֶבְ / יוֹן
   יוֹן is accented closed long (like בָּר of מִדְבָּר).
   אֶבְ is pretonic closed short (like מִד of מִדְבָּר).
   בְ has silent *shewa* because it closes the syllable.

3. כָּבֵד   כָּ / בֵד
   בֵד is ACL (like בָּר of דְּבָר). כָּ is POL (like דְּ of דְּבָר).
   כָּ has *dagesh lene*; only *dagesh lene* can begin a word.

4. הַקּוֹל   הַקְ / קוֹל
   ק has *dagesh forte* (it is not a *begadkephat*); there are two קs.
   קוֹל is ACL (like בָּר of מִדְבָּר).
   הַק is PCS (like מִד of מִדְבָּר).

5. לְבָב   לְ / בָב.   בָב is ACL. לְ is POL.
   Both בs lack *dagesh lene* due to a preceding vowel.

6. לְבָבוֹת   לְבָ / בוֹת. בוֹת is ACL. לְבָ is POL.
   בs lack *dagesh lene* due to a preceding vowel or vocal *shewa*.
   לְ has vocal *shewa* (SPP) because silent *shewa* cannot begin a word.

7. לְבּוֹת   לְבּ / בוֹת.
   בוֹת is ACL; לְבּ is PCS.
   בּ has *dagesh forte* because it follows a vowel.

8. בַּיִת   בַּ / יִת.
   בַּ is AOS. יִת is post-tonic (like לֶךְ of מֶלֶךְ).
   בַּ has *dagesh lene*; only *dagesh lene* can begin a word.

2.13 Vocabulary.

1   אָב   *n.m.* father (1210)

2   אָדָם   *n.m.* humankind, a man, person (551*)

3   אֲדָמָה   *n.f.* ground, earth (222)

4   אָח   *n.m.* brother (629)

5   אָחוֹת   *n.f.* sister (119)

6   אִישׁ   *n.m.* man, husband, each (2199)

7   אֵם   *n.f.* mother (220)

8   אֵשׁ   *n.f/m.* fire (376)

9   אִשָּׁה   *n.f.* woman, wife (781)

10   בֵּן / בֶּן   *n.m.* son (of) (4941)

11   בַּת   *n.f.* daughter (of) (587)

12   גּוֹי   *n.m.* nation, people (560)

13   כֹּל   *n.m.* all, every, whole, any (5415)

14   עִיר   *n.f.* city (1088)

15   עָפָר   *n.m.* dust, dry earth (110)

16   קָהָל   *n.m.* assembly, company, congregation (123)

17   שֵׁבֶט   *n.m.* rod, tribe, staff, scepter (190)

18   שָׁנָה   *n.f.* year (878)

Prefixed words. These attach to the front of the next word.

19   הַ־ / הָ   *art.* the (24,058-), e.g. *he+pataḥ+dagesh* as in הַשָּׁנָה, *the year,* or before gutturals it may be *he+qametz* as in הָאֵשׁ, *the fire.*[4]

20   וְ / וּ / וָ   *cj.* and (50,524), e.g. וְשָׁנָה, *and* a year.

21   בְּ   *prp.* in, with, by, at, among, into, when (15,559), e.g. בְּשָׁנָה, *in* a year.

22   כְּ   *prp.* like, as, according to, when (3053), e.g. כְּאֵשׁ, *like* a fire.

23   לְ   *prp.* to, for, regarding, belonging to (20,321), e.g. לְאִשָּׁה, *for* a wife.

art. = article	*n.m.* = noun masculine
cj. = conjunction	*n.f.* = noun feminine
prp. = preposition	*n.f/m.* = noun (may be masculine or feminine)

---

[4] Further variations on the vowel of the article are discussed in 5.4.1.

2.14   Learning Activities on the CD.

The first thing to 'do is to memorize the syllable principles in 2.6.1 so that you can easily recognize these abbreviations:

for nouns – ACL, AOS, AQH;

for all – POL, PCS, SPP, PSV.

Then go to the CD for practice and exercises. The learning activities in this chapter include syllabifying words and practice reading, especially with ch. 2 vocabulary.

1   Syllabification practice.

When a Hebrew word appears, try to determine where it divides into syllables and how the syllables conform to the syllable principles. Then click to see the answers. Syllables will be labeled with the abbreviations mentioned above and in 2.6.1. Remember to account for *dagesh forte* and double the letter appropriately. Do these to practice and gain confidence for doing the exercises.

The words appear on a scroll background. At the top are abbreviations of the syllable principles (ACL, AOS, AQH, POL, PCS, SPP, PCS) and three feather quills, all of which are dragable. Click on a quill and while holding the button down drag it to where the word should be divided into syllables. If a letter has a *dagesh forte*, place the quill right on the *dagesh* to help remember the letter is doubled and is in two different syllables. Then select and drag the syllable abbreviations to label the syllables. The answer will appear below for comparison. All the labels and quills will be reset when you go to the next practice item.

2   Syllabification Exercise.

Divide the words into syllables and label them with the abbreviations for the accent principles. The exercise is in the workbook. Answers are available in a separate document on the CD.

3   Learn ch. 2 vocabulary.

4   Practice Readings: Proper nouns.

Practice reading proper nouns. There are several lists of names. In each case you will first review the names in English. Then click to see the names in Hebrew and click again to see the answer.

5   Practice Readings: Genesis names and kinship terms.

These readings use proper names from Genesis plus the personal and kinship terms from ch. 2 vocabulary, e.g. "Isaac is a father."

6   Practice Readings: Vocabulary.

Practice reading ch. 2 vocabulary that have been inserted into English sentences. The answer gives the entire sentence in English with an appropriate gloss for the Hebrew vocabulary item.

chapter three

Nouns Part One:
Gender, Number, State

3.1   Focus.

In this chapter you are to learn:

the meanings of gender, number, and state,

the connecting symbol *maqqef*, ־, e.g. in דְּבַר־מֶלֶךְ

the ten noun endings,

that nouns can be formed with the prefixes מ, ת, and א, and

the assimilation of *nun*.

Perhaps the most common definition of nouns is a list: "a noun is a person, place, thing, or idea." All languages use nouns but may have different categories for spelling them. Hebrew nouns are similar to, but not the same as, English nouns.

Hebrew has three numbers (singular, dual, and plural), two genders (masculine and feminine) and two states (absolute and construct) which are indicated by a grand total of only ten noun endings. English has number and, to a limited degree, also has gender. But there is no direct comparison for *state* in English.

Think of noun endings as including accent or lack of accent. The rest of the word responds by changing vowel length according to the syllable principles.

3.2   Roots, lexemes, and morphemes; the anatomy of Hebrew words.

Hebrew words are generally built around three consonants, called radicals or root letters. We will use R_1, R_2 and R_3 to refer to the 1st, 2nd, and 3rd root letters. Pretend that the word *cover* was a Hebrew root כבר, *KBR*. We could then build the following words: *kāḇār* "a cover"; *kāḇar* "he covered"; *kāḇūr* a "covered" thing; *tiḵbōr* "she will cover"; *kōḇēr* "covering." In each case you see the root letters *KBR*. Compare שָׁפַט *to judge*, מִשְׁפָּט *law or custom*, and שׁוֹפֵט *a judge*. In each case you see the root letters שׁפט. While English may change the vowels in a word, like s*i*ng, s*a*ng, and s*u*ng, most English morphemes are added to the end of a word or lexeme, like jump*ing*, jump*s*, jump*ed*. (Morphemes are the parts like *–ing* that can be transferred to other words; lexemes are items like *jump*.) Hebrew regularly changes the inside vowels, either because of the morpheme or due to the syllable principles.

For certain practical reasons, many Hebrew dictionaries arrange their entries according to the root letters. But it may not feel practical at first to look for a word under a heading that is different from its spelling in a text (like looking up מִשְׁפָּט under שׁפט). To determine a word's root you must be able to separate it from prefixes or suffixes or infixes. As we look at adding morphemes to Hebrew roots, be thinking also about how to subtract them from words in order to find the root.

3.3   The three characteristics of Hebrew nouns: gender, number, and state.

3.3.1   Gender.

(a) **The digest version.** English has three genders, *he*, *she,* and *it*, or masculine, feminine, and neuter. Hebrew has only masculine and feminine, there is no *it*. In Hebrew a day is *he*; a year is *she*.

(b) **The extended version.** Gender is a category of grammar. The gender of a noun is determined by what pronoun can replace it. Except for personal nouns, like father or mother, gender is mostly a distant memory in English, but consider the word *ship*. "*She* is a beauty" may refer to the U.S.S. Enterprise because in English *ship* is a feminine noun (though in Russian, for example, *ship* is a masculine noun). Hebrew does not have the neuter category *it*. So all nouns, whether personal or impersonal, are referred to as *he* or *she* in Hebrew. But we will translate impersonal nouns as *it*. In linguistic terms, masculine and feminine do not mean male and female, they are merely *marked* (usu. fem.) or *unmarked* (usu. masc.). For example, feminine noun forms in Hebrew are sometimes used for abstract concepts.

There are two different sets of noun endings. Most masculine nouns use one set and most feminine nouns use the other set. Some, however, take their endings from what seems to us to be the "wrong" set and are called irregular. Noun gender is also important to other parts of speech. For example, an adjective that describes a noun will be spelled in the same gender as the noun.

3.3.2   Number.

(a) **The digest version**. English has two numbers: singular and plural. Hebrew has three numbers: singular, dual, and plural. Dual is used for natural pairs.

(b) **The extended version**. When we think of numbers we tend to think of countable objects. *Singular* is one; *plural* is more than one. But the grammatical category of number is more complex. English and Hebrew both have *collectives*, singular forms referring to something with many members, e.g. a *crowd*, or a *people*. Hebrew also has *composites*, plural forms referring to one thing with many components. The plural form פָּנִים means *face*. Plural spellings are sometimes used for abstract concepts, e.g. כִּפֻּרִים means atonement. At this point, just expand your thinking of grammatical number beyond countable objects.

3.3.3 State.

Hebrew differs from English in the grammatical category of state. Hebrew has two states: **absolute and construct**. We may view the absolute state as "normal." The construct state is a relationship, in that a construct noun is related to the following word. That relationship can often be translated with *of*. For example, in *the word of the Lord*, *word* is in construct with *the Lord*, which is in the absolute state. The meaning of *word* is narrowed down, or determined, by *the Lord*, i.e. the word of the Lord vs. the word of the *servant*. A common use is possessive, e.g. *the harp of David* or *David's harp*.

Being in the construct state does not limit the role a noun can perform. *Word* would be in the absolute state and be the verb's subject in "the *word* is favorable." *Word* would still be the subject, but be in the construct state, in "the *word of* the Lord is favorable." Construct nouns can be strung together. In *the Lord of all of the earth*, *Lord* is in construct with *all*; and *all* is in construct with *earth*.

Besides being connected to the next word in meaning, construct nouns (of the types covered in this chapter) are also connected in pronunciation. The construct nouns do not have an accent of their own. So their last syllable is pretonic as if the entire following word were the accented syllable.

The noun in the construct state is called either the construct noun, or by the Latin, *nomen regens*. The following word or suffix that modifies it is called either the *nomen rectum* or the genitive noun.

3.3.4 The Genitive *Case?*!

English still has cases in its pronouns, that is, different forms for different functions in a sentence, e.g. *we*, *us*, *our*. Once upon a time, Hebrew had different case endings for its nouns. We call those cases nominative, accusative, and genitive. Biblical Hebrew does not have case endings but, like English, relies on word order.

The noun modifying a construct noun used to be in the genitive case. It is still often called "the genitive noun," since this easier to say than "the noun modifying the construct noun" and it avoids using Latin terms. Also many publications use the terminology of cases. *Nominative* refers to the subject of a verb. *Genitive* refers to the object of a preposition (ch. 5) or the word modifying a construct noun. *Accusative* refers to almost everything else, including the object of a verb; accusatives are adverbial.

3.4 *Maqqef⁻* a connecting symbol, e.g. דְּבַר־מֶלֶךְ.

A *maqqef*, a raised horizontal line, indicates that two words are pronounced closely together. It may appear between a verb and a preposition, or a particle and a verb, and in other situations. **It may or may not appear after construct nouns.**

3.5   The ten noun endings.

The charts show construct forms with a *maqqef* and the accent on the following word (e.g. fw ־דְּבַר). The symbol Ø represents that there is no ending.

Masculine.

Singular	absolute	Ø ֫	דָּבָר	word
	construct	fw־Ø	fw־דְּבַר	word of
Plural	absolute	◌ִים	דְּבָרִים	words
	construct	fw־◌ֵי	fw־דִּבְרֵי	words of

Feminine.

Singular	absolute	◌ָה / ◌ֶת	מַלְכָּה	queen
	construct	fw־◌ַת	fw־מַלְכַּת	queen of
Plural	absolute	◌וֹת	מְלָכוֹת	queens
	construct	fw־◌וֹת	fw־מַלְכוֹת	queens of

Dual endings on both masculine and feminine nouns.

absolute	◌ַיִם	יָדַיִם	(two) hands
construct	fw־◌ֵי	fw־יְדֵי	(two) hands of

3.6   The noun endings and the syllable principles.

The syllable principles explain the vowel changes when the noun endings are added. This especially helps distinguish construct and absolute forms.

3.6.1 **Masculine nouns** of the *milra*, or דָּבָר-type.

It will be easiest to understand the vowel changes to know that the underlying historical form was *דַבַּר. So when you see a *qametz*, it is a lengthened *patah*; when you see a *shewa*, it is a shortened *patah* (not a shortened *qametz*).

דָּבָר masc. sg. ab.	The ending is Ø (nothing), but the last syllable is accented. בָר is accented closed long (ACL). דָּ is pretonic open long (POL).
fw־דְּבַר masc. sg. cs.	The ending is Ø, but the accent is on the following word. דְבַר is pretonic closed short (PCS). דְ takes *shewa* in problem position (SPP).
דְּבָרִים masc. pl. ab.	The ending ◌ִים has the accent and needs a consonant. רִים is accented closed long (ACL). דְבָ is pretonic open long (POL). דְ takes *shewa* in problem position (SPP).
fw־דִּבְרֵי masc. pl. cs.	The ending ◌ֵי needs a consonant and is pretonic. רֵי is pretonic open long (POL). דְבְ בְ takes *shewa* in problem position (SPP). דִ Two vocal *shewas* in a row generate a *hireq* (PSV).

3.6.2 Feminine nouns.

Feminine forms involve a couple more rules. First the loss of final ת.[1] Most feminine forms were and are marked with *tav*, but it has usually dropped away in the singular absolute form. A *he* is written as a *mater*, leaving הָ. This AQH syllable is a clue that it is feminine. (Some feminine singular absolute forms do end with ת, e.g. דַּעַת, מִשְׁמֶרֶת, מַמְלָכוּת, and חַטָּאת. You distinguish their state by vowel changes or by context.)

The next rule is that morphological interests can override the syllable principles. The feminine plural morpheme is וֹת whether accented or not. In the construct it is pretonic closed yet still long. You must look to the preceding syllable to distinguish the absolute and construct states (see 3.7.2).

The underlying form of the word is *מַלְכַּת, which survives in the sg. cs.

מַלְכָּה fem. sg. ab.	כָּה מַלְ	AQH (accented *qametz-he*, explained above). is pretonic closed short (PCS).
fw מַלְכַּת־ fem. sg. cs.	כַּת מַלְ מַ	is pretonic closed short (PCS). לְ has *shewa* in problem position (SPP). מַ prefers its original *patah* (PSV).
מַלְכוֹת fem. pl. ab.	כוֹת מָלְ מַ	is accented closed long (ACL). is pretonic open long (POL). מַ has *shewa* in problem position (SPP). (מַלְ could have worked but the common דְּבָרִים pattern is imposed.)
fw מַלְכוֹת־ fem. pl. cs.	כוֹת מַלְ מַ	is pretonic closed, but the fem. pl. morpheme is long. לְ has *shewa* in problem position (SPP). מַ prefers its original *patah* (PSV).

N.B. The feminine plural may be written without *vav*, מַלְכֹת or מְלָכֹת.

3.7 Distinguishing State when the ab. and cs. forms have the same ending.

To distinguish the state of masc. singulars and of fem. plurals, apply the syllable principles. Watch these closely: POL, PCS, SPP, because *maqqef* is not always used. The vowel class may vary but the same syllable principles apply.

3.7.1 Masculine Singular ab. and cs. Compare these forms with no ending.

A-class

דָּבָר is ab.   בָר is accented closed long. דָּ is pretonic open long.

דְּבַר is cs.   דְּבַר־ is pretonic closed short, so it is construct.

דְּ has *shewa* in problem position.

---

[1] New Englanders may drop final *r*, as in "sneak*uhs*" instead of sneakers (tennis shoes). Many people drop certain final *d*'s, e.g. "life-size" instead of "life-size*d*," or "first come, first serve" instead of "first come, first serve*d*." The former should mean that the first to arrive do the serving.

I-class

שָׂדֶה is ab.   דֶה is accented open short (like מֶ of מֶלֶךְ; the ה is a *mater*).

שָׂ is pretonic open long.

שְׂדֵה is cs.   שְׂדֵה־ is pretonic open long (like דְ of דְּבַר; ה is a *mater*).

שְׂ has *shewa* in problem position.

U-class

כֹּל is ab.   כֹּל is accented closed long (like בַר of דְּבַר).

כָּל is cs.   כָּל־ is pretonic closed short (like דְּבַר of דְּבַר־).

For some masc. sg. nouns (with PCS syllables), you must focus on R₂ and R₃.

מִדְבָּר is ab.   בָּר is **accented closed long**. מִדְ is pretonic closed short.

מִדְבַּר is cs.   בַּר־ is **closed short** so it is **pretonic** and it is **construct**.

מִדְ has *shewa* in problem position, preceded by a short *ḥireq*.

The key clue for these is whether their final syllable follows the accent rules or the pretonic rules.

3.7.2 Feminine Plural ab. and cs., both ending in וֹת or ֹת.

The feminine plural ending is defined by its long *o* vowel, so it does not reduce in construct when it is pretonic and closed. The preceding syllable has the clue; if open long, it is absolute; but a *shewa* results from problem position when in construct.

מְלָכוֹת is ab.   כוֹת is accented closed long.

מְלָ is open long, so it is pretonic and it is absolute.

מַלְכוֹת is cs.   כוֹת is pretonic closed; the long morpheme has priority.

The key clue: לְ **has *shewa*, so it is in problem position and is construct.**

Compare also:

מִשְׁפָּחוֹת is ab.   פָּ is pretonic open long, so it is absolute.

מִשְׁפְּחוֹת is cs.   פְּ has *shewa* so it is problem position and it is construct.[2]

Some fem. pl. words have a pretonic closed short syllable, so their absolute and construct forms are identical and you must **judge based on context.**

מִצְוֹת is ab.   וֹת (*vōt* with consonantal *vav*)[3] is accented closed long.

מִצְ is **pretonic closed short**.

מִצְוֹת is cs.   וֹת is pretonic closed but stays long (morpheme priority).

מִצְ has *shewa* **in problem position**, preceded by a short *ḥireq*.[4]

---

[2] The מ is a prefix which stays with R₁ as a unit, מִשְׁ. Two *shewas* in a row often mean there is a prefix.

[3] The ו is consonantal in מִצְוֹת. Since there is a *shewa* under the צ, closing the syllable מִצְ, the ו cannot be a *ḥolem-vav*; it must be consonantal because only consonants can begin syllables.

[4] Compare also מַעֲלָה. Its structure is like מִצְוָה but the guttural takes a composite *shewa*. Its plural absolute and construct forms look alike מַעֲלוֹת.

3.7.3   Lexical Interests – long vowels as part of the word.

Some words have a vested interest in a long vowel as well as the radicals. It resists reduction, like the morpheme וֹת. Most often it is an *u*-class or *i*-class vowel written with ו or י in its lexical form: ◌וֹ, ◌וּ, or ◌ִי. To distinguish their absolute and construct forms, focus on whether R₁ has pretonic or distant syllable characteristics.

אָדוֹן is ab.   אָ is **open long**, so it is **pretonic** and therefore absolute.

אֲדוֹן is cs.   אֲ has *shewa,* so it is **problem position**, therefore construct.
(דוֹן is pretonic closed but still long due to its lexical nature.)

קָצִיר is ab.   קָ is **pretonic open long**, therefore absolute.

קְצִיר is cs.   קְ has *shewa* **in problem position**, therefore construct.
(צִיר is pretonic closed yet long due to its lexical nature.)

3.8   Dual.

Masculine and feminine nouns use the same dual endings. The dual absolute has a *millel* accent ◌ַ֫יִם; the dual construct is pretonic open long, fw◌ֵ֫י, like the masculine plural construct. The dual is used for two of something, most commonly things naturally occurring in pairs but also two units of measurement.

sg. ab.	dual ab.	translation	dual cs.	translation
יָד	יָדַ֫יִם	a pair of hands	fwיְדֵ֫י	hands of
רֶ֫גֶל	רַגְלַ֫יִם	a pair of feet	fwרַגְלֵ֫י	feet of
כָּנָף	כְּנָפַ֫יִם	a pair of wings		
יוֹם	יוֹמַ֫יִם	two days		
שָׁנָה	שְׁנָתַ֫יִם	two years		

The dual of a word for something occurring in pairs may be used as the plural. Six כְּנָפַ֫יִם is six wings not six pairs of (= 12) wings.

Some words without a dual sense are spelled with dual endings, e.g.:

מַ֫יִם "water,"   שָׁמַ֫יִם "heaven(s),"   מִצְרַ֫יִם "Egypt,"   צָהֳרַ֫יִם "noon."

3.9   Gender confusion and irregular plurals.

Generally one set of endings is applied to masculine nouns and the other to feminine nouns, as in דָּבָר and מַלְכָּה. But some words switch; they are irregular. Some feminine nouns lack הָ◌ or ת in the singular; they are unmarked (have ø). Masculine nouns ending in הָ◌, like שָׂדֶה and a few others, use וֹת◌ for the plural.

pl. ab.	sg. ab.		pl. ab.	sg. ab.	
יָדוֹת	יָד	fem.	שָׂדוֹת	שָׂדֶה	masc.
שָׁנִים	שָׁנָה	fem.	מַרְאוֹת	מַרְאֶה	masc.
עָרִים	עִיר	fem.	אָבוֹת	אָב	masc.

So the noun endings are helpful for determining gender but you need to rely on the dictionary to be sure. Learn the gender of the vocabulary for each chapter.

3.10   Determining roots.

Some Hebrew dictionaries list their nouns by their singular absolute form, called **the lexical form**, others list nouns by root (verbs are always listed by root). That is, some dictionaries would list מִשְׁפָּט in its lexical form under the מs; other dictionaries list מִשְׁפָּט under the root letters שׁפט, *to judge*, along with other nouns from the same root. For most of the examples in this chapter, determining a word's root is as simple as removing the ending and vowels. Alas, but it is not always so easy!

As מִשְׁפָּט shows, sometimes a prefix has been added to the beginning. At other times a נ can no longer be seen due to assimilation (1.8.6). Chapter 4 includes other possibilities. Here we visit prefixes and *nun*.

3.10.1   Prefixes: א, מ, and ת.

Hebrew can make nouns by adding a prefix, most commonly מ, but also ת or א. The prefix tends to form a syllable with R₁. The prefix + R₁ unit stays together even before vocal *shewa*, e.g. fwמִשְׁפְּטֵי. Normally *shewas* and short vowels alternate in distant syllables, but the prefix + R₁ unit is an extra feature. Seeing two *shewas* in a row is often a clue that a prefix has been added to the root. Having learned the syllable principles trains you to spot variations which are to be understood as clues that something else has also happened (remember: clues, not "exceptions").

pl. cs.	pl. ab.	sg. cs.	sg. ab.	root	gender
fwמִשְׁפְּטֵי	מִשְׁפָּטִים	fwמִשְׁפַּט	מִשְׁפָּט	שׁפט	masc.
fwמִשְׁפְּחוֹת	מִשְׁפָּחוֹת	⁵fwמִשְׁפַּחַת	מִשְׁפָּחָה	שׁפח	fem.
fwמִצְוֺת	מִצְוֺת	fwמִצְוַת	מִצְוָה	צוה	fem.

3.10.2   The Assimilation of *Nun*.

When נ ends a syllable inside of a word (*nun* over a silent *shewa*, נְ) it turns into a copy of the next consonant and is then written as a *dagesh forte* in that letter. This can happen in English: in + mobile = immobile.

(a) Prefix and R₁ = נ.

Hebrew builds the noun *gift* from the root נתן, *to give*, with a prefixed מ.

מַנְתָּן ← נתן + מ.

The נ, now over silent *shewa*, assimilates into the ת as a *dagesh forte*.

מַנְתָּן ← מַתְּתָן ← מַתָּן.

Compare:

fwמַטּוֹת	מַטּוֹת	fwמַטֵּה	מַטֶּה	נטה	masc.
fwמַטּוֹת	מַטּוֹת	fwמַטַּת	מַטָּה	נטה	fem.

---

⁵ This form added an accent in the construct form; it is a segolate pattern, cf. 4.5.1.

(b) **R₂ = נ.**

אִשָּׁה, *woman*, looks as though it is related to אִישׁ, but it is actually related to אֱנוֹשׁ, *man*, from the root, אנשׁ. The *nun* assimilated: אַנְשָׁה ← אִשְׁשָׁה ← אִשָּׁה.

Sometimes the *dagesh forte* cannot survive. בַּת *daughter* comes from בנת. *Nun* assimilates into *tav* but the *tav* cannot hold the *dagesh forte* because no vowel follows it. Still, the assimilated *nun* protects the short vowel, hence בַּת. (It is only בָּת_{AT} with a pausal accent.) Being accented closed *short* and having only two letters clues you in that something extra has happened. (Dictionaries may list בַּת under בַּת or בֵּן.)

Knowing the root helps you understand the different forms of these two common feminine nouns. But in a practical sense, you need to just learn these irregular forms.

pl. cs.	pl. ab.	sg. cs.	sg. ab.	root
fw‑בְּנוֹת	בָּנוֹת	fw‑בַּת	בַּת	בנת
fw‑נְשֵׁי	נָשִׁים	fw‑אֵשֶׁת	אִשָּׁה	אנשׁ

Dagesh forte **can signal an assimilated *nun* or the same letter doubled.**

A short vowel in an accented closed syllable can signal a lost root letter.

3.11 Summary.

Here again are the noun endings, the main point of the chapter.

Dual both	fem. pl.	fem. sg.	masc. pl.	masc. si.	
◌ַ֫יִם	◌וֹת	◌ָה / ◌ַת	◌ִ֫ים	Ø	absolute
fw‑◌ַ֫י	fw‑◌וֹת	fw‑◌ַת	fw‑◌ֵ֫י	fw‑Ø	construct

On our sample words they look like this:

יָדַ֫יִם	מַלְכוֹת	מַלְכָּה	דְּבָרִים	דָּבָר	absolute
fw‑יְדֵי	fw‑מַלְכוֹת	fw‑מַלְכַּת	fw‑דִּבְרֵי	fw‑דְּבַר	construct

Notes.

Some nouns take their singular and plural endings from different lists.

Feminine singular words may use ◌ַת, ◌ָה, or Ø.

Feminine plurals may be written defectively ◌ֹת instead of ◌וֹת.

Construct nouns may or may not have *maqqef*. *Maqqef* does not equal *construct*.

Without *maqqef* or distinct endings, the construct can usually be recognized by observing the syllable principles. Sometimes you must rely on context.

Morphological interests, e.g. ◌וֹת, or lexical interests, e.g. אָדוֹן, may override the syllable principles by maintaining a long vowel.

If the lexical form of a noun or adjective includes ◌וֹ, ◌וּ, ◌ִי, or ◌ֵי,[6] they are likely to always stay long, but may be written defectively, ◌ֹ, ◌ֻ, ◌ִ, or ◌ֵ.

---

[6] There are several historical reasons why many *ḥolem vavs* stay long. Some grammars call these historically long vowels; others call them unchangeably long (although they can change).

3.12   Vocabulary.

1	אֹזֶן	*n.f.* ear (188)
2	1 אַף	*cj.* also, even, how much more/less (133)
3	2 אַף	*n.m.* nose, anger (277)
4	אֵת / אֶת־	*prt.* (an untranslatable particle often indicating the direct object, i.e. what receives the verb's action) (10987)
5	אַתְּ	*prn.* you (fem. sg.) (67)
6	אַתָּה	*prn.* you (masc. sg.) (749)
7	אַתֶּם	*prn.* you (masc. pl.) (283)
8	אַתֵּנָה	*prn.* you (fem. pl.) (4)
9	הֵם	*prn.* they (mascc. pl.) (565)
10	הֵנָּה	*prn.* they (fem. pl.) (31*)
11	זֹאת	*prn.* this (fem. sg.) (605) (pl. = אֵלֶּה)
12	זֶה	*prn.* this (masc. sg.) (1178) (pl. = אֵלֶּה)
13	יָד	*n.f.* hand, power (1627)
14	יָמִין	*n.f.* right (hand), south (141)
15	כָּנָף	*n.f.* wing, skirt, corner (111)
16	כַּף	*n.f.* palm, sole, hollow, pan (195)
17	לֵבָב / לֵב	*n.m.* mind/heart, will (854*)
18	לָשׁוֹן	*n.m/f.* tongue, language (117)
19	עַיִן	*n.f.* eye, appearance, spring (900)
20	פֶּה	*n.m.* mouth (498) (*construct* פִּי)
21	פָּנֶה / פָּנִים	*n.m/f.* face (2126) (always plural)
22	פַּעַם	*n.f.* step, pace, once, occasion (118)
23	רֶגֶל	*n.f.* foot (251)
24	וֹ	*suffix* his, him, e.g. לְשׁוֹנוֹ his tongue, אַפּוֹ his anger, לוֹ to him

The suffixed pronoun וֹ attaches to the end of the word it describes. It attaches to the construct form of a noun. The suffixes do not follow accent rules but the noun will still follow the syllable principles.

You learned the other personal pronouns in ch. 1. Here is the full list.

1cs	אֲנִי	I		1cp	אֲנַחְנוּ	we
2ms	אַתָּה	you		2mp	אַתֶּם	you
2fs	אַתְּ	you		2fp	אַתֵּנָה	you
3ms	הוּא	he		3mp	הֵם	they
3fs	הִיא	she		3fp	הֵנָּה	they

You need to be able to write the pronoun forms from memory. They will be the basis for learning pronominal suffixes and verb endings in chs. 6, 10, and 15.

3.13   Learning Activities on the CD.

First memorize the noun endings (3.5). Second, be sure you understand how the noun endings and syllable principles interact (3.6). Some learners may do best to begin by copying out the endings; others may want to begin with the practice parsing.

1   Grammar Illustration: noun forms.

The ten noun endings are attached to דבר, מלכה, and יד, and the syllable principles are applied. Watch the illustrations with your book open to 3.5–6.

2   Copying Exercise.

In the workbook, copy the paradigms for דָּבָר, מַלְכָּה, and יָד, noting the accent positions and syllable structures.

3   Practice Parsing.

Practice recognizing the noun endings. Try to parse (identify gender, number, state, and lexical form of) the nouns that appear, then click for the answers. The nouns are from chs. 1–2 vocabulary; they include forms with the 3ms pronominal suffix (from ch. 3 vocabulary). The random button gives variety while the up and down buttons allow you to compare other forms of the same word. There are 142 entries. Remember, this is practice. Do enough to be confident of your recognition of the endings. Then go to the exercises and prove how well you have learned.

If you select that the word has a 3ms suffix, the entry for state will automatically become "cs" for construct state. Similarly any entry in the the suffix field will be erased if you select "ab" for absolute state.

4   Review words with irregular endings.

Review the chart in your workbook of your vocabulary words which have irregular spellings (especially irregular plurals). You may want to refer to this chart when doing your practice readings or exercises.

5   Practice Readings.

Short phrases and sentences made of vocabulary words plus personal names from Genesis and a few other proper nouns. You will need to decipher the names based on sound. But take note that מִצְרַיִם is Egypt. Select proper nouns (that have not already appeared in the learning exercises) are marked by a double asterisk **.

6   Translation Exercise.

Translate Hebrew phrases (like those in the practice readings) as well as Bible verses. Vocabulary helps are provided, but you need to know the vocabulary from chs. 1–2 and must figure out proper nouns or guess by transliterating.

7   Parsing Exercise.

Parse Hebrew nouns which appear in the translation exercise.

8   Learn ch. 3 vocabulary.

chapter four

Nouns Part Two:
More Noun Patterns

4.1   Focus.

In this chapter you are to learn:

no more noun endings,

   the **geminate** and **segolate** noun patterns, and

   the peculiar behaviors of the "weak" letters נ, ו, י, and gutturals,

       in order to parse nouns and determine their roots.

Certain noun patterns and "weak" consonants produce differences from the patterns of דָּבָר and מַלְכָּה. When the syllable principles put the "weak" consonants in certain positions, their peculiar behaviors are triggered. The results may differ from the syllable principles. To figure out the root, we ask what we must "undo" to restore the syllable principles. First read the summary in 4.8.1 for the core of what to get from the chapter. Each topic has three parts: **what?**, **why?**, and **examples**. Focus on **what** happens. The "**why**" explains the what; the **examples** illustrate it.

4.2   Weak letters overview (cf. 1.8).

In the following discussions, R_1 = G means the 1st radical is a guttural, R_2 = ו/י means the 2nd radical is *vav* or *yod*, R_3 = נ means the 3rd radical is a *nun*, etc.

(a) **Nun**. *Nun* closing a syllable inside of a word assimilates as a *dagesh forte*.

(b) ו **and** י. **They drop out or become vowels**, i.e. contract into diphthongs. Original unaccented ַו → וֹ (*aw* → *ô*). Original unaccented ַי → יֵ (*ay* → *ê*).

(c) **Gutturals and** ר. *Dagesh* **Problem:** refusing to take *dagesh forte*.
   Solution 1: Compensatory lengthening. For א, ע, and ר, the preceding vowel
       usually lengthens (e.g. ַ to ָ, ִ to ֵ).
   Solution 2: Semi-doubling (or virtual doubling). For ה and ח, we treat them as
       if doubled to keep the vowel short. (It does not really double but may be
       viewed as partially doubling.)

(d) **Gutturals.** *Shewa* **Problem:** rejecting vocal (and sometimes silent) *shewa*.
   Solution: They take composite *shewa*, ֲ, ֱ, or ֳ.

37

4.3   *Nun* **assimilation.** אַף **from** אנף**.**

(a) **What?**   When you only see two radicals, especially as an accented closed short syllable, the missing root letter may be an assimilated *nun*.

(b) **Why?**   *Nun*, closing a syllable within a word, assimilates into the next letter as a *dagesh forte*, e.g. אַנְפִּים ← אַפִּים. Without an ending there is no vowel after the פ, so the *dagesh* drops out, e.g. אַף, but its influence is felt in keeping the short vowel. (In older days, R_3 had a case ending vowel which maintained the doubling.)

(c) **Examples:** $R_2 = $ נ.   Prefix plus $R_1 = $ נ.

Word	What happened	Root	Word	What happened	Root
אִשָּׁה	אַנְשָׁה ← אַשְׁשָׁה ←	אנש	מַתָּן	מַנְתָּן ← מַתְּתָן ←	נתן
בַּת	בַּנְת ← בַּתְּת ←	בנת	מִטָּה	מַנְטֶה ← מַטְּטֶה ←	נטה
אַף	אַנְף ← אַפְּף ←	אנף			

N.B. Always be suspicious of an initial מ, ת, or א, as possibly a prefix.

4.4   **Geminates. $R_2 = R_3$ with no vowel between.** כַּף **from** כפף**.**

The 2nd and 3rd root letters of a geminate are the same letter, so R_2 becomes *dagesh forte*. R_1 and R_2 form a syllable package and prefer a particular vowel class.

(a) **What?**   When you only see two radicals, especially as an accented closed short syllable, finding the root may mean doubling the last radical: e.g. כַּף, from כפף.

(b) **Why?**   Only a following vowel can keep a letter doubled. Two consonants ending a word cannot be pronounced, e.g. ḥuqq rather than ḥuq. So with an ending you see *dagesh forte*, but in the singular forms with no ending, the *dagesh* drops out. (In older days, R_3 had a case ending, keeping it doubled.)

N.B. $R_2 = $ נ creates the same situation because assimilation creates a geminate (doubled) pattern. Geminates are far more common than roots with $R_2 = $ נ, so while restoring a *nun* may be the answer to finding the root, first try a geminate root.

(c) **Examples:** Here are basic examples of the absolute forms. Observe the loss of the doubled radical so that you can be prepared to add it back in to the root.

Word	What happened	Root	Word	What happened	Root	
כַּף , כַּף	כַּפְף ←	כפף	עַם, עָם	עַמְם ←	עמם	sg
כַּפּוֹת	כַּפְפוֹת ←		עַמִּים	עַמְמִים ←		pl
עֵת	עִתְת ←	עתת	צֵל	צְלְל ←	צלל	sg
עִתִּים	עִתְתִים ←		צְלָלִים	צְלְלִים ←		pl
חֹק	חָקְק ←	חקק	תֹּם	תָּמְם ←	תמם	sg
חֻקִּים	חָקְקִים ←		—	—		pl

4.4.1 Geminate vowel length and the lexical form.

(a) **What?** When looking for the lexical form of a geminate in the dictionary, focus on the vowel class; do not get hung up on the particular vowel.

(b) **Why?** In the lexical form, *i*-class and *u*-class geminates may have a long vowel, but with a plural ending or pronominal suffix, geminates have a short vowel in the $R_1 + R_2$ unit. It is PCS, e.g. חֻקִּים = קִים / חֻק, or has SPP preceded by its short vowel, e.g. חֻקִּי = fw‾קִי / חֻק. (Feminine geminates do not end in הָ.)

(c) **Examples:**

suffix	pl. cs.	pl. ab.	sg. ab. **lexical form**	root
עִתּוֹ	fw‾עִתֵּי	עִתִּים	עֵת	עתת
חֻקּוֹ	fw‾חֻקֵּי	חֻקִּים	חֹק	חקק
כַּפּוֹ	fw‾כַּפּוֹת	כַּפּוֹת	כַּף	כפף

4.4.2 Geminate vowel length in singular forms.

(a) **What?** Singular absolute and construct forms of geminates may be the same, requiring you to judge by context.

(b) **Why?** While there is no *dagesh*, its effect survives in the ab. forms of some *a*-class geminates by keeping a short vowel, כַּף, unless there is a pausal accent, כָּף. But many singular absolute *a*-class geminates are regularly long. Dictionaries tend to list all *a*-class geminates with a short vowel in the singular absolute, but in actual texts it is not so, e.g. they list עַם, יַ, חַג, and גַּן but you find עָם, יָם, חָג, and גָּן.

The *i*-class and *u*-class words are accented closed long in the absolute and usually pretonic closed short in the construct. But sometimes their construct forms take an accent so we find a long vowel, e.g. fw‾עֹז.

(c) **Examples:**

sg. cs.	sg. ab.	root	sg. cs.	sg. ab.	root
fw‾כַּף	כָּף or כַּף	כפף	fw‾עֵת or עֶת‾	עֵת	עתת
fw‾עַם	עָם or עַם[1]	עמם	fw‾שֶׁן or שֵׁן‾	שֵׁן	שנן
fw‾גַּן	גָּן	גנן	fw‾חֻק	חֹק	חקק
			fw‾עֹז	עֹז	עזז

---

[1] Usually עַם; the construct form עַ precedes numbers, which is normally an absolute position. Other geminates have this regular behavior, e.g. פַּר, *bull*, but פַּר אֶחָד, *one bull*.

4.4.3   Geminate with $R_2 = R_3 =$ G.

Geminate roots that end with two gutturals need to apply the solutions to the *dagesh* problem. Sometimes they write both R_2 and R_3.

Word	What happened	Root	form
fẘ הָרֲרֵי֫־	fẘ הָרֲרֵי֫ ← הַרֲרֵי֫ ← fẘ הַרְרֵי֫	הרר	pl cs
OR fẘ הַרֲרֵי֫־	fẘ הַרֲרֵי֫ ←		

In רֵי֫ הָרֲ, רֵ is POL and הָ has *qametz(!)* in problem position. It should have *shewa* preceded by a short vowel, הַרְ. *Resh* tries to become a *dagesh* but this is rejected by the next *resh*. Applying *compensatory lengthening*, the *patah* lengthens to *qametz*.

4.5   Segolates. Words like מֶ֫לֶךְ and פֶּ֫עַם.

Historically, segolates have an $R_1 + R_2$ package, like geminates. But they solve the problem of having no ending by inserting a vowel under R_2. The name *segolate* comes from the *segol* that is usually under R_2, like מֶ֫לֶךְ. (The name is a little misleading since they will have a *patah* if R_2 is a guttural, like פֶּ֫עַם.)

(a) **What?**

Without an ending, the singular construct and absolute forms have a *millel* accent (not on the last syllable) and look exactly alike, requiring you to judge based on context. *I*-class and *u*-class vowels in the accented open syllable may be long.

The דְּבָרִים pattern takes over in the plural absolutes.

The $R_1 + R_2$ package is preserved in plural constructs, in dual forms, and with suffixes (and also in related feminine forms that end in הֶָ֫, e.g. מַלְכָּה).

Sometimes they are called *qaṭl*-, *qiṭl*-, and *quṭl*- forms to represent the class of the theme vowel (*qṭl* is often used to represent root letters in paradigms).

(b) **Why?** R_3 used to lead the case endings which are now gone. Since Hebrew syllables must begin with a consonant, R_2 broke away from R_1 to make a syllable with R_3. But R_1 kept the accent. In the case of *a*-class words, the vowel under R_1 changed to match the *segol* under R_2.

(Using חֹ֫דֶשׁ as an example: With a case ending it was *ḥod-šu*; without, it was an unpronounceable *ḥodš*. Move R_2 and add a vowel, *ḥo-deš*. A-class words make R_1's vowel similar: *nap-šu → nap-š → na-peš → ne-peš*.)

(c) **Examples:**

suffix	pl. cs.	pl. ab.	sg. cs.	sg. ab.	root	class
מַלְכּוֹ	fẘ מַלְכֵי֫־	מְלָכִים	fẘ מֶ֫לֶךְ־	מֶ֫לֶךְ	מלך	*a*-class
חֶלְקוֹ	fẘ חֶלְקֵי֫־	חֲלָקִים	fẘ חֵ֫לֶק־	חֵ֫לֶק	חלק	
קִבְרוֹ	fẘ קִבְרֵי֫־	קְבָרִים	fẘ קֶ֫בֶר־	קֶ֫בֶר	קבר	*i*-class
חָדְשׁוֹ	fẘ חָדְשֵׁי֫־	חֳדָשִׁים	fẘ חֹ֫דֶשׁ־	חֹ֫דֶשׁ	חדש	*u*-class

The R$_1$ + R$_2$ package is also preserved in the dual:

feet	fw אֶזְנֵי־ רַגְלֵי	רַגְלַיִם	ears	fw אָזְנֵי־	אָזְנַיִם

Here is a more detailed look at the forms of מֶלֶךְ. Observe that the singular absolute and construct forms are identical, since *maqqef* is not always used.

sg. ab.	מֶלֶךְ	The masc. sg. has no ending, like דְּבַר, but it is *millel*; מֶ is **accented open short (AOS)**.
sg. cs.	fw מֶלֶךְ־	Again no ending, like דְּבַר־, but **singular segolates retain an accent in construct**.
pl. ab.	מְלָכִים	כִים R$_3$ leads an ACL syllable. The pattern of the *milra* words, e.g. דְּבָרִים, imposes itself on the segolate plurals (POL, SPP).
pl. cs.	fw מַלְכֵי־	כֵי R$_3$ leads a pretonic open long syllable (POL). מַלְ has *shewa* in problem position (SPP). מַ prefers its original *patah* for its short vowel (PSV).
sg. with suffix	מַלְכּוֹ	כּוֹ R$_3$ leads a syllable; the suffix demands an accent regardless of syllabic structure. מַלְ is PCS, preserving original *patah*.

4.5.1 Segolates with R$_1$ or R$_2$ = G. Gutturals take composite *shewa*.

suffix	pl. cs.	pl. ab.	sg. cs.	sg. ab.	root
נַעֲרוֹ	fw נַעֲרֵי־	נְעָרִים	fw נַעַר־	נַעַר	נער
אַרְצוֹ	fw אַרְצוֹת־	אֲרָצוֹת	fw אֶרֶץ־	אֶרֶץ	ארץ
חָדְשׁוֹ	fw חָדְשֵׁי־	חֳדָשִׁים	fw חֹדֶשׁ־	חֹדֶשׁ	חדש
אָהֳלוֹ	fw אָהֳלֵי־	אֹהָלִים	fw אֹהֶל־	אֹהֶל	אהל

4.5.2 Feminine singular ending ת.

Segolates account for most feminine nouns retaining ת in the singular absolute, e.g. סֹלֶת ,צָרַעַת ,דַּעַת ,מִשְׁמֶרֶת ,דֶּלֶת, and.

4.6 Pausal Accents.

Pausal accents lengthen the accented vowel of dual forms, e.g. אׇזְנָיִם ,רַגְלָיִם, and *a*-class singular segolates, e.g. אֶרֶץ vs. אָרֶץ. While the main pausal accents are *atnah*, ⃝ and *sof pasuq*, :⃝⃝, pausal forms can appear with a few other accents. These lengthened vowels help you to pause appropriately when reading Hebrew aloud, like punctuation in English. For more on the values of recognizing pauses, see ch. 23.

4.7   **Weak Consonants *Vav* and *Yod*.**

A *vav* or *yod* over silent *shewa* contracts into a diphthong, but it is usually still visible as a *matre*. It can drop out entirely, making it harder to discern the root. As a word's first letter, all initial *vavs* have become *yods*.[2]

4.7.1   **R_1 = י/ו.**   מוֹשָׁב from יָשַׁב.

(a) **What?**   In words beginning with מוֹ, מוּ, מֵי, תּוֹ, תּוּ, or תֵּי , the *mem* or *tav* is often a prefix while the *vav* or *yod* was R_1. Be ready to remove a prefix and look up a root beginning with *yod, even if you can see that R_1 was vav.*

> (א can be a prefix. But, beginning a noun, אַ and אִ are almost always R_1 and R_2.)

(b) **Why?**   A prefix + R_1 makes a closed syllable, as in מִדְבָּר, or fẘ. So when R_1, either ו or י, is over silent *shewa*, this triggers the weak letter behaviors.

Original unaccented וְ becomes וֹ (*aw → ô*). The *vav* is now a *mater*.

Original unaccented יְ became יֵ (*ay → ê*). The *yod* is now a *mater*.

(c) **Examples:**

Word	What happened	Original root	Root in dictionary
מוֹשָׁב	מ + ושב ← מַוְשָׁב ←	ושב	ישב
fẘמוֹשַׁב	fẘ מַוְשַׁב ← מ + ושב ←	ושב	ישב
fẘמוֹעֲדֵי	fẘ מַוְעֲדֵי ← מ + ועד ←	ועד	יעד
תּוֹרָה	ת + ורה ← תַּוְרָה ←	ורה	ירה
מֵישָׁרִים	מ + ישר ← מַיְשָׁרִים ←	ישר	ישר

Do not think of words like fẘמוֹשָׁב, with a distant open long syllable, as an "exception" to the syllable principles. The syllable principles apply first and then cause the weak letter rule to kick in (י/ו over *shewa*). It is your clue to the root.

To parse masculine singular absolute and construct forms, focus on R_2 and R_3. מוֹשָׁב is absolute (שָׁב is ACL); מוֹשַׁב is construct (שַׁב is PCS).

With feminine plurals you must judge by context. תּוֹרוֹת is the plural absolute and construct of תּוֹרָה, found under ירה in the dictionary. (Remember, *holem* may be defective. These are the same: תֹּרֹת, תּוֹרֹת, תּוֹרוֹת.)

N.B. In ch. 8 we will find that *holem* can follow R_1 to make the participle.

4.7.2   **R_2 = י/ו.**   אוֹר from אור; סֵסִים from סוס.

R_2 = ו or י usually becomes vocalic in nouns and typically lingers on as a *mater*. Sometimes they are consonantal in a segolate style pattern (4.7.3).

---

[2] A few personal names, the conjunction וְ, and the word וָו "socket, nail" begin with *vav*.

(a) **What?** When you see only two root consonants with a *mater* י or ו in between, the י or ו is probably R_2. Sometimes, however, the *mater* drops out.

(b) **Why?** R_2 = ו or י morphs into a long vowel when it sits atop a silent *shewa*; the contraction occurs in all syllable positions. First the syllable principles apply, making closed short syllables, then the contraction occurs, making them long. The resulting variation from the syllable principles is the clue to the root. Thus fw אוּרֵי־ has POL רֵי־, but או does not have *shewa* in problem position. The root is אור.

(c) **Examples:**

suffix	pl. cs.	pl. ab.	sg. cs.	sg. ab.	root
אוֹרוֹ	fw אוּרֵי־	אוֹרִים	fw אוֹר־	אוֹר	אור
סוּסוֹ	fw סוּסֵי־	סָסִים	fw סוּס־	סוּס	סוס
עִירוֹ	fw עָרֵי־	עָרִים	fw עִיר־	עִיר	עור
—	fw סִירוֹת־	סִירוֹת	fw סִיר־	סִיר	סיר
שִׁירוֹ	fw שִׁירֵי־	שִׁירִים	fw שִׁיר־	שִׁיר	שיר
מְקֹמוֹ	fw מְקֹמוֹת־	מְקוֹמוֹת	fw מְקוֹם־	מָקוֹם	קום

מָקוֹם reminds you to be on the lookout for prefixed מ, ת, or א.

Pay the most attention to the vowel class. The long vowel can change, e.g. אוֹר and אוֹרִים, but is almost always in the same vowel class. It does not, of course, reduce to *shewa* because *shewa* under *vav* or *yod* triggers contraction and lengthens it. Other historical forces may also make vowels long.

4.7.3 Segolate style R_2 = י/ו. עַיִן and עֵין from עין.

(a) **What?** R_2 = י or ו remains consonantal in the singular absolute in a segolate fashion (*millel* accent), but contracts in the singular construct or with an ending.

(b) **Why?** With the case endings gone, a vowel is added after R_2 to begin a syllable with R_3, while R_1 keeps the accent, e.g. עַיִן. (The vowel added after R_2 is called an anaptyptic vowel.) Otherwise, the accent shifts down and the ו or י responds to silent *shewa* by contracting, e.g. *his eye*, עַיְנוֹ ← עֵינוֹ.

(c) **Examples:**

Word	What happened	Root	Word	What happened	Root
עַיִן	← עַיְן		מָוֶת	← מַוְת	
fw עֵין	← fw עַיְן־	עין	fw מוֹת	← fw מַוְת־	מות
fw עֵינֵי־	← fw עַיְנֵי־		fw מוֹתֵי־	← fw מַוְתֵי־	
עֵינוֹ	← עַיְנוֹ		מוֹתוֹ	← מַוְתוֹ	

(Some words, like מָוֶת, *death*, have a long vowel under R_1 with all accents, not just pausal accents.)

4.7.4 R_3 = ﬠ/י ≠ ה. **Whether you see** ה**,** ו**,** י**, or** ø**, they are in dictionaries as** R_3 = ה**.** R_3 = ﬠ/י **are usually replaced by** *mater* ה**, or lost when endings are added.**

Generally, R_3 = ﬠ/י drop out. For example, the *segol* in שָׂדֶה reveals an original י; ה is a *mater*. For nouns like שָׁנָה, the feminine *a*-vowel overrides any other preference. The *mater* ה is absent in the plural forms.

pl. cs.	pl. ab.	sg. cs.	sg. ab.	*lexical*
fw⁻שְׂדֵי / fw⁻שְׂדוֹת	שָׂדוֹת	fw⁻שְׂדֵה	שָׂדֶה	שדה
fw⁻שְׁנֵי	שָׁנִים	fw⁻שְׁנַת	שָׁנָה	שנה

R_3 = י **sometimes survives.**[3] **You see the** י**, but look it up as having final** ה**.**

Typically, R_1's vowel is reduced to *shewa*:   שְׁבִי and ,בְּכִי ,חֲלִי ,כְּלִי ,פְּרִי.

Many give R_1 a full vowel in pause: שֶׁבִי and ,בֶּכִי ,חֳלִי ,כֶּלִי ,פֶּרִי.[4]

Some words with irregular plurals may have been originally R_3 = י.

Memorize אָב **and** אָח**.** (A dictionary *may* have אח under אחה).

suffix	pl. cs.	pl. ab.	sg. cs.	sg. ab.	root
אָבִיו	fw⁻אֲבוֹת	אָבוֹת	fw⁻אֲבִי	אָב	אבי
אָחִיו	fw⁻אֲחֵי	אַחִים	fw⁻אֲחִי	אָח	אחי

4.8   **Summary.**

A few basic principles "run the show" for Hebrew morphology, but there are some *extra* rules. Syllable principles are primary; weak letter rules are secondary. Use the weak letter rules to diagnose variations in syllable structure or words with too few radicals, working back to the syllable principles. Focus your review in 4.8.1.

4.8.1   **What you see.**

From a recognition standpoint, this chapter boils down to a few statements:

(a)   ATM rule. Be suspicious of מ, ת, or א starting a word. They could be prefixes.

(b)   Final ה may be the feminine singular morpheme or R_3 (originally R_3 = ﬠ/י).

     ◌ָה is feminine; ◌ֶה is masculine.

(c)   If you see *ḥolem* after the first consonant,

     it could be R_1 = ו becoming *ḥolem* after a prefix (or a participle pattern, ch. 8).

(d)   Absolute and construct singular forms of segolates and geminates look the same. Judge by context.

---

[3] R_3 = י survives in 48 such words. 47 are masculine. The one exception, לְחִי / לֶחִי, means "chin, cheek, jawbone." Feminine gender is commonly used for parts of the body. R_3 = ו rarely survives but dictionaries often list these words with a final ה. In the Bible most words with surviving R_3 = ו are Aramaic or other Semitic loan words; perhaps a dozen are rare Hebrew words. About half of the "Hebrew" ones refer to plants or animals.

[4] A few always have a vowel in the absolute state. The word חֲצִי "half (of)" is usually in construct, but in the absolute state it is usually חֵצִי. The dictionaries will list it as חֲצִי. Caution: do not rely on computer programs to parse these correctly; you will need to look at the context.

(e) If you can see only two radicals, you may need to

restore $R_2 = R_3$

restore $R_2 = $ נ (less common than $R_2 = R_3$)

restore $R_2 = $ י/ו (which has usually remained as a *mater*)

restore $R_3 = $ ה (a *mater* which was lost when endings were added).

4.8.2   Knowing why helps you make choices.

The loss of the case endings mattered to words with an $R_1 + R_2$ syllable unit:

Geminates (*qall-, qill-, qull-*)

lose R_3 without an ending and

put *dagesh forte* in R_3 with an ending,

but if $R_2 = R_3$ is guttural, then it cannot double, requiring either

compensatory lengthening of the preceding vowel or

semi-doubling (virtual doubling) of the guttural.

They may keep an accent in the construct singular.

$R_2 = $ *nun* nouns may

lose *nun* without an ending (or rather, *nun* mutates into R_3, then R_3 is lost) and

put *dagesh forte* in R_3 with an ending.

Segolates (*qaṭl-, qiṭl-,* and *quṭl-*)

add *segol* or *pataḥ* (with gutturals) to make an $R_2 + R_3$ syllable,

while R_1 keeps the accent in both the absolute and construct singular.

A-class segolates take *segol* after R_1 but restore their *a*-class vowel whenever R_1

and R_2 can reunite because of endings or due to a pausal accent.

Plural absolutes use the דְּבָרִים pattern.

Segolate styled $R_2 = $ י/ו nouns

add *segol* or *ḥireq* to make an $R_2 + R_3$ syllable in the singular absolute,

but contract when lacking an accent (unable to stand over silent *shewa*).

$R_1 = $ ו words: without a prefix, *vav* became *yod*.

$R_1 = $ ו words: with a prefix, *vav* becomes *ḥolem* (sometimes *shureq*).

$R_1 = $ י words: with a prefix, *yod* becomes *ṣere yod*.

$R_2 = $ י/ו words: י/ו becomes vocalic, usually staying as a *mater*.

$R_3 = $ י/ו words: י/ו is usually replaced by a *mater he* or lost when there is an ending.

Words retaining $R_3 = $ י/ו are listed under $R_3 = $ ה in dictionaries.

Words retaining $R_3 = $ י usually have vocal *shewa* under R_1.

**Especially with segolates and geminates, computer programs are unreliable in classifying construct state.

4.8.3   Summary of application.

Although there are other clues besides variation in syllable structure, when you do encounter variations from the underlying syllable principles these mutations are often clues to a morpheme or to the root. Remember: **clues not exceptions**. These examples focus on the root.

fw‑מִשְׁפְּטֵי   Two *shewas* in a row: a clue that a prefix was added.
Remove the prefixed מ; the root is שׁפט.

כַּף   Accented closed *short*: a clue that R$_2$ = R$_3$, a geminate.
Restore R$_2$ = R$_3$; the root is כפף.
(The accent could have lengthened the vowel.)

אַף   Accented closed *short*: a clue that R$_2$ = נ assimilated into R$_3$.
Restore R$_2$ = נ; the root is אנף. (Geminates are more common.)
(The accent could have lengthened the vowel.)

מֵישָׁרִים   Lacks *shewa* in problem position: a clue to contraction, R$_1$ = י.
Remove the prefix. Restore consonantal י. The root is ישׁר.

fw‑מוֹשַׁב   Lacks *shewa* in problem position: a clue to contraction, R$_1$ = ו.
Remove prefix; restore ו; see the root ישׁב in the lexicon/dictionary.

fw‑אוּרֵי   Lacks *shewa* in problem position: a clue to R$_2$ = ו/י.
Restore *mater* to consonant; the root is אור.

fw‑בֵּית, fw‑אוֹר   Pretonic closed *long*: a clue to contraction.
Restore *mater* to consonant; the roots are בית and אור.

בְּכִי   Ends in י, also monosyllabic: clues to R$_3$ = י ≠ ה.
The original root is בכי, but the dictionary may have it under בכה.

fw‑חֹדֶשׁ   Accented open *long*: a clue that it is a segolate
and its construct and absolute forms are identical.

אֶרֶץ, רַגְלָיִם   Accented open *long* a-class: a clue to pause.

4.9   Vocabulary.

1	אָהֵב	*vb.* to love (217), *he loves* or *he loved***
2	אוֹר	*n.f.* light (120)
3	אֵל / אֱלֹהִים	*n.m.* God, god(s) (2839)
4	אֲשֶׁר	*prt.* who, which, that (5503)
5	הַר⁵	*n.m.* mountain, hill country (558)
6	חָדָשׁ	*adj.* new (53)
7	חֹדֶשׁ	*n.m.* new moon, month (283)
8	יוֹם	*n.m.* day (2301)
9	יָם	*n.m.* sea, west (396)
10	כִּי	*cj.* that, because, when, indeed (4487)
11	לֹא / לוֹא	*prt.* not, no (5193)
12	לַיְלָה / לַיִל	*n.m.* night (235*)
13	לָכֵן	*cj.* therefore (לְ + כֵּן) (201)
14	מְאֹד	*adv.* very, exceedingly, quite (300)
15	מַיִם	*n.m.* water(s) (585) *construct* מֵי
16	עֵד	*n.m.* witness (69)
17	עוֹד / עֹד	*adv.* yet, still, again, continuance (491)
18	עוֹלָם	*n.m.* forever, always, ancient (439)
19	עֵץ	*n.m.* tree, wood(s) (330)
20	עֵת	*n.f/m.* time (297)
21	שֵׁם	*n.m.* name (864)
22	שָׁמַיִם	*n.m.* heaven, sky (421)

**Note: The actual form אָהֵב means *he loves* or *he loved*. The lexical form of most verbs is called the Qal perfect third masculine singular form (ch. 10). We use the English infinitive to emphasize the concept that the verb means and not give the false impression that the form is always in a particular time frame or verb tense.

---

⁵ The most common form of the singular absolute is הַר, as it usually occurs with the article, הָהָר. On the article before guttural letters, see further in ch. 5.

4.10   Learning Activities on the CD.

On the one hand this chapter is a chance to keep practicing the noun endings learned in ch. 3. On the other hand it is like a tutorial in the weak consonants.

1   Grammar Illustration: Noun Formations.

Watch illustrations of noun formations that are described in the chapter.

2   Copying Exercise.

A fill-in-the-blank activity reviewing the summary in 4.8.1.

3   Practice Parsing.

Try to parse the nouns that appear, then click for the answers. The items include most nouns and adjectives from chs. 1–22, including forms with the 3ms pronominal suffix, a total of 657 items. Use the Random button for variety in practice. Use the Next buttons to see other forms of the same word. Because of the large number of entries, this Learning Activity can be used to review the noun endings at any time without merely repeating something you have done before.

On entering roots from the on-screeen type pad. Be sure to use final forms of letters for R_3. Note that roots which are $R_3 = $ י/ו ≠ ה are given as $R_3 = $ ה, e.g. שָׂדֶה as שׂדה, since this is how they are commonly listed in a dictionary. All $R_2 = $ ו roots expect simple ו for the answer. (The וֹ and וּ will be used for verbs.)

4   Parsing Exercises.

There are two sets of parsing exercises. The first set is based on previous vocabulary words. The second set includes words you have not had before.

5   Practice Readings: Pronouns and Construct Forms. 21 items.

This section drills on pronouns and construct forms of kinship terms.

6   Practice Readings: 3ms suffix. 20 items.

This section consists of vocabulary words with the suffix וֹ. Try to recognize the vocabulary word and translate with the suffix.

7   Practice Readings: Phrases. 75 items.

This section has short phrases from Bible verses using the vocabulary from chs. 1–3. The meanings of any words you have not had as vocabulary are provided in parentheses. Names are marked as (PN) for personal name, (GN) for geographic name, or (N) for other kinds of proper nouns. The LORD's name, יְהוָֹה, pronounced *'adonay*, is marked as (DN) for divine name.

8   Translation Exercise.

Translate verses from the Hebrew Bible. Vocabulary helps are provided as in the practice readings.

9   Learn ch. 4 vocabulary.

chapter five

Prepositions, Conjunction, Article, Interrogative, Direct Object

5.1   Focus.

In this chapter you are to learn several small words with similar spelling concerns:

the prepositions used 100+ times in the Hebrew Bible,

the conjunction וּ in its various forms: וְ, וָ, וּ,

the so-called direct object indicator אֵת / אֶת־,

the definite article, *the*: הַ◌, Gהַ, Gהָ, Gהֶ,

that inseparable prepositions replace the ה of the article, and

the interrogative particle, הֲ (הַ before א, ע, or vocal *shewa*, rarely הֶ).

For the most part, learning these is little more than learning vocabulary. The chapter explains when different vowels are used with the conjunction, inseparable prepositions, article, and interrogative particle. Focus on recognition; you can use the explanations for reference later.

5.2   Prepositions.

A preposition relates a noun (its object) to another word in the sentence. It occurs before its object, in *pre*-position. Prepositions may be spatial words (*on, over, in, by,* or *among*) or indicate many other kinds of relationships (*according to, by means of*).

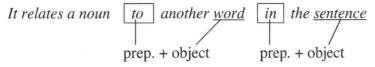

It relates a noun to *another word* in *the sentence*

prep. + object   prep. + object

A preposition's meaning depends heavily on the words it relates together. An English gloss in the vocabulary list will not work for every occurrence of the Hebrew preposition. For example, תַּחַת is commonly glossed *below* or *under*, but when someone is תַּחַת הָהָר, they are *at the foot of* the mountain. It takes practice. As you read texts and learn other vocabulary you may wish to learn combinations, e.g. a verb plus a certain preposition has a particular meaning.

Prepositions are typically patterned like construct nouns. You can analyze their form for practice, but are well served by simply treating them as vocabulary items.

5.2.1   Independent Prepositions.

Many prepositions occur as independent words in a sentence.

אֵצֶל	beside
בֵּין / בֵּינוֹת	between
בְּעַד	away from, on behalf of, behind, through
לִפְנֵי	before, in the presence of
מֵעַל	upwards, above
תַּחַת	below, under, instead of

(In form compare בֵּית־ to בֵּין; מֶלֶךְ־ to תַּחַת, דִּבְרֵי to לִפְנֵי; דְּבַר to בְּעַד.)

5.2.2   *Maqqef* prepositions.

Some prepositions almost always attach to their object with a *maqqef* (as PCS syllables). Without *maqqef*, they typically keep their short vowel.

אֶל / אֶל־	to, towards, into, against, unto
אֶת / אֶת־	with, beside
עַד / עַד־ / עֲדֵי־	as far as, even to, up to, until, while, as long as
עַל / עַל־	on, upon, on the basis of, according to, on account of, above, by, onto
עִם / עִם־	with, against (e.g. fight with = fight against)

Some prepositions that are normally independent are occasionally joined to the following word with a *maqqef*: אֵצֶל־, בֵּין־, בְּעַד־.

5.2.3   The Preposition מִן (מִן, מִ◌, מִן־).

The preposition מִן may be joined to its object by *maqqef* or directly attached. If attached, the *nun* assimilates (1.8.6) into the next letter as a *dagesh forte*, unless the next letter is a guttural. Now you have to watch out for מ not only as a prefix used to make nouns but also as a preposition.

Maqqef; no assimilation–	מִן־חֶבְרוֹן	from Hebron
Nun assimilates–	מִכָּל־ ← מִנְכָּל־	from all of…
Compensatory lengthening[1]	מֵעֵדֶן ← מִנְעֵדֶן	from Eden
Semi/virtual-doubling–	מִחוּץ ← מִנְחוּץ	from the outside (= outside)

The preposition מִן can indicate separation in space, *from, out of, away from*, or separation in degree, *than, more than*. (Chapter 7 deals with the comparative use, *more than*.)

---

[1] מִן normally takes *maqqef* before ח. Compensatory lengthening before א and ר is normal for מִן. Semi-doubling is only expressed in מְחוּט, מִחוּץ, and מִהְיֹת (מִן plus the infinitive of היה, *to be*).

5.2.4 Compound Prepositions.

Hebrew may make prepositions by combining two (or more) prepositions or a preposition plus another word. These occur as independent words.

לְ + פְּנֵי	לִפְנֵי	before
מִן + אַחַר	מֵאַחֲרֵי / מֵאַחַר	away from, from after
מִן + אֶת	מֵאֵת	out of, from (beside)
מִן + חוּץ	מִחוּץ	outside, around
מִן + עַל	מֵעַל	from upon, from over
מִן + עִם	מֵעִם	from with, beside, away from
מִן + פְּנֵי	מִפְּנֵי	from before, because
מִן + תַּחַת	מִתַּחַת	(from) beneath,
בְּ + תּוֹךְ	בְּתוֹךְ	in the midst of
מִן־ + תּוֹךְ	מִן־תּוֹךְ	from the midst of
לְ + נֶגֶד	לְנֶגֶד	in front of, before
מִן + נֶגֶד	מִנֶּגֶד	across from, opposite of, away from

5.3 Inseparable Prepositions and conjunction וּ.

The prepositions בְּ, כְּ, and לְ are called inseparable prepositions because they always attach to another word. So does the conjunction וּ. The different vowels that בְּ, כְּ, לְ, and וּ can take are explained below, but **for recognition you can focus on the consonants**. Whenever וּ begins a word, it is always[2] the conjunction. The main problems with recognizing the inseparable prepositions are possibly confusing them for a word's first root letter and when they replace the הַ of the article (5.4.2).

5.3.1 Normally *shewa* in problem position.

Originally each had a short *a*-vowel. Since they are attached to another word, which bears the accent, they usually have *shewa* in problem position, וְ, לְ, כְּ, בְּ.

5.3.2 Pretonic Position, possibly POL *qametz* or SPP.

In pretonic position they *may* take pretonic open long *qametz*. They are pretonic before monosyllabic words, suffixes (ch. 6), and singular segolates:

;בָּהֶן ,בָּזֶה	;לָמַיִם ,לָאִישׁ ,לָזֹאת
;כָּכֶם ,כָּזֶה	.וָמַיִם ,וָאִישׁ ,וָרַע

Because it is so much more common for them to be in problem position, they normally take *shewa* even in pretonic position:

.וְכֶסֶף ,לְאִישׁ ,בְּאֶרֶץ ,כְּמֶלֶךְ

---

[2] Since originally R₁ = וּ words have switched to an initial יּ. See 4.7 *n*.1 for rare exceptions.

5.3.3 Alternating *shewas* and vowels.

(a) *Shewa* before a vowel.

If a word's first consonant has an unaccented full vowel, they take *shewa*:

Problem position: וְדָבָר, לְדָבָר, כְּדָבָר, בְּדָבָר

Distant: וּדְבָרֵי, לִדְבָרֵי, כִּדְבָרֵי, בִּדְבָרֵי

(b) Vowel before *shewa*.

If the word begins with *shewa* a short vowel must be created (cf. 2.4.6) If there are no special interests, a *ḥireq* is used, as in fw דְּבָרֵי :

בִּשְׁבִי, בִּבְכִי, לִדְבָרִים, כִּדְבָרִים, בִּדְבָרִים

(c) Special Interests before *shewa*.

First letter *yod* becomes vocalic, יִ ← יְ, e.g.: בִּימֵי ← בְיְמֵי ← בְּ + יְמֵי :

בִּימֵי "in the days of"   וִימֵי "and the days of"

לִימִין "at the right hand of"   כִּידֵי "like the hands of"

Matching short vowel. Composite *shewas* (under gutturals) require the short vowel in the same vowel class as the composite *shewa*, e.g.:

וַאֲדָמָה,	כַּחֲלוֹם,	בַּחֲלוֹם	◌ֲ◌
וֶאֱמֶת,	לֶאֱמֶת,	בֶּאֱמֶת	◌ֱ◌
וָחֳלָיִים,	לָחֳלִי,	בָּחֳלָיִים	◌ֳ◌

Vav conjunction becomes וּ. Before simple *shewa*, *vav* is in position for a vowel. It becomes וּ, e.g. וּדְבָרִים, unless it is before *yod* (as above). It is the only syllable in Hebrew that does not begin with a consonant.

5.3.4 וּ before *BuMP* letters, בּוּמַ"ף.

The labial letters (those formed with the lips), בּ, מ, and פּ also affect the conjunction. וּ becomes וּ before בּ, מ, and פּ, e.g. וּמֶלֶךְ, וּפְנֵי, וּבֵין.[3]

5.3.5 Quiescent *aleph*.

Aleph quiesces and the vowel under the preposition lengthens in forms of אֱלֹהִים, e.g. לֵאלֹהִים.

5.3.6 Recognition.
These vowel variations do not much affect your recognition of the conjunction and inseparable prepositions. When the inseparable prepositions replace part of the article (next), the vowels are more important.

5.4 The Form of the Article, הַ◌, "the."

The article attaches directly to the word it modifies. Its basic form is הַ◌, *he-pataḥ-dagesh forte*. But words beginning with gutturals as well as preceding inseparable prepositions cause variations.

---

[3] There is a rare instance of consonantal וּ before בּ in Gen 1:2 and Jer 4:23 in the phrase תֹּהוּ וָבֹהוּ "formless and void."

5.4.1   The Article (הַ◌) before gutturals and ר: Gהָ, Gהֶ, or Gהֶ.

The gutturals' usual solutions to the *dagesh* problem, **compensatory lengthening** and **semi-doubling (or virtual doubling),** are a bit more complicated with the article. The article's vowel depends also on what vowel is with the guttural and whether it is accented. With a couple of exceptions, the article is generally (1) הָ before א, ע, and ר, (2) הֶ before הָ and חָ, and (3) הַ before ה and ח with vowels other than *qametz*. As long as the article's ה survives, *recognizing* the article is not too difficult. This chart is **for reference**. There are rare exceptions.

	before *qametz*	before another vowel		before *qametz*	before another vowel	
א/ר	הָרֹ הָאֹ	הָרֹ הָאֹ	acc.	הֶחָ	הַח	ח
	הָרָ הָאָ	הָרָ הָאָ	unacc.	הֶחָ	הַח	
ע	הָעֹ	הָעֹ	acc.	הֶהָ	הַה[4]	ה
	הֶעָ	הָעָ	unacc.	הֶהָ	הַה	

Before א, ר, or ע, the article is הָ, except before unaccented עָ, it is הֶעָ.

Before ה, or ח, without ◌ the article is הַ.

Before הָ, or חָ, the article is הֶ, except before accented הָ, it is הֶהָ.

5.4.2   Inseparable prepositions before the article replace the ה.

When a ה is preceded by vocal *shewa*, the ה usually drops out. So, when inseparable prepositions precede the article, the ה drops out, e.g. לַ◌ ← לְהַ◌. Without ה, the *pataḥ* and *dagesh forte* are the clues to the article's presence.

But, if the word begins with a guttural, then the *dagesh* is rejected and the *pataḥ* may be gone as well. So it is possible for a word to be articular but not have the *he*, the *pataḥ*, or *dagesh forte*, e.g.:

> *in the city*   בָּעִיר[5] ← בְּהָעִיר   (cp. בְּעִיר *in a city*; הָעִיר *the city*).

When the article has *segol* (before הֶ, חֶ, הֶ, and עֶ) and then loses the ה, it may seem the toughest to recognize. But when the inseparable prepositions take *segol*, it is usually the article (unless it is matching a *ḥaṭaph segol*; cp. 5.3.3.c):

בֶּעָרִים	*in the cities,*	לֶעָרִים	*to the cities,*	כֶּעָרִים	*like the cities;*
בֶּעָפָר	*in the dust,*	לֶחֶרֶב	*at/by the sword,*	כֶּחָג	*like the festival.*

---

[4] Except **regularly** before the 3mp pronoun הָהֵם, הָהֵמָּה.

[5] Recall that the inseparable prepositions may have pretonic open long *qametz* (5.3.2). As a result there are some situations where you must rely on context to clarify. But it is not recommended that you rely on parsing guides or computer programs for these.

5.4.3   Recognition.

From the standpoint of recognition, we may make the following generalizations:

(a)   Inseparable preposition **with *shewa* or *ḥireq* – not articular**.

(b)   Inseparable preposition **with *segol* – articular**, except before *ḥaṭaph segol*.

(c)   Inseparable preposition **with an *a*-vowel – usually articular**.

  Exception 1: before R$_1$ gutturals with *ḥaṭaph pataḥ*, e.g. בַּחֲלֹם,[6]

  Exception 2: pretonic prepositions may have open long *qametz* (cf. 5.3.3).

(d)   ה before a substantive (noun, adj., pronoun) is usually the article (not to be confused with R$_1$ = ה). It may be the interrogative particle (5.6) when ה has the "wrong" vowel (for an article) before a guttural (usually *pataḥ* before א or ע).

5.5   The Article and Definiteness.

Hebrew has a definite article, "the," but not an indefinite article, "a/an." The article is *one* way that Hebrew expresses definiteness. **A Hebrew noun is definite**

 1) if it has the article,

 2) if it is in construct with a definite noun,

 3) if it has a pronominal suffix, or

 4) if it is a proper noun.

5.6   Interrogative particle הֲ, sometimes הַ (rarely הֶ).

The interrogative particle ה turns a sentence into a question or makes a clause conditional (e.g. *whether…*). It is attached directly to the first word of the clause.

The normal form (89%) of the interrogative particle is הֲ. About half the time, it is attached to לֹא. Sometimes (11%) it is spelled הַ, mostly before א or ע or vocal *shewa*. (Composite *shewas* upgrade to a full vowel when followed by vocal *shewa*.)

The article does not take *pataḥ* before א or ע, so הָאַף has the article; הַאַף has the interrogative. Since *he-pataḥ* normally distinguishes the article, these are tough to recognize. Only interrogative ה can be put on a verb or adverb; the article cannot.[7]

5.6.1   Examples of the interrogative particle:

הֲלוֹא־אָח עֵשָׂו לְיַעֲקֹב	-1-	Was not Esau Jacob's brother?
הֲלֹא כָל־הָאָרֶץ לְפָנֶיךָ	-2-	Isn't the whole land before you?
הֲתַחַת אֱלֹהִים אָנֹכִי	-3-	Am I in the place of God?
(alive) הַעוֹד אָבִי חָי	-4-	Is my father still alive?
(you will obey) הֲתִשְׁמֹר מִצְוֹתוֹ אִם־לֹא	-5-	[…to know what is in your heart] *whether* you will obey his commands or not.

---

[6] Rarely these can be articular; but trust to context rather than parsing guides.

[7] An adverb, like הַעוֹד, must have the interrogative. Parsing aids are often unreliable for these. The rare form הֶ occurs before gutturals with *qametz* or *qametz ḥatuph*, but these cases are not on nouns.

5.7   אֵת / אֶת־, The "direct object indicator."

The particle אֵת / אֶת־ and the preposition אֵת / אֶת־ look the same, **except** when pronominal suffixes are added (ch. 6). (Both are prepositions.) The forms אֵת and אֶת־ relate only to accent and pronunciation, not to function.

This particle is primarily used before a verb's definite direct object. The direct object of a verb receives the action in the verb or is otherwise the aim of the verbal notion (examples 1–2). The subject of a passive verb receives its action, e.g. *the soccer ball* was kicked. In English, the performer of the action, the *agent*, may be indicated with a preposition, e.g. "the soccer ball was kicked *by Carl.*" The particle אֵת / אֶת־ is also used to mark the agent of passive verbs (example 3) or to specify its understood impersonal subject (example 4).

5.7.1   **Examples of the particle אֵת / אֶת־.**

וּבְנֵי יִשְׂרָאֵל אָכְלוּ (they ate) אֶת־הַמָּן   *-1-*   And the Israelites ate (the) manna.

וַיֶּאֱהַב יַעֲקֹב אֶת־רָחֵל (he loved)   *-2-*   Jacob loved Rachel.

וַתִּמָּלֵא הָאָרֶץ אֶת־הַמָּיִם (it was filled)   *-3-*   The land was filled *by* the water.

וַיֻּגַּד לְרִבְקָה (it was reported)   *-4-*   It was reported to Rebeka,
אֶת־דִּבְרֵי עֵשָׂו   *namely*, the words of Esau.

5.8   **Vocabulary: mostly prepositions used 100+ times in the Bible.**

1	הֲ, הַ [8]	*prt.*	interrogative particle (661+)
2	אַחַר / אַחֲרֵי	*adv.*	behind, after(wards) (718*)
3	אֶל	*prp.*	to, toward, against, at, unto, concerning (5518)
4	אֵת / אֶת־	*prp.*	with, beside (890)
5	בֵּין / בֵּינוֹת	*prp.*	between, interval (409)
6	בַּעַד / בְּעַד־	*prp.*	through, on behalf of, behind (104)
7	לִפְנֵי	*prp.*	before, in the presence of (לְ + פָּנֶה) (1126)
8	מֵאֵת	*prp.*	out of, from (beside) (מִן + אֵת) (180)
9	מִן / מִ⬚ / מִן־	*prp.*	from, out of, since, (more) than (7529)
10	מַעַל	*prp.*	upwards, above (140)
11	מֵעַל	*prp.*	from upon, from (beside) (מִן + עַל) (311)
12	עַד / עֲדֵי־	*prp.*	as far as, even to, until (1263)
13	עַל	*prp.*	on, over, against, on account of, to (5777)
14	עִם	*prp.*	with, near, besides (1084)
15	תּוֹךְ (תָּוֶךְ)	*n.m.*	midst of (420) (*almost always in construct and compound*)
16	תַּחַת	*prp.*	below, under, instead of (510)
17	בּוֹא	*vb.*	to come/go in, enter, come to (2592)

---

[8] The form is הָ before gutturals with *qametz* or before composite *shewa*.

5.9   Summary.

A preposition relates a noun (its object) to another word in the sentence.

When מִן attaches directly to its object, the *nun* assimilates unless the word begins with a guttural. Then compensatory lengthening or semi-doubling applies.

Inseparable prepositions and the conjunction וֹ normally have *shewa*;

they may have a pretonic open long *qametz*;

they have a vowel before a *shewa*,

typically *hireq* (if followed by *yod* then בְּיִ ← בִּי),

or the short vowel corresponding to the class of a following composite *shewa*.

וֹ becomes וּ before *shewa* and before labials, במף.

A Hebrew noun is definite if it (1) has the article, (2) is in construct, (3) has a pronominal suffix, or (4) is a proper noun.

The article הַ becomes הָ, הַ, or הֶ before gutturals due to the *dagesh* problem.

Before א, ר, or ע, the article is הָ, except before unaccented עָ, it is הֶעָ.

Before ח, or ה, without ָ the article is הַ.

Before הָ, or חָ, the article is הֶ, except before accented הָ, it is הֶהָ.

Inseparable prepositions replace the ה of the article.

An inseparable preposition

with *shewa* or *hireq* is not articular,

with *segol* is articular – *except* before *hataph segol*, e.g. לֶאֱמֶת,

with an *a*-vowel is usually articular,

– *except* before *hataph patah*, e.g. בַּחֲלֹם, and

– *except* pretonic prepositions may have *qametz* but no *dagesh*.

The interrogative particle הֲ (הַ before א or ע or a vocal *shewa*) turns a sentence into a question or makes a clause conditional (e.g. *whether…*). It is attached directly to the first word of the clause.

5.10   Learning activities on the CD.

You will need to learn this chapter's vocabulary in order to do the exercises.

1   Grammar Illustrations.

2   Article Identification. Identify if a noun is articular (cf. 5.4.3). 25 items.

3   Parsing Exercise.

4   Practice Readings Pt. 1 (using chs. 1–4 vocabulary). 76 items.

The divine name will no longer be marked by (DN).

5   Learn ch. 5 vocabulary.

6   Practice Readings Pt. 2 (using chs. 1–5 vocabulary). 51 items.

7   Translation Exercise.

chapter six

Pronouns,
Pronominal Suffixes
on Substantives and Prepositions

6.1   Focus.

In this chapter you are to learn:

to **recognize the forms of pronominal suffixes,**

based on the independent pronouns already learned as vocabulary.

Like English, Hebrew uses different forms for the pronouns as subject and object (*we*, *us*). When the subject of a sentence, Hebrew pronouns are independent words. For all other functions, Hebrew pronouns are suffixes on other words.

Generally, the suffixes derive from part of the independent pronouns and are best learned by comparison. The three lists in 6.2 are the heart of the chapter. Study across the rows. They are similar enough to achieve a **basic recognition** quickly. Most of the remainder of the chapter illustrates how they are put onto different types of nouns and on prepositions, following the syllable principles. The many charts are there for reference, not to imply a need for large amounts of rote memorization. The basic issue of vowel changes due to the syllable principles is briefly illustrated in the grammar illustration on the CD.

In comparing suffixes to the independent pronoun, note that the ת of the independent pronouns has been replaced by כ in the suffixes. The 3fs suffix is better compared to the noun's fem. singular ה, but will usually have a *qametz* ָה or a *mappiq* הּ, because it is not a *mater*. The most important distinction between suffixes is that type 2 suffixes have a י as part of a connecting vowel, signaling that it is attached to a plural noun, adjective, or participle.

A few notes included in 6.2.1 and 6.2.2 refer to the upcoming participles and infinitives so that all the suffix information will be in one place for future reference. For now, just skip over those notes about participles and infinitives. They will be repeated in ch. 8.

Pronominal suffixes are usually translated (1) with the possessive, דְּבָרוֹ, *his word*, (2) as an object, לוֹ, *to him*, or (3) with *of*, כֻּלּוֹ, *all of it*. But judge by context for good English idiom if in some situations these do not make for good writing style.

6.2 Pronouns and Pronominal suffixes.

From the independent pronoun, certain **basic parts** are used to form the suffixes. Gray letters in the basic parts column may be omitted or altered (ה changes to כ).

Type 2	Type P	Type 1	Indep. Pronoun			
on plurals, prepositions	alt. type for prepositions	on sg., inf., prepositions	**Basic parts**			
◌ַי, ◌ָֽי AT	◌ָנִי	◌ִי	נִי	אֲנִי	1cs	me, my
◌ֶיךָ	◌ָךְ, ◌ָֽךְ AT	◌ְךָ, ◌ֶ֫ךָ	◌ָ֑ךְ ← כ	אַתָּה	2ms	you, your
◌ַ֫יִךְ, ◌ָֽיִךְ AT	◌ָךְ, ◌ֵךְ	◌ֵךְ	◌ֵ֑ךְ ← כ	אַתְּ	2fs	you, your
◌ָיו	◌הוּ	◌וֹ, ◌ֵהוּ, ◌ ו	◌הוּ	הוּא	3ms	him, his
◌ֶ֫יהָ	◌ָ֫הּ	◌ָהּ	(cp. fem. noun) ◌ָ֫ה	הִיא	3fs	her, her
◌ֵ֫ינוּ	◌ֵ֫נוּ	◌ֵ֫נוּ	נוּ	אֲנַ֫חְנוּ	1cp	us, our
◌ֵיכֶם	◌ְכֶם	◌ְכֶם	◌ֶם ← כם	אַתֶּם	2mp	you, your
◌ֵיכֶן	◌ְכֶן	◌ְכֶן	◌ֶן ← כן	אַתֵּ֫נָה	2fp[1]	you, your
◌ֵיהֶם	◌ָהֶם	◌ָם, הֶם	◌ֶם	הֵם	3mp	them, their
◌ֵיהֶן	◌ָהֶן, ◌ָהֵ֫נָה	◌ָן, הֶן, נה	◌ֶן	הֵ֫נָה	3fp	them, their

6.2.1 General Notes:

(a) **Type 1 suffixes are used on the sg. cs. forms** of nouns, adjectives, and participles as well as on infinitives (ch. 8) and some prepositions. Variants in the 3ms form relate to a noun's structure.

(b) **Type 2 suffixes are used on the pl. cs. forms** of nouns, adjectives, and participles as well as on some prepositions. The ◌ֵי of the masc. pl. cs. is absorbed, or replaced, by the ◌ֵי of the type 2 suffixes.

(c) **The Type P list, for prepositions only**, has a large variety of connecting vowels that may be used (hence no vowel under the box). Note esp. the 1cs form.

(d) Prepositions may take their suffixes from any of the three lists; but each preposition is consistent in which list it uses.

(e) The pausal forms listed (with the *aṭnaḥ*, ◌̣) are used a significant percentage of the time; 20% of 1cs forms and 30% of 2fs forms on plural nouns are pausal.

---

[1] An alternate form, ◌ְכֵ֫נָה appears 4x in Ezekiel. The 2fp suffix is only used 19x in the Bible.

6.2.2 Notes on Type 1 suffix forms.

1cs *Ptc. & inf.* (ch. 8) may also use the Type P נִי◌, e.g. פָנַי, פָנֵי, פָנֵי.

2ms The vocal *shewa* may be composite with gutturals, זַרְעֲךָ. On a few *inf.* it has a *mater he*, כָה◌. On prepositions it may be ךָ◌.

2fs Some nouns use a different connecting vowel: פִּיך, אָבִיך, אָחִיך, and כַלָּך.

3ms וֹ◌ is the most common. It sometimes has ה as its *mater*, כֻּלֹּה.

וֵהוּ◌ is used primarily with masc. nouns or *ptc.* ending in ה (שָׂדֵהוּ) from שָׂדֶה)[2]

וֹ◌ is used with nouns having a י in their construct forms: פִּיו, אָבִיו, אָחִיו.

1cp Variations in connecting vowel: פִּינוּ, אָבִינוּ, אָחִינוּ, and כֻּלָּנוּ.

2mp & 2fp In כֶם◌ and כֶן◌ the *shewa* is vocal (no *dagesh lene*).

3mp & 3fp הֶם◌ & הֶן◌ go on פֶּה, אָב, אָח, and a few R₃ ≠ ה = י words.

6.2.3 Specific Notes on Type 2 suffix forms.

3mp The 3mp suffix on feminine plural nouns and irregular masculine plurals is frequently Type 1, i.e. וֹתָם◌.

6.2.4 Recognition. Focus on similarities of form and the distinctive *yod* of Type 2 suffixes on plural nouns.

Review the forms of the pronominal suffixes for 15 minutes (pondering their similarities and differences) before finishing this chapter. Copying the suffix lists while reciting the independent pronoun is a good way to review.

6.3 The independent (subject) pronouns.

There are also a few alternate forms of the independent pronoun that you have not had as vocabulary items.

1cs	אֲנִי, אֹנכִי	I	1cp[3]	אֲנַחְנוּ	we
2ms	אַתָּה	you	2mp	אַתֶּם	you
2fs	אַתְּ	you	2fp[4]	אַתֵּנָה	you
3ms	הוּא	he	3mp	הֵם, הֵמָּה	they
3fs	הִיא, הוּא[5]	she	3fp[6]	הֵנָּה	they

---

[2] Cp. the common words מַחֲנֶה, מַרְאֶה, מַעֲשֶׂה, and קָצֶה. The *mater* ה of R₃ = י ≠ ה disappears when suffixed. This ending is used on a few nouns from weak roots, רֵע, מֶרַע, מִין, אוּר, מוֹט, מִן, and פִּילֶגֶשׁ.

[3] There is also a rare 1cp form נַחְנוּ.

[4] אַתֵּן occurs once as a 2fp form.

[5] The form הוּא (pronounced הִיא) occurs only in Torah. The consonants are an archaic spelling.

[6] The 3fp form הֵן, which might be expected by comparison to the 3mp form הֵם, does occur in post-Biblical Hebrew, but occurs only as a pronominal suffix in Biblical Hebrew.

6.4 **Attaching and translating the suffixes.**

The suffixes establish where the accent goes (though they do not follow noun accent rules). A chain reaction follows based on the syllable principles. For example, *my word*, דְּבָרִי, has POL (pretonic open long) *qametz*, preceded by SPP (*shewa* in problem position) דְּבָ. However, vowels that are long due to special interests do not reduce: (1) long as part of the lexeme, e.g. אָדוֹן, (2) diphthongs, e.g. וֹ ← וַ, and (3) the fem. pl. morpheme וֹת. Typically, these involve וֹ, יֵ or יִ.

On *nouns and substantival adjectives (and participles)*, suffixes are often translated with the possessive pronoun in English.

דְּבָרוֹ *his word*   חֲכָמֶיךָ *your wise ones*   רֹכְבוֹ *its rider*

Sometimes the word *of* (often used with construct forms) is preferable.

שְׁנֵיהֶם *two of them* כֻּלָּנוּ *all of us*

Suffixes become the object of a preposition: לוֹ *to him*, עִמּוֹ *with him*.

Suffixes do not interrupt the construct relationship.

הַר־קָדְשׁוֹ   = *his holy mountain* (not *the mountain of his holiness*)

A common mistake for new students is to translate the noun and suffix with the same number, e.g. דְּבָרֵנוּ mistakenly as *our words*, when *our word* is correct.

6.5 **The suffixes attached to words of various patterns.**

The rest of the chapter illustrates how the pronominal suffixes attach to different noun patterns. They demonstrate how the pieces go together as a point of reference.

6.5.₁ **Suffixes on דָּבָר-type masculine nouns, adjectives, and participles.**

(a)   **Masculine singular**   **Masculine plural**

my word	דְּבָ רִי	ִי	1cs	my words	דְּבָ רַי	ַי	1cs
your word	דְּבָ רְךָ	ְךָ	2ms	your words	דְּבָ רֶיךָ	ֶיךָ	2ms
your word	דְּבָ רֵךְ	ֵךְ	2fs	your words	דְּבָ רַיִךְ	ַיִךְ	2fs
his word	דְּבָ רוֹ	וֹ	3ms	his words	דְּבָ רָיו	ָיו	3ms
her word	דְּבָ רָהּ	ָהּ	3fs	her words	דְּבָ רֶיהָ	ֶיהָ	3fs
our word	דְּבָ רֵנוּ	ֵנוּ	1cp	our words	דְּבָ רֵינוּ	ֵינוּ	1cp
your word	דְּבַר כֶם	ְכֶם	2mp	your words	דִּבְרֵי כֶם	ֵיכֶם	2mp
your word	דְּבַר כֶן	ְכֶן	2fp	your words	דִּבְרֵי כֶן	ֵיכֶן	2fp
their word	דְּבָ רָם	ָם	3mp	their words	דִּבְרֵי הֶם	ֵיהֶם	3mp
their word	דְּבָ רָן	ָן	3fp	their words	דִּבְרֵי הֶן	ֵיהֶן	3fp

דְּבָ   Note POL (pretonic open long) בָ, with SPP (*shewa* in problem position) דְּ.

דִּבְרֵי   Note POL רֵי, and דִּבְ with SPP and PSV (preceded by a short vowel).

6.5.2 Feminine nouns.

(a) Singular of שָׁנָה and צְדָקָה

my year	שָׁנָ תִי	צִדְקָ תִי	ָתִי	1cs
your year	שָׁנָ תְךָ	צִדְקָ תְךָ	ָתְךָ	2ms
your year	שָׁנָ תֵךְ	צִדְקָ תֵךְ	ָתֵךְ	2fs
his year	שָׁנָ תוֹ	צִדְקָ תוֹ	ָתוֹ	3ms
her year	שָׁנָ תָהּ	צִדְקָ תָהּ	ָתָהּ	3fs
our year	שָׁנָ תֵנוּ	צִדְקָ תֵנוּ	ָתֵנוּ	1cp
your year	שְׁנַתְ כֶם	צִדְקַתְ כֶם	ָתְכֶם	2mp
your year	שְׁנַתְ כֶן	צִדְקַתְ כֶן	ָתְכֶן	2fp
their year	שָׁנָ תָם	צִדְקָ תָם	ָתָם	3mp
their year	שָׁנָ תָן	צִדְקָ תָן	ָתָן	3fp

Feminine ת splits away from תָ to lead the suffixed syllable.

שָׁנָ is POL (pretonic open long) with SPP (*shewa* in problem position).

צִדְקָ has POL קָ, and צִדְ with SPP and PSV.

(b) Feminine plural of שָׁנָה and צְדָקָה

my years	שָׁנוֹ תַי	צִדְקוֹ תַי	ַי	1cs
your years	שָׁנוֹ תֶיךָ	צִדְקוֹ תֶיךָ	ֶיךָ	2ms
your years	שָׁנוֹ תַיִךְ	צִדְקוֹ תַיִךְ	ַיִךְ	2fs
his years	שָׁנוֹ תָיו	צִדְקוֹ תָיו	ָיו	3ms
her years	שָׁנוֹ תֶיהָ	צִדְקוֹ תֶיהָ	ֶיהָ	3fs
our years	שָׁנוֹ תֵינוּ	צִדְקוֹ תֵינוּ	ֵינוּ	1cp
your years	שְׁנוֹתֵי כֶם	צִדְקוֹתֵי כֶם	ֵיכֶם	2mp
your years	שְׁנוֹתֵי כֶן	צִדְקוֹתֵי כֶן	ֵיכֶן	2fp
their years	שְׁנוֹתֵי הֶם	צִדְקוֹתֵי הֶם	ֵיהֶם	3mp
their years	שְׁנוֹתֵי הֶן	צִדְקוֹתֵי הֶן	ֵיהֶן	3fp

שָׁנוֹ is POL with SPP.

צִדְקוֹ has POL קוֹ, and צִדְ with SPP and PSV.

צִדְקוֹתֵי has POL תֵי. The feminine plural morpheme stays long, קוֹ.

צִדְ has SPP and PSV.

6.5.3 R₃ = ' ≠ ה.

Masculine nouns ending in הֶ, e.g. שָׂדֶה, were originally R₃ = '. These have a few variations. The *mater* ה is gone. The 2fs connecting vowel is different. The 3ms suffix is וֹ or הוּ, which is still very comparable to the independent pronoun, as is the 3mp suffix, which may be הֶם.

Words with ' in their lexical form, e.g. פְּרִי (*fruit*), retain it with suffixes.

(a) **R₃ = ' ≠ ה singular.**

מַעֲשֶׂה	שָׂדֶה	אָח	אָב	פְּרִי	פֶּה		
—	שָׂדִי	אָחִי	אָבִי	פִּרְיִי	פִּי	יִ	1cs
מַעֲשֶׂךָ	שָׂדְךָ	אָחִיךָ	אָבִיךָ	פֶּרְיְךָ	פִּיךָ	ךָ	2ms
—	—	אָחִיךְ	אָבִיךְ	פֶּרְיֵךְ	פִּיךְ	ֵךְ	2fs
מַעֲשֵׂהוּ	שָׂדֵהוּ	אָחִיו	אָבִיו	פִּרְיוֹ	פִּיו	וֹ	3ms
—	שָׂדָהּ	אָחִיהָ	אָבִיהָ	פִּרְיָהּ	פִּיהָ	הָ	3fs
מַעֲשֵׂנוּ	—	אָחִינוּ	אָבִינוּ	—	פִּינוּ	נוּ	1cp
—	—	אֲחִיכֶם	אֲבִיכֶם	פֶּרְיְכֶם	פִּיכֶם	כֶם	2mp
—	—	—	אֲבִיכֶן	—	—	כֶן	2fp
—	שָׂדָם	אֲחִיהֶם	אֲבִיהֶם	פִּרְיָם	פִּיהֶם	ם	3mp
—	שָׂדָן	—	אֲבִיהֶן	פִּרְיָן	פִּיהֶן	ן	3fp

(b) **R₃ = ' ≠ ה plural.**

מַעֲשֵׂי	שָׂדַי	אַחַי	אֲבוֹתַי		
מַעֲשַׂי	שָׂדַי	אַחַי	אֲבוֹתַי	יַ	1cs
מַעֲשֶׂיךָ	שָׂדֶיךָ	אַחֶיךָ	אֲבוֹתֶיךָ	ֶיךָ	2ms
מַעֲשַׂיִךְ	—	אַחַיִךְ	—	ַיִךְ	2fs
מַעֲשָׂיו	—	אֶחָיו	אֲבוֹתָיו	ָיו	3ms
—	שְׂדוֹתֶיהָ	אַחֶיהָ	—	ֶיהָ	3fs
מַעֲשֵׂינוּ	שְׂדוֹתֵינוּ	אַחֵינוּ	אֲבוֹתֵינוּ	ֵינוּ	1cp
מַעֲשֵׂיכֶם	שְׂדוֹתֵיכֶם	אֲחֵיכֶם	אֲבוֹתֵיכֶם	ֵיכֶם	2mp
—	—	—	—	ֵיכֶן	2fp
מַעֲשֵׂיהֶם	שְׂדוֹתֵיהֶם	אֲחֵיהֶם	אֲבוֹתָם	ֵיהֶם	3mp
—	—	—	—	ֵיהֶן	3fp

6.5.4 Segolate nouns.

(a) Singular segolates.

With suffixes, singular segolates maintain their original pretonic closed short syllable with characteristic vowel.

	a-class מֶלֶךְ	*u*-class קֹדֶשׁ	*i*-class סֵפֶר		
my king	מַלְכִּי	קָדְשִׁי	סִפְרִי	◌ִי	1cs
your king	מַלְכְּךָ	קָדְשְׁךָ	סִפְרְךָ	◌ְךָ	2ms
your king	מַלְכֵּךְ	קָדְשֵׁךְ	סִפְרֵךְ	◌ֵךְ	2fs
his king	מַלְכּוֹ	קָדְשׁוֹ	סִפְרוֹ	◌וֹ	3ms
her king	מַלְכָּהּ	קָדְשָׁהּ	סִפְרָהּ	◌ָהּ	3fs
our king	מַלְכֵּנוּ	קָדְשֵׁנוּ	סִפְרֵינוּ	◌ֵנוּ	1cp
your king	מַלְכְּכֶם	קָדְשְׁכֶם	סִפְרְכֶם	◌ְכֶם	2mp
your king	מַלְכְּכֶן	קָדְשְׁכֶן	סִפְרְכֶן	◌ְכֶן	2fp
their king	מַלְכָּם	קָדְשָׁם	סִפְרָם	◌ָם	3mp
their king	מַלְכָּן	קָדְשָׁן	סִפְרָן	◌ָן	3fp

(b) Plural segolates.

The pattern of דְּבָרִים is imposed on the plurals. The *yod* of the type 2 suffixes helps indicate that the nouns are plural. When the 2nd and 3rd plural endings move R$_1$ and R$_2$ together again, they retain their characteristic vowel.

my kings	מְלָכַי	קָדָשַׁי	סְפָרַי	◌ַי	1cs
your kings	מְלָכֶיךָ	קָדָשֶׁיךָ	סְפָרֶיךָ	◌ֶיךָ	2ms
your kings	מְלָכַיִךְ	קָדָשַׁיִךְ	סְפָרַיִךְ	◌ַיִךְ	2fs
his kings	מְלָכָיו	קָדָשָׁיו	סְפָרָיו	◌ָיו	3ms
her kings	מְלָכֶיהָ	קָדָשֶׁיהָ	סְפָרֶיהָ	◌ֶיהָ	3fs
our kings	מְלָכֵינוּ	קָדָשֵׁינוּ	סְפָרֵינוּ	◌ֵינוּ	1cp
your kings	מַלְכֵיכֶם	קָדְשֵׁיכֶם	סִפְרֵיכֶם	◌ֵיכֶם	2mp
your kings	מַלְכֵיכֶן	קָדְשֵׁיכֶן	סִפְרֵיכֶן	◌ֵיכֶן	2fp
their kings	מַלְכֵיהֶם	קָדְשֵׁיהֶם	סִפְרֵיהֶם	◌ֵיהֶם	3mp
their kings	מַלְכֵיהֶן	קָדְשֵׁיהֶן	סִפְרֵיהֶן	◌ֵיהֶן	3fp

6.5.5   Geminate nouns and prepositions.

(a) Singular.

With suffixes, geminate nouns have a *dagesh* in R_2 and also retain their $R_1 + R_2$ syllable with characteristic vowel. The prepositions עִם and אֶת have geminate roots and do the same. The prepositions themselves should not be considered singular since prepositions do not have number. The direct object particle אֵת is not geminate but is included here to show the differences between the particle and preposition.

D.O. particle אֶת־, אֵת	preposition אֶת־, אֵת	preposition עִם	sg. noun עַם		
אֹתִי	אִתִּי	עִמִּי, עִמָּדִי[7]	עַמִּי	◌ִי	1cs
אֹתְךָ, אֹתָךְ	אִתְּךָ, אִתָּךְ	עִמְּךָ, עִמָּךְ	עַמְּךָ, עַמֶּךָ	◌ְךָ	2ms
אֹתָךְ	אִתָּךְ	עִמָּךְ	עַמֵּךְ	◌ֵךְ	2fs
אֹתוֹ	אִתּוֹ	עִמּוֹ	עַמּוֹ	◌וֹ	3ms
אֹתָהּ	אִתָּהּ	עִמָּהּ	עַמָּהּ	◌ָהּ	3fs
אֹתָ֫נוּ	אִתָּ֫נוּ	עִמָּ֫נוּ	עַמֵּ֫נוּ	◌ֵנוּ	1cp
אֶתְכֶם	אִתְּכֶם	עִמְּכֶם	עַמְּכֶם	◌ְכֶם	2mp
—	—	—	עַמְּכֶן	◌ְכֶן	2fp
אֹתָם, אֶתְהֶם	אִתָּם	עִמָּם, עִמָּהֶם	עַמָּם	◌ָם	3mp
אֹתָן, אֶתְהֶן	—	—	עַמָּן	◌ָן	3fp

(b) Plural.

No geminate noun in the Bible expresses the full set of pronominal suffixes on plural nouns. This sample is illustrative of how they form.

צַד	חֹק	שַׂר	עַם		
—	חֻקַּי	שָׂרַי	עַמַּי	◌ַי	1cs
—	חֻקֶּ֫יךָ	—	עַמֶּ֫יךָ	◌ֶ֫יךָ	2ms
—	—	שָׂרַ֫יִךְ	—	◌ַ֫יִךְ	2fs
צָדָיו	חֻקָּיו	שָׂרָיו	עַמָּיו	◌ָיו	3ms
צָדֶ֫יהָ	—	שָׂרֶ֫יהָ	עַמֶּ֫יהָ	◌ֶ֫יהָ	3fs
—	—	שָׂרֵ֫ינוּ	—	◌ֵ֫ינוּ	1cp
צָדֵיכֶם	—	שָׂרֵיכֶם	—	◌ֵיכֶם	2mp

---

[7] The longer form, עִמָּדִי, predominates in older texts while the shorter form, עִמִּי, predominates in later texts.

6.5.6   Prepositions.

Prepositions can take suffixes from any of the lists. Each is consistent in which suffixes it uses. You simply need to be able to recognize the person and number of the suffix. The use of type 2 suffixes does not mean that a preposition should be understood as plural; prepositions do not have number.

Note the longer forms of כ and מִן, כְּמֹו‎ and מִמֶּנ.

The 3ms suffix on מִן, מִמֶּנּוּ < מִמֶּנְהוּ‎, looks identical to the 1cp מִמֶּנּוּ < מִמֶּנְנוּ.

Type 2		P type		Type 1		
עַל	אֶל	מִן	כ	ל	ב	
עָלַי, עָלָי	אֵלַי, אֵלָי	מִמֶּנִּי, מִנִּי	כָּמֹונִי	לִי	בִּי	1cs
עָלֶיךָ	אֵלֶיךָ	מִמְּךָ	כָּמֹוךָ	לְךָ, לָךְ	בְּךָ, בָּךְ	2ms
עָלַיִךְ	אֵלַיִךְ	מִמֵּךְ	כָּמֹוךְ	לָךְ	בָּךְ	2fs
עָלָיו	אֵלָיו	מִמֶּנּוּ	כָּמֹוהוּ	לֹו	בֹּו	3ms
עָלֶיהָ	אֵלֶיהָ	מִמֶּנָּה	כָּמֹוהָ	לָהּ	בָּהּ	3fs
עָלֵינוּ	אֵלֵינוּ	מִמֶּנּוּ	כָּמֹונוּ	לָנוּ	בָּנוּ	1cp
עֲלֵיכֶם	אֲלֵיכֶם	מִכֶּם	כָּכֶם	לָכֶם	בָּכֶם	2mp
עֲלֵיכֶן	אֲלֵיכֶן	מִכֶּן	כָּכֶן	לָכֶן	בָּכֶן	2fp
עֲלֵיהֶם	אֲלֵיהֶם	מֵהֶם	כָּהֶם	לָהֶם	בָּהֶם	3mp
עֲלֵיהֶן	אֲלֵיהֶן	מֵהֶן	כָּהֶן, כָּהֵנָּה	לָהֶן	בָּהֶן	3fp

6.5.7   Miscellaneous.

R_2 = י/ו nouns contract as in the construct forms.

absolute	construct	suffixed
מָוֶת, *áwe* ← *aw*	מֹות, *ô* ← *aw*	מֹותֹו
עַיִן, *áyi* ← *ay*	עֵין, *ê* ← *ay*	עֵינֹו

R_2 = נ nouns

absolute	construct	suffixed
אִשָּׁה	אֵשֶׁת	אִשְׁתֹּו
בַּת	בַּת	בִּתֹּו

Compare the preposition אֶל and noun אֵל: אֵלַי is *to me*; אֵלִי is *my God*.

6.6   Summary.

Review the chart at 6.2. It is the essence of the chapter. See also the grammar illustration on the CD.

6.7   Vocabulary.

1	אָמַר	*vb.* to say (5316), *he (has) said*
2	וַיֹּאמֶר	*vb.* (and) he said (2076)
3	לֵאמֹר	*inf.* saying, (or quotation marks); *(Qal inf.* ל + אָמַר) (939)
4	טוֹב	*adj.* good (530)
5	יָצַר	*vb.* to form, mold (pottery) (63), *he (has) formed*
6	יָשָׁר	*adj.* straight, right (119)
7	מִשְׁמֶרֶת	*n.f.* guard, watch, obligation, duty (78)
8	עָשָׂה	*vb.* to do, make, perform (2632), *he did/made, he has done/made*
9	צַדִּיק	*adj.* just, righteous (206)
10	צֶדֶק	*n.m.* rightness, righteousness, justice, integrity (123)
11	צְדָקָה	*n.f.* righteousness (159)
12	קָדוֹשׁ	*adj.* holy (117)
13	קֹדֶשׁ	*n.m.* holiness, sacredness (470)
14	קָטָן	*adj.* small, young (27)
15	קָטֹן	*adj.* small, insignificant; *vb.* be small (74)
16	רַב	*adj.* many (419)
17	רֹב	*n.m.* multitude, abundance (150)
18	רַע	*adj.* bad, evil, *as subst.* distress, calamity, evil (312)
19	רָעָה	*n.f.* evil, harm, misery, distress (354)
20	רָשָׁע	*adj.* wicked, criminal, guilty (264)
21	שָׁמַר	*vb.* to guard, watch, keep (469), *he (has) watched*
22	שֹׁמֵר	*ptc.* watchman, watch, guard, keeping (107)

6.8   Learning activities on the CD.

1   Grammar Illustration. Review the pronoun paradigms in color. Also watch examples of how vowels change based on the syllable principles.

2   Learning to recognize the forms. Copy the chart in 6.2 row by row, reciting out loud the independent pronoun and the suffixes as you copy them.

3   Practice Parsing. Parse nouns and suffixes. 694 items.

The items include all forms of nouns and prepositions from chs. 1–5 that occur in the Bible with suffixes. (Roots are not given in the answers for prepositions.)

4   Practice Readings. Chs. 1–5 vocabulary plus וַיֹּאמֶר and לֵאמֹר from ch. 6.

Observe the pronominal suffixes carefully and pay special attention to the number (singular or plural) of the nouns to which they may be attached.

5   Parsing Exercise.

6   Translation Exercise.

7   Learn ch. 6 vocabulary.

chapter seven

Adjectives

7.1   Focus.

In this chapter you are to learn:

> *no new endings*,
>
> **three adjective positions**: **attributive, predicate, and substantival**,
>
> that adjectives agree with their nouns in gender and number,
>
> that agreeing in definiteness, or not, helps determine position,
>
> the four ways for a noun to be definite,
>
> **the comparative use of מִן**, and
>
> **the demonstrative adjectives and pronouns**.

Holy Cow! vs. Cow of holiness.

Sometimes nouns in a construct chain should be rendered with an English adjective. The type of "of" in הַר הַקֹּדֶשׁ, "mountain of holiness," means mountain "characterized by" holiness, i.e. the *holy* mountain. But besides the noun קֹדֶשׁ, *holiness*, there is the adjective קָדוֹשׁ, *holy*. And though קָדוֹשׁ describes neither cows nor mountains in the Bible, adjectives are the most common means for describing the qualities of nouns.

Adjectives modify (describe) nouns or function as nouns. Adjectives can function in three ways: attributively, *the holy mountain*; predicately, *the mountain is holy*; or substantively, *the Holy (One)*. Adjectives use the noun endings you have already learned to indicate gender and number.

7.2   Three adjective positions.

Great Scott! vs. Scott is Great.

(a) **Attributive**. Adjectives may describe nouns in more than one way. They may be attributive, e.g. the *good* book, the *dangerous* criminal, the *easy* test.

(b) **Predicate**. Or they may function as a predicate, e.g. the book *is good*; the criminal *is dangerous*; the test *is easy*.

Scott, the Great!

(c) **Substantival** adjectives stand in the place of nouns, e.g. the *good*, the *bad*, and the *ugly*. The *wicked* will perish.

7.3   Adjectives are *agree*able.

An adjective has the same gender and number as the noun that it describes or replaces. We say that the adjective *agrees* with the noun. Adjectives can change gender (to match their noun); nouns do not change gender.

7.3.1   Agreeing in Gender.

Adjectives agree with their nouns in actual gender rather than in form. The noun spelling may be "irregular," but the adjective spelling is regular.

masculine		feminine	
דְּבָרִים טוֹבִים	good words	שָׁנָה טוֹבָה	a good year
אָבוֹת זְקֵנִים	old fathers	הָעִיר גְּדֹלָה	the city is large
		שָׁנִים רַבּוֹת	many years

7.3.2   Agreeing in Number.

Adjectives generally match their nouns as singular or plural (as above, 7.3.1).

Adjectives may be plural after collective nouns.

עַם־קְדֹשִׁים   holy people

Adjectives may be singular after plural nouns which are singular in sense.

הָאֱלֹהִים הַקָּדוֹשׁ   the holy God

Adjectives use plural endings on the *rare* occasions that they modify dual nouns.

7.3.3   Agreeing in Definiteness.

Agreement or disagreement in definiteness helps indicate whether an adjective is attributive or predicate. (A substantival adjective may be either definite or indefinite and is distinguished by the lack of a noun to modify.)

An adjective is made definite by the article. But a noun is definite if it: (1) has the article, (2) is in construct with a definite noun, (3) has a pronominal suffix (a type of being in construct), or (4) is a proper noun.

7.4   Position.

7.4.1   Attributive adjective (*Great Scott*).

An attributive adj. follows its noun, agreeing in gender, number, and definiteness.

אִישׁ טוֹב	a good man	הָאִישׁ הַטּוֹב	the good man
אִשָּׁה טוֹבָה	a good woman	הָאִשָּׁה הַטּוֹבָה	the good woman
אֲנָשִׁים טֹבִים	good men	הָאֲנָשִׁים הַטֹּבִים	the good men
נָשִׁים טֹבוֹת	good women	הַנָּשִׁים הַטֹּבוֹת	the good women

These also agree in definiteness, but only the adjective has the article.

בְּנָהּ הַקָּטָן	her younger son	(*determined by suffix*)
הָמָן הָרָע	evil Haman	(*proper noun*)
מַעֲשֵׂה יְהוָה הַגָּדֹל	the LORD's great work	(*determined by construct*)

7.4.2 Predicate adjectives *(Scott is Great).*

(a) Predicate adjectives agree with their nouns in gender and number but are never definite. The predicate adjective may precede or follow its noun.

גָּדוֹל הָרָעָב	the famine was severe
הָרָעָב גָּדוֹל	the famine was severe
טוֹבָה הָאָרֶץ	the land is good
הָאָרֶץ טוֹבָה	the land is good
הָעָם רָב	the people are many
רָב הָעָם	the people are many
טוֹבָה אֶרֶץ	a land is good
אֶרֶץ טוֹבָה	a land is good /a good land

(The time frame of the translation depends on the context.)

(b) Ambiguity of position.

Predicate adjectives are never definite (attributive adjectives are not definite when their noun is not definite). When both noun and adjective are not definite, predicate position is clear if the adjective precedes the noun.

גָּדוֹל עָם	a people is great

If an indefinite adjective follows an indefinite noun, the adjective could be either attributive or predicate. It will usually be attributive; context will clarify.

עָם גָּדוֹל	a great people *or* a people is great
עָנָן כָּבֵד	a thick cloud *or* a cloud was thick

7.4.3 Substantival *(Scott, the Great).*

Sometimes an adjective acts as a noun. It has the gender and number of the noun it replaces. It may be definite or indefinite, in the absolute state or construct.

הַקָּדוֹשׁ	The Holy *One*
קְדוֹשׁ יִשְׂרָאֵל	The Holy *One* of Israel
גְּדֹלֵי הָעִיר	The important *men* of the city
וְשֵׁם הַקְּטַנָּה מִיכַל	The name of the younger *daughter* was Michal.

7.4.4 Adjusting to the sense.

You can make adjustments to fit the context, such as supplying or deleting the article, or changing the number in order to represent a class of persons.

Text:	טוֹב יְשַׁלֶּם אֶת־צַדִּיקִים *(it repays)*
Substantival טוֹב:	*a* good *thing* = benefit(s).
Substantival צַדִּיקִים:	righteous *people* = the righteous.
Translate:	Benefit repays the righteous.

7.5   Construct chains.

Adjectives do not interrupt construct chains. Attributive adjectives follow the end of the chain even when modifying a noun in the front or the middle of the construct chain.

בְּנֵי־יִשַׁי הַגְּדֹלִים   the sons of Jesse, the older
= the older sons of Jesse

עַל־תְּנוּךְ (lobe) אֹזֶן בָּנָיו הַיְמָנִית   on the lobe of the ear of his sons, the right one
= on his sons' right ear lobe

7.6   Adverbial use of adjectives.

Sometimes adjectives should be translated as adverbs in English.

וַיָּבֹא (he came) יַעֲקֹב שָׁלֵם (safe) שְׁכֶם   Jacob came *safely* to Shechem.

7.7   Comparisons.

(a) Context may indicate a comparative sense.

וְשֵׁם הַקְּטַנָּה   the name of the *small* = the *younger* (daughter)'s name.

(b) Comparisons with the preposition מִן.

מִן makes comparisons of degree, i.e. "more than." One noun has its adjective's quality to a greater degree than another noun following מִן.

זְקֵנִים הַמְּלָכִים מֵהַמְּלָכוֹת   The kings are older than the queens.

קְטַנּוֹת הַמְּלָכוֹת מֵהַמְּלָכִים   The queens are younger than the kings.

הַטּוֹב מִמֶּךָ   The one who is better than you

(c) But not every מִן following an adjective is comparative.

עַם־רָב מִיִשְׂרָאֵל   many people from Israel

7.8   Demonstratives. (A little bit of **this** and a little bit of **that**.)

The demonstratives, *this* and *that*, may be used as adjectives or pronouns.
The *near* demonstrative:

זֶה	this	masc. sg.		אֵלֶּה	these	masc. pl.
זֹאת	this	fem. sg.			these	fem. pl.

The *far* demonstratives, "that/those," are the third person independent pronouns.

הוּא	that	masc. sg.		הֵמָּה, הֵם	those	masc. pl.
הִיא	that	fem. sg.		הֵנָּה	those	fem. pl.

7.8.1　Demonstrative adjectives.

Used as attributive adjectives, the demonstratives are articular and follow any other adjectives that may be describing the noun.

הַמֶּלֶךְ הַזֶּה	this king
הַמֶּלֶךְ הַהוּא	that king
הָאָרֶץ הַזֹּאת	this land
הָאָרֶץ הַהִיא	that land

הַמֶּלֶךְ הַטֹּב הַזֶּה	this good king
הַמֶּלֶךְ הַטֹּב הַהוּא	that good king
הָאָרֶץ הַטֹּבָה הַזֹּאת	this good land
הָאָרֶץ הַטֹּבָה הַהִיא	that good land

הַמְּלָכִים הַטֹּבִים הָאֵלֶּה	these good kings
הַמְּלָכִים הַטֹּבִים הָהֵם	those good kings
הָאֲרָצֹת הַטֹּבוֹת הָאֵלֶּה	these good lands
הָאֲרָצֹת הַטֹּבוֹת הָהֵנָּה	those good lands

7.8.2　Demonstrative pronouns.

As pronouns, the demonstratives may be used for any noun function: subject (1), direct object (2), or object of a preposition (3).

(they shall stand) אֵלֶּה יַעֲמֹדוּ	-1-	*these* shall stand...
זֹאת (you have done) כִּי עָשִׂיתָ	-2-	because you have done *this*
מִזֶּה (he departed) נָסְעוּ	-3-	he departed from *this* (place)

In predicate position the demonstratives are pronouns.

זֶה הָאִישׁ	this is the man	אֵלֶּה הַמְּלָכִים	these are the kings
זֹאת הָאָרֶץ	this is the land	אֵלֶּה הַמְּלָכוֹת	these are the queens

Depending on context, the 3rd person pronouns may be translated as personal pronouns or as the far demonstrative.

הוּא הָאִישׁ	that is the man he is the man	הֵם הַמְּלָכִים	those are the kings they are the kings
הִיא הָאָרֶץ	that is the land it is the land	הֵנָּה הַמְּלָכוֹת	those are the queens they are the queens

7.9 Summary.

Adjectives agree with their nouns in gender and number.

Attributive adj. (great Scott) agree in definiteness and follow their noun.

Predicate adj. (Scott is great) are indefinite and usually precede their noun.

Substantival adj. (Scott, the Great) function as a noun.

A noun is definite if it: (1) has the article, (2) is in construct with a definite noun, (3) has a pronominal suffix, or (4) is a proper noun.

Adjectives do not interrupt construct chains.

מִן makes comparisons of degree. (Do not always translate מִן as "from.")

Demonstrative adjectives follow other adjectives.

Adjective position Summary.

Attributive: **A**fter the noun and with the **A**rticle *if* the noun is definite.

Predicate: usually **P**recedes the noun and has *no article*.

Substantival: as a **N**oun when **N**o Noun.

7.10 Vocabulary.

1	אִין / אַיִן	*subs.* not, there is not (790)
2	אָכַל	*vb.* to eat (820), *he ate/has eaten*
3	אָרַר	*vb.* to curse (63), *he (has) cursed*
4	דַּעַת	*inf. cs.* to know (*Qal infinitive construct of* יָדַע) (51)
5	דַּעַת	*n.f.* knowledge (88)
6	הִנֵּה / הֵן	*prt.* Look! See here! Take note! (indicates point of view or awareness) (1147*)
7	יָדַע	*vb.* to know (956), *he knows/knew*
8	יֵשׁ	*subs.* there is (138)
9	כַּאֲשֶׁר	*cj.* as, just as, according as, when (511)
10	כָּבֵד	*adj.* heavy, honorable; *vb.* be honored, heavy, weighty (155)
11	כָּבוֹד	*n.m.* honor, glory, abundance (200)
12	כֹּהֵן	*n.m.* priest (750)
13	לֶכֶת	*inf. cs.* to walk (*Qal infinitive construct of* הָלַךְ) (136)
14	נָבִיא	*n.m.* prophet (317)
15	נָטָה	*vb.* to stretch out, extend, bend (216), *he (has) stretched out*
16	עָנָן	*n.m.* cloud, cloud-mass (87)
17	צֵל	*n.m.* shadow, shade, protection (53)
18	קַחַת	*inf. cs.* to take, receive (*Qal infinitive construct of* לָקַח) (49)
19	שֶׁ / שְׁ / שַׁ	*prt.* who, which, that (143)
20	תֵּת	*inf. cs.* to give (*Qal infinitive construct of* נָתַן) (161)

7.11 **Learning activities on the CD.**

Adjectives use the same endings that you learned for nouns. You need the most practice at recognizing and translating adjective positions and translating the demonstratives, as well as the comparative use of מִן.

1 **Practice Readings: Adj. Position.** Old kings and young queens.

The first activity has 464 combinations using the nouns אִישׁ, מַלְכָּה, מֶלֶךְ and אִשָּׁה, the adjectives זָקֵן, קָטָן (for *young*), טוֹב and רָשָׁע, the preposition מִן, the article and the demonstratives. The random button will give you some variety, while the up and down buttons go through sets based on two nouns and adjectives. There is no need to do every one. Practice until you catch on.

2 **Practice Readings** (using chs. 1–6 vocabulary).

The Practice Readings, taken from the Bible, emphasize adjectives and recent vocabulary. Pay special attention to adjective position, demonstrative pronouns, and the use of מִן.

3 **Parsing Exercise.**

Parse nouns and pronominal suffixes attached to nouns or prepositions.

4 **Translation Exercise.**

5 **Learn ch. 7 vocabulary.**

chapter eight

Participles, Infinitive Construct

8.1   Focus.

In this chapter you are to learn:

that participles are verbal adjectives and infinitives are verbal nouns,

the Qal active and passive participle patterns E☐☐ֹ and E☐וֹ☐☐,

the Qal infinitive construct, ☐ֹ☐ְ / ☐ָ☐ֶ / ☐ְ☐ָ, and S☐ָ☐ְ,

(The "E" represents a noun ending; the "S" represents a pronominal suffix.)

and weak verb behaviors.

Verbs come in several stems, or spelling patterns, called *binyanim* (בְּנְיָנִים). This chapter covers the basic stem, called the Qal stem. (The dictionary form of a verb is the Qal perfect (ch 10) 3ms form, typically ☐ַ☐ָ or ☐ָ☐ָ, e.g. שָׁמַר or עָשָׂה.)

Participles.

As adjectives, participles use the noun endings to indicate gender and number and can occur in attributive or predicate positions or be substantival.

E☐☐ֹ,   Qal active ptc.,   שֹׁמֵר   *keeping, one who keeps/watches, a guard.*

E☐וֹ☐☐,   Qal passive ptc.,   שָׁמוּר   *kept, being kept/watched, what is kept.*

Infinitive constructs.

Infinitive constructs are verbal nouns, often translated with *to* or *-ing*. They do not use endings but they do jobs that nouns do and a couple of other jobs as well.

☐ֹ☐ְ / ☐ָ☐ֶ / ☐ְ☐ָ,   Qal infinitive construct, e.g. כְּתֹב *to write, writing.*

8.2   Qal active participle, E☐☐ֹ.

The Qal active participle is marked by a long *o*-vowel, *ḥolem vav* or *ḥolem*, after R₁. It is pretonic open long in the absolute, but it does not reduce in construct because it has a morphological commitment to the long *ḥolem*. It acts with a verbal behavior in that R₂ has a vocal *shewa* when R₃ has to lead an ending (cf. 2.10).

Qal active	Feminine		Masculine	
participle	plural	singular	plural	singular
absolute	שֹׁמְרוֹת	שֹׁמֶרֶת, שֹׁמְרָה	שֹׁמְרִים	שֹׁמֵר
construct	fw‾שֹׁמְרוֹת	fw‾שֹׁמֶרֶת	fw‾שֹׁמְרֵי	fw‾שֹׁמֵר

8.3   Qal passive participle, ⬛⬜וֹ⬜⬜.

The Qal passive participle is marked by an *u*-class vowel between R$_2$ and R$_3$; typically it is *shureq* but sometimes *qibbuṣ*. It follows the noun accent principles, but the וֹ morpheme does not reduce. Construct forms are *rare*.

Qal passive participle	Feminine		Masculine	
	plural	singular	plural	singular
absolute	שְׁמוּרוֹת	שְׁמוּרָה	שְׁמוּרִים	שָׁמוּר
construct	fwֹ שְׁמוּרוֹת	fwֹ שְׁמוּרַת	fwֹ שְׁמוּרֵי	fwֹ שְׁמוּר

8.4   Participle functions.

8.4.1   Substantival.

(a) A participle can act as a noun, with or without the article. Examples 1–2 are active; examples 3–4 are passive.

(he raised) וַיָּקֶם יְהוָה שֹׁפְטִים	-1-	The LORD raised up *judges*.
לְשֹׁמְרֵי מִצְוֹתָי	-2-	…to *those who keep* my commandments.
הֶעָשׂוּי לָכֶם בְּמִצְרָיִם	-3-	…*the [thing] done* to you in Egypt.
בֶּן־הָאֲהוּבָה	-4-	the son of *the loved [wife]*.

(b) Some participles are quite standardized in their roles as nouns:

Enemy   אֹיֵב (only as subst. ptc.);   Potter   יָצַר → יוֹצֵר *to form*

Inhabitant   יָשַׁב → יוֹשֵׁב *to dwell*;   Shepherd   רָעָה → רֹעֶה *to pasture*

(c) Participles may be in apposition to a noun. Apposition is when two or more nouns have the same referent (refer to the same thing) and have the same function in the sentence (e.g. both are subject).

יְהוָה אֱלֹהֵי הַשָּׁמַיִם שֹׁמֵר הַבְּרִית (the covenant)

O LORD, God of heaven, *Keeper of* the covenant…

8.4.2   Attributive.

(a) Active participles with the article may be best translated as a relative clause in English, i.e. translate the article as *that, who, which*.

יְהוָה הָאֹמֵר אֵלַי	-5-	the LORD *who said* to me
הָאִישׁ הָעֹשֶׂה זֹאת	-6-	the man *who did* this

(b) Only *rarely* will an active participle without the article translate well as an attributive adjective.

כְּאֵשׁ אֹכֶלֶת	-7-	like a *consuming* fire

(c) Passive participles are more easily translated as adjectives and may be attributive with or without the article.

וְיָדוֹ הַנְּטוּיָה	-8-	his *stretched out* hand
בְּיָד נְטוּיָה	-9-	with *an outstretched* hand

8.4.3   Predicate and verbal. Predicate participles do not have the article.

(a) Without the article, active participles translate well as participles in English. They usually indicate continuous or progressive action in whatever time frame the surrounding context establishes.

עֵלִי שֹׁמֵר אֶת־פִּיהָ   *-10-*   Eli *was watching* her mouth.

כִּי יֹדֵעַ אֱלֹהִים   *-11-*   For God *knows*…

(b) Without the article, predicate position passive participles may often be translated with adjectives or passive participles.

אֲרוּרָה הָאֲדָמָה   *-12-*   *Cursed* is the ground.

8.4.4   Participle translation summary (generalized).

With article: Active: substantival or relative clause.

Passive: substantival or attributive adjective.

Without article: Active: substantival or participial (*-ing, -ed*).

Passive: substantival or adj. (attributive or predicate).

8.5   Weak verb participles (i.e. verbs with consonants which have extra rules).

8.5.1   R$_2$ = G.

Gutturals take composite *shewa* instead of simple *shewa*: אֹהֲבֵי ,אֹהֲבִים.

8.5.2   R$_3$ = י ≠ ה

Like שָׂדֶה (4.7.4), participles whose masculine singular forms end in ֶה were originally R$_3$ = י not ה. Adding endings to the active forms eliminates the *mater* ה. In the passive forms the original י prevails.

עָשָׂה   lexical form, Qal verb *to do, make, perform.*

עֹשֶׂה   Qal act. ptc.   *doing/making, one who does/makes,*

עָשׂוּי   Qal pass. ptc. *thing done, prepared*

fem. pl.	fem. sg.	masc. pl.	masc. sg.	ab. forms
עֹשׂוֹת	עֹשָׂה	עֹשִׂים	עֹשֶׂה	Qal act. ptc.
עֲשׂוּיֹת	עֲשׂוּיָה	עֲשׂוּיִם	עָשׂוּי	Qal pass. ptc.

8.5.3   R$_2$ = ו/י (also called hollow verbs).

The Qal active participles of R$_2$ = ו/י roots lose R$_2$ and **do not use *holem*** after R$_1$. They have *qametz*, like בוא, (except for אֹיֵב, *enemy*, and מֵת, *dead*).

Qal active	Feminine		Masculine	
participle	plural	singular	plural	singular
absolute	בָּאוֹת	בָּאָה	בָּאִים	בָּא
construct	—	fw בָּאַת	fw בָּאֵי	fw בָּא

To tell these apart from nouns which lose a radical, remember R$_2$ = ו/י nouns keep a *mater*, and *a*-class geminates can put *dagesh* in R$_3$.

There are only 10 passive participles of R$_2$ = ו/י roots. They usually have *shureq*, e.g. mp שׁוּבֵי.

8.5.4 $R_2 = R_3$, Geminates.

No problems. These roots write R_2 and R_3, e.g. שׁוֹדֵד, from שָׁדַד *to destroy*.

8.6   Infinitive construct.

Infinitives are verbal nouns often translated with *to* or *-ing*.

8.6.1   ◻◌ֹ◻, ◻◌ַ◻, or ◻◌ֵ◻: Qal infinitive construct, strong verbs.

The pattern for strong verbs is **monosyllabic** ◻◌ֹ◻, ◻◌ַ◻, or ◻◌ֵ◻, e.g. כְּתֹב *to write*. Most infinitives use *holem* after R_2 but some use *patah* or *tsere*. In particular, the *shewa* under R_1 is characteristic of the Qal infinitive construct.

8.6.2   Infinitive construct functions.

87% of all infinitive constructs are objects of a preposition, most often לְ or בְּ. With לְ the infinitive frequently indicates purpose. With בְּ the infinitive is frequently translated temporally, *when*.

לִשְׁמֹר אֶת־אֲרוֹן (ark) יְהוָה	-1-	...*to keep* the ark of the LORD
לִשְׁמֹר לַעֲשׂוֹת אֶת־כָּל־מִצְוֹתָיו	-2-	...*to be careful to do* all his commands
בִּשְׁמוֹר יוֹאָב אֶל־הָעִיר	-3-	*when* Joab *watched* the city

About 6% are preceded by a temporal indicator like יוֹם or אַחֲרֵי.

בְּיוֹם שְׁמֹעַ אִישָׁהּ	-4-	on the day of the *hearing* of her husband (= on the day her husband hears...)

An **infinitive complement** completes the meaning of another word, such as an adjective or a verb, e.g. better *to serve*, better *to give*.

טוֹב לָלֶכֶת	-5-	it is good *to go* ...
טוֹב לָתֵת	-6-	it is good *to give* ...

8.7   Weak verbs, Qal infinitive construct.

8.7.1   **Gutturals.** On their own, gutturals cause no major issues.

G◌ֹ◻ R_3 = G may (or may not) take a furtive *patah*.

◻◌ְG R_1 = G takes composite *shewa* instead of simple *shewa*.

8.7.2 $R_3 = $ י ≠ ה: ◻◌ֹות

The lexical form looks as if $R_3 = $ ה, but these originally $R_3 = $ י/ו verbs mutate into ◻◌ֹות in the inf. cs. The obvious difficulty is that it looks a like a feminine plural noun or like $R_3 = $ ת. The signal is *shewa* under R_1, e.g. עֲשׂוֹת from עָשָׂה.

8.7.3 $R_2 = $ י/ו. ◻וֹ◻, ◻וּ◻, ◻ִי◻ (also called hollow verbs).

The lexical form of $R_2 = $ י/ו verbs is the infinitive construct, unlike most verbs which use the Qal perfect (ch 10), e.g. the lexical form בוֹא is the infinitive construct. Since $R_2 = $ י/ו becomes a long vowel, there can be no characteristic *shewa* under R_1. Also the infinitive's vowel is the preference of the root's R_2. R_2 is usually present as a *mater* but may disappear, e.g. בֹא instead of בוֹא, שֵׁב instead of שׁוּב.

8.7.4   **Losing R_1. R_1 = י and נָתַן, הָלַךְ, other R_1 = נ and לקח.**

$$ \Box\underline{\Box}\underline{\Box} \mathsf{T} / \Box\underline{\Box}\underline{\Box} \mathsf{T} = \mathsf{T}R_3R_2 / \mathsf{T}R_3R_2 $$

These roots lose R_1, add ת, and use a segolate pattern. As we learn verbs we will find that הָלַךְ acts like R_1 = י verbs and לקח acts like R_1 = נ verbs. The easiest approach to these infinitives:

   1) to learn the infinitives of הָלַךְ, נָתַן, and לָקַח as vocabulary (cp. ch. 7),

   2) to realize that all R_1 = י verbs lose R_1 and watch out for תֶֶ_ / תֶ__, and

   3) to be wary that sometimes it is an R_1 = נ verb that has lost R_1.

So, all R_1 = י verbs lose R_1:   דַּעַת is the infinitive construct of   יָדַע, *to know*.

הָלַךְ loses R_1:   לֶכֶת is the infinitive construct of   הָלַךְ, *to walk*.

נתן loses both נs: תֵּת is the infinitive construct of   נָתַן, *to give*.

לקח loses R_1:   קַחַת is the infinitive construct of   לָקַח, *to take*.

   Most R_1 = נ verbs preserve the נ. Thus נְפוֹל is easy to recognize as the infinitive of נָפַל. (N.B. נשא, נגש, נגע, נפח, and נטע lose R_1.)

8.7.5   **Quiescent א.**

   In the common words יָצָא and נָשָׂא, after R_1 is lost and ת is added at the end, the א quiesces, so the *segols* merge into a long *ṣere*, צֵאת ← צֶאֶת and שֵׂאת ← שֶׂאֶת.

   Preceded by a preposition, R_1 = א often quiesces, resulting in a long vowel under the preposition, most commonly in לֵאמֹר, for לְ + אֱמֹר.

8.7.6   **Geminate infinitives: $\Box\dot{\Box}$, $R_2\dot{R_1}$.**

   Geminate infinitives usually write R_1 + *ḥolem* + R_2, e.g. סֹב *to surround*. Occasionally they write R_2 and R_3, סְבֹב *to surround*.

8.7.7   **Paragogic ה.**

   Some infinitive constructs add הָ at the end, (or a ת like R_1 = weak roots).

$$ \text{אֲהָבָה} = \text{אהב} + \text{הָ} \qquad\qquad \text{אַהֲבַת} = \text{אהב} + \text{ת} $$

8.8   **Pronominal suffixes on infinitives and participles.**

8.8.1   **Pronominal suffixes on infinitives: S$\Box\Box$.**

The infinitive construct uses Type 1 suffixes like singular nouns (6.2).

The suffix may indicate either the performer or receiver of the action.

The *o*-vowel *may* shift, becoming short *qametz ḥatuph* under R_1: שָׁמְרוֹ ← שָׁמֹר + וֹ.

       לְשָׁמְרָהּ = לְ + שָׁמֹר + הָהּ   *-1-*   *to keep it*

       וּלְאָכְלְכֶם = לְ + אָכֹל + כֶם   *-2-*   *and for your eating [= for your food]*

       בִּנְטוֹתִי = בְּ + נְטֹת + יִ   *-3-*   *When I stretch [my hand against Egypt]*

Geminates. Suffixes allow *dagesh* in geminate roots (unless R_2 = G).:

       תֻּמִּי = תמם + יִ

8.8.2   Pronominal suffixes on participles.

The suffix indicates the receiver of the action. Participles take pronominal suffixes like nouns: Type 1 endings for the singular and type 2 for the plural.

שֹׁפְטִי	my judge	שֹׁפְטֵיכֶם	your judges
שֹׁמְרֶךָ	the one who keeps you	כָּל־אֹכְלַיִךְ	all who devour you
כָּל־יוֹדְעוֹ	each one who knew him	אֹכְלָיו	the ones who eat it

1cs suffix.   Ptc. and inf. cs. may use the Type P 1cs suffix נִי◌, e.g. עֹשֵׂנִי *my maker*.

3ms suffix.   Masc. ptc. (or nouns) ending in ה use הוּ◌, e.g. עֹשֵׂהוּ *his maker*.

8.9   Summary.

Participle translation summary (generalized).

Ptc. with article: Active: substantival or relative clause.

Passive: substantival or attributive adjective.

Ptc. without article: Active: substantival or participial (*-ing, -ed*).

Passive: substantival or adj. (attributive or predicate).

93% of infinitive constructs are immediately preceded by a preposition or a temporal indicator like יוֹם or אַחֲרֵי.

ל + infinitive frequently indicates purpose.

בְּ + infinitive is frequently temporal, *when*.

◌ֹ◌◌ֵ◌ַ: Qal active ptc., שֹׁמֵר keeping, one who keeps/watches, keeper/guard.

◌ֵ◌וּ◌◌: Qal passive ptc., שָׁמוּר kept, being kept/watched, what is kept.

◌ְ◌◌ֹ, ◌ְ◌◌ַ, or ◌ֶ◌◌: Qal infinitive construct, כְּתֹב *to write, writing*.

◌ָ◌◌ְS: Infinitives with suffixes: The *o-vowel may* shift: שָׁמְרוֹ → וֹ + שְׁמֹר

R₃ = י ≠ ה

Endings exclude *mater* ה in the active ptc.: עֹשֶׂה, עֹשִׂים, עֹשָׂה, עֹשׂוֹת.

The original י survives in the passive ptc.: עֲשׂוּי, עֲשׂוּיִם, עֲשׂוּיָה, עֲשׂוּיֹת.

Qal infinitive construct: ◌◌וֹת .

R₂ = ו/י

Active participles lose R₂ and use *qametz* under R₁: בָּא, בָּאִים, בָּאָה, בָּאוֹת.

Qal infinitive construct: ◌וֹ◌, ◌וּ◌, ◌יִ◌.

Infinitives losing R₁: ◌ֵ◌ת / ◌ֶ◌ת.

All R₁ = י verbs lose R₁; watch out for ◌ֵ◌ת / ◌ֶ◌ת.

לֶכֶת is the infinitive construct of הָלַךְ, *to walk*.

תֵּת is the infinitive construct of נָתַן, *to give*.

קַחַת is the infinitive construct of לָקַח, *to take*.

Some R₁ = נ verbs lose the נ.

Quiescent א: יצא from צֵאת → צֵאת; ל + אֱמֹר → לֵאמֹר

8.10   Vocabulary.

1	אֶחָד / אַחַת	*n.m./n.f.* one (976*)
2	שְׁנַיִם / שְׁתַּיִם	*n.m./n.f.* two (769)
3	שָׁלֹשׁ	*n.m.* three; pl. thirty (606*)
4	אַרְבַּע	*n.m.* four, pl. forty (466*)
5	חָמֵשׁ	*n.m.* five, pl. fifty (508*)
6	שֵׁשׁ	*n.m.* six, pl. sixty (274*)
7	שֶׁבַע	*n.m.* seven, pl. seventy (490*)
8	שְׁמֹנֶה	*n.m.* eight; pl. eighty (147*)
9	תֵּשַׁע	*n.m.* nine, pl. ninety (78*)
10	עֶשֶׂר / עָשָׂר	*n.m.* ten, x-teen; pl. twenty (829*)
11	מֵאָה	*n.m.* hundred (583)
12	אֶלֶף	*n.m.* thousand, cattle (496)
13	חֲצִי־ / חֵצִי	*n.m.* half (125)
14	שֵׁנִי	*adj.* second (156)
15	אֵיךְ	*adv.* how (61)
16	הָלַךְ	*vb.* to walk, go, come (1554), *he went/has gone*
17	לָמָּה / לָמָה	*prn.* why? (178)
18	לָקַח	*vb.* to take, receive (976), *he took/has taken*
19	מַדּוּעַ	*adv.* why (72)
20	מַה־⌷ / מָה / מֶה	*prn.* what?, what! (571)
21	נָתַן	*vb.* to give, put, set, exchange, grant, yield, dedicate (2014), *he gave/has given*

N.B. The numbers used for counting are called cardinal numbers.

N.B. You learned some infinitives in the vocabulary of ch. 7. Remember that לֶכֶת and הָלַךְ are two forms of the same word, as are קַחַת and לָקַח and also תֵּת and נָתַן.

8.11   Learning activities on the CD.

In this chapter you are to learn to translate participles and infinitive constructs. You may want to keep your grammar open to the chapter summary while doing the practice readings. Keep comparing the participle position to the translation technique. Watch out for pronominal suffixes, especially on infinitives, since this causes a shift in the *o*-vowel back to the first radical.

1   Learn the forms.

Copy the forms of the participle and infinitive.

2   Practice Parsing. 203 items.

Parse participles and infinitive constructs with and without pronominal suffixes. The participles and infinitives are of verbs from previous vocabulary. Use the random button and practice long enough to be sure you recognize the forms.

3   Practice Readings Part A (using chs. 1–7 vocabulary). 79 items.

This first set focuses on incorporating the vocabulary from ch. 7.

4   Practice Readings Part B (using chs. 1–7 vocabulary). 20 items.

This second set focuses on participles and infinitives.

5   Parsing Exercise.

Parse participles and infinitive constructs with and without pronominal suffixes.

6   Translation Exercise.

Translate verses from the Hebrew Bible. Vocabulary helps are provided.

7   Learn ch. 8 vocabulary.

chapter nine

Selected Words,
Numbers

9.1 Focus.

This chapter illustrates special words and numbers. Approach these primarily as vocabulary items; use the discussions for reference. A few glosses may be learned for each of the special vocabulary items, but you will find, when reading actual texts, that these need to be adapted to fit the context. Memorize the basic glosses. Read the discussions for illustration purposes and future reference.

9.2 יֵשׁ / יֶשׁ־ *There is/are; is/are.* **Particle of existence.**

יֵשׁ expresses existence or presence. The examples include declarative statements (1), questions (2–3), and לְ indicating possession (3–4). A pronominal suffix on יֵשׁ may act as a subject for a participle.

יֵשׁ־אֱלֹהִים שֹׁפְטִים בָּאָרֶץ	-1- *There is* a God who judges in the earth.
הֲיֵשׁ יְהוָה בְּקִרְבֵּנוּ	-2- *Is* the LORD in our midst?
הֲיֵשׁ לָכֶם אָח	-3- Do you have a brother?
	(= Is there to you a brother?)
כָּל־יֶשׁ־לוֹ	-4- everything which is his
	(= all *there is* to him)

9.3 אֵין / אַיִן *There is not/ not.* **A particle of negation.**

אַיִן is mostly used for noun clauses, including participle clauses. אֵין indicates absence or non-existence. The examples include declarative statements (1–2) and לְ for possession (3). A pronominal suffix on אֵין may act as a subject for a participle (4). (In contrast, לֹא is used with interrogative הֲ, single words, and verbal clauses.)

וְאָדָם אַיִן לַעֲבֹד (to work) אֶת־הָאֲדָמָה	-1- There was no human to work the soil.
אֵין בּוֹ מָיִם	-2- There was no water in it.
אֵין לוֹ בֵּן	-3- He had no son.
אֵינֶנִּי נֹתֵן לָכֶם תֶּבֶן (straw)	-4- I am not giving you straw.

9.4   הֵן / הִנֵּה *See here! Notice…, realize(d)*, **or point of view.**

הִנֵּה indicates awareness or calls for attention. Its translation must be sensitive to the context. The key parts of the context are who is speaking to whom, and which is having, or is to have, the הִנֵּה–experience. In dialogue, a speaker may use הִנֵּה to call another's attention to something, as in "Hey!" "Look here," or "you see." הִנֵּה may be translated as an exclamation, "Wow!" to show the speaker's own reaction. For the perspective of a character in a story, it may best be translated with a verb, "he realized." הִנֵּה may take a pronominal suffix, meaning *here I am* or *here you are*. The pronominal suffix may also act like a subject for a participle or a nominal clause. With a participle, the action is often impending in the near future. Chapter 29 further illustrates the uses of הִנֵּה.

וַיֹּאמֶר אַבְרָהָם אַבְרָהָם	*-1-*	He called, "Abraham, Abraham."
וַיֹּאמֶר הִנֵּנִי		And he said, "Here I am."
הִנְנִי רֹפֵא (ptc. healing) לָךְ	*-2-*	See here, I am going to heal you.
הִנָּךְ יָפָה (beautiful)	*-3-*	Wow, you are beautiful!
וְהִנֵּה הַסְּנֶה (bush) בֹּעֵר (burning) בָּאֵשׁ	*-4-*	He *realized* that the bush was burning.

Consider the context of example 4. Exod 3:2 begins with the narrator telling the audience that "The Angel of the LORD appeared to him as a fire's flame from the middle of the bush." So the audience knows about the burning bush, but Moses does not. As we picture the story on our mental movie screen, we see the burning bush and know its nature, then we widen the perspective and see Moses enter the scene. By saying וַיַּרְא *he looked*, the narrator has us see Moses look at the bush. Then וְהִנֵּה pictures Moses becoming aware of and intrigued by the bush. A movie director could translate this וְהִנֵּה by showing an expression of interest on the character's face.

9.5   הָ, **Directional** ה **or terminative** ה.

Sometimes הָ indicates *direction toward*, not the feminine morpheme. You can tell them apart because the lexical form of the noun does not have הָ, because it is either masculine or an unmarked feminine, like עִיר. In the extremely rare cases when it is on marked feminine nouns, it goes on the construct form, e.g. הָתָה. Also, directional הָ typically goes on a noun which is a place or direction, or sometimes a time reference.

to the land/ground אַרְצָה	to Egypt מִצְרָיְמָה (מִצְרַיִם Egypt)
eastward קֵדְמָה (קֶדֶם east)	from year[1] to year מִיָּמִים יָמִימָה

---

[1] In this expression, the plural of *day*, יוֹם, means *year*.

9.6   אֲשֶׁר, שֶׁ;[2] **relative pronouns,** *that, whom, which, when, one who.*

The translation of אֲשֶׁר and שֶׁ must be adjusted as the person or thing indicated by the pronoun (its antecedent or head) performs or receives the action of a verb or acts substantively. Your instincts will generally lead you in the right direction. There may be elements in the אֲשֶׁר clause which repeat a prior element in the sentence; the repetition is usually unnecessary in English (cf. #4). See further in ch. 29.

יְהוָה אֱלֹהֵי הַשָּׁמַיִם אֲשֶׁר לְקָחַנִי מִבֵּית אָבִי…   -1-   The LORD, God of heaven *who* took me from my father's house…

וַיֹּאמֶר לַאֲשֶׁר עַל־בֵּיתוֹ   -2-   He said to *the one who was* over his household (= his steward).

כַּחוֹל (sand) שֶׁעַל־שְׂפַת הַיָּם   -3-   …like sand *which is* on the edge[3] of the sea.

וַיֹּאמֶר אֲנִי יוֹסֵף אֲחִיכֶם אֲשֶׁר־מְכַרְתֶּם אֹתִי מִצְרָיְמָה   -4-   He said, "I am Joseph, your brother, *whom* you sold ~~me~~ to Egypt."

9.6.1   אֲשֶׁר **in combinations.**

אֲשֶׁר may combine with prepositions or conjunctions. Because of its frequency you should learn כַּאֲשֶׁר; the others are for reference.

כַּאֲשֶׁר	as, even as, when		יַעַן אֲשֶׁר	because of
בַּאֲשֶׁר	in that, inasmuch, where		עַד אֲשֶׁר	unto which = until
מֵאֲשֶׁר	from where(ever), as for		תַּחַת אֲשֶׁר	under which = on account of

9.6.2   הַ□ , כִּי , אֲשֶׁר. **That's how to say** *that.*

You have encountered these terms already; this list serves as reference.

כִּי, meaning *that,* usually follows a finite verb of *thinking, saying,* or *perceiving.*

אֲשֶׁר, meaning *that,* usually follows a noun and is followed by a verb.

הַ□, the article, meaning *that,* usually follows a noun and is followed by a ptc. or inf.

9.7   מַה־□ / מָה / מֶה.

The forms מָה and מֶה appear before gutturals since they reject *dagesh.*

מַה is usually an interrogative meaning "what?"

מַה may also be used as an emphatic "How!"

מַה is sometimes used indefinitely, "whatever."

Prepositions may combine with מַה. Due to its frequency you should learn לָמָה. The others are included for reference.

לָמָה	why?		כַּמָה	how many?		עַד־מָה	how long?
בַּמָה	how?			how long?		עַל־מָה	why?

---

[2] There are additional rare relative pronouns זוּ, זוֹ, and זֶה.

[3] Notice the semantic range of שָׂפָה, the *lip* of the sea is its *edge* or *rim.*

9.8   Numbers.

You should be able to *recognize* the construct forms and feminine forms. Constructs have the normal vowel changes due to the shift of accent. Feminine forms are marked by הָ and תְ. But *learn* the other forms of *one*, *two*, and *first*.

Cardinal numbers, used for counting, usually do not match the gender of the nouns they describe,[4] except for numbers one and two.

Ordinal numbers indicate position, e.g. third. They are marked by יִ or יתִ, e.g. שְׁלִישִׁי (masc.), שְׁלִישִׁית (fem.). They follow their nouns and agree in gender.

9.8.1   Cardinal and ordinal numbers 1–10.

	Cardinal numbers					Ordinal numbers	
	masc. ab.	masc. cs.	fem. ab.	fem. cs.		masc.	fem.
1	אֶחָד	אַחַד	אַחַת	אַחַת	1st	רִאשׁוֹן	רִאשׁוֹנָה
2	שְׁנַיִם	שְׁנֵי	שְׁתַּיִם	שְׁתֵּי	2nd	שֵׁנִי	שֵׁנִית
3	שָׁלֹשׁ	שְׁלֹשׁ	שְׁלֹשָׁה	שְׁלֹשֶׁת	3rd	שְׁלִישִׁי	שְׁלִישִׁית
4	אַרְבַּע	אַרְבַּע	אַרְבָּעָה	אַרְבַּעַת	4th	רְבִיעִי	רְבִיעִית
5	חָמֵשׁ	חֲמֵשׁ	חֲמִשָּׁה	חֲמֵשֶׁת	5th	חֲמִישִׁי	חֲמִישִׁית
6	שֵׁשׁ	שֵׁשׁ	שִׁשָּׁה	שֵׁשֶׁת	6th	שִׁשִּׁי	שִׁשִּׁית
7	שֶׁבַע	שְׁבַע	שִׁבְעָה	שִׁבְעַת	7th	שְׁבִיעִי	שְׁבִיעִית
8	שְׁמֹנֶה	שְׁמֹנֶה	שְׁמֹנָה	שְׁמֹנַת	8th	שְׁמִינִי	שְׁמִינִית
9	תֵּשַׁע	תְּשַׁע	תִּשְׁעָה	תִּשְׁעַת	9th	תְּשִׁיעִי	תְּשִׁיעִית
10	עֶשֶׂר	עֶשֶׂר	עֲשָׂרָה	עֲשֶׂרֶת	10th	עֲשִׂירִי	עֲשִׂירִית

9.8.2   Teens and tens.

The teens combine *ten* with *one* through *nine*. The tens, 20–90, are indicated by plural forms of the cardinal numbers, except 20 is the plural of 10.

	with masc. nouns	with fem. nouns		tens, 20–90
11	אַחַד עָשָׂר עַשְׁתֵּי עָשָׂר	אַחַת עֶשְׂרֵה עַשְׁתֵּי עֶשְׂרֵה		
12	שְׁנֵי עָשָׂר שְׁנַיִם עָשָׂר	שְׁתֵּי עֶשְׂרֵה שְׁתֵּים עֶשְׂרֵה	20	עֶשְׂרִים
13	שְׁלֹשָׁה עָשָׂר	שְׁלֹשׁ עֶשְׂרֵה	30	שְׁלֹשִׁים
14	אַרְבָּעָה עָשָׂר	אַרְבַּע עֶשְׂרֵה	40	אַרְבָּעִים
15	חֲמִשָּׁה עָשָׂר	חֲמֵשׁ עֶשְׂרֵה	50	חֲמִשִּׁים
16	שִׁשָּׁה עָשָׂר	שֵׁשׁ עֶשְׂרֵה	60	שִׁשִּׁים
17	שִׁבְעָה עָשָׂר	שְׁבַע עֶשְׂרֵה	70	שִׁבְעִים
18	שְׁמֹנָה עָשָׂר	שְׁמֹנֶה עֶשְׂרֵה	80	שְׁמֹנִים
19	תִּשְׁעָה עָשָׂר	תְּשַׁע עֶשְׂרֵה	90	תִּשְׁעִים

---

[4] Some grammarians say they do match in gender, but are spelled irregularly.

9.8.3   Twenty-one to ninety-nine.

Numbers, such as forty-two, are usually joined by וֹ, e.g. forty and two,

אַרְבָּעִים וּשְׁתַּיִם forty-two

אַרְבַּע וּשְׁלֹשִׁים thirty-four

עֶשְׂרִים וְחָמֵשׁ twenty-five

9.8.4   Hundreds, thousands, and beyond.

Two hundreds, two thousands, and twenty thousand may be indicated by dual forms.

מֵאָה 100	מָאתַיִם 200	מֵאוֹת hundreds (in 300–900)
אֶלֶף 1000	אַלְפַּיִם 2000	אֲלָפִים thousands (in 3000–9000)
רְבָבָה 10,000	רִבּוֹתַיִם 20,000	רִבּוֹת ten thousands (in 30,000–90,000)

9.8.5   Singular nouns understood as plural.

Some nouns with numbers more than one are singular in form.

אַרְבָּעִים וּשְׁתַּיִם עִיר forty-two cities

אַרְבַּע וּשְׁלֹשִׁים שָׁנָה thirty-four years

9.9   Summary.

This chapter consists of the use of special vocabulary.

יֵשׁ is a particle of existence, often translated *there is/are*.

אֵין is a negative particle, often translated *not* or *there is not*.

הֵן/הִנֵּה indicates point of view, awareness, or calls for attention.

אֲשֶׁר and שֶׁ are relative pronouns – *who*, *which*, *that*. Prepositions may combine with אֲשֶׁר, e.g. כַּאֲשֶׁר, *as, even as, when*.

מֶה / מָה / מַה־◌ means *what?* or *how!* and occasionally *whatever*. It may combine with prepositions, e.g. לָמָּה, *why?* (= *for what?*).

הָ◌, Directional ◌ָה ה. may indicate *direction toward*.

Numbers. Having learned the masculine singular absolute forms in the last chapter's vocabulary, you should be able to *recognize* the construct and feminine forms.

The counting numbers, called cardinal numbers, generally *do not match the gender* of the nouns they describe (only *one* and *two* do).

The tens are indicated by plural forms, e.g. שְׁלֹשִׁים is thirty.

Ordinals indicate position, e.g. 2nd, 3rd. They are marked by ◌ִי, שְׁלִישִׁי (masc.), or שְׁלִישִׁית, ◌ִית (fem.). They follow their nouns and agree in gender.

9.10   Vocabulary.

1	אֶבֶן	*n.f.* stone (276)
2	אָדוֹן	*n.m.* master, superior, lord (335)
3	אוֹת	*n.m.* sign, symbol, pledge, omen; **(not the D.O. indicator) (79)
4	אֲרוֹן	*n.m/f.* ark, chest (202)
5	בְּרִית	*n.m.* covenant (287)
6	חָנָה	*vb.* to camp, bend down (143), *he (has) camped*
7	חֶרֶב	*n.f.* sword (413)
8	כָּתַב	*vb.* to write (225), *he wrote/has written*
9	לֶחֶם	*n.m.* bread, food (340)
10	מַחֲנֶה	*n.m.* camp, encampment (215)
11	מָלֵא	*vb.* be full (252), *it is/was full*
12	מָלֵא	*adj.* full (61)
13	מָקוֹם	*n.m.* place, standing place (401)
14	עֵדָה	*n.f.* congregation (149*)
15	עָוֹן	*n.m.* wrongdoing, guilt (from)/punishment (for) iniquity (233)
16	פֹּה	*adv.* here (82)
17	קֵץ	*n.m.* end (67)
18	קָצֶה	*n.m.* end, edge (92)
19	קֶרֶב	*n.m.* midst, inner, innards (227)
20	שָׁם	*adv.* there (835)

9.11   Learning activities on the CD.

This chapter has no new morphemes and no new parts of speech. It illustrates the use of certain vocabulary. Normally the exercises use only the vocabulary of previous chapters, but in this case you will need to learn ch. 9 vocabulary for the second set of practice readings and translation exercises.

1   **Practice Readings Pt A** (using ch. 1–8 vocabulary). 50 items.

2   **Translation Exercise.**

3   **Morphology review.** Practice writing Unit 1 morphology.

You can practice parsing by going to the previous chapters on the CD.

4   **Learn ch. 9 vocabulary.**

5   **Practice Readings Pt B** (using chs. 1–9 vocabulary). 50 items.

6   **Translation Exercise.**

You have learned enough now to read paragraphs, not just assorted verses.
Section One: misc.   Section Two: Josh 3:16–4:2, 5–6.
Section Three: Num 14:1–8.

chapter ten

Introduction to Verbs;
Qal Perfect

10.1 Focus.

In this chapter you are to learn:

the **9 endings of the perfect verb** by comparison to the pronoun and noun,

the **syllabic structure of the Qal perfect**, including its "identity badge,"

the difference between **stative** and **fientive** verbs, and

that the Hebrew verb system is not tense based like English.

The English verb may indicate tense, or time, with words, e.g. *will, have, has been*; suffixes, e.g. love*s*, love*d*; or vowel changes, e.g. s*i*ng, s*a*ng, s*u*ng. Hebrew lacks words like *will* and *had*. When it uses suffixes or changes vowels, it does so for different reasons than English.

This chapter introduces the Qal perfect conjugation. A verbal conjugation is a set of spellings that indicate the person, number, and gender of a verb's subject, e.g. *we, she, you*. Hebrew has two major conjugations, one with suffixes (endings) only, one with prefixes and some suffixes. Sometimes they are called the *suffixed* and *prefixed* conjugations, but most often the *perfect* and *imperfect*. These terms refer to verbal aspect. As an overgeneralization, the perfect conjugation views action as complete and the imperfect as incomplete (*n.b.* not complete*d* and incomplete*d*). The time frame of a verb depends on its form, the context, and whether it describes a state or an action, that is, whether it is *stative* or *fientive*.

The perfect verb has three main components. The endings signal person, gender, and number. The theme vowel, which is R_2's vowel, may help signal whether it is stative or fientive. R_1's syllable signals the stem; we call it the stem's ID badge.

כָּ תַ֫ בְ תָּ

Ending	Theme vowel	R_1's syllable
indicates subject's person, gender, & number	may indicate stative vs. fientive	indicates stem/binyan

10.2   The Qal Perfect Paradigm.

The paradigms on the next page are the heart of the chapter and reveal several basic things. (1) The endings come from the independent pronoun or the noun. (2) There may be a difference between fientive and stative verbs in spelling and (3) possibly in translation. (4) The vowel under R_1 is consistent among all the lists.

A verb's accented syllable need not follow the noun accent rules. But once the endings establish the accent, the other syllable principles apply and shape the verb.

10.2.1   The ID badge. The Qal syllabic structure and R_1: ⱻ◻◌̇◌̣ or Ė◻◻◌̣.

ⱻ◻◌̇◌̣   קָטַ֫לְנוּ R_1 usually has pretonic open long *qametz*.

Ė◻◻◌̣   קְטַלְתֶּ֫ם   With the accent on תֶּ֫ם, R_1 takes *shewa* in problem position.

Because of the syllable principles, **Qal perfect R_1 has *qametz* or *shewa*.** The other verbal stems treat R_1 differently, so this is the Qal perfect's unique signature. A stem's unique traits are sometimes called principal parts, stem characteristics, stem distinctives, or other similar terms. We will call it a stem's ID badge. These traits typically involve R_1 and identify the verb's stem.

10.2.2   *The Syllabic structure* and R_2 and R_3.

(a)   *If* the suffix has only one consonant, *or if* there is no suffix,

then R_2 and R_3 are together with the accent and a full vowel. R_1 has POL *qametz*.

קָטַ֫ל, קָטַ֫לְנוּ, קָטַ֫לְתָּ, קָטַ֫לְתְ, קָטַ֫לְתִּי

(b)   *If* the suffix begins with a vowel,

then R_3 goes with that vowel and R_2 takes vocal *shewa* (cp. 2.10). Since *shewa* is not a syllable, R_1 is still pretonic open long. A pausal accent on R_2 gives it a long vowel.

קָ טְ לוּ, קָ טְ לָה   קָ טְלוּ, קָ טְלָה

(c)   *If* the suffix has two consonants,

then the suffix is "heavy" enough to take the accent. R_2 and R_3 form a PCS syllable, while R_1 now takes vocal *shewa* in problem position.

קְטַל תֶּ֫ן, קְטַל תֶּ֫ם

(d)   The other verbal stems treat R_2 and R_3 the same way as either קָטַל or כָּבֵד.

10.2.3   Types of Verb (stative or fientive) or Verbal *Aktionsart*

Stative verbs describe a state or condition while fientive verbs describe an action. They may use a different theme vowel in the Qal perfect. Fientive (action) verbs use an *a*-class theme vowel under R_2, like קָטַל. Stative verbs usually use a combination of *i*-class and *a*-class vowels, like כָּבֵד, or use an *i*-class or an *u*-class theme vowel throughout. The rest stays the same. You will read more about translation below.

Memorize the paradigms for קָטַל and כָּבֵד. (The Qal perfect 3ms form is the lexical form for most verbs.) Reciting the pronoun with each form is helpful.

10.2.4 The Qal Perfect Paradigm.

(a) Fientive (showing syllabic structure).

	translation	Qal perfect	Perfect Endings	Pronoun/ Noun	
1cs	I (have) killed	קָ טַ֫ ל תִּי	תִּי	אָנֹכִי	1cs
2ms	you (have) killed	קָ טַ֫ ל תָּ	תָּ	אַתָּה	2ms
2fs	you (have) killed	קָ טַ֫ ל תְּ¹	תְּ	אַתְּ	2fs
3ms	he (has) killed	קָ טַ֫ ל	Ø	דָּבָרØ	3ms
3fs	she (has) killed	קָ טְלָה	◌ָה	מַלְכָּה	3fs
1cp	we (have) killed	קָ טַ֫ ל נוּ	נוּ	אֲנַחְנוּ	1cp
2mp	you (have) killed	קְטַל תֶּ֫ם	תֶּם	אַתֶּם	2mp
2fp	you (have) killed	קְטַל תֶּ֫ן	תֶּן	אַתֵּנָה	2fp
3cp	they (have) killed	קָ טְלוּ	וּ²		3cp

(b) Stative (similar to fientives but a different theme vowel under R₂.)

	translation	*a/i*-class	*i*-class	*u*-class
1cs	I am/was honored	כָּבַ֫דְתִּי	מָלֵאתִי	יָכֹ֫לְתִּי
2ms	you are/were honored	כָּבַ֫דְתָּ	מָלֵאתָ	יָכֹ֫לְתָּ
2fs	you are/were honored	כָּבַ֫דְתְּ	מָלֵאת	יָכֹ֫לְתְּ
3ms	he is/was honored	כָּבֵ֫ד	מָלֵא	יָכֹל
3fs	she is/was honored	כָּבְדָה³	מָלְאָה	יָכְלָה
1cp	we are/were honored	כָּבַ֫דְנוּ	מָלֵאנוּ	יָכֹ֫לְנוּ
2mp	you are/were honored	כְּבַדְתֶּ֫ם	מְלֵאתֶ֫ם	יְכָלְתֶּ֫ם
2fp	you are/were honored	כְּבַדְתֶּ֫ן	מְלֵאתֶ֫ן	יְכָלְתֶּ֫ן
3cp	they are/were honored	כָּבְדוּ	מָלְאוּ	יָכְלוּ

---

¹ This is an unusual form, with a *dagesh* following a *shewa* and a second *shewa* under the last letter. Cp. 2.7 *n.* 1. Historically, the ת was followed by a vowel.

² This long *ū* vowel also came from a plural noun marker, but it is no longer in Biblical Hebrew.

³ The *metheg* (2.9) with the *qametz* under R₁ כָּ indicates it is an open syllable. It is not always written.

10.3   The theme vowel.

The theme vowel can help distinguish whether a verb is stative or fientive, but it is not determinative. Most stative verbs are like כָּבֵד and only use a different theme vowel in their lexical form, the 3ms Qal perfect (but see below for 3fs and 3cp). However, gutturals can influence the vowel choice. The verb יָדַע *to know* is stative but the theme vowel does not show it. Usually you can tell by the dictionary entry; stative verbs are usually glossed as "*be X.*"

10.3.₁   The theme vowel and pausal forms.

Pausal accents tend to lengthen vowels. In the Qal perfect, this means that R₂ will have a long vowel, except for the 2mp and 2fp forms, which have the accent on their ending. Pausing also restores the accent to R₂ for the 3fs and 3cp forms. Note that the pausal forms reveal that all the third person forms of כָּבֵד are *i*-class.

	fientive contextual	fientive **pausal**	stative contextual	stative **pausal**
1cs	קָטַ֫לְתִּי	קָטָ֫לְתִּי	כָּבַ֫דְתִּי	כָּבָ֫דְתִּי
2ms	קָטַ֫לְתָּ	קָטָ֫לְתָּ	כָּבַ֫דְתָּ	כָּבָ֫דְתָּ
2fs	קָטַ֫לְתְּ	קָטָ֫לְתְּ	כָּבַ֫דְתְּ	כָּבָ֫דְתְּ
3ms	קָטַ֫ל	קָטָ֫ל	כָּבֵד	כָּבֵ֫ד
3fs	קָטְלָה	קָטָ֫לָה	כָּבְדָה	כָּבֵ֫דָה
1cp	קָטַ֫לְנוּ	קָטָ֫לְנוּ	כָּבַ֫דְנוּ	כָּבָ֫דְנוּ
2mp	קְטַלְתֶּ֫ם	קְטַלְתֶּ֫ם	כְּבַדְתֶּ֫ם	כְּבַדְתֶּ֫ם
2fp	קְטַלְתֶּ֫ן	קְטַלְתֶּ֫ן	כְּבַדְתֶּ֫ן	כְּבַדְתֶּ֫ן
3cp	קָטְלוּ	קָטָ֫לוּ	כָּבְדוּ	כָּבֵ֫דוּ

Pausal forms of verbs are more common in poetry and speech than narrative. Observing them in speech can increase the sense of drama in a dialogue (cf. ch. 23).

(Pausal forms also lengthen the vowel in the 3fs and 3cp forms of *i*-class and *u*-class statives, e.g. יִכְלָה, מָלְאוּ, מָלְאָה, and יִכְלוּ.)

10.3.₂   For future reference.

Some verbal stems have a mixed theme vowel in the perfect like כָּבֵד, while other stems have *a*-class perfects, like קָטַל. We will learn those stems by making comparisons to כָּבֵד and קָטַל.

10.4   The verb and *maqqef*.

Sometimes the verb is joined to another word by *maqqef*: אָמַר־לִי *he said to me*. It is a pronunciation issue, indicating the words are to be read closely together. (The verb with *maqqef* is not in construct.)

10.5 Stative or Fientive and Time frame.

Fientive verbs describe an action, motion, or process, such as: כָּתַב *to write*, שָׁבַר *to break*, קָטַל *to kill*, קָבַר *to bury*. Fientive verbs may take a direct object which receives the action of the verb, e.g. he (has) killed *the enemy*, they (have) broke(n) *the pottery*. These are called **transitive** verbs. Fientive verbs which do not take a direct object, like *he walked*, are called **intransitive** verbs.

Stative verbs describe a condition or state of being, such as: כָּבֵד *to be fat* or *honored* (i.e. have social weight), זָקֵן *to be old*, or יָכֹל *to be able*. Stative verbs can be **transitive**. The stative verb אָהֵב (*he loves*) takes a direct object (but the direct object is not affected like the object of a fientive verb).

The perfect conjugation sees the verbal situation as complete. A state can be complete in the present or in the past. So *stative verbs* in the *perfect* conjugation may be either past or present time. זָקְנָה can present a state complete in the present, *she is old*, or in the past, *she was old*. כָּבֵד can present a state complete in the present, *he is honored*, or in the past, *he was honored*. A future state will typically be expressed by the *imperfect* (incomplete) conjugation (ch 12), e.g. *he will be honored* (יִכְבַּד).

As an action is not complete in the present, *fientive verbs* in the *perfect* conjugation typically express an action in the past. Where in the past depends on context, such that כָּתְבוּ might sometimes be rendered *they wrote* and at other times *they have written*. The *imperfect* (יִכְתְּבוּ) may express present or future actions, both viewed as incomplete, e.g. they *are writing* or they *will write*.

Aspect, type, and context can combine as follows, though this introductory chart does not have all the possibilities.

	Fientive	Stative
Perfect (complete)	**past** (past action viewed as complete or as a whole)	**past** (past state viewed as complete) **present** (a state is complete in the present)
Imperfect (not complete)	**present** (an action in progress is incomplete) **future** (future action viewed as incomplete)	**future** (state viewed as incomplete in the future)

10.6 *Vav* plus perfect: wᵉqatal / *vav* plus perfect consecutive.

The perfect preceded by וְ is sometimes called a *wᵉqatal* form (וְקָטַל) or a perfect consecutive.[4] In this construction it may have other functions. Chiefly they are to continue the character of the preceding verb (whatever its form may be) or to advance it in a logical consequence, such as beginning an apodosis (if... then...). We will meet these uses as we learn the other verb forms and will revisit them in ch. 31.

---

[4] Some people refer to it as a *vav* consecutive plus the perfect.

10.7   Translation.

10.7.1   Subject in the verb.

The subject is included in the verb and may not be explicitly stated elsewhere.

עָשָׂה אֶת־הָאָדָם   He had made humankind.

If the subject is explicitly stated, the pronoun in English is usually unnecessary.

וְשָׁמַר יְהוָה אֱלֹהֶיךָ לָךְ   The LORD your God ~~he~~ protected you.

If the subject is stated and the Hebrew pronoun is used with the verb, this is often for emphasis and so it may be useful to repeat the pronoun in English.

הֲלֹא הוּא אָמַר־לִי אֲחֹתִי הִוא   "Didn't he *himself* say to me,
                                                'she is my sister'?"

Since Hebrew has no neuter, the masculine and feminine third person singular forms may be translated *it* as fits the context.

10.7.2   Object of the verb.

What is translated as the direct object in English may be the object of a preposition in Hebrew, rather than be marked by אֵת.

וְשָׁמַר יְהוָה אֱלֹהֶיךָ לָךְ   The LORD your God protected *you.*

10.7.3   Time frame, genre, and context.

As mentioned, Qal perfect statives and fientives may be translated differently in English. For example, the stative perfect may be present but not the fientive perfect. You will need to judge by context. These illustrations are not exhaustive but point out some important considerations about context.

(a)   Speech/dialogue.

The **perfect stative** is usually present in speech.

אָהַבְתִּי אֶת־אֲדֹנִי   -1-   "I *love* my master"
                                          Exod 21:5

וַיֹּאמֶר אַהֲרֹן ...   -2-   Aaron said,
אַתָּה יָדַעְתָּ אֶת־הָעָם...   "You yourself *know* the people..."
                                          Exod 32:22

The **perfect fientive** is often simple past time in speech.

וַיֹּאמֶר הָאָדָם ...   -3-   The man said,
הִוא נָתְנָה־לִי מִן־הָעֵץ ...   "She *gave* to me from the tree."
                                          Gen 3:12

The English perfect may be chosen to focus on the results of the action.

שָׁמַעְתִּי אֶת־תְּפִלָּתֶךָ   -4-   "I *have heard* your prayer."
                                          1Ki 9:3

(b) Poetry.

The **perfect stative** is often present in poetry, as in speech.

-5-   אָהַבְתָּ רָּע מִטּוֹב   You *love* evil more than good
Ps 52:5

-6-   אֲנִי יָדַעְתִּי כִּי־גָדוֹל יְהוָה   I *know* that the LORD is great.
Ps 135:5

The **perfect fientive** may be simple past time in poetry.

-7-   ... נָתַתָּה לּוֹ   [He asked life from you.] You *gave* it to him.
Ps 21:5

-8-   לֹא שָׁמְרוּ בְּרִית אֱלֹהִים   they *did* not *keep* God's covenant
Ps 78:10

The English perfect may be chosen to focus on the results of the action.

-9-   וְהָאָרֶץ נָתַן לִבְנֵי־אָדָם   The earth he *has given* to the sons of men.
Ps 115:16

In this way a perfect fientive can serve in a context which focuses on the present even though a perfect fientive cannot be present tense like the stative fientive.

(c) Narrative.

In narrative it will be quite normal for the perfect stative to be past time and the perfect fientive to be perfective in English. This is because the perfect verb form is usually in a kind of background clause. A Hebrew storyteller narrates the story's past events in sentences with the verb first, using a verb form called the preterite (ch. 12).

So the main action line of the Jonah story, for example, comes in these verb-first preterite clauses, "There was a storm…, the sailors were afraid…, they called to their gods…, they tossed cargo overboard." At that point, the author wants us to see not the next thing but something going on at the same time. Jonah is asleep during the frenzied actions of the sailors. So he switches to a noun-first construction and a perfect verb. The perfect fientive should be translated with a past perfect in English.

-10-   ... וְיוֹנָה יָרַד   But Jonah *had gone down* [into the ship]
Jon 1:5

This syntactic clue breaks the sequence of events. How this change affects the hearers' mental picture of a story depends on the story line. In this case it is a change in scene, from above deck to below deck. Sometimes it has a freeze frame effect while the narrator points out some detail in the existing scene.

A stative verb in such a background clause is typically simple past time.

-11-   וְיִשְׂרָאֵל אָהַב אֶת־יוֹסֵף   Israel loved Joseph [more than all his sons]
Gen 37:3

The preceding examples are not exhaustive nor are you expected to master them now. Focus on learning the forms and the basic translation options. The practice readings and exercises will familiarize you with more examples.

10.8   A sneak peek at the verb system.

10.8.1   Stems/*Binyanim*.

The Qal is the first of seven verbal stems, or **binyanim**, which use the subject spellings from the perfect and imperfect conjugations. There are three basic parts to the spellings of verbs: (1) the suffixes or prefixes indicating the subject (i.e. perfect or imperfect conjugation), (2) the theme vowel, and (3) the identifying characteristic of the stem, or its **identity badge**, which always involves R₁.

The names of the other six stems come from their 3ms perfect form of the verb *pa'al*, (פָּעַל *to do*): Niphal (נִפְעַל), Piel (פִּעֵל), Hitpael (הִתְפַּעֵל), Pual (פֻּעַל), Hiphil (הִפְעִיל), and Hophal (הָפְעַל). These six stems are called the **derived stems.**

In the cases of the Niphal, Hiphil, and Hophal, it is easy to see the prefixes (נ and ה) which characterize each *binyan* in the stem names. The Piel, Hitpael, and Pual normally double the second radical, but פֻּעַל has a guttural for R₂, which cannot double, obscuring this feature in the name.

So in the derived stems, the first radical joins either a prefix (נ or ה) or a doubled R₂ in making the identifying feature of the *binyan*. That syllable, including a characteristic vowel, constitutes the stem's ID badge. The behaviors of R₂ and R₃ are otherwise controlled by the endings and are comparable to קָטַל or כָּבֵד. Learning the derived stems mainly involves learning their pretonic syllable, i.e. asking the question, "what happens to R₁?"

10.8.2   Voice, the direction of the action.

Active voice indicates the subject performs the action (*he hit* the ball). **Passive voice** indicates the subject receives the action (*he was hit* by the ball). **Reflexive voice** indicates the subject somehow performs and receives the action (they *stared at one another*). Qal, Piel, and Hiphil verbs are active voice. Niphal and Hophal verbs may be passive or reflexive. Pual verbs are passive; and Hitpael verbs are reflexive.

	preform. נ	Double R₂			preformative ה	
Qal	Niphal	Piel	Pual	Hitpael	Hiphil	Hophal
Active	Pass., Refl.	Active	Passive	Reflexive	Active	Pass., Refl.

The Qal and Niphal represent the basic or normal meaning of the root word. The Qal gives the active, כָּתַב *to write*, the Niphal gives the passive, נִכְתַּב *to be written*. The D-stems (Piel, Pual, and Hitpael) share a core notion but differ in voice, likewise the H-stems (Hiphil and Hophal). The meanings in the D-stems and the H-stems may be viewed as variations on the Qal and Niphal. Stative and fientive roots are affected differently by the derived stems. We will learn those meanings later. For now note that it is good practice to distinguish fientives and statives in the Qal.

10.9   Summary.

Qal Perfect ID badge: Ḃ◌◌ָ or Ė◌◌◌ַ

Qal perfect R₁ has pretonic open long *qametz* or *shewa* in problem position.

Qal perfect pausal	Qal perfect contextual	Qal perfect pausal	Qal perfect contextual	Perfect Suffixes	Pronoun/ Noun	
כָּבַ֫דְתִּי	כָּבַ֫דְתִּי	קָטַ֫לְתִּי	קָטַ֫לְתִּי	תִּי	אָנֹכִי	1cs
כָּבַ֫דְתָּ	כָּבַ֫דְתָּ	קָטַ֫לְתָּ	קָטַ֫לְתָּ	תָּ	אַתָּה	2ms
כָּבַ֫דְתְּ	כָּבַ֫דְתְּ	קָטַ֫לְתְּ	קָטַ֫לְתְּ	תְּ	אַתְּ	2fs
כָּבֵ֫ד	כָּבֵד	קָטָ֫ל	קָטַל	Ø	דָּבָרØ	3ms
כָּבֵ֫דָה	כָּבְדָה	קָטָ֫לָה	קָטְלָה	◌ָה	מַלְכָּה	3fs
כָּבַ֫דְנוּ	כָּבַ֫דְנוּ	קָטַ֫לְנוּ	קָטַ֫לְנוּ	נוּ	אֲנַ֫חְנוּ	1cp
כְּבַדְתֶּ֫ם	כְּבַדְתֶּ֫ם	קְטַלְתֶּ֫ם	קְטַלְתֶּ֫ם	תֶּם	אַתֶּם	2mp
כְּבַדְתֶּ֫ן	כְּבַדְתֶּ֫ן	קְטַלְתֶּ֫ן	קְטַלְתֶּ֫ן	תֶּן	אַתֶּ֫נָה	2fp
כָּבְד֫וּ	כָּבְד֫וּ	קָטְל֫וּ	קָטְל֫וּ	וּ		3cp

Qal perfect fientives generally have an *a*-class theme vowel under R₂.

Most Qal perfect stative verbs have a mixed *a/i*-class theme vowel or an *i*-class or *u*-class theme vowel throughout.

Verb Type and Time frame; basic options.

	Fientive	Stative
Perfect (complete)	**past** (past action viewed as complete or as a whole)	**past** (past state viewed as complete) **present** (a state is complete in the present)
Imperfect (not complete)	**present** (an action in progress is incomplete) **future** (future action viewed as incomplete)	**future** (future state viewed as incomplete)

A *vav* plus perfect consecutive, or *wᵉqatal* form (וְקָטַל) typically continues the character of the preceding verb.

10.10 **Vocabulary**. Frequent adverbs and conjunctions. Select weak verbs.

1	אָז	*adv.*	then, at that time, thereupon (141)
2	אַךְ	*adv.*	surely, only, however (161)
3	גַּם	*adv.*	also (769)
4	כֹּה	*adv.*	thus, here (577)
5	כֵּן	*adv.*	thus, so (741)
6	רַק	*adv.*	only, surely (109)
7	אוֹ	*cj.*	or (321)
8	אִם	*cj.*	if, when, or (1070)
9	יַעַן	*cj.*	on account of (100)
10	כִּי אִם	*cj.*	except, but only (156)
11	לְמַעַן	*cj.*	in order that, on account of (272)
12	עַל־כֵּן	*cj.*	therefore (161)
13	פֶּן	*cj.*	lest (133)
14	בּוֹשׁ	*vb.*	be ashamed (125)
15	בָּחַר	*vb.*	to choose (172)
16	גָּלָה	*vb.*	to uncover, depart (into exile) (187)
17	מוּת	*vb.*	to die (845)
18	מָצָא	*vb.*	to find (457)
19	סָבַב	*vb.*	to surround, turn, go around (163)
20	עָזַב	*vb.*	to abandon, forsake, leave (214)
21	קוּם	*vb.*	to arise, rise, stand up (627)
22	שָׁמַע	*vb.*	to hear, obey (1165)
23	תָּמַם / תַּם	*vb.*	be complete, finished (64)

10.11 **Learning activities on the CD.**

1 **Grammar Illustration.** Watch the Qal perfect be formed by adding pronoun or noun parts to the verbal root and then adding the theme vowel and the stem ID badge.

2 **Practice Parsing: Sets A, B, C, D.**

Set A. Focus on endings. Parse Qal pf. verbs from chs. 1–9 vocabulary. 12 items.

Set B. Focus on the root. Parse Qal pf. verbs not from past vocabulary. 12 items.

Set C. Focus on the stem. Parse Qal pf. verbs that are Qal or Non-Qal. 12 items.

Set D. Review. Parse verbs including ptc. and inf. cs. 15 items.

3 **Parsing Exercise.**

4 **Practice Reading** (using vocabulary from chs. 1–9). 57 items.

5 **Translation Exercise.**

Section One: misc. Section Two: 1Sam 26:5–9.

6 **Learn ch. 10 vocabulary.**

chapter eleven

Qal Perfect: Weak Verbs

11.1   Focus.

In this chapter you are to learn:

no new verb endings,

to apply the weak letter behaviors to the structure of the Qal perfect.

Weak verbs have letters that follow extra rules. After those rules are followed a root letter may be missing or R_1's syllable may differ from the strong verb, that is, the stem's ID badge may look disguised. As a strategy, when you see a pattern that does not match the strong verb, ask which consonantal peculiarity caused the change. Read the discussions to answer that question. Focus on the principles involved and on the places that differ most from the strong verb. The variations are your clues to the root.

We will compile a list of characteristics of the weak roots and call them Alias Profiles (11.5). At this point, they will help you identify the type of weak root and when the other verb stems are added they will help you identify the stem as well.

11.2   Review: Extra Rule letters (weak consonants).

The weak consonants are נ, ו, and י, and the gutturals. Additionally, geminate roots ($R_2 = R_3$) are weak and have extra rules. Though unique in having *dagesh lene*, *begadkephat* letters are not considered weak because these letters are still written and do not affect the vowels. Weak letters affect the vowels, disappear, or both.

Summary of issues (cp. chs. 1, 4, and 8).

נ   Over silent *shewa*, נְ tends to assimilate in the next letter as *dagesh*, ◻ּ◻ ← ◻ְנ◻.

י/ו   י and ו tend to become vocalic or drop out and prefer certain vowel classes.

G   Gutturals – א, ה, ח, & ע – reject simple *shewa*, preferring composite *shewa*.

א   Aleph also quiesces (is written but not pronounced) when closing a syllable.

$R_3 = $ י ≠ ה   The ה of the lexical form leads one to think of these as gutturals, but the ה is a *mater*; י was the real root letter.

$R_2 = R_3$ Geminate verbs usually do not permit a vowel between R_2 and R_3.

Geminate verbs and $R_2 = $ י/ו involve the greatest structural differences from the pattern in the strong verb. The others have only minor variations for the Qal perfect.

11.3   Gutturals, *nun*, and final *yod*: minor variations.

You can scan these quickly to see their similarity to קָטַל or כָּבֵד, then read the discussions to confirm the few places which differ. R_1 still displays the Qal perfect's identity badge, either a pretonic open long *qametz* or *shewa* in problem position.

	strong	$R_1 = G$	$R_2 = G$	$R_3 = G$	$R_3 = א$	$R_3 = א$
1cs	קָטַ֫לְתִּי	עָמַ֫דְתִּי	בָּחַ֫רְתִּי	שָׁמַ֫עְתִּי	מָלֵ֫אתִי	מָצָ֫אתִי
2ms	קָטַ֫לְתָּ	עָמַ֫דְתָּ	בָּחַ֫רְתָּ	שָׁמַ֫עְתָּ	מָלֵ֫אתָ	מָצָ֫אתָ
2fs	קָטַ֫לְתְּ	עָמַ֫דְתְּ	בָּחַ֫רְתְּ	שָׁמַ֫עַתְּ **	מָלֵאת	מָצָאת
3ms	קָטַל	עָמַד	בָּחַר	שָׁמַע	מָלֵא	מָצָא
3fs	קָטְלָה	עָמְדָה	בָּחֲרָה *	שָׁמְעָה	מָלְאָה	מָצְאָה
1cp	קָטַ֫לְנוּ	עָמַ֫דְנוּ	בָּחַ֫רְנוּ	שָׁמַ֫עְנוּ	מָלֵ֫אנוּ	מָצָ֫אנוּ
2mp	קְטַלְתֶּ֫ם	עֲמַדְתֶּ֫ם *	בְּחַרְתֶּ֫ם	שְׁמַעְתֶּ֫ם	מְלֵאתֶ֫ם	מְצָאתֶ֫ם
2fp	קְטַלְתֶּ֫ן	עֲמַדְתֶּ֫ן *	בְּחַרְתֶּ֫ן	שְׁמַעְתֶּ֫ן	מְלֵאתֶ֫ן	מְצָאתֶ֫ן
3cp	קָטְלוּ	עָמְדוּ	בָּחֲרוּ *	שָׁמְעוּ	מָלְאוּ	מָצְאוּ

	strong	Doubly Weak	$R_3 = י \neq ה$	$R_3 = נ$	* $R_3 = נ$ (נתן)
1cs	קָטַ֫לְתִּי	עָשִׂ֫יתִי	גָּלִ֫יתִי	זָקַ֫נְתִּי	נָתַ֫תִּי
2ms	קָטַ֫לְתָּ	עָשִׂ֫יתָ	גָּלִ֫יתָ	זָקַ֫נְתָּ	נָתַ֫תָּ
2fs	קָטַ֫לְתְּ	עָשִׂ֫ית	גָּלִ֫ית	זָקַ֫נְתְּ	נָתַ֫תְּ
3ms	קָטַל	עָשָׂה	גָּלָה **	זָקֵן	נָתַן
3fs	קָטְלָה	עָשְׂתָה	גָּלְתָה **	זָקְנָה	נָתְנָה
1cp	קָטַ֫לְנוּ	עָשִׂ֫ינוּ	גָּלִ֫ינוּ	זָקַ֫נּוּ **	נָתַ֫נּוּ
2mp	קְטַלְתֶּ֫ם	עֲשִׂיתֶ֫ם	גְּלִיתֶ֫ם	—	נְתַתֶּ֫ם
2fp	קְטַלְתֶּ֫ן	עֲשִׂיתֶ֫ן	גְּלִיתֶ֫ן	—	נְתַתֶּ֫ן
3cp	קָטְלוּ	עָשׂוּ	גָּלוּ **	זָקְנוּ	נָתְנוּ

11.3.1   Gutturals (א, ה, ח, and ע).

The gutturals' main issue in the Qal perfect is an easily recognized change of simple *shewa* to composite *shewa*. The 2fs forms when $R_3 = ח$ or $ע$ have an extra rule (see below). (*Dagesh forte* is a not an issue since it is not part of the Qal paradigm.)

(*a*) R₁ = G.   The second person plural endings move the accent so R₁ is in problem position, taking composite *shewa*: עֲזַבְתֶּן, עֲזַבְתֶּם.

(*b*) R₂ = G.   The 3fs and 3cp contextual forms call for vocal *shewa*. R₂ = G insists on composite *shewa*: בָּחֲרָה, בָּחֲרוּ (no problem in pause בָּחָרוּ).

(*c*) **R₃ = G (ה or ע).**   Gutturals can usually tolerate silent *shewa* under R₃.[1]

The **2fs forms** call for a vocal *shewa* under R₃. ה and ע should insist on *ḥataph pataḥ* instead. But **yet another rule** is applied. The unusual cluster of *shewas* and *dagesh* of 2fs forms (קָטַלְתְּ) upgrade it to a full *pataḥ*[2] (e.g. שָׁמַעְתְּ ← שָׁמַעַתְּ; לָקַחַתְּ ← לָקַחְתְּ). Though **rare** (only 32 times), it is a true variation from the pattern.

(*d*) R₃ = א.   The *aleph* quiesces and a preceding vowel is always long. Stative roots use *ṣere* for the theme vowel. Fientive roots use *qametz*. Since the suffixes now follow a vowel, ת does not take *dagesh lene*: מָצָאת, מָצָאתָ, etc.

11.3.2 *Nun.*

Over a silent *shewa*, *nun* often assimilates into the following consonant (unless a guttural), appearing as a *dagesh forte*. In the Qal perfect only R₃ takes silent *shewa*.

(*a*) R₃ = נ (except נתן).   Generally, R₃ = נ does accept silent *shewa* in the Qal perfect. But it assimilates into the *nun* of the 1cp suffix נו, a very rare form.

(*b*) R₃ = נ (נתן).   For the common root נתן, R₃ = נ assimilates into the ending, both ת and נ: נָתַתִּי, נָתַנּוּ, etc. Distinguish 3cp נָתְנוּ from 1cp נָתַנּוּ ← נָתְנְוּ.

11.3.3 **R₃ = י ≠ ה; final ה is a *mater lectionis*, originally R₃ = י.**

(*a*) The original *yod* is still used for the first and second persons as part of a *ḥireq yod*, גָּלִיתָ , גָּלִיתִי etc. Following a vowel, ת does not take *dagesh lene*.

(*b*) In the third persons, the *yod* is gone and the theme vowel, if present, is *a*-class. The 3ms ends in *mater* הָ. The 3fs ends in תָה to be distinct from the 3ms. Do not confuse it with 2ms תָ.[3] The 3cp suffix וּ attaches directly to R₂, e.g. גָּלוּ.[4] Remember to look all of these up in the dictionary under roots with a final ה.

11.3.4 **Doubly Weak Verbs.**

Verbs with more than one special needs consonant are called doubly weak. For example, עָשָׂה is both R₁ = G and R₃ = י ≠ ה, showing both the original R₃ = י and a *ḥataph pataḥ* under R₁ in the second person plural forms, e.g. עֲשִׂיתֶן , עֲשִׂיתֶם.

---

[1] The 1cp forms will have composite *shewa* if a pronominal suffix is added (ch. 15).

[2] This is similar to the interrogative particle הֲ. It is upgraded to *pataḥ* when followed by vocal *shewa* (5.6). We will see this behavior again in the imperfect paradigm, when a guttural requires a *ḥataph pataḥ* but is then changed to full *pataḥ* by a following vocal *shewa*.

[3] Rarely 2ms תָ is written with a *mater* תָה; context will clarify in these few cases.

[4] Except in rare cases where the original *yod* survives and behaves like the strong verb.

11.4   Disruptive roots.

Two root types shake up the verb's structure, $R_2 = R_3$ and $R_2 = $ י/ו. These alter the normal arrangement of three root consonants, distorting the identity badge of the Qal perfect, namely R_1 being in a pretonic open long syllable.

11.4.1 $R_2 = R_3$, Geminates.

From geminate nouns we learned that without a suffix, R_3 disappears, e.g. כַּף and כָּף. With a suffix, R_3 survives with a *dagesh forte*, e.g. כַּפּוֹת or כַּפּוֹ. R_3 is also lost from the Qal perfect 3ms, e.g. תַּם and תָּם (looking a lot like a noun), but survives with a *dagesh forte* in the 3fs and 3cp, e.g. תַּמָּה and תַּמּוּ. This geminate behavior is not new, but R_1 no longer has POL *qametz*, which is new for Qal perfect.

Also new, the 1st and 2nd persons preserve R_2 and R_3 by adding *holem* before the ending, e.g. תַּמּוֹתִי, תַּמּוֹתָ, etc. So R_1 is not POL, it is pretonic closed short. Do not mistake the *holem* connecting vowel for a root letter;[5] it is a clue to geminate roots.

There are a few variations in geminate behavior as can be seen in the following paradigms for ארר, סבב, and תמם. When R_2 is a guttural, it cannot double and the preceding vowel is lengthened (compensatory lengthening).[6]

	doubly weak	fientive (usually)	stative (usually)
1cs	אֲרוֹתִי	סַבּוֹתִי	תַּמּוֹתִי
2ms	אֲרוֹתָ	סַבּוֹתָ	תַּמּוֹתָ
2fs	אֲרוֹת	סַבּוֹת	תַּמּוֹת
3ms	אָרַר	סָבַב	תַּם
3fs	אֲרָרָה	סָבְבָה	תַּמָּה
1cp	אֲרוֹנוּ	סַבּוֹנוּ	תַּמּוֹנוּ
2mp	אֲרוֹתֶם	סַבּוֹתֶם	תַּמּוֹתֶם
2fp	אֲרוֹתֶן	סַבּוֹתֶן	תַּמּוֹתֶן
3cp	אָרְרוּ	סָבְבוּ	תַּמּוּ

Most often, undoing a *dagesh forte* restores the root as $R_2 = R_3$. The connecting *holem* is a special clue. With no ending, 3ms forms like תַּם signal by the short vowel that a *dagesh forte* needs to be restored and then undone to find $R_2 = R_3$.

11.4.2 $R_2 = $ י/ו.

As in the noun, R_2 *vav* and *yod* often become vocalic or drop out. With R_2 gone, R_1 forms a syllable with R_3, except when R_3 begins a syllable with a vocalic suffix (3fs and 3cp). They are distinct from geminates by the lack of *dagesh forte* throughout and the long vowel in the 3ms. $R_2 = $ י/ו should be restored to find the root.

---

[5] Only two verbs, each occurring once in the Hebrew Bible, preserve final *waw*.
[6] Semi-doubling is applied in the few cases where $R_2 = R_3 = $ ח.

	a-class קום	*a*-class שים	*a*-class בוא	*u*-class בוש	mixed type מות
1cs	קַ֫מְתִּי	שַׂ֫מְתִּי	בָּ֫אתִי	בֹּ֫שְׁתִּי	מַ֫תִּי
2ms	קַ֫מְתָּ	שַׂ֫מְתָּ	בָּ֫אתָ	בֹּ֫שְׁתָּ	מַ֫תָּה
2fs	קַמְתְּ	שַׂמְתְּ	בָּאת	בֹּשְׁתְּ	מַתְּ
3ms	קָם	שָׂם	בָּא	בּוֹשׁ	מֵת
3fs	קָ֫מָה	שָׂ֫מָה	בָּאָה	בּוֹשָׁה	מֵ֫תָה
1cp	קַ֫מְנוּ	שַׂ֫מְנוּ	בָּאנוּ	בֹּ֫שְׁנוּ	מַ֫תְנוּ
2mp	קַמְתֶּם	שַׂמְתֶּם	בָּאתֶם	בֹּשְׁתֶּם	מַתֶּם
2fp	קַמְתֶּן	שַׂמְתֶּן	בָּאתֶן	בֹּשְׁתֶּן	מַתֶּן
3cp	קָ֫מוּ	שָׂ֫מוּ	בָּאוּ	בּוֹשׁוּ	מֵ֫תוּ

Notes. The *u*-class may use *ḥolem vav* or just *ḥolem*.

Only בוש, טוב, and אור (rare) are *u*-class; מות (common) is the only mixed type.

When R_3 = ת, it assimilates into the ת of the endings as a *dagesh forte*.

Watch the accent. קָ֫מָה is 3fs pf.; קָמָ֫ה is the fem. sg. ab. ptc.

Be ready to look these up in the dictionary with either *vav* or *yod* as R_2. The lexical form is the Qal infinitive, which reveals the original *vav* or *yod* of R_2.

11.5 Summary. Alias Profiles for Qal Perfect.

From a recognition standpoint, the main problem is when you can only see two radicals. You then need to undo and restore $R_2 = R_3$, R_3 = י ≠ ה, R_2 = י/ו (or R_3 = נ for נתן). In the chart, "V" stands for vocalic ending; "C" stands for consonantal ending.

structure	example	root
⬚ַ⬚	תַּם	$R_2 = R_3$
⬚⬚	מֵת / בֹּשׁ / קָם	R_2 = י/ו
V⬚ַ⬚	תַּמּוּ	$R_2 = R_3$
V⬚ָ⬚	קָמָה / קָמוּ	R_2 = י/ו
	גָּלָה / גָּלוּ	R_3=י≠ה
V⬚⬚ / V⬚ַ⬚	מֵתוּ / בֹּשׁוּ	R_2 = י/ו

structure	example	root
C⬚וֹ⬚	אָרוֹת / תַּמּוֹת	$R_2 = R_3$
C⬚ַ֫⬚	גָּלִית	R_3=י≠ה
C⬚⬚	בֹּשְׁתְּ / קַמְתְּ	R_2 = י/ו
Cת	נָתַתִּי	נתן
⬚ַ⬚תָה	גָּלְתָה	R_3=י≠ה

n.b. ⬚⬚ *e.g.* סֹב *can be* $R_2 = R_3$ *inf. cs.*

Clue: 3ms accented closed short – alias $R_2 = R_3$.

Clue: 2 root letters with a long vowel and no dagesh – alias R_2 = י/ו (⬚ָ⬚ possible ptc.)

Clue: *dagesh forte* before a vocalic ending – alias $R_2 = R_3$.

Clue: ו before a consonantal ending – alias $R_2 = R_3$.

Clue: י⬚ before the ending – alias R_3 = י ≠ ה.

Clue: 2 root letters with vocalic ending & POL *qametz* – alias R_2 = י/ו or R_3 = י ≠ ה.

R_3 = G (ה or ע). An extra rule for 2fs creates a full *pataḥ* under R_3: שָׁמַ֫עַתְּ.

R_3 ≠ ה = י 3fs ends in תָה.

11.6   Vocabulary.

Some words in Hebrew have homonyms (more than one word spelled the same way). Dictionaries number them to keep them separate. This list includes meanings for two of the verbs עָנָה and one of the verbs קָרָא (the other is in ch. 18).

1	בָּכָה	*vb.*	to weep (114)
2	הָיָה	*vb.*	be(come), happen (3576)
3	זָעַק	*vb.*	to cry out, call (73)
4	חָיָה	*vb.*	to live (283)
5	חַי	*adj.*	alive (254)
6	חַיָּה	*n.f.*	animal (living thing), life (107)
7	חַיִּים	*n.m.*	life (140)
8	יָעַץ	*vb.*	to advise, counsel (80)
9	לָמַד	*vb.*	to learn, train in (87)
10	מִסְפָּר	*n.m.*	number, recounting (retelling) (134)
11	סָפַר	*vb.*	to count; Piel to recount, declare, report (107)
12	סֵפֶר	*n.m.*	document, book, writing (191)
13	סֹפֵר / סוֹפֵר	*n.m.*	scribe, secretary (54)
14	1 עָנָה	*vb.*	to answer, respond (316)
15	2 עָנָה	*vb.*	to be oppressed, be humble (79)
16	עָנִי	*adj.*	poor, afflicted, humble (80)
17	עֵצָה	*n.f.*	counsel, advice (87)
18	1 קָרָא	*vb.*	to call, proclaim, read aloud, name (739)
19	שָׁאַל	*vb.*	to ask (176)
20	שִׁיר	*vb.*	to sing (88)
21	שִׁיר	*n.m.*	song (78)

11.7   Learning Activities on the CD.

1   Grammar Illustration: Qal perfect weak verbs.

2   Practice Parsing: Sets A, B, C, D. Keep your book open to 11.5.

Set A. Focus on weak roots. Parse Qal pf. weak verbs (from chs. 1–10). 15 items.

Set B. Focus on the root. Parse Qal pf. verbs not from past vocabulary. 15 items.

Set C. Focus on the stem. Parse perfect verbs that are Qal or Non-Qal. 17 items.

Set D. Review. Parse verbs including ptc. and inf. cs. 15 items.

3   Parsing Exercise.

4   Practice Reading (using vocabulary from chs. 1–10). 60 items.

5   Translation Exercise.

Section One: Misc. Section Two: 1Sam 26:10–13. Section Three: Num 14:9–11.

6   Learn ch. 11 vocabulary.

chapter twelve

Qal Imperfect and Preterite: Strong Verbs

12.1 Focus.

In this chapter you are to learn:

the ten imperfect affixes,

the **syllabic structure and ID badge of the Qal imperfect,**

the common marker of the preterite, and

the common translation values of the imperfect and preterite.

The imperfect conjugation uses prefixes and some suffixes to indicate the person, gender, and number of the subject. Prefixes and suffixes are also called affixes. These spellings will be the basis for determining the subject of the imperfect, preterite, and volitional (ch. 14) verbs.

In appearance, the Qal imperfect basically adds these affixes to the infinitive construct. The first radical joins the prefix to make a pretonic closed short syllable with *ḥireq* – which is the ID badge of the Qal imperfect. For example, the infinitive construct of the fientive verb כָּתַב is כְּתֹב. Add an imperfect prefix יִכְתֹּב = יְ + כְּתֹב. The infinitive construct of the stative verb לָמַד is לְמַד. Add an imperfect prefix יִלְמַד = יְ + לְמַד. Some Qal imperfects of weak roots use an *i*-class theme vowel. נָתַן will be our example.

The derived stems (chs. 16–20) have either an *a*-class or an *i*-class theme vowel, so we will use יְלַמֵּד (from לָמַד) and יִתֵּן (from נָתַן) as standards for comparison. The ID badges for the derived stems are also in the syllable which is formed with R₁.

The **imperfect** conjugation is used for incomplete aspect. Typically, English may translate the imperfect fientive as present or future and the imperfect stative as future. The **preterite** conveys past time. The preterite is spelled like the imperfect but is most often marked by וַ, *vav-pataḥ-dagesh forte* at the beginning. It may move the accent up one position in comparison to the imperfect.

12.2   The Qal imperfect fientive strong verb (contextual forms).

1cs	I (will) kill	אֶקְטֹל
2ms	you (will) kill	תִּקְטֹל
2fs	you (will) kill	תִּקְטְלִי
3ms	he (will) kill	יִקְטֹל
3fs	she (will) kill	תִּקְטֹל
1cp	we (will) kill	נִקְטֹל
2mp[1]	you (will) kill	תִּקְטְלוּ
2fp	you (will) kill	תִּקְטֹלְנָה
3mp	they (will) kill	יִקְטְלוּ
3fp	they (will) kill	תִּקְטֹלְנָה

> Qal Imperfect ID badge:
>
> R$_1$ + Prefix with short *i*-class
>
> ☐☐☐ִP

(a) Syllabic structure.

If there is no suffix **or** there is a consonantal suffix,

then R$_2$ joins R$_3$ with a full vowel and the accent

   and R$_1$ joins the prefix in a PCS *i*-class syllable, e.g. תִּקְטֹל or תִּקְטֹלְנָה.

If there is a vocalic suffix,

then R$_3$ must join the suffix **and** R$_2$ takes vocal *shewa*, staying with R$_3$

   and R$_1$ joins the prefix in a PCS *i*-class syllable, e.g. תִּקְטְלוּ or תִּקְטְלִי.

   But in pause R$_2$ keeps the accent and a full vowel, e.g. תִּקְטֹלוּ or תִּקְטֹלִי.

(b) Notes on the Qal Imperfect.

The 1cs short *i*-class vowel is *segol* due to the *aleph*.

Look-alikes: 2ms and 3fs look alike. 2fp and 3fp look alike. Judge by context.

The most important elements for parsing are the affixes and the behavior of R$_1$. The affixes will remain the same in the other stems, but R$_1$'s syllable will differ.

12.3   Theme vowels.

On the following page לָמַד and נָתַן provide examples of the *a*-class and *i*-class paradigms. Note that the theme vowel does not affect parsing. The theme vowel may distinguish between fientive and stative roots or reveal pause. Paying attention to pauses can add drama to reading the text (ch. 23). The derived stems are either *a*-class or *i*-class, so learning these now has value beyond this chapter. The first syllable is offset to emphasize the stem's ID badge. The נתן paradigm is given twice to show the syllabic structure before *nun* assimilates and also the actual spellings.

---

[1] The 2mp and 3mp may also be spelled תִּקְטְלוּן and יִקְטְלוּן. The meaning of this paragogic *nun* is debated.

Qal Imperfect

(a) Contextual forms.

	u-class	a-class	i-class (some weak roots)	
	fientives	statives	structure	spelling
1cs	אֶק טֹל	אֶל מַד	אֶנ תֵּן	אֶתֵּן
2ms	תִּק טֹל	תִּל מַד	תִּנ תֵּן	תִּתֵּן
2fs	תִּק טְלִי	תִּל מְדִי	תִּנ תְּנִי	תִּתְּנִי
3ms	יִק טֹל	יִל מַד	יִנ תֵּן	יִתֵּן
3fs	תִּק טֹל	תִּל מַד	תִּנ תֵּן	תִּתֵּן
1cp	נִק טֹל	נִל מַד	נִנ תֵּן	נִתֵּן
2mp	תִּק טְלוּ	תִּל מְדוּ	תִּנ תְּנוּ	תִּתְּנוּ
2fp	תִּק טֹלְנָה	תִּל מַדְנָה	תִּנ תֵּנָּה	תִּתֵּנָּה
3mp	יִק טְלוּ	יִל מְדוּ	יִנ תְּנוּ	יִתְּנוּ
3fp	תִּק טֹלְנָה	תִּל מַדְנָה	תִּנ תֵּנָּה	תִּתֵּנָּה

(b) Pausal forms.

2fs, 2mp, and 3mp (forms with a vocalic ending): R$_2$ has a full vowel with the accent.

A-class paradigm: *patah* lengthens to *qametz*.

	u-class	a-class	i-class	
1cs	אֶק טֹל	אֶל מָד	אֶנ תֵּן	אֶתֵּן
2ms	תִּק טֹל	תִּל מָד	תִּנ תֵּן	תִּתֵּן
2fs	תִּק טֹלִי	תִּל מָדִי	תִּנ תֵּנִי	תִּתֵּנִי
3ms	יִק טֹל	יִל מָד	יִנ תֵּן	יִתֵּן
3fs	תִּק טֹל	תִּל מָד	תִּנ תֵּן	תִּתֵּן
1cp	נִק טֹל	נִל מָד	נִנ תֵּן	נִתֵּן
2mp	תִּק טֹלוּ	תִּל מָדוּ	תִּנ תֵּנוּ	תִּתֵּנוּ
2fp	תִּק טֹלְנָה	תִּל מָדְנָה	תִּנ תֵּנָּה	תִּתֵּנָּה
3mp	יִק טֹלוּ	יִל מָדוּ	יִנ תֵּנוּ	יִתֵּנוּ
3fp	תִּק טֹלְנָה	תִּל מָדְנָה	תִּנ תֵּנָּה	תִּתֵּנָּה

12.4   Preterite.

The preterite is a form for past time action. It is an archaic form surviving in Hebrew with a special form of the conjunction, וַ◌, *vav-paṭaḥ-dagesh forte* (except for compensatory lengthening before א, as וָא). The prefixes, suffixes, and theme vowels are the same as the imperfect for strong roots. In some forms of the preterite the accent is placed one syllable toward the beginning of the word (which produces a distinct form for certain weak roots).

	Qal Imperfect	Qal Preterite	
1cs	אֶכְתֹּב	וָאֶכְתֹּב	I wrote
2ms	תִּכְתֹּב	וַתִּכְתֹּב	you wrote
2fs	תִּכְתְּבִי	וַתִּכְתְּבִי	you wrote
3ms	יִכְתֹּב	וַיִּכְתֹּב	he wrote
3fs	תִּכְתֹּב	וַתִּכְתֹּב	she wrote
1cp	נִכְתֹּב	וַנִּכְתֹּב	we wrote
2mp	תִּכְתְּבוּ	וַתִּכְתְּבוּ	you wrote
2fp	תִּכְתֹּבְנָה	וַתִּכְתֹּבְנָה	you wrote
3mp	יִכְתְּבוּ	וַיִּכְתְּבוּ	they wrote
3fp	תִּכְתֹּבְנָה	וַתִּכְתֹּבְנָה	they wrote

On rare occasions in poetry or in dialogue, a preterite will be used without the conjunction and looks like an imperfect. In such cases you will have to judge by context, though accent may be a tip.

12.4.1   A Preterite by any other name.

The preterite was not always properly understood and therefore has been called a lot of names. Be aware of the different terminology that publications may use:

Vav conversive with imperfect: It was once thought that the conjunction "converted" the imperfect into a perfect, recognizing that these "imperfects" should be translated as past time, like some perfects.

Vav consecutive with imperfect: This title recognized that the *vav* does not "convert" the imperfect, but this form usually relates a consecutive set of events in the past and usually begins with *vav*.

Vav plus **imperfect consecutive**: This title recognizes that the verb form itself is responsible for indicating events in past time. The *vav* usually happens to be there with this verb form, which is like the imperfect in spelling.

Vayyiqtol: This title simply describes וַ◌, *vay-*, plus the Qal 3ms imperfect, *yiqtol*, and so is less prejudiced in its title (but only truly descriptive of the Qal).

Preterite, or *vav* plus preterite: This title refers to the function that the verb normally performs and is also used with other Semitic languages. (Hebrew once had several prefixed conjugations which came to look alike. Cp. 31.5 n. 3)

The title "*vav* conversive" is fading out of use. But you may run across any of these titles in books or journals; all refer to the same thing from different viewpoints.

12.5   Narrative and the preterite.

The preterite is the backbone of narrative. As the most common verb form, the preterite gives the main sequence of events, moving the story line along in simple past time, and serves as the framework that other syntactical structures spin off of.

Story lines commonly begin with a perfect verb and are continued by preterites. For example, Exodus 3 begins with a noun-first construction, with a perfect verb plus participle.

> 3:1   ...וּמֹשֶׁה הָיָה רֹעֶה   Moses *had been pasturing* [the flock of Jethro...]

With past time established, a series of preterites gives the sequence of action.

> 3:1   ...וַיִּנְהַג אֶת־הַצֹּאן   He *drove* the flock [west of the desert]
>
> ...וַיָּבֹא אֶל־הַר   He *came* to the mountain [of God, at Horeb]
>
> etc.   etc.

It is also common to begin with וַיְהִי,[2] the *vayyiqtol* form of הִיה, especially with a temporal modifier, e.g.

> Ruth 1:1   וַיְהִי בִּימֵי   It happened in the days of...
> 1Ki 22:2   וַיְהִי בַּשָּׁנָה הַשְּׁלִישִׁית   It happened in the third year...

Once the main line of preterites is established, changing the word order sets off a clause. *Vayyiqtol* forms, having the conjunction, are always verb-first constructions. Switching to a noun (or adj. etc.)-first construction precludes using a *vayyiqtol*. This variation presents various kinds of background material or contrasting information (cf. 10.7.3 *c.*). Note how the perfects in Gen 31 give background to the main story line carried by the preterites.

> 18   preterite   ...וַיִּנְהַג   He *drove* away [all his livestock...]
>
> אֲשֶׁר + pf.   אֲשֶׁר רָכָשׁ   which he *had acquired*...
>
> 19   Noun 1st + pf.   וְלָבָן הָלַךְ   Laban *had gone* [to shear sheep...]
>
> preterite   וַתִּגְנֹב רָחֵל   Then Rachel *stole* [the household gods]

The preterite can convey more than simple past time, but its main job is to say, "and then [he/she] *X*-ed."

---

[2] The scribes frequently leave out the *dagesh forte* from the *yod* of this common form.

12.6   Time frame and the imperfect.

The imperfect may be **present** time. In this line of poetry, the imperfect expresses a general truth, Ps 116:1:

אָהַבְתִּי   I love [him]

כִּי־יִשְׁמַע יְהוָה אֶת־קוֹלִי   for the LORD *hears* my voice.

The imperfect can indicate **future** time, here occurring in speech (1Chr 16:18). Note that the sentence is not verb first.

לְךָ אֶתֵּן אֶרֶץ־כְּנָעַן   To you I *will give* the land of Canaan.

The imperfect can also be used for a **past habitual** action (also called iterative), that is, an action that was done again and again. It is not viewed as complete on any particular occasion. Compare De 11:10.

begins noun clause	כִּי הָאָרֶץ...	Indeed the land [is not like the land of Egypt]
אֲשֶׁר + perfect	אֲשֶׁר יְצָאתֶם	which you *have gone* out from
אֲשֶׁר + imperfect	אֲשֶׁר תִּזְרַע ³	where you *used to sow* seed

The imperfect can be used with an imperative sense. As in English, "You will X" can be either future time or used to give commands, as in Exod 12:18:

[In the 1st month, on the 14th day, at evening]

תֹּאכְלוּ מַצֹּת   you shall eat matzah-bread...

12.7   Summary.

Memorize the spellings of the Qal imperfect.

Learn the translation options in order to start developing the art of translation. Because the imperfect conveys **incomplete aspect**, it may be used for a **future** event or state, an action occurring in the **present** or a **general truth** (fientive or stative), or a **past habitual** action – depending on syntax and context.

The **preterite** looks very much like the imperfect. It is most often preceded by ‍וַ, *vav-patah-dagesh forte*, and may move the accent forward. The preterite usually conveys the **past action** line of events in a story, *and then they X-ed.*

The **Qal imperfect ID badge** is that R_1 joins the prefix with an *i*-class vowel (*hireq* or *segol*) in a pretonic closed short syllable.

The Qal imperfect has verbs with theme vowels in all three vowel classes: most fientive verbs use *holem*, most stative verbs use an *a*-class vowel, while נָתַן and $R_3 = $ ‍י ≠ ה verbs use an *i*-class vowel.

Looking ahead. Except for the Qal's *hireq* under the prefix, the prefixes, suffixes, and theme vowels transfer to the other *binyanim*. The Niphal, Piel, Hitpael, and Hiphil follow the theme vowel pattern in יִתֵּן. The Pual and Hophal follow יְלֻמַּד.

---

³ זרע, *to sow*, is fientive not stative. It has an *a*-class vowel because of the preference of the guttural ע.

12.8   Vocabulary.

1	אָחַז	*vb.*	to grasp, take hold (63)
2	אָסַף	*vb.*	to gather, collect, remove (200)
3	גָּנַב	*vb.*	to steal (40)
4	זָבַח	*vb.*	to slaughter; Piel to sacrifice (134)
5	זֶבַח	*n.m.*	sacrifice (162)
6	יָטַב	*vb.*	be good, pleasing (117)
7	יָכֹל	*vb.*	be able, prevail, endure (193)
8	יָרֵא	*vb.*	be afraid (317)
9	יָשַׁב	*vb.*	to sit, dwell, (יֹשֵׁב = ptc. inhabitant; שֶׁבֶת = inf. cs.) (1088)
10	מִזְבֵּחַ	*n.m.*	altar (403)
11	מִשְׁכָּן	*n.m.*	dwelling (place), abode (139)
12	נָפַל	*vb.*	to fall, get down (435)
13	עָבַר	*vb.*	to pass over/through/by (553)
14	עֵבֶר	*n.m.*	side, edge, area on the other side (92)
15	רָאָה	*vb.*	to see (1311)
16	שִׂים	*vb.*	to put, place, set (588)
17	שׁוּב	*vb.*	to turn back, return; (1075)
18	שָׁכַן	*vb.*	to dwell, settle (130)
19	שָׁלַח	*vb.*	to send, stretch out (847)
20	שָׁתָה	*vb.*	to drink (217)

12.9   היה. Since all the root letters of the common verb הָיָה are weak, its paradigms are included here for reference. The verb חָיָה follows the same pattern.

1cs	אֶהְיֶה	וָאֱהִי / וָאֶהְיֶה	I was
2ms	תִּהְיֶה	וַתְּהִי	you were
2fs	—	וַתְּהִיִי	you were
3ms	יִהְיֶה	וַיְהִי	he was
3fs	תִּהְיֶה	וַתְּהִי	she was
1cp	נִהְיֶה	וַנְּהִי / וַנִּהְיֶה	we were
2mp	תִּהְיוּ	וַתִּהְיוּ	you were
2fp	—	—	you were
3mp	יִהְיוּ	וַיִּהְיוּ	they were
3fp	תִּהְיֶינָה	וַתִּהְיֶין	they were

12.10   Learning Activities on the CD.

1   Grammar Illustration.

Watch the Qal imperfect constructed by starting with the infinitive construct and adding the imperfect affixes with the Qal stem ID badge.

2   Learn Paradigms.

Copy and recite the Qal imperfect paradigms of קטל, למד, and נתן as often as it takes to learn them (cf. 12.3.a).

3   Practice Parsing: Sets A, B, C, D.

Set A. Focus on affixes. Parse Qal impf. weak verbs (from chs. 1–11). 20 items.

Set B. Focus on the root. Parse Qal impf. verbs (beside chs. 1–11). 20 items.

Set C. Focus on the stem. Parse verbs that are Qal or Non-Qal. 20 items.

Set D. Review. Parse all types of Qal verbs. 20 items.

4   Parsing Exercise.

5   Practice Reading (using vocabulary from chs. 1–11). 70 items.

6   Translation Exercise.

Section One: misc. Section Two: 1Sam 26:14–17. Section Three: 1Ki 3:18–24.

7   Learn ch. 12 vocabulary.

chapter thirteen

Qal Imperfect and Preterite: Weak Verbs

13.1   Focus.

In this chapter you are to learn:

> *no new affixes* and *no new weak consonant behaviors*, but
>
> to **diagnose** the weak consonant behaviors in the Qal imperfect.

Wherever certain conditions are created by a word pattern, they trigger the weak letter behaviors. Focus on the principles involved rather than on learning new patterns for every type of root. Observe how much is similar to what you have already learned and **focus most on situations that obscure the root**. The variations, or aliases to the Qal identity, result from normal Hebrew behaviors. The Alias Profiles summary (13.7.1) organizes these by what happens to the prefix and R_1.

13.1.2   Weak letter review.

Try to recall the specific behavior based on these prompts.

נ   assimilation.

י/ו   may become vocalic; may drop out; vowel preferences.

Gutturals   *shewa* problem; *dagesh* problem; vowel preferences.

א   quiesces; also guttural behaviors.

$R_3 = $ י $ \neq $ ה

$R_2 = R_3$ **Geminates** may not allow a vowel between R_2 and R_3.

If you cannot recall the full sets of conditions and behaviors, *review before going on.*

13.1.3   Structural Review.

Qal imperfect. ⊞☐☐ְP; Qal preterite. ⊞☐☐ְṔ֫ו

R_1 joins an imperfect prefix, making a PCS syllable, with *ḥireq* (or *segol* for 1cs).

R_3 closes a syllable when there is no ending or when there is a consonantal ending.

R_2 takes vocal *shewa*, staying with the accented syllable when the ending is vocalic.

Most weak letter rules apply to syllable closing R_1 and R_3,

Preterites may move the accent up and usually begin with ☐ו.

As will always be true, $R_2 = $ י/ו and geminates require special attention.

The question: undoing what weak letter rule will restore the impf. pattern?

13.2   *Nun.*

When נ closes a syllable, i.e. is over silent *shewa*, it may assimilate into the next letter as *dagesh forte*. The Qal imperfect pattern puts R_1 over silent *shewa*. This is the main issue for roots with *nun* in the Qal imperfect. We have already seen this with נתן. But watch for the copycats.

(a)   **R_1 = נ.** R_1 = נ assimilates into R_2, e.g. תִּתֵּן. But if R_2 is a guttural, the נ almost always survives, e.g. תִּנְאַף.[1]

(b)   **R_2 = נ.** No problems. R_2 does not close a syllable.

(c)   **R_3 = נ.** R_3 = נ assimilates into the 2/3 fp ending. This is very rare.

(d)   **Copycats.**

     The ל of לקח assimilates like an R_1 = נ, e.g. תִּקַּח.

     Some verbs which are both R_1 = י & R_2 = צ behave as R_1 = נ.[2]

(e)   **Paradigms.**

	R_3 = נ & R_1 = נ	R_3 = נ	R_2 = נ	R_1 = נ	R_1 = י & R_2 = צ
1cs	אֶתֵּן	אֶשָּׁכֹן	אֶגְנֹב	אֶפֹּל	אֶצֹּג
2ms	תִּתֵּן	תִּשָּׁכֹן	תִּגְנֹב	תִּפֹּל	תִּצֹּג
2fs	תִּתְּנִי	תִּשָּׁכְנִי	תִּגְנְבִי	תִּפְּלִי	תִּצְּגִי
3ms	יִתֵּן	יִשָּׁכֹן	יִגְנֹב	יִפֹּל	יִצֹּג
3fs	תִּתֵּן	תִּשָּׁכֹן	תִּגְנֹב	תִּפֹּל	תִּצֹּג
1cp	נִתֵּן	נִשָּׁכֹן	נִגְנֹב	נִפֹּל	נִצֹּג
2mp	תִּתְּנוּ	תִּשָּׁכְנוּ	תִּגְנְבוּ	תִּפְּלוּ	תִּצְּגוּ
2fp	תִּתֵּנָּה	תִּשָּׁכֹנָּה	תִּגְנֹבְנָה	תִּפֹּלְנָה	תִּצֹּגְנָה
3mp	יִתְּנוּ	יִשָּׁכְנוּ	יִגְנְבוּ	יִפְּלוּ	יִצְּגוּ
3fp	תִּתֵּנָּה	תִּשָּׁכֹנָּה	תִּגְנֹבְנָה	תִּפֹּלְנָה	תִּצֹּגְנָה

13.2.1   Main issue: ☐P alias for Qal impf. ID: ☐☐☐P.

   ☐P R_1 = נ/לקח/R_3י   **Alias:** ☐☐P ← ☐☐נְP

About the "alias" line. We need always to watch R_1 which in turn affects the prefix. So our first point of reference is the prefix and first visible radical. These are listed to the left, in this case ☐P standing for a prefix with a *hireq* and the first visible radical with a *dagesh forte*. Next is the type of root, here R_1 = נ/לקח/R_3י meaning R_1 = נ verbs and verbs that act like them, i.e. לקח and some verbs R_1 = י & R_2 = צ. Last it gives its structure with boxes for all visible radicals: ☐☐P.

---

[1] For *nun* surviving before a guttural, cf. תִּנְאַף, וַיִּנְהַג, יִנְעַם, יִנְחֲלוּ. But compare תֵּחַת ← תֶּחֱחַת, showing that compensatory lengthening is possible.

[2] יצת, יצע, and יצג; some forms of יצק and יצר; but not יצא.

13.3 Gutturals prefer *a*-class vowels and resist *shewa*.

(a) Minor issues.

Gutturals often have composite *shewa* instead of simple *shewa*. R_3 or R_2 gutturals may require an *a*-class theme vowel. The theme vowel is not part of the Qal ID badge. Stem identity involves R_1: prefix + short *i*-vowel + R_1 = Qal imperfect.

(b) Primary Issues. R_1 gutturals change the vowel with the prefix.

Prefix with *a*-class vowel. □□G̱P

Historically, the Qal imperfect had an *a*-class vowel with the prefix. In pretonic closed syllables, the *a*-vowel changed to *i*-class, hence □□□̣P. But the gutturals' vowel preference was able to keep the *a*-vowel. Plus the gutturals want composite *shewa* and in one setting even get a full *patah* (13.3.2).

Prefix with *holem* and R_1 = א. □□א̇P

You have already learned וַיֹּאמֶר as a vocabulary word. By analogy you should recognize as Qal other R_1 = א verbs with a *holem* after the prefix.

13.3.1 R_3 = G or R_2 = G.

(a) R_3 = ע/ח usually accept silent *shewa* and prefer an *a*-class theme vowel rather than the *holem* commonly used by fientive verbs.

(b) R_3 = א. The א quiesces, typically lengthening the theme vowel: יִקְרָא, אֶמְצָא .

(c) $R_3 \neq$ ה. These are really R_3 = י; see below.

(d) R_2 = G (א, ה, ח, ע). Possible vowel preference. *Shewa* problem.

The verb may (or may not) take an *a*-class theme vowel.

They take composite *shewa* instead of silent *shewa* (2fs, 2mp, 3mp), e.g.

תִּשְׁחֲטוּ , וְיִשְׁאֲלוּ (but תִּמְאָסוּ in pause).

(e) **Paradigms.** Negligible changes in the Qal impf.

	R_3 = א	R_3 = G	R_2 = G
1cs	אֶמְצָא	אֶשְׁלַח	אֶבְחַר
2ms	תִּמְצָא	תִּשְׁלַח	תִּבְחַר
2fs	תִּמְצְאִי	תִּשְׁלְחִי	תִּבְחֲרִי
3ms	יִמְצָא	יִשְׁלַח	יִבְחַר
3fs	תִּמְצָא	תִּשְׁלַח	תִּבְחַר
1cp	נִמְצָא	נִשְׁלַח	נִבְחַר
2mp	תִּמְצְאוּ	תִּשְׁלְחוּ	תִּבְחֲרוּ
2fp	תִּמְצֶאנָה	תִּשְׁלַחְנָה	תִּבְחַרְנָה
3mp	יִמְצְאוּ	יִשְׁלְחוּ	יִבְחֲרוּ
3fp	תִּמְצֶאנָה	תִּשְׁלַחְנָה	תִּבְחַרְנָה

13.3.2 R_1 = G. Extra rules: יַעֲמְדוּ and אֹמַר.

(a) R_1 = ה, ח, ע, and sometimes א. *Shewa* problem and vowel preferences.

The usual result is E☐☐G̱P̱ or E☐☐G̱P̱ (1cs & R_1 = א prefer G̱P̱).

In forms with vocalic suffixes, R_2's vocal *shewa* upgrades R_1's composite *shewa* to a full vowel, e.g. תַּעֲמְדוּ. (Cp. to the Qal pf. 2fs שָׁמַעַתְּ ← שָׁמַעַתְּ ← שְׁמַעַתְּ).

(b) R_1 = א.

If the theme vowel is not *holem*, then R_1 = א verbs usually use *holem* after the impf. prefix and R_1 = א quiesces. אמר and אכל are the most common.[3]

For 1cs forms, where the prefix is א, R_1 = א drops out: אֹכֵל ← אֹאכֵל. It then looks like the Qal act. ptc., אֹכֵל, but the theme vowel is different.

(c)   **Paradigms**. R_1 = G changes the vowel under the prefix.

	R_1 = G.	R_1 = א	R_1 = א	R_1 = א
1cs	אֶעֱמֹד	אֶאֱסֹף	אֹמַר **	וָאֹמַר **
2ms	תַּעֲמֹד	תַּאֱסֹף	תֹּאמַר	וַתֹּאמַר
2fs	תַּעַמְדִי **	תַּאַסְפִי **	תֹּאמְרִי	וַתֹּאמְרִי
3ms	יַעֲמֹד	יַאֱסֹף	יֹאמַר	וַיֹּאמֶר
3fs	תַּעֲמֹד	תַּאֱסֹף	תֹּאמַר	וַתֹּאמֶר
1cp	נַעֲמֹד	נַאֱסֹף	נֹאמַר	וַנֹּאמֶר
2mp	תַּעַמְדוּ **	תַּאַסְפוּ **	תֹּאמְרוּ	וַתֹּאמְרוּ
2fp	תַּעֲמֹדְנָה	תַּאֱסֹפְנָה	תֹּאמַרְנָה	וַתֹּאמַרְנָה
3mp	יַעַמְדוּ **	יַאַסְפוּ **	יֹאמְרוּ	וַיֹּאמְרוּ
3fp	תַּעֲמֹדְנָה	תַּאֱסֹפְנָה	תֹּאמַרְנָה	וַתֹּאמַרְנָה

13.3.3   **Main issues: G̱P̱ and א̇P aliases for Qal impf. ID: ☐☐☐̣P.**

G̱P̱   **R_1 = G Alias: ☐☐G̱P̱ or V☐☐G̱P̱**

א̇P   **R_1 = א Alias: ☐☐א̇P and 1cs ☐☐̣א**

13.4   ו and י have vowel preferences, may drop out or become vocalic.

13.4.1 R_3 = י ≠ ה.[4]

The י gives the *i*-class theme vowel while the ה is a *mater*. The י itself survives before consonantal suffixes (2/3fp).[5] But vocalic suffixes replace it altogether.[6] **The preterite's shift of accent also results in the loss of R_3.** The Qal imperfect of נתן is used for comparison since it also has an *i*-class theme vowel, but it is shown with its *nuns* not assimilated in order to reveal the structure.

---

[3] Cp. אבד, אבה, אחז, and אפה.

[4] The few R_3 = ו verbs have acted like R_3 = י ≠ ה. Twice the R_3 = ו behaves as a regular consonant.

[5] In the Qal perfect 1st and 2nd persons, the י survived before consonantal suffixes: גָּלִיתָ, גָּלִיתִי, etc.

[6] In the Qal perfect 3fs and 3cp, the vocalic endings replaced R_3 = י, e.g. גָּלָה, גָּלוּ, etc. Sometimes the י survives (mostly in pausal forms), יִשְׁלָיוּ, יִשְׁתָּיוּ, יִבְכָּיוּ, יֶאֱתָיוּ, although תִּגְבָּהוּ, יִגְבָּהוּ, and וְאֶהֱמָיָה.

	cp. *i*-class	Impf. R$_3$ = י ≠ ה	preterite R$_3$ = י ≠ ה	
1cs	אֶתֵּן	אֶשְׁתֶּה	וָאֶשְׁתְּ	וָאֶבְכֶּה
2ms	תִּתֵּן	תִּשְׁתֶּה	וַתֵּשְׁתְּ	וַתֵּבְךְּ
2fs	תִּתְּנִי	תִּשְׁתִּי	וַתִּשְׁתִּי	וַתִּבְכִּי
3ms	יִתֵּן	יִשְׁתֶּה	וַיֵּשְׁתְּ	וַיֵּבְךְּ
3fs	תִּתֵּן	תִּשְׁתֶּה	וַתֵּשְׁתְּ	וַתֵּבְךְּ
1cp	נִתֵּן	נִשְׁתֶּה	וַנֵּשְׁתְּ	וַנֵּבְךְּ
2mp	תִּתְּנוּ	תִּשְׁתּוּ	וַתִּשְׁתּוּ	וַתִּבְכּוּ
2fp	תִּתֵּנָּה	תִּשְׁתֶּינָה	וַתִּשְׁתֶּינָה	וַתִּבְכֶּינָה
3mp	יִתְּנוּ	יִשְׁתּוּ	וַיִּשְׁתּוּ	וַיִּבְכּוּ
3fp	תִּתֵּנָּה	תִּשְׁתֶּינָה	וַתִּשְׁתֶּינָה	וַתִּבְכֶּינָה

13.4.2   **R$_1$ = י/ה.** **Major structural changes** as R$_1$ contracts into a vowel.

(a)   The impf. pattern puts R$_1$ over silent *shewa*. Silent *shewa* makes י contract into a vowel. R$_1$ is now part of a pretonic open long vowel; it may not be written as a *mater*.

     usually יִיטַב but also יִטַב: P□□ ← Pי□□

     seldom יִישֵׁב usually יֵשֵׁב: P□□ ← Pֵי□□ ← Pִי□□.[7]

(b)   **Special cases.**   (For R$_1$ = י & R$_2$ = צ roots see above at R$_1$ = נ, 13.2)

יכל   R$_1$ appears as ו and has a stative *a*-class theme vowel: יוּכַל.

הלך   This R$_1$ = ה behaves as an *i*-class R$_1$ = י: יֵלֵךְ.

(c)   **Paradigms.**

	נתן	ישב		יתב	יכל	הלך
1cs	אֶתֵּן	אֵשֵׁב	וָאֵשֵׁב	אִיתַב	אוּכַל	אֵלֵךְ
2ms	תִּתֵּן	תֵּשֵׁב	וַתֵּשֵׁב	תִּיתַב	תּוּכַל	תֵּלֵךְ
2fs	תִּתְּנִי	תֵּשְׁבִי	וַתֵּשְׁבִי	תִּיתְבִי	תּוּכְלִי	תֵּלְכִי
3ms	יִתֵּן	יֵשֵׁב	וַיֵּשֵׁב	יִיתַב	יוּכַל	יֵלֵךְ
3fs	תִּתֵּן	תֵּשֵׁב	וַתֵּשֵׁב	תִּיתַב	תּוּכַל	תֵּלֵךְ
1cp	נִתֵּן	נֵשֵׁב	וַנֵּשֵׁב	נִיתַב	נוּכַל	נֵלֵךְ
2mp	תִּתְּנוּ	תֵּשְׁבוּ	וַתֵּשְׁבוּ	תִּיתְבוּ	תּוּכְלוּ	תֵּלְכוּ
2fp	תִּתֵּנָּה	תֵּשַׁבְנָה	וַתֵּשַׁבְנָה	תִּיתַבְנָה	תּוּכַלְנָה	תֵּלַכְנָה
3mp	יִתְּנוּ	יֵשְׁבוּ	וַיֵּשְׁבוּ	יִיתְבוּ	יוּכְלוּ	יֵלְכוּ
3fp	תִּתֵּנָּה	תֵּשַׁבְנָה	וַתֵּשַׁבְנָה	תִּיתַבְנָה	תּוּכַלְנָה	תֵּלַכְנָה

---

[7] R$_1$ = ו has become *yod*. Originally R$_1$ = י roots are all stative and place a *ḥireq* under the prefix. Most originally R$_1$ = ו roots are fientive and place a *ṣere* under the prefix. If they are *a*-class due to having a guttural for R$_2$ or R$_3$, they may place a *ḥireq* under the prefix.

(d) **R₁ = ʾ Advanced reference information on theme vowel behavior**.

R_1 = ʾ verbs use an *a*-class theme vowel if stative or if a fientive has a guttural for R_2 or R_3: אֲדַע, אִיעַץ, יִישַׁר, יִיטַב. Otherwise R_1 = ʾ/ח fientives are *i*-class but use an *a*-class theme vowel for feminine plurals.

13.4.3 R_2 = ʾ/ח. **Major structural changes** as R_2 becomes vocalic.

R_2 becomes a vowel, causing a collapse of the syllabic structure.

R_1 moves over to begin a syllable and cannot join the prefix. If R_1 has the accent, the prefix will be pretonic open long. We learned with R_1 = G that the Qal imperfect prefix used to have an *a*-vowel; we see it again here as a POL *qametz*, יָקוּמוּ, יָקוּם.[8]

The prefix may have *shewa* in problem position when a connecting vowel is used before *a consonantal suffix*: תְּשׁוּבֶ֫ינָה. We will show this pattern as S☐☐☐P.

The preterite shifts the accent to the prefix when there is no suffix. This may reduce the vowel between R_1 and R_3, noted most by the absence of a *mater*: וַיָּ֫קָם.

	שׁוּב		שִׂים		בּוֹא	
	Impf.	Preterite	Impf.	Preterite	Impf.	Preterite
1cs	אָשׁוּב	וָאָשֻׁב	אָשִׂים	וָאָשִׂ֫ים	אָבוֹא	וָאָבוֹא
2ms	תָּשׁוּב	וַתָּ֫שָׁב	תָּשִׂים	וַתָּ֫שֶׂם	תָּבוֹא	וַתָּבוֹא
2fs	תָּשׁוּבִי	וַתָּשֻׁ֫בִי	תָּשִׂ֫ימִי	וַתָּשִׂ֫ימִי	תָּבוֹאִי	וַתָּבוֹאִי
3ms	יָשׁוּב	וַיָּ֫שָׁב	יָשִׂים	וַיָּ֫שֶׂם	יָבוֹא	וַיָּבוֹא
3fs	תָּשׁוּב	וַתָּ֫שָׁב	תָּשִׂים	וַתָּ֫שֶׂם	תָּבוֹא	וַתָּבוֹא
1cp	נָשׁוּב	וַנָּ֫שָׁב	נָשִׂים	וַנָּ֫שֶׂם	נָבוֹא	וַנָּבוֹא
2mp	תָּשׁ֫וּבוּ תָּשֻׁ֫בוּ	וַתָּשֻׁ֫בוּ	תָּשִׂ֫ימוּ	וַתָּשִׂ֫ימוּ	תָּבֹ֫אוּ	וַתָּבֹ֫אוּ
2fp	תְּשׁוּבֶ֫ינָה תְּשֻׁבְנָה	וַתְּשׁוּבֶ֫ינָה וַתְּשֻׁבְנָה	תְּשִׂימֶ֫נָה	וַתְּשִׂימֶ֫נָה	תָּבֹ֫אנָה תָּבֹ֫אינָה	וַתָּבֹ֫אנָה וַתָּבֹ֫אינָה
3mp	יָשׁ֫וּבוּ תָּשֻׁ֫בוּ	וַיָּשֻׁ֫בוּ	יָשִׂ֫ימוּ	וַיָּשִׂ֫ימוּ	יָבֹ֫אוּ	וַיָּבֹ֫אוּ
3fp	תְּשׁוּבֶ֫ינָה תְּשֻׁבְנָה	וַתְּשׁוּבֶ֫ינָה וַתְּשֻׁבְנָה	תְּשִׂימֶ֫נָה	וַתְּשִׂימֶ֫נָה	תָּבֹ֫אנָה תָּבֹ֫אינָה	וַתָּבֹ֫אנָה וַתָּבֹ֫אינָה

13.4.4   **Main issues: Aliases for Qal impf. ID: ☐☐☐ִP.**

☐ָP R_2 = ʾ/ח **Alias:** ☐☐ָP

☐ָP R_2 = ʾ/ח **Alias:** S̆☐☐ָP

☐ֵP R_1 = ʾ / הלך **Alias:** ☐☐ֵP   or R_3 ≠ ה **Alias:** ☐ֵ☐P וַ   or שׁבֵP **Alias** from בּוֹשׁ

☐ִ P R_3 = ʾ ≠ ה **Alias:** ☐☐ִP / Cʾ☐☐ִP / ☐☐ִP וַ / G☐ִP וַ

---

[8] The original *a*-class vowel with the Qal imperfect prefix changed to *ḥireq* in closed syllables.

13.5 Geminates, $R_2 = R_3$. Major structural changes. Two options.

Geminates do not permit a vowel between R_2 and R_3. So R_2 assimilates into R_3, but R_3 cannot hold a *dagesh forte*, unless there is a suffix. And R_1 must have a vowel.[9] This means that the prefix will be either pretonic open long (option A) or in order to keep the syllable closed, R_1 will double with a *dagesh forte* (option B).

(a) Option A.

R_1 joins R_2, usually giving the prefix a pretonic open long vowel. Statives tend to have an *a*-class theme vowel and use *sere* under the prefix, like תמם, while fientives have *holem* as the theme vowel and use *qametz* under the prefix, like סבב.

(b) Option B.

As seen with סבב, the same root may spelled in more than one way. The second way of treating geminates preserves the Qal imperfect ID of the prefix joining R_1 with an *i*-class vowel. It does this by doubling R_1 with a *dagesh*. **These look deceptively like $R_1 = $ ‍נ verbs.**

	תמם Opt. A	סבב Opt. A	סבב Opt. B
1cs	אֶתַּם	אָסֹב	אֶסֹּב
2ms	תֵּתַּם	תָּסֹב	תִּסֹּב
2fs	תֵּתַּמִּי	תָּסֹבִּי	תִּסֹּבִּי
3ms	יֵתַּם	יָסֹב	יִסֹּב
3fs	תֵּתַּם	תָּסֹב	תִּסֹּב
1cp	נֵתַּם	נָסֹב	נִסֹּב
2mp	תֵּתַּמּוּ	תָּסֹבּוּ	תִּסֹּבּוּ
2fp	תְּתַמֶּינָה[10]	תְּסֻבֶּינָה	תִּסֹּבֶּינָה
3mp	יֵתַּמּוּ	יָסֹבּוּ	יִסֹּבּוּ
3fp	תְּתַמֶּינָה	תְּסֻבֶּינָה	תִּסֹּבֶּינָה

13.5.1 Main issues: ☐☐P, ☐☐P, and ☐☐P aliases for Qal impf. ID: ☐☐☐P;

☐P $R_2 = R_3$ Alias: ☐☐P   ☐P $R_2 = R_3$ Alias: ☐☐P

☐P $R_2 = R_3$ Alias: ☐☐P   ☐P $R_2 = R_3$ Alias: E☐☐P

13.6 Doubly weak נטה: only one radical remains in the preterite.

The ‍נ assimilates into R_2. R_3 is lost due to the shift of accent. With no vowel after R_2, it cannot hold the *dagesh*. The result is just וַיֵּט for the 3ms.

---

[9] If $R_2 = R_3 = $ G, then in forms with suffixes, R_1 will have *shewa*, יְרֵעוּ from רעע, but this only happens five times in the Bible.

[10] For forms with consonantal suffixes (2/3fp), the prefix has *shewa* in problem position, but this only happens twice in the Bible.

13.7   Summary.

Despite the many types of weak roots, parsing may seem easy at this point because we have only learned the Qal stem. The biggest practical problem is when only two root letters are visible, deciding whether to restore an assimilated *nun* or geminate or a lost *vav* or *yod*: $R_1 = $ נ, $R_2 = R_3$, $R_1 = $ י, $R_2 = $ י/ו or $R_3 = $ י $\neq$ ה. In short, if there were only Qal verbs, your main concern would be to find the root by (1) adding *nun* at the beginning, (2) adding a copy of the second radical at the end, or (3) adding a *yod* or *vav* in just about any position.

For the purpose of figuring out the root, those three issues will continue through the derived stems as well. But there will also be the problem of determining the stem. So we will need to watch the behaviors of R_1, the prefix, and their vowels. The alias profiles help you do this for the prefixed conjugations (imperfect and preterite) by (1) listing the characteristics of the prefix and R_1, (2) correlating these with the stems, and (3) providing brief notes about which root types are possible or likely. You should memorize the identifying characteristics of the strong verb, its ID badge, but practice parsing with your book open to the alias profiles. The alias profiles concentrate on situations where a root letter is not visible. Gutturals are only included when they do not match the stem's identifying characteristics (ID badge) for the strong root (not e.g. for taking composite *shewa* or affecting the theme vowel).

13.7.1   Alias Profiles.

□ִP	·P □ְP יְP	Qal	□□·P : $R_1 = $ נ/לקח/ה/R_3צי or $R_2 = R_3$ $R_3 \neq $ ה : □□ְP / Cיְ□□P / □□ְP ֶו / G□ְP ֶו $R_1 = $ י (e.g. ירא)
□ֵP	□ֵP	Qal	$R_1 = $ י/הלך, $R_2 = R_3$, $R_3 = $ י $\neq$ ה pret., נטה, בוש
□ַP	GP	Qal	Qal (*i*-class theme when also $R_2 = $ י or $R_3 = $ י $\neq$ ה)
□ֹP	□□ֹP	Qal	$R_2 = $ י/ו or $R_2 = R_3$
□ֹP	[11]Sֹ□□P	Qal	$R_2 = $ י/ו or $R_2 = R_3$
□וּP	וּכלP	Qal	יכל
אP	□□ֹP	Qal	$R_1 = $ א (1cs א deletes $R_1 = $ א, אֹמַר)

13.7.2   Notes on Qal Imperfect with *nun* type assimilation and loss of $R_3 = $ י $\neq$ ה.

תִּפֹּל ← תִּנְפֹּל   E□□·P ← E□□ְנP. Assimilation of נ. (*Dagesh* in R_2).

תִּצֹּג ← תִּיְצֹג   E□□·P ← E□□יְP. $R_1 = $ י & $R_2 = $ צ behaving as $R_1 = $ נ.

תָּסֹב ← תָסֹב $R_2 = R_3$ Option B, looking like $R_1 = $ נ.

יִשְׁתּוּ   Vocalic suffix deletes $R_3 = $ י $\neq$ ה.

וַיֵּשְׁתְּ   Preterite loss of $R_3 = $ י $\neq$ ה.

---

[11] This happens with the heavy fp ending, but in the Alias Proiles the "S" is for the more common pronominal suffix (ch. 15), which also pulls the accent down, putting the prefix in problem position.

13.7.3 Notes on Qal Imperfect with open long vowels under the prefix.

Most often this indicates $R_1 = $ י/ן, $R_2 = $ י/ן, or $R_2 = R_3$.

תִּיטַב	$R_1 = $ י $\rightarrow$ vocalic (original $R_1 = $ י).	(י still visible)
וַתֵּשֶׁב / תֵּשֵׁב	$R_1 = $ י $\rightarrow$ vocalic (original $R_1 = $ ן).	(Prefix- P̱; *i*-class theme)
תֵּלֵךְ	הלך acts like $R_1 = $ י.	(Prefix- P̱; *i*-class theme)
תּוּכַל	$R_1 = $ י (originally ן) > vocalic.	(ן still visible; $R_1 = $ ן > י)
תֵּתַמּוּ / תֵּתַם	$R_2 = R_3$ Opt. A.	(Prefix- P̱; R_2 not *mater*, poss. *dagesh*)
וַתָּשָׁב / תָּשׁוּב	$R_2 = $ י/ן becomes vocalic.	(Prefix- P̱; R_2 may be *mater*)
תָּסֹבּוּ / תָּסֹב	$R_2 = R_3$ Opt. A.	(Prefix- P̱; R_2 not *mater*, poss. *dagesh*)

13.7.4 Misc. Notes.

$R_1 = $ G usually have ⬜⬜G̱P̱ or ⬜⬜G̱P̱. A vocal *shewa* under R_2 upgrades R_1's composite *shewa* to a full vowel, e.g. ו⬜⬜G̱P̱ and ו⬜⬜G̱P̱.

Preterite $R_3 = $ י $\neq$ ה roots lose R_3 altogether, e.g. וַתֵּבְךְּ, וַיֵּשְׁתְּ.

$R_2 = $ י/ן preterites usually lose the *mater*, e.g. וַיָּקֻמוּ, וַיָּקָם.

13.8 Vocabulary. Words primarily related to negation, perception, and good/evil.

1	אַל	*adv.* not, no (in prohibitions) (729)
2	בַּל	*adv.* not, no (73)
3	בִּלְתִּי	*adv.* except, not, so as not to (לְבִלְתִּי) (112)
4	נָא	*prt.* please (particle of entreaty) (405)
5	בִּין	*vb.* to understand, discern, perceive (171)
6	זָכַר	*vb.* to remember (235)
7	חָשַׁב	*vb.* to reckon, account (124)
8	מַחֲשָׁבָה	*n.f.* thought, device (56)
9	מַרְאֶה	*n.m.* vision, appearance, sight (103)
10	נָבַט	*vb.* *Pi., Hi. to look at, regard (70)
11	פָּקַד	*vb.* to note, count, appoint, attend to = inspect/punish/reward; Hi. to appoint; Ni. to be noticed, missed (304)
12	שָׁכַח	*vb.* to forget (102)
13	חָטָא	*vb.* to do wrongly, sin (240)
14	חַטָּאת	*n.f.* sin, sin offering (298)
15	חֶרְפָּה	*n.f.* reproach (73)
16	טָמֵא	*vb.* be(come) unclean (162)
17	פֶּשַׁע	*n.m.* violation, transgression, guilt of/punishment for/offering for transgression (93)
18	רָעַע	*vb.* be/do evil, displeasing, harmful (98)

13.9   **Learning Activities on the CD.**

1   **Grammar Illustrations** of Qal imperfect weak verbs.

2   **Practice Parsing: Sets A, B, C, D, E.**

Set A. Qal impf. and preterite of roots with *nun* or gutturals. 20 items.

Set B. Qal impf. and preterite of roots with *vav*, *yod*, or $R_2 = R_3$. 25 items.

Set C. Qal impf. and preterite of roots from chs. 1–12 vocabulary. 25 items.

Set D. Qal impf. and preterite of roots not from chs. 1–12 vocabulary. 25 items.

Set E. Review. Parse all types of Qal verbs. 25 items.

3   **Parsing Exercise.**

4   **Practice Reading** (using vocabulary from chs. 1–12). 72 items.

5   **Translation Exercise.**

Section One: misc.   Section Two: 1Sam 26:18–21.

Section Three: Num 14:12–15.   Section Four: 2Sam 12:21–23.

6   **Learn ch. 13 vocabulary.**

chapter fourteen

Qal Volitional Forms, Infinitive Absolute

14.1 Focus.

In this chapter you are to learn:

the use and spelling of the Qal infinitive absolute, קָטוֹל, קָטֹֽם,

negation,

the meanings of volitional verbs, and

to parse volitional verbs based in part on knowing the imperfect.

Volitional verbs indicate the will, or volition, of the speaker. The cohortative (1st person), imperative (2nd person), and jussive (3rd person) are all based on the imperfect spellings. Compared to the imperfect, (1) cohortatives add הָ; (2) imperatives erase the prefix; and (3) the jussives move the accent up one position (cp. preterite forms).

In chapter 10 we learned that *vav* plus the perfect may be consecutive to whatever verb form it follows (10.6). If a volitional verb is followed by *vav* + perfect, the perfect may be continuing the volitional notion. Following an imperfect, *vav* + perfect may be sequential in future time.

Whereas the infinitive construct commonly fills noun functions, the primary function of the infinitive absolute is adverbial. Over half the time it appears with a verb of the same root to focus on the mood of the verb. These uses, called paronomastic, can usually be translated by words like *certainly, really,* or *actually.* The infinitive absolute is similar to the infinitive construct in form but has pretonic open long *qametz* under R₁, קָטֹל. Its pattern usually does not change for weak roots.

Hebrew has several words for negation, as you learned in last chapter's vocabulary. We review the situations in which they are used, but generally just knowing the vocabulary leads you to a good translation. Take special note, however, of אַל vs. לֹא with the prefixed forms.

14.2   Cohortative (coh.). First Person Volitional. אֶ◻◻◻ָה or נְ◻◻◻ָה

The cohortative is formed by adding ◌ָה onto the first person imperfect:

אֶקְטְלָה = אֶקְטְלָה + ◌ָה (or אֶקְטֹלָה) *let me…* or *I should/intend to…*

נִקְטְלָה = נִקְטְלָה + ◌ָה (or נִקְטֹלָה) *let us…* or *we should…*

Keep identifiers distinct. The cohortative is marked by the ◌ָה suffix with a first person prefix, e.g. א or נ. The Qal ID badge is the prefix + short *i*-vowel + R₁. Together they make the Qal cohortatives: אֶ◻◻◻ָה or נִ◻◻◻ָה.

14.2.₁ Weak root Cohortatives.

Being based on the imperfect, weak root cohortatives act the same as imperfect weak forms. This section serves as **review and reference**. Notice the consistency of a first person prefix, א or נ, and the ◌ָה ending.

R₁ = נ. *Nun* over silent *shewa* assimilates as *dagesh*.

(נתן) אֶתְּנָה ← אֶתְּנָה   (נתן) נִתְּנָה ← נִתְּנָה

R₁ = י. *Yod* over silent *shewa* becomes vocalic; it may not be written as a *mater*.

(ישב) אִיעֵצָה ← אִיעֵצָה   (יעץ) אֵשְׁבָה ← אֵשְׁבָה

The *i*-class vowel[1] under the א keeps the coh. distinct from the R₁ = א Qal pf. 3fs, אָמְרָה.

R₂ = י/ו. י/ו become vocalic. R₁ begins the syllable, leaving the prefix POL *qametz*.

(מות) אָמוּתָה (בוא) אָבוֹאָה (סור) אָסֻרָה (שים) אָשִׂימָה

The theme vowel helps keep these coh. distinct from the R₁ = א Qal pf. 3fs, אָמְרָה.

R₁ = א. Some R₁ = א roots take *holem* after the prefix; R₁ = א drops out after the imperfect prefix א.

נאכְלָה   אֹמְרָה ← אֹמְרָה

אֹמְרָה looks identical to a Qal ptc. fem. sg. ab. You must judge by context; both are rare.

R₁ = G. Gutturals may or may not tolerate silent *shewa*.

אֶעְבְּרָה cp. אֶעֶבְרָה   נַעְבְּרָה cp. נַעַבְרָה

Typically gutturals prefer composite *shewa*. But followed by vocal *shewa*, the guttural gets upgraded to a full vowel, cp. 3mp impf. יַעַמְדוּ and 2fs perfect שָׁמַעַתְּ.

R₂ = G. Gutturals prefer composite *shewa* in the contextual forms: נִבְחֲרָה.

R₃ = י ≠ ה. Rarely cohortative, the original *yod* **may** survive:[2] אֶהֱמָיָה (המה).

R₂ = R₃. Also rare, a *dagesh forte* may not appear.

נָבֹזָה (בזז; an option A geminate)   נִדְמָה (דמם; an option B geminate)

---

[1] Some R₁ = א verbs have *holem*, e.g. אֹמְרָה which looks like a fem. si. Qal act. ptc. The verb יכל, *be able*, restores a ו, e.g. נוּכְלָה.

[2] R₃ = י ≠ ה cohortative forms are rare. If the *yod* drops out, ◌ָה distinguishes the cohortative from the imperfect, which has ◌ֶה.

14.3 **Imperative** (imv.). Second Person Volitional. ◻◻ְ◻ָ or E◻ְ◻ְ◻.

The imperative forms look like the imperfect forms, but with the prefix deleted. This means that the 2ms imv. is usually identical to the inf. cs. with the ◻◻ְ◻ָ pattern. As with the inf. cs., the theme vowel may be *u*-class, *a*-class, or *i*-class. We can tell them apart because the inf. cs. is normally preceded by a preposition or time word.

When the prefix is removed from the 2fs or 2mp forms, those with a vocalic ending, that leaves two *shewas* in a row, וּ◻ְ◻ְ◻ַ. To solve the pronunciation problem, the first becomes a *hireq*, as in the E◻ְ◻ִ◻ pattern. This is not an issue for the 2fp imv. because its ending begins with a consonant, allowing it to keep a full vowel with R₂.

Compare the imperatives to the imperfect forms.

Endings		*u*-class		*a*-class		*i*-class	
		Imv.	Impf.	Imv.	Impf.	Imv.	Impf.
ø	ms	קְטֹל	תִּקְטֹל	שְׁמַע	תִּשְׁמַע	בְּכֵה	תִּבְכֶּה
◻ִי	fs	קִטְלִי	תִּקְטְלִי	שִׁמְעִי	תִּשְׁמְעִי	בְּכִי	תִּבְכִּי
◻וּ	mp	קִטְלוּ	תִּקְטְלוּ	שִׁמְעוּ	תִּשְׁמְעוּ	בְּכוּ	תִּבְכּוּ
◻ְנָה	fp	קְטֹלְנָה	תִּקְטֹלְנָה	שְׁמַעְנָה	תִּשְׁמַעְנָה	בְּכֶינָה	תִּבְכֶּינָה

(a) Notes on spelling.

קִטְלוּ The *hireq* under R₁ keeps the mp imv. distinct form the Qal pf. 3cp with POL *qametz* under R₁, קָטְלוּ.

קְרֶאןָ The fp may not have the *mater he*. The fp imv. is rare.

(b) Notes on use.

Said *by* a person with authority, an imperative is a command; said *to* a person of authority, an imperative is a request. In both cases, the imperative represents the wish of the speaker.

14.3.₁ Paragogic ◻ָה on ms imv.[3]

The ms imv. sometimes adds ◻ָה, called a **paragogic** ה. In strong roots this usually shifts the *o* vowel to R₁ as *qametz hatuph* (cp. 8.8.1) but some use *hireq*. Paragogic ה occurs most with weak roots which have lost a radical or in the Psalms.

strong		R₁ = י & הלך		other weak		
ms Imv.	root	ms Imv.	root	ms Imv.	root	
זָכְרָה	זכר	רְדָה	ירד	תְּנָה	נתן	R₁ = נ
שָׁמְעָה	שמע	הֲבָה	יהב	שׁוּבָה	שוב	R₂ = ו/י
		לְכָה	הלך	אָרָה	ארר	R₂ = R₃

---

[3] Paragogic ◻ָה may be inconsistently tagged in a computer program.

14.3.2 Weak root imperatives.

(a) **R₁** = נ and **R₁** = י.

A missing **R₁** = נ or י is generally not restored[4] in the imperative. Remember, לקח acts like **R₁** = נ and הלך acts like **R₁** = י.

	נתן		לקח	ידע			הלך	ירא
	Imv.	Impf.	Imv.	Imv.	Impf.		Imv.	Imv.
2ms	תֵּן	תֵּתֵן ← תִּנְתֵּן	קַח	דַּע	דַּע ← תֵּדַע	תִּידַע	לֵךְ	יְרָא
2fs	תְּנִי	תֵּתְנִי ← תִּנְתְּנִי	קְחִי	דְּעִי	דְּעִי ← תֵּדְעִי	תִּידְעִי	לְכִי	—
2mp	תְּנוּ	תֵּתְנוּ ← תִּנְתְּנוּ	קְחוּ	דְּעוּ	דְּעוּ ← תֵּדְעוּ	תִּידְעוּ	לְכוּ	יְראוּ
2fp	—		—	—			לֵכְנָה	—

(b) **R₂** = י/ו are vocalic as in the imperfect.

	Imv.	Impf.	Imv.	Impf.	Imv.	Impf.
2ms	שֵׁב / שׁוּב	תֵּשׁוּב	שִׂים	תֵּשִׂים	בֹּא / בוֹא	תֵּבוֹא
2fs	שְׁבִי / שׁוּבִי	תֵּשׁוּבִי	שִׂמִי	תֵּשִׂימִי	בֹּאִי / בוֹאִי	תֵּבוֹאִי
2mp	שְׁבוּ / שׁוּבוּ	תֵּשׁוּבוּ	שִׂמוּ	תֵּשִׂימוּ	בֹּאוּ	תֵּבוֹאוּ
2fp	שֹׁבְנָה	תֵּשֹׁבְן	—	—	—	—

The mp imv. of **R₂** = י/ו roots can usually be distinguished from the Qal pf. 3cp in that the perfect usually has *qametz* under R₁, שָׁבוּ, שָׂמוּ, and בָּאוּ. In some cases the Qal pf. also uses *holem*, e.g. בֹּשׁוּ, and so context must determine if it is pf. 3cp or imv. mp.

(c) **R₂** = **R₃** Geminates.

Note *dagesh forte* in R₃ with a vocalic suffix. Without a suffix R₃ is lost.

	Imv.	Impf.	Imv.	Imv.
2ms	סֹב	תֵּסֹב	—	אֲרָה
2fs	סֹבִּי	תֵּסֹבִּי	רָנִּי	—
2mp	סֹבּוּ	תֵּסֹבּוּ	רָנּוּ	אֲרוּ
2fp	—	תֵּסֻבֶּינָה	—	—

(d) **R₃** = י ≠ ה.

The imperatives display the standard behaviors of verbs appearing to be **R₃** = ה. Without a suffix (ms), the *mater he* is used with an *i*-class vowel under R₂. With a vocalic suffix (fs, mp), a *mater he* cannot be used; the suffix attaches directly to R₂. With a consonantal suffix (fp), the original *yod* survives.

---

[4] A few times **R₁** = נ is restored, e.g. נְטֵה, נִפְלוּ. Except for roots also R₂ = י/ו which do not lose the נ in the impf., the 11 ms imv. of נְטֵה account for half of those restoring נ.

	Imv.	Impf.	Imv.	Impf.	Imv.	Impf.
2ms	שְׁתֵה	תִּשְׁתֶּה	רְאֵה	תִּרְאֶה	עֲשֵׂה	תַּעֲשֶׂה
2fs	—	תִּשְׁתִּי	רְאִי	תִּרְאִי	עֲשִׂי	תַּעֲשִׂי
2mp	שְׁתוּ	תִּשְׁתּוּ	רְאוּ	תִּרְאוּ	עֲשׂוּ	תַּעֲשׂוּ
2fp	—	תִּשְׁתֶּינָה	רְאֶינָה	תִּרְאֶינָה	—	תַּעֲשֶׂינָה

(e) **R₁ = G/א** or **R₂ = G**.

These simply prefer composite *shewa* in place of a simple *shewa*.

	Imv.	Impf.	Imv.	Impf.	Imv.	Impf.	Imv.	Impf.
2ms	אֱחֹז	תֶּאֱחֹז	עֲבֹר	תַּעֲבֹר	אֱסֹף	תֶּאֱסֹף	אֱמֹר	תֹּאמַר
2fs	אֶחֱזִי	—	עִבְרִי	תַּעֲבוּרִי	אִסְפִי	תֶּאֱסְפִי	אִמְרִי	תֹּאמְרִי
2mp	אֶחֱזוּ	—	עִבְרוּ	תַּעֲבְרוּ	אִסְפוּ	—	אִמְרוּ	תֹּאמְרוּ
2fp	—	—	—	—	—	—	אֱמֹרְנָה	תֹּאמַרְנָה

(f) **R₃ = G/א**. R₃ = G accepts silent *shewa*.

Syllable-closing *aleph* quiesces, lengthening the vowel in the ms imv.

	Imv.	Impf.	Imv.	Impf.
2ms	שְׁמַע	תִּשְׁמַע	קְרָא	תִּקְרָא
2fs	שִׁמְעִי	—	—	תִּקְרְאִי
2mp	שִׁמְעוּ	תִּשְׁמְעוּ	קִרְאוּ	תִּקְרְאוּ
2fp	שְׁמַעְנָה	—	קְרֶאןָ	תִּקְרֶאנָה

14.4 Jussive. Volitional verbs mostly in the third persons.

Jussives indicate the will or desire of the speaker with regard to things or third parties. They can often be translated with *let...* or *may...*, e.g., *let my prayer come before you*, or *may the* L*ORD* *bless him*.

In form they can be compared to the imperfect or to the preterite without the ⬚וַ. The different accent position produces a distinct form in R₃ = י ≠ ה and R₂ = י/ו roots. Lacking a suffix, the 3ms and 3fs R₃ = י ≠ ה lose both the *mater he* and the vowel of R₂ (cp. וַיֵּשְׁתְּ 13.4.1). R₂ = י/ו are more likely to be written without *matres lectionis*, but this is not a dependable feature for distinguishing the imperfect and jussive.

You must primarily rely on context to decide if a prefixed form is jussive. The weak verb examples below have slightly different looks. Study them to be sure that you can recognize person, number, and root.

14.4.1 Compare the jussive to the imperfect and preterite.

The jussive of most verbs looks like the imperfect.

	Impf.	Jussive	Preterite	root
3ms	יִקְטֹל	יִקְטֹל	וַיִּקְטֹל	קטל
3fs	תִּקְטֹל	תִּקְטֹל	וַתִּקְטֹל	

The jussive's similarity to the preterite is clear with $R_3 = $ י ≠ ה and $R_2 = $ י/ו.

	Impf.	Jussive	Preterite	root	Impf.	Jussive	Preterite	root
3ms	יַעֲשֶׂה	יַעַשׂ	וַיַּעַשׂ	עשה	יָשׁוּב	יָשֹׁב	וַיָּשָׁב	שׁוּב
3fs	תַּעֲשֶׂה	תַּעַשׂ	וַתַּעַשׂ		תָּשׁוּב	תָּשֹׁב	וַתָּשָׁב	
3ms	יִשְׁתֶּה	יֵשְׁתְּ	וַיֵּשְׁתְּ	שׁתה	יָשִׂים	יָשֵׂם	וַיָּשֶׂם	שׂים
3fs	תִּשְׁתֶּה	תֵּשְׁתְּ	וַתֵּשְׁתְּ		תָּשִׂים	תָּשֵׂם	וַתָּשֶׂם	
3ms	יִהְיֶה	יְהִי	וַיְהִי	היה	יָבוֹא	יָבֹא	וַיָּבוֹא	בוֹא
3fs	תִּהְיֶה	תְּהִי	וַתְּהִי		תָּבוֹא	תָּבֹא	וַתָּבוֹא	

Distinct jussive forms are also known as short forms or apocopated forms. They can occur in the first and second persons also, but are primarily third person.

14.5 Negation.

לֹא is used with the imperfect, perfect, adjectives, and nominal clauses.

אַל is used with the jussive and cohortative.

There are also short forms, or jussives, in the second persons. In the various resources you may use, some will call these second person forms juss. + אַל. Others will call them impf. + אַל.

Imperative forms are not negated in Hebrew. Hebrew can express two kinds of negative commands.

Impf. + לֹא expresses an abiding prohibition.

Juss./Impf. + אַל expresses a temporary prohibition.

14.5.1 Impf. + לֹא.

The particle לֹא is used with the imperfect either for simple **negation** (Jer 11:11, 1Sam 12:15) or to express **prohibitions** (negative commands) of an enduring nature (Exod 20:14–15). That is, they are permanent prohibitions, expressing a principle that should not be violated, rather than a temporary situation.

Jer 11:11	וְלֹא אֶשְׁמַע אֲלֵיהֶם	I will not listen to them.
1Sam 12:15	וְאִם־לֹא תִשְׁמְעוּ	And if you will not listen
	בְּקוֹל יְהוָה	to the voice of the LORD…
Exod 20:14–15	לֹא תִּנְאָף	Do not commit adultery.
	לֹא תִּגְנֹב	Do not steal.

14.5.2 Juss. + אַל; Coh. + אַל.

The particle אַל is used to negate the volitionals (except the imperative). The Jussive + אַל indicates a prohibition that is temporary, or for a particular occasion.[5] When Jeremiah says not to listen to the prophets (Jer 23:16), he does not mean to never ever listen to prophets, but rather that they should not listen to these particular prophets who are not telling the truth. The cohortative (2Sam 24:14) is rarely negated.

Jer 23:16	אַל־תִּשְׁמְעוּ עַל־דִּבְרֵי הַנְּבִאִים	Do not listen to the words of the prophets (who…)
Gen 22:12	אַל־תַּעַשׂ לוֹ מְאוּמָה	Do not do anything to him.
2Sam 24:14	וּבְיַד־אָדָם אַל־אֶפֹּלָה	Let me not fall into the hand of man.

14.5.3 Terminology. Jussive vs. Imperfect in the 2nd person. For reference.

In most cases the imperfect and jussive look alike. Distinct jussive forms occur when $R_3 = $ י ≠ ה or $R_2 = $ ו/י because the different accent produces a shorter form. Most often אַל occurs with the shortened form of these verbal roots. However, some resources and computer programs reserve the term jussive to third person forms. They apply the label imperfect to second person prefixed forms + אַל or any second person prefixed form that is volitional. Other resources recognize these as jussives.

14.5.4 Negation Summary.

Generally, knowing the vocabulary will lead you to a good translation. For exegesis, you should distinguish between impf. + לֹא and juss./impf. + אַל.

לֹא for negating imperfect, perfect, adjectives, participles, and nominal clauses.

Impf. + לֹא for permanent prohibitions.

אַל for negating jussives (and short imperfects) and cohortatives.

Juss./Impf. + אַל for temporary or situational prohibitions.

בִּלְתִּי/לְבִלְתִּי for negating infinitive constructs (also בְּלִי, מִבְּלִי, בְּלֹא).

בַּל for negating imperfect, perfect, participle, and infinitive construct.

Used mostly in poetry, בַּל is much less common than לֹא.

14.6 נָא. Particle of politeness.

Using the particle נָא may be a polite way of asking for consideration. It occurs mostly after volitional verbs or after אַל in negative constructions. In English, you can often use the word *please* for the same effect.

---

[5] Lev. 10:9 uses juss. + אַל for a prohibition against priests drinking alcohol on the occasion(s) of coming to the tent of meeting. It is called a perpetual statute later in the verse, meaning that it is always prohibited on those occasions; but is not a prohibition against drinking any alcohol on any occasion.

14.7   Infinitive Construct (inf. cs.) review.

You have already learned the Qal infinitive construct, ☐☐☐ , e.g. כְּתֹב *to write* (8.6 & 7). In the strong verb and some weak verbs, the infinitive construct often has the same form as the masc. sg. imperative and is worthy of review here. In context they are not hard to tell apart, since the infinitive construct follows a preposition or time word in the vast majority of cases.

(a) Observe the monosyllabic pattern in the following forms, regardless of the theme vowel. When there are three radicals, the first takes *shewa* to be monosyllabic. Also, $R_2 = $ י/ו roots are monosyllabic because R_2 becomes vocalic. Geminates may follow the pattern of the strong verb or drop R_3.

strong	$R_2 = G$	$R_1 = G/$א	$R_3 = G$	$R_1 = $נ	$R_2 = $ו	$R_2 = $י	$R_2 = R_3$
קְטֹל	בְּחֹר	עֲבֹר	שְׁמֹעַ	נְפֹל	בּוֹא	שׂוֹם	סֹב / סְבֹב
לְמֹד		אֱסֹף		(see below)	שׁוּב	רִיב	צַר

(b) The forms below add ה on the end. As you learned in 8.7, $R_3 = $ י $\neq$ ה roots use the ending וֹת. Some $R_1 = $ נ verbs follow the pattern in the strong verb above; others have lost the *nun* and add ה. Along with $R_1 = $ י roots, they have a segolate formation.

$R_1 = $נ		$R_1 = $י		$R_3 = $ י $\neq$ ה	
גֶּשֶׁת	תֵּת (נתן)	שֶׁבֶת	צֵאת	עֲשׂוֹת	הֱיֹת / הֱיוֹת
שְׂאֵת	קַחַת (לקח)	דַּעַת	לֶכֶת (הלך)	שְׁתוֹת	

14.8   Infinitive Absolute (inf. ab.), ☐ָ☐☐ / ☐ָ☐וֹ☐.

The Qal infinitive absolute pattern is a very consistent ☐ָ☐☐, e.g. קָטֹל. The ☐ָ☐☐ pattern holds throughout most weak roots. $R_3 = G$ typically take furtive *pataḥ*. $R_1 = $ נ and $R_1 = $ י roots retain their first radical. Geminates often write both R_2 and R_3. The *holem* of the infinitive absolute usually becomes the vowel for $R_2 = $ י/ו roots. However, $R_3 = $ י $\neq$ ה roots may use either *mater vav* or *mater he* for the *holem*.

strong	$R_2 = G$	$R_1 = G/$א	$R_3 = G$	$R_2 = $ו	$R_2 = $י	$R_2 = R_3$
קָטֹל	בָּחֹר	עָבֹר	שָׁמֹעַ	בּוֹא	שׁוֹם	סֹב / סָבֹב
לָמֹד		אָסֹף		שׁוֹב	רוֹב / רִיב	

$R_1 = $נ		$R_1 = $י		$R_3 = $ י $\neq$ ה	
נָפֹל	נָתֹן	יָשֹׁב	יָצֹא	רָאֹה / רָאוֹ (ראה)	
נָשֹׂא	לָקֹח	יָדֹעַ	הָלֹךְ	הָיֹה / הָיוֹ (היה)	

14.8.1 Infinitive Absolute functions.

A slight majority of infinitive absolutes occur with a finite verb of the same root. These are called **paronomastic**. This construction usually heightens the verb's mood, i.e. its degree of reality, expressing certainty or emphasizing non-real mood. It can often be translated with adverbs such as *surely*, *certainly*, or *clearly*.

שָׁתוֹ תִשְׁתּוּ   -1-   You *surely ought to* drink.
Jer 25:28

עָשֹׂה אֶעֱשֶׂה עִמְּךָ חֶסֶד   -2-   I will *surely deal* with you kindly.
2Sam 9:7

The infinitive absolute may also fill noun functions and very often acts adverbially, describing verbs of different roots. See further in ch. 30.

14.9 Verbal sequences.

14.9.1 Volitional verbs as purpose/intention.

Volitional verbs express the will of the speaker. This is not limited to giving commands and making requests. This can include stating the speaker's intention or indicating a purpose (*so that, in order that*). This function often occurs in a sequence of volitional verbs.

...וּקְחוּ (imv. לקח) אֶת־אֲבִיכֶם   -1-   Get your father...
וּבֹאוּ (imv. בוא) אֵלָי   And come to me
וְאֶתְּנָה (coh. נתן) לָכֶם אֶת־טוּב   *so I will give* you the best of the land
וְאִכְלוּ (imv. אכל) אֶת־חֵלֶב   *so that* you may eat the fat
Gen 45:18

עַתָּה חָכְמָה וּמַדָּע תֶּן־לִי (imv.)   -2-   Give me now wisdom and insight
וְאֵצְאָה (coh. יצא) לִפְנֵי הָעָם־הַזֶּה   *in order that I may go out* before this people
2Chr 1:10

14.9.2 Perfect consecutive, *vav* + perfect.

The *vav* plus perfect may continue a previously established framework. It may be sequential to or a consequence of the preceding verb. Once the volitional mode has been established by an imperative or jussive, it may be continued by a *vav* plus perfect. The *vav* + perfect may also continue the verbal frame of an imperfect.

עֲמֹד (imv.) בְּשַׁעַר בֵּית יְהוָה   -3-   Stand at the gate of the LORD's house
וְקָרָאתָ שָּׁם   *and call out* there/to call out there...
Jer 7:2

אִם־שָׁמוֹעַ תִּשְׁמְעוּ בְּקֹלִי   -4-   If you will actually obey my voice,
וּשְׁמַרְתֶּם אֶת־בְּרִיתִי   *and will keep* my covenant
Exod 19:5

14.10   Summary.

Volitional verbs indicate the will, or volition, of the speaker.

Volitional verb spellings are similar to the imperfect.

1st person,   cohortative,   אָ◻◻◻ָה or נְ◻◻◻ָה, *let me, let us.*

אֶקְטְלָה, נִקְטְלָה

2nd person,   imperative,   ◻◻◻ָ◻, command, request, purpose, or intention.

קְטֹל, קִטְלִי, קִטְלוּ, קְטֹלְנָה

A suffix called a paragogic *he*, ◻ָה, appears on some weak roots

(R_1 = נ, R_1 = י, R_2 = י/ו, R_2 = R_3) masc. sg. imperatives.

3rd person,   jussive,   ◻◻◻ָ◻, *let X...* or *may X....*

They look like the imperfect or like preterites without ◻וַ.

R_3 = י ≠ ה lose both the *mater he* and the vowel of R_2.

R_2 = י/ו are more likely to be written without vowel letters.

There are also second person jussives and a few first person jussives.

Negation Summary. (Knowing the vocabulary generally leads to a good translation.)

לֹא for negating impf., pf., adj., ptc., and nominal clauses.

אַל for negating jussives (and short imperfects) and cohortatives.

** **Impf. +** לֹא for permanent prohibitions.

** **Juss./Impf. +** אַל for temporary or situational prohibitions.

בִּלְתִּי/לְבִלְתִּי for negating infinitive constructs (also בְּלִי, מִבְּלִי, בְּלֹא).

בַּל for negating imperfect, perfect, participle, and infinitive construct.

Used mostly in poetry, בַּל is much less common than לֹא.

נָא, the particle of politeness, can often be translated *please.*

Infinitive Absolute (inf. ab.). קָ◻ֹ◻ .

The pattern holds in most weak roots.

R_3 = י ≠ ה may use either *mater vav* or *mater he* for the *ḥolem.*

The perfect consecutive, *vav* + perfect, may continue a previously established framework, i.e. continue a previously established volitional sense or be sequential to the imperfect in future time.

14.11 **Vocabulary**. Words primarily related to travel.

1	בָּרַח	*vb.* to flee (63)
2	דָּרַךְ	*vb.* to tread, march, bend (a bow) (63)
3	דֶּרֶךְ	*n.m.* way, road, manner (712)
4	דָּרַשׁ	*vb.* to seek, resort to (165)
5	יָצָא	*vb.* to go/come out; inf. cs. צֵאת (1076)
6	יָרַד	*vb.* to go/come down; inf. cs. רֶדֶת (382)
7	כָּשַׁל	*vb.* to stumble, stagger (65)
8	נָגַשׁ	*vb.* to draw near, approach; inf. cs. גֶּשֶׁת (125)
9	נוּס	*vb.* to flee, escape (160)
10	נָסַע	*vb.* to set out, drive (flocks), journey (146)
11	נָשָׂא	*vb.* to lift, bear, carry; inf. cs. שֵׂאת (659);
12	סָבִיב	*adv.* round about, circuit (338)
13	סוּר	*vb.* to turn aside (298)
14	עָלָה	*vb.* to go up, ascend (894)
15	פּוּץ	*vb.* be dispersed, scattered (65)
16	פָּנָה	*vb.* to turn, look (134)
17	פָּרַשׂ	*vb.* to spread out (67)
18	קָרַב	*vb.* to approach, draw near (280)
19	רוּץ	*vb.* to run (104)

14.12 **Learning Activities on the CD.**

1 **Grammar Illustrations** of Qal imperative verbs.

2 **Practice Parsing: Sets A, B, C.**

Set A. Practice parsing Qal volitional verbs from chs. 1–13 vocabulary. 30 items.

Set B. Practice parsing Qal volitional verbs not from your vocabulary. 22 items.

Set C. Parse all types of Qal verbs from chs. 1–13 vocabulary. 50 items.

3 **Parsing Exercise.**

4 **Practice Reading** (using vocabulary from chs. 1–13). 72 items.

5 **Translation Exercise.**

Section One: misc. Section Two: 1Sam 26:22–25.

Section Three: Num 14:16–20. Section Four: 2Sam 7:1–7.

6 **Learn ch. 14 vocabulary.**

chapter fifteen

Pronominal Suffixes on Verbs

15.1 Focus.

In this chapter you are to learn:

to recognize pronominal suffixes on verbs.

The direct object of a verb may be expressed by a pronominal suffix on the verb. There are nine perfect and ten imperfect verb forms on which to put the ten pronominal suffixes. Besides variations in the pronouns, that could make up to 190 combinations – for the strong verb. You can readily see that rote memorization of all particulars is an undesirable approach. *The best strategy, as always, is to think in terms of the* **syllable principles and comparison** *to what you should already know.*

Like pronominal suffixes on nouns, the forms of the suffixes on verbs may be **compared to** the ends of **the independent pronouns**. Indeed they are nearly identical to the forms used with nouns and prepositions. When attached to verbs the accent moves and the *syllable principles* lengthen and shorten vowels accordingly.

(Participles and infinitives employ the pronominal suffixes used with nouns, cf. chs. 6 and 8).

15.2 Pronominal suffixes on verbs.

Compare the suffixes to the independent pronoun in the chart below. As before, the ת of the second person is replaced by כ in the suffixes. The 3fs suffix is best compared to the ה of the feminine singular noun, but the pronoun will usually have a *mappiq* or have a *qametz* underneath. Verb forms ending in a consonant often require a connecting vowel, usually *pataḥ* or *qametz* for perfect verbs and *ṣere* or *segol* for imperfect verbs. **Other than differences in connecting vowels, the forms of the suffixes are essentially the same.**

For purposes of recognition, **learn the forms that occur on verbs ending in vowels** and simply be prepared for there to be a connecting vowel for verb forms ending in consonants. In addition you should learn a few alternate forms using *nun* listed below (far left).

Pronominal suffixes for verbs. (E.g. *he guarded me/you/etc.*)

suffix on Impf. verbs w/final cons.	suffix on Pf. verbs w/final cons.	suffix on verbs with final vowel	Basic parts	indep. pron.		obj. pron.
נִֽי, נִֽי	נִֽי	נִי	נִי	אֲנִי	1cs	me
ךָֽ, ךָ	ךָ	ךָ	ךָ → תָ	אַתָּה	2ms	you
ךְ	ֵךְ, ָךְ	ךְ	ךְ → תְ	אַתְּ	2fs	you
ֵהוּ, נֽוּ	ֵהוּ, וֹ	ו, הוּ	הוּ	הוּא	3ms	him
ֶהָ, ָהּ, ֶנָּה	ָהּ	הָ	הָ	הִיא	3fs	her
ֵנוּ, נֽוּ	נֽוּ	נוּ	נוּ	נַחְנוּ	1cp	us
ְכֶם	ְכֶם	כֶם	כֶם → תֶם	אַתֶּם	2mp	you
ְכֶן	ְכֶן	כֶן	כֶן → תֶן	אַתֵּנָה	2fp	you
ֵם	ָם	ֵם, הֶם	הֶם	הֵם	3mp	them
ֵן	ָן	ן	ן	הֵנָּה	3fp	them

All the essential information of the chapter is in this chart. The rest of the chapter provides illustrations to confirm how they attach. Explanations are provided, but remember, your **focus** is **on recognition**.

15.3   Attaching the suffixes to Qal Perfect strong verb.

Remember the Qal perfect ID badge (strong verb). R_1 has pretonic open long *qametz* or *shewa* in propretonic problem position.

(a) Qal Perfect strong verb, 3rd persons.

With pronominal suffixes, all third person perfect forms share the feature that R_3 begins a syllable with the accent. Consequently, R_2 has pretonic open long *qametz*, while R_1 has *shewa* in problem position.

The 3ms perfect adds a connecting vowel to R_3. The 3fs perfect uses its original form שָׁמְרַת. Feminine singular nouns also preserved their original ת with pronominal suffixes and in the construct.

(b) Qal Perfect strong verb, 1st and 2nd persons.

With pronominal suffixes, the first and second persons place the accent after R_3. Thus $R_2 + R_3$ form a pretonic closed short syllable, and R_1 is in problem position with *shewa*. In the following charts, **observe** that the suffixes may be recognized based on knowing the independent pronoun, while the verb follows the pretonic rules.

Minor note on the **2mp.** On the *very rare* occasion that the 2mp perfect of any stem has a pronominal suffix, it is also based on an older ending, תוּם, yet the *mem* drops out, hence, שְׁמַרְתּֽוּנוּ.

(c) **3ʳᵈ person Qal perfect plus suffixes**   SↃↃↃ.

suffix		Qal Pf. 3ms שָׁמַר	Qal Pf. 3fs שְׁמָרָה	Qal Pf. 3cp שָׁמְרוּ
1cs	נִי	שְׁמָרַנִי	שְׁמָרַתְנִי	שְׁמָרוּנִי
2ms	ךָ	שְׁמָרְךָ	שְׁמָרַתְךָ	שְׁמָרוּךָ
2fs	ךְ	שְׁמָרֵךְ	שְׁמָרַתֶךְ	שְׁמָרוּךְ
3ms	ו, הוּ	שְׁמָרוֹ, שְׁמָרַהוּ	שְׁמָרַתּוּ[1], שְׁמָרַתְהוּ	שְׁמָרוּהוּ
3fs	הָ	שְׁמָרָהּ	שְׁמָרַתָּה[2]	שְׁמָרוּהָ
1cp	נוּ	שְׁמָרָנוּ	שְׁמָרַתְנוּ	שְׁמָרוּנוּ
2mp	כֶם	—	—	—
2fp	כֶן	—	—	—
3mp	ם	שְׁמָרָם	שְׁמָרַתַם	שְׁמָרוּם
3fp	ן	שְׁמָרָן	שְׁמָרַתַן	שְׁמָרוּן

(d) **1ˢᵗ and 2ⁿᵈ person Qal perfect plus suffixes**   SĚↃↃↃ

suffix		2ms שָׁמַרְתָּ	2fs שָׁמַרְתְּ	1cs שָׁמַרְתִּי	1cp שָׁמַרְנוּ
1cs	נִי	שְׁמַרְתַּנִי	שְׁמַרְתִּינִי	—	—
2ms	ךָ	—	—	שְׁמַרְתִּיךָ	שְׁמַרְנוּךָ
2fs	ךְ	—	—	שְׁמַרְתִּיךְ	—
3ms	הוּ / ו	שְׁמַרְתָּהוּ / שְׁמַרְתּוֹ	שְׁמַרְתִּידהוּ	שְׁמַרְתִּיהוּ / שְׁמַרְתִּיו	שְׁמַרְנָהוּ
3fs	הָ	שְׁמַרְתָּהּ	שְׁמַרְתִּיהָ	שְׁמַרְתִּיהָ	שְׁמַרְנוּהָ
1cp	נוּ	שְׁמַרְתָּנוּ	שְׁמַרְתִּינוּ	—	—
2mp	כֶם	—	—	—	—
2fp	כֶן	—	—	—	—
3mp	ם	שְׁמַרְתָּם	שְׁמַרְתִּים	שְׁמַרְתִּים	שְׁמַרְנוּם
3fp	ן	שְׁמַרְתָּן	שְׁמַרְתִּין	שְׁמַרְתִּין	—

2ms. The 2ms ending, תָּ, is תַ before a 1cs suffix, except in pausal forms, e.g. תַנִי. Before a 3ms suffix, ו, the *a*-vowel contracts, ַו → וֹ , שְׁמַרְתּוֹ.

2fs. The 2fs perfect uses an older form with *hireq yod*, תִי.[3] The 2fs and 1cs perfects with third person pronominal suffixes are easily confused due to the תִי-syllable. You must judge by context, *but note that the 2fs perfect plus suffix is rare.*

---

[1] This form represents an assimilation of ה into ת: ַתְהוּ → ַתּוּ.

[2] This form represents an assimilation of ה into ת: ַתְהָ → ַתָּ → ַתָּה. The *he* on the end is a *mater*.

[3] The archaic spelling may occur without a suffix, but with the familiar vowel pointing, e.g. קָטַלְתִּי.

15.4   Attaching the suffixes to Qal Perfect weak roots.

Weak roots vary little from the strong verb when adding pronominal suffixes.

R_1 = י and R_1 = נ pose no problem since both accept vocal *shewa*.

R_1 = G simply asks for composite *shewa* instead of vocal *shewa*.

R_2 = נ and R_2 = G are non-issues since R_2 always has a full vowel.

R_3 = נ and R_3 = G are non-issues since they usually accept *shewa*.

The most significant variations are R_2 = י/ו, R_2 = R_3, and R_3 = י ≠ ה.

(a) R_2 = י/ו. This group is almost entirely limited to the root שִׂים.

If the verb ending or pronominal suffix begins with a vowel, R_3 must begin that syllable and has the accent. Consequently, R_1 has pretonic open long *qametz*, since R_2 has dropped out, שָׂמַנִי, שָׂמָה.

If the verb ending or pronominal suffix begins with a consonant, R_3 and R_1 form a PCS syllable with *pataḥ*, since R_2 has dropped out.   שַׂמְתָּם, שַׂמְתִּיךָ, שַׂמְתִּיו

(b) R_2 = R_3.

Geminates **may** write all three radicals and behave like the strong verb, e.g. סְבָבֻהוּ, *they surrounded him*, סְבָבוּנִי *they surrounded me*.

Geminates **may** write R_2 as *dagesh forte* in R_3; then R_1 and R_2 form a PCS syllable, סַבּוּנִי, *they surrounded me*.

Geminates **may** add a *holem* connecting vowel between R_3 and the endings of the perfect conjugation, אָרוֹתִיהָ, *I cursed her/it*.

(c) R_3 = י ≠ ה.

The first and second persons behave much like the strong verb (with original *yod* surviving): רְאִיתִיו, *I saw him* (וְרְאִי is POL with SPP).

The **3cp** form, with or without pronominal suffixes, drops the *mater he* due to the vocalic ending of the perfect paradigm, רָאוּךָ, *they saw you*.

The **3ms** verb adds a connecting vowel as in the strong verb, which then obliterates the *mater he*, e.g. רָאָם, *he saw them*.

The **3fs** form is quite rare, e.g. רָאַתְךָ, *she/it saw you*.

15.5   Attaching the suffixes to Qal Imperfect and related forms.

(a)   *Nun forms of the suffixes.* The imperfect may also use alternative suffix forms with *nun*, sometimes called an energic *nun*. In the 2ms suffix the *nun* has assimilated into the *kaph*, ־ֶּךָ ← ־ֶנְךָ; the 3ms ־ֶנּוּ comes from ־ֶנְהוּ. That makes it identical to the 1cp forms, but the first person forms are rare.

־ֵנִי	1cs	me		־ֶּךָ	2ms	you	־ֶנּוּ	3ms	him
־ֶנּוּ	1cp	us					־ֶנָּה	3fs	her

(b) Qal imperfect plus suffixes: S◌̂◌◌◌P, Ṡ◌◌◌P.

suffix		Qal Impf. 3ms יִשְׁמֹר	Qal Impf. 3mp יִשְׁמְרוּ
1cs	נִי	יִשְׁמְרֵנִי, יִשְׁמְרֵנִי	יִשְׁמְרוּנִי
2ms	ךָ	יִשְׁמָרְךָ, יִשְׁמְרֶךָ	יִשְׁמְרוּךָ
2fs	ךְ	יִשְׁמְרֵךְ	יִשְׁמְרוּךְ
3ms	ו, הוּ	יִשְׁמְרֵהוּ, יִשְׁמְרֶנּוּ	יִשְׁמְרוּהוּ
3fs	הָ	יִשְׁמְרֶהָ, יִשְׁמְרֶנָּה	יִשְׁמְרוּהָ
1cp	נוּ	יִשְׁמְרֵנוּ	יִשְׁמְרוּנוּ
2mp	כֶם	יִשְׁמָרְכֶם	יִשְׁמְרוּכֶם
2fp	כֶן	יִשְׁמָרְכֶן	יִשְׁמְרוּכֶן
3mp	ם, ◌מוֹ	יִשְׁמְרֵם	יִשְׁמְרוּם
3fp	ן	יִשְׁמְרֵן	יִשְׁמְרוּן
		and similarly for 1cs, 2ms, 3fs, 1cp	and similarly for 2fs, 2mp

(c) **Notes.**

With the 2mp, 2fp, and (sometimes) 2ms pronominal suffixes without a full connecting vowel, e.g. יִשְׁמָרְךָ, יִשְׁמָרְכֶם, יִשְׁמָרְכֶן, the *qametz* is *qametz ḥaṭuph*.

The 2fp and 3fp imperfect verbs are not used with pronominal suffixes; instead the 2mp and 3mp forms are used as common forms.

Where the imperfect lacks an ending (1cs, 2ms, 3ms, 3fs, 1cp), an *i*-class connecting vowel or *shewa* is added. (The perfect uses an *a*-class connecting vowel.) This moves the accent to R_3's vowel. Similarly, imperfect forms with a vocalic suffix move the accent to R_3. R_2 will typically take vocal *shewa* such that it stays in the accented syllable and keeps the R_1 + prefix package together e.g. יִשְׁמְרֵנִי,[4] *he (will) guard(s) me*, יִתְּנֵנִי, *he (will) give(s) me*, יִשְׁמָרוּךָ, *they (will) guard you*. However, *a*-class verbs regularly give pretonic open long *qametz*, תִּשְׁמָעֵנִי, יִשְׁמָעוּךָ. Either way, they should be easy to recognize.

15.6   Attaching the suffixes to Qal Imperfect weak roots.

Again the only significant issues relate to $R_2 = $ י/ו, $R_2 = R_3$, and $R_3 = $ י $\neq$ ה.

(a) $R_2 = $ י/ו.

R_3 begins a syllable due either to the imperfect paradigm (2fs, 2mp, 3mp) or the connecting vowel of the pronominal suffixes. Since R_2 becomes vocalic, R_1 is pretonic open long, while the prefix has vocal *shewa* in propretonic problem position: תְּשִׂימֵנוּ *you set us*, יְשִׂמֵהוּ *he set him* (שׂים).

---

[4] Cp. יִשְׁמְרוּ and כָּתְבוּ.

(b) **R₂ = R₃**.

This pattern is dominated by the frequency of חָנַן, *to have mercy*. R₃ leads the accented syllable. R₂, represented as a *dagesh forte* in R₃, closes a PCS syllable with an *u*-class vowel, יְחָנֵּנוּ (חנן), יְסַבּוּהוּ (סבב).

Some geminates double R₁ instead, יִקְבֶהוּ (קבב).

(c) **R₃ = י ≠ ה**.

The *mater he* disappears when the connecting vowel of the pronominal suffixes is added, יַעֲנֵנוּ, תַּעֲנְךָ, יִרְאֶהָ, וַיִּרְאוּהָ, וַיַּעֲשֵׂהוּ, תַּעֲשֶׂהָ.

15.7 Imperatives: S☐☐☐, SE☐☐☐, or S☐☐☐.

The imperatives are based on the same pattern as the imperfect. There is one change in the ms imperative, as also in the infinitive construct. When a pronominal suffix is added, the *o*-vowel may shift from R₂ to R₁ and reduces to (pretonic closed short) *qametz ḥatuf*. (Remember, 93% of infinitive constructs are preceded by a preposition or word for time, cf. 8.6.2, while imperative forms occur when someone directly addresses another. They are easily distinguished in real sentences.)

	ms Imv.			Inf. cs.	
no suff	שְׁמֹר	Keep!	no suff	שְׁמֹר	to keep
3ms suff	שָׁמְרֵהוּ	Keep him!	3ms suff	שָׁמְרוֹ	his keeping/
1cs suff	שָׁמְרֵנִי	Keep me!			keeping him

The masculine plural imperatives behave as the imperfect. *I*- and *u*-class roots maintain *shewa* under R₂ and have a *ḥireq* under R₁, שִׁמְרוּ ← שְׁמְרוּ. *A*-class roots have pretonic open long *qametz* under R₂ and *shewa* in problem position under R₁. Compare the imperfect תִּשְׁמְעוּהָ to the imperative שְׁמָעוּנִי.

	2mp Imv.			2mp Imv.	
no suff	שִׁמְרוּ	Keep!	no suff	שִׁמְעוּ	Listen!
3ms suff	שִׁמְרוּהוּ	Keep him!	3ms suff	—	—
3fs suff	שִׁמְרוּהָ	Keep her!	3fs suff	שְׁמָעֶנָּה	Hear it!
1cs suff	שִׁמְרוּנִי	Keep me!	1cs suff	שְׁמָעוּנִי	Hear me!

15.8 Summary.

See the chart in 15.2.

Looking ahead, the pronominal suffixes attach to the derived stem verbs, which you are about to learn, very similarly to the way they do to the Qal. If the verb form does not end in a vowel, a connecting vowel is added. The syllable principles apply but the identifying characteristics of the derived stems are more stable than in the Qal.

15.9   Vocabulary. Words primarily related to speaking and selling.

In preparation for the derived stems (chs. 16–22), the vocabulary includes several verbs which do not occur in the Qal. The list includes these abbreviations:

Ni. = Niphal   Pi. = Piel   Hi. = Hiphil   Hit. = Hitpael

An asterisk precedes the stem abbreviation if the root does not occur in the Qal. They have been given the vowels of the Qal perfect 3ms for their lexical form, even if they do not occur in the Qal.

1	בָּרַךְ	*vb.* *Pi. to bless; Hi. to cause to kneel (327)
2	בְּרָכָה	*n.f.* blessing (69)
3	דָּבַר	*vb.* *Pi. to speak (1141*)
4	הָלַל	*vb.* be boastful; Pi. to praise (146)
5	הָמוֹן	*n.m/f.* sound, murmur, tumult (86)
6	יָדָה	*vb.* to shoot; Pi. to cast; Hit. to confess, praise; Hi. to laud, praise (111)
7	מָכַר	*vb.* to sell (80)
8	מְלָאכָה	*n.f.* work, wares, craftsmanship (167)
9	מַעֲשֶׂה	*n.m.* deed, work (235)
10	נְאֻם	*n.m.* utterance of, declaration of (376) (always in construct)
11	נָבָא	*vb.* *Ni., Hi. to prophesy (115)
12	נָגַד	*vb.* *Hi. to declare (371)
13	נַחֲלָה	*n.f.* possession, property (222)
14	עָבַד	*vb.* to work, serve (289)
15	עֶבֶד	*n.m.* servant, slave (803)
16	עֲבֹדָה	*n.f.* service, labor, work (145)
17	קוֹל	*n.m.* voice, sound (505)
18	קָנָה	*vb.* to acquire, buy, get (85)
19	שָׁבַע	*vb.* *Ni. to swear, take an oath (186)
20	תָּקַע	*vb.* to give a blow/blast (on a horn), clap, thrust, drive (70)

15.10   Learning Activities on the CD.

1   Practice Parsing: Sets A, B, C, D, E.

Set A. Perfect verbs with pronominal suffixes. 20 items.

Set B. Imperfect and preterite verbs with pronominal suffixes. 20 items.

Set C. Imperative verbs with pronominal suffixes. 20 items.

Set D. Inf. cs. and ptc. pronominal suffixes. 20 items.

Set E. Review of verbs with pronominal suffixes. 15 items.

2   Parsing Exercise (Part A).

3   Practice Reading (using vocabulary from chs. 1–14). 70 items.

4   Translation Exercise (Section One) **and Parsing Exercise** (Part B).
Selected verses with verbs appearing in Parsing Exercise B.

5   Translation Exercise.
Section Two: Num 14:21–24.

6   Learn ch. 15 vocabulary.

chapter sixteen

Derived Stems: Infinitives and Participles

16.1 Focus.

In this chapter you are to learn:

the nine patterns that characterize the six derived stems,

their application in infinitives and participles, and

that D-stem and H-stem participles have preformative *mem*.

Chapter 10 previewed the verbal stems, or *binyanim*.[1] This chapter formally introduces them. There are nine patterns that characterize these six stems (three have two patterns). After these are learned, there will be virtually no more morphological pieces to learn. The following chapters will simply cover how these patterns combine with the verbal conjugations (pf., impf., etc.) and how they trigger weak letter behaviors. *As always, our strategy is to think in terms of the syllable principles and comparison to what you* should *already know.*

Syntactically, we will introduce some of the basic relationships between the stems. These generalizations can help infer a verb's meaning from the Qal, but a lexicon is really the most important resource for the meanings of verbs in different stems. Also, not all verbs occur in the Qal. Some vocabulary should be learned in terms of their different stems' meanings.

Infinitives and participles in the derived stems function as they do in the Qal.

16.2 The derived stems (*binyanim*).

The names of the derived stems come from each stem's 3ms perfect form of the verb *pa'al*, (פָּעַל *to do*): Niphal (נִפְעַל), Piel (פִּעֵל), Hitpael (הִתְפַּעֵל), Pual (פֻּעַל), Hiphil (הִפְעִיל), and Hophal (הָפְעַל). The Piel, Pual, and Hitpael are sometimes called the D-stems, or doubling stems, because they double R_2 (even though you cannot see it in the *'ayin* of פעל). The Hiphil and Hophal, also called the H-stems, use a preformative ה. (The Hitpael is a D-stem not an H-stem, despite the ה.) The Niphal, N-stem, has a preformative נ.

---

[1] Both of these terms are used in scholarly literature.

There are three basic groups among the *binyanim* (stems). The stems in each group tend to share a common element of meaning but differ in voice. Voice indicates the direction of the action. **Active voice** indicates that the subject performs the action (*he hit* the ball). **Passive voice** indicates that the subject receives the action (*he was hit* by the ball). **Reflexive voice** indicates that the action somehow pertains back to the subject who performs it, e.g. *they stared at one another*.

	preform. נ	Double R$_2$			preformative ה	
Qal	Niphal	Piel	Pual	Hitpael	Hiphil	Hophal
Active	Pass., Refl.	Active	Pass.	Reflexive	Active	Pass., Refl.

The derived stems treat fientive and stative verbs differently. In addition, they can be used to make verbs out of adjectives and nouns. We will use the active voice Piel to illustrate the D-stems and the Hiphil for the H-stems. As a reminder, fientive verbs involve an activity. Stative verbs describe a state, quality, or attribute.

Fientive (activity)   קָטַל to kill,   כָּתַב to write,

                         שָׁבַר to break,   קָבַר to bury.

Stative (quality)   כָּבֵד to be heavy,   זָקֵן to be old,   לָמֵד to learn,

                         מָלֵא to be full,   קָטֹן to be small.

16.2.1 Basic uses of the Niphal, the N-stem.

(a) **Passive of the Qal.** Often the Qal represents the basic or normal meaning of the root word and the Niphal gives the passive voice of the same meaning.

root	Qal	Niphal
מצא	to find	to be found
כתב	to write	to be written, or to be recorded

(b) **Reflexive or Middle.** The Niphal can give a reflexive or "middle" meaning, where the subject is somehow involved in both performing and receiving the action.

root	Qal	Niphal
יעץ	to counsel	to consult with
סגר	to shut	to shut oneself in

(c) **Of stative roots.** Verbs that are stative in the Qal *rarely* occur in the Niphal. The Niphal may make them *ingressive*.

root	Qal	Niphal
קדשׁ	be holy	to be (treated as) holy, (or *reflexive*) to demonstrate oneself as holy.
בער 2	be stupid	(*ingressive*) to become stupid/stupefied

(d) **No connection to the Qal.** Sometimes the Niphal describes a condition or state and the root is not used or not attested in the Qal. (Passive meanings, emphasizing the resulting condition, are often similar to stative notions.)

root	Qal	Niphal
כּוּן	—	to be firm, fixed, established, prepared

Sometimes the difference between the Qal and Niphal is difficult to articulate. A dictionary may give the same English gloss for both Qal and Niphal. These examples are beginning guides to the derived stems.

16.2.2 Basic uses of the D-stems, represented by the Piel.

(a) **Factitive** of stative verbs. The Piel indicates that the quality or state indicated by the stative root is made to be the case, or made into a *fact*.

root	Qal	Piel
כבד	to be heavy/honored	to give honor to
טהר	to be clean	to make clean/to cleanse

(b) **Denominative.** The Piel makes a verb out of a noun or adjective.

noun		Piel
תּוֹעֵבָה	abomination	regard as abomination/to abhor
דָּבָר	word	to speak

(c) **Plurative** of fientive verbs.[2] The action in some way involves plurality.

root	Qal	Piel
שׁבר	to break (in two)	to break to pieces/to shatter
קבר	to bury	to bury (a host)

(d) **No Qal connection.** Some verbs have no Qal counterpart or nominal source.

root	Qal	Piel
בקשׁ	—	to seek

16.2.3 Basic uses of the H-stems, represented by the Hiphil.

(a) **Factitive** of stative verbs. The Hiphil may also be factitive. Rarely does a stative root occur in both Piel and Hiphil.

root	Qal	Hiphil
כבד	to be heavy/honored	to fatten
חזק	to be/grow strong	to strengthen, or to repair (said of walls)

---

[2] Before the nature of plurative verbs was learned from other languages, the Piel was often called *intensive*, a label still in use. Goetze has shown the inadequacy of the term (A. Goetze, "The So-called Intensive of the Semitic Languages," JAOS 62 [1942]). See also 26.1.

(b) **Denominative.**

noun		Hiphil
אֹזֶן	ear	to listen
אוֹר	light	to give light

(c) **Causative** of fientive verbs. The subject causes the action to occur.

root	Qal	Hiphil
שׁקה	to drink	to give a drink to (someone) to water (the ground)
בוא	to come	to cause to come/to bring

(d) **Connection to Niphal.** Some verbs which occur in the Niphal but not the Qal have a counterpart in the Hiphil. There can be a variety of kinds of connections and explanations. This example is comparable to the factitive of a stative verb.

root	Niphal	Hiphil
כון	to be firm, fixed, established, prepared	to establish, prepare

16.2.4 Summary of stem functions.

The specific functions of the stems can be further explored. These examples illustrate: (1) that it matters whether the root is stative or fientive, (2) that you need to learn some vocabulary by the different stems' meanings, and (3) that you will need to use a dictionary to get more familiar with the meanings of the derived stems. The following summary is a helpful start.

basic meaning		Qal	Active
	pref. נ	Niphal	Pass./Refl.
factitive (of statives)	Double R₂	Piel	Active
denominative (of adj./nouns)		Hitpael	Refl.
plurative (of fientives)		Pual	Passive
factitive (of statives)	pref ה	Hiphil	Active
denominative (of adj./nouns)			
causative (of fientives)		Hophal	Pass./Refl.

16.3 The identity badges of the derived stems.

Sometimes the stem's name (from its 3ms pf.) reveals its characteristics, but not always, for four reasons: (1) פָּעַל is a weak verb and cannot take *dagesh forte* in R₂ for the D-stems, (2) three stems do not use the perfect's pattern for their other verb forms, (3) in some forms the preformative נ or ה of the Niphal, Hiphil, or Hophal drops out, and (4) the 3ms forms are unable to reveal variations in the theme vowel that may occur throughout certain conjugations.

16.3.₁ Derived stem ID badges.

A stem's identity badge always involves R_1. In the derived stems, R_1 joins a prefix or a doubled R_2, which in turn affects the prefix. So for any verb form we look at the behavior of R_1 and the prefix, if present. It is as if every verb wears an identifying badge on R_1. **Memorize these 9 patterns.** In the chart, the "P" stands for any prefix letter; the $\mathbb{P}$ is in outline form if there may not be a prefix on some forms. Patterns on the right are for perfects. In the Ni. it is also for infinitives and participles.

Niphal	□□◌ִP	□□◌ַנ
Piel	□◌ִ□◌ְּℙ	□◌ִ□
Hitpael	□◌ִ□◌ְּתְהP	
Pual	□◌ִ□◌ֻ ℙ	
Hiphil	□□◌ְ ℙ	□□◌ִ ה
Hophal	□□◌ְ ָ P	

16.4 Derived stem ID badges in their infinitive forms.

The derived stems use the same form for the infinitive construct and infinitive absolute, except for the Niphal. The Niphal may (or may not) use the form on the right for its infinitive absolute. Observe how they use the ID badges listed above.

Piel	קַטֵּל	Niphal	הִקָּטֵל	נִקְטֹל
Hitpael	הִתְקַטֵּל	Hiphil	הַקְטִיל	
Pual	קֻטֹּל	Hophal	הָקְטֵל	

16.4.₁ The structure of the derived stem infinitives.

The Hiphil and Piel are the most common infinitives besides the Qal. The Niphal is infrequent and the Pual and Hophal are rare. Because the infinitives display the stem ID badges so clearly, learning them has value well beyond their frequency.

Niphal infinitive.

□□◌ַנ   Inf. ab.

R_1 joins the Niphal's נ to make a PCS syllable with *ḥireq*.

R_2 has an *u*-class theme vowel, *ḥolem*.

□□◌ִ◌ָה   Inf. cs. or ab.

R_1 has pretonic open long *qametz*.

נ would have *shewa* in problem position so it has assimilated into R_1 as *dagesh*.

ה is a place holder to make the syllable to keep the assimilation of נ into R_1.

R_2 has an *i*-class theme vowel, *ṣere*.

Piel infinitive.

□ַּ□ֵּ□   Inf. cs. or ab.

R₁ joins doubled R₂ with *patah*.

R₂ has an *i*-class theme vowel, *sere*.

Hitpael infinitive.

□ַּ□ֵ□ְתִה   Inf. cs. or ab.

R₁ joins doubled R₂ with *patah*.

הְתִ is added in front; note the *shewa* in problem position.

R₂ has an *i*-class theme vowel, *sere*.

Pual infinitive.

□ֻּ□□   Inf. cs. or ab.

R₁ joins doubled R₂ with *qibbus*.

R₂ has an *u*-class theme vowel, *holem*.

Hiphil infinitive.

□ִ□ְקַה   Inf. cs. or □□ְקַה inf. ab.

R₁ joins ה with PCS *patah*.

R₂ has *hireq yod* (or at least an *i*-class vowel for weak roots).

Hophal infinitive.

□□□ְקָה / □□□ְקָה / □□וּה   Inf. cs. or ab.

R₁ joins ה in a PCS syllable with an *u*-class vowel.

R₂ may have an *a*-class theme vowel, *patah*, or an *i*-class vowel, *sere*.

16.5   Infinitive Functions.

There are no new functions to learn. Infinitives act the same regardless of stem. What the stem affects is the meaning of the lexeme.

16.5.1   Infinitive Absolutes.

If the infinitive is paronomastic, it focuses on the mood or modality of the verb (14.8.1), often translated by words like *certainly* or *surely*. An infinitive absolute may also act adverbially, often stating the manner of the action (ch 30).

16.5.2   Infinitive Constructs.

The infinitive construct and infinitive absolute are identical in form in most of the derived stems. Note that in context, 96% of infinitive constructs in the Bible are immediately preceded by:

1) a preposition (esp. לְ),

2) a temporal indicator, e.g. שָׁנָה, אָז, עֵת, יוֹם, אַחַר, אַחֲרֵי, or

3) a purpose/cause indicator, e.g. יַעַן.

Most of the remaining 4% are used as complements, completing the meaning of another word, such as like to _____, able to _____, willing to _____, refuse to _____, add to _____, know how to _____, seek to _____, sufficient to _____.

The infinitive construct is a verbal noun. It may be the object of a preposition or a verb. Rarely, it is even the subject of a verb. It often expresses purpose or temporal notions (see further in ch. 30).

     purpose: לִשְׁמֹר *in order to guard…*

     temporal: וַיְהִי כִשְׁמֹעַ *it happened when [someone] heard.*

16.5.3   Infinitive Construct with pronominal suffixes.

Infinitive constructs use the same pronominal suffixes as singular nouns. With pronominal suffixes the accent is on R_3. So, typical of verbs, R_2 takes vocal *shewa*, staying with the accented syllable. The Hiphil retains its *ḥireq-yod* (or at least *ḥireq*), a pretonic open long syllable. The stem ID badges are unchanged.

    Niphal הִקָּטְלוֹ   Piel   קַטְּלוֹ

    Hiphil הַקְטִילוֹ   Hitpael הִתְקַטְּלוֹ

16.6   Derived stem participles.
16.6.1   Function.

Derived stem participles function like Qal participles (8.4). They are verbal adjectives using the noun endings to show agreement in gender and number with what they modify. They agree or differ in definiteness to show attributive or predicate position and may be used substantively.

Active participles (including the Hitpael) with the article are almost always to be translated substantively or as a relative clause. Without the article, they may be substantival or translated with an English participle (*-ing, -ed*). The passive participles are most often to be translated as adjectives or substantively, but sometimes as English participles with *-ing* or *-ed*. Judge by context.

16.6.2   Spellings.

Derived stem participles are comprised of a preformative מ (except for the Niphal) plus the stem's ID badge plus the noun endings. The מ replaces the ה of the Hiphil, Hophal, and Hitpael. The Qal, Piel, and Hitpael participles have an *i*-class theme vowel under R_2 which reduces to *shewa* when endings are added, such that R_2 stays with the accented syllable. The Hiphil participle has *ḥireq-yod*, which does not reduce. The passive participles, the Niphal, Pual, and Hophal participles, are *a*-class. Their theme vowel becomes pretonic open long when the noun endings are added. Many feminine singular participles employ a תֶ ending in a segolate pattern תֶ◌ֶ◌, or תַ◌ַ◌ with gutturals.

16.6.3   ID badges in strong verb participles.

➤ **Qal participle.**   (About 70% of biblical participles.)

□□וֹ□	Active ptc.: *ḥolem* after R$_1$.
□וֹ□□ / E□וֹ□□	Passive ptc.: *u*-vowel after R$_2$; R$_1$ is POL *qametz* or SPP.

➤ **Niphal participle.**   (About 8% of biblical participles.)

נ□□□	Pattern: E + □□□נ ID Badge: נ with *hireq* joins R$_1$. R$_2$ gets *qametz* (except fem. sg. ת–forms). The *a*-class theme vowel follows noun accent rules.

ALL D- AND H-STEM PARTICIPLES HAVE PREFORMATIVE מ.

➤ **Piel participle.**   (About 8% of biblical participles.)

מ□·□□	Pattern: E + □·□□ + מ ID Badge: vocal *shewa – patah – dagesh*. מ in problem position with *shewa*. R$_1$ joins doubled R$_2$ (unless guttural) with *patah*.

➤ **Hitpael participle.**   (About 2% of biblical participles.)

מ□·□ת□	Pattern: E + □·□ת□ + מ. ID Badge: מת plus *patah – dagesh*. מ replaces ה and joins ת, i.e. מת. R$_1$ joins doubled R$_2$ (unless R$_2$ is guttural) with *patah*.

➤ **Pual participle.**   (About 2% of biblical participles.)

מ□·□□	Pattern: E + □·□□ + מ ID Badge: מ plus vocal *shewa – qibbuṣ – dagesh*. מ in problem position with *shewa*. R$_1$ joins doubled R$_2$ (unless R$_2$ is guttural) with *qibbuṣ*. R$_2$ is *a* class (except fem. sg. contextual ת–forms).

➤ **Hiphil participle.**   (About 9% of biblical participles.)

מ□□י□	Pattern: E + □□□י□ + מ ID Badge: Prefix has *patah*. R$_2$ has *hireq yod*. מ replaces ה, joining R$_1$ with *patah*. מ□□י□. R$_2$ has *hireq yod* (or an *i*-class vowel for weak roots).

➤ **Hophal participle.**   (About 1% of biblical participles.)

מ□□□	Pattern: E + □□□ה + מ ID Badge: Prefix has *qametz hatuph* (or an *u*-vowel). מ replaces ה and joins R$_1$ for a pretonic closed short syllable with *qametz hatuph* מ□□□. R$_2$ is *a* class (except fem. sg. contextual ת–forms).

16.6.4 Derived stem participle paradigms.

Observe closely the combination of pieces in the participles. To the root have been added the noun endings, stem ID badges, and preformative מ (or נ for Niphal).

	Niphal	Piel	Hitpael	Pual	Hiphil	Hophal
	נּ□□□	P□ֵ·□□	P□ַ·□תְּ□□	P□·□□	P□ְ□□	P□□□
ms	נִקְטָל	מְקַטֵּל	מִתְקַטֵּל	מְקֻטָּל	מַקְטִיל	מָקְטָל
fs	נִקְטֶלֶת	מְקַטֶּלֶת	מִתְקַטֶּלֶת	מְקֻטֶּלֶת	מַקְטֶלֶת	מָקְטֶלֶת
mp	נִקְטָלִים	מְקַטְּלִים	מִתְקַטְּלִים	מְקֻטָּלִים	מַקְטִילִים	מָקְטָלִים
fp	נִקְטָלוֹת	מְקַטְּלוֹת	מִתְקַטְּלוֹת	מְקֻטָּלוֹת	מַקְטִילוֹת	מָקְטָלוֹת

16.7 Summary.

The six derived stems have nine core patterns. These ID badges combine with the conjugations already learned for the Qal to produce the various verb forms.

The infinitives represent the basic patterns of most verb forms.

The participles add the noun endings. And except for Qal and Niphal, all participles have preformative מ (which follows the syllable principles).

The use of infinitives and participles is the same as described in the Qal.

Memorize this chart.

Niphal	□□ָ·P	נּ□□□
Piel	P□□·□□	□·□□
Hitpael	P□תַ·□□□	
Pual	P□□·□□	
Hiphil	P□□ְ□□	ה□□□
Hophal	P□□ֳ□□	

16.8   Vocabulary. Primarily words related to buildings.

1   אֹהֶל   *n.m.* tent (348)

2   אוֹצָר   *n.m.* treasury, storehouse (79)

3   בַּיִת   *n.m.* house (2047); *irregular plural forms: בָּתִּים and fw בָּתֵּי־

4   בָּנָה   *vb.* to build (377)

5   דֶּלֶת   *n.f.* door (88)

6   הֵיכָל   *n.m.* palace, temple (80)

7   חוֹמָה   *n.f.* wall (133)

8   חָצֵר   *n.m.* court, enclosure, village (192)

9   כּוּן   *vb.* *Ni. be established, firm, prepared; Hi. to prepare, establish, provide (219)

10   מִקְדָּשׁ   *n.m.* sanctuary (75)

11   סָגַר   *vb.* to shut, close; Pi., Hi. to deliver up (91)

12   עַמּוּד   *n.m.* pillar, column (112)

13   פֵּאָה   *n.f.* corner, side (86)

14   פָּתַח   *vb.* to open (136)

15   פֶּתַח   *n.m.* doorway, opening, entrance (164)

16   קִיר   *n.m.* wall (73)

17   שַׁעַר   *n.m/f.* gate (373)

16.9   Learning Activities on the CD.

1   Grammar Illustration. Forming infinitives and participles.

2   Learn forms. Copy the chart from 16.3.1.

3   Explore Stem Meanings.
     Look up the meanings of the selected words in different stems in the dictionary. Reflect on the degree to which knowing the general function of the stem helps.

4   Practice Parsing: derived stem infinitives and participles. 97 items.

5   Parsing and Translation Exercise: Section One
     (includes derived stem infinitives).

6   Parsing and Translation Exercise: Section Two
     (includes derived stem participles).

7   Practice Reading (using vocabulary from chs. 1–15). 67 items.

8   Translation Exercise: Section Three: 2Chr 34:1–4. See Workbook appendix.

9   Learn ch. 16 vocabulary.

chapter seventeen

I-class Imperfects:
Niphal, Piel, Hitpael, Hiphil

17.1   Focus.

In this chapter you are to learn:

no new spellings and no new functions, but

to recognize the stem ID badges which have been inserted into the imperfect paradigm with *i*-class theme vowels (comparing them to יִתֵּן).

The Niphal, Piel, Hitpael, and Hiphil imperfects are built by combining their ID badges (ch 16) with the imperfect affixes and an *i*-class theme vowel, similar to יִתֵּן. The Niphal, Piel, and Hitpael use *ṣere* while the Hiphil uses *ḥireq yod*.

R₂ & R₃ pattern	R₁ ID badge	Stem
יִתֵּן +	□□ֵּP	Niphal
	□□ֵּP	Piel
	□□ֵּתְP	Hitpael
	□□ֵP	Hiphil

As with the Qal we may also view the derived stem imperfects as a combination of the imperfect affixes and the stem's infinitive construct. The imperfect's prefixes precede any stem prefixes. The imperfect prefixes take vowels as dictated by the syllable principles and will replace a stem's ה.[1]

Niphal Impf.	Ni. Inf.	Impf. prefix	Piel Impf.	Piel Inf.	Impf. prefix
□□ֵּP =	הִקָּטֵל	+ P	□□ֵּP =	קַטֵּל	+ P
תִּקָּטֵל =	הִקָּטֵל	+ ת	תְּקַטֵּל =	קַטֵּל	+ ת

Hiphil Impf.	Hi. Inf.	Impf. prefix	Hitpael Impf.	Hit. Inf.	Impf. prefix
□ִי□ֵP =	הַקְטִיל	+ P	□□ֵתְP =	הִתְקַטֵּל	+ P
תַּקְטִיל =	הַקְטִיל	+ ת	תִּתְקַטֵּל =	הִתְקַטֵּל	+ ת

---

[1] Just as the inseparable prepositions replace the ה of the article, cp. 5.4.2.

17.2   *I*-class prefixed conjugations.

(a) **The Parts.** Compare the Qal of יִתֵּן to the pieces of the Niphal, Piel, and Hitpael.

	Qal *i*-class	Ni./Pi./Hit.	Niphal	Piel	Hitpael
	R_1 joins prefix w/ *ḥireq*	R_2 & R_3	R_1 POL *qametz* R_1's dagesh = נ joined to prefix	R_1 joins doubled R_2 + pref.	R_1 joins doubled R_2 + תְ P
	⬜⬜ְ⬜ְּP		⬜⬜ִ⬜ָּ֜P	⬜⬜ִ⬜ְP	⬜⬜ִ⬜ְתְP
1cs	אֶ תֵּן	טֵל +	אֶקָּ	אֲקַ	אֶתְקַ
2ms	תִּ תֵּן	טֵל +	תִּקָּ	תְּקַ	תִּתְקַ
2fs	תִּ תְּנִי	טְלִי +	תִּקָּ	תְּקַ	תִּתְקַ
3ms	יִ תֵּן	טֵל +	יִקָּ	יְקַ	יִתְקַ
3fs	תִּ תֵּן	טֵל +	תִּקָּ	תְּקַ	תִּתְקַ
1cp	נִ תֵּן	טֵל +	נִקָּ	נְקַ	נִתְקַ
2mp	תִּ תְּנוּ	טְלוּ +	תִּקָּ	תְּקַ	תִּתְקַ
2fp	תִּ תֵּנָּה	טְלֶנָה +	תִּקָּ	תְּקַ	תִּתְקַ
3mp	יִ תְּנוּ	טְלוּ +	יִקָּ	יְקַ	יִתְקַ
3fp	תִּ תֵּנָּה	טְלֶנָה +	תִּקָּ	תְּקַ	תִּתְקַ
Coh. 1cs	אֶ תְּנָה	טְלָה +	אֶקָּ	אֲקַ	אֶתְקַ
Coh. 1cp	נִ תְּנָה	טְלָה +	נִקָּ	נְקַ	נִתְקַ
Juss. 3ms	יִ תֵּן	טֵל +	יִקָּ	יְקַ	יִתְקַ
Juss. 3fs	תִּ תֵּן	טֵל +	תִּקָּ	תְּקַ	תִּתְקַ
Juss. 3mp	יִ תְּנוּ	טְלוּ +	יִקָּ	יְקַ	יִתְקַ
Juss. 3fp	תִּ תֵּנָּה	טְלֶנָה +	תִּקָּ	תְּקַ	תִּתְקַ

Notes.

The theme vowel of the 2fp and 3fp varies, typically *patah* in Niphal, תִּקָּטֵלְנָה, *sere* in the Piel, תְּקַטֵּלְנָה, but either in the Hitpael.

Pausal forms have a long vowel under R_2, so the only differences are to forms with a vocalic suffix, e.g. תִּתְקַטֵּלוּ, תְּקַטֵּלוּ, תִּתֵּנוּ.

The preterite typically begins with *vav-patah-dagesh* but otherwise looks like the imperfect, or more precisely, like the jussive.

(b) **The Parts.** Compare the Qal pausal forms of יִתֵּן to the pieces of the Hiphil. The Hiphil normally uses *ḥireq yod* where the other *i*-class imperfects use *ṣere*.

	Qal *i*-type pausal R₁ joins prefix w/ *ḥireq* □□□ִP	Hiphil contextual = pausal R₁ joins prefix w/ *pataḥ* (ה replaced by prefix) □ִי□□P
1cs	אֶ תֵּ ן	אַקְ טִיל
2ms	תִּ תֵּ ן	תַּקְ טִיל
2fs	תִּ תֵּ נִי	תַּקְ טִי לִי
3ms	יִ תֵּ ן	יַקְ טִיל
3fs	תִּ תֵּ ן	תַּקְ טִיל
1cp	נִ תֵּ ן	נַקְ טִיל
2mp	תִּ תֵּ נוּ	תַּקְ טִי לוּ
2fp	תִּ תֵּ נָּה	תַּקְ טֵלְ נָה
3mp	יִ תֵּ נוּ	יַקְ טִי לוּ
3fp	תִּ תֵּ נָּה	תַּקְ טֵלְ נָה
Coh. 1cs	אֶ תְּ נָה	אַקְ טִי לָה
Coh. 1cp	נִ תְּ נָה	נַקְ טִי לָה
Juss. 3ms	יִ תֵּ ן	יַקְ טֵל
Juss. 3fs	תִּ תֵּ ן	תַּקְ טֵל
Juss. 3mp	יִ תְּ נוּ	יַקְ טִי לוּ
Juss. 3fp	תִּ תֵּ נָּה	תַּקְ טֵלְ נָה

Notes.

The preterite looks like the jussive with *vav-pataḥ-dagesh*.

Though there can be minor variation in the theme vowel, simply swapping the ID badge creates the new paradigm. The consonants stay the same, but the set of marks attached to R₁ (including its syllabic tie to the prefix or possible *dagesh* in R₂) identifies the verb's stem.

(c) *I*-class imperfect paradigms.

	Qal *i*-class	Niphal	Piel	Hitpael	Hiphil
1cs	אֶתֵּן	אֶקָּטֵל	אֲקַטֵּל	אֶתְקַטֵּל	אַקְטִיל
2ms	תִּתֵּן	תִּקָּטֵל	תְּקַטֵּל	תִּתְקַטֵּל	תַּקְטִיל
2fs	תִּתְּנִי	תִּקָּטְלִי	תְּקַטְּלִי	תִּתְקַטְּלִי	תַּקְטִילִי
3ms	יִתֵּן	יִקָּטֵל	יְקַטֵּל	יִתְקַטֵּל	יַקְטִיל
3fs	תִּתֵּן	תִּקָּטֵל	תְּקַטֵּל	תִּתְקַטֵּל	תַּקְטִיל
1cp	נִתֵּן	נִקָּטֵל	נְקַטֵּל	נִתְקַטֵּל	נַקְטִיל
2mp	תִּתְּנוּ	תִּקָּטְלוּ	תְּקַטְּלוּ	תִּתְקַטְּלוּ	תַּקְטִילוּ
2fp	תִּתֵּנָּה	תִּקָּטַלְנָה	תְּקַטֵּלְנָה	תִּתְקַטֵּלְנָה	תַּקְטֵלְנָה
3mp	יִתְּנוּ	יִקָּטְלוּ	יְקַטְּלוּ	יִתְקַטְּלוּ	יַקְטִילוּ
3fp	תִּתֵּנָּה	תִּקָּטַלְנָה	תְּקַטֵּלְנָה	תִּתְקַטֵּלְנָה	תַּקְטֵלְנָה
Coh. 1cs	אֶתְּנָה	אֶקָּטְלָה	אֲקַטְּלָה	אֶתְקַטְּלָה	אַקְטִילָה
Coh. 1cp	נִתְּנָה	נִקָּטְלָה	נְקַטְּלָה	נִתְקַטְּלָה	נַקְטִילָה
Juss. 3ms	יִתֵּן	יִקָּטֵל	יְקַטֵּל	יִתְקַטֵּל	יַקְטֵל
Juss. 3fs	תִּתֵּן	תִּקָּטֵל	תְּקַטֵּל	תִּתְקַטֵּל	תַּקְטֵל
Juss. 3mp	יִתְּנוּ	יִקָּטְלוּ	יְקַטְּלוּ	יִתְקַטְּלוּ	יַקְטֵֿילוּ
Juss. 3fp	תִּתֵּנָּה	תִּקָּטֵלְנָה	תְּקַטֵּלְנָה	תִּתְקַטֵּלְנָה	תַּקְטֵלְנָה

Note: Hitpael 2/3 fem. pl may be *a*- or *i*-class.

17.3 Loss of *dagesh* in *D*-stems. **

Certain letters may lose their *dagesh* in the doubling stems when they have a vocal *shewa*. Vocal *shewa* appears under R₂ when R₃ has a vocalic suffix (e.g. 2fs, 2mp, 3mp impf. or with pronominal suffixes). The loss of the *dagesh forte* in these circumstances is most frequent with ק and the sibilants ס, צ, שׂ, and שׁ, but may occur with others as well, such as ו, י, ל, מ and נ, (i.e. with about half the alphabet).

17.4 Pronominal suffixes.

With pronominal suffixes the accent is on R₃. Typically, R₂ takes vocal *shewa*, staying with the accented syllable. The Hiphil retains its *ḥireq-yod* (or at least *ḥireq*), a pretonic open long syllable. Stem ID badges are unchanged. (Niphal and Hitpael imperfects rarely have pronominal suffixes.)

17.5 Imperatives.

We may build the imperative forms by starting with the imperfects and removing the prefix. The ה of the Hitpael and Hiphil is restored. The Niphal, as with its infinitive, adds ה at the front to keep its R₁ ID badge. R₁'s *dagesh* and *qametz* mark it as Niphal; do not mistake it for a Hiphil, Hophal, or Hitpael.

I-class imperatives compared to imperfects.

	Niphal		Piel	
2ms	הִקָּטֵל ←	תִּקָּטֵל	קַטֵּל ←	תְּקַטֵּל
2fs	הִקָּטְלִי ←	תִּקָּטְלִי	קַטְּלִי ←	תְּקַטְּלִי
2mp	הִקָּטְלוּ ←	תִּקָּטְלוּ	קַטְּלוּ ←	תְּקַטְּלוּ
2fp	—	—	קַטֵּלְנָה ←	תְּקַטֵּלְנָה

	Hiphil		Hitpael	
2ms	הַקְטֵל ←	תַּקְטִיל	הִתְקַטֵּל ←	תִּתְקַטֵּל
2fs	הַקְטִילִי ←	תַּקְטִילִי	הִתְקַטְּלִי ←	תִּתְקַטְּלִי
2mp	הַקְטִילוּ ←	תַּקְטִילוּ	הִתְקַטְּלוּ ←	תִּתְקַטְּלוּ
2fp	הַקְטֵלְנָה ←	תַּקְטֵלְנָה	—	—

Notes.

As in the Qal, the ms imv. looks like the infinitive construct. But as infinitive constructs are usually preceded by a preposition or word for time, they are easy to tell apart in an actual sentence.

17.6   Summary.

There are no new functions or morphological pieces. Review the chart in 17.2.c. Look for the stem's ID badge in the imperfect paradigm, which you already know.

17.7   Vocabulary. Primarily words related to emotions.

1	בָּעַר	*vb.* to burn, purge	(87*)
2	חֲלוֹם	*n.m.* dream	(65)
3	חֵמָה	*n.f.* heat, rage, venom	(125)
4	חֵן	*n.m.* favor, grace	(69)
5	חָנַן	*vb.* to show favor, be gracious	(77)
6	חֶסֶד	*n.m.* loyal love, kindness	(249)
7	חָפֵץ	*vb.* to delight in	(74)
8	חָרָה	*vb.* to burn, be kindled, angry, upset	(93)
9	מָאַס	*vb.* to reject, refuse, despise	(74)
10	נָחַם	*vb.* *Ni. be sorry, to change one's mind; Pi. to comfort	(108)
11	שָׂמַח	*vb.* be glad, rejoice	(156)
12	שִׂמְחָה	*n.f.* joy, gladness	(94)
13	שָׂנֵא	*vb.* to hate	(148)
14	שָׂרַף	*vb.* to burn	(117)
15	תּוֹעֵבָה	*n.f.* disgust, abhorrence, abomination	(118)

17.8   Review of R₁ ID badges.

Niphal

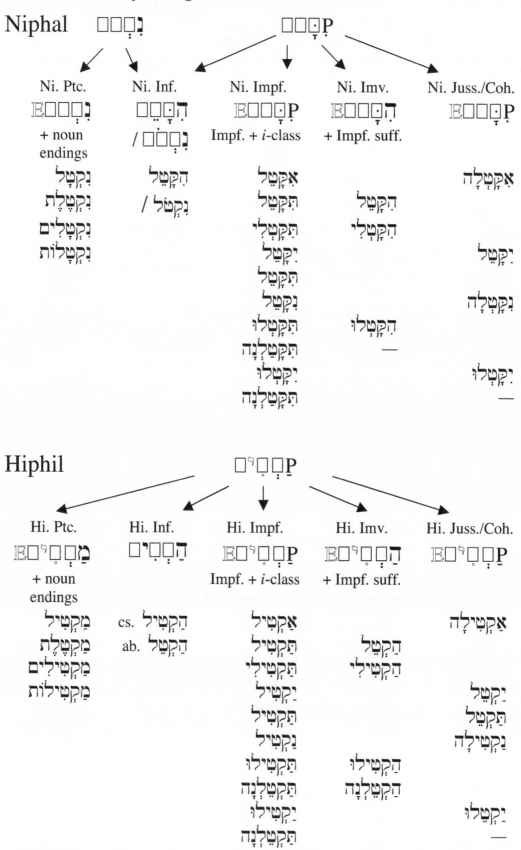

Ni. Ptc.	Ni. Inf.	Ni. Impf.	Ni. Imv.	Ni. Juss./Coh.
נִ□□□E + noun endings	הִ□□□ֵ / נִ□□□E	E□□□ֵP Impf. + *i*-class	הִ□□□ֵE + Impf. suff.	E□□□ֵP

Hiphil

Hi. Ptc.	Hi. Inf.	Hi. Impf.	Hi. Imv.	Hi. Juss./Coh.
מַ□י□E + noun endings	הַ□י□	E□י□P Impf. + *i*-class	הַ□י□E + Impf. suff.	E□□□P

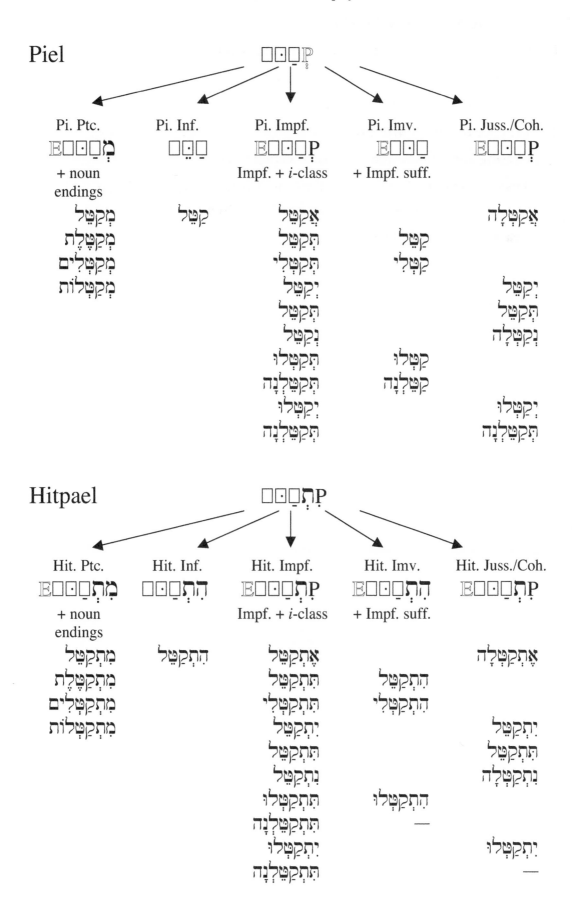

Piel

Pi. Ptc.	Pi. Inf.	Pi. Impf.	Pi. Imv.	Pi. Juss./Coh.
+ noun endings		Impf. + *i*-class	+ Impf. suff.	
מְקַטֵּל	קַטֵּל	אֲקַטֵּל		אֲקַטְּלָה
מְקַטֶּלֶת		תְּקַטֵּל	קַטֵּל	
מְקַטְּלִים		תְּקַטְּלִי	קַטְּלִי	
מְקַטְּלוֹת		יְקַטֵּל		יְקַטֵּל
		תְּקַטֵּל		תְּקַטֵּל
		נְקַטֵּל		נְקַטְּלָה
		תְּקַטְּלוּ	קַטְּלוּ	
		תְּקַטֵּלְנָה	קַטֵּלְנָה	
		יְקַטְּלוּ		יְקַטְּלוּ
		תְּקַטֵּלְנָה		תְּקַטֵּלְנָה

Hitpael

Hit. Ptc.	Hit. Inf.	Hit. Impf.	Hit. Imv.	Hit. Juss./Coh.
+ noun endings	הִתְקַטֵּל	Impf. + *i*-class	+ Impf. suff.	
מִתְקַטֵּל	הִתְקַטֵּל	אֶתְקַטֵּל		אֶתְקַטְּלָה
מִתְקַטֶּלֶת		תִּתְקַטֵּל	הִתְקַטֵּל	
מִתְקַטְּלִים		תִּתְקַטְּלִי	הִתְקַטְּלִי	
מִתְקַטְּלוֹת		יִתְקַטֵּל		יִתְקַטֵּל
		תִּתְקַטֵּל		תִּתְקַטֵּל
		נִתְקַטֵּל		נִתְקַטְּלָה
		תִּתְקַטְּלוּ	הִתְקַטְּלוּ	
		תִּתְקַטֵּלְנָה	—	
		יִתְקַטְּלוּ		יִתְקַטְּלוּ
		תִּתְקַטֵּלְנָה		—

17.9   Learning Activities on the CD.

1   **Grammar Illustration.** Forming *i*-class imperfects.

2   **Learn forms.** Copy the chart from 17.2.c.

3   **Practice Readings** (primarily building recent vocabulary). 34 items.

4   **Practice Readings with Practice Parsing.** 25 items plus verb parsing.

5   **Parsing and Translation Exercise: Section One.**

6   **Translation Exercise: Sections Two and Three.** See Workbook appendix.
     Section Two: 2Chr 34:5–8.   Section Three: Neh 8:1–3.

7   **Learn ch. 17 vocabulary.**

chapter eighteen

I-class Imperfects:
R_3 = Weak, R_2 = G, R_1 = G,
R_2 = נ, R_1 = נ

18.1 Focus.

In this chapter you are to learn:

> *no new endings and no new weak consonant behaviors*, but
>
> to diagnose weak consonant behaviors in the *i*-class imperfects.

The weak consonant behaviors are triggered by their syllabic positions, which are determined by the stem patterns. Several of the weak letters cause no problems in these paradigms. The discussions cover the weak letters in each position, noting if they cause little or no change. Focus most on the issues in the chart below and items in the chapter marked **. You may want to refer to the Alias Profiles as you read. R_3 weak behaviors in all the derived stems are the same as in the Qal, since the stems' ID badges do not involve R_3. The toughest of these is the loss of R_3 = י ≠ ה.

Nun assimilation is triggered by R_1 = נ Hiphil imperfects. Gutturals reject the *dagesh forte* of the doubling stems in R_2 position and of the Niphal in R_1 position. R_1 = G Hiphils tend to take composite *shewa* instead of simple *shewa*. While there are some vowel changes, observe the consistency of the vowel class. Besides reviewing R_3 = י ≠ ה, the chapter's most essential elements are these:

R_2 = G	Piel	𝔼□G̣P̣ → 𝔼□G̱P̣	
			Hit. 𝔼□ḡḤP̣ → 𝔼□G̣ḤP̣ / 𝔼□G̱ḤP̣
R_1 = G	Niphal	𝔼□ḡP̣ → 𝔼□ḡGP	
R_1 = נ	Hiphil	𝔼□ˢ□□P̣ → 𝔼□ˢ□P̣	

18.2 R_3 = weak; same old, same old.

R_3 weaknesses are the same in the derived stems as in the Qal. Their manifestation depends on the syllable structure created by the ending and the accent. Displaying the stems in groups according to syllabic structure emphasizes the similarity of behavior. *Pay special attention to situations in which a radical is somehow "lost" or a stem ID Badge is altered.*

18.2.1 R₃ = ' ≠ ה.

Vowel preference is a non-issue, since both the original R₃ = ' as well as the stems prefer an *i*-class vowel.

No suffix: ' is replaced by *mater* ה and preceded by an *i*-class vowel.

Vocalic suffixes: ' is replaced by a vocalic suffix (most of the time).

Consonantal suffix: ' is preserved in the 2/3 fp forms.

Preterite and jussive:** With the accent on the prefix, there is normally no trace of R₃ = ' when there is no ending, that is, there is no *mater lectionis* ה and no vowel. In the Piel and Hitpael, this means the *dagesh* cannot survive in R₂. Focus on the vowel pattern of R₁ and the prefix.

		Qal	Niphal	Piel	Hitpael	Hiphil
No suffix	3ms	יִגְלֶה	יִגָּלֶה	יְגַלֶּה	יִתְגַּלֶּה	יַגְלֶה
Vowel suff.	3mp	יִגְלוּ	יִגָּלוּ	יְגַלּוּ	יִתְגַּלוּ	יַגְלוּ
Cons. suff.	3fp	תִּגְלֶינָה	תִּגָּלֶינָה	תְּגַלֶּינָה	—	תַּגְלֶינָה
preterite	3ms	וַיִּגֶל	וַיַּרְא'[1]	* וַיְגַל [2]	* וַיִּתְגַּל	* וַיֶּגֶל * וַיַּעַל

18.2.2 R₃ = נ.

These are virtually a **non-issue** because the *nun* only assimilates into the *nun* of 2/3 fp forms and these are *extremely rare*.[3]

18.2.3 R₃ = Guttural.

Vowel preference may call for *furtive pataḥ* or an *a*-class theme vowel. These are virtually a **non-issue** since R₃ gutturals usually accept silent *shewa* and usually accept their vowel environment.

		Niphal	Piel	Hitpael	Hiphil
No suffix	3ms	יִבָּקַע	יְבַקַּע	יִתְבַּקַּע	יַבְקִיעַ
Vowel suff.	3mp	יִבָּקְעוּ	יְבַקְּעוּ	יִתְבַּקְּעוּ	יַבְקִיעוּ
Cons. suff.	3fp	—	תְּבַקַּעְנָה	—	תַּבְקַעְנָה

When closing a syllable, א quiesces as in the Qal. But since these paradigms call for a long theme vowel, it makes almost no difference.[4]

---

[1] The *nun* of the Niphal could not assimilate into the guttural, so the prefix vowel is lengthened. Only the root ראה occurs in the Niphal preterite with frequency.

[2] Piel preterites do not take *dagesh forte* in the *yod* prefix of a 3ms or 3mp form.

[3] R₃ always has a vowel or vocal *shewa* with a pronominal suffix, so R₃ = נ would not assimilate. The 2/3 fp forms of R₃ = נ verbs occur only three times. And in two of these the *dagesh* is not written.

[4] If the *aleph* has required an *a*-class theme vowel, it will be *qametz* even in the contextual forms.

18.3   R$_2$ = weak.

18.3.$_1$ R$_2$ = Guttural.

(a) Prefixing stems.

These are virtually a **non-issue** for the Niphal and Hiphil since R$_2$ usually has a full vowel. When vocalic endings would call for a vocal *shewa* under R$_2$ in the Niphal, they will have a composite *shewa*: תִּלָּחֲמוּ.

(b) Doubling stems.**

Gutturals refuse the *dagesh forte* called for by these stems. The classic solutions are compensatory lengthening of the preceding vowel for א, ע, and ר and semi-doubling for ה and ח. These solutions are not applied consistently.[5] It is simplest to be prepared to find any of the gutturals applying either solution: compensatory lengthening or virtual (semi-)doubling.

		Niphal	Piel	Piel	Hitpael	Hiphil
No suffix	3ms	יִנָּחֵם	יְנַחֵם	יְבָרֵךְ	יִתְנָחֵם	יַשְׁחִית
Vowel suff.	3mp	יִנָּחֲמוּ	יְנַחֲמוּ	יְבָרְכוּ	יִתְנָחֲמוּ	יַשְׁחִיתוּ
Cons. suff.	3fp	—	—	—	—	—
preterite	3ms	וַיִּנָּחֵם	וַיְנַחֵם	וַיְבָרֵךְ	וַיִּתְנָחֵם	וַיַּשְׁחֵת

18.3.$_2$ R$_2$ = נ.

This is a **non-issue** because R$_2$ never closes a syllable.

18.4   R$_1$ = weak.

18.4.$_1$ R$_1$ = G.

(a) Prefixing stems.

Hiphil. R$_1$ = G is a **minor issue** in the Hiphil as R$_1$ = G usually takes composite *shewa* instead of simple *shewa*: תַּעֲבִירוּ, וַיַּעֲבֵר, etc. (Do not look for *hireq yod* to identify the Hiphil. Some Hiphils, especially preterites, use *sere* or another *i*-vowel. To identify the stem, you need to look at its ID badge by R$_1$.)

Confusable forms** (*a*-class under prefix and *i*-class theme):

Qal R$_1$ = G imperfects also take *patah* under the prefix and composite *shewa* under R$_1$. Most Hiphil verbs can be distinguished by the *i*-class theme vowel of the Hiphil. But R$_3$ = י ≠ ה and R$_2$ = י verbs are *i*-class in the Qal imperfect. Verbs like עשׂה and חיל חיל look the same in Qal and Hiphil: וַיָּחֶל, וַיַּעַשׂ, יַעֲשֶׂה.

Niphal.** All gutturals and ר reject R$_1$'s *dagesh forte* and lengthen the preceding vowel to *sere*. R$_1$ is still marked by POL *qametz*: יֵעָשֶׂה, יֵחָשֵׁב, יֵהָפֵךְ, יֵאָכֵל.

(b) Doubling stems.

R$_1$ = G is a **non-issue** in the Piel and Hitpael since R$_1$ gets a full *a*-class vowel.

---

[5] In the Piel, ע usually opts for semi-doubling rather than compensatory lengthening.

18.4.2 $R_1 = $ נ.

(a) Prefixing stems.

Hiphil.** $R_1 = $ נ closes a syllable and assimilates into R_2 as *dagesh*.[6]

וַיַּגֵּד ← וַיַּ֨גֵּ֬ד;   וַיַּגִּידוּ ← וַיַּ֨גִּ֬ידוּ

Niphal. R_1 gets a full vowel in the Niphal, so these are a **non-issue**.

(b) $R_1 = $ נ & $R_3 = $ ה in the Hiphil.**

If $R_1 = $ נ and $R_3 = $ י ≠ ה also, then R_2 may be the only letter written. In preterites, the loss of the final syllable means the *dagesh* that was the $R_1 = $ נ must drop out.

root	3ms Impf.	3ms Pret.	3mp Pret.	1cp Impf. + pr. suff.
נטה	יַטֶּה	וַיֵּט	וַיַּטּוּ	
נכה	יַכֶּה	וַיַּךְ	וַיַּכּוּ	נַכֶּנּוּ

The Qal behaved similarly. וַיֵּט is Qal. וַיַּט is Hiphil. The vowel class under the prefix is your clue. נכה, *to strike* (ch. 20 vocabulary), does not occur in the Qal.

(c) Doubling stems.

$R_1 = $ נ is a **non-issue** in the Piel and Hitpael since R_1 gets a full vowel.

18.6   For reference. A special Hitpael Problem: Metathesis or Assimilation of ת.

The Hitpael's ת may switch places with R_1 (metathesis) or assimilate into R_1.

Metathesis with Sibilants.

With R_1 sibilants (ס, צ, שׂ, שׁ) the sibilant and the ת switch places.

(סתר) תִּתְסַתָּר ← תִּסְתַּתָּר   (שמר) יִתְשַׁמֵּר ← יִשְׁתַּמֵּר

Further, when the sibilant is צ (very rare), the ת becomes a ט.

(צדק) נִתְצַדָּק ← נִצְתַּדָּק ← נִצְטַדָּק

Assimilation with Dentals.

With R_1 dentals (ד, ט, ת) the ת assimilates as *dagesh forte* because of their similarity in sound (a few times it assimilates into נ in late books).

(דמה) אֶתְדַּמֶּה ← אֶדַּמֶּה   (טמא) תִּתְטַמָּאוּ ← תִּטַּמָּאוּ

The Hitpael is an uncommon stem and these special problem roots account for only about 5% of all Hitpael verbs. The beginning student will likely rely on reference works to at least double check the parsing of the above.

---

[6] If $R_2 = $ G, then the *nun* survives over silent *shewa*. Another oddity is that נוה in the Hiphil usually has a *dagesh forte* in the נ of jussive and preterite forms: וַתַּנַּח, וַיַּנִּיחוּ.

For future reference, here is a list of the most common roots in the Hitpael (none of which begin with sibilants and only one of which begins with a dental):

פלל	to pray, intercede (80)	אבל	to mourn (19)
הלך	to walk about, live (64)	אוה	to desire, lust after (19)
יצב	to station oneself (48)	חנן	to seek/implore favor (17)
נבא	to prophesy (28)	טמא	to defile oneself (15)
חזק	to strengthen oneself (27)	נדב	to volunteer (14)
קדש	to keep oneself apart/consecrated (24)	גרה	to provoke (12)
הלל	to boast (23)	חתן	to marry (11)
יחש	to enroll/be enrolled by genealogy (20)	ידה	to thank, confess (11)

18.7   Summary.
18.7.1   General Summary.

Gutturals.

R_3 = G   Ni., Hi., Pi., Hit.: R_3 = G accept silent *shewa*, a non-issue.

R_2 = G   Ni., Hi.: R_2 = G accepts the *i*-class vowel, a non-issue.

Pi., Hit.: R_2 = G rejects *dagesh forte*, a **major issue**.

Solution: compensatory lengthening or virtual doubling.

R_1 = G   Pi., Hit.: R_1 = G has a full *a*-class vowel, a non-issue.

Hi.: R_1 = G has composite *shewa*, a *minor issue*.

Ni.: R_1 = G/ר reject *dagesh forte*, a **major issue**.

Solution: compensatory lengthening.

Nun.

R_3 = נ   Ni., Hi., Pi., Hit.: Assimilates into fp נָה, so rare a non-issue.

R_2 = נ   Ni., Hi., Pi., Hit.: R_2 never closes a syllable, a non-issue.

R_1 = נ   Ni., Pi. Hit.: R_1 has a vowel, a non-issue.

Hi.: R_1 = נ assimilates as *dagesh forte* into R_2, a **major issue**.

Yod.

R_3 = י ≠ ה   Ni., Hi., Pi., Hit.: a **major issue** (but identical to Qal behavior).

No suffix: י is replaced by *mater* ה and preceded by an *i*-class vowel.

Vocalic suffixes: י is replaced by a vocalic suffix (most of the time).

Consonantal suffix: י is preserved (2/3 fp forms).

Preterite and jussive: accent shifts, when there is no ending, then there is no trace of R_3 (no *mater* and no vowel).

Preterite Pi. and Hit.: no *dagesh* in R_2 since R_3 and vowel are gone.

R_3 = י ≠ ה & R_1 = נ   (נטה, נכה)

Preterite Hi. and Qal: no *dagesh* in R_2 since R_3 and vowel are gone.

18.7.2 Focused Summary.

(a) Piel and Hitpael R_2 = G rejects *dagesh forte*.

   Solution: compensatory lengthening or virtual doubling.

Piel □□ְ□ַP →	$\begin{array}{l} \Box\Box G\underset{..}{\Box}P \\ \Box\Box G\Box P \end{array}$	Hit. □□ְ□ַתְP →	$\begin{array}{l} \Box\Box G\Box תְP \\ \Box\Box G\Box תְP \end{array}$

Notice particularly: R_1 still has an *a*-class vowel and

   the prefix before R_1 has *shewa* in problem position.

(b) Niphal R_1 = G/ה reject *dagesh forte*. Solution: compensatory lengthening.

Niphal □□ִ□ָP →	□□ִGP

Notice particularly: R_1 still has POL *qametz* and

   the prefix still has an *i*-class vowel.

(c) Hiphil R_1 = נ assimilates as *dagesh forte* into R_2.

Hiphil □□ַיְ□□P →	□□ַיְ□P

Notice particularly: R_1 has still joined the prefix with *pataḥ*.

   Always account for *dagesh forte*. Syllabically □□ַיְ□P is □□ַיְ□□P.

18.7.3 Alias Profiles.

Recognizing stem identities for prefixed paradigms now involves:

			Notes
□P	□ְP		If □□P then R_1 = נ/לקח/R_3יצ or $R_2 = R_3$
	□ֵP □יְP	Qal	R_3 = י ≠ ה : □□ְP / Cיְ□□P / □□ְP וְ / G□ְP וְ
			R_1 = י (e.g. ירא)
	□ָP□	Ni.	If P = ה, then inf. or imv.
	□תְ□P□	Hit.	
□P	□P	Qal	R_1 = י/הלך, $R_2 = R_3$, R_3 = י ≠ ה pret./juss., בוש, נטה
	GP	Ni.	If P = ה, then inf. or imv.
□P	GP	Qal/Hi.	(Qal has *i*-class theme only if R_3 = י ≠ ה or R_2 = י)
	□ְP , □P	Hi.	If P = ה, then inf. or imv. □□P R_1 = נ (rarely R_3יצ)
□ָP	□□ָP	Qal	R_2 = י/ו or $R_2 = R_3$; (*I*-class theme only when R_2 = י)
□P	Ś□□P	Qal	R_2 = י/ו or $R_2 = R_3$; (*I*-class theme only when R_2 = י)
	□ַ□P	Piel	Pi. □□ְP; G□ְP / G□ַP; □□ֵP וְ is R_3 = י ≠ ה
□וP	□וכַלP	Qal	יכל
אP	□□אP	Qal	R_1 = א (1cs א deletes R_1 = א, אמר)

18.8 **Vocabulary**. Words primarily related to gathering/splitting and measuring.

1	אַמָּה	*n.f.* cubit, forearm (249)	
2	אָסַר	*vb.* to bind, tie, harness (73)	
3	אֹרֶךְ	*n.m.* length (95)	
4	יַחְדָּו	*adv.* together (96)	
5	יָסַף	*vb.* to add; Hi. to add to, repeat, increase, (213)	
6	יָתַר	*vb.* *Ni. to remain, be left over; Hi. to leave, leave over (106)	
7	יֶתֶר	*n.m.* remainder, excess (97)	
8	בַּד / לְבַד	*n.m.* alone, separate (161)	
9	קָבַץ	*vb.* to gather, collect, assemble (127)	
10	קָרָא 2	*vb.* *Ni., Hi. to meet, encounter, befall, happen (136)	
11	קָרַע	*vb.* to tear, rend (63)	
12	שָׁאַר	*vb.* *Ni. to remain, be left over; Hi. to leave over, spare (133)	
13	שְׁאֵרִית	*n.f.* remainder, the rest, remnant (66)	
14	שָׁבַר	*vb.* to break; Pi. to shatter (148)	
15	צָוָה	*vb.* *Pi. to order, command, charge (496)	

N.B. Chapter 11 included 1 קָרָא *to call, proclaim, read.*

18.9 **Learning Activities on the CD.**

1 **Grammar Illustration.**

2 **Practice Readings with Practice Parsing.** 45 items plus verb parsing.
Keep your textbook open to the Alias Profiles, 18.7.3.

3 **Parsing and Translation Exercise: Section One.**

4 **Translation Exercise: Sections Two and Three.** See workbook appendix.
Section Two: 2Chr 34:9–12.   Section Three: Neh 8:4–6.

5 **Learn ch. 18 vocabulary.**

chapter nineteen

I-class Imperfects:
R_2 = ʾ/ı, R_1 = ʾ/ı, R_2 = R_3
Weak Imv., Inf., & Ptc.

19.1 Focus.

In this chapter you are to learn:

no new endings,

no new weak consonant behaviors, but

to diagnose weak consonant behaviors in the *i*-class imperfects.

Vav and *yod* tend to drop out or become diphthongs; geminates dislike having a vowel between R_2 and R_3. Besides weak letter behaviors, roots that are R_2 = ʾ/ı or R_2 = R_3 may employ alternate patterns in place of the doubling stems.

The Polel, Hitpolel, and Polal are alternate patterns to the Piel, Hitpael, and Pual. Their ID badge is a *ḥolem* after R_1 and the repetition of R_3. There are 304 verbs (from 62 roots) in these stems in the Bible. In addition, there are several other more rare alternate stem patterns. They are primarily mentioned for reference and so that you may recognize these terms in other reading.

Focus on diagnosing R_1 = ʾ/ı, R_2 = ʾ/ı and R_2 = R_3 roots. This will complete the weak roots for *i*-class imperfects. The real trouble spots are R_2 = ʾ/ı in both the Hiphil and Niphal, R_1 = ʾ/ı in the Hiphil, and R_2 = R_3 in both the Hiphil and Niphal.

R_2 = ʾ/ı	Ni.	□□ֵP →	□וֹ·P	Hi.	□ֹ□P / śₑ□ֹ□P
R_1 = ʾ/ı		——		Hi.	□ֹ□ִיP / □ֹ□וֹP
R_2 = R_3	Ni.	□□ֵP →	□ֵP, □Gᴾ	Hi.	□ֵP, □ֵP / śₑ□□P

The imperatives, infinitives, and participles each follow all the same weak behaviors as the imperfects, as confirmed by the paradigms later in this chapter.

You may want to refer to the Alias Profiles as you read through the chapter. Your goal is to understand how a change resulted from a stem and weak letter.

169

19.2   R₂ = י/ו.

(a) **Prefixing stems.**

Niphal.

R₂ = ו contracts with the preceding *qametz* to form וֹ (*āw → ô*).

$$P\Box\hat{\Box}\Box \leftarrow P\Box\hat{\Box}\Box \qquad (כון תִּכָּוֵן \leftarrow תִּכּוֹן)$$

The result looks like R₁ = נ Qal impf., יִפֹּל ← יִנְפֹּל, but the Qal rarely has *holem-vav*. Of R₂ = ו roots, only כון and מוט occur with any frequency; R₂ = י does not occur.

Hiphil.

The prefix becomes *qametz* (POL) or takes *shewa* (SPP). Here is why. R₂ = י/ו drops out and is replaced by the Hiphil's *hireq-(yod)*. R₁ must then lead a syllable, so the prefix becomes pretonic open long with *qametz*, תָּבִיא (Hi. בוא). Or it has *shewa* in problem position, תְּבִיאֵנִי, when the accent shifts due to a pronominal suffix.

$$\text{E}\Box^{?}\hat{\Box}\Box\text{P} \rightarrow \text{E}R_3{}^{?}\hat{R}_1\text{P} \qquad תְּשֶׁבְנָה, וַיְּשִׁיבוּ, תָּשִׁיב.$$
$$\text{SE}\hat{\Box}^{?}\Box\Box\text{P} \rightarrow \text{SE}\hat{R}_3{}^{?}R_1\text{P} \qquad תְּשִׁיבֵנוּ, וַיְּשִׁיבֵהוּ.$$

A *yod* is usually written for the imperfect but not for the jussive or preterite, especially if there is no ending. But it is still an *i*-class vowel.[1]

	Imperfect	Jussive	Preterite
	תָּשִׁיב	יָשֵׁב	וַיָּשֶׁב

Confusable forms.

R₂ = י Qal imperfects also have *qametz* under the prefix and an *i*-class vowel after R₁. So יָבִין and וַיָּבֶן could be either the Qal or Hiphil of בין. You must judge based on context.

(Statistically speaking, if the root is truly R₂ = י, then most are Qal and few are Hiphil. Qal impf. R₂ = ו roots are almost always *u*-class, תָּבוֹא, תָּשׁוּב.)

(b) **Doubling stems.**

Piel and Hitpael.

These are **sometimes a non-issue** since ו and י may remain consonantal and take *dagesh forte* as called for by these stems, e.g. Piel: נִחֵיָה, יְצַוֶּה; Hitpael: וַיִּתְאַוֶּה.

But R₂ = י/ו (and R₂ = R₃) *may use alternate patterns* (see 19.6).

19.3   R₁ = י/ו

(a) **Prefixing stems.**

Niphal.

A **non-issue**. R₁ gets a full vowel in the Niphal, so original R₁ = ו[2] remains consonantal, taking the *dagesh* and *qametz* characteristic of the Niphal:

$$(יעץ) וַיִּוָּעֵץ \quad (ידע) יִוָּדַע \quad (ילד) יִוָּלֵד$$

---

[1] If R₃ is a guttural, the jussive and preterite forms take *patah* rather than *segol* or *hireq*.

[2] R₁ = י occurs only once or twice.

Hiphil.

$R_1 = $ ו contracts with the preceding *pataḥ* to form וֹ (*aw* → *ô*).

P⬜יוֹ⬜ ⬜ ← P⬜וְ⬜י⬜   יֹסִיף ←, יַוְסִיף   יוֹסִפוּ ← יֹסִיף

N.B. הלך behaves as $R_1 = $ ו, e.g. וַיֹּלֶךְ, יֹלֶךְ.

$R_1 = $ י contracts with the preceding *pataḥ* to form *ṣere* (*ay* → *ê*).

P⬜י⬜יֵ⬜ ⬜ ← P⬜יְ⬜י⬜   יֵיטִבוּ ← יִיטִבוּ   וַיֵּיטֶב ← וַיִּיטֶב

(A few $R_1 = $ י & $R_2 = $ צ behave $R_1 = $ נ).

Confusable forms.

In theory, a $R_1 = $ י Qal active participle looks like a $R_1 = $ י Hiphil jussive (either may write *ḥolem* or *ḥolem-vav*). Context will clarify; the potential confusion arises primarily when considering theoretical possibilities.

Hi. impf.	Hi. juss.	Qal ptc.
יֹסִיף	יֹסֵף	יֹסֵף

(b) Doubling stems.

Piel and Hitpael. $R_1 = $ י/ו are virtually a **non-issue** in the Piel and Hitpael since R_1 gets a full vowel. For the few originally $R_1 = $ ו roots occurring in the Hitpael, the original *vav* survives, e.g. אֶתְוַדַּע (ידע).

19.4 $R_2 = R_3$: generally a major issue.

(a) Prefixing stems.

Niphal and Hiphil (see full paradigms on 337 and 341).

No suffix: R_2 cannot maintain *dagesh*. R_1 may double in Hiphil.

Ni.: יִמַּס (מסס), תֵּחֵל (חלל), יֵגַּל (גלל).

Hi.: וַיָּסֶב (סבב), יַתֵּם (תמם), וַיָּדֶק (דקק), .

Vocalic suffixes: R_3 typically has *dagesh* representing R_2. R_1 begins a syllable.

Ni.: R_1 joins R_2 with *pataḥ*, יִסַּבּוּ (סבב).

Hi.: R_1 joins R_2 with *ṣere*. The prefix is POL or joins a doubled R_1, PCS:

וַיָּסֹבּוּ (סבב), וַיָּחֵלּוּ (חלל), וַיַּכּתוּ (כתת).

The Niphals have an *i*-class vowel under the prefix; the Hiphils keep an *a*-class vowel under the prefix.[3]

(b) Doubling stems.

Piel and Hitpael.

These are *sometimes a non-issue* and will behave as the strong verb, doubling R_2 with *dagesh* and still writing R_3: אֲהַלֵּל, וַתְּחַלְלוּ, וַתְּחַלֵּלְנָה; יִתְפַּלֵּל, וַיִּתְפַּלְלוּ.

But $R_2 = R_3$ (and $R_2 = $ י/ו) **may generate alternate patterns**, see 19.6.

---

[3] With pronominal suffixes, the accent moves down, so the Hiphil prefix may reduce to *shewa* (SPP). This does not occur in the Niphal and only 9 times in the Hiphil, e.g. אֲשִׁמֵּם (שמם), וַיְסִבֵּנִי (סבב).

19.5 Participles, Infinitives, and Imperatives of weak roots.

The same weak behaviors also appear in the inf., imv., and ptc. Some types of weak roots are rare in certain stems, so we have given preference to forms that actually occur. Scan the lists for the stem ID badges; problem spots are marked *.

19.5.1 Participles, Infinitives, and Imperatives of weak roots with י/ו or G.

Niphal □□□ִP / נִ□□□

נִ□□□P	R₃ = י ≠ ה	R₂ = י/ו	R₁ = י/ו	R₃ = G	R₂ = G	R₁ = G
Inf. cs.	הִגָּלוֹת	הִכּוֹן	הִוָּלֵד	הִנָּבֵא	הִלָּחֵם	הֵאָסֵף
Imv. ms	הִגָּלֵה	הִכּוֹן	—	הִנָּבֵא	הִלָּחֵם	הֵאָסֵף
Imv. mp	הִגָּלוּ	הִכּוֹנוּ	הִוָּשְׁעוּ	הִנָּבְאוּ	הִלָּחֲמוּ	הֵאָסְפוּ
Ptc. ms	נִגְלֶה	נָכוֹן *	נוֹתָר *	נִמְצָא	נִלְחָם	נֶאֱסָף
Ptc. mp	נִגְלִים	נְכוֹנִים *	נוֹתָרִים *	נִמְצָאִים	נִלְחָמִים	נֶאֱסָפִים

Hiphil □□□ַP

E□□יַ□□P	R₃ = י ≠ ה	R₂ = י/ו	* R₁ = י/ו	R₃ = G	R₂ = G	R₁ = G
Inf. cs.	הַגְלוֹת	הָבִיא	הוֹצִיא	הַשְׁלִיחַ	הַשְׁחִית	הַחֲזִיק
Imv. ms	הַגְלֵה	הָבֵא	הוֹצֵא	הַשְׁלַח	הַשְׁחֵת	הַחֲזֵק
Imv. mp	הַגְלוּ	הָבִיאוּ	הוֹצִיאוּ	הַשְׁלִיחוּ	הַשְׁחִיתוּ	הַחֲזִיקוּ
Ptc. ms	מַגְלֶה	מֵבִיא *	מוֹצִיא	מַשְׁלִיחַ	מַשְׁחִית	מַחֲזִיק
Ptc. mp	מַגְלִים	מְבִיאִים *	מוֹצִיאִים	מַשְׁלִיחִים	מַשְׁחִיתִים	מַחֲזִיקִים

Piel □□□ַ

E□□□ַP	R₃ = י ≠ ה	R₂ = י/ו	R₁ = י/ו	R₃ = G	R₂ = G	R₁ = G
Inf. cs.	גַּלּוֹת	צַוֹּת, קַיֵּם	יַסֵּר	שַׁלַּח	נַחֵם	חַזֵּק
Imv. ms	גַּלֵּה	צַוֵּה / צַו *	יַסֵּר	שַׁלַּח	מַהֵר	חַזֵּק
Imv. mp	גַּלּוּ	צַוּוּ	יַסְּרוּ	שַׁלְּחוּ	מַהֲרוּ	חַזְּקוּ
Ptc. ms	מְגַלֶּה	מְצַוֶּה	(f) מְיַלֶּדֶת	מְשַׁלֵּחַ	מְנַחֵם	מְחַזֵּק
Ptc. mp	מְגַלִּים	—	(f) מְיַלְּדֹת	מְשַׁלְּחִים	מְנַחֲמִים	מְחַזְּקִים

Hitpael □□□תְ□P

E□□□תְ□P	R₃ = י ≠ ה	R₂ = י/ו	R₁ = י/ו	R₃ = G	R₂ = G	R₁ = G
Inf. cs.	הִתְגַּלּוֹת	—	הִתְיַצֵּב	הִתְנַשֵּׂא	הִתְנַחֵם	הִתְהַלֵּךְ
Imv. ms	הִתְגַּל	—	הִתְיַצֵּב	—	הִתְפָּאֵר	הִתְהַלֵּךְ
Imv. mp	הִתְגַּלּוּ	—	הִתְיַצְּבוּ	הִתְפַּתְּחוּ	הִטַּהֲרוּ	הִתְהַלְּכוּ
Ptc. ms	מִתְגַּלֶּה	מִתְאַוֶּה	מִתְוַדֶּה	מִתְנַשֵּׂא	מִתְנַחֵם	מִתְהַלֵּךְ
Ptc. mp	מִתְגַּלִּים	מִתְאַוִּים	מִתְוַדִּים	מִתְנַשְּׂאִים	מִתְנַחֲמִים	מִתְהַלְּכִים

19.5.2 Niphal and Hiphil R$_2$ = R$_3$; Hiphil R$_1$ = נ.

The R$_1$ = נ Hiphils are the most common of these. Niphal geminates are rare.

	Niphal	Hiphil	Hiphil	Hiphil
	R$_2$ = R$_3$	R$_2$ = R$_3$	R$_1$ = נ	R$_1$ = נ & R$_3$=י≠ה
Inf. cs.	הֵחֵל	הָסֵב	הַגִּיד	הַכּוֹת
Imv. ms	—	הָסֵב	הַגִּידָה	הַךְ
Imv. mp	הִבָּרוּ	הָסֵבּוּ	הַגִּידוּ	הַכּוּ
Ptc. ms	נָמֵס	מֵסֵב / מֵרַע *	מַגִּיד	מַכֶּה
Ptc. pl	נְשַׁמּוֹת	מְרֵעִים *	מַגִּידִים	מַכִּים

19.5.3 Notes.

Hiphil and Hitpael imperatives restore their ה (since the imperfect prefixes no longer replace it).

Niphal imperatives also uses preformative ה, as in its infinitive.

Piel R$_3$ = י ≠ ה imperative masculine singular may lose R$_3$, e.g. צַו (צוה).

ו contracts to וֹ in the Ni. R$_2$ = ו, the Hi. R$_1$ = י (original ו) and the Ni. ptc. R$_1$ = י

י contracts to ◌ in the Hi. R$_1$ = י (original י)

Hiphil ptc. of both the R$_2$ = י/ו and the R$_2$ = R$_3$ have *ṣere* under the preformative מ.

Niphal ptc. of both the R$_2$ = י/ו and the R$_2$ = R$_3$ have *qametz* under the stem's נ.

Hiphil and Niphal ptc. of R$_2$ = י/ו and R$_2$ = R$_3$ have *shewa* in problem position if there is an ending.

You must stay conscious of what letters can be a prefix. מַכֶּה might easily be confused as a Pi. imv. from a root מכה. After finding no such root, you would need to reanalyze it with מ as a prefix. Fortunately, even for unknown words, the number of options in any case is relatively small and context will provide clues. The more vocabulary you know the easier it will be also.

19.6 Additional doubling patterns.

There are some alternate patterns for the doubling stems, especially for R$_2$ = י/ו and R$_2$ = R$_3$ roots. Their names come from the resulting patterns, still using the root פעל as the base, but their meanings are like those of the stems you have already learned. The forms are rare but you should be familiar with the terms so that you recognize them when used in dictionaries or other works.

Meaning like Piel	Meaning like Hitpael	Meaning like Pual
Polel	Hitpolel	Polal
Pilpel	Hitpalpel	Polpal
Poel	Hitpoel	Poal
Palal		Pulal

19.6.1 Polel, Hitpolel, Polal.

These are the most common alternatives to the doubling stems. They are marked by *holem* after R_1 and repetition of the last radical. They are used mostly for geminates, like סבב, e.g. יְסוֹבֵב, or $R_2 = $ ו/י, like קוּם below.

	Polel	Hitpolel	Polal
Impf. 3ms	יְקוֹמֵם	יִתְקוֹמֵם	יְקוֹמַם
Impf. 3mp	יְקוֹמְמוּ	יִתְקוֹמְמוּ	יְקוֹמְמוּ
Impf. 3fp	יְקוֹמֵמְנָה	יִתְקוֹמֵמְנָה	יְקוֹמַמְנָה
Imv. ms	קוֹמֵם	הִתְקוֹמֵם	
Imv. mp	קוֹמְמוּ	הִתְקוֹמְמוּ	
Inf. cs.	קוֹמֵם	הִתְקוֹמֵם	
Ptc.	מְקוֹמֵם	מִתְקוֹמֵם	מְקוֹמָם

The other alternative doubling patterns will be discussed in ch. 22.

19.7 Summary.

19.7.1 General Summary.

(a) $R_2 = $ ו/י. Pi., Hit.: ו and י often take *dagesh forte*, a non-issue,

but note that alternate patterns may be used (19.6).

Ni.: $R_2 = $ ו contracts to וֹ, a **major issue**, but infrequent (cp. כון and מוט).

Hi. $R_2 = $ ו/י drops out, a **major issue**.

Prefix becomes open long or takes *shewa* in problem position.

Jussives and preterites have no *yod* with the theme vowel.

(b) $R_1 = $ ו/י. Ni., Pi., Hit.: R_1 has a vowel, orig. ו survives, a *minor issue*.

Hi.: R_1 closes a syllable, a **major issue**.

ו contracts to *holem(-vav)*; י contracts to *ṣere(-yod)*.

(c) $R_2 = R_3$. Pi., Hit.: may use **alt. patterns**.

Ni. Hi.: may lose R_3, a **major issue**. Hi. R_1 may double.

19.7.2 Focused Summary.

$R_2 = $ ו/י	Ni.	□□◌ְP → □וֹ◌ְP	Hi.	□ְ◌□□ְP → □ְ◌ִ◌P / ŠĒ□ְ◌P
$R_1 = $ ו/י	Ni.	—	Hi.	□ְ◌□□ְP → □ְ◌ִ◌P / □ְ◌וֹP
$R_2 = R_3$	Ni.	□□◌ְP → □◌ְP / □G̊P	Hi.	□ְ◌□□ְP → □◌ְP, V□◌ְP / Š̊□□ְP

19.7.3 Alias profiles.

The alias profiles are arranged by what you see with R_1 and the prefix. Review your understanding of weak forms by explaining how the strong verb pattern interacted with the weak letters to produce these aliases. You should know the strong verb ID badges without a reference chart.

			Notes
□ַP	□ִP	Qal	If □□P then $R_1 = $ נ/לקח/R_3=יצ or $R_2 = R_3$
	□ָP		$R_3 = $ י $\neq$ ה : □□P / Cי□□P / □□P׳ / G□P׳
	יP		$R_1 = $ י (e.g. ירא, mater yod may be omitted, e.g. וַיִּרְאוּ)
	□ִP	Ni.	□□ִP $R_2 = R_3$; □וֹ□P $R_2 = $ ו (usu. כון, Qal $\neq$ וֹ); V□□ִP $R_3 = $ י $\neq$ ה	If P = ה, then inf. or imv.
	יֹ□P		
	□ָ□P		
	□תָּP	Hit.	(□□וֹ□תָּP Hitpolel)
□ֶP	□ֵP	Qal	$R_1 = $ י/הלך, $R_2 = R_3$, $R_3 = $ י $\neq$ ה pret./juss., בוש, נטה
	GP	Ni.	□GP $R_2 = R_3$	If P = ה, then inf. or imv.
	GP		□וֹGP $R_1 = $ G & $R_2 = $ ו
	□ֵמ	Hi. ptc.	□□ֵמ $R_2 = R_3$ or $R_2 = $ ו/י
	יP	Hi.	$\leftarrow$ □□יP $R_1 = $ י
□ַP	GP	Qal/Hi.	(Qal has *i*-class theme only if $R_3 = $ י $\neq$ ה or $R_2 = $ י)
	□ֵP	Hi.	If P = ה, then inf. or imv.
	□ִP		□□P $R_1 = $ נ (rarely R_3=יצ)
□ָP	□ָP	Qal	$R_2 = $ ו/י or $R_2 = R_3$; (*I*-class theme only when $R_2 = $ י)
		Hi.	$R_2 = $ ו/י or $R_2 = R_3$; (*I*-class theme 98%)
□וֹP	□וֹP	Hi.	$\leftarrow$ □□וֹP $R_1 = $ י/הלך
אP	□□אP	Qal	$R_1 = $ א (1cs א deletes $R_1 = $ א, אֹמַר)
□וP	יוכל P	Qal	יכל
□ֶP	Ś□□ֶP	Qal/Hi.	$R_2 = $ ו/י or $R_2 = R_3$ (n.b. E□□ֶP) (Qal only has *i*-class theme if $R_2 = $ י)
	□Pa□	Piel	Pi. □□ֶP; G□ֵP / G□ֵP; □□ֵP׳ is $R_3 = $ י $\neq$ ה
	□ֵמe	Hi. ptc.	□□ֵמ $R_2 = R_3$ or $R_2 = $ ו/י (ptc. + ending)
	□□וֹ□P	Polel/ Polal	$R_2 = $ ו/י or $R_2 = R_3$
	□□וֹ□תָּP	Hitpolel	$R_2 = $ ו/י or $R_2 = R_3$

19.8   Vocabulary. Words primarily relating to health and death.

1	אָבַד	*vb.*	to perish (185)
2	בּוֹר	*n.m.*	pit, cistern, well, *fig.* the grave (67)
3	הָרַג	*vb.*	to kill (167)
4	חָלָה	*vb.*	be sick, weak; Pi. to entreat (75)
5	כָּרַת	*vb.*	to cut (off/down), make a treaty (289)
6	לִין / לוּן	*vb.*	to lodge (71)
7	מָוֶת	*n.m.*	death (153)
8	נָגַע	*vb.*	to touch, reach, strike (150)
9	עוּר	*vb.*	to wake up, rouse oneself (80)
10	צָלַח	*vb.*	be successful, prosper (65)
11	צָרָה	*n.f.*	distress, straits (70)
12	קָבַר	*vb.*	to bury (133)
13	קֶבֶר	*n.m.*	grave, tomb (67)
14	שָׂבַע	*vb.*	be sated, satisfied (97)
15	שְׁאוֹל	*n.f/m.*	Sheol, netherworld (65)
16	שָׁכַב	*vb.*	to lie down (213)
17	שָׁכַם	*vb.*	*Hi. to rise early (65)
18	שָׁלוֹם	*n.m.*	health, wholeness, intact, sound, safety, deliverance (237)
19	שָׁלֵם	*vb.*	be complete, sound (116)
20	תָּמִים	*adj.*	complete, whole, wholesome (91)

19.9   Learning Activities on the CD.

1   Grammar Illustration.

2   Practice Readings with Practice Parsing. 30 items plus verb parsing.
Keep your textbook open to the Alias Profiles, 19.7.3.

3   Parsing and Translation Exercise: Section One.

4   Translation Exercise: Sections Two and Three. See Workbook appendix.
Section Two: 2Chr 34:14–18.   Section Three: Neh 8:7–9.

5   Learn ch. 19 vocabulary.

chapter twenty

A-class Imperfects:
Pual, Hophal

20.1 Focus.

In this chapter you are to learn:

no new spellings and no new functions, but

to recognize the stem ID badges which have been inserted into the imperfect paradigm with *a*-class theme vowels (comparing them to יְלַמֵּד).

The Pual and Hophal imperfects are built by combining their stem ID badges (ch. 16) with the imperfect affixes and an *a*-class theme vowel, similar to יְלַמֵּד. They are not very common stems (about 250 prefixed forms). The weak roots use various *u*-class vowels as an alias to their ID badge.

The Key: an *u*-vowel with R_1 is Pual; an *u*-vowel with the prefix is Hophal.

R_2 & R_3 pattern	R_1 ID badge	Stem
יְלַמֵּד +	☐☐ּ☐P	Pual
	☐☐ָ☐P	Hophal

20.2 Pual. ☐☐ּ☐P **(vocal *shewa–qibbuṣ–dagesh*).**

R_2 is doubled (unless a guttural). R_1 joins the doubled R_2 in a pretonic closed short syllable with a *qibbuṣ* or, more rarely, a *qametz ḥaṭuph*. The prefix of the imperfect takes *shewa* in problem position.

Gutturals.

Compensatory lengthening for R_2 = א, ע, or ר. The *dagesh* will be rejected and the *qibbuṣ* will lengthen to *holem* to compensate, e.g. תְּבֹרַךְ (ברך).

Semi-doubling for ה (ח does not occur). The *qibbuṣ* remains but the *dagesh* is gone due to semi-doubling, e.g. יְרֻחַם (רחם).

Geminates also take a *holem* after R_1 and no *dagesh* in R_2, e.g. יְחוֹלְלוּ (חלל).

R_2 = ו/י take *dagesh forte* as in the strong verb (unless it is Polal).

R_1 = **weak** verbs present no issues in the Pual.

20.3　Hophal. $\square\square\square P$, $\square\square P$, $\square\square$וP.

The imperfect prefix replaces the Hophal's preformative ה[1] and joins R_1 to make a pretonic closed short syllable with an *u*-class vowel: *qametz ḥaṭuph*, *qibbuṣ*, or *shureq*. The basic ID Badge for all Hophal imperfects and preterites is an *u*-class vowel appearing with the imperfect prefix. Strong verbs normally use *qametz ḥaṭuph*. The most common Hophal forms are weak roots, using *qibbuṣ* or *shureq*.

(a)　$R_1 = $ נ and some geminates use *qibbuṣ*.

Geminates may or may not double R_1 in compensation for the loss of R_3. Remember, the *u*-vowel is with the prefix, so יֻגַּד is Hophal not Pual.

		Form	Options (* = correct)
$\square\square P$	← $\square\square$גP ← $\mathbb{R}_2 R_2 \square P$	יֻגַּד	גדד or נגד*
		יֻכַּת	כתת* or נכת
		תֻּפַר	פרר*
		יָחְקוּ	נחק or חקק*

(b)　$R_1 = $ י/ח, $R_2 = $ י/ח, and some geminates use *shureq*.

		Form	Options (* = correct)
$\square\square$וP	← $\square\square$וP ← $\square$ח/יP ← $\mathbb{R}_2 R_2 \square P$	יוּמַת	מתת,* or מות, ימת
		אוּבַל	בלל ,ביל,* or יבל
		יוּדַק	דקק* ,דיק, or דדק
		יוּבָא	בוא or יבא*

Besides the Hophal, only the Qal impf. of יכל has ו after the prefix.

(c)　Gutturals.

Gutturals present few problems in the Hophal. Generally, they require a composite *shewa* instead of simple *shewa*, e.g. יָעֳמַד. But **a following vocal shewa upgrades R_1 to a full vowel**, e.g. תָעָבְדֵם (with 3mp pr. suffix).

20.4　$R_3 = $ Weak Pual and Hophal.

R_3 gutturals are no problem since they prefer these paradigms' *a*-class theme vowel.

$R_3 = $ נ presents no problems.

$R_3 = $ י ≠ ה take an *i*-class vowel under R_2 as preferred by the original י, e.g. תֻּעֲנֶה, while vocalic suffixes obliterate R_3 entirely, e.g. וַיְכֻלּוּ.

---

[1] The prefix would have SPP before the ה, but a vocal *shewa* and following ה tend to drop out, e.g. $\square P$ ← $\square$הP, as with the Hiphil and Hitpael as well as the ה of the article before inseparable prepositions.

20.5   **The Parts.** Compare the Qal forms of יִלְמַד to the Pual and Hophal.

	Qal *a*-type R₁ joins prefix	Pu. & Ho. R₂ & R₃	Pual R₁ joins doubled R₂ + pref.	Hophal R₁ joins pref.
	□□□ַP		□□·□ַP	□□□ַP
1cs	אֶלְ מַד	טַל +	אֲקֻטַּל	אָקְטַל
2ms	תִּלְ מַד	טַל +	תְּקֻטַּל	תָּקְטַל
2fs	תִּלְ מְדִי	טְלִי +	תְּקֻטְּלִי	תָּקְטְלִי
3ms	יִלְ מַד	טַל +	יְקֻטַּל	יָקְטַל
3fs	תִּלְ מַד	טַל +	תְּקֻטַּל	תָּקְטַל
1cp	נִלְ מַד	טַל +	נְקֻטַּל	נָקְטַל
2mp	תִּלְ מְדוּ	טְלוּ +	תְּקֻטְּלוּ	תָּקְטְלוּ
2fp	תִּלְ מַדְנָה	טַלְנָה +	תְּקֻטַּלְנָה	תָּקְטַלְנָה
3mp	יִלְ מְדוּ	טְלוּ +	יְקֻטְּלוּ	יָקְטְלוּ
3fp	תִּלְ מַדְנָה	טַלְנָה +	תְּקֻטַּלְנָה	תָּקְטַלְנָה

94% of Pual and Hophal imperfects and preterites are third person forms. There are no cohortative or jussive Puals or Hophals in the Bible. There are no Pual imperatives and only two Hophal imperatives. (With the prefix removed, the ה survives in the Hophal imperative: הֻשְׁכְּבָה ← הָשְׁכְּבָה [שכב], הֻפְנוּ [פנה] ← הָפְנוּ).

20.6   **The variety of *u*-vowels in the Pual and Hophal.**

N.B. If an *u*-vowel is with the prefix, it is Hophal, if it is with R₁ it is Pual.

	Pual		Hophal		
1cs	אֲקֻטַּל	אֲבָרֵךְ	אָקְטַל	אוּמַת	אֻגַּד
2ms	תְּקֻטַּל	תְּבָרֵךְ	תָּקְטַל	תּוּמַת	תֻּגַּד
2fs	תְּקֻטְּלִי	תְּבָרְכִי	תָּקְטְלִי	תּוּמְתִי	תֻּגְּדִי
3ms	יְקֻטַּל	יְבָרֵךְ	יָקְטַל	יוּמַת	יֻגַּד
3fs	תְּקֻטַּל	תְּבָרֵךְ	תָּקְטַל	תּוּמַת	תֻּגַּד
1cp	נְקֻטַּל	נְבָרֵךְ	נָקְטַל	נוּמַת	נֻגַּד
2mp	תְּקֻטְּלוּ	תְּבָרְכוּ	תָּקְטְלוּ	תּוּמְתוּ	תֻּגְּדוּ
2fp	תְּקֻטַּלְנָה	תְּבָרַכְנָה	תָּקְטַלְנָה	תּוּמַתְנָה	תֻּגַּדְנָה
3mp	יְקֻטְּלוּ	יְבָרְכוּ	יָקְטְלוּ	יוּמְתוּ	יֻגְּדוּ
3fp	תְּקֻטַּלְנָה	תְּבָרַכְנָה	תָּקְטַלְנָה	תּוּמַתְנָה	תֻּגַּדְנָה

20.7 Advanced Information. Qal Passive.

In addition to the Niphal, Pual, and Hophal passive stems, there are remnants of a Qal Passive in the Bible. We have already encountered this with the Qal Passive participle, but there are also survivors among the finite verb forms. The Qal Passive imperfect and preterite are characterized by an *u*-class vowel after the prefix: P□□□ or P□□ִ. Most occurrences happen to be $R_1 = $ נ and therefore the נ (or ל of לקח) assimilates into R_2 as *dagesh*. The result looks remarkably like a Hophal imperfect (or a Pual perfect), e.g. יֻתַּן, תֻּקַּח. There are few Qal passives and not all cases are agreed upon by scholars. Most likely, you will rely on other resources to help you with these forms when reading the Bible, but you need to know what those resources are referring to. Qal Passives are archaic forms that give a meaning which is passive to the normal meaning of the Qal. It has been mostly replaced by the Niphal.

20.8 Vocabulary. Words primarily related to war.

1	אֹיֵב	*ptc.* enemy (285)
2	בָּקַשׁ	*vb.* *Pi. to seek (225)
3	הָפַךְ	*vb.* to turn, overturn, change (95)
4	חָלָל	*adj.* pierced, fatally wounded, slain (94)
5	יָרַשׁ	*vb.* to take possession of, inherit, dispossess (232)
6	לָחַם	*vb.* to fight; Ni. to do battle (171)
7	לָכַד	*vb.* to capture, seize, take (121)
8	מִלְחָמָה	*n.f.* battle, war (319)
9	נָכָה	*vb.* *Ni. to be smitten; Hi. to smite (501); Hi. pret. = וַיַּךְ
10	צָבָא	*n.m.* army, host, warfare, service (487)
11	צַר	*n.m.* adversary (73)
12	קֶשֶׁת	*n.f.* bow (76); (The verb דרך describes bending a bow.)
13	רָדַף	*vb.* to pursue, persecute (144)
14	רֶכֶב	*n.m.* chariot(ry), upper millstone (120)
15	שָׁחַת	*vb.* *Ni. to be marred, spoiled; Hi. to act corruptly (152)
16	שָׁלַךְ	*vb.* *Hi. to throw (125)
17	שָׁלָל	*n.m.* plunder, booty, spoil (74)
18	שָׁמַד	*vb.* Ni. to be destroyed, exterminated (90)
19	שָׁמֵם	*vb.* be devastated, appalled, desolated (92)
20	תָּפַשׂ	*vb.* to seize, grasp, wield (65)

20.9 Summary. Alias Profiles for prefixed conjugations.

□ִP	⊡ִP		If □□ִP then $R_1 = $ נ/לקח/$R_3 = $ יצ or $R_2 = R_3$
	□ִP	Qal	$R_3 = $ י ≠ ה : □□ִP / C□ֵ□ִP / □□ִP וַ / G□ִP וַ
	יִP		$R_1 = $ י (e.g. ירא, mater yod may be omitted, e.g. וַיִּרְאוּ)
	□ִ□P	Ni.	□□ִP $R_2 = R_3$; □וֹ□ִP $R_2 = $ ו (usu. כון, Qal ≠ i); V□ֶ□ִP $R_3 = $ י ≠ ה	If P = ה, then inf. or imv.
	וֹ□ִP			
	□ַ□ִP			
	□ְתָ□P	Hit.	(□□וֹ□ְתָ□P Hitpolel)
□ֵP	□ֵP	Qal	$R_1 = $ י / הלך, $R_2 = R_3$, $R_3 = $ י ≠ ה pret./juss., or בּוֹשׁ
	G□ֵP G□ֵP	Ni.	□G□ֵP $R_2 = R_3$ □וֹG□ֵP $R_1 = $ G & $R_2 = $ ו	If P = ה, then inf. or imv.
	□ֵמ	Hi. ptc.	□□ֵמ $R_2 = R_3$ or $R_2 = $ י/ו
	יֵP	Hi.	$R_1 = $ י
□ֵP	G□ֵP	Qal/Hi.	(Qal has *i*-class theme only if $R_3 = $ י ≠ ה or $R_2 = $ י)
	□ִ□ֵP	Hi.	If P = ה, then inf. or imv. □□ֵP $R_1 = $ נ (rarely $R_3 = $ יצ)
	⊡ֵP		
□ַ□P	□ַ□P	Qal	$R_2 = $ י/ו or $R_2 = R_3$; (*I*-class theme only when $R_2 = $ י)
		Hi.	$R_2 = $ י/ו or $R_2 = R_3$; (*I*-class theme 98%)
□P u/o	וP / P / ָP	Ho.	□□ָP / □□ָP ← □□ֻ□ָP or $\mathbb{R}_2 R_2$□ָP □□וֹP ← □□וּ□ָP or י/ו□ָP or $\mathbb{R}_2 R_2$□ָP □□G□ָP / V□□G□ָP
	לוּכַל P	Qal	יכל
□וֹP	□וֹP	Hi.	← □□וֹP $R_1 = $ י/הלך
אַP	□□אַP	Qal	$R_1 = $ א (1cs א deletes $R_1 = $ א, אֹמַר)
□ַP	Ŝ□□ַP	Qal/Hi.	$R_2 = $ י/ו or $R_2 = R_3$ (n.b. E□□P) (Qal only has *i*-class theme if $R_2 = $ י)
	□ַP a	Piel	□ִ□ַP ; G□ַP / G□ַP ; □□ַP וַ is $R_3 = $ י ≠ ה
	□ַP u/o	Pual	ה□□ַP / V□□ַP $R_3 = $ י ≠ ה □G□ַP / □ה□ַP ;
	□ַמ e	Hi. ptc.	□□ַמ $R_2 = $ י/ו or $R_2 = R_3$ (ptc. + ending)
	□□וֹ□ַP	Polel/Polal	$R_2 = $ י/ו or $R_2 = R_3$
	□□וֹ□ְתַP	Hitpolel	$R_2 = $ י/ו or $R_2 = R_3$

20.10   **Learning Activities on the CD.**

1   **Grammar Illustration.**

2   **Practice Parsing.**
Identify whether the verb is Pual or Hophal. 42 items.

3   **Practice Readings with Practice Parsing.** 53 items plus verb parsing.
Keep your textbook open to the Alias Profiles, 20.9.

4   **Parsing and Translation Exercise: Section One.**

5   **Translation Exercise: Sections Two and Three.** See workbook appendix.
Section Two: 2Chr 34:19–22.   Section Three: Neh 8:10–12.

6   **Learn ch. 20 vocabulary.**

chapter twenty-one

*Derived stems: Perfects:
Strong verbs, R₃ = weak*

21.1   Focus.

In this chapter you are to learn:

no new spellings and no new functions, but

to recognize the stem ID badges inserted into the perfect paradigm, and

to recognize derived stem perfects which are R_3 = weak.

In this chapter we add the suffixes of the perfect conjugation to the derived stems. Three stems use different identity markers in the perfect than in the other conjugations. You learned these with the other ID badges in 16.3.1:

Niphal נ□□,   Piel □□·□,   Hiphil ה□□·□

Since the names of the stems are based on their perfect 3ms forms, the stem names should help you remember these ID badges. Just remember the theme vowel is on the name but is not part of the ID badge. The Piel, Hitpael, and Hiphil ID badges are added to the pattern of כָּבֵד, though the Hiphil uses *ḥireq yod* for the theme vowel. The Niphal, Pual, and Hophal ID badges for R_1 are added to the pattern of קְטַל.

R_2 & R_3 pattern	R_1 ID badge	Stem	R_2 & R_3 pattern	R_1 ID badge	Stem
כָּבֵד +	□□·□	Piel	קְטַל +	נ□□	Niphal
	הִתְ□·□	Hitpael		□·□	Pual
	ה□□·□	Hiphil		הָ□□	Hophal

Building and recognizing the derived stem perfects is straightforward. Neither the stems nor the perfect conjugation are new material.

R_3 = weak behaviors are the same in all seven stems and of little consequence. R_3 = G and R_3 = נ usually accept silent *shewa*, though א quiesces. The first and second persons of R_3 = י ≠ ה verbs reveal the original י, e.g. גָּלִיתִי, while vocalic suffixes replace *matres*, e.g. גָּלוּ.

21.2   Stem ID badges in the Perfect strong verb and R₃ = weak.

➤ **Qal perfect ID badge.**   ⬜⬜◌̣◌̄   ⬜⬜◌̣

R_1 has a pretonic open long *qametz* OR

R_1 has a vocal *shewa* in problem position

       (with the heavy endings or pronominal suffixes).

Fientive theme vowel: *a*-class.

Stative theme vowel: mixed *i/a*, *ḥolem*, or *ṣere* for R₃ = **א**.

➤ **Niphal perfect ID badge.**   ⬜⬜◌̣נ

R_1 joins a prefixed **נ** to make a pretonic closed short syllable with *ḥireq*.

Theme vowel: *a*-class.

➤ **Piel perfect ID badge.**   ⬜◌·◌̣

R_1 joins a doubled R_2 to make a pretonic closed short syllable with *ḥireq*.

Theme vowel: mixed *i/a*.

➤ **Hitpael perfect ID badge.**[1]   ⬜◌·◌̣הִת

R_1 joins a doubled R_2 (unless R_2 is guttural) to make a pretonic closed short syllable

       with *pataḥ* and הִת is added in front.

Theme vowel: mixed *i/a*.

➤ **Pual perfect ID badge.**[2]   ⬜◌·◌̦

R_1 joins a doubled R_2 to make a pretonic closed short syllable with *qibbuṣ*.

Theme vowel: *a*-class.

➤ **Hiphil perfect ID badge.**   ⬜⬜◌̣הִ

R_1 joins a prefixed **ה** to make a pretonic closed short syllable with *ḥireq*.

Theme vowel: mixed *i/a*.

Third persons use *ḥireq yod* for the *i*-class theme vowel: ⬜◌̣◌̣הִי.

➤ **Hophal perfect ID badge.**[3]   ⬜⬜◌̣הָ

R_1 joins a prefixed **ה** to make a pretonic closed short syllable with *qametz ḥaṭuph*.

Theme vowel: *a*-class.

Sometimes the hophal perfect (even for the strong verb) takes *qibbuṣ* ⬜⬜◌̣הֻ, so focus

       on the vowel class. The **ה** prefix has an *u*-class vowel.

---

[1] There are only 137 Hitpael perfects in the Bible.
[2] There are only 146 Pual perfects in the Bible. (Only two other Puals in the Bible lack a prefix.)
[3] There are only 109 Hophal perfects in the Bible.

21.3   **Compare the Qal of כָּבֵד to the Piel, Hitpael, and Hiphil.**

(a)   **The parts.** This chart shows how to put the pieces together to build the forms.

	Qal R₁ POL or SPP	Pi./Hit./Hi. R₂ & R₃ contextual	Piel R₁ joins doubled R₂	Hitpael R₁ joins doubled R₂ + pref. הִתְ	Hiphil R₁ joins pref. ה
1cs	כָּ בַּדְתִּי	טַלְתִּי	קַ טַּ	הִתְ קַ טַּ	הִקְ
2ms	כָּ בַּדְתָּ	טַלְתָּ	קַ טַּ	הִתְ קַ טַּ	הִקְ
2fs	כָּ בַּדְתְּ	טַלְתְּ	קַ טַּ	הִתְ קַ טַּ	הִקְ
3ms	כָּ בֵּד	טֵל	קַ טַּ	הִתְ קַ טַּ	see *(b & c)*
3fs	כָּ בְדָה	טְלָה	קַ טַּ	הִתְ קַ טַּ	see *(b & c)*
1cp	כָּ בַּדְנוּ	טַלְנוּ	קַ טַּ	הִתְ קַ טַּ	הִקְ
2mp	כִּ בַדְתֶּם	טַלְתֶּם	קַ טַּ	הִתְ קַ טַּ	הִקְ
2fp	כִּ בַדְתֶּן	טַלְתֶּן	קַ טַּ	הִתְ קַ טַּ	הִקְ
3cp	כָּ בְדוּ	טְלוּ	קַ טַּ	הִתְ קַ טַּ	see *(b & c)*

(b)   **Mixed *a/i*-class perfects:** *a*-class 1st and 2nd persons, *i*-class 3rd persons.

	Qal	Piel	Hitpael	Hiphil
1cs	כָּבַ֫דְתִּי	קִטַּ֫לְתִּי	הִתְקַטַּ֫לְתִּי	הִקְטַ֫לְתִּי
2ms	כָּבַ֫דְתָּ	קִטַּ֫לְתָּ	הִתְקַטַּ֫לְתָּ	הִקְטַ֫לְתָּ
2fs	כָּבַ֫דְתְּ	קִטַּ֫לְתְּ	הִתְקַטַּ֫לְתְּ	הִקְטַ֫לְתְּ
3ms	כָּבֵד	קִטֵּל	הִתְקַטֵּל	הִקְטִיל
3fs	כָּבְ֫דָה	קִטְּלָה	הִתְקַטְּלָה	הִקְטִ֫ילָה
1cp	כָּבַ֫דְנוּ	קִטַּ֫לְנוּ	הִתְקַטַּ֫לְנוּ	הִקְטַ֫לְנוּ
2mp	כְּבַדְתֶּ֫ם	קִטַּלְתֶּ֫ם	הִתְקַטַּלְתֶּ֫ם	הִקְטַלְתֶּ֫ם
2fp	כְּבַדְתֶּ֫ן	קִטַּלְתֶּ֫ן	הִתְקַטַּלְתֶּ֫ן	הִקְטַלְתֶּ֫ן
3cp	כָּבְ֫דוּ	קִטְּלוּ	הִתְקַטְּלוּ	הִקְטִ֫ילוּ

(c)   N.B. the Hiphil 3rd persons use *ḥireq yod* in both contextual and pausal forms.

	3ms	3fs	3cp	*a*-class 1cs, etc.
Hiphil	הִקְטִיל	הִקְטִילָה	הִקְטִילוּ	הִקְטַ֫לְתִּי
Qal pausal	כָּבֵ֫ד	כָּבֵ֫דָה	כָּבֵ֫דוּ	כָּבַ֫דְתִּי
Piel pausal	קִטֵּ֫ל	קִטֵּ֫לָה	קִטֵּ֫לוּ	קִטַּ֫לְתִּי

21.4   Compare the Qal of קָטַל to the Niphal, Pual, and Hophal.

(a)   **The Parts.** This chart shows how to put the pieces together to build the forms.

	Qal/Ni/Pu/Ho R$_2$ & R$_3$ contextual	Qal R$_1$ POL or SPP	Niphal R$_1$ joins pref. נ	Pual R$_1$ joins doubled R$_2$	Hophal R$_1$ joins preform. הָ
1cs	טַּ֫לְתִּי	קָ	נִקְ	קֻטַּ	הֻקְ
2ms	טַּ֫לְתָּ	קָ	נִקְ	קֻטַּ	הֻקְ
2fs	טַּ֫לְתְּ	קָ	נִקְ	קֻטַּ	הֻקְ
3ms	טַל	קָ	נִקְ	קֻטַּ	הֻקְ
3fs	טְלָה	קָ	נִקְ	קֻטַּ	הֻקְ
1cp	טַּ֫לְנוּ	קָ	נִקְ	קֻטַּ	הֻקְ
2mp	טַלְתֶּ֫ם	קְ	נִקְ	קֻטַּ	הֻקְ
2fp	טַלְתֶּ֫ן	קְ	נִקְ	קֻטַּ	הֻקְ
3cp	טְלוּ	קָ	נִקְ	קֻטַּ	הֻקְ

(b)   **A-class perfects.**

	Qal	Niphal	Pual	Hophal
1cs	קָטַ֫לְתִּי	נִקְטַ֫לְתִּי	קֻטַּ֫לְתִּי	הֻקְטַ֫לְתִּי
2ms	קָטַ֫לְתָּ	נִקְטַ֫לְתָּ	קֻטַּ֫לְתָּ	הֻקְטַ֫לְתָּ
2fs	קָטַ֫לְתְּ	נִקְטַ֫לְתְּ	קֻטַּ֫לְתְּ	הֻקְטַ֫לְתְּ
3ms	קָטַל	נִקְטַל	קֻטַּל	הֻקְטַל
3fs	קָטְלָה	נִקְטְלָה	קֻטְּלָה	הֻקְטְלָה
1cp	קָטַ֫לְנוּ	נִקְטַ֫לְנוּ	קֻטַּ֫לְנוּ	הֻקְטַ֫לְנוּ
2mp	קְטַלְתֶּ֫ם	נִקְטַלְתֶּ֫ם	קֻטַּלְתֶּ֫ם	הֻקְטַלְתֶּ֫ם
2fp	קְטַלְתֶּ֫ן	נִקְטַלְתֶּ֫ן	קֻטַּלְתֶּ֫ן	הֻקְטַלְתֶּ֫ן
3cp	קָטְלוּ	נִקְטְלוּ	קֻטְּלוּ	הֻקְטְלוּ

(c)   Pausal accents lengthen the theme vowel, except the heavy endings (2mp, 2fp).

	1cs	3cp	2mp
Niphal	נִקְטָ֫לְתִּי	נִקְטָ֫לוּ	נִקְטַלְתֶּ֫ם
Pual	קֻטָּ֫לְתִּי	קֻטָּ֫לוּ	קֻטַּלְתֶּ֫ם
Hophal	הֻקְטָ֫לְתִּי	הֻקְטָ֫לוּ	הֻקְטַלְתֶּ֫ם

21.5   R₃ = weak.

21.5.₁   R₃ = G (except א). No problems.

R₃ is not doubled in any paradigm and R₃ = G can take *shewa*, so there are no real problems. The gutturals' preference for *a*-class vowels may result in 3ms Piel or Hitpael forms with *pataḥ*, e.g. בִּקַּע, or *furtive pataḥ* in the Hiphil 3ʳᵈ persons, e.g. הִשְׁמִיעַ (or Piel pausal forms צִמֵּחַ). All the other persons and stems are already *a*-class in the perfect.

21.5.₂   R₃ = א.

א quiesces when closing a syllable as R₃ and the preceding vowel is long. In the derived stems, *aleph* prefers *ṣere* like the Qal stative root מָלֵא. Only the Niphal and Pual 3ʳᵈ persons remain *a*-class; their first and second persons are *i*-class. The Piel, Hitpael, and Hiphil become entirely *i*-class, e.g.:

stem	3ms	2ms
Piel	רִפֵּא	רִפֵּאתָ
Hitpael	הִתְרַפֵּא	הִתְרַפֵּאתָ
Hiphil	הִמְצִיא	הִמְצֵאתָ
Niphal	נִמְצָא	נִמְצֵאתָ
Pual	רֻפָּא	—

21.5.₃   R₃ = נ.

R₃ closes a syllable but נ only assimilates into the 1cp ending נוּ. It does not assimilate into a suffixed ת (except for נתן). As you can see, R₃ = נ is rarely an issue.

stem	1cs	1cp	stem	1cs	1cp
Niphal	נִשְׁעַנְתִּי	נִשְׁעַנּוּ	Piel	שִׁכַּנְתִּי	—
Hiphil	הֶאֱמַנְתִּי	הֵכַנּוּ (כון)	Hitpael	הִתְחַנַּנְתִּי	—
Hophal	(3ms only)		Pual	(3ms only)	

21.5.₄   R₃ = י ≠ ה.

All the derived stems behave in the same way as the Qal for R₃ = י ≠ ה. If there is a consonantal suffix (1ˢᵗ and 2ⁿᵈ persons), then the original R₃ = י is written and preceded by an *i*-vowel. If there is no ending, as with the 3ms, then a *mater* ה is written, preceded by an *i*-vowel. If there is a vocalic suffix, as with the 3cp, it replaces R₃ altogether. The 3fs replaces it with a ת in order to add the 3fs ending.

	Qal	Niphal	Piel	Hitpael	Pual	Hiphil	Hophal
1cs	גָּלִיתִי	נִגְלֵיתִי	גִּלִּיתִי	הִתְגַּלֵּיתִי	גֻּלֵּיתִי	הִגְלֵיתִי	הָגְלֵיתִי
3ms	גָּלָה	נִגְלָה	גִּלָּה	הִתְגַּלָּה	גֻּלָּה	הִגְלָה	הָגְלָה
3fs	גָּלְתָה	נִגְלְתָה	גִּלְּתָה	הִתְגַּלְּתָה	גֻּלְּתָה	הִגְלְתָה	הָגְלְתָה
3cp	גָּלוּ	נִגְלוּ	גִּלּוּ	הִתְגַּלּוּ	גֻּלּוּ	הִגְלוּ	הָגְלוּ

21.6 Vocabulary. Words primarily relating to reliability or covering.

1	אָוֶן	*n.m.* trouble, deception, wickedness, false cult (81)
2	אָמַן	*vb.* *Hi. to believe in; Ni. to prove reliable, faithful (97)
3	אֱמֶת	*n.f.* truth, reliability, firmness (127)
4	בָּטַח	*vb.* to trust, be confident in (120*)
5	גִּבּוֹר	*adj.* strong, mighty (160)
6	גְּבוּרָה	*n.f.* strength (62)
7	הֶבֶל	*n.m/f.* futility, vapor (73)
8	חָזַק	*vb.* be(come) strong, firm; Hi. to prevail, seize (290)
9	חַיִל	*n.m.* strength, wealth, army (246)
10	כֹּחַ	*n.m.* strength, power (126)
11	כָּסָה	*vb.* to cover, conceal (153)
12	נָצַב	*vb.* *Ni. to take one's stand; Hi. to station, set up (74)
13	סָתַר	*vb.* *Hi. to hide, conceal; Ni. be hidden, hide oneself (82)
14	עֹז	*n.m.* strength, might, fortified (76)
15	עָמַד	*vb.* to stand, arise (524)
16	שִׁית	*vb.* to put, set, fix, set up as, ordain (86)
17	שֶׁקֶר	*n.m.* deception, falsehood (113)

21.7 Learning Activities on the CD.

1 **Grammar Illustration.**

2 **Practice Parsing.** 30 items focused on derived stem perfects.

3 **Practice Readings with Practice Parsing.** 38 items plus verb parsing.

4 **Parsing and Translation Exercise: Section One.**

5 **Translation Exercise: Sections Two and Three.** See workbook appendix.
   Section Two: 2Chr 34:23–28.   Section Three: Neh 8:13–15.

6 **Learn ch. 21 vocabulary.**

chapter twenty-two

Derived Stems: Perfects:
R_1 = Weak, R_2 = Weak, R_2 = R_3;
Rare Stems

22.1 Focus.

In this chapter you are to learn:

no new endings and *no new weak consonant behaviors*, but

to diagnose R_1 and R_2 weak consonant behaviors in derived stem perfects,

and to be aware of the alternate doubling stems.

The Piel, Hitpael, and Pual join R_1 to a doubled R_2 and have few changes in the derived stems (watch for R_2 = G). The Niphal, Hiphil, and Hophal join R_1 to a prefix. Their weak perfects make small changes to the prefix vowel (focus on its class).

The Polel, Hitpolel, and Polal are alternatives to the Piel, Hitpael, and Pual. Some other rare stems are listed at the end of the chapter for reference.

As with the prefixed conjugations, we will compile these alterations into Alias Profiles, which you can refer to while practicing parsing. Besides derived stem perfects, the Alias Profiles will include other forms without the imperfect prefixes, such as imperatives and infinitives.

22.2 Gutturals.
22.2.1 R_1 = G.

(a) Doubling Stems: no problems.

R_1 = G is no problem for the doubling stems, since R_1 always gets a full vowel.

Piel	□□◌	→ □□G	חִזַּקְתִּי	חִזַּקְתֶּם	חִזְּקוּ
Hitpael	□□◌הִתְ◌	→ □□Gהִתְ◌	הִתְחַזַּקְתִּי	הִתְחַזַּקְתֶּם	הִתְחַזְּקוּ
Pual	□□◌	→ □□G	אֻסַּף	אֻסְּפוּ	

(b) Prefixing stems: composite *shewa*, vowel preference.

The pattern of the prefixing stems puts R_1 over a silent *shewa*. But gutturals often call for a composite *shewa* of the same vowel class as the prefix. In the Niphal and Hiphil, the guttural may change the prefix vowel to *pataḥ* for 1ˢᵗ or 2ⁿᵈ persons.

Niphal	□□□נֶ	→ □□Gֶנֶ or □□Gֲנַ	נֶעֱבַרְתְּ,	נַעֲשָׂה
Hiphil	□◌□□הֶ	→ □◌□Gֱהֶ or □◌□Gֲהַ	הֶעֱמַדְתְּ / הַעֲמַדְתָּ	
Hophal	□□□הָ	→ □□Gהָ	הָחֳרְבָה	(rare)

189

(c) Pattern Break.

The 3fs and 3cp Niphal[1] perfect may have a full vowel under R₁, due to a following vocal *shewa*, e.g.

נֶעֶשְׂתָה ← נֶעְשְׂתָה ← נֶעְשְׂתָה (עשׂה)   נֶאֶסְפוּ ← נֶאֶסְפוּ ← נֶאְסְפוּ

(d) Confusable forms.

Qal impf. 1cp נַעֲשֶׂה, נַעֲבֹד and Ni. pf. 3ms נַעֲשָׂה.

Both of these have no suffix and a נ prefix with *pataḥ* due to R₁ = G. But the Qal impf. does not have an *a*-class theme vowel when R₁ = G.

22.2.₂ R₂ = G.

(a) Doubling Stems: compensatory lengthening or semi-doubling.

Gutturals and ר reject *dagesh forte*, so R₂ = G is a problem for the doubling stems. The solutions are usually stated as semi- (virtual) doubling for ה and ח and compensatory lengthening of the preceding short vowel for א, ע, and ר. But be prepared for any guttural to apply either solution, since they are not consistent.[2] This is the same behavior we saw in R₂ = G imperfects for the doubling stems.

(b) Confusable forms.

When compensatory lengthening is applied, R₁ is pretonic open long. The Pual's *u*-class vowel is a long *ḥolem* after R₁, making the Pual perfect 3ms and 3fs[3] look like a Qal ptc., except that the Pual has an *a*-class theme vowel.

Qal	□□ָ□		בָּרַח	ptc. □□̇□ קֹרֵא
Piel	□□ּ□	→ □G□	בֵּרַךְ	
Pual	□□ֻ□	→ □G□̇	קֹרָא	

(c) Prefixing stems: no problems.

Since R₁ closes a syllable, R₂ usually has a full vowel – no problems. The Niphal contextual forms of the 3fs and 3cp call for vocal *shewa* under R₂; the guttural requires composite *shewa*.

Niphal	נִ□□ָ□ָה	→ נִ□G□ָה	נִשְׁאֲרָה	נִבְהֲלוּ
Hiphil	הִ□□ִי□ָה	→ הִ□G□ָה	הִמְעִיטָה	הִתְעִיבוּ

Hophal: 3fs and 3cp do not occur in R₂ = G.

---

[1] The rule is that a composite *shewa* upgrades to a full vowel when followed by a vocal *shewa*. In theory, it would happen in the Hophal if these forms were in the Bible. It does not happen in the Hiphil, since the *ḥireq(-yod)* theme vowel of the Hiphil is used even in the contextual forms. We saw a similar upgrading of a *ḥataph* vowel to a full vowel in R₃ = G Qal pf.: שָׁמַעַתְּ ← שָׁמַעַתְּ ← שְׁמַעַתְּ.

[2] The solutions are applied haphazardly. ר produces compensatory lengthening the most consistently, then א. While they normally generate *ṣere* in the Piel, the guttural preference for *a*-class vowels sometimes generates *pataḥ* (or rarely *qametz*) under R₁. ח is rather consistent in semi-doubling (except its one Pual form). But ה sometimes warrants compensatory lengthening, though semi-doubling is its usual behavior. ע is entirely inconsistent.

[3] There are only 17 such Puals in the Bible.

22.2.3 Main issues: Aliases for derived stem perfects with gutturals.

☐☐Gֶ   **Alias for Ni. Pf.**   ☐☐Gֶה   **Alias for Hi. Pf.**

☐☐Gַ   **Alias for Ni. Pf.**   ☐☐Gַה   **Alias for Hi. Pf.**

☐Gֳ   **Alias for Pi. Pf.**   ☐Gֹ   **Alias for Pu. Pf.**

22.3 *Nun.*

22.3.₁ R₁ = נ.

(a) Doubling Stems: no problems.

R₁ has a full vowel in the doubling stems so there are no problems.

(b) Prefixing stems: assimilation.

R₁ = נ assimilates into R₂ as a *dagesh forte*.

Niphal   ☐☐נְ   →   ☐☐נִּ   →   ☐☐ נִ   נִצַּבְתָּ (נצב)

Hiphil   ☐ִ☐הְ   →   ☐ִ☐הִּ   →   ☐ִ☐ הִ   הִגַּדְתָּ (נגד)

Hophal   ☐☐הָ   →   ☐☐הֻּ   →   ☐☐ הָ   הֻגַּד (נגד) (נכה) הֻכֵּיתִי

(c) Inconsistent additional rule.

If R₂ is a guttural then R₁ = נ cannot assimilate as a *dagesh*, so it often survives as נ over silent *shewa*. However, when R₂ = ח in the Niphal, semi-doubling is applied (21x with the root נחם), making it look like a Piel perfect R₁ = נ & R₂ = ח.

Niphal   ☐☐נְ   →   ☐חֶםנִ   →   נֹחַם   →   נֻחַם   נִחַמְתָּם, נִחַמְתִּי

(d) Confusable forms.

The Niphal and Hiphil R₁ = נ perfects can be confused with the Piel perfect if the prefixed ה or נ is thought to be a root letter. For example:

נִחַמְתִּי Ni. pf. 1cs of נחם   looks like Pi. pf. 1cs   נחם

נִצַּבְתָּ Ni. pf. 2ms of נצב   looks like Pi. pf. 2ms   נצב

נִקַּמְתִּי Ni. pf. 1cs of נקם   looks like Pi. pf. 1cs   נקם

הִגַּדְתָּ Hi. pf. 2ms of נגד   looks like Pi. pf. 2ms   הגד (not a real root)

(e) R₁ = י & R₂ = צ acting like R₁ = נ. (These are **rare**.)

As with the Qal, if R₁ = י and R₂ = צ, then the י may behave as R₁ = נ.

Niphal נִצְּתוּ (יצת)   Hiphil הִצַּתִּי, הִצִּיתוּ (יצת).

22.3.₂ R₂ = נ: no problems.

R₂ does not close a syllable in the prefixing stems and נ accepts the *dagesh forte* of the doubling stems.

22.3.₃ Main issues: Aliases for derived stem perfects with *nun*:

☐ִ☐הָ   **Alias for Ho. Pf.**   R₁ = נ   נֹחַם   **Alias for Ni. Pf.** נחם (or Pi. Pf.)

☐ִ☐נ   **Alias for Ni. Pf.**   R₁ = נ / R₁ = י & R₂ = צ

☐ִ☐ה   **Alias for Hi. Pf.**   R₁ = נ / R₁ = י & R₂ = צ

22.4   *Vav* and *Yod*.

22.4.1 $R_1 = $ ‏י/ו‎.

Remember that all originally $R_1 = $ ‏ו‎ words become $R_1 = $ ‏י‎ when R_1 is the first letter of a word. They must be looked up in the dictionary as $R_1 = $ ‏י‎ even when you find words preserving the ‏ו‎ as a consonant or part of a diphthong.

(a) Doubling Stems.

After accounting for ‏ו‎ to become ‏י‎, there are **no other problems,** since R_1 always gets a full vowel in the doubling stems.

Piel	‏סִ□□‎	→ ‏יִ□□‎	‏יִסַּד‎
Hit.	‏הִתְסַ□□‎	→ ‏הִתְוַ□□‎	‏הִתְוַדָה‎ (‏ידה‎)
		→ ‏הִתְיַ□□‎	‏הִתְיַצְבוּ‎ (‏יצב‎)
Pual	‏סֻ□□‎	→ ‏יֻ□□‎	‏יֻסַּד‎

(b) Prefixing stems.

R_1 is placed over a silent *shewa*, triggering the formation of diphthongs. In the Hiphil, the diphthong depends on whether R_1 was originally ‏ו‎ or ‏י‎.[4]

Niphal	‏נִ□□□‎	→ ‏נְ□□□‎	→ ‏נו□□‎	‏נוֹדַע‎ (‏ידע‎)
Hiphil	‏הִ□□□‎	→ ‏הַו□□‎	→ ‏הו□□‎	‏הוֹלִיד‎ (‏ילד‎)
		→ ‏הַי□□‎	→ ‏הֵ□□‎	‏הֵיטַבְתָּ‎, ‏הֵטַבְנוּ‎ (‏יטב‎)
Hophal	‏הָ□□□‎	→ ‏הָו□□‎	→ ‏הו□□‎	‏הוּרַדְתָּ‎ (‏ירד‎)

For recognition purposes, the main things to realize are that the ‏וֹ‎ or ‏וּ‎ comes from R_1 and must be looked up in the dictionary as $R_1 = $ ‏י‎, and also to not confuse this ‏וֹ‎ with the Qal ptc. Here the same information is arranged by the resulting vowel contraction.

Ni. ‏נְ□□‎ → ‏נוֹ□□‎ Hi. ‏הַו□□‎ → ‏הוֹ□□‎	Hi. ‏הַי□□‎ → ‏הֵי□□‎ ‏הֵ□□‎	Ho. ‏הָו□□‎ → ‏הוּ□□‎

22.4.2 $R_2 = $ ‏י/ו‎.

$R_2 = $ ‏י/ו‎ change the pattern of the prefixing stems by pulling R_1 away from the prefix. In the doubling stems, these roots may comply with the normal pattern or use a new kind of pattern: Polel, Polal, or Hitpolel (see 22.8).

---

[4] There are no originally $R_1 = $ ‏י‎ Hophals. Niphals of $R_1 = $ ‏י‎ roots are very rare and contract like other Niphals into ‏נו□□‎, e.g. ‏נוֹשַׁנְתֶּם‎ (‏ישׁן‎). Originally $R_1 = $ ‏י‎ verbs are stative. On the rare occasions that statives are put into the "passive" stems, the nuance is other than passive.

(a) Doubling Stems.

The doubling stems *may* double the ו or י as a consonant, which means there are **no problems** (but see 22.8). This is generally limited to R_2 = ו and by far the most common root is צוה.

Piel	□ִ□ַ□	→	□ַוִ□	צִוָּה, צִוִּיתִי
Hit.	הִתְ□ַ□ֵ□	→	הִתְ□ַוָּ□	(אוה) הִתְאַוִּיתִי
Pual	□ֻ□ַ□	→	□ֻיָּ□	צֻוָּה, צֻוֵּיתִי

(b) Prefixing stems.

R_2 = י/ו drop out, so R_1 must begin a syllable and cannot join the prefix. As a result, the prefix will either be pretonic open long or have composite *shewa* in problem position if there is a heavy ending (2mp, 2fp) or pronominal suffix. Unfortunately, the theme vowel and prefix vowel vary. **For these you must rely heavily on recognizing the stem prefix, נ or ה, and that a root letter is missing.**

Niphal	נִ□ְ□ַ□	→	נָ□ֹ□	נָפֹצוּ (פוץ)
		→	נְ□ֹ□É	נְפוֹצֹתֶם (פוץ)
Hiphil	הִ□ְ□ַ□	→	הֵ□ִ□	(בוא) הֵבֵאתָ, הֵבִיאוּ, הֵנַפְתָּ (נוף)
		→	הֱ□□É	הֲבֵיאָךְ, הֲבֵאתֶם (קום) הֲקִימֹתִי,
Hophal	הָ□ְ□ַ□	→	הוּ□□	(כון) הוּכַן, הוּבָא (בוא)
		→	הָ□□	(סוג) הָסַג; (כון) הֲכֵן, הָבֵאתָה (בוא)

The Niphal tends to generate a *holem* theme vowel, while the prefix tends to be POL *qametz* or have *shewa* in problem position. (היה accepts the Niphal pattern: נְהָיְתָה, נִהְיָה.) Further, Niphals may add a *holem* connecting vowel before the suffix of the perfect.

The Hiphil's theme vowel may be *hireq(-yod)*, *ṣere*, or an *a*-class vowel. The prefix tends to have POL *ṣere* or composite *shewa* in problem position, *ḥaṭaph pataḥ* or *ḥaṭaph segol*. Hiphils may also add a *holem* before the perfect's suffix.

The Hophal takes an *a*-class theme vowel. The prefix vowel is POL *shureq* or *qibbuṣ*. The result, הוּ□□ or הָ□□, looks like the Hophal perfect of a R_1 = י/ו root.

22.4.3 Main issues: Aliases for derived stem perfects with R_1 = י/ו or R_2 = י/ו.

הֵ□□	**Alias for Hi. Pf.** R_2 = י/ו or R_1 = י	□□ִיֵ□	**Alias for Hi. Pf.** R_1 = י
הֱ□□É	**Alias for Hi. Pf.** R_2 = י/ו	□□וֹה	**Alias for Hi. Pf.** R_1 = י
נָ□ֹ□	**Alias for Ni. Pf.** R_2 = י/ו	□□וֹנ	**Alias for Ni. Pf.** R_1 = י
נְ□ֹ□É	**Alias for Ni. Pf.** R_2 = י/ו		
הוּ□□	**Alias for Ho. Pf.** R_2 = י/ו or R_1 = י		
הָ□□	**Alias for Ho. Pf.** R_2 = י/ו		

22.5 $R_2 = R_3$.

(a) Doubling Stems.

These may have **no problems**, writing a *dagesh forte* in R_2 and still writing R_3. However, like the $R_2 = $ י/ו verbs, they may be put into a new kind of pattern (22.8).

(b) Prefixing stems.

Geminates do not permit a vowel between R_2 and R_3, so R_1 and R_2 stay together. That means that R_1 will not join the prefix, making it pretonic open long or leaving it with *shewa* in problem position. R_3 often adds *holem* before consonantal suffixes.

	Niphal	Hiphil	Hophal
1cs	נְקַלֹּתִי (קלל)	הַחִלֹּתִי (חלל)	—
2ms	—	הַחִלֹּותָ (חלל)	—
2fs	נְחַלֹּתְ (חלל)	הֲדִקֹּות (דקק)	—
3ms	נָסַב (סבב)	הֵחֵל (חלל)	הוּחַל (חלל)
3fs	נָשַׁמָּה (שמם)	הֵחֵלָּה (חלל)	—
2mp	נְמַקֹּתֶם (מקק)	—	—
3cp	נָשַׁמּוּ (שמם)	הֵחֵלּוּ (חלל)	הָמַכּוּ (מכך)

There can be some minor variations in the theme vowel for some roots.

22.5.1   Main issues: Aliases for derived stem perfects with $R_2 = R_3$.

נְ□□   **Alias for Ni. Pf.** $R_2 = R_3$ הֵ□□   **Alias for Hi. Pf.** $R_2 = R_3$

□Gְנ   **Alias for Ni. Pf.** $R_2 = R_3$ (rare)   □Gֵה   **Alias for Hi. Pf.** $R_2 = R_3$ (rare)

נְ□·E   **Alias for Ni. Pf.** $R_2 = R_3$ (rare)   הֵ□·E   **Alias for Hi. Pf.** $R_2 = R_3$ (rare)

הוּ□□   **Alias for Ho. Pf.** $R_2 = R_3$ (rare)   הָ□·   **Alias for Ho. Pf.** $R_2 = R_3$ (1x)

22.6   **Hishtaphel of** חוה, *to bow down*, *prostrate oneself*, *worship*.

Although used only with one root, it is a common root, meaning *to bow down, worship*. (Older resources may call this a Hitpael of שׁחו.)

Pret. 3ms וַיִּשְׁתַּחוּ   Pret. 3mp וַיִּשְׁתַּחֲווּ   Inf. cs. הִשְׁתַּחֲוֺת

Ptc. mp ab. מִשְׁתַּחֲוִים   Pf. 2ms הִשְׁתַּחֲוִיתָ   Pf. 3cp הִשְׁתַּחֲווּ

22.7   **For reference. Hitpael peculiar behavior.**

Remember that the Hitpael has a peculiar behavior of its own. The ת of the Hitpael prefix הִת may assimilate into or switch places with R_1. These are **very rare** in the perfect. For full reference list of Hitpael odd behaviors see 18.6.

Sibilants.

ת and $R_1 = $ שׁ switch places: וְהִשְׁתַּנִּית from שׁנה.

ת and $R_1 = $ צ switch places, then the ת becomes a ט: הִצְטַיְּדְנוּ from ציד.

Dentals.

ת assimilates as *dagesh forte* into $R_1 = $ ט: הִטֲּהָרוּ from טהר.

22.8   Polel, Hitpolel, Polal

Geminates and $R_2 = $ י/ו tend to switch patterns instead of using the Piel, Hitpael, and Pual. Typically, they add a *holem* after R_1 and repeat the last radical (without the doubling stems' *dagesh*). The Polel is an *a/i*-mixed theme vowel paradigm, like the Piel. So its 14 *a*-class 1st and 2nd person forms look just like the rare Polal would look.

	Polel	Hitpolel	Polal
1cs	קוֹמַמְתִּי	הִתְקוֹמַמְתִּי	קוֹמַמְתִּי
2ms	קוֹמַמְתָּ	הִתְקוֹמַמְתָּ	קוֹמַמְתָּ
2fs	קוֹמַמְתְּ	הִתְקוֹמַמְתְּ	קוֹמַמְתְּ
3ms	קוֹמֵם	הִתְקוֹמֵם	קוֹמַם
3fs	קוֹמְמָה	הִתְקוֹמְמָה	קוֹמְמָה
1cp	קוֹמַמְנוּ	הִתְקוֹמַמְנוּ	קוֹמַמְנוּ
2mp	קוֹמַמְתֶּם	הִתְקוֹמַמְתֶּם	קוֹמַמְתֶּם
2fp	קוֹמַמְתֶּן	הִתְקוֹמַמְתֶּן	קוֹמַמְתֶּן
3cp	קוֹמְמוּ	הִתְקוֹמְמוּ	קוֹמְמוּ

22.9   Reference Information. Additional doubling patterns.

There are more alternate patterns for the doubling stems besides the Polel, Hitpolel, and Polal. The forms are **rare** but you should be aware of the terms so that you recognize them when used in dictionaries or other works.

Meaning like Piel	Meaning like Hitpael	Meaning like Pual
Polel	Hitpolel	Polal
Pilpel	Hitpalpel	Polpal
Poel	Hitpoel	Poal

22.9.1   Additional doubling patterns.

Here are some samples of the additional patterns, for future reference. The **Poel, Poal,** and **Hitpoel** use the same vowel pattern as the Polel, Polal, and Hitpolel but have tri-consonantal roots that are not geminate or $R_2 = $ י/ו. (Some sources call all of these Poel, Poal, and Hitpoel, including geminates and $R_2 = $ י/ו.)

Poel	1Sam 21:3	יוֹדַעְתִּי	Poel pf. 1cs ידע *to make know*
	Is 40:24	שֹׁרֵשׁ	Poel pf. 3ms שרשׁ *to take root*
	Ps 77:18 (17)	זֹרְמוּ	Poel pf. 3cp זרם *to pour out*
	Amos 5:11	בּוֹשַׁסְכֶם	Poel inf. cs. בשׁס *to trample* + 2mp suff
	Ps 101:5	מְלוֹשְׁנִי	Poel ptc. ms cs לשׁן *make talk/slander*
Hitpoel	Is 52:5	מְנֹאָץ	Hitpoel ptc. ms ab נאץ *to despise*
	Jer 25:16	הִתְגֹּעֲשׁוּ	Hitpoel pf. 3cp געשׁ *to shake*
	Jer 46:8	יִתְגֹּעֲשׁוּ	Hitpoel impf. 3mp געשׁ *to shake*
Poal	Jer 12:2	שֹׁרָשׁוּ	Poal perf 3cp שרשׁ *to take root*

22.9.2 The **Pilpel**, **Polpal**, and **Hitpalpel** are patterns of geminate or $R_2 = $ ו/י roots which repeat both the first and last radicals.

Pilpel	גִּלְגֵּל *to roll*	קִלְקֵל *to shake up*	כִּלְכֵּל *to sustain*
Hitpalpel	הִתְגַּלְגֵּל	הִתְקַלְקֵל	
Polpal			כֻּלְכַּל

22.9.3 The **Palal/Palel** and **Pulal** patterns involve four root letters due to repeating the 3rd radical.

Palal/Palel   Prov 1:33 שַׁאֲנַן; Job 3:18 שַׁאֲנַנוּ *to be at ease.*

Pulal   The root אמל *to fail* (15x in pf.) as in אֻמְלָלוּ ,אֻמְלַל.

22.9.4   Additional patterns.

There are a few other minor patterns. As with the preceding minor patterns it is not necessary to learn them, just to know that some strange patterns exist and rely on your dictionary or other tools when they are encountered.

22.10   Summary: Alias Profiles.

Most changes in weak stem perfects are in the prefixing stems: Niphal, Hiphil, and Hophal. But the prefix and its vowel class almost always indicate the stem. A נ prefix indicates Niphal; a ה prefix with an *i*-class or *a*-class vowel indicates Hiphil; a ה prefix with an *u*-class vowel indicates Hophal. However, a ה prefix with a *holem* could be either Hiphil or Hophal. If you know the form is a perfect (by looking at the ending), then focus on these factors for determining the stem.

(The ID badges of the strong verb are not repeated. The Hitpael weak forms are not listed because the perfect suffix and the הִתְ prefix are normally clear indicators of the stem and conjugation.)

הֶ☐ i/a	Hi. Pf.
הוֹ	Hi. Pf. $R_1 = $ י Ho. Pf. $R_1 = $ י [5]
הֻ☐ u	Ho. Pf.
נ☐	Ni. Pf.
נֶחֱם	Ni. Pf. or Pi. Pf.
☐G☐	Pi. Pf.
☐G☐	Pu. Pf. (cp. Qal act. ptc.)
☐☐וֹ☐	Polel, Polal

---

[5] Because there are only two Hophal verbs in the Bible that follow this pattern, this Hophal option is omitted from the Alias Profiles that follow.

22.10.1 Alias Profiles for Perfect Weak verbs.

When only two radicals remain visible, then to restore the root we need to add either (1) a *nun*, usually R_1 (rarely R_3), (2) $R_2 = R_3$, or (3) a *vav* or *yod* in any position. If we know that a form is perfect (due to the ending), we can find a clue to the root based on the vowel with the prefix. (Some of the rarest changes are omitted.)

הָ i/a	הֵ◻◻	Hi. Pf. $R_1 = $ נ $ / R_1 = $ י $ \& R_2 = $ צ
	הֵי◻◻	Hi. Pf. $R_1 = $ י
	הֵ◻◻	Hi. Pf. $R_2 = $ י/ת $ / R_1 = $ י $ / R_2 = R_3$
	הֱ◻◻Ė	Hi. Pf. $R_2 = $ י/ת $ / R_2 = R_3$
	הֵG◻◻	Hi. Pf. $R_1 = $ G (including 3ms)
	הֶG◻◻	Hi. Pf. $R_1 = $ G (but not 3ms)
הֹו◻◻	הֹו◻◻	Hi. Pf. $R_1 = $ י (or בוֹש)
הָ u	הוֹ◻◻	Ho. Pf. $R_2 = $ י/ת $ / R_1 = $ י (or rarely $R_2 = R_3$)
	הָ◻◻	Ho. Pf. $R_1 = $ נ
	הָ◻◻	Ho. Pf. $R_2 = $ י/ת
נ◻	נ◻◻	Ni. Pf. $R_1 = $ נ $ / R_1 = $ י $ \& R_2 = $ צ (cf. Pi. pf./ Qal 1cp impf.)
	נG◻◻	Ni. Pf. $R_1 = $ G
	נG◻◻	Ni. Pf. $R_1 = $ G
	נ◻◻	Ni. Pf. $R_2 = R_3$
	נ◻וֹ◻	Ni. Pf. $R_2 = $ ו
	נוֹ◻◻	Ni. Pf. $R_1 = $ י
	נֱוֹ◻Ė	Ni. Pf. $R_2 = $ י/ת
נחם	נחם	Ni. Pf. or Pi. Pf.
◻G◻	◻G◻	Pi. Pf.
◻Gֹ◻	◻Gֹ◻	Pu. Pf. (rare; cp. Qal act. ptc. which is normally *i*-class)
◻וֹ	◻◻וֹ◻	Polel, Polal (cp. Qal act. ptc. which rarely uses וֹ)

To this list we will add the Qal perfect weak verbs (ch. 11) and notes about Niphal participles (see p. 204).

22.11 **Vocabulary.** Primarily words related to ruling and legal matters.

1	חֹק	*n.m.*	statute, decree (131)
2	כִּסֵּא	*n.m.*	throne, honored seat (alt. כִּסֵּה) (135)
3	מַלְאָךְ	*n.m.*	messenger, angel (213)
4	מָלַךְ	*vb.*	to reign, be(come) king (350)
5	מַלְכוּת	*n.f.*	reign, kingdom, royalty (91)
6	מַמְלָכָה	*n.f.*	kingdom, dominion (117)
7	מָשַׁח	*vb.*	to anoint, smear (70)
8	מָשַׁל	*vb.*	to rule (81)
9	נָשִׂיא	*n.m.*	chief, prince (130)
10	פָּלַל	*vb.*	*Hit. to pray; Pi. to mediate, arbitrate (84)
11	פַּרְעֹה	*n.m.*	Pharaoh, (Egyptian) king (274)
12	רִיב	*vb.*	to contend, strive (72)
13	רִיב	*n.m.*	strife, dispute (62)
14	רֹעֶה	*ptc.*	shepherd (100)
15	רָעָה	*vb.*	to shepherd, to pasture, to feed (167)
16	שַׂר	*n.m.*	chief, official, prince (425)
17	שָׁפַט	*vb.*	to judge, give justice (204)
18	שֹׁפֵט	*ptc.*	judge (68)

22.12 **Learning Activities on the CD.**

1 **Grammar Illustration.**

2 **Practice Parsing.** 50 items.
You may want to keep your book open to the Alias Profiles (cp. Excursus A).

3 **Practice Readings with Practice Parsing** (chs. 1–21 vocabulary). 35 items.

4 **Parsing and Translation Exercise: Section One.**

5 **Learn ch. 22 vocabulary.**

6 **Practice Readings with Practice Parsing** (chs. 1–22 vocabulary). 38 items.

7 **Translation Exercise.** See workbook appendix.
Section Two: 2Chr 34:29–33.   Section Three: Neh 8:16–18.

8 **Translation and Parsing Review Exercise.**

Excursus A: Sorting through Forms:
Stem ID Badges and Alias Profiles

A.1   **Sorting through forms.**

When we parse verbs, we ask *what is at the end*? If we identify a noun ending, we know it is a participle. If we identify a perfect ending, we know it is a perfect. In either case we look to the beginning to find out the stem by the behavior of R_r which wears the stem's ID badge, or an Alias. If there is an imperfect ending or no ending, we look to the beginning for an imperfect prefix or participle's מ. And we continue to identify the stem by the behavior of R_r which wears the stem's ID badge, or an Alias.

But we should still think through forms that are not perfects, but do not have imperfect prefixes or preformative מ. The main problems are with (1) forms that have no ending or a וֹ ending, e.g. 3ms pf., ms imv., and inf. as well as 3cp pf. and mp imv., (2) forms which could be either a perfect or a participle, e.g. Ni. 3ms pf. and ms ptc., and (3) forms with a תָ ending, e.g. some ms imv.

A.2   **Perfects, Imperatives, and Infinitives.** Forms with no ending or a וֹ ending.

We can usually distinguish perfects and imperatives that use the same endings (3ms pf. and ms imv.; 3cp pf. and mp imv.) by recalling their ID badges (ch. 16). Remember, three stems have two patterns, reserving one for the perfect. Since the Bible has no Pual and only 2 Hophal imperatives, we may focus first on the Niphal, Piel, and Hiphil, the three stems which use a different pattern for their perfects.

	Imv. ms/inf.	3ms Pf.	Imv. mp	3mp Pf.
Niphal	הִ◻◻◻ֵ	נִ◻◻◻	הִ◻◻◻וּ	נִ◻◻◻וּ
Piel	◻◻ּ◻	◻ּ◻◻	◻◻ּ◻וּ	◻ּ◻◻וּ
Hiphil	הַ◻◻◻ֵ	הִ◻◻◻	הַ◻◻◻וּ	הִ◻◻◻וּ

After the stem ID badges are identified and kept straight, the imperatives should not be confused with the perfects even in the weak roots. Piel perfect weak roots do not use an *a*-class vowel under R_1. The only Hiphil perfect weak roots that can use an *a*-class vowel under the prefixed ה are $R_1 = G$, but these never do so in the 3rd persons. Nor could any Niphal perfect weak root be confused with a Niphal imperative, due to the different prefix. Qal imperatives that have an ending can be distinguished from the perfect by the vowel under R_1. The mp imv. is קִטְלוּ while the 3cp pf. is קָטְלוּ. The Qal ms imv. is monosyllabic, e.g. קְטֹל.

It is still the case that Hitpael 3ms perfects, ms imperatives, and infinitives are the same form. But this is not a common stem and in actual practice context will make them hard to confuse. From the context your most expected clues are that the infinitive construct usually follows a preposition, the imperative is usually an address in direct speech, and the 3ms perfect describes something as a third party.

A.3   Perfects and Participles.

Certain Qal and Niphal forms may be either perfects or participles. The list of forms which may be either is not as long as it first looks. It basically includes Qal $R_2 = $ ׳/ו and Niphals. Weak participles in the Niphal have the same characteristics as weak perfects in the Niphal. Most of the time they can be distinguished by their accent or theme vowel.

	Pf. 3ms	Ptc. ms	Pf. 3fs	Ptc. fs
Qal $R_2 = $ ׳/ו	בָּא	בָּא	בָּאָה	בָּאָה
Qal $R_2 = $ ׳/ו	מֵת	מֵת	מֵתָה	מֵתָה
Ni. $R_3 = $ א/ה	נִמְצָא	נִמְצָא	נִמְצָאָה	נִמְצָאָה
Ni. strong	נִקְטֵל	fw̌ נִקְטָל־	נִקְטְלָה	fw̌ נִקְטֶלֶת־
Ni. strong	נִקְטַל	נִקְטָל	נִקְטְלָה	נִקְטָלָה
Ni. $R_1 = $ ׳	נוֹתַר	נוֹתָר	נוֹתְרָה	נוֹתָרָה
Ni. $R_1 = $ נ	נִצַּב	נִצָּב	נִצְּבָה	נִצָּבָה
Ni. $R_1 = $ G	נֶאֱמַן	נֶאֱמָן	נֶאֶמְנָה	נֶאֱמָנָה
Ni. $R_2 = R_3$	נָקַל / נָסַב	נָמֵס / נָבָּר	נָשַׁמָּה	נְשַׁמָּה

The participles are accented like nouns. They have the accent on the last syllable. So the Niphal masculine singular participles have an accented closed long (ACL) *qametz*, while the 3ms perfects have *patah*. Feminine singular participles have a pretonic open long (POL) *qametz* under R_2, while the 3fs perfects give R_2 a vocal *shewa*. (In addition, a lot of feminine participles use a segolate formation, תֶ◌ֶ◌ֶ, instead of ◌ָה.) In theory, Niphal participles in construct look like perfects because the participle becomes pretonic closed short with *patah*, like the perfect. This can happen but is extremely rare. It is more common for pausal forms of the perfect to lengthen the theme vowel under R_2 and look like a participle, but this happens less than a dozen times (at the ends of poetic lines).

Because the Alias Profiles focus on R_1 and determining stem, we will add the participle option to the appropriate lines of the Qal and Niphal, but they can usually be distinguished by the accent rules. The forms that must truly be distinguished by context are the Qal $R_2 = $ ׳/ו and the Niphal $R_3 = $ G for which 3ms pf. = ms ptc. In the case of the $R_3 = $ א/ה Niphals, the 3ms perfect has long *qametz* because of the silent letter at the end, looking just like the participle. Also, unfortunately, the Qal imperfect 1cp forms of $R_3 = $ א roots look identical to them, because they also have an *a*-class theme vowel and R_1 joins a נ prefix with a *hireq*.

A.4   Forms with הָ.

There are several endings which consist of הָ: (1) the feminine singular noun ending, also used on participles, (2) the 3fs perfect verb ending, (3) directional הָ on nouns, (4) cohortative, and (5) paragogic הָ, occurring mostly on masculine singular imperatives of weak roots or imperatives in requests, and on some weak infinitives.

We have already discussed the הָ ending on perfects and participles. The directional הָ is distinguished by being on nouns of place. The cohortative appears on first person prefixed verbs. Paragogic הָ appears about 50 times on infinitives and about 250 times on imperatives. The presence of the paragogic הָ on weak imperatives helps keep them distinct from weak infinitives that add ת at the end.

root	Inf. cs.	ms Imv. + par ה	root	Inf. cs.	ms Imv. + par ה
יָרַד	רֶדֶת	רְדָה	הָלַךְ	לֶכֶת	לְכָה
נָתַן	תֵּת	תְּנָה	לָקַח	קַחַת	קְחָה
נָגַשׁ	גֶּשֶׁת	גְּשָׁה	קוּם	קוּם	קוּמָה

The main clue that these are Qal imperatives with paragogic הָ is that they are monosyllabic. The infinitives with paragogic הָ can be distinguished from imperatives in that infinitives are usually preceded by prepositions.

The derived stem imperatives that have הָ (mostly Hiphil) can be distinguished from their perfects by their ID badge at R_1. The number of derived stem infinitives that have paragogic הָ is so small that they need not be considered here.

Occasionally a strong root in the Qal has paragogic הָ. This can result in a vowel change at R_1. Most often it changes to the expected *hireq*, e.g. שִׁמְעָה. But a few times it will be *shewa* in problem position, e.g. שְׁמָעָה. Or, like the infinitive with a pronominal suffix, it will move the *u*-class vowel back to R_1, e.g. כָּרְתָה, זָכְרָה. These latter are so rare that we will not include them in the Alias Profiles. Paragogic הָ also occurs on some preterites, but the conjunction clearly marks them as such.

A.5   Review of other confusable forms.

(a)   וֹת ending.

Infinitives of $R_3 = $ י $\neq$ ה verbs end in וֹת, which can be confused for a feminine plural noun or participle ending, until the beginning of the verb is analyzed. The participle and infinitive should not be confused in the derived stems because the participles have preformative מ for the D-stems and H-stems and a prefixed נ for the Niphal (the Ni. inf. is הֵָ for these roots). The Qal participles ◌ֹ◌ֵ◌ and ◌◌וֹ◌ are also clearly distinguished from the infinitives. But you do need to keep in mind that וֹת is an infinitive ending and not exclusively a feminine plural ending.

(b) Inseparable prepositions and attached מִן.

The inseparable prepositions (בְּ, כְּ, and לְ) may at times be confused for R_1.

The attached preposition מִן, having lost the *nun*, might be mistaken for the participle preformative of the D-stems and H-stems. But the preposition only has *ṣere* before a guttural, while the participle prefix never has *ḥireq* and only has *ṣere* before Hiphil $R_1 = $ י or $R_2 = $ ו/י (and a very few $R_2 = R_3$).

(c) Imperfect and stem prefixes.

The imperfect prefixes and R_1 may at times be confused. For example, The Niphal and Hiphil $R_1 = $ נ perfects can be confused with the Piel perfect if the prefixed ה or נ is thought to be a root letter, e.g. נִצַּבְתָּ, נִקַמְתִּי, or הִגַּדְתָּ.

Or the Qal active participle and Hiphil jussive of an R_1 root look alike, יֹסֵף. For the Qal ptc., the י is R_1; for the Hiphil jussive, the י is a prefix. But context will easily clarify.

Always be alert for מ, א, י, ת, נ, and ה as either a root letter or a prefix.

(d) 1cs Pronominal suffix.

The 1cs pronominal suffix יִ◌ may at times be confused with the 2fs imperfect suffix. Or if it is on a word ending in ת, i.e. תִי◌, it might be mistaken for the 1cs perfect suffix.

These are mainly theoretical considerations. The 1cs suffix on finite verbs is נִי◌ with a connecting vowel. It is יִ◌ only on infinitives and participles. When on an infinitive it may look like a feminine singular imperative, but since infinitives are preceded by prepositions or time words, this is never a problem in context. The 1cs suffix יִ◌ attaches to a ת primarily on infinitives ending in וֹת◌, i.e. $R_3 = $ י $≠$ ה, making them look a little like $R_2 = $ ו/י or $R_2 = R_3$ perfects that add a *holem* before the perfect suffix. These three things help you identify it as an infinitive: (1) the root is usually a common $R_3 = $ י $≠$ ה root, (2) the ID badge for the stem almost always clarifies that it is not a perfect, and (3) infinitives are usually signaled by a preceding preposition. So only a bare handful of Qal participles which are also $R_2 = $ ו/י could be confused before context is considered.

(e) Qal impf. 1cp and Niphal pf. 3ms.

Both of these have no suffix and a נ prefix. When the Qal takes an *a*-class theme vowel ($R_3 = $ G), they look alike: נִמְצָא, נִשְׁמַע. But these are not common forms. The Qal impf. of $R_3 = $ י $≠$ ה has an *i*-class theme vowel but the Niphal is *a*-class. When the Qal 1cp impf. or coh. is also $R_1 = $ נ, it can even look like a Piel perfect, נִפְּלָה, but these are also rare.

A.6   The process of parsing.

The stem ID badges and Alias Profiles are all about the process of parsing verbs. To parse verbs you need to identify their endings and prefixes, if any, and their stem, based primarily on R_1's syllable structure. A noun ending indicates the verb is a participle. A perfect ending indicates the verb is a perfect. A couple of imperfect endings indicate if it may be an imperfect, preterite, or imperative. And sometimes there is no ending. In each case you must also look at the beginning of the verb for any prefix, which may then tell you whether the verb is imperfect or preterite, imperative, infinitive, or even 3ms perfect. And you must look at R_1's syllable and environment, because the stem's identity centers on R_1. In short we ask:

What is at the end?

What is at the beginning?

What is the behavior of R_1?

When we are answering these questions, we need to know some things without reference to helps (or our reading speed will be too slow to be effective). We need to solidly know the noun endings, the perfect and imperfect conjugations, the common mark of the preterite, that D-stem and H-stem ptc. have preformative מ, that Niphal ptc. use a prefixed נ, and the Qal ptc. and inf. identifiers. We need to solidly know the syllable principles and weak consonant rules. We need to solidly know the stem ID badges for the strong verb and which ID badges are used for which conjugations. And we need to be able to recognize the pronominal suffixes based on knowing the independent pronoun.

When looking at the ending we need to know that some forms have more than one possibility (which will be cleared up when we look at the beginning of the form):

נות   fem. pl. noun/ptc. or inf. cs. of $R_3 = $ י $\neq$ ה

הָ   fem. sg. noun/ptc. or 3fs pf. or cohortative or directional or paragogic

∅   3ms pf. or ms imv. or ms ptc. or inf. or impf.

ו   3cp pf. or mp imv./impf./pret.

When looking at the beginning we need to watch for whether מ, א, י, ת, נ, or ה is a root letter or a prefix. And we need to know to expect an infinitive construct to normally be preceded by a preposition or word for time.

The Alias Profiles can help us to review weak forms or to practice parsing. They are arranged on the assumption that you can tell (from the ending and/or prefix) whether a verb is based on the prefixed conjugation or the perfect or participle. They provide recognition points related to R_1 and any prefix in order to identify the stem and possible root types.

Alias Profiles for Perfect verbs and some ptc. and inf.

הִ‍‍‍‍‍ₐ/ᵢ	הֵ□□	Hi. Pf. $R_1 = $ נ / $R_1 = $ י & $R_2 = $ צ
	הִי□□	Hi. Pf. $R_1 = $ י
	הֵ□□	Hi. Pf. $R_2 = $ י/ו or $R_1 = $ י or $R_2 = R_3$
	Éהֱ□□	Hi. Pf. $R_2 = $ י/ו or $R_2 = R_3$ (also Śהֱ□□)
	הֶ□Gₐ	Hi. Pf. $R_1 = $ G (incl. 3ms)
	הֶ□Gₐ	Hi. Pf. $R_1 = $ G (but not 3ms)
הוֹ□□	הוֹ□□	Hi. Pf. $R_1 = $ י (or בוֹשׁ)
הֻₐ	הוּ□□	Ho. Pf. $R_2 = $ י/ו or $R_1 = $ י (or rarely $R_2 = R_3$)
	הֳ□□	Ho. Pf. $R_1 = $ נ
	הֳ□□	Ho. Pf. $R_2 = $ י/ו
נ□	נִ□□	Ni. Pf./Ptc. $R_1 = $ נ / $R_1 = $ י & $R_2 = $ צ (cf. Pi. pf./ Qal 1cp impf.)
	נֶ□Gₐ	Ni. Pf./Ptc. $R_1 = $ G
	נֶ□Gₐ	Ni. Pf./Ptc. $R_1 = $ G
	נָ□□	Ni. Pf./Ptc. $R_2 = R_3$
	נָ□וֹ□	Ni. Pf./Ptc. $R_2 = $ ו
	נוֹ□□	Ni. Pf./Ptc. $R_1 = $ י
	Éנָ□וֹ□	Ni. Pf./Ptc. $R_2 = $ י/ו
	נֶ□□א	Ni. 3ms Pf. = ms Ptc. (cp. Qal 1cp impf.)

Ni. ptc. ms □□ָ֫□נִ / fw □□ַ□נִ
Ni. pf. 3ms □□ָ□נִ / □□ַ□נ

נֶחָם	נֶחָם	Ni. Pf. or Pi. Pf.
É□□□		Cp. Pi. Pf. and cp. Qal imv.
□G□	□G□	Pi. Pf.
□G□	□G□	Pu. Pf. (rare; cp. Qal act. ptc. which is normally *i*-class)
□וֹ	□□וֹ□	Polel, Polal Pf. (cp. Qal act. ptc. which rarely uses וֹ)

Qal perfect weak.

structure	example	root
□ַ□	תַּם	$R_2 = R_3$
□□	מֵת / בֹּשׁ / קָם	$R_2 = $ י/ו
V□ַ□	תַּמּוּ	$R_2 = R_3$
V□ָ□	קָמְה / קָמוּ	$R_2 = $ י/ו
	גָּלָה / גָּלוּ	$R_3 = $ י ≠ ה
V□ֹ□ / V□ַ□	מֵתוּ / בֹּשׁוּ	$R_2 = $ י/ו

structure	example	root
C□□וֹ	אָרוֹת / תַּמּוֹת	$R_2 = R_3$
C□□ִי	גָּלִיתָ	$R_3 = $ י ≠ ה
C□□	בֹּשְׁתָּ / קַמְתָּ	$R_2 = $ י/ו
Cנת	נָתַתִּי	נתן
□□תְ□ה	גָּלְתָה	$R_3 = $ י ≠ ה
□□ַ pf./ptc. □ו□/□י□ inf./imv. $R_2 = $ י/ו		
n.b. □□ *e.g.* סֹב *can be* $R_2 = R_3$ *inf. cs.*		

Alias Profiles for Prefixed verbs, imperatives, and some ptc.

□̣P	⊡P	Qal	If □□P then $R_1 = $ לקח/נ/R_3 = יצ or $R_2 = R_3$
	□̣P		$R_3 = $ י $\neq$ ה : □ְ□̣P / C י□ְ□̣P / □ְ□̣P ו / G□□P ו
	י̣P		$R_1 = $ י (e.g. ירא, mater yod may be omitted, e.g. ויראו)
□̣P	⊡̣P	Ni.	□□̣P $R_2 = R_3$;	If P = ה, then inf. or imv.
	ו̇⊡̣P		□ו̇□̣P $R_2 = $ ו (usu. כון, Qal $\neq$ ו̇);	
	⊡̣P		V□ָ□̣P $R_3 = $ י $\neq$ ה	
	□ְתָ̣P	Hit.	(□□ו̇□ְתָ̣P Hitpolel)	
□ֵP	□ֵP	Qal	$R_1 = $ י / הלך, $R_2 = R_3$, $R_3 = $ י $\neq$ ה pret./juss., נטה, בוש
	GP	Ni.	□GP $R_2 = R_3$	If P = ה, then inf. or imv.
	G̣P		□ו̇GP $R_1 = $ G & $R_2 = $ ו	
	מֵ□	Hi. ptc.	□□מֵ□ $R_2 = R_3$ or $R_2 = $ ו/י	
	י̣P	Hi.	$R_1 = $ י	
□ֵP	GP	Qal/Hi.	(Qal has *i*-class theme only if $R_3 = $ י $\neq$ ה or $R_2 = $ י)
	□ֵP	Hi.	If P = ה, then inf. or imv.	
	⊡ֵP		□⊡ֵP $R_1 = $ נ (rarely R_3 יצ); נטה = ויט; נכה = ויך	
□ָP	□ָP	Qal	$R_2 = $ ו/י or $R_2 = R_3$; (*I*-class theme only when $R_2 = $ י)
		Hi.	$R_2 = $ ו/י or $R_2 = R_3$; (*I*-class theme 98%)
□ָP u/o	ו̇P / ֹP / ָP	Ho.	□□ְP / □□⊡P $\leftarrow$ □□ֻ̇P or $\mathbb{R}_2 R_2$□ְP
			□□ו̇P $\leftarrow$ □□ְוP or □ו/י□P or $\mathbb{R}_2 R_2$□ְP
			□□GP / V□ָ□GP
	ו̇כלP	Qal	יכל
□ו̇P	□ו̇P	Hi.	$\leftarrow$ □□ְוP $R_1 = $ י / הלך
אֵP	□□אֵP	Qal	$R_1 = $ א (1cs א deletes $R_1 = $ א, אמר)
□ֵ̣P	S̆□□ֵ̣P	Qal/Hi.	$R_2 = $ ו/י or $R_2 = R_3$ (n.b. E□⊡P) (Qal only has *i*-class theme if $R_2 = $ י)
	□ַP a :	Piel	□ֵ□ַP ; G□ַP / G□ַ̣P ; □□ַ̇P ו $R_3 = $ י $\neq$ ה
	□P u/o :	Pual	ה□ֻ□ַP / V□□ַP $R_3 = $ י $\neq$ ה □Gֻ□ַP / □הֻ□ַP ;
	מֵ□ e	Hi. ptc.	□□מֵ□ $R_2 = $ ו/י or $R_2 = R_3$ (ptc. + ending)
	□□ו̇□ֵP	Polel/ Polal	$R_2 = $ ו/י or $R_2 = R_3$
	□□ו̇□ְתָP	Hitpolel	$R_2 = $ ו/י or $R_2 = R_3$

Excursus B
Introduction to Chapters 23–32:
A Syntax Sampler

Meaning arises from combinations. Lexemes (3.2), grammatical forms, syntax, and larger discourse features combine to create meaning in language. The meaning of a verb, for example, is a combination of the lexeme plus the verbal stem plus the conjugation plus other features in the context. The first three combine to construct the verb form in its sentence, but then the verb's specific time frame usually depends on the context (10.7.3 and 12.6). Also, what a given word specifically refers to depends on various combinations. The meaning of *delivered* is different in *she delivered the letters* and in *she delivered the baby*. And it is different in *she delivered the baby* based on whether *she* is the mother or the obstetrician. Similarly, the referent of יָלַד, usually listed in the dictionary as *bear a child*, will differ depending on whether the subject is the mother or the father.

Meaning arises from combinations. Some parts of the meaning are specifically indicated by forms or words (grammar and vocabulary). Other parts come from a combination of factors often lumped together in that conglomerate loosely referred to as *context*. Now that you have learned the forms of Biblical Hebrew and have built up a stock of vocabulary, what you need to do most is read texts and learn to observe the context well, seeing more and more how the pieces make up the whole.

In this section we study topics other than morphology, with many of the topics falling under the heading of syntax. These chapters will make you aware of how various elements in the context can interact in the process of creating meaning. The more aware you are of what can be involved, the better you will be able to ask questions about how a particular text works. The better the questions that you ask, the better the answers you will find.

Mastery of Hebrew syntax is beyond the scope of a first year grammar. But you should also learn to ask questions of the material in reference works, whether dictionaries or advanced grammars. Reference works should not be approached with the basic question *"What does X mean?"* But rather *"What does X mean in relationship to A, B, and/or C?"* Language is very flexible, using a fairly small number of forms to create a nearly limitless range of expression. The combinations are what multiply a language's ability to be expressive.

Dictionaries are arranged under the headings of words, but the words have meaning in a context based on combinations between the word and other elements. Even if you select an English translation from the dictionary because "it just feels right" in the passage you are studying, you are at least subconsciously comparing your passage to the information available in the dictionary in order to make the choice. Advanced grammars and syntax works are also arranged according to topics. And those elements have meaning in contexts based on combinations with other factors. The more specific you can be about comparing an actual text to the information in reference works, the better your translation and exegesis will be.

The next set of chapters are not only an introduction to assorted topics on syntax, they are an introduction to reference works on syntax. They are not an introduction in the sense of providing synopses and reviews of advanced grammars. Rather they try to model how to think about and utilize the information in those reference works. Your expectation should not be that when you look in a reference work you will find "the answer." Sometimes when you consult a reference work you find exactly what you want; sometimes you can infer the information you want from what you find; and sometimes you realize that you need to dig deeper. Neither dictionaries nor advanced grammars are or can be exhaustive. Language is more flexible than any resource has room to describe. They give you a start and can help you learn to think about how the Hebrew language works. You make the best use of their counsel by approaching them with questions about how words or elements of syntax relate to other parts of the context.

Most of the chapters in this section cover one or two main topics, such as a part of speech, a verbal stem, or a conjugation. The topic is divided into sections of common uses with examples such as you may find in reference works. Then the chapter discusses how certain uses are conditioned by the combinations they are in. Learning this material is not a matter of learning to recite lists of options, but learning to see the relevant connections that help you select or infer the right option when you do research. We say *infer* because a passage that you study may employ a use for something that is not directly covered in the reference list's general overview.

Our chief resource for this will be *A Guide to Biblical Hebrew Syntax* by Bill T. Arnold and John H. Choi (Cambridge: Cambridge University Press, 2003), an excellent next step in your Hebrew training. We will refer to portions of Arnold and Choi by the abbreviation *AC* followed by the page number. Sections will be cited with the symbol §.

At the same time, the most important thing for you to be doing is reading Hebrew texts. The Workbook Appendix includes 2Chr 34 and Neh 8 as options (they have a high percentage of derived stem forms and can also be integrated throughout chs. 16–22). But chapters 23–32 are not tied to those passages and may be used as supplemental reading to any Hebrew passage because they emphasize general skills on common topics. They may also be read in any order.

These chapters also do not include vocabulary lists. Eleven additional vocabulary lists appear in Appendix A. These 216 words comprise the rest of the words used 50 or more times in the Bible. Lists 23–29 group words based on topics like most of the earlier lists. Lists 30–32 give words used 50–60 times in the Bible, while the words in list 33 are used more than 50 times only because they are so common from Exod 25 through Num 10. Programs vary in their first year vocabulary goals, so the CD also includes a list of these same words strictly according to frequency for instructors to assign as they see fit.

The first two chapters in this unit are not strictly on syntax. Chapter 23 looks at the use of pause in storytelling to add drama. Its main purpose is to remind that we are not attempting to merely decode Hebrew data, we are reading great literature. Chapter 24 illustrates issues in lexicography. Its goal is not to make you a lexicographer but to give you perspective on how to use and evaluate the information found in dictionaries. Chapters 25–31 sample topics in syntax. Chapter 32 considers how to translate the verb system in poetry and is offered as a beginning step in this genre.

As you read extended texts of Biblical Hebrew, these chapters train you to see relationships between various elements of the text, how words bring meaning to the sentences and how they interact with other elements in order to create meaning. The exposure to these interrelationships should help you learn to ask good questions about what texts mean and how to use reference works such as dictionaries or reference grammars and works about syntax.

chapter twenty-three

Pauses and Drama

23.1 Focus.

The main purpose of this chapter is to remind us that the Bible is great literature – in Hebrew. Thus far we have focused on the spellings of word forms. A hidden danger is to miss seeing the larger picture of narrative texts as great stories, as dramatic and powerful. So we pause here, less to learn a new skill and more to renew our vision of reading Hebrew texts. We do not come to these texts simply to decode them but to enter into them.

23.2 On Drama in Literature.

Paying close attention, teacher John Keating marks out a chart on the chalkboard while a high school student reads from chapter one of a literature textbook, explaining how to assess the greatness of a poem by graphing its importance and perfection. The students take careful notes as their school has conditioned them to do. The reading of the essay is punctuated by the flourished striking of the chalk. Finally the teacher delivers his viewpoint with a smile, or perhaps a smirk, shocking his students by placing the value of the essay somewhat lower than rubbish, "Excrement!" Having thus rendered his opinion of the essay, he proceeds to tell his students to "Rip it out!" The students' conditioning to compliance edges out their sense of the responsible use of resources. They dismember their textbooks and deposit the requisite pages in the trashcan. Thus Robin Williams' character in *Dead Poets Society*[1] begins to teach his pupils that there is more to literature than clinical analysis and graphs. Literature is about passion, about that for which humans live. He desires that his students be drawn into the deep meanings in good literature, connecting the life in literature with their own lives.

---

[1] *Dead Poets Society*, Touchstone Pictures, 1989.

Biblical narrative, like narrative generally, is comprised of many parts: plot, characters, organizing structures such as chiasmus, etc., which it may in fact be helpful to graph. Understanding Biblical Hebrew narrative does involve different steps like translating, evaluating text critical issues, doing lexical studies and syntactical analysis, examining rhetorical structures, and other elements. But the whole involves more than the pieces.

This chapter focuses on one element of the storytelling process, namely pause. But our end goal is larger than this element. As a whole, the narrative constitutes a story, a story that was told and is to be retold. Narratives are stories to be experienced in the telling and in the hearing. We focus on pauses with a view toward the drama they bring to stories. We also give general consideration to the process of hearing and visualizing the story. For these stories are great literature – in Hebrew, a compelling drama that invites us into dialogue with the lives of others and their God.

23.3   Indicators of pause.

One aspect of pausing deals with keeping phrases as distinct pieces. A college speech instructor might call this blocking the text and advise students to print out the text being read not in paragraphs, but in blocks, or units of phrases that belong together. Then they should think about what they want to achieve with the emotion in their voices and gestures to support the content of the text. The Masoretes have blocked the text for us with the accents. The major disjunctive accents do not necessarily correspond to clauses, but usually mark off chunks of text that are in some way a sense unit. These are very helpful for planning oral delivery.

In addition, the Masoretes indicated pauses through pausal forms and some uses of *dagesh*. Pausal forms are distinct from contextual forms, not in how they are parsed but in how they are spoken. *Begadkephat* letters are also affected by pausing, and *dagesh lene* is the result of stopping, or pausing. The Masoretes were at pains to preserve an oral reading tradition. They added the vowels and other marks with a concern for how to *read* this great and moving literature.

Pausal forms represent vocal intonation, reflecting the strength of an accent and length of a vowel when the speaker pauses. Biblical Hebrew is a stress-based language whose forms take shape in response to the placement or shifting of the accent, as expressed in the syllable principles throughout the morphology section. The differences in vowels are a by-product of how Hebrew was spoken.

The *maqqef* also reflects concern for the orality of the text, though as a kind of opposite to pause. While it follows many construct nouns, its job is not to indicate the construct state. Many, perhaps most, construct nouns are not marked by *maqqef* and the Masoretes employ *maqqef* more often in other situations, such as joining a verb to a particle or preposition. The *maqqef* itself is not performing different jobs.

Maqqef simply indicates close association *in speech* (just as the different vowels of construct nouns result from the effect *in speech* of moving the accent).

Pausing has a reflex in vocal stress, producing distinct forms in some types of words: verbs with *a*-class theme vowels, verbs with vocalic endings (regardless of the class of theme vowel), dual nouns, certain geminate or segolate nouns, and some pronominal suffixes, as in the following examples.

	contextual	pausal
Qal pf. 1cs	שָׁמַ֫רְתִּי	שָׁמָ֫רְתִּי
Qal pf. 3fs	שָׁמְרָה	שָׁמָ֫רָה
Qal impf. 3ms	יִגְדַּל	יִגְדָּ֫ל
Qal impf. 3mp	יִכְתְּבוּ	יִכְתֹּ֫בוּ
Ni. pf. 3ms	נִכְרַת	נִכְרָ֫ת
segolate noun	אֶ֫רֶץ	אָ֫רֶץ
geminate noun	כַּף	כָּף
3ʳᵈ *yod* noun	בְּלִי	בֶּ֫כִי
dual	רַגְלַ֫יִם	רַגְלָ֫יִם
2ms pr. suffix	ךָ֫ / ְךָ	ךָ֫ / ֶ֫ךָ
1cs pr. suffix	ִ֫י	ָ֫י
pronoun	אֲנִי, אַתָּה	אָ֫נִי, אָ֫תָּה

Pausal forms seldom affect parsing and so may be given little attention in beginning grammars. Pausal forms get little attention in commentaries, since they do not generally affect parsing and are not then considered *exegetically* significant. Likewise any homiletic significance is usually overlooked.

Dagesh can also indicate pause or the lack thereof. Typical rules for describing *dagesh* include: (1) *dagesh forte* follows a vowel (within a word), while (2) *dagesh lene* follows a consonant, and (3) *dagesh forte* cannot begin a word while (4) *dagesh lene* begins a word unless the previous word ends in a vowel. But in fact, *dagesh lene* can appear after a word ending in a vowel and *dagesh forte* can begin words. The deciding factor is pause or the lack thereof.

The more complete rule for *dagesh lene* is that it follows a stop, which is either a consonant or a pause. If the speaker has paused, breath has stopped, even if the previous word ended in a vowel. So a *begadkephat* letter beginning the next word cannot be spirantic and will have *dagesh lene*. Further, if a word ending in a vowel is very closely related *in speech* to the next word, i.e. said rapidly together with it, that following word may begin with *dagesh forte*. We turn now to examples of these features in discourse and their contribution to the drama of the stories.

(a) Dagesh lene after a vowel.

In Gen 39:9, Joseph rebuffs the advances of Potiphar's wife with these words, וְלֹא־חָשַׂךְ מִמֶּ֫נִּי מְא֔וּמָה כִּי אִם־אוֹתָ֖ךְ בַּאֲשֶׁר אַתְּ־אִשְׁתּ֑וֹ. The word כִּי has a *dagesh lene* although the previous word, מְא֔וּמָה, ends in a vowel (the ה is a *mater lectionis*). Thus we hear and retell the story "…He has not withheld from me anything *(pause)* except you, since you are his wife."

The pause is dramatic and influences how we verbalize and visualize the story line. Our reading (in Hebrew or English) should not be a flat monotone but reflect the shocked insistence of Joseph's protest as he clarifies that his answer is a very final "no." He concludes a series of statements about the kindness and trust he has received from his master with the sweeping statement, said with conviction, loyalty, and protest, that "he has not withheld from me anything." It becomes easy in our mind's eye to see Joseph make a sweeping gesture at מְא֔וּמָה (*anything*), then change his facial expression and tone as he *pauses* before saying, כִּי אִם־אוֹתָ֖ךְ, "except you." In our mind's eye, we might even see him point to her as he said it.

In 2Samuel 7, King David remarks to Nathan that while he dwells in a cedar-paneled palace, the ark of the LORD sits in a tent. Reading his intent, Nathan responds (vs 3), כָּל אֲשֶׁר בִּלְבָבְךָ לֵךְ עֲשֵׂה כִּי יְהוָה עִמָּךְ. We note that כִּי with a *dagesh lene* follows a vowel, which indicates a pause. Also the suffix on the final word עִמָּךְ is a second *masculine* singular pausal form (though it is identical to the 2fs form, Nathan is not calling David a woman). But the 2ms suffix on לְבָב (*heart/mind*) is not pausal. Nathan is not depicted as pausing after "Everything which is on your mind." Rather he proceeds directly on to the verbs and then pauses, "Everything which is on your mind go do, (pause) because the LORD is with you."

(b) Dagesh forte beginning a word.

The LORD sends Nathan to David to ask, הַאַתָּה תִּבְנֶה־לִּי בַ֫יִת לְשִׁבְתִּי (vs 5), "Are you going to build me a house to dwell in?" Observe several reading cues. The verb תִּבְנֶה begins with *dagesh lene*, though the preceding word ends with a vowel. And *maqqef* joins the verb to a preposition beginning with a *dagesh forte*.[2] The English reader might emphasize *build* and *house*, stressing the impossibility of building a structure to house the God of heaven and earth. But the Hebrew reader is directed otherwise. The *dagesh lene* beginning תִּבְנֶה־ indicates a brief pause at אַתָּה (*you*). The *maqqef* and *dagesh* in the following *lamed* require that the reader cannot linger on תִּבְנֶה־ (*build*) but must proceed on to ־לִּי (*for me*). The emphasis is not on the action but on the agent, on who will do the building. For it is not David who will

---

[2] *Lamed* cannot take *dagesh lene* so it looks like a *dagesh forte*, since those are the only two *dageshes* we have met so far. This *dagesh* results from the close association of the two words in pronunciation (cf. Joüon-Muraoka, p. 80f).

build the LORD a בַּיִת (*house*), meaning a temple. Rather, it is the LORD (vs 11) who will build David a בַּיִת (*house*), meaning a dynasty. We are not merely concerned with the play on the word בַּיִת; we want to *hear* Nathan and *be assured* like David.

(c) Pausal forms.

Pausing is natural at the completion of a sentence. Consequently there is a major pause at the end of every Hebrew verse and usually one in the middle as well, whether in narrative, poetry, or speech. They are the most dramatic in speech, helping to mark off clauses and phrases occurring within a verse.

In Judges 3, however, we hear the narrator pause while relating the action-packed adventure of Ehud. Having been made subservient to Moab for their sins, the Israelites have cried out to the LORD. The LORD's deliverer is not so much imposing as he is clever. Being left-handed, he has concealed a weapon where a right-handed person would not, and he has gained a private audience with the Moabite king by pretending to have a secret divine word, seemingly received at the shrine in Gilgal.

Before we come to the narrator's use of a pausal form, we have occasion to observe how the narrator's use of time increases the drama and excitement in the story. At the beginning, narrative time moves quickly. Ehud brings the tribute to Eglon, dismisses the couriers, then returns from the idols at Gilgal, and is suddenly in the king's court again. Narrative time slows down for the assassination scene. His actions must occur quickly, but we get the narrative equivalent of shooting a movie scene in slow motion, "Ehud stretched out his left hand. He took the dagger from his right thigh. And thrust it into his belly." We even get a gory close-up shot of the hilt going in after the blade and Eglon's blubber folding up over it, as well as the odoriferous information that this triggered some of Eglon's bodily functions. The narrator pauses on this event by giving us so much detail. (If we were watching this as a movie, the theme music would kick in and continue through Ehud's escape.)

After Ehud has locked the doors and left, Eglon's courtiers are waiting, assuming their king is going to the bathroom. They wait to the point that it is embarrassing. But he kept not opening the doors so they finally got a key to unlock them. The narrator pauses on the next word וַיִּפְתָּחוּ, "and they opened." This pause, combined with the following הִנֵּה, gives extra drama to the story. הִנֵּה indicates awareness, often the moment of coming to realize something. In this passage we have the narrative equivalent of watching a detective show or police drama where the investigators are looking through a house. As viewers, we have seen the crime and know there is a body to be found. There is a brief pause when they put their hand on *that* doorknob, our pausal וַיִּפְתָּחוּ, and perhaps the background music cuts out or changes. Then the door opens and הִנֵּה, shock, sudden awareness – we see the body sprawled out. The action sequence is spectacular in any case, but the pausal form *they opened*, followed by הִנֵּה, heightens the drama a bit more.

In Ruth 3:9 we find a pausal form at an unusual place in speech. Following her mother-in-law's instructions, Ruth has come to Boaz, who has fallen asleep after celebrating a hearty harvest party. She has pulled back his skirt enough to uncover his feet and lain down to wait. He stirs (perhaps his feet have gotten cold) and wakes to discover a woman near his feet. He warily asks her, "Who are you?" And she responds, אָנֹכִי רוּת אֲמָתֶךָ וּפָרַשְׂתָּ כְנָפֶ֙ךָ֙ עַל־אֲמָתְךָ כִּי גֹאֵל אָתָּה׃. "I am Ruth, your maidservant; So spread your *kānāp* over your maidservant; since you are a kinsman redeemer." As indicated by the *dagesh lene* in כִּי which follows a vowel, there is a brief pause after the 2ⁿᵈ "*your maidservant*," אֲמָתְךָ. Interestingly though, this אֲמָתְךָ (*'ămāt^ekắ*) is not a pausal form, whereas the first occurrence of the term is pausal, אֲמָתֶךָ (*'ămātékā*).

Further, the word כְנָפֶךָ is pausal but does not occur in a pausal position. It is in the middle of the clause and lacks any reason in syntax or accent to be pausal. Jöuon correctly identifies it as a pausal form, but attributes this to mimicking the first אֲמָתֶךָ, which, he says, is pausal due to the accent *zaqqef*, ◌̇.³ We credit Jöuon for noticing the form but disagree with his explanation. If similarity with the first and pausal אֲמָתֶךָ (*'ămātékā*) were the issue, then we would expect the 2ⁿᵈ אֲמָתְךָ (*'ămāt^ekắ*), which is also accented with *zaqqef*, to be pausal like the first. Instead, we should *hear* Ruth emphasize the word כְנָפֶךָ in her reply to Boaz. Those listening to the story being told, or read, are directed by this emphasis back to an earlier occurrence of the term in Ruth 2:12. Boaz had blessed her by the LORD under whose כָּנָף (*wing*) she had taken refuge. She now asks Boaz to symbolically spread his כָּנָף (*skirt*) over her. Likewise the pause at the first אֲמָתֶךָ may carry emphasis; Ruth accords herself a higher social standing as compared with earlier references to herself as נָכְרִי and שִׁפְחָה.⁴ The play on the word כָּנָף in 3:9 and 2:12 has not gone unnoticed by commentators on the written text, but the *vocal* emphasis adds drama to the mental movie screen on which the *hearer* imagines the story.

(d) Pause indicated by repetition of וַיֹּאמֶר.

A pause may also be indicated by the repetition of וַיֹּאמֶר without a change of speaker. In 1Kings 3, Solomon's wisdom in governance is tested as two prostitutes stand before him disputing whose son has died and whose lives. The first tells her story, explaining how the other woman switched infants in the middle of the night, substituting a dead son for a living one. The other woman denies this with the claim לֹא כִּי בְּנֵךְ הַמֵּת וּבְנִי הֶחָי. The next speech is not introduced with a preterite (not with וַתֹּאמֶר), but rather a participle, וְזֹאת אֹמֶרֶת. The participle indicates that it is

---

³ Paul Jöuon, *Ruth* (Rome: Pontifical Biblical Institute, 1993), p. 73.
⁴ For references to the discussion on whether Ruth intends to make a distinction in her social status, see Katherine Doob Sakenfeld, *Ruth* (Louisville, John Knox Press, 1999), p. 58.

while the second woman issues her denial that the first cuts in with the same denunciation, לֹא כִּי בְּנֵךְ הַמֵּת וּבְנִי הֶחָי.

While we are here, we should note that *dagesh lene* in בְּנֵךְ indicates a pause following לֹא כִּי. The כִּי, however, has no *dagesh lene* following לֹא, since the two are a package. The final word of the quotation, הֶחָי, is pausal. In addition to these clues the line must be read with the intensity of an anguished mother; לֹא כִּי No! בְּנֵךְ הַמֵּת וּבְנִי הֶחָי Your son is the dead one! My son is the living!

After he hears their claims, the king's speech is introduced by וַיֹּאמֶר הַמֶּלֶךְ in verse 23. He summarizes the case by quoting their identical and competing claims. Then the king's speech is again introduced with וַיֹּאמֶר הַמֶּלֶךְ in verse 24. The audience already knows the speaker, do they not? The repetition of וַיֹּאמֶר signals an even greater pause than a pausal form or *dagesh lene* following a vowel; it indicates a gap of time between the two utterances. He is the same speaker, but this is a new speech act, hence the repetition of וַיֹּאמֶר. Combined with his next words this adds great drama to how we visualize the story.

The ladies are speaking at the same time, perhaps yelling, "My son …," "No! Your son…" In this commotion, the king speaks to his court, summarizing the scant evidence, "This one says… but this one says…" Then he falls silent, thinking. In the following silence, at least from the king, the courtiers and listeners to the story wonder what he will do, for the case surely seems impossible to decide from the available evidence. If we were making this into a movie, we might muffle the background noises and center on the king, while keeping the movements of the plaintiffs in the frame. Solomon is "in a zone" and makes a decision.

Finally he speaks, again introduced by וַיֹּאמֶר, a new speech act from the same speaker. His words seem entirely foreign to the setting and surely bring silence to the whole court, קְחוּ לִי־חָרֶב, "Fetch me a sword." The brooding silence between the speech acts amplifies the suspense. Into that gap, the king speaks with command, an emphasis on the word *sword* echoing ominously. The shock value of the order derives partly from its terseness, but the use of *maqqef* and the pausal form further emphasize this deadly object with no obvious or desirable connection to this case.

It is very common for the imperative of לקח to be joined to a following לְ with *maqqef*, and other than this instance, it is always the case when the speaker refers to himself with לִי.[5] In these, the Masoretes preserve a diction in which the verb and preposition are a tight unit, "Get-me X;" "Get-yourself Y." But here, and only here,

---

[5] Plural imperatives of לקח joined to a following לְ with *maqqef*: Gen 45:19; Num 16:6; 2Ki 2:20; 3:15; Job 42:8. Plural imperatives of לקח not joined to a following לְ with *maqqef*: Exod 5:11; 9:8; 12:21; Josh 3:12; 4:2; 1Ki 3:24; Jer 29:6. All singular imperatives of לקח followed by לְ are joined to it with *maqqef* except one instance with an intervening paragogic he. Joining the verb to a following לְ with *maqqef* is fairly common in the indicative as well.

the preposition ל and its object are joined by *maqqef* not to the preceding verb קְ
but to the following direct object of the verb, to חָ֫רֶב. While the lack of *maqqef* after
the verb may not indicate a pause, its placement is a variation and it moves us on to
the shock word חָ֫רֶב. While חָ֫רֶב must be pausal by virtue of ending the sentence,
this vocal emphasis certainly fits the mood of the scene. We can convey the effect in
English with the slightest hesitation after the imperative, while running the rest of the
words together and emphasizing the last, "Fetch me-a-**sword**."

With no indication of the sword's purpose, the pause on "sword" rings
portentously in our ears. For what purpose a sword? The king is silent. We might
presume silence in the court while we see the next action – they brought him a
sword. Then the king speaks again, indicating the sword's use. וַיֹּ֫אמֶר הַמֶּ֫לֶךְ,
"Cleave the living child in two. Give half to the one and half to the other." The
petitioners, courtiers, and listeners to the story are shocked alike, as intended by the
king, and by the narrator. Such words would shock in any case, but our sense of the
total drama is increased by our perception of gaps of time between actions and
pauses in speech.

(e) Accent marks.

Since pause is integrally bound up with accent, we can also look to accent marks
for Masoretic clues to pause. Since all beginning Hebrew students must learn the
vowels and *dagesh*, we have begun with these as indicators of pause. Learning the
full accent system would yet seem a daunting task. However, we may focus on a
small number of the heavier accents in narrative.

In addition to *sof pasuq* which ends every verse :☐☐, the most significant accent
marks for these purposes are: *aṭnaḥ* ☐, *zaqqef parvum* ☐, *zaqqef magnum* ☐, *rebia* ☐,
segolta ☐ and *shalshelet* ☐. A word of caution – pause is not simply a matter of the
accent system. Except for *sof pasuq* and *aṭnaḥ*, pausal forms are optional with the
other accents. So pausal forms and *dagesh lene* after a word ending with a vowel
continue to be important and independent reading clues.

The following selection from Ruth 1:11–13 is Naomi's second plea with her
daughters-in-law to remain in Moab. The accent marks are included with the
Hebrew. At least a minor pause is envisioned for every *sof pasuq*, *aṭnaḥ*, *zaqqef*, and
rebia. Correspondingly, the text is laid out to begin a new line after each of these
accents. Four of these breaks are also signaled by *dagesh lene* after a vowel or by a
pausal form. Of course, noticing the pauses is only a part of reading dramatically.
Her first attempt to encourage them to return to their homes and hope for a husband
in Moab has failed. Among other concerns, she voices that their prospects for
marriage are slim to none if they go with her. There is something missing in print
that is brought to life when reading in our best dramatic voice, a voice which can be

informed by the Masoretic accents. We hear her incredulity and can easily punctuate her pauses with a mental picture of her pacing, looking first to the one, then to the other.

שֹׁ֥בְנָה בְנֹתַ֖י	"Return, my daughters.
לָ֥מָּה תֵלַ֖כְנָה עִמִּ֑י	Why go with me?
הַֽעֽוֹד־לִ֤י בָנִים֙ בְּֽמֵעַ֔י	Are there still sons in my womb…
וְהָי֥וּ לָכֶ֖ם לַאֲנָשִֽׁים:	…that would become your husbands?
12 שֹׁ֤בְנָה בְנֹתַי֙ לֵ֔כְןָ	"Return, my daughters. Go!
כִּ֥י[6] זָקַ֖נְתִּי מִהְי֣וֹת לְאִ֑ישׁ	Indeed, I'm too old to have a husband.
כִּ֤י אָמַ֙רְתִּי֙ יֶשׁ־לִ֣י תִקְוָ֔ה	If I say, 'There's hope for me…
גַּ֣ם[7] הָיִ֤יתִי הַלַּ֙יְלָה֙ לְאִ֔ישׁ	even that I would have a husband tonight…
וְגַ֖ם יָלַ֥דְתִּי בָנִֽים:	and what's more bear *sons*,'
13 הֲלָהֵ֣ן ׀ תְּשַׂבֵּ֗רְנָה	"Would you hold off for them[8]
עַ֚ד אֲשֶׁ֣ר יִגְדָּ֔לוּ[9]	until they were grown?
הֲלָהֵן֙ תֵּֽעָגֵ֔נָה	Would you lock yourselves away for them
לְבִלְתִּ֖י הֱי֣וֹת לְאִ֑ישׁ	to avoid getting married?
אַ֣ל בְּנֹתַ֗י	No my daughters,
כִּֽי־[10]מַר־לִ֤י מְאֹד֙ מִכֶּ֔ם	indeed [life] is more bitter for me than for you…
כִּֽי־יָצְאָ֥ה בִ֖י יַד־יְהוָֽה:	since the hand of the Lord has gone out against me."

23.4 On the value of noting pauses.

The text was originally written in consonants only; the long vowels of pausal forms and the *dagesh* are secondary. And postulating, for example, that Naomi is pacing in Ruth 1:11–13 is speculation. These elements do not affect exegesis in the way that lexical studies or text critical work might. So why bother?

(a) Form.

Pause is part of a larger issue of vocal intonation, which reminds us of the form of the literature. It is a story to be *told*; this form is the embodiment of God's word. God's message is not simply an enduring religious principle to be extracted from a text; God's message comes as a package and the package helps convey the message.

---

[6] The *dagesh lene* in כִּי is preceded by a vowel in לֵכְןָ which would demonstrate (even without the accent mark) that the Masoretes understood a pause between them.

[7] Note that גַּם with *dagesh lene* is preceded by תִקְוָה which ends in a vowel (ה is a *mater*).

[8] Or "therefore, would you hold off." לָהֵן may be a conjunction, "therefore," or the preposition plus pronominal suffix (either a copying error for לָהֶם or the Aramaic form of the 2mp).

[9] Although not with *atnaḥ* or *sof pasuq*, יִגְדָּלוּ is a pausal form.

[10] Note that כִּי with *dagesh lene* is preceded by בְּנֹתַי which ends in a vowel.

Yes, we may still notice word plays or benefit from lexical studies or text critical work without an ear for pause in storytelling. But the point in studying the pieces is not to dissect the story and display its constituent elements on glass slides. At that point the lab animal is dead. We want to integrate our findings into an appreciation for a living, breathing story. Attending to pause, which is to consider how to communicate the story, helps bring us to the whole.

(b) Homiletics and teaching.

Something is amiss if we study narrative, that is *story*, while overlooking *storytelling*. Herein, a sensitivity to reading the text with feeling has homiletic significance. At the most basic level, being schooled in the nuances of reading the Hebrew text should help students avoid dull and monotonous public readings of the English text. Better yet, attending to these signals can provide a basis for describing the drama of the stories to an audience which does not read Hebrew. We can be tutored by the Masoretes, harvesting valuable information from masters of Hebrew literature. As great acting draws us more deeply into a movie, these literary clues draw us more deeply into the story.

It is true that the vowels and other signs were not originally written; however, the reading tradition was not invented *ad hoc* or in a vacuum. While the Masoretes were not infallible, they were of no small skill and we rely on them heavily for a great many matters related to the Hebrew Bible. With pausal forms and *dagesh* they are shooting flares across our bow. "Take note, there is great drama here; read with feeling and intensity so that your listeners can experience the life of the story."

This is still a text-based approach. We do not advocate inventing wholly new things or trying to fill in gaps deliberately left by the narrator. Speculating on romantic interests in Boaz' and Ruth's minds at their first encounter in Ruth 2 may be good fodder for creative writing, but is invention rather than interpretation. Yet whether we read or listen to Mark Twain or Tom Clancy, we inevitably create some picture in our minds of the unfolding action. There is room for us to imagine some details differently, as long as we let the storyteller control the scene. In the same way, we can read Hebrew syntax as camera directions, imagine different visual effects when narrative time slows down, and listen for pauses and emphasis in the characters' voices while staying true to the story as written. We can help others see and hear the story more vividly, and hopefully entice and train them through this modeling into more engrossed private readings of the English Bible.

(c) Affect.

If one thinks strictly of exegetical tasks, the exegete may say that whether the story is retold well or not, the story line is the same, and therefore exegesis will arrive at the same big ideas. However, story is not merely a cognitive exercise.

Listening for the pauses is part of a larger process of entering into the story in order to be moved and altered by it. We project action on our mental movie screen and experience the emotion of the drama in a joint strategy to let concepts and values penetrate our psyche and our worldview. The story as a whole contains a large affective element which supports the teachings it contains.

(d) Application.

While application may not be a direct result of noticing pausal forms, affect relates to application. A story cannot be reduced to a single proposition or big idea. The story form is the vehicle for applications and the stuff of reflective contemplation. Biblical narratives are not exegetical problems to conquer; they are invitations to a conversation with the lives of others and their God. In that conversation we are to be conquered by the story.

We need to think in terms of story as well as principles. We find an example in science fiction from Star Trek: The Next Generation. The 2nd episode of season 5, *Darmok*, presents Captain Picard and crew with a cross-cultural communication barrier. Although the computer translates the words into English, they find that the Tamarians communicate with reference to stories from their culture. The Tamarian Captain and First Officer disagree on whether they should proceed like one story or another. Their Captain thinks this encounter should be like "Darmok and Jalag at Tanagra." The first officer objects, "Zima, at Anso! Zima and Bakor... Mirab, his sails unfurled." By the end, Picard can tell the Tamarian First Officer how things turned out, "Shaka, when the walls fell." To them, the reference to a story scene conveys what happened.

Similarly, while the Bible could simply say, "do not harden your hearts," Psalm 95:8ff says not to harden them "as at Meribah, As in the time at Massah in the wilderness" and goes on to refer to more of the story. The story helps the message sink in. As the Tamarian Captain describes his plan, "Darmok and Jalag at Tanagra," Psalm 95 warns its hearers with "Israel, in the wilderness, when they provoked God." The affective element is part of application. We can cite a principle, e.g. "Do not covet." Or we can say, "Eve, when she ate the forbidden fruit." The story package, affectively well told, is part of application taking hold.

In summary, Biblical Hebrew narratives are great literature – in Hebrew – not merely exegetical problems to solve. Learning pausal forms and paying close attention to "rule-breaking" uses of *dagesh* can contribute to homiletical skills. Particularly in speech, these clues from the Masoretes inform the Hebrew reader of subtleties that aid in entering into the drama of the story.

23.5   Summary.

(a) The principal point of the chapter has been to remind us how intriguing the Biblical stories are, that all the little pieces we work on are directed to a larger goal. Do pay attention to the pieces. Connect them to the larger whole. And retell them well.

(b) Reading signals.

Pauses in reading may be indicated by major accents, pausal forms, or *dagesh lene* following a vowel. *Maqqef* and *dagesh forte* beginning a word indicate a close connection in speech.

The speed of narrative time can vary. Long events or sequences can be quickly summarized, or lots of detail can put narrative time into slow motion. The repetition of וַיֹּאמֶר when the same character is speaking also indicates a pause in narrative action.

The major accents are *sof pasuq* :◻◻, *aṭnaḥ* ◻, *zaqqef parvum* ◻̇, *zaqqef magnum* ◻̈, *rebia* ◻̇, *segolta* ◻̊, and *shalshelet* ◻̊.

chapter twenty-four

*Lexicography:
Semantic Combinations
and the Meaning of* פָּקַד

24.1   Focus.

Your vocabulary lists have included Hebrew words and corresponding English words. Glossaries and dictionaries do the same. The English words are not truly definitions; they are glosses, words that could be used in English, depending on the circumstances. But a particular English gloss cannot be used in any and every situation. The purpose of this chapter is to help you observe the circumstances that affect a word's meaning or translation.

Meaning in language is not a mere matter of stringing words together but arises from the combination of words, grammar, syntax, and larger discourse features. This chapter uses the verb פָּקַד to illustrate ways in which words, or lexemes, combine with other elements to create meanings. As a result you should be better able to make use of a Hebrew dictionary and to make translation decisions.

Approach dictionaries with more questions in mind than "what does this word mean?" Ask about the circumstances in which the word is used and compare the entries in the dictionary to each other and the Hebrew text you are studying.

First we will present some basic theoretical foundations for lexical studies; then we will illustrate many of the issues with the word פָּקַד. The purpose is not to become expert on פָּקַד but to display issues in lexical studies.

24.2   Theoretical Issues.

A dictionary consists of a list of words; each entry of the list has more words in explanation. From these obvious features we may ask several questions and make several observations. How do words mean more than one thing in the dictionary, but only one thing in a sentence? And why do speakers choose the words they choose?

(a)   Word choices; Paradigmatic relationships and references to reality.

As a list of words, a dictionary represents a pool of words available to speakers in the language community. Aside from occasionally inventing a word, or borrowing one from another language, speakers choose from those they know in keeping with their use by the language community. Speakers may choose their words because certain words best represent something in the real world they wish to describe. *The brown horse ran through the green meadow*. If a brown horse ran through a green meadow, then *the blue pig floated over the gray mountain* will not do at all to communicate the reality that the speaker wants to describe. The meanings of words are constrained by the baggage that the speaking community has attached to them. If *pig* means *horse*, it's not English. If *dog* means *fish*, it's not English; it's דָג.

On the other hand, words do not correspond simplistically to realities. One could also say *the chestnut stallion galloped across the lush meadow* and still refer to the same reality as *the brown horse ran through the green meadow*. These sentences, or utterances,[1] do not say the same thing; but they might refer to the same reality.[2]

Since more than one expression may refer to the same reality, it follows that speakers may choose their words in order to be distinct from a similar description. Some people (unfamiliar with horse terminology) may describe a horse as walking, running, or even jogging, while other people will differentiate trotting, cantering, galloping, etc. A cook might be complimented for a *good* meal, or for a meal that is not just good but *fabulous*. The descriptions come from the same type of words but distinguish (in this case) a matter of degree. But different words do not always have distinct referents. After one speaker has complimented the cook for an *excellent* main dish, another guest may agree by saying it is *wonderful*. The first speaker chooses *excellent* over *good* in order to make a stronger compliment. The second speaker chooses *wonderful* for stylistic variation rather than for any "exegetical" significance as to whether *wonderful* is better than or otherwise different from *excellent* in meaning.

Speakers choose their words from an existing set of words partly because of what the words can correspond to and partly to differentiate from words of similar meaning, though more than one expression may suit their purpose equally well.

A group of words which are related by sharing a piece of meaning comprise a **semantic field**. The larger pool of words used by the language community can be divided into various levels of semantic fields, e.g. verbs of motion, verbs of motion of living creatures, verbs of motion of horses. Words that can meaningfully replace each other in a sentence are in a **paradigmatic** relationship, e.g. verbs that can describe horse movements are in a paradigmatic relationship with each other.

---

[1] The term *sentence* has a technical meaning which includes a subject and a predicate. The term *utterance* is broader and includes meaningful communication, spoken or written, even if it is not a sentence. In this chapter, we may use *sentence* with the broader meaning of an *utterance*. Similarly, we are using *speaker* to mean someone making an *utterance*, including written expressions.

[2] Non-equestrians might lump several horse colors under "brown."

A word is considered to be a **sign** or a **symbol**. As an approach to the meaning of words, **signification** deals with how the words (signs) in a language relate to each other. The reality[3] to which a word refers is its **referent**. As an approach to the meaning of words, **denotation** deals with how words specify their referents.

(b) Words as containers of potential meaning; semantic components.

Although words do point to realities, words do not correspond to realities in a one-to-one fashion. Just as the same reality may be pointed to by different words, the same word can point to more than one reality. That is why entries in a dictionary have more than one explanation. The dictionary must account for the meaning of *letter* in *the mail carrier brought five letters* and in *'horse' has five letters. Letter* may refer to a character of the alphabet or to a piece of correspondence. As an entry in the dictionary, *letter* may have either meaning. But put into a sentence, it has only one meaning.[4] In a sentence, a word is in relationships with other language elements. Those relationships point to each word's meaning as intended by the speaker.

The potential meanings that a word may have are together called its **semantic range**. The actual meaning of a word in a sentence is called its **specific use** or **semantic use**. The pieces of meaning which make up its semantic range or which can be employed for a specific use are called its **semantic components**.

Approaching the meaning of a word in terms of its semantic components (called **componential analysis**) has some usefulness as well as limitations. We may understand certain *horse* terms by listing their semantic components. *Stallion, mare, colt, filly*, and *foal* can be distinguished based on gender and age. In the following chart, + means the word has that component, x means the word may have that component, - means the word does not have that component.

	horse	male	female	adult
stallion	+	+	-	+
mare	+	-	+	+
colt	+	+	-	-
filly	+	-	+	-
foal	+	x	x	- -[5]

Approaching word meaning through componential analysis is more useful with nouns and adjectives than other parts of speech. Still, viewing words as a collection of semantic pieces can provide a handle for describing how words supply meaning.

---

[3] The "reality" may be a fictional reality, also known as the world of the discourse. For example, terms like *orc, dwarf,* and *elf* refer to specific "realities" within the discourse world of J.R.R. Tolkien's Middle Earth (J.R.R. Tolkien, *The Lord of the Rings*, New York: Ballantine, 1965).

[4] Sometimes a speaker may intend more than one meaning, called a *double entendre*, such as in making a joke which depends on a play on words.

[5] A foal is a newborn.

For example, *throne* has semantic components including *chair* and *royalty*. In a sentence like *the throne of England said today...*, we understand that chairs do not talk, so the semantic component of royalty is promoted; the referent of *throne* is actually the Queen.[6] In contrast, the semantic piece of *royalty* is deleted or used ironically in a sentence like *he's upstairs on the throne*. As a crass or comical way of referring to someone using the toilet, the *chair* component has been modified while any *royalty* component may come from distorting the idea that *a man's home is his castle*. Thinking of semantic components helps us describe what has happened.

(c) Meaning from combinations: the whole is more than the pieces.

So we can view words as containers of potential meaning, like buckets with semantic pieces inside. The word is chosen because it has semantic pieces that can point to the reality the speaker wants to communicate (its correspondence value). And it is chosen in distinction from other available words (its paradigmatic contrast). Once a word is put into a sentence,[7] the context points to which semantic pieces are being used. Context clarifies that the mail carrier brought five pieces of correspondence, not five characters of the alphabet.

Consider the meaning of *dust* in *dust the house*. Using *dust* as a verb means there is an activity involving dust. Saying *dust the house* (instead of *dust the crops*) indicates that *dusting* means removing the dust (not putting it on). Just as *the house* points to the proper meaning of *dust*, *dust* points to the proper meaning of *the house*. *Dust the house* means [Remove] dust [from items inside] the house. This sentence focuses on the results to be achieved. In order to actually remove the dust, *dusting* includes picking up small items and wiping flat surfaces with a cloth. *Dusting* may point to a reality that includes these activities, but the word *dusting* does not "mean" *picking up small items and wiping flat surfaces with a cloth*. On the one hand *dust the house* means more than *an activity involving dust* plus *the house*. On the other hand, the individual words in *dust the house* do not denote all of the realities to which the phrase points.

(d) Translation and dictionaries: glosses vs. definitions.

Glosses are words in one language that could be used to translate a word from another language. Definitions are descriptions of meaning. For example the Hebrew word רוּץ can be glossed in English as *run*. But רוּץ and *run* are not the same thing; *run* does not define רוּץ. The definition of *run* might be: fast bi-pedal motion in which both feet come off the ground at the same time and move in a left, right, left, right sequence. This would contrast with the definition of *skip* as: fast bi-pedal

---

[6] This is called metonymy, where one thing stands for another.

[7] Again, we may use the sentence for convenient reference, but relationships outside the immediate sentence, or utterance, may be the key elements.

motion in which both feet come off the ground at the same time in the sequence left, right, right, left, left, etc. *Run* also contrasts with *jog* and *walk*, but includes *sprint*, relationships which could be indicated by defining the semantic components of these words. However, *run* means something altogether different in *my nose is running*, *her hose are running*, *she is running for office* or *the river is running*. רוּץ is not "defined" by *run*, but *run* can be used to gloss רוּץ under the correct circumstances. Under other circumstances, *run* would not be an acceptable gloss for רוּץ and רוּץ would not be an acceptable gloss for *run*. When you use a Hebrew dictionary, you must come with the knowledge that it gives glosses rather than definitions and come with the question, "under what circumstances is this gloss useable?" The entries in a dictionary rarely answer that question directly. Instead they may provide examples, on the basis of which you can answer the question indirectly.

(e) *Dictionaries and information.*

Dictionaries do not merely include a list of glosses. They often supply additional information. Dictionaries may include information about the semantic field. For example, *The New International Dictionary of Old Testament Theology and Exegesis*[8] refers to related words in its entries and includes indices to semantic fields in vol. 5. *The Dictionary of Classical Hebrew*[9] (*DCH*) also identifies parallel and opposite terms in its entries.

Dictionaries may also give contextual clues. A dictionary may distinguish meanings by noting when a verb or noun is used with one or another preposition or in other combinations. These combinations may be called syntagmemes or collocations. *DCH* is probably the most deliberate in including syntactic information, but most of the dictionaries will include some.

Whatever dictionary you use, you need to come to it with questions about the word in the passage(s) you are looking up. How is the word related to its context? What kinds of relationships is it in? How does this compare to the kinds of examples given in the dictionary entry? Although you use a dictionary as a reference tool, remember that the dictionary is not the Bible, even metaphorically speaking. It is a collection of opinions. The more important thing is a meaningful comparison of your word in its context to a similar construction with a clear meaning.

---

[8] Willem A. VanGemeren, ed., *The New International Dictionary of Old Testament Theology and Exegesis* (Grand Rapids: Zondervan, 1997). This dictionary is complete in 5 vols.
[9] David J. A. Clines, ed., *The Dictionary of Classical Hebrew* (Sheffield: Sheffield Academic Press, 1993-).

24.3   Semantic Combinations and the Meaning of פָּקַד.

This treatment of פָּקַד intends to demonstrate the interplay of words and other elements to create meaning. To some degree it will be helpful to identify the basic meaning, or focal components, of פָּקַד. פָּקַד involves taking note of something. It may mean taking note of someone or something and often implies taking an action corresponding to an assessment of the situation. פָּקַד can also note that one thing is to be associated with another (as in placing or assigning). The various specific uses of the word, however specialized, seem derivable from these features.

Our discussion will treat first those meanings that center on taking note of something and secondly on those related to assigning. The discussions will include formulaic ways of describing the syntactic environment in which a meaning occurs. For example,

(Qal) פָּקַד + D. O. /sin/ + עַל + /person/

means a Qal form of פָּקַד occurring with a direct object which is a word in the semantic field of *sin* and a phrase consisting of the preposition עַל with a person as its object. The order of the elements can vary. For example, the prepositional phrase may come before the direct object.

24.3.1   Assessing and acting: punishing or assisting.

This section shows how different syntax, such as the type of direct object and prepositional phrase and other contextual elements, helps to signal a word's meaning. It also illustrates the difference between a gloss and what a word means.

The King James Version often translated פָּקַד with the word *visit*, a translation that no longer works in English. פָּקַד can contribute the semantic pieces of taking note of something in the sense of inspecting and assessing it. It also carries the implication of acting based on that assessment. פָּקַד may refer to acts of punishing (the implication of noting one's sin against them) or assisting (noting someone for blessing). So it may be glossed *inspect*, *assess*, *punish*, or *assist*. Either *punish* or *assist* may be chosen when the emphasis is on the implied action. But these two different "meanings" also depend on the syntactic environment of פָּקַד.

(a) **Punishing:** Qal פָּקַד + D. O. /sin/ + עַל + /person/[10]

The most common construction used for punishing is the Qal of פָּקַד with a direct object which is some sin or evil, and the preposition עַל plus the person punished. Jer 36:31 is a typical example.

---

[10] 2Sam 3:8 (the only case where God is not the agent); Exod 20:5; 32:34 (2nd); 34:7; Lev 18:25; Num 14:18; De 5:9; Is 13:11; 26:21; Jer 6:6; 21:14; 23:2 (2nd); 25:12; 36:31; Hos 1:4; 2:15 (Eng 13); 4:9, 14; 12:3; Amos 3:2, 14 (1st). Hos 4:14 has a clause indicating sins as the direct object.

Jer 36:31   אֶת־עֲוֹנָם   וְעַל־עֲבָדָיו   עָלָיו   וּפָקַדְתִּי

| D.O. indicator | and against | against | I will take note |
| + their iniquity | his servants | him | |

I will[11] note their iniquity against him and his servants.

In English, we usually change the verb to *punish* and then turn the object of the preposition into a direct object and turn the direct object into a preposition's object.

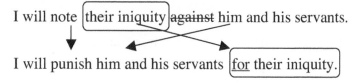

But *punish* is only a gloss in English. פקד does not "mean" *punish*. To describe the same reality, we could choose other glosses. Instead of *punish* we could use *hold accountable for*. Or we could stay closer to the meaning of פקד and translate *take note (of your sin against you), account (your sin against you), hold (your sin against you)* or *call (your sin to account against you)*. Each of these represents the pieces in the פקד-bucket, which includes taking note of something and implies an action. But פקד would not then "mean" *hold* or *call*, etc., just as פקד does not "mean" *punish*. It is simply used in a setting where the referent of the entire construction can be described in English by the semantic pieces in the word *punish*. That setting involves taking note of someone's wrongdoing and acting to their disadvantage, i.e. noting /sins/ against someone: Qal פקד + D. O. /sin/ + עַל + /person/.

Looking at a dictionary entry or studying a word necessitates making comparisons. Compare the formula expressed above in Jer 36:31 to Hos 1:4.

Hos 1:4   עַל־בֵּית יֵהוּ   אֶת־דְּמֵי יִזְרְעֶאל   וּפָקַדְתִּי

| against the house | D.O. indicator + | I will take note |
| of Jehu | the blood of Jezreel | |

I will call the blood of Jezreel to account against the house of Jehu.

Strictly speaking, the direct object *blood* is not in the semantic field of /sin/. And *house*, when separated from a context, is not considered a /person/. However, the construct plus "genitive," *blood of Jezreel*, stands for *bloodshed at Jezreel* and refers to a wrong act. And the *house of Jehu* refers not to his domicile but to Jehu's line, or extended family. Thus all the right parts of the formula are present. Hos 1:4 is directly comparable to the formula in Jer 36:31 when we recognize that the word for sin may be replaced by another expression of sin.[12]

---

[11] וּפָקַדְתִּי is a perfect consecutive, carrying on the future time frame already established by the context.

[12] Other expressions of sin: Jer 21:14 *the fruit of your deeds*; Hos 2:15 (Eng 13) *the days of the Baals*; 4:9 *their ways*, 14 *harlotry*.

Punishment passages demonstrate that several syntactic combinations can produce the same meaning. The key thing is for the context to combine the three elements: פָקַד, the sin noted, and the person punished. The person punished may not be the object of the preposition עַל. These three may also be brought together by having the /person/ occur as a pronominal suffix on the word for sin. For example:

Hos 8:13   וְיִפְקֹד חַטֹּאותָם   *He will call their sin to account.*

We can observe that in these passages,[13] the person(s) have already been discussed (i.e. fronted[14] in the paragraph) which is why they can be referred back to by a pronoun. Apparently this paragraph structure makes the prepositional phrase with עַל optional. On the one hand, these varied constructions show that the most common formula (Qal פָקַד + D. O. /sin/ + עַל + /personal/) is not the only way to describe punishing, and on the other hand they show that the same *functions* of the direct object and the עַל phrase are handled elsewhere in the discourse.[15]

Rather than say that פָקַד has a certain meaning and may or may not be collocated with עַל, the thing to do is compare the circumstances under which פָקַד conveys that meaning. This example also warns you to look for the same functions being performed, but not always the same grammatical or lexical items.

(b) **Assisting:** Qal פָקַד + D. O. /person/ + context.

A different syntactical construction is used when helping rather than punishing someone. In these, the Qal of פָקַד usually takes a personal[16] direct object and the context describes the benefits received. The meaning of פָקַד is still *to take note of* with an implied action, but the context of giving benefits can justify English glosses such as *assist*, *attend to*, or sometimes *provide for*.

Gen 21:1	דִּבֵּר	כַּאֲשֶׁר	יְהוָה	וַיַּעַשׂ	... אֶת־שָׂרָה	פָקַד	וַיהוָה
	he had said	just as	the LORD	and he did	D.O. + Sara	he took note of	The LORD

The LORD attended to Sara and did just as he had said (i.e. she conceived).

Both the context and the syntax (the person is the direct object rather than the object of עַל) indicate פָקַד's meaning in the sentence.

---

[13] Jer 14:10; Hos 8:13; 9:9; Ps 89:33 (Eng 32).

[14] That is, the paragraph began with reference to the person, marking that person as the topic of the paragraph. "Fronting" may also be called "topicalizing."

[15] There are a few other variations. In 1Sam 15:2 the sinning agent is noted in a relative clause which itself functions as the direct object specifying the sin. In addition, the person punished becomes the subject of a passive verb in Jer 6:6 in the MT (but the Septuagint suggests that the text should be different). The sin also may be identified in a relative clause describing the person in the prepositional phrase begun by עַל (Jer 9:24 [Eng 25]; 30:20; Zeph 1:8, 9, 12). Is 10:12 places the /sin/ in the עַל phrase, which also includes the person being punished.

[16] Gen 21:1; 50:24, 25; Exod 3:16; 4:31; 13:19; 1Sam 2:21; Jer 15:15; 27:22; 29:10; Zeph 2:7; Ps 106:4; Ruth 1:6; Jer 32:5. In Jer 32:5 the good thing, getting out of prison, is implied. Twice the direct object is impersonal. Ps 80:15 (Eng 14) concerns a vine which represents Israel. In Ps 65:10 (Eng 9) God attends to the earth, giving it fertility.

(c) **Assisting, Punishing, or Inspecting:** Qal פקד + context.

In future time constructions, פקד may refer to punishing or assisting as indicated by the context. These state that God will take notice of someone in the future, with either punishment or restoration implied by the larger discourse units.[17] But פקד may refer to other actions besides punishing or assisting. Some sort of inspection is often involved and/or an intent to act in a certain manner.[18] A variety of glosses can be used, depending on the nature of the implied activity. *Inspect* or *assess* may be adequate.[19] For example, when Jesse sends David with provisions for his brothers, he instructs,

1Sam 17:18 לְשָׁלוֹם תִּפְקֹד וְאֶת־אַחֶיךָ
regarding welfare | Notice! | your brothers

Assess your brothers regarding welfare. = See how your brothers are doing.

24.3.2 Counting vs. Mustering.

Again distinguishing a gloss from a word's meaning, this section considers how a word relates to other words with similar meaning as well as how it refers to reality. It also illustrates that language changes over time.

A special form of notation is counting. פקד frequently means *to count*, especially counting people.[20] Because it is used in military contexts it is often translated *muster*. How does the word relate to the reality? Many things may be happening in the reality being described, but the sentence only refers to some of those features. English *muster* means to assemble troops for inspection, roll call, or service. Does פקד "mean" *muster*? Or does it simply mean *count*, and happens to be

---

[17] Exod 32:34; Is 24:22 (Ni.); Jer 6:15; 49:8; 50:3; Ezek 38:8 (Ni.); Ps 59:6 (5). With עַל + /person/ it refers to punishment. The context may state offenses. Frequently the contexts indicate the punishments or means of punishment: Is 24:21, 22; 27:1; 29:6 (Ni.); Jer 5:9, 29; 9:8; 11:22; 27:8; 29:32; 44:13 (2x), 29; 46:25; 50:18 (1st and 2nd) (using אֶל); 51:44; Zech 10:3 (1st), similarly Jer 51: 47, 52, and Amos 3:14 (2nd), which concern an altar rather than a person. On one occasion, Is 26:14, there is neither a direct object nor a prepositional phrase but the context indicates the judgment and פקד is followed by a verb with a pronominal suffix representing who is punished.

[18] Judg 15:1; 1Sam 17:18; 2Ki 9:34; Is 27:3; Jer 23:2 (1st); Ezek 23:21; Zech 10:3 (2nd); 11:16; Ps 17:3; Prov 19:23 (Ni.); Job 5:24; 7:18; 31:14; and possibly Is 26:16.

[19] Still the KJV's common *visit* no longer works. An exception to this may be Judg 15:1 where Samson goes to "visit" his wife. But considering that he brings a young goat (as a gift for his father-in-law?) and wants to come (בוא) to his wife in her room, an implication that he wants to act in accordance with the marital situation is quite likely.

[20] Qal finite verb: Num 1:3, 19, 44 (2nd), 49; 3:15 (2nd), 16, 39 (2nd), 42; 4:23, 29, 30, 34, 37 (2nd), 45 (2nd), 46 (2nd) 49 (1st); 26:63 (2nd), 64 (2nd); Josh 8:10; 1Sam 11:8; 13:15; 15:4; 14:17 (2nd); 2Sam 18:1; 1Ki 20:15 (1st & 2nd), 26; 2Ki 3:6; Qal inf. constr.: Exod 30:12 (2nd & 3rd); 2Sam 24:4; Qal imv. Num 3:15 (1st), 40; 1Sam 14:17 (1st); 2Sam 24:2; Qal pass. ptc.: Exod 30:12 (1st), 13, 14; 38:21 (1st), 25, 26; Num 1: 21, 22, 23, 25, 27, 29, 31, 33, 35, 37, 39, 41, 44 (1st), 45, 46; 2: 4, 6, 8, 9, 11, 13, 15, 16, 19, 21, 24, 26, 28, 30, 31, 32 (1st & 2nd); 3:22 (1st & 2nd), 34, 39 (1st); 43; 4:36, 37 (1st), 38, 40, 41 (1st), 42, 45 (1st), 46 (1st), 48, 49 (2nd); 7:2; 14:29; 26:7, 18, 22, 25, 27, 34, 37, 41, 43, 47, 50, 51, 54, 57, 62 (1st), 63 (1st), 64 (1st), 1Chr 23:24; Pual: Exod 38:21 (2nd); Num 4:49 (2nd); 26:64 (2nd); Hot.: Num 1:47; 2:33; 26:62; 1Ki 20:27; Hit.: Judg 20:15 (1st & 2nd), 17; 21:9 (all pertaining to the war on Benjamin); Piel ptc.: Is 13:4. Possibly also Ezek 38:8, a Niphal.

used in contexts where fighters are being called on and counted? To address the question we must consider the relation between פקד and other words in the language system as well as between פקד and the events of military preparation.[21]

(a) פקד *and other words for counting,* ספר *and* מנה.

By way of comparison, the verb ספר occurs 35 times in the Qal and Niphal with a meaning related to *counting.* ספר usually counts objects or time spans. It is said of people seven times, either that they cannot "be counted"[22] or when they are registered or counted in a census.[23] The close association with being registered raises the question of whether ספר refers only to *counting.*[24] But its rarity shows that it is not the default word for *counting*, especially for counting people.

מנה is also used for counting and for assigning but occurs only 36 times. Fifteen times מנה means *to appoint, assign*, a meaning shared by פקד. But these uses of מנה have a predominantly late distribution and foreign audience or setting.[25] This may indicate changes in the language over time (diachronic developments), i.e. מנה appears to move into the semantic space of פקד. But for most of Biblical Hebrew, we observe that מנה and ספר are not the common words for counting. Paradigmatically, פקד is the default word for counting people. Now then, if people are counted at the time of a muster, does the word for counting them mean *muster*?

(b) פקד *and other elements of military preparation.*

We should also observe other words used in the process of getting troops together for battle. Though not all occur in the same passage, we see that troops may be summoned (צעק or Pi. שמע) with the implication that they actually respond and assemble. They may be assembled (אסף), counted (פקד or מנה), outfitted (כלכל) and arranged for battle (ערך).

Next consider some military contexts in which פקד appears. 1Sam 15:4 initially uses שמע (Pi.) for calling the troops together, then פקד for counting them, followed by their numbers. In 1Ki 20:25 Ben-hadad's Aramean servants advise him to מנה an army like his previous one. He then counts out the new army in verse 26, the action now indicated by the narrator with פקד. In verse 27, the Israelites are both counted (פקד) and then outfitted (כלכל). The context focuses on having an equivalently

---

[21] It is beyond the scope of this illustration to adequately consider the cognate languages. Akkadian *paqādu*, for example, has a military meaning. Stephen Kaufman remarks that "The wide range of meanings of this verb in the various Semitic languages allows for the possibility of various mutual influences." *The Akkadian Influences on Aramaic* (Chicago: University of Chicago Press, 1974), p. 79.

[22] Gen 16:10; 1Ki 3:8.

[23] 2Sam 24:10; Ps 87:6; 1Chr 21:2; 23:3; 2Chr 2:17.

[24] Perhaps it is related to *marking down.*

[25] Is 65:12; Jonah 1:17; 4:6, 7, 8; Ps 61:7; Job 7:3; Dan 1:5, 10, 11; 2:24, 49; 3:12; Ezra 7:25; 1Chr 9:29. It is likewise a late setting for most of the uses of ספר for counting people, but the sample is too small to be significant.

sized army rather than on roll call. Either *tallying up* or *counting off* the army could convey the sense well.

In Judges 20:11 and 14, the forces of Israel and Benjamin are assembled, an action indicated by אָסַף, the most common word for assembling (i.e. *mustering*) troops. Then in verses 15 and 17 each force is counted (פָּקַד) and their total numbers indicated. With the people already assembled, פָּקַד properly refers to counting.

In 1Sam 24:2, David sends Joab, commander of the army, throughout the tribes to פָּקַד the people. As a result, David would know the number of the people. Surely, פָּקַד means *count* rather than *muster* in this passage, because the people are not assembled.

פָּקַד seems to not mean calling the troops together, or assembling them, or outfitting them. And even though military preparation may be involved, we frequently are told the *numbers* of the people. This certainly suggests that actual *counting* has occurred. The English word *muster* may seem to work, but it is not certain that פָּקַד actually has the same technical meaning as *muster*. The call and assembly of these "troops" does not specifically refer to the roll call of a standing army, it often means blowing the shofar and hoping able-bodied farmers show up with some tool that can be used to hit people. After they are assembled (as indicated by אָסַף), then they are *counted*, indicated by פָּקַד, to see how many have come.

24.3.3 Missing? and Empty?

This section again illustrates the difference between a gloss and a word's meaning and the relationship between a word and the reality to which it refers.

According to the dictionaries, פָּקַד can be glossed *miss* or *be missing*.[26] The Niphal is used for the sense of *be missing* and both the Niphal and the Qal for *miss*. 1Sam 20:18 offers an interesting example. David plans to skip a feast at the palace for fear of king Saul. But Jonathan says,

מָחָר חֹדֶשׁ וְנִפְקַדְתָּ כִּי יִפָּקֵד מוֹשָׁבֶךָ

Most translations render Jonathan's warning to David, "Tomorrow is the new moon, so *you will be missed because your seat will be empty*." Does פָּקַד now mean *miss* and *empty*? This no doubt reflects the reality that Jonathan anticipated. Yet one may also say, "you will be *noticed* because your seat will be *noteworthy*." This example at least raises the question as to whether the English *miss* works so well in some passages that we confuse our workable gloss with the meaning of the Hebrew term. Or perhaps *miss* derived from *being conspicuous by virtue of absence* when the context shows that one's presence is expected. And as a result *miss* has become part of its meaning.

---

[26] Num 31:49; Judg. 21:3; 1Sam 20:6, 18 (2x), 25, 27; 25:7, 15, 21; 2Sam 2:30; 1Ki 20:39; 2Ki 10:19 (2x); Is 34:16; Jer 3:16; 23:4; and possibly Is 38:10.

24.3.4 Assigning.

This section illustrates how factors not expressed in words relate to word meaning. It also provides an example of the role of syntax.

פָּקַד may also note one thing or person for a relationship to another person or thing, typically a relationship of oversight or placement. So פָּקַד can be glossed *to appoint* or *assign*, or *to put* or *to place*. The dictionaries recognize that both the Qal and the Hiphil can be glossed as *assign*, but may not explain a difference between them. We must turn to context. The Qal and Hiphil uses of פָּקַד, meaning *assign*, can be explained on the basis of existing authority structures.

(a) Assigning responsibility in an existing authority structure:

Qal פָּקַד + D. O. /person/ + prep. עַל or אֵת + /person/

Persons who already have authority are given a responsibility over other people[27] in the Qal. In Gen 40:4, Joseph has already been promoted in responsibilities in the prison. When Pharaoh's butler and baker are thrown in jail,

וַיִּפְקֹד שַׂר הַטַּבָּחִים אֶת־יוֹסֵף אִתָּם

The captain of the guard assigned Joseph to them.

The general structure is the Qal of פָּקַד with a personal direct object who is assigned over person(s) indicated by the prepositions אֵת or עַל.[28] The group for which a person has oversight or responsibility may be implied by the context rather than mentioned in the sentence.[29] Notice how similar this construction is to that for punishing; it differs in the type of word which fills the direct object role.

Qal פָּקַד + D. O. /impersonal/ + עַל + /person/

People are also assigned a responsibility or duty within their existing authority[30] in the Qal. The general structure is the Qal of פָּקַד with an impersonal direct object (often an infinitive)[31] assigned in relation to a person, indicated by the preposition

---

[27] Gen 40:4; Num 3:10; 27:16; De 20:9; Jer 13:21; 49:19; 50:44 ; 51:27.

[28] There are too few occurrences to establish different nuances for the prepositions, but it may depend on the level of parity between the person given the assignment and the others involved. אֵת would reflect more parity, e.g. *assign with/to*; עַל would reflect more subordination, e.g. *assign over*. אֶל is used in Jer 49:19 (= 50:44) if this is not a mistake for עַל. Curiously, the five cases of אֶל with פָּקַד occur in Jer 46–50 (46:25; 49:19 = 50:44; and twice in 50:18). A different nuance or a diachronic shift in preposition usage? An idiolect of Jeremiah's or a scribe's copying problem?

[29] As in Num 3:10 and De 20:9.

[30] Num 4:27, 32; Job 34:13; 36:23; Ezra 1:2; 2Chr 36:23.

[31] The impersonal direct object is expressed by a noun or infinitive phrase. The Numbers references refer to tabernacle objects and the Gershonites' or Merarites' duty to care for them. The Job references refer to אֶרֶץ as a sphere of authority and to דֶּרֶךְ as a sphere of behavior, these being construed as duties or parameters of authority for God in rhetorical questions. The reference in Ezra and its repetition in 2Chr uses לִבְנוֹת לוֹ בַיִת in the slot for direct object.

עַל. In Ezra 1:2 Cyrus claims that God has given him the earth's kingdoms and furthermore,

וְהוּא־פָקַד עָלַי לִבְנוֹת־לוֹ בַיִת בִּירוּשָׁלִָם

he assigned to me to build him a house in Jerusalem.

As with punishment passages, the preposition עַל may be omitted if its function is otherwise handled by the context. For example, Num 4 discusses the duties of the Gershonites and the Merarites. In verse 27, the Gershonites are the object of the preposition עַל, but not the Merarites in verse 32. As verse 29 begins with בְּנֵי מְרָרִי, the Merarites are fronted as the topic of a paragraph, something not true of the Gershonites in the preceding unit.

(b) Assigning new authority:

Hiphil פָקַד + D. O. /person/ + prep. + /person or place/

Initial investments of authority are indicated by the Hiphil. The general structure is the Hiphil of פָקַד with a personal direct object assigned in relation to objects and places[32] or to people.[33] After defeating Judah, Nebuchadnezzar appoints Gedaliah as governor.

וַיַּפְקֵד עֲלֵיהֶם אֶת־גְּדַלְיָהוּ 2Ki 25:22

He appointed Gedaliah over them.

The verb פָקַד places the person (direct object) in relation to the object, place, or person(s) by means of a preposition, עַל or בְּ.[34] If פָקַד occurs in a relative clause modifying the person(s), then the prepositional phrase is not needed.[35]

The choice between using the Qal or Hiphil of פָקַד appears to depend on whether the person already had authority or not. For example, the jailer appoints Joseph over Pharaoh's baker and cup bearer with the Qal of פָקַד (Gen 40:4). The jailer had already given Joseph responsibility over the prisoners (Gen 39:22), so this represents no new investment of authority, merely an assignment within an existing structure. The contexts show that the rest of the cases where the Qal is used may be qualified in the same way. Potiphar, however, invested Joseph with authority over

---

[32] Gen 39:4, 5; 41:34; Num 1:50; Josh 10:18; 2Ki 7:17; Is 62:6; Esth 2:3; and those concerning Gedaliah: Jer 40:5, 7; 41:2, 18.

[33] Jer 1:10; Ps 109:6; 1Chr 26:32; and those concerning Gedaliah: 2Ki 25:22, 23; Jer 40:11; 41:10.

[34] For the Gedaliah passages, בְּ is used for places and עַל for people. In 2Ki 25:23 the reference to people is missing and so there is no preposition, although עַל would be expected. Elsewhere עַל is used for both persons and places, with two exceptions. Esth 2:3 uses בְּ for *in the provinces*. That is, the appointees do not have oversight of the provinces but rather a responsibility to fulfill within the provinces. In Jer 37:21, Jeremiah is the direct object and is assigned/placed in (בְּ) the court of the guardhouse. As such we might suggest he is treated as an object and that this verse is part of placing rather than assigning. Once לְ relates the person to a task. In 1Ki 11:28 לְ occurs with the infrequent סֵבֶל which, as a word referring to a task, differs from the other examples in this category.

[35] Cf. Jer 41:10.

his possessions with the Hiphil of פקד (Gen 39:4). This is a first-time event and the Hiphil is the consistent choice for such.[36]

New categories of assignment are also given in the Hiphil even to persons already having certain responsibilities. For example, in 2Ki 7:17 the king gives his steward the specific responsibility of overseeing the gate when the starving people of Samaria were permitted to go out and plunder the enemy camp. Even though it is presupposed that the steward already had other responsibilities, the peculiarity of the situation suggests that this duty represented a categorically new assignment. Similarly in Josh 10:18, the singular task of monitoring five kings, who have become trapped in a cave, is assigned to some soldiers with the Hiphil.

The distinction appears to be maintained in passive constructions and with participles. The Hophal participles all refer to persons appointed to oversee specific temple refurbishing projects, under either Joash or Josiah.[37] As specific projects, they can be understood as specially assigned tasks. So where a Hiphil would be expected in a construction with a finite verb, the Hophal participle is used rather than the Qal. The Qal participles refer to army officers in passages where the positions are not being set up at the time.[38] The three Niphal references, which would be considered passive to the Qal usages, do not appear to assign new categories of duty.[39] Since the newness of the assignment is part of the background information, rather than the sentences themselves, this explanation of the difference between the Qal and Hiphil of פקד must remain an inference.

(c) *Assigning calamity:* פקד + D.O. /calamity/ + על + /person/

Separate from the issue of responsibilities, פקד notes or appoints a calamity on people, once with the Hiphil and twice in the Qal.[40] There are not enough examples to determine the difference between the stems. Sending a calamity can be considered a punishment, but this way of saying it differs from the earlier punishment constructions. Compare how word meaning interacts with syntax.

פקד + D.O. /calamity/ + על + /person/	= appoint a calamity against someone
פקד + D.O. /sin/ + על + /person/	= call sin to account against someone
פקד + D.O. /person/ + על + /person/	= assign someone over a person
פקד + D.O. /task/ + על + /person/	= assign a task to a person

Often verb meanings come from the verb plus a preposition. In the case of פקד, its meaning also depends on the nature of the direct object.

---

[36] If an original investment of authority is redescribed or quoted at a later time, the Hiphil is still used, as in Gen 39:5 and Num 1:50.

[37] 2Ki 12:12 (Eng 11) Qere, 2Ki 22:5, 9, and 2Chr 34:10, 12, and 17.

[38] Num 31:14, 48 and 2Ki 22:9 = 2Chr 23:14.

[39] In Num 16:29 the subject is the fate [פְּקֻדַּת] of all men. In Neh 7:1 the gatekeepers, singers, and Levites were appointed while in Neh 12:44 the ambiguous "men," probably Levites, were appointed.

[40] Lev 26:16; Jer 15:3; Zeph 3:7.

24.4   Take note: a word about core meanings.

We have found it useful to present פָּקַד as having a core meaning *to take note*. Looking at it this way makes it easy to ask the question whether פָּקַד means *to be noted* or *to miss*, whether it means *to punish* or is simply used in a context of punishing, whether it means *to muster* or just *to count*. This perspective can also be useful as a memory device for learning word meanings. But its usefulness is limited. Do not make it a rigid approach to looking for word meaning. Even when different word meanings seem explainable as having derived from a root meaning, this may not be useful or may even be misleading. For example, what good does it really do for you to look at counting as a form of notation or to explain assigning as noting a task for someone? The idea of a core meaning can help you think about semantic components, but do not get mired down by trying to connect every application of a word to a core meaning.

24.5   Summary.

Fortunately, few words involve all the issues that פָּקַד does. Our treatment is designed to illustrate several principles about word meaning. The main point is that you not simply use dictionaries to answer the question, "what does this word mean?" You need to know what the word means "here," in a particular text, involving many relationships. So you need to have several questions in mind, questions that lead to analyzing the examples in a dictionary and making good comparisons to actual texts. Getting good answers starts with asking good questions, like:

Under what circumstances can a certain gloss be used?

How does this word relate to other words in the language?

Is there a significant modifier which signals or limits the meaning of this word?

How do the semantic pieces of this word relate to the reality being referred to by the sentence?

What syntactical structure is the word in?

Can the syntactical structure vary, i.e. can it involve the same elements in a different way?

Are any larger discourse features affecting the meaning or the choice of the word?

Has the meaning or syntactic construction of the word changed over time?

It is easy to think of a dictionary as something you go to to find "the answer." But you will get better answers if the dictionary is something you go to expecting to ask more questions.

chapter twenty-five

Noun Syntax

25.1 Focus.

What roles can a noun perform? Translating a construct noun plus its modifying genitive with "of" does not always work best. And sometimes there seems to be a noun sitting around in the sentence with no clear indicator of its function; it is not the subject, direct object, or object of a preposition. What jobs can it perform?

To talk about these roles, grammarians create labels and lists. Given the inherent flexibility of language and the space limits of any publication, no list is exhaustive. They are not the answer to the question, *what are all the things that nouns can do?*, although they familiarize us with common functions. Rather the lists are guides to illustrate the roles nouns can play and help us think about the relationships that nouns can be in. The important thing is to understand those relationships. The labels are simply our tools.

25.2 Nominative. *AC 6–7 §2.1*

(a) Subject.

The subject is what the sentence is about. The subject performs the action of an active verb and receives the action of a passive verb.

בָּרָא אֱלֹהִים אֵת הַשָּׁמַיִם	-1-	*God* created the heavens... Gen 1:1
וְנִפְקְחוּ עֵינֵיכֶם	-2-	Your *eyes* will be opened Gen 3:5

(b) Predicate Nominative.[1]

In copulative sentences (sentences that couple two things together) with a form of הָיָה or in nominal clauses, both the subject and predicate are in the nominative.

יהוה מֶלֶךְ	-3-	The LORD is *king*. Ps. 10:16
וַיְהִי־הֶבֶל רֹעֵה צֹאן וְקַיִן הָיָה עֹבֵד אֲדָמָה	-4-	Abel was a *shepherd* of the flock. But Cain was a *worker* of the ground. Gen 4:2

---

[1] Historically these may have been accusative, but the terminology typically bows to English usage.

239

(c) Vocative.

The vocative is a form of address. A vocative noun normally has the article.

בֶּן־מִי אַתָּה הַנָּעַר   -5-   Whose son are you, *young man?*
1Sam 17:58

הוֹשִׁיעָה הַמֶּלֶךְ   -6-   Help, *O king.*
2Sam 14:4

(d) Nominative Absolute.

A nominative absolute serves to focus attention on something before saying a sentence about it. It also goes by the term focus marker or *casus pendens* (case pending, i.e. here is something that will be mentioned, wait to see how). The noun in the nominative absolute is usually referred to by a pronoun in the following sentence.

הָאִשָּׁה אֲשֶׁר נָתַתָּה עִמָּדִי   -7-   The *woman*, whom you gave to me,
הִוא נָתְנָה־לִי מִן־הָעֵץ   she gave to me from the tree
Gen 3:12

יְהוָה הוּא הָאֱלֹהִים   -8-   The LORD, he is God
1Ki 18:39

25.3   Accusative. *AC 13–21 §2.3.*

Accusatives are adverbial from a Semitic perspective. From an English perspective, we divide them into direct objects and other adverbial uses.

25.3.1   Direct Objects. *AC 14–18 §2.3.1.*

The nature of the accusative of direct object depends on the verb. For example, the action in the verb may affect the direct object or effect the direct object, that is, bring it about.

(a) Affected.

וַיַּךְ אֶת־הַסֶּלַע בְּמַטֵּהוּ   -1-   [Moses] struck *the rock* with his staff.
Num 20:11

(b) Effected.

עָשׂוּ לָהֶם עֲצַבִּים   -2-   They made *idols* for themselves.
Hos 8:4

In the first example, the rock already exists and an action happens to it. In the next example, the idols did not already exist, only raw materials. The rock is affected; the idols are effected.

(c) Internal.

Another relationship is created when the direct object is based on the same root as the verb. These may also be called cognate accusatives. They are abstract nouns of action, usually indefinite, and often best translated adverbially.

וַיִּירְאוּ הָאֲנָשִׁים יִרְאָה גְדוֹלָה   -3-   The men feared a great *fear.*
= The men became very afraid.
Jon 1:10

(d) Double accusatives.

The meaning of some verbs may permit or require two direct objects. The causative meanings of the Hiphil and Piel stems particularly lend themselves to double accusatives.

וַיִּבְנֶה אֶת־הָאֲבָנִים מִזְבֵּחַ   -4-   He built the *stones* into an *altar*.
1Ki 18:32

לִמַּדְתִּי אֶתְכֶם חֻקִּים   -5-   I have taught *you statutes*.
De 4:5

The so-called direct object indicator marks an object of these verbs, "he built *stones*" and "I have taught *you*." But each has another object, "he built *an altar*" and "I have taught *statutes*."

The title *double accusative* does not signal any new use of the accusative, only that the verb takes two accusatives. In 1Ki 18:32, *stones* are an **affected** direct object (they already exist) and *altar* is an **effected** direct object (it is brought into being, or brought into shape). Other relationships can exist between the two direct objects besides these. When you encounter them, the main question is not *what do accusatives do* but rather *how does the meaning in this noun relate to the meaning in the verb*? Remember too, that Hebrew may use a preposition where English uses a direct object (10.6.2).

25.3.2 Other adverbial uses. *AC 18–21 §2.3.2.*

Hebrew sentences sometimes have nouns that are not nominative or the direct object of the verb and whose role is not indicated by a preposition. In a word-for-word translation, they can seem rather awkward. They are adverbial, meaning they describe some circumstance related to the verb. Often they should by translated with prepositional phrases in English. Arnold and Choi list 7 categories:

(a) Place (where something happens).

(b) Time (when something happens).

(c) Manner (how something happens).

(d) State (a characteristic of the verb's subject).

(e) Specification (clarifies or further explains the verbal action).

(f) Material (what was used in the action).

(g) Product (what was produced by the action).

The adverbial nature generally depends on the meaning of the noun. That is, a noun with a meaning related to time, e.g. לַיְלָה, will by used as an adverbial accusative of time, not manner or place.

וַיַּעַן כָּל־הָעָם קוֹל אֶחָד	-6-	All the people answered *one voice* Exod 24:3
וַיֵּרְדוּ כָל־יִשְׂרָאֵל הַפְּלִשְׁתִּים	-7-	All Israel went down *the Philistines* 1Sam 13:20
חָלָה אֶת־רַגְלָיו	-8-	he was sick *his feet* 1Ki 15:23
וַיִּיצֶר יְהוָה אֱלֹהִים אֶת־הָאָדָם עָפָר מִן־הָאֲדָמָה	-9-	The LORD God formed the man *dirt clods* from the ground Gen 2:7

In example 6, *one voice* describes the way in which the people answered, so we call it an adverbial accusative of manner and translate "answered *with* one voice."

In example 7, *the Philistines* describes whom they went to meet, so we call it an adverbial accusative of place and translate "went down *to* the Philistines."

In example 8, *his feet* explains precisely where he was sick, so we call it an adverbial accusative of specification and translate "sick *in* his feet."

In example 9, *dirt clods* identifies what was used to make humans, so we call it an adverbial accusative of material and translate "formed the man *out of* dirt clods."

The titles provide a handle for describing the relationships that exist between certain kinds of verbs and certain kinds of nouns. They are not functions of an independent thing called *case*. An intransitive verb like יָרַד, *to go down*, could not be modified by an adverbial accusative of material. In example 9, *dirt clods* are not what was used to make humans *because* עָפָר is an adverbial accusative of material; rather we call it an adverbial accusative of material *because* it was the stuff used to make humans.

25.4   Genitive; going beyond "of." *AC 8–13 §2.2.*

Genitive refers to the object of a preposition[2] or the word modifying a construct noun. Arnold and Choi provide 13 labels for describing the use of genitives in construct relationships. Remember that the labels are really describing the relationship between the "genitive" noun and the construct noun that it modifies. That relationship depends not on the "genitive case" but on the meanings of the two words involved. Such lists go beyond translating with "of" and illustrate the common ways that words of various types may be related in a construct relationship.

(a) Possessive (who owns the construct noun) or **possessed** (what is owned by the construct noun).

הֵיכָל יהוה	temple of *the LORD* – possessive.
בַּעַל בַּיִת	owner of *the house* – possessed.

---

[2] When it is the object of a preposition, the syntax of genitives is usually described under the headings of the prepositions (*AC 95–126 §4.1*) rather than under the genitive case.

(b) **Relationship** (someone associated with the construct noun, often by kinship).

בְּנֵי מֶלֶךְ   sons of *the king*, or the *king's* sons

אָחִי   *my* brother

(c) **Subjective** (the performer of the action implied by the construct noun).

יֵשַׁע אֱלֹהִים   the salvation of (i.e. performed by) *God*

(d) **Objective** (the recipient of the action implied by the construct noun).

יִרְאַת יהוה   the fear of *the LORD* (i.e. the LORD is feared)

(e) **Attributive** (gives a quality or attribute of the construct noun).

הַר־קָדְשׁוֹ   his[3] mountain of *holiness* = his holy mountain

(f) **Specification**, (the genitive noun is typified by a quality in the construct adj.).

טֹבַת מַרְאֶה   good of *appearance* = good looking = beautiful

(g) **Cause** (the cause of the construct or what is caused by the construct).

רוּחַ חָכְמָה וּבִינָה   the spirit of (= which gives) *wisdom and insight*

חוֹלַת אַהֲבָה   sick of (= due to) *love*

(h) **Purpose** (the intended use of the construct noun).

צֹאן טִבְחָה   sheep of (= intended for) *slaughter*

(i) **Means** (the impersonal[4] instrument or means by which the action implied by the construct is performed).

שְׂרֻפוֹת אֵשׁ   burned of (= by) *fire*

(j) **Material** (the material that the construct noun is made of).

אֲרוֹן עֵץ   an ark of *wood*

(k) **Measure** (something measured by a number or quantity in the construct).

שְׁנֵי בָנִים   two ~~of~~ *sons*

בְּכָל־לְבַבְכֶם   with all of *your mind*

(l) **Explicative** (a specific member of a category represented by the construct).

נְהַר־פְּרָת   the river ~~of~~ *Euphrates*

(m) **Superlative** (the best part of what the construct noun refers to).

מִבְחַר קְבָרֵנוּ   the choic*est* of our gravesites

מֶלֶךְ מְלָכִים   the king of *kings* = the greatest king

---

[3] Pronominal suffixes do not interrupt the construct chain, cf. 6.4.

[4] When personal, it is called a genitive of agency or subjective genitive.

25.5   Examples.

וַיְהִי דְּבַר־יְהוָה אֶל־יוֹנָה	*-1-*	The word of *the LORD* came to Jonah
בֶּן־אֲמִתַּי לֵאמֹר	*-2-*	son of *Amittai*, saying,
		Jon 1:1
קוּם לֵךְ אֶל־נִינְוֵה הָעִיר הַגְּדוֹלָה	*-3-*	Get up, go to Ninevah, the great city.
וּקְרָא עָלֶיהָ	*-4-*	And cry out against it.
כִּי־עָלְתָה רָעָתָם לְפָנָי		for their *wickedness* has come up before me.
		Jon 1:2
וַיָּקָם יוֹנָה לִבְרֹחַ תַּרְשִׁישָׁה מִלִּפְנֵי יְהוָה	*-5-*	But Jonah got up to flee *to Tarshish* away from the LORD
וַיֵּרֶד יָפוֹ	*-6-*	He went down *to Joppa*
וַיִּמְצָא אֳנִיָּה בָּאָה תַרְשִׁי	*-7-*	He found a *ship* going *to Tarshish*
וַיִּתֵּן שְׂכָרָהּ	*-8-*	He gave (= paid) its *fare*
		Jon 1:3
– – – – –		– – – – –
וַיִּקְרַב אֵלָיו רַב הַחֹבֵל	*-9-*	The captain *of the ship* approached him
		Jon 1:6

In example 1, *the LORD* modifies a construct noun, telling who communicated the word, so we call it a subjective genitive. This views *word* as a noun of action.

In example 2, *Amittai* modifies a construct noun identifying to whom Jonah, the son, is related. So we call it a genitive of relationship.

In example 3, *the great city*, is in apposition to Nineveh. **Apposition** means that two nouns are simply next to each other (juxtaposed) and refer to the same thing with the same syntax. For more on apposition see *AC 21–24*.

In example 4, *wickedness* is a subject nominative of the verb עָלָה.

In example 5, *Tarshish* is marked by directional הָ, cf. 9.5.

In example 6, *Joppa* is an adverbial accusative of place.

In example 7, *ship* is the direct object of the verb מָצָא. And *Tarshish* is an adverbial accusative of place.

In example 8, *fare* is the direct object of the verb נתן.

In example 9, *the ship* does not precisely fit any of the categories listed for the genitive. One might be tempted to call it a genitive of possession, specifically that *the ship* is the possession of the captain. But the captain probably does not own the ship; he just runs it. At this point you might expand your definition of possession to include using something. Or you can look at *captain* as implying action and call it an objective genitive, though this is questionable. Or you can make up a new title, like *genitive of subordination*. The *ship*, implying also the ship's crew, maintenance, and functions, is subordinate to the *captain*, the noun in construct.

In addition, *ship* in example 7 does not neatly fit the direct object categories. *He found a ship*. The *ship* is not affected by Jonah finding it. And it is certainly not effected by Jonah finding it. The same might be said of the *statutes* taught by Moses in De 4:5 (25.3.1.d). These observations bring us to the main point of the chapter, the contributions and limits of labels.

25.6   On the use of syntactic labels.

Remember what case is – case is the *relationship* between a noun and another word in a sentence. So these functions are the result of the interaction between more than one word. They do not first exist independently as linguistic items that are then applied to nouns. They are not like morphemes, spellings that can be transferred from noun to noun. There is no independently existing adverbial accusative of X, or genitive of Y, waiting for the speaker or writer to apply to any noun. The speaker may decide to use the construct form, but does not think, "I had better use the genitive of Z." Case functions do not exist as independent items that can be applied to any noun. But words in sentences do not exist in isolation; the relationships between words do exist. Describing them with syntactic labels helps to illustrate the ways in which Hebrew works.

While *captain of the ship* may make sense to us regardless of its syntactic label, the word *of* does not always work to render the relationship in a construct chain. And going through a sentence word by word brings us to nouns which do not have their role marked in the way that English might use prepositions or adverbial morphemes. Then (or when commentaries refer to these labels) consulting a list of adverbial accusatives feels much more useful.

When consulting the lists, do not simply look at the titles. A key element of linguistic inquiry is making comparisons. You need to compare the type of noun involved and the type of word to which it is related in your text to those in the examples. When you find examples similar to your text, this will guide you in understanding and translating whatever text you are working on.

To test your understanding of a title, try to make a translation of your text based on that category. Such an exercise will quickly reveal that some categories will not work. Using רַב־הַחֹבֵל, captain of the ship, as an example:

If it were an attributive genitive, it would be – the shiply captain.

If it were a genitive of cause, it would be – the one made captain by the ship.

If it were a purpose genitive, it would be – the captain intended for a ship.

If it were an explicative genitive, it would be – the captain which is the ship, or the captain named Ship.

If it were an objective genitive, it would mean the captain does some sort of shipping activity. (This tag assumes you can view *captain* as a noun of action, which is debatable.) And so forth. However, just because one syntactic category may seem to make a sensible translation in English does not guarantee that it is the correct one.

We do not say, "because it is X therefore it means Y," but rather, "because it means Y, therefore we call it X." So we would not want to say, "Because it is a genitive of possession, *captain of the ship* means that the captain owns the ship," since in fact, the captain may not own the ship.

Lists of case functions, whether here or in advanced reference grammars, are not exhaustive. The syntactic relationships can be grouped together or subdivided at different levels, and each publication is under its own space limitations. Finding an exact parallel is reassuring because you know that your analysis is backed up by other examples. Not finding an exact parallel to your text is not necessarily a failure to succeed. Finding a partial parallel and reflecting on how your text is specifically different is success when you come to realize the relationship between the words in your text. It is acceptable to "make up" a new title that describes the relationship more specifically than those in a reference list. It is only giving up after not finding an exact parallel that is a failure to succeed.

And thinking that the objective is merely to memorize a list of titles and their meanings is one pathway to this error. That makes the lists of labels the masters and us the servants, trying to figure out "which one it is." The goal is to be able to think correctly about relationships between words, to make comparisons between different texts by noting the types of words involved and to make linguistic decisions based on linguistic comparisons. The labels are our servants; they help us to think about the relationships between words.

25.7   Summary.

Syntactic labels are to be our servants not our masters.

Linguistic analysis requires making comparisons and distinctions between different types of words and interrelationships.

Nominative refers to subjects, predicate nominatives, and words "outside" the syntax of the clause, such as vocatives and nominative absolutes.

Accusatives are the other nouns not marked by a preposition and not modifying a construct noun; they are adverbials, including direct objects.

Genitives are nouns modifying construct nouns or the objects of prepositions.

Apposition refers to a noun juxtaposed to another (not in the construct relationship and typically agreeing in gender, number, and definiteness) giving further specification of the first noun.

When "of" does not make a good translation of a construct plus "genitive" noun, consider how the two ideas may be related and look for similar relationships in a reference list of genitive noun functions.

When a noun's function is not marked by a preposition or a construct noun, consider how it relates to the verb and translate accordingly.

chapter twenty-six

Verb Syntax:
The Piel

26.1   Focus.

Chapter 16 formally introduced the verbal stems and some basic relationships between them.

basic meaning		Qal	Active
	pref. **ִנ**	Niphal	Pass./Refl.
factitive (of statives)	Double R$_2$	Piel	Active
denominative (of adj./nouns)		Hitpael	Refl.
plurative (of fientives)		Pual	Passive
factitive (of statives)	pref **ה**	Hiphil	Active
denominative (of adj./nouns)			
causative (of fientives)		Hophal	Pass./Refl.

These generalizations can help infer a verb's meaning from the Qal but are not to be rigidly applied. The syntactic labels are again descriptors of the combination of more than one element and so can be further divided into more categories.

This chapter looks in particular at the Piel stem, but its larger purpose is to guide you in how to use reference lists of the functions of any of the verbal stems. We will look at the categories of the Piel and Pual in Arnold and Choi and balance the use of labels against the initial caution they quote from Stephen Kaufman, "it is pointless to try to find a single…explanation to account for all the transformative power of the D-stem. It is simply a form."[1]

The Piel was once misunderstood as "intensive." For a brief history on corrections to this notion see Waltke and O'Connor §24.1.[2]

---

[1] Stephen A. Kaufman, "Semitics: Directions and Re-Directions," in *The Study of the Ancient Near East in the Twenty-First Century: The William Foxwell Albright Centennial Conference*, Jerrold S. Cooper and Glenn M. Schwartz, eds. (Winona Lake: Eisenbrauns, 1996), pp. 273–82.
[2] Bruce Waltke and Michael O'Connor, *An Introduction to Biblical Hebrew Syntax* (Winona Lake: Eisenbrauns, 1990), pp. 396–400.

26.2   Piel and Pual. *AC 41–47 §3.1.3–4.*

(a) Factitive/resultative (turns stative and some intransitive fientives into transitive verbs). In contrast to the Hiphil, which primarily causes an action to occur, the Piel indicates a cause which produces a state.

root	Qal	Piel
כבד	to be heavy/honored	to give honor to
טהר	to be clean	to make clean/to cleanse
גדל	to be great	to make great, exalt

Piel

אֲטַהֵר אֶתְכֶם	-1-	I will *cleanse* them. Ezek 36:33
וַתְּכַבֵּד אֶת־בָּנֶיךָ מִמֶּנִּי	-2-	You *honor* your sons more than me. 1Sam 2:29
וַיְגַדֵּל יְהוָה אֶת־שְׁלֹמֹה	-3-	The LORD *made* Solomon *great*. 1Chr 29:25

Pual

וְשׁוֹמֵר תּוֹכַחַת יְכֻבָּד	-4-	The one who attends to reproof will *be honored*. Prov 13:18
אַתְּ אֶרֶץ לֹא מְטֹהָרָה	-5-	You are a land not *cleansed*. Ezek 22:24

(b) Denominative (*makes a verb out of a noun or adjective*).

noun		Piel
דָּבָר	word	to speak
זֶמֶר	praise song	sing praise
כֹּפֶר	price for ransom	to ransom, pay for

Piel

וַיְדַבֵּר	-6-	he said
זַמְּרוּ לַיהוָה בְּכִנּוֹר	-7-	*Sing praises* to the LORD on the lyre. Ps 98:5

Pual

בְּחֶסֶד וֶאֱמֶת יְכֻפַּר עָוֹן	-8-	By faithfulness and truth, iniquity *is paid for*. Prov 16:6

(c) Frequentitive/Plurative (*pluralizes the action of a fientive verb*).

The action of the Qal becomes in some way plural, perhaps through repetition or in result.

verb		Piel
שָׁאַל	ask	ask repeatedly = *beg*, or consult regularly
הָלַךְ	walk	walk around, go about

Piel

| וַיְהַלֵּךְ אַט | -9- | He *walked about* dejectedly.
1Ki 21:27 |

| וְנוֹעַ יָנוּעוּ בָנָיו וְשִׁאֵלוּ | -10- | Let his children wander and *beg*.
Ps 109:10 |

(d) **Declarative** *(recognizes or declares a condition).*

The declarative Piel "involves some kind of proclamation, delocution or estimative assessment, although the precise nature of these verbs and their relationship to the factitive is debated" (*AC 45*).

root		Piel
טמא	Qal: to be unclean	to declare unclean
צדק	noun: righteousness Qal: be in the right, justified	to declare righteous, to demonstrate as righteous
גאל	*no Qal*	to declare defiled

Piel

| טִמֵּא יְטַמְּאֶנּוּ הַכֹּהֵן | -11- | The priest shall *declare* him *unclean*.
Lev 13:44 |

| חָפַצְתִּי צַדְּקֶךָּ | -12- | I desire *to justify* you.
Job 33:32 |

Pual

| וַיְגֹאֲלוּ מִן־הַכְּהֻנָּה | -13- | They were *considered unclean* for the priesthood.
Ezra 2:62 |

Being clean, unclean, or righteous is a separate issue from being declared clean, unclean, or righteous. In such a case the verb does not express making someone clean, unclean, or just. For example, Lev 13:44 first identifies that the person is unclean, טָמֵא הוּא, then instructs the priest to declare him unclean (Piel טמא). The declaration may recognize the status as legally or socially effective, but does not bring it about.

(e) **Misc.**

Some Piel verbs have no counterpart in the Qal and their meaning appears to be simple active like the Qal, e.g. בִּקֵּשׁ *to seek*.

A high percentage of Puals are participles which "denote a thing or person for or in which a new condition has been attained" (*AC 46*).

| וְהִנֵּה יָדוֹ מְצֹרַעַת כַּשָּׁלֶג | -14- | Now his hand was *leprous* like snow.
Exod 4:6 |

26.3   On titles for verb stem syntax.

These titles, factitive, resultative, denominative, plurative (or frequentative), and declarative, are used regularly in works on syntax. Observe that the titles themselves are of different kinds. "Denominative" merely says that the verb comes from a noun or adjective. It does not identify what it does to the meaning in the way that the title "plurative" indicates something done to the meaning of verb.

In a certain sense, the denominative is like the factitive. Adjectives and stative verbs are similar, with one of their pieces of meaning being an attribute or quality. Nouns, especially abstract nouns, can also have an attribute or quality as a piece of their meaning. The D-stems make a verbal sense out of that attribute or quality.

But this is a rather vague and general description. Consider the English denominative *dust*. Using *dust* as a verb simply indicates an activity involving dust. The specific activity depends on other factors.

Dust the house = (Remove) dust (from items in) the house (but not the floor).

Dust the crops = (Apply fertilizer/pesticide) dust (to) crops (by aerial spraying).

Many Piel verbs can be described as bringing about a state or quality, so they are titled factitive. But others cannot. Of those that cannot, several can be described as recognizing that state or quality, or making it be recognized in an abstract sense (e.g. judicially or socially). They can be lumped together and called declarative. Some call these delocutives, grouping them together by the observation that locution, or speech, is involved. The title *delocutive* emphasizes the manner (speech); the title *declarative* emphasizes the abstract result.

But these titles do not cover everything, and not every use of a root is the same. The Piel of צדק may be declarative, as in example 12 of 26.2, but it may reveal the righteous status or make it appear to be so (settings which are not delocutive). In Jer 3:11 God charges that "faithless Israel has *proven to be* more *righteous* (Piel צדק) than treacherous Judah." Ezek 16:52 uses the Qal of צדק to say "*they are* more *right* than you," then again refers to this situation with a Piel infinitive of צדק, "when you *made* your sister *righteous*" (= *made* your sister *appear righteous* by comparison). Locution is involved in Job 32:2 when Elihu is angry with Job for *justifying* himself before God. In that case it refers to Job's oral defense but does not establish his legal standing in the way that the judge's decision would declare him "not guilty."

Similarly, in the Qal טהר means to be clean, and the Piel of טהר can be used in a declarative sense.

וְטִהַר הַכֹּהֵן אֶת־הַנֶּגַע   *-1-*   The priest shall pronounce the infected person clean.
Lev 13:13

But the Piel of טהר can also be used in a factitive sense.

וְטִהַרְתָּ אֹתָם	-2-	[Take the Levites] and sanctify them. Num 8:6
וּמְטַהֵר כֶּסֶף	-3-	and a purifier of silver Mal 3:3
לְטַהֵר הָאָרֶץ וְהַבָּיִת	-4-	to purify the land and the temple 2Chr 34:8

Often the factitive uses of טהר are abstract, e.g. a ceremony to atone for something and so to make it clean or sacred. But as example 3 shows, the cleansing can be physical, the specific referent dependent on the item being cleaned; *cleaning* silver means to refine or purify it.

Especially when the referents are considered – refining metal, asserting social acceptability due to health status, or performing a ceremony to make something religiously sacred – then attempting to enumerate "all the transformative power of the D-stem" rapidly fails. It would be like trying to spell out the meaning of the English morpheme *–ify*, in various manifestations like *identify*, *verify*, *sanctify*, *glorify*, *stupefy*, *magnify*, *justify*, etc. We could make some broad generalizations but the resulting referent depends on more than just the morpheme *–ify*.

So too, attempting to explain the wide variety of referents as semantic pieces of the D-stems tries to put too much of the meaning which results from root and context into the stem morpheme. We can say that in the broadest sense, the D-stems either "verb*ify*" certain qualities or pluralize certain actions. It is not simply a matter of there being a Piel of X, existing as an independent category which can then be applied to any verb. In each case the specific nuance arises from combination with other factors. So it can even be argued that the different stems of a verbal root should be considered distinct and separate words, but this does not entirely eliminate the usefulness of considering the stems to be modifying (a) core root idea(s).

In a practical sense, discussion of the verb stems under syntax headings, like factitive, is useful for illustrating some of the more common ways in which the stems are used. The more space a publication has, the more subcategories it can present. The discussions assist you in evaluating the role of the stem and the resultant meaning of the word. But the dictionaries, identifying the meaning of the verb in different stems, remain crucial. And both types of reference works are best used by asking how the word you are studying compares in many circumstances and relationships with the examples in the reference works. The meaning has arisen from combinations, so only asking the question "what does this item mean?" will inevitably overlook important considerations.

This perspective, developed by using the Piel for illustration, extends to other stems as well. Consider again English denominatives. One cannot predict in advance what they will mean. *Book it. Table it. Tag it. Dust the X.* Likewise many sayings could be understood in different ways and become the basic material for jokes and humor. Peggy Parish made part of her career writing the *Amelia Bedelia* books (New York: Harper Collins, 1963-) in which Amelia carries out such comedic misunderstandings as *dusting* the house by spreading dusting powder all over everything and wondering why her employers do not *undust* their house, as she does hers. Or *drawing the curtains* – with a paper and pencil; *putting the lights out* – on the laundry line; *dressing the chicken* – in clothes. Language is fluid and always changing. Somebody tries a form or word for a specific referent, and if the speaking community comes to recognize it, then that is what it means. The same is true with the Hebrew Piel.

The principle extends beyond the Piel. The Niphal, for example, does something to remove focus from the agent of a verb's action. Active verbs generally become passive (he was hit), middle (the door opens), or reflexive (I dress myself). Stative verbs often become ingressive in the Niphal, e.g. בער *to be stupid* (Qal) and *to become stupid/stupefied* (Niphal) (16.2.1). But they do not always become ingressive, e.g. קדש, *be treated as holy* or *demonstrate oneself as holy*. Speakers try one of a limited number of forms for a meaning, and if the community accepts it, then that is what it means. Something does suggest to the speaker to try one stem or another. But simply asking the question, "What does this stem mean?" can make the matter sound far more rigid and static than language really can be, as if it has always done the same things in the same ways without other influences. The question can be useful, but with the wrong perspective on the fluidity of language, the question is misleading.

26.4   Summary.

The D-stems facilitate linking a quality in the semantic components of the verb to other elements; the resultant meaning arises from the combination of the many elements, not just the verb and the stem.

The broadest categories of effect of the D-stems are (1) factitive and denominative and (2) plurative. More specific groups can be identified and may be helpful for comparison; but the more specifically the effect is described the more likely it is to include other elements of the context.

chapter twenty-seven

Verb Syntax:
Participles

27.1   Focus.

The meaning of a participle results from a combination of several elements. Participles are built by combining a root with a verb stem and a participle morpheme. Syntax or context then indicates whether it plays the role of adjective, noun, or verb. And if it acts as a verb, then the surrounding context establishes its time frame.

This chapter focuses on the participle's verbal uses and the effect of context on the time frame.

27.2   Participle functions (Cp. 8.4 and *AC 77–83 §3.4.3*).

27.2.₁   Substantival.

(a) A participle can act as a noun. As such it may be employed in any of the noun syntax categories or be in the construct state. Arnold and Choi observe that as a noun, the participle most often has the article, though it may be omitted, especially in poetry (*AC 82*).

(b) Participles in construct with another noun have an additional syntax relationship not seen in other genitives (25.4). The genitive modifying the construct participle may tell the place of the activity in the participle. This is especially true of verbs of motion like בוא and יצא (*AC 82*).

יוֹרְדֵי־בוֹר	-1-	those *who go down to* the pit Is 38:18
כֹּל בָּאֵי שַׁעַר־עִירוֹ	-2-	all *who entered*[1] the gates of his city Gen 23:10
כֹּל יֹצְאֵי הַתֵּבָה	-3-	all *who came*[1] *out of* the ark Gen 9:10

Active participles in the construct are often followed by the recipient of the action (objective genitive). Passive participles in the construct are often followed by the performer of the action (subjective genitive) or by a genitive of specification.

---

[1] Context establishes a past time frame.

(c) Some participles have essentially become nouns, "most denoting vocations or other identifying roles" *(AC 82)*.[2]

יוֹצֵר	Potter	אוֹיֵב	Enemy
יוֹשֵׁב	Inhabitant	רֹעֶה	Shepherd
שֹׁפֵט	Judge	סֹפֵר	Scribe

27.2.2 Attributive. The attributive participle "ascribes a quality to a noun" *(AC 78)*. It typically agrees with the noun it modifies in gender, number, and definiteness.

(a) A participle can act as an adjective. Passive participles translate as an adjective in English more commonly than active participles. Passive participles may "connote a completed action" *(AC 78)* as in example *3*, or an inherent quality as in *4* and *5*.[3]

לֵב שֹׁמֵעַ	-1-	a *listening* heart (= sensitive mind) 1Ki 3:9
וּבִזְרֹועַ נְטוּיָה	-2-	and with an *outstretched* arm De 4:34
הַכֹּהֲנִים הַמְּשֻׁחִים	-3-	the *anointed* priests Num 3:3
כָּל־עֵץ נֶחְמָד לְמַרְאֶה	-4-	every tree *desirable/pleasing* in appearance Gen 2:9
מַה־נּוֹרָא הַמָּקוֹם	-5-	How *awesome* is this place. Gen 28:17

(b) Participles may be best translated by a relative clause. This is especially the case with active participles with the article (8.4.2).

מִבְּכוֹר פַּרְעֹה הַיֹּשֵׁב עַל־כִּסְאוֹ	-6-	from the firstborn of Pharaoh who sits on his throne Exod 11:5
הַיּוֹם הַבָּא	-7-	the day that is coming/has come Jer 47:7
לֻחֹת אֶבֶן כְּתֻבִים בְּאֶצְבַּע אֱלֹהִים	-8-	tablets of stone which were inscribed by the finger of God. Exod 31:18

27.2.3 Predicate. The predicate participle "expresses an assertion about a noun or pronoun in a nominal clause, i.e. a clause without a finite verb" *(AC 79)*.

The predicate participle agrees with the noun it modifies in gender and number but is never definite. The time frame of the participle depends on the context,

---

[2] Words like שֹׁפֵט, *judge*, are clearly participles, since the root is regularly used as a verb. It is debated whether some words vocalized in the *qōtēl* pattern, like אוֹיֵב, כֹּהֵן or יֶגֶב should be called participles since the root does not occur in the verb. As a result some words will be called participles in some reference works but be called nouns in other reference works.

[3] "The participle of the reflexive or passive stems, especially the *Niphal*, correspond occasionally to an English *-ible* or *-able* term or a Latin gerundive... for example, נוֹרָא ... 'to be feared, terrible.'" (Waltke and O'Connor, p. 620).

expressing a "durative or progressive action or condition that may occur in past, present or future time" (*AC 79*). The subject of the participle is often a pronoun and may be expressed by a pronominal suffix on יֵשׁ, אַיִן, or הִנֵּה.

Arnold and Choi give several examples of participles in past, present, and future time frames. We have placed in separate headings the examples with הִנֵּה and היה.

(a) Present.

אָנֹכִי בֹּרַחַת	-1-	I *am fleeing* Gen 16:8
לֹא־כֵן אֲנַחְנוּ עֹשִׂים	-2-	We *are not doing* what is right 2Ki 7:9
כִּי יֹדֵעַ אֱלֹהִים	-3-	For God *knows* Gen 3:5
דּוֹר הֹלֵךְ וְדוֹר בָּא וְהָאָרֶץ לְעוֹלָם עֹמָדֶת	-4-	A generation *goes* and a generation *comes*; but the earth *remains* forever Ecc 1:4

(b) Past.

וְנָהָר יֹצֵא מֵעֵדֶן	-5-	A river *was flowing* out from Eden. Gen 2:10
וַאֲשֶׁר־הוּא עֹשֶׂה יְהוָה מַצְלִיחַ	-6-	Whatever he was doing, the LORD *was prospering*. Gen 39:23
וַאֲדֹנִיָּה בֶן־חַגִּית מִתְנַשֵּׂא	-7-	Adonijah, son of Haggith, *was advancing* himself. 1Ki 1:5
וְלוֹט יֹשֵׁב בְּשַׁעַר־סְדֹם	-8-	Lot *was sitting* in the gate of Sodom. Gen 19:1
לְסִיחֹן מֶלֶךְ הָאֱמֹרִי אֲשֶׁר יוֹשֵׁב בְּחֶשְׁבּוֹן	-9-	…to Sihon, king of the Amorites, who *was living* at Heshbon. De 3:2

(c) Future.

כִּי לְיָמִים עוֹד שִׁבְעָה אָנֹכִי מַמְטִיר עַל־הָאָרֶץ	-10-	For in yet seven days, I *will send rain* on the earth Gen 7:4
לַמּוֹעֵד הַזֶּה כָּעֵת חַיָּה אַתְּ חֹבֶקֶת בֵּן	-11-	At this season, in due time, you *shall embrace* a son (or *will be embracing*) 2Ki 4:16
אֲשֶׁר הָאֱלֹהִים עֹשֶׂה הִרְאָה אֶת־פַּרְעֹה	-12-	That which God *is about to do*, he has shown Pharaoh. Gen 41:28
כִּי־מַשְׁחִתִים אֲנַחְנוּ אֶת־הַמָּקוֹם הַזֶּה	-13-	For we *are about to destroy* this place. Gen 19:13

(d) **With הִנֵּה**, the predicate participle may indicate immediate or impending action.

הִנֵּה פְלִשְׁתִּים נִלְחָמִים בִּקְעִילָה	-14-	Hey, the Philistines *are fighting* against Keilah. 1Sam 23:1
וְהִנֵּה אֹרְחַת יִשְׁמְעֵאלִים בָּאָה מִגִּלְעָד	-15-	Lo and behold, a caravan of Ishmaelites *was coming* along from Gilead. Gen 37:25
וְהִנֵּה שְׁלֹשָׁה אֲנָשִׁים נִצָּבִים עָלָיו	-16-	Right there, three men *were standing* alongside him. Gen 18:2
וְהִנֵּה אֲנַחְנוּ מְאַלְּמִים אֲלֻמִּים בְּתוֹךְ הַשָּׂדֶה	-17-	Get this! We *were binding* sheaves in the middle of the field. Gen 37:3
וַאֲנִי הִנְנִי מֵבִיא אֶת־הַמַּבּוּל מַיִם	-18-	And I, even I, *am going to bring* a flood of water [on the earth]. Gen 6:17
הִנְּךָ שֹׁכֵב עִם־אֲבֹתֶיךָ	-19-	See here, you are *about to lay to rest* with your forefathers. De 31:16
הִנְנִי נֹתְנוֹ בְּיָדְךָ הַיּוֹם	-20-	Look, I *will deliver* it into your hand today. 1Ki 20:13

(e) **With היה.**

וַיְהִי הֵם מְרִיקִים שַׂקֵּיהֶם	-21-	They were *emptying* their sacks. Gen 42:35
וּמֹשֶׁה הָיָה רֹעֶה אֶת־צֹאן יִתְרוֹ חֹתְנוֹ	-22-	Moses was *pasturing* the flock of Jethro his father-in-law. Exod 3:1
הַבָּקָר הָיוּ חֹרְשׁוֹת וְהָאֲתֹנוֹת רֹעוֹת עַל־יְדֵיהֶם	-23-	The oxen were *plowing* and the donkeys were *feeding* beside them Job 1:14
מַמְרִים הֱיִיתֶם עִם־יְהוָה מִיּוֹם דַּעְתִּי אֶתְכֶם	-24-	You have been *rebelling* against the LORD since the day I knew you. De 9:24
וָאֱהִי צָם וּמִתְפַּלֵּל לִפְנֵי אֱלֹהֵי הַשָּׁמָיִם	-25-	And I was *fasting* and *praying* before the God of heaven. Neh 1:4
וְכִסֵּא דָוִד יִהְיֶה נָכוֹן לִפְנֵי יְהוָה עַד־עוֹלָם	-26-	And the throne of David will be *established* before the LORD forever. 1Ki 2:45

27.3 Observations.

One goal of this section is to train you to make good observations and look for interrelationships. We have used Arnold and Choi's predicate participle illustrations extensively in this chapter as an occasion to discuss interacting with reference works.

Though we have grouped them under separate headings here, you would notice in Arnold and Choi that the sections illustrating participles in the present, past, and future each include special mention of the participle with הִנֵּה and the sections on the past and future also note using the participle with היה. By doing this they are pointing out to you the combinations that are important in creating meaning.

Now let us make further observations beyond the issue of time frame. Excluding the constructions with היה, all the examples of the participle in present (1–4 and 14) or future (10–13 and 18–20) time frames are from speech.[4] All of the examples in a past time frame without הִנֵּה or היה are from narration.

Waltke and O'Connor's work, which is about four times as long as Arnold and Choi's, has 44 examples of the predicate participle, besides their sections on the use of the participle with היה and other finite verbs.[5] There too, every example of the participle in past time is in narration and every example in present and future time is in speech. This observation should reinforce the importance of attending to genre and to always be cognizant of whether you are reading narrative, poetry, or speech.

So you read that *context* establishes the time frame of the participle and you can observe by the examples that a major setting for a participle to be in past time is the background clause in narrative. You can also observe that a major setting for present and future time participles is in speech. Though you turn to that section of the reference work to learn something about the participle, you should be learning something about narrative and speech at the same time – at least if you come to the reference work from a perspective that asks multiple questions of any text you study.

(a) Some observations on participles in narration.

Not only are the past time examples from narration, they are also not verb-first constructions. You will recall (12.5) that preterite forms are the backbone of narrative, moving the action along in past time. Because the preterite normally is joined to the conjunction ו, the verb must be first in the sentence. Hebrew narrative uses variation from this word order to make background statements. When a participle is used in these background clauses, the participle represents something going on in the same time frame as the main narrative, which is past time. This observation about the participle can be set in contrast to other non–preterite clauses in narration.

---

[4] Admittedly, example 4, Eccl 1:4, could be considered a proverb.
[5] Waltke and O'Connor, pp. 624–631.

Nominal clause. A noun clause without a participle would also present a condition that is true in the same (past) time frame as the narrative. Observe in 1Ki 1:3–4:

| *preterite* | וַיָּבִאוּ | They brought [her to the king] … |
| *nominal* | וְהַנַּעֲרָה יָפָה עַד־מְאֹד | Now the girl was very beautiful. |

Similarly in Judges 3:17:

| *preterite* | וַיַּקְרֵב אֶת־הַמִּנְחָה | He brought the tribute [to Eglon]… |
| *nominal* | וְעֶגְלוֹן אִישׁ בָּרִיא מְאֹד | By the way, Eglon was very obese. |

Perfect Stative Verb. The stative perfect can be present time since a state is complete in the present. So a background clause with a perfect stative verb could also present a condition that is true in the same (past) time frame as the narrative, as illustrated by 2Sam 19:31–32:

| *preterite* | וַיַּעֲבֹר אֶת־הַמֶּלֶךְ הַיַּרְדֵּן | He went along with the king to the Jordan |
| *nominal* | וּבַרְזִלַּי זָקֵן מְאֹד | Now Barzillai was very old. |

Perfect Fientive Verb. But a background clause with a perfect fientive verb would be a step farther back, as illustrated (in 12.5) from Gen 31:18–19:

preterite	וַיִּנְהַג	He *drove* away all his livestock…
אֲשֶׁר + *pf.*	אֲשֶׁר רָכָשׁ	which he *had acquired*…
Noun 1ˢᵗ + *pf.*	וְלָבָן הָלַךְ	Laban *had gone* to shear sheep…
preterite	וַתִּגְנֹב רָחֵל	Then Rachel *stole* the household gods.

Imperfect Verb. Such a background clause with an imperfect often indicates an imperfective action in the past (also called past habitual), as illustrated by Gen 2:6.

| Noun 1ˢᵗ + *impf.* | וְאֵד יַעֲלֶה מִן־הָאָרֶץ | A mist *used to rise* from the ground. |

We are not exhausting the possible nuances of background statements. But this discussion should illustrate that just as it is useful in lexicography to consider the meanings of a word in relation to similar words, so too in syntactical studies, it is important to consider the meaning of one construction in relation to similar constructions. A background statement in narration supplies to the participle a past time frame. The active participle supplies to the story, as you see it in your mind's eye, an ongoing action that is concurrent to the main action of the story. A passive participle conveys a condition concurrent to the main action of the story.

(b) **Some observations on participles in speech.**

The present time frame of participles in speech may be contrasted to the past time frame of participles in narration by Josh 7:21–22. In Josh 7:21 we come into the middle of Achan's story of taking forbidden items from Jericho. Even though it is direct speech, he is telling a story, or narrating, so we find the preterite carrying the story line.

| *preterite* | וָאֶחְמְדֵם וָאֶקָּחֵם | …then I coveted them and took them. |

He then stops the story and turns to matters as they stand. הִנֵּה helps to shift the focus from the story of the past to awareness of something in the present. He says,

| *pass. ptc.* | וְהִנָּם טְמוּנִים בָּאָרֶץ בְּתוֹךְ הָאָהֳלִי | You know what[6] – they *are hidden* in the ground in my tent |
| *nominal* | וְהַכֶּסֶף תַּחְתֶּיהָ | and the silver is beneath it. |

Being in speech gives the participle its present time frame. Joshua 7:22 returns us to the main narrative, conveying the action line with preterites.

| *preterite* | וַיִּשְׁלַח יְהוֹשֻׁעַ מַלְאָכִים | Joshua sent messengers. |
| *preterite* | וַיָּרֻצוּ הָאֹהֱלָה | They ran to the tent. |

Now הִנֵּה helps to shift the focus to the perspective of the messengers as they discover the goods. Being in past narration gives the participle a past time frame.

| *pass. ptc.* | וְהִנֵּה טְמוּנָה בְּאָהֳלוֹ | And sure enough, [it] *was hidden* in his tent |
| *nominal* | וְהַכֶּסֶף תַּחְתֶּיהָ | with the silver beneath it. |

If a speaker is telling a story about what has happened, then we call it narration. Whether it is the narrative voice of a book or narration from the direct speech of a character, that is where we find past time participles in background clauses. Otherwise in speech, the speaker is often describing things as they are, i.e. conversing in present time, or perhaps saying how things will be. So the predicate participle in speech usually informs of current or future circumstances as in examples 1–3 and 10–11 above.

What then about Gen 37:3 (example 17 in 27.3.2)? It is in speech, but it is translated past time even though it is not preceded by a preterite. We observe that Joseph is beginning to tell the story of his dream, so it is narration. On the other hand, a present tense translation works because English will also allow the context to establish the time frame. The fact that he is telling a dream lets the readers or listeners know the time frame; it is still safe to translate, "so there we are binding sheaves in the middle of the field…" It sets the stage for telling the story.

---

[6] A very free translation of הִנֵּה.

In Hebrew, הִנֵּה brings us into the perspective of the dream and the participle paints a picture of the action going on when the dream story begins. These make it vivid in the telling. In English, a creative translation of הִנֵּה and dramatic tone of voice, together with the participle, also paints a vivid picture. After all, the larger goal is not merely to translate or apply syntactic labels, but to enter into the story or draw your audience into it.

English also permits using a present tense form and letting context indicate the future time frame. Before looking at the Hebrew examples, consider these:

"The check is in the mail."

The speaker may still be on the phone with the creditor and has not actually written the check yet, but intends to immediately.

"Where are you going?" "I am going to the store."

Now what I in fact may be doing is putting on my shoes, an action which prompts the question, and then the response, "I am going to the store." This can be viewed from several angles. We could say that *am going*, the present participle construction, can also be used for future time. Or we can say that the sentence expands the meaning of *going* to include the preparation to go. Or we could say that the referent action, which is obviously in the future, is so real to the speaker as to use the present. Or we could say that the present participle is used for intention for the immediate future. We might even affirm more than one of these viewpoints at the same time. But however we describe this use of this morpheme, we should recognize that there is a close connection between the present time and what is envisioned or intended for the (near) future. The use of the present for a referent clearly in the future makes the portrayal more vivid in conveying the viewpoint of the speaker (whether that viewpoint is intention or certitude, etc.).

Now look again at example 20 (of 27.2.3), but translated in the present.

הִנְנִי נֹתְנוֹ בְיָדְךָ הַיּוֹם   *-20-*   Look, I *am delivering* it into your hand today.
1Ki 20:13

The context still indicates that the action will occur in the future but the present tense translation still makes sense. The point is not to quibble over whether these participles "should" be *translated* present or future (either is fine), but rather to point out the options and constraints. In some cases, the referent is in the future; and the progressive nature of the participle lends immediacy to its depiction. This is why many of the future time examples are translated *about to do X*. And this is also why Arnold and Choi aptly say in footnote 100:

The announcement of imminent action, which has already in fact begun to take place, is a powerful literary tool in the hands of the Old Testament prophets. Announcements of judgment frequently use this future *predicate participle* for rhetorical effect (*AC 81*).

We may add that this is very common with הִנֵּה, so that the combination הִנֵּה plus pronominal suffix (e.g. הִנְנִי) plus participle is often effectively rendered, "Look here, I am about to *X*," or "I hereby *X*," or "I am hereby *X*-ing" Having a translation formula is not so much the point as serving the larger drama of the text.

(c) **Participles and היה.**

Background clauses can use a participle alone, but a main clause needs a finite verb. In these constructions, active participles contribute the durative notion while the form of היה specifies the time frame. (See the examples above at 27.2.3.*e*.)

Participles may also be used as substantives or attributive adjectives in clauses with היה.

27.4   **Special participle use of הלך.**

The participle of הלך followed by a participle or an adjective can have a unique function. The construction *going on and being X* (the participle of הלך plus conjunction וְ plus participle/adjective) means *being increasingly X*, or *to be more and more X*, as in Jonah 1:11 and 13.

> כִּי הַיָּם הוֹלֵךְ וְסֹעֵר   For the sea was getting stormier and stormier.
>
>   *or*
>
>   For the sea was raging more and more.

This use occurs rarely enough that it may not be mentioned in a reference grammar on syntax; however, it is likely to be mentioned in your dictionary.

27.5   Summary.

Participles may be used as substantives or as attributive or predicate adjectives.

The genitive modifying the construct participle may tell the place of the activity in the participle (a "genitive" function not mentioned under noun syntax in ch. 25).

Active participles in the construct are often followed by the recipient of the action (objective genitive). Passive participles in the construct are often followed by the performer of the action (subjective genitive) or by a genitive of specification.

The time frame of a predicate participle depends on its context. Background statements in narrative are a common setting for past time; speech is a common setting for present or future time. With הִנֵּה the ptc. may indicate action in the near future.

The agent of the participle is often a pronoun or suffix on יֵשׁ, אֵין or הִנֵּה. (The agent is the performer of the action even if not a grammatical subject.)

The ptc. הֹלֵךְ may indicate the increasing nature of a following וֹ plus ptc./adj.

When consulting reference works, you need to consider more than the single category under which you find an item discussed. You must consider the relationships it is in. Your analysis should rely most on comparison to Biblical Hebrew examples in similar relationships.

chapter twenty-eight

Clausal Syntax in Narrative;
Movies in the Mind

28.1   Focus.

This chapter identifies basic functions of preterite clauses (*AC 84–87*) and non-verb-first clauses in narrative (*AC 164–167, 182–184*), and encourages you to connect the clauses to the larger drama of the story created by these constructions.

The backbone of a Hebrew narrative is the preterite. Preterite verbs move the basic action of the story along and act as a default type of construction. Because the preterite is a frozen form combining the conjunction with this otherwise archaic verb form, it is always first in the sentence. Sentences in narrative which are not verb first are marked, or distinguished by their word order. These non-preterite sentences can function in several ways. So too, the preterite can have more than one function. This chapter focuses on clausal constructions in narrative with the goal of not merely identifying their functions but connecting the role of clauses to the drama of the story.

To help us enter into the story we will use some basic camera or movie terminology. The biblical narratives are great stories, designed for reading aloud – storytelling through speaking. Listeners, or readers, play out the story on a mental movie screen. The story, as it is told, invites us to imagine a certain background, brings characters onto the stage, and guides the actions that play there. To help bridge the gap between an ancient oral society and one with television and 100-million-dollar epic movies, the clausal structure of Hebrew narrative can be thought of as a storyboard with various stage directions. As with *Drama in the Pauses* (ch. 23), we want to attend to the details of clauses, without losing sight of the bigger picture. These are great Hebrew stories and are great in Hebrew. Let our understanding of the pieces breathe life into the stories. Let us learn not just to label clause structures, but to describe the stories vividly to others.

28.2   Review.

In chapter 10 we learned that we must consider several factors when translating Hebrew verbs into English tenses: aspect, type, and context.

(a) Narrative genre.

A Hebrew storyteller narrates the story's past events in sentences with the verb-first, using a preterite verb. The main action line of the Jonah story, for example, comes in these verb-first clauses. There was a storm (וַיְהִי); the sailors were afraid (וַיִּירְאוּ); they called to their gods (וַיִּזְעָקוּ); they tossed cargo overboard (וַיָּטִלוּ). At that point, the author wants us to see not the next thing but something going on at the same time. Jonah is asleep during the frenzied actions of the sailors. So he switches to a noun-first construction and a perfect verb.

וְיוֹנָה יָרַד... But Jonah *had gone down* (into the ship) Jon 1:5

This syntactic clue suspends the sequence of events. How this change affects the hearers' mental picture of the story depends on the story line. In this case it is a change in scene, from above deck to below deck.

(b) Background clauses in narrative.

In chapter 27 we contrasted various non-verb-first clauses in narrative (27.3.*a*).

Nominal clause. A noun clause (without a verb or participle) presents a condition that is true in the same (past) time frame as the narrative.

Perfect Stative Verb. A background clause with a perfect stative verb could also present a condition that is true in the same (past) time frame as the narrative.

Perfect Fientive Verb. But a background clause with a perfect fientive verb would be a step farther back, as perfective in English, e.g. have *X*-ed.

Imperfect Verb. Such a background clause with an imperfect often indicates a past habitual action.

28.3 Main line and off-line structures.

Various labels are used to describe clause structure in narrative. Preterites have been called main line structures or paratactic structures, while noun-first constructions have been called off-line structures or hypotactic structures. These can be further labeled to describe their contribution to the narrative. The labels are generated by the meanings of the clauses in relation to the main paragraph.

Do not think in terms of Bible verses but rather in terms of clauses. A verse may have several clauses. It is useful to print the text one clause at a time in order to display the sequence of clauses. Marking a photocopy of the text to visually divide the clauses is quicker, and you may develop different marks for different clauses.

28.3.₁ Preterites *AC 84–87 §3.5.1*. **Main line or Paratactic clauses.**

The preterite (or *vayyiqtol* or *vav* plus imperfect consecutive, cf. 12.4.1) most commonly conveys a succession of events in the past. The past time frame is often first established by a non-preterite construction.

(a) *Sequential* (indicating an action or situation subsequent to the previous).

Refer to the previous page, 28.2*a*, for examples of the sequential use of the preterite in Jonah 1. It is often best to not translate the conjunction *vav* but rather view it as the period used to end the preceding sentence.

(b) *Consequential* (indicating a logical result from a previous action or situation).

וַיְהִי יְהוָה אֶת־יוֹסֵף	*-1-*	The LORD was with Joseph.
וַיְהִי אִישׁ מַצְלִיחַ		*And so* he became a successful man.
		Gen 39:2

(c) Sometimes the "next event" of the sequence depends on (rather than merely follows) the prior event. More important than debating whether to call them sequential or consequential (or create a new category) is having the freedom to translate accordingly. In 1Sam 17:49, the stone sinking into Goliath's head and Goliath's fall are not the abstract logical results of the previous, but these next actions in the sequence are the consequence of being hit in the head with a sling stone.

וַיִּשְׁלַח דָּוִד	*-2-*	David stretched out [his hand...]
וַיִּקַּח		He took [a stone...]
וַיְקַלַּע		*Then* he slung (it)
וַיַּךְ		*And* it struck [the Philistine...]
וַתִּטְבַּע		*so that* [the stone] embedded [in his forehead.]
וַיִּפֹּל		*And then* he fell...
		1Sam 17:49

Translating *then*, *and*, *so that*, or *and then* is more a part of story telling than simply trying to decide how to translate the *vav*. Do not be rigid in translating the conjunction with the preterite, but let the story line itself interact with your rendition. (Though some works will refer to types of *vav*, e.g. conjunctive, disjunctive, etc., it is really the relationship between the thoughts in the clauses that you are translating rather than the *vav*.)

(d) *Summary* (summarizes the previous or following scene in the story).

A preterite, or even a short series of preterites, may summarize the previous or following scene.

וַיֶּחֱזַק דָּוִד מִן־הַפְּלִשְׁתִּי	*-3-*	*Thus* David prevailed over the Philistine
בַּקֶּלַע וּבָאֶבֶן		with a sling and stone.
וַיַּךְ אֶת־הַפְּלִשְׁתִּי וַיְמִיתֵהוּ		He struck the Philistine and killed him.
וְחֶרֶב אֵין בְּיַד־דָּוִד		But there was no sword in David's hand.
		1Sam 17:50

The first lines of 1Sam 17:50 summarize the previous scene. While we could argue that *prevailing over the Philistine* is logically subsequent to him falling in verse 49, it is obvious that *he struck...and killed him* cannot be sequential but summarizes (recapitulates) the previous scene.

(e) Narratival (begins a narrative or scene, especially וַיְהִי).

While the other uses also occur in narrative, they typically follow something else in a series, so this title is applied to preterites which actually begin a story or scene in a story. Using וַיְהִי to start a story or scene is quite common (cp. 12.5).

וַיְהִי אִישׁ אֶחָד מִן־	-4-	There was a certain man from …
		1Sam 1:1
וַיֵּרָא אֵלָיו יְהוָה	-5-	The LORD appeared to him [by the oaks of Mamre]
		Gen 18:1

(f) Epexegetical (clarifies, paraphrases, or specifies the clause that precedes it).

Arnold and Choi note that the preterite may repeat or give more specification to the preceding clause (*AC 86–87*).

אֲבָל אִשָּׁה־אַלְמָנָה אָנִי	-6-	Truly I am a widow.
וַיָּמָת אִישִׁי		My husband died.
		2Sam 14:5
וְלֹא־זָכַר שַׂר־הַמַּשְׁקִים אֶת־יוֹסֵף	-7-	The chief cupbearer did not remember Joseph.
וַיִּשְׁכָּחֵהוּ		He forgot him.
		Gen 40:23
וַיַּעֲשׂוּ בְנֵי־יִשְׂרָאֵל אֶת־הָרַע	-8-	The Israelites did what was evil [in the LORD's eyes],
וַיִּשְׁכְּחוּ אֶת־יְהוָה אֱלֹהֵיהֶם		that is, they forgot the LORD their God
וַיַּעַבְדוּ אֶת־הַבְּעָלִים		but rather they served the Baals [and the Asheroth].
		Judg 3:7

(g) Dependent (the action occurs within the scope of a preceding temporal phrase)

A temporal phrase (without a verb) may precede a preterite. In such cases the action in the preterite is understood to happen in that time frame; thus it is dependent on the phrase for the time of its action.

בִּשְׁנַת־מוֹת הַמֶּלֶךְ עֻזִּיָּהוּ	-9-	In the year King Uzziah died,
וָאֶרְאֶה אֶת־אֲדֹנָי		I saw the Lord [sitting on a throne]…
		Is 6:1

(h) Etc.

There are many more nuances that preterite verbs can have in other settings. These nuances are based on the story line.

28.3.2 Interruptions in verb sequences; background clauses *AC 92–94 §3.5.4.* Also called off-line or hypotactic clauses.

(a) Distinct subject (a successive action by a different subject).

Arnold and Choi list several examples of interruptions in verbal (i.e. preterite) sequences. We have seen several already (28.2b). This category is "a seemingly successive action performed by a different subject, thereby placing emphasis on an agent who is distinct from the agent of the main verb, and, in effect, presenting an opposition of subjects" (*AC 92*).

-10- וַיְשַׁלַּח אֶת־הָעָם נֹשְׂאֵי הַמִּנְחָה	…He dismissed the people who were transporting the tribute. Judg 3:18
וְהוּא שָׁב מִן־הַפְּסִילִים	But (then) he turned back from the idols [which were at Gilgal]… Judg 3:19

Noun-first clauses in narrative, especially those which specify the subject (a known character), the place (setting), the time, or a combination of these often do more than mark emphasis on a distinct subject. They may mark a break in the scenes of the story. In these cases they are not simply parenthetical information supplementing an action in a preterite line; they can help to divide the larger narrative into its scenes or constituent parts.

(b) Etc.

Besides the various time frames which background statements may have, there are a variety of possible relationships between the type of information in these non-verb-first clauses and other elements of the story. They can set the stage for the story or section of the story to begin, describe the circumstances of another action, introduce new characters, present contrasting information, or perform other functions. These types of relationships involve more than word order and verbal aspect; they involve the structure of how story information is presented.

28.4 Envisioning the story. Your mental movie screen.

The verbs and clause structure perform such functions as moving the action along (at different speeds), expanding on circumstances, or focusing our attention on something, etc. We need to know what clauses are doing, but we do not want to just assign labels to them. The most important question is not, "What kind of clause is this?" Answer: "This noun-first clause is a circumstantial clause." The more important question is, "What does this do for the story?" Breaking down these clauses must not keep us from seeing that they add up to something bigger. To help with this, we can view clausal information as stage or camera directions.

The story of "Special Agent" Ehud makes for a great action movie. The first set of preterites move the story rapidly along and establish the setting for Ehud's private plot. Judges 3:12:

וַיֹּסִ֙פוּ֙ בְּנֵ֣י יִשְׂרָאֵ֔ל לַעֲשֹׂ֥ות הָרַ֖ע בְּעֵינֵ֥י יְהוָ֑ה	Then the Israelites again did the evil in the LORD's sight.
וַיְחַזֵּ֣ק יְהוָ֗ה אֶת־עֶגְל֤וֹן מֶֽלֶךְ־מוֹאָב֙ עַל־יִשְׂרָאֵ֔ל	So the LORD strengthened Eglon, king of Moab over Israel
עַ֛ל כִּי־עָשׂ֥וּ אֶת־הָרַ֖ע בְּעֵינֵ֥י יְהוָֽה׃	because they had done what was evil in the LORD's sight.

The first clause should have us see Israel worshipping idols and also feel the distaste of it. The second clause is summary of what follows. It gives the big picture, like the title of the chapter selection on a DVD menu, while the following will fill in some details. The subordinate causal clause reemphasizes why this happened.

Then narrative time moves quickly with a series of preterites. *He* (Eglon) *gathered* (וַיֶּאֱסֹף) allies; *he went* (וַיֵּלֶךְ); *he struck* (וַיַּךְ) Israel; *they served* (וַיַּעַבְדוּ) … 18 years. *Then they cried out* (וַיִּזְעֲקוּ) to the LORD. So *the LORD raised* (וַיָּקֶם) *up* a deliverer. We should know the cycle from earlier in the book; these verses rapidly fill in some particulars.

Then a series of appositional phrases describe the deliverer. They serve the purpose of characterization. We learn his name, family, and tribe. We find out that he is left-handed, described as *bound with respect to his right hand,*[1] an important detail for later in the story. This literary technique is called foreshadowing. Its role in the story is to prepare you to understand how a later scene will work. These appositional phrases supply information without changing the clausal structure; they are still part of the preterite sentence.

Another preterite follows; *the Israelites sent* (וַיִּשְׁלְחוּ) tribute under his charge to Eglon. This clause also acts as a summary for the coming scene. The next preterite, וַיַּעַשׂ, is not sequential to this summary וַיִּשְׁלְחוּ *they sent*; however, it is part of a series of events. The chapter on the DVD menu is *they sent tribute*. The movie might even show tribute being collected for transport. But the specific scene for Ehud starts with וַיַּעַשׂ, Ehud *made* himself a dagger. You can translate "had made" if you like, but it is not necessary; you could just as well start a new paragraph. This is because the story simply asks you to next start seeing Ehud and then merges this thread of the story with the larger preparations for paying tribute.

---

[1] We, the modern audience, do not really know if the phrase אִטֵּ֖ר יַד־יְמִינ֑וֹ, *bound with respect to his right hand* (a genitive of specification) simply means he was left-handed, or that he was left-handed because he had been trained that way by binding the right hand (something done elsewhere in the Near East) or because his right hand or arm was malformed or injured. The original audience knew and we can envision the story successfully either way.

The scene with Ehud then uses non-preterite clauses to direct the cameras and focus the audience's attention. The topic of the nominal clauses is the dagger. Because they are nominal clauses, they are in the same time as the previous preterite (27.3a), so we know to use a simple past. We can label it circumstantial. But in our mind's eye, we need to see the camera zoom in on the blade. *It had two edges.* We see it turning to expose both edges. Our view starts at the tip and slowly brings the rest of the blade into view. *It was a (short) cubit long.* An impressive skewer. (Perhaps we see him wave and thrust it, testing its balance.) To convey this to an audience, you might compare it to James Bond being given a special device.

After the blade has been held up for the audience to appreciate its potential, we see Ehud strap (וַיַּחְגֹּר) it under his garments onto his *right* thigh. We now connect this to the description that he was *bound with regard to his right hand.* The weapon's hiding place is related to handedness (and to evading detection by guards).

Now that Ehud is ready, the next verb is a singular preterite with Ehud as the subject but with a group of people implied. *He brought* (וַיַּקְרֵב) *the tribute to Eglon, King of Moab.* The story has now brought together two threads, Ehud's personal preparation and the previous statement that *they sent* tribute under his charge. A lot of activity is assumed in this telling: the packing, the journey, the arrival, the presentation. This way of saying it has jumped the scene to the presentation.

Next, we hear another noun-first background clause. The cameras focus on Eglon – perhaps initially on his face, then backing away – but only so far as to see his frame filling the picture. וְעֶגְלוֹן אִישׁ בָּרִיא מְאֹד׃ *Now Eglon was a man who was very obese* (or *Now Eglon – he was fat to the max*). This too is foreshadowing.

After lingering on the magnitude of Eglon's size, וַיְהִי starts a new scene, so the camera cuts to a new setting, perhaps using a fade-through technique. The וַיְהִי clause tells us that the time frame is after the tribute has been delivered. And we are back to the action line with the preterite (וַיְשַׁלַּח) *he dismissed* the people, the tribute bearers. A noun-first clause shows his simultaneous contrasting action. *But he turned back* from the idols which were at Gilgal. And through this ruse, he gains audience with king Eglon.

We have earlier described how narrative time slows down for the assassination scene, suggesting slow-motion camera technique. We also considered the dramatic use of the pausal form וַיִּפְתָּחוּ and the particle הִנֵּה. See 23.3c.

You might observe that the preterites are generally saying, *next thing,* whether we call them sequential, consequential, summary, or something else. The story sequence is not the same as the sequence of history. In history, Ehud "had made" the dagger first, before the tribute was sent. If we called וַיַּעַשׂ by a name like *pluperfect,* that title would indicate something about when the action occurred in relation to another action in the story. But it would not actually mean that the preterite has the value of a pluperfect. The preterite, *and then he X-ed*, conveys the story scene. In the story line, Ehud "made" the dagger next. The sense that he *had made* the dagger arises from the chronological sequence of events (not the sequence of scenes) and the preterite happens to be the point where we find ourselves making a decision about translation. *Viewing* the story does not have this problem. Thus thinking about the story like a movie, making scene changes and using camera techniques, not only makes a bridge to modern culture, but also helps us think properly about narrative. Again the meaning arises from combinations; we organize syntax material around certain forms because that is where we find ourselves wrestling with the nuances of translation.

28.5   Summary.

(a) Preterite clauses (Main line or Paratactic clauses).

The preterite most commonly conveys a succession of events in the past. The past time frame is often first established by a non-preterite construction.

Sequential (indicating an action or situation subsequent to the previous).

Consequential (indicating a logical result from previous action or situation).

Summary (summarizes the previous or following scene in the story).

Narratival (begins a narrative or scene, especially וַיְהִי).

Epexegetical (clarifies, paraphrases, or specifies the clause that precedes it).

Dependent (the action occurs within the scope of a preceding temporal phrase).

Etc. There are many more nuances that preterite verbs can have resulting from combinations of a variety of factors, such as continuing the nuance of a prior verb form or accounting for the type of verbal root or context.

(b) Background clauses (off-line or hypotactic clauses).

See 27.3a for examples of time frames.

Distinct subject (a successive action by a different subject or emphasizing the subject's action as different from others).

Etc. There are a variety of possible relationships between the type of information in noun-first clauses and other elements of the story. They can set the stage for the story to begin, describe the circumstances of another action, introduce new characters, present contrasting information, or perform other functions.

(c) Seeing the stories.

More than just labeling clauses, we want to know how the clausal structure contributes to the story. We want to learn to see and retell how the action moves, how the scenes shift, etc. Using "movie" language is a tool for both.

chapter twenty-nine

Particles
הִנֵּה *and* אֲשֶׁר

29.1   Focus.

We continue the theme of looking at meaning as it arises from combinations, using the particles אֲשֶׁר and הִנֵּה. We are using the word *particle* in a general sense, little words that do not have paradigms. Particles do not derive from a root in the way that nouns and verbs do.

A dictionary will approach these particles from a lexical perspective, suggesting glosses that may be used in English translation. But they may be sparse on the settings in which they are used. We highly recommend consulting Arnold and Choi and other syntax reference works for examples of how various particles function.[1] The categories assigned to the particles in reference works may be viewed as translation advice for when the particles occur in similar circumstances.

We will discuss these particles as having a base meaning that interacts with the context. We will emphasize how larger discourse features affect their meaning.

29.2   אֲשֶׁר. Cp. 9.6; *AC 172–175; 184–186.*

אֲשֶׁר introduces a clause that is either substantival or relative. Most of the time אֲשֶׁר refers back to a noun and is easily translated by *who*, *which*, *that*, or *where*, depending on its antecedent. Sometimes its antecedent is only implied.

(a) **Substantival.** Arnold and Choi illustrate that an אֲשֶׁר clause can fulfill the function of a nominative (1), accusative (2), or genitive (3) noun under the heading of substantival clauses (*AC 171–173*).

טוֹב אֲשֶׁר לֹא־תִדֹּר	-1-	*That* you do not vow is better… Ecc 5:4
וַיָּשֶׂם דָּנִיֵּאל עַל־לִבּוֹ אֲשֶׁר לֹא־יִתְגָּאַל	-2-	Daniel set [on] his mind *that* he would not defile himself Dan 1:8
כָּל־יְמֵי אֲשֶׁר הַנֶּגַע בּוֹ	-3-	All the days ~~of~~ *that* the infection is in him Lev 13:46

---

[1] Chapter four of Arnold and Choi illustrates the uses of prepositions (95–126), adverbs (127–42), conjunctions (143–56), the particles of existence/nonexistence (156–61).

(b) **Relative clause.** Frequently אֲשֶׁר relates a clause back to a noun. Often that noun, its antecedent, is represented again by a pronoun in the relative clause. English usually does not tolerate this redundancy, though it can be helpful for identifying the antecedent. See 9.6 to review or *AC 184–185*.

A special use in a relative clause (not covered in ch. 9) is **paronomasia**. "The repetition of a word in both the main clause and in the relative clause can be used to express a sense of indeterminateness" (*AC 185–186*).

וַאֲנִי הוֹלֵךְ	-4-	While I am going *wherever* I will go
עַל אֲשֶׁר־אֲנִי הוֹלֵךְ		2Sam 15:20
וַיֵּצְאוּ מִקְּעִלָה	-5-	They went out from Keilah
וַיִּתְהַלְּכוּ בַּאֲשֶׁר יִתְהַלָּכוּ		and went about *wherever* they could go.
		1Sam 23:13

(c) **Clause functions.** The *content* of an אֲשֶׁר clause can fulfill several functions in the discourse. Arnold and Choi classify relative clauses into two types. The *limiting* clause makes "a distinction between more than one member of a group or class," while the *nonlimiting* clause "marks a general attribute of the antecedent without setting it off against other members of its 'class'" (*AC 184*). אֲשֶׁר also appears in other kinds of clauses such as final, result, and causal clauses (*AC ch. 5*). אֲשֶׁר is merely the relative pronoun while the clause function stems from its content and the larger discourse. For example, Waltke and O'Connor include אֲשֶׁר שָׁכְבָה עָלָיו (1Ki 3:19) as an example of a causal clause, translating "*because* she lay on top of him."[2] The clause content gives the cause of death, but אֲשֶׁר is just the relative pronoun modifying בֵּן (*whom*) or perhaps לַיְלָה (*when*).

וַיָּמָת בֶּן־הָאִשָּׁה הַזֹּאת	-6-	This woman's son, *whom* she lay on ~~him~~, died at night.
לָיְלָה אֲשֶׁר שָׁכְבָה עָלָיו		1Ki 3:19

Similarly they cite De 4:10 as an example of a final clause, translating אֲשֶׁר as *in order that* they learn.[3] Again, אֲשֶׁר itself is simply a relative pronoun. The notion of *purpose* (for learning) arises from the combination of other elements.

וְאַשְׁמִעֵם אֶת־דְּבָרָי	-7-	And I will make them hear my words,
אֲשֶׁר יִלְמְדוּן לְיִרְאָה אֹתִי		*which* they should learn in order to fear me…
		De 4:10

אֲשֶׁר serves to identify something about דְּבָרָי. The content of the clause identifies the intention for which they were given. "As a rule אֲשֶׁר is a mere connecting link."[4]

---

[2] Waltke and O'Connor, p. 640.
[3] Waltke and O'Connor, p. 639.
[4] Francis Brown, S. R. Driver, Charles A. Briggs. *The New Brown-Driver-Briggs Hebrew and English Lexicon of the Old Testament*, revised. Peabody, MA: Hendricksen, 1996, p. 81.

29.3   הִנֵּה. Cp. 9.4; *AC 157–161*.

הִנֵּה is called a deictic particle; it points something out or presents something. הִנֵּה may be called presentative. In a basic sense, הִנֵּה indicates a realization or calls for attention. It differs from יֵשׁ, which primarily affirms the existence or the presence of something. הִנֵּה points out something with the suggestion of implications. This general concept is applied in multiple ways, depending on the context. To account for contextual features, approach the rendering of הִנֵּה with these questions:

1) Who is talking to whom?

2) Who is having, or is expected to have, the הִנֵּה experience?

3) Why is this phrase highlighted?

Who is talking to whom?

Is the speaker a character in the story or is it the narrator? This is basically the same as asking whether הִנֵּה occurs in reported speech or as part of the narrative. But a character in a story may become a narrator, who briefly tells a story. Asking who the speaker is works hand in hand with asking who is addressed. Is it another character in the story or is it the narrator's general audience? This leads directly to the next question.

Who is having, or is expected to have, the הִנֵּה experience?

Is the speaker describing their own realization (their own הִנֵּה experience), calling for the attention of the person they are addressing (asking or directing them to have a הִנֵּה experience) or directing the audience to share the perspective (the הִנֵּה experience) of a third party, such as a character in a story? It is also possible that the speaker and the addressee are to share the realization. These questions about the setting of הִנֵּה help us to think through the next question.

Why is this phrase highlighted?

By pointing at something, הִנֵּה highlights it. This is called giving it focus or saliency. הִנֵּה does not give each phrase a particular level of focus, that is, הִנֵּה does not assign the same specific level of urgency, surprise, or importance to every phrase. Rather הִנֵּה marks something as significant *relative* to the surrounding context. But the bigger question is why. Why does highlighting it (giving it relative saliency) accomplish the speaker's goal with respect to the addressee?

A few preliminary notes.

These examples include הִנֵּה and וְהִנֵּה but not הֵן, although הֵן is very similar and many of these things apply to it as well.[5] There are some different settings in

---

[5] Are הִנֵּה and הֵן the same? They are very similar. But while הִנֵּה commonly occurs with participles as verbal elements, הֵן does not. Whether הֵן cannot do so, is another question, but the preference for הִנֵּה when participles are used may point to a difference between the two.

which הִנֵּה and וְהִנֵּה occur. הִנֵּה commonly begins reported speech (e.g. following forms of אָמַר) while וְהִנֵּה often occurs when narrating (e.g. she looked... וְהִנֵּה etc.). Since it is quite rare for reported speech to begin with *vav*, it is not remarkable that הִנֵּה begins reported speech without *vav*. It is also not remarkable for *vav* to appear between clauses in narration. And in both cases the particle הִנֵּה is deictic/presentative. Even though syntactically there may be labels that apply to one and not to the other, הִנֵּה and וְהִנֵּה are treated together below.[6]

It is worth repeating that glosses that work in English do not establish the *meaning* of the Hebrew particle. There are many occasions in which הִנֵּה can be sensibly *translated* by "if/when" in conditional sentences. The gloss works in English because of the protasis-apodosis type of relationship between the clauses, not because הִנֵּה has the *meaning* of these conjunctions. Its meaning is probably more like "here is the case and in such a case...(then)." This can be sensibly translated as "if...(then)" or "let's suppose X, (then)" or in other ways. Likewise, at times an interjection may work well in an English rendering, but this does not mean that הִנֵּה is an interjection in Hebrew.

Analyzing הִנֵּה clauses is a multifaceted task. Trying to identify a core meaning or to suggest English glosses for הִנֵּה is a lexical task. Trying to classify clause functions and identify different circumstances or uses of הִנֵּה and וְהִנֵּה is a syntactical task. Trying to account for speaker, addressee, and relative saliency is a task of discourse analysis. They are interrelated issues rather than isolated issues. So keep in mind which type of information a resource (dictionary, syntax book, etc.) focuses on. The following examples give dynamic translations in an attempt to account for the larger discourse functions.

(a) **Examples in speech, with הִנֵּה for the addressee's experience.**

The following 4 examples have similar syntax but different purposes in conversation. Each case is an example of reported speech from one character in the story to another using הִנֵּנִי, which may be considered a standardized expression. In each case the speaker presents himself to the addressee so that the addressee realizes something about the speaker's presence. But they are used for different strategies. The speaker responds to being directly addressed in examples 1 and 2, to being indirectly addressed in example 3, and is not responding to an address in example 4.

-1- וַיֹּאמֶר יִצְחָק אֶל־אַבְרָהָם אָבִיו	Isaac spoke to his father Abraham.
וַיֹּאמֶר אָבִי	He said, "Dad?"
וַיֹּאמֶר הִנֶּנִּי בְנִי	And he said, "*Yes*, son."
	Gen 22:7

---

[6] That is, וְהִנֵּה is not treated as an additional particle, but simply as הִנֵּה which happens to have the conjunction.

וַיִּקְרָא יְהוָה אֶל־שְׁמוּאֵל	-2-	The LORD called to Samuel.
וַיֹּאמֶר הִנֵּנִי		And he responded, "*Right here.*"
וַיָּרָץ אֶל־עֵלִי		Then he ran to Eli
וַיֹּאמֶר הִנְנִי כִּי־קָרָאתָ לִּי		and said, "*I'm here...* because you called me."
		1Sam 3:4–5
אֶת־מִי אֶשְׁלַח וּמִי יֵלֶךְ־לָנוּ	-3-	"Whom shall I send? Who will go for us?"
וָאֹמַר הִנְנִי שְׁלָחֵנִי		Then I said, "*Hey, me.* Send me."
		Is 6:8
הִנְנִי עֲנוּ בִי נֶגֶד יְהוָה	-4-	"*Here I am.* Bear witness against me before the LORD."
		1Sam 12:3

In example 1, Abraham is verifying that he is paying attention. Isaac knows exactly where Abraham is and Abraham knows this. In 1Sam 3:4, from example 2, Samuel does not know whether the other party (assumed to be Eli) already knows where he (Samuel) is or whether Eli is looking for him. In the rhetoric of example 3, Isaiah is not directly addressed, but presents himself as a volunteer. In example 4, Samuel has already been talking and the people listening to him. הִנְנִי serves to present himself as the new topic of conversation, which constitutes a challenge. Perhaps "here I am" would work in each case if the only question were translation. But for public reading one must consider more subtle nuances, such as tone of voice (whether reading the Hebrew or reading English based on your study of the Hebrew), or choosing other colloquial expressions that fit the mood better.

In the next two examples it is clear that the parties are already paying attention to each other. The speaker is highlighting something that the other should especially note. This can work to set out an idea that the speaker will go on to talk about.

וַיֹּאמֶר אֱלֹהִים	-5-	Next God said,
הִנֵּה נָתַתִּי לָכֶם אֶת־כָּל־עֵשֶׂב		"*Now look around here*; I hereby give you every plant [bearing seed...]
לָכֶם יִהְיֶה לְאָכְלָה		It shall be for your food."
		Gen 1:29
וַיֹּאמֶר הִנֵּה הָאֵשׁ וְהָעֵצִים	-6-	He said, "*Um*, here's the fire and the wood–
וְאַיֵּה הַשֶּׂה לְעֹלָה		so where's the lamb for an offering?"
		Gen 22:7

(b) **In speech with הִנֵּה expressing a supposition to consider, perhaps jointly.**

Making a distinction between the speaker and addressee having the הִנֵּה experience should not be rigid. This can already be argued for example 6. Isaac is noticing and wondering, and he wants Abraham to notice the same thing in order to grasp why he asks the question. So too in other cases, the speaker may be wanting to think together with the person who is addressed.

וַיֹּאמֶר דָּוִד ... אֶל־כָּל־עֲבָדָיו	-7-	David said to Abishai and all his servants,
הִנֵּה בְנִי ... מְבַקֵּשׁ אֶת־נַפְשִׁי		"*Seeing that* my son seeks my life,
וְאַף כִּי־עַתָּה בֶּן־הַיְמִינִי		how much more now, this Benjaminite?"
		2Sam 16:11
וַיֹּאמֶר לוֹ הִנֵּה־נָא	-8-	He said to him, "*Please consider*–
אִישׁ־אֱלֹהִים בָּעִיר הַזֹּאת...		There's a man of God in this city…
עַתָּה נֵלְכָה שָּׁם...		let's go there now."
וַיֹּאמֶר שָׁאוּל לְנַעֲרוֹ		Saul said to his servant,
וְהִנֵּה נֵלֵךְ וּמַה־נָּבִיא לָאִישׁ...		And *supposing* we go, what will we bring to the man?"
וַיֹּאמֶר הִנֵּה		He said, "*Hey*, I've got ¼ shekel of silver."
נִמְצָא בְיָדִי רֶבַע שֶׁקֶל כָּסֶף		1Sam 9:6–8

Note especially the second הִנֵּה in 1Sam 9:6–8. Saul uses *vav* plus הִנֵּה to begin speech, which is very rare, because he is continuing the thought already expressed by his servant. Although the speaker is asking the other party to give attention to a certain idea, where הִנֵּה introduces a supposition it is less important to ask who is having, or is to have the הִנֵּה experience.

(c) **In speech with הִנֵּה expressing the speaker's experience.**

הִנֵּה may signal the speaker's perspective or reaction, drawing the listener into their emotion or reaction. The nuance depends on what the speaker is reacting to and how they are reacting. Translation need not be restricted to "lo" or "behold." For a movie, rather than a translation, perhaps an actor might simply gesture.

הִנָּךְ יָפָה	-9-	*Wow*, you are beautiful!
		Song 4:1
הִנֵּה אָנֹכִי הוֹלֵךְ לָמוּת	-10-	[Esau said,] "*Oy!* I am going to die."
		Gen 25:32
וָאָקֻם בַּבֹּקֶר לְהֵינִיק אֶת־בְּנִי	-11-	"I rose in the morning to nurse my son
וְהִנֵּה־מֵת		and, *oh my*, he was dead.
וָאֶתְבּוֹנֵן אֵלָיו בַּבֹּקֶר		Then I examined him in the morning
וְהִנֵּה לֹא־הָיָה בְנִי		and realized he was not my son
אֲשֶׁר יָלָדְתִּי		to whom I had given birth."
		1Ki 3:21
וָאֵרֶא בַּחֲלֹמִי	-12-	"I saw in my dream –
וְהִנֵּה שֶׁבַע שִׁבֳּלִים		(*gesture*) – seven ears…"
		Gen 41:22
וָאֶרְאֶה	-13-	"I looked
וְהִנֵּה חֹר־אֶחָד בַּקִּיר		and *noticed* – there was one hole in the wall."
		Ezek 8:7
כִּי רָאִינוּ אֶת־הָאָרֶץ	-14-	"For we have seen the land,
וְהִנֵּה טוֹבָה מְאֹד		and *indeed* it is very good."
		Judg 18:9

(d) In narration with הִנֵּה expressing the perspective of a character.

The narrator may use הִנֵּה to change the point of view to that of a character in the story. The audience should see it through the character's eyes.

וּפַרְעֹה חֹלֵם וְהִנֵּה -15-	Pharaoh was dreaming. *And this is what he saw*—
עֹמֵד עַל־הַיְאֹר	he was standing by the Nile. Gen 41:1
וַיִּשָּׂא עֵינָיו וַיַּרְא -16-	He lifted up his eyes and looked—
וְהִנֵּה־אִישׁ עֹמֵד לְנֶגְדּוֹ	*there was* a man standing opposite him. Josh 5:13
וַיַּרְא וְהִנֵּה הַסְּנֶה בֹּעֵר בָּאֵשׁ -17-	He looked and was *intrigued* that the bush was burning. Exod 3:2
וַיָּרֻצוּ הָאֹהֱלָה -18-	They ran to the tent.
וְהִנֵּה טְמוּנָה בְּאָהֳלוֹ	And *sure enough*, it was hidden in his tent. Josh 7:22

(e) In narration with הִנֵּה appealing to the audience.

The narrator may highlight some circumstance, not making the scene come from a character's viewpoint, but like having the camera zoom in or focus on something. The view may expand to involve characters who also observe it, but the storytelling presents the facts first, then the characters. Under the narrator's direction, the audience sees it without the "camera" taking the character's point of view.

וַתַּעַל שִׁכְבַת הַטָּל -19-	Then the dew dried up and
וְהִנֵּה עַל־פְּנֵי הַמִּדְבָּר דַּק מְחֻסְפָּס	*there*, on the surface of the ground, was a thin flakelike thing… Ex16:14

In the next example, in Numbers 12 the narrator first presents Miriam to the audience, then focuses in on her leprous condition. The first הִנֵּה has the audience take in the fact that Miriam is leprous. Next Aaron is brought into the scene, still unaware, and then we see him realize her condition. This second הִנֵּה is like the previous category, where the narrator wants the audience to see the perspective of the character even though the audience already knows the information.

וְהֶעָנָן סָר מֵעַל הָאֹהֶל -20-	When the cloud left the tent—
וְהִנֵּה מִרְיָם מְצֹרַעַת כַּשָּׁלֶג	there, *look*, Miriam was leprous, like snow.
וַיִּפֶן אַהֲרֹן אֶל־מִרְיָם	Then Aaron turned toward Miriam
וְהִנֵּה מְצֹרָעַת	and *was shocked* to see her leprous. Num 12:10

29.4   Logical connections in the content. *AC 160–161.*

Since הִנֵּה may present an idea on which the following clause comments, there can be a variety of logical connections between the content of the two clauses.

-21- וַיָּשָׁב רְאוּבֵן אֶל־הַבּוֹר	Reuben returned to the pit.
וְהִנֵּה אֵין־יוֹסֵף בַּבּוֹר	And – *horrors* – no Joseph in the pit.
וַיִּקְרַע אֶת־בְּגָדָיו	Then he tore his clothes.
	Gen 37:29

The fact that Joseph was not in the pit is the cause for Reuben to tear his clothes. You might translate *because Joseph was not in the pit*. Even though הִנֵּה does not "mean" *because*, הִנֵּה points to the cause (yet with emotion). Other logical relationships are possible.

29.5   Summary.

אֲשֶׁר and הִנֵּה may each be viewed as having a general meaning, אֲשֶׁר a nominalizer and הִנֵּה an attention getter. הִנֵּה in particular can be quite versatile in contributing functions to communication events.

Reference works contain many kinds of information. Sometimes that information mostly teaches about Hebrew; sometimes it mostly gives translation advice or suggestions.

For reflection and discussion: Are אֲשֶׁר and הִנֵּה of the same type? Is a wide range of translation options more appropriate for one and less for the other? Why?

chapter thirty

Verb Syntax:
Infinitives

30.1   Focus.

The chapter surveys the many roles that the infinitive construct and infinitive absolute may play. The discussions attempt to portray the most common uses and to illustrate understanding a rare construction of the infinitive absolute by means of comparison.

30.2   On history.

The names infinitive absolute and infinitive construct give the impression that these forms are related. That impression may be strengthened by observing the *shewa* under R₁ for the Qal infinitive construct and pretonic open long *qametz* under R₁ for the Qal infinitive absolute. They appear to be variant forms based on the accent rules' response to their syntactical positions, construct or absolute. While this impression contributed to their names, it is in fact false. The two forms come from historically different sources. So we do not understand one in light of the other, but treat them as unrelated.

30.3   Infinitive Construct. Cp. 8.6–8.8.1, 16.5, and *AC 67–73*.

The infinitive construct is a verbal noun, essentially conveying the verbal idea of the root. Its actual role depends on its syntax. It can occur in any noun position: nominative (1), accusative (2), or genitive (3). The infinitive construct may take pronominal suffixes, which may be the performer (3) or receiver (4) of the action.

עֲנוֹשׁ לַצַּדִּיק לֹא־טוֹב	-1-	*To impose* a fine on the innocent is not good. Prov 17:26
לֹא אֵדַע צֵאת וָבֹא	-2-	I do not know (how) *to go out* and *come* in (= *I am inexperienced*) 1Ki 3:7
כִּימֵי צֵאתְךָ מֵאֶרֶץ מִצְרָיִם	-3-	As in the days *when you came* from the land of Egypt Mic 7:15
לְשָׁמְרָהּ	-4-	*...to keep it.* Gen 2:15

Its most common role is as the object of a preposition (about 87%). In context, 96% of infinitive constructs are immediately preceded by: (1) a preposition, esp. לְ, (2) a temporal indicator, e.g. שָׁנָה, אָז, עֵת, יוֹם, אַחַר, אַחֲרֵי, or (3) an indicator of purpose or cause, e.g. יַעַן. Most of the remaining 4% are used as complements, completing the meaning of another word, such as *seek to X, sufficient to X*. Most exceptions to these generalizations are in Jeremiah, Ezekiel, Daniel, Ezra, and Chronicles.

(a) Infinitive constructs occur as objects of these prepositions.

לְ	4529	עַד	151	עַל	17	תַּחַת	2
בְּ	726	לְמַעַן	65	בַּעֲבוּר	8	נֶגֶד	1
כְּ	251	אַחֲרֵי	55	אֶל	3	עִם	1
מִן	184						

(b) Infinitive constructs occur after these adverbs.

יַעַן	26[1]	*because*		טֶרֶם	2	*before*
עוֹד	8	*still*		אָז	1	*then*
אִם	4	*if*		תְּמוֹל	1	*previously*
אַחַר	3	*after*				

(c) The common uses of those frequently combined with the infinitive construct:

אַחֲרֵי temporal – prior to the main verb; transl.: *after* (AC 70)

בְּ temporal – same time as the main verb; transl.: *as, when, while* (AC 69)

   causal – transl.: *because, since*

כְּ temporal – immediately preceding the main verb; transl.: *as soon as, when* (AC 69)

לְ purpose – transl.: *in order to* (AC 71)

   result – transl.: *so that* (AC 71)

   temporal imminence – transl.: *about to, soon to, at the point of* (AC 72)

   specification – transl.: *by ___-ing* (AC 72)

מִן partitive – transl.: *from*

   comparative – transl.: *than*

   causal – transl.: *because*

   temporal – transl.: *from, since*

עַד temporal – at the end of the main verb's action; transl.: *until* (AC 70)

לְמַעַן purpose – transl.: *in order to* (AC 71)

30.3.1 In addition to the uses above, Arnold and Choi illustrate five uses of the infinitive construct with prepositions and another use in expressions of obligation.

---

[1] These are mostly in Ezekiel.

(a) Temporal. *AC 69–70.*

וַיְהִי בְּבוֹאָם בְּשׁוּב דָּוִד מֵהַכּוֹת אֶת־הַפְּלִשְׁתִּי	-6-	It happened *when they came*, while David returned from striking the Philistine. 1Sam 18:6
וַיְהִי כִרְאוֹת הַמֶּלֶךְ אֶת־אֶסְתֵּר	-7-	It happened *as soon as* the king saw Esther... Est 5:2
לֹא אוּכַל לַעֲשׂוֹת דָּבָר עַד־בֹּאֶךָ	-8-	I am not able *to do* anything until you come. Gen 19:22
וַיָּשָׁב יוֹסֵף אַחֲרֵי קָבְרוֹ אֶת־אָבִיו	-9-	Joseph returned... *after he buried* his father. Gen 50:14

(b) Purpose. *AC 71.*

וַיָּבֵא אֶל־הָאָדָם לִרְאוֹת מַה־יִּקְרָא־לוֹ	-10-	He brought [each] to the man *to see* what he would call it, Gen 2:19
וְאוֹתָנוּ הוֹצִיא מִשָּׁם לְמַעַן הָבִיא אֹתָנוּ לָתֶת לָנוּ אֶת־הָאָרֶץ	-11-	But as for us, he brought us from there in order *to bring* us [here] *to give* us the land... De 6:23

(c) Result. *AC 71.*

וַיְגָרֶשׁ שְׁלֹמֹה אֶת־אֶבְיָתָר לְמַלֵּא אֶת־דְּבַר יְהוָה	-12-	Solomon banished Abiathar [from being priest] and *so fulfilled* the word of the Lord 1Ki 2:27
וַיְקַטְּרוּ לֵאלֹהִים אֲחֵרִים לְמַעַן הַכְעִיסֵנִי	-13-	They burned incense to other gods *so that they angered* me... 2Ki 22:17

(d) Imminence. *AC 72.*

וַיְהִי הַשֶּׁמֶשׁ לָבוֹא	-14-	It happened as the sun was *about to set*... Gen 12:15

(e) Specification. *AC 72–73.*

הָלַךְ אַחֲרַי בְּכָל־לְבָבוֹ לַעֲשׂוֹת רַק הַיָּשָׁר בְּעֵינָי	-15-	he followed me with all his heart *by doing* only what was just in my sight 1Ki 14:8

(f) Obligation. *AC 71–72.*

וְעָלַי לָתֶת לְךָ עֲשָׂרָה כָסֶף	-16-	It would have been on me (= I would have had) *to give* you 10 silver pieces. 2Sam 18:11
אֵין לָבוֹא אֶל־שַׁעַר הַמֶּלֶךְ	-17-	None [were] *to enter* the gate of the king [clothed in sackcloth] Est 4:2

30.4   Infinitive Absolute. Cp. 14.8 and *AC 73–77*.

The most common use (about 55%) of the infinitive absolute is for emphasis (*AC 74–76*) in paronomastic constructions (i.e. with a finite verb of the same root). The infinitive absolute can perform a wide variety of functions. It may act as a noun in nominative, accusative, or genitive relationships (*AC 74*), as a substitute for a verb (*AC 77*), or adverbially, often noting the manner of the main verb's action (*AC 76*).

It is helpful to consider both the grammatical roles of the infinitive absolute and the constructions in which it occurs. There are about 870 infinitive absolutes in the Bible.[2] About 466 of these are paronomastic, with a decided preponderance of these in speech.[3] Around 107 occur in a paired relationship. The approximately 297 remaining infinitive absolutes may occur independently or in lists. Some questions may be raised about the infinitive absolute with *vav* and about paronomastic infinitive absolutes which follow the main verb rather than precede it.

Besides giving you pointers for handling infinitive absolutes, this discussion provides the occasion to consider again how language elements work in combinations, how they relate to the referent, and what kind of questions to ask of grammatical resources. We will also consider how English glosses influence us.

(a) Paronomastic. What sort of emphasis?

The paronomastic infinitive absolute adds emphasis to the verb, which can be translated by words like *surely, certainly, definitely, indeed, clearly,* or *in fact.* These translations understand the infinitive absolute to emphasize the mood of a verb of the same root. Some works use the word *intensive* to describe the infinitive absolute. This has been understood in different ways. The question is whether the emphasis of the paronomastic infinitive absolute adds information about the referent or the mood of the speaker, that is, the modality of the main verb.

Consider these different expressions which have the same referent:

We are going to London and then to Edinburgh.

We *really* are going to London and then to Edinburgh.

The referent does not change, but something changes. The second example insists on the reality of the statement. Perhaps the speaker thinks the destination will be questioned and adds *really*. The context may even clarify that the travel plans were unexpected. *We're* really *going to London – I got a great deal on airline tickets.* Not every word in a sentence is telling you more information about the referent. Some words carry information about the speaker's perspective or mood.

---

[2] This does not include the 14 uses of the adverb מַהֵר, which may be viewed as an infinitive absolute. Since infinitive absolutes may act as imperatives, the matter of counting them is also complicated by the fact that in some stems and roots, infinitive absolutes are identical in form to imperatives.

[3] There are a handful in narration: Gen. 20:18; 27:30; Exod 13:19 (1st); Lev 10:16; Num 11:32; Josh 17:13; Judg 1:28; 7:19 (1st); 1Sam 1:10; Ezek 1:3; 2Chr 28:19.

Now consider the meaning of וּבָכֹה תִבְכֶּה. The root בכה means *to weep*. What does it mean with the infinitive absolute? Does it say something about the weeping? For example, 1Sam 1:10:

וְהִיא מָרַת נָפֶשׁ וַתִּתְפַּלֵּל עַל־יְהוָה וּבָכֹה תִבְכֶּה

She was distressed within. She prayed to the LORD and wept *bitterly*.

Or does it provide another kind of information (since weeping might be considered an unexpected feast day activity)?

She was distressed within and prayed to the LORD. *In fact*, she was weeping.

The English glosses both appear to work. That means that how well an English gloss works is not the sole measure of whether it is correct. How might we decide?

We turn to comparisons. Is 30:19 assures the people who long for the LORD that he will be gracious to them and hear their cry. He says to the people in Zion, בָּכוֹ לֹא־תִבְכֶּה. Does he promise them "you will not weep *bitterly*"– meaning that they may weep *mildly*? Or is the promise that "you will not weep, *at all*"? In the first understanding, the infinitive absolute says something about the referent, about the weeping. In the second understanding, it emphasizes something else. The projected future is hard to envision, so the assurance of the promise is strengthened.

One way to say *weep bitterly* is to combine מרר, *be bitter*, with בכה, as in Is 22:4 אֲמָרֵר בַּבֶּכִי, *let me be bitter with weeping* (= *let me weep bitterly*). Another is to use גָּדוֹל מְאֹד, as in 2Sam 13:36 בָּכוּ בְכִי גָּדוֹל מְאֹד (*the king and his servants*) *wept very bitterly*, or perhaps *very profusely*. So Hebrew is not limited to one way of saying *weep bitterly*. But is the infinitive absolute one of them?

Consider other paronomastic infinitive absolutes. What would the "intensive" meaning of מוֹת be? To *die suddenly*? *Die painfully*? *Theatrically*? But to emphasize that a certain crime or decree warrants capital punishment, מוֹת יוּמָת means *he must be executed*. The infinitive absolute מוֹת does not say something more about the referent (the person is not more dead). But it is emphatic about the intent of the law. Most of the time it is not hard to find the contextual reason for emphasis of the verbal mood. Often the mood is emphasized because what the sentence is about is contrary to the expectation of the speaker or the other party.[4]

Of the paronomastic uses of the infinitive absolute, about 29% are in predictions, promises, threats, and statements of intent. Another 25% emphasize the fact or reality of an action. About 24.5% are volitional, mostly imperative or jussive. A sizeable minority of these are forms of מוֹת יוּמָת. Nearly 14.5% are in conditional statements, i.e. *if such and such is the case*. And roughly 7% are interrogative, generally in rhetorical questions.

---

[4] Cp. Gen 26:28; 43:7; Exod 11:1; 19:13; Num 22:37; 35:26; Ju 15:2, 13; 2Sam 17:11; 1Ki 3:26; 8:13; Is 40:30; Jer 7:5; 14:19; 22:10; Mic 2:12; Nah 3:13; 2Chr 18:27, and many others.

(b) **Pairings.**

An infinitive absolute may be part of a pair of words connected by *vav* and together modifying the main verb (about 44% in narration). The pair almost always follows the main verb and may or may not consist of two infinitive absolutes.

וַיֵּשֶׁב הָעָם לֶאֱכֹל וְשָׁתוֹ	-1-	The people sat down to eat and *drink*. Exod 32:6
וַיֵּלֶךְ הָלוֹךְ וְאָכֹל	-2-	He went along, *walking* and *eating*. Judg 14:9
וָאֲדַבֵּר ... הַשְׁכֵּם וְדַבֵּר	-3-	I spoke, *rising early* and *speaking*. Jer 7:13
הַבַּיִת אֲשֶׁר־אֲנִי בוֹנֶה גָּדוֹל וְהַפְלֵא	-4-	the house which I am about to build will be great and *wonderful*. 2Chr 2:8
וְרָעוּ אֶתְכֶם דֵּעָה וְהַשְׂכֵּיל	-5-	They will pasture you on knowledge and *understanding*. Jer 3:15

About two thirds of these pairings include an infinitive absolute based on the same root as the main verb; i.e. they are paronomastic. But unpaired paronomastic infinitive absolutes almost always precede the main verb. The pair serves a different purpose, as seen in the forms of עוד in Jer 11:7:

כִּי הָעֵד הַעִדֹתִי בַּאֲבוֹתֵיכֶם בְּיוֹם הַעֲלוֹתִי אוֹתָם
מֵאֶרֶץ מִצְרַיִם וְעַד־הַיּוֹם הַזֶּה הַשְׁכֵּם וְהָעֵד לֵאמֹר

I *certainly warned* your fathers on the day I brought them up from the
land of Egypt, even unto this day, rising early and *warning*, saying, ...

The infinitive absolute in the pairing, וְהָעֵד, is not emphasizing the mood, because that role is played by the paronomastic הָעֵד before the main verb. In a pairing the infinitive absolute is adverbial even if based on the same root as the main verb. Compare 2Ki 2:11: וַיְהִי הֵמָּה הֹלְכִים הָלוֹךְ וְדַבֵּר, *they were going along, walking and talking*. The narrator is not trying to convince us that they were *actually walking*. Rather, the storyteller wants you to picture Elijah and Elisha as walking and talking, i.e. engrossed in conversation. Then הִנֵּה, a flaming chariot rushes in to divide them. Often the effect is to say *both A and B* at the same time; the infinitive simply sets out the abstract concept rather than specifies the subject as would a finite verb. The infinitive absolute may be paired with nouns, adjectives, or various verb forms.

The most common word in these pairings is הלך. Like the participle of הלך, this root may (but does not always) convey the sense of increasing, such as increasing in the quality of a following item in the pair.

וַיֵּלֶךְ הָלוֹךְ וָרָב	-6-	He continued, growing greater and greater. 1Sam 14:19
וַיֵּלֶךְ הָלוֹךְ וְגָדֵל	-7-	He continued to become richer and richer. Gen 26:13

(c) Individually or in lists.

These infinitive absolutes are not tied to the main verb nor involved in a pairing. With some frequency they occur in lists or sequences. Here the infinitive absolute functions in its greatest variety. About 33% of these act as nouns (8–9). 22% express the manner of or otherwise explicate the main action (10–12), 20% indicate degree or measure (adverbial or adjectival), particularly cases of הַרְבֵּה and הֵיטֵב (13–16). And 18% can be translated as imperative or jussive verbs (17–19) though their function in Hebrew may actually be more like a nominative absolute (25.2d).

לָקַחַת מוּסַר הַשְׂכֵּל	-8-	to receive instruction in *wisdom* Prov 1:3
רַחֵם תִּזְכּוֹר	-9-	Remember *mercy*. Hab 3:2
מָחַצְתָּ רֹּאשׁ מִבֵּית רָשָׁע עָרוֹת יְסוֹד עַד־צַוָּאר	-10-	You struck the chief from the house of the wicked – *splitting open* from thigh to neck. Hab 3:13
הַאֶבְכֶּה בַּחֹדֶשׁ הַחֲמִשִׁי הִנָּזֵר כַּאֲשֶׁר עָשִׂיתִי	-11-	Should I weep in the fifth month, *fasting* as I have done? Zech 7:3
רָאוֹת רַבּוֹת וְלֹא תִשְׁמֹר פָּקוֹחַ אָזְנַיִם וְלֹא יִשְׁמָע	-12-	*seeing* much, you do not observe (with) *open* ears, but no one hears Is 42:20
יֵהוּא יַעַבְדֶנּוּ הַרְבֵּה	-13-	Jehu will serve him *much*. 2Ki 10:18
וְדָרְשׁוּ הַשֹּׁפְטִים הֵיטֵב	-14-	The judges shall investigate *thoroughly*. De 19:18
שְׂכָרְךָ הַרְבֵּה מְאֹד	-15-	Your reward will be very *great*. Gen 15:1
וְעֵצִים הַרְבֵּה	-16-	and *much* wood Is 30:33
זָכוֹר אֶת־יוֹם הַשַּׁבָּת	-17-	*Remember* the Sabbath day. Exod 20:8
הָלוֹךְ וְאָמַרְתָּ	-18-	*Go* and say... Jer 39:16
הִמּוֹל לוֹ כָל־זָכָר	-19-	*Let* all his males *be circumcised* Exod 12:48

The infinitive absolute may appear in lists. The list in Is 59:4 gives the manner in which people present court cases. Is 59:13 lists Israel's iniquities as a series of abstract nouns expanding the last clause of the previous verse.

אֵין־קֹרֵא בְצֶדֶק	-20-	No one pleads justly.
וְאֵין נִשְׁפָּט בֶּאֱמוּנָה		No one presents a case honestly:
בָּטוֹחַ עַל־תֹּהוּ וְדַבֶּר־שָׁוְא		*trusting* confusion, *speaking* lies,
הָרוֹ עָמָל וְהוֹלֵיד אָוֶן		*conceiving* mischief and *bearing* iniquity.
		Is 59:4
וַעֲוֺנֺתֵינוּ יְדַעֲנוּם	-21-	we know our iniquities:
פָּשֹׁעַ וְכַחֵשׁ בַּיהוָה		*transgressing*, *denying* the LORD,
וְנָסוֹג מֵאַחַר אֱלֹהֵינוּ		*turning* from our God…
דַּבֶּר־עֹשֶׁק וְסָרָה		*speaking* (of) oppression and revolt
הֹרוֹ וְהֹגוֹ מִלֵּב דִּבְרֵי־שָׁקֶר		*conceiving* and *mulling over* deceitful words from the mind.
		Is 59:12-13

When infinitive absolutes act as nouns, English may use a gerund, with *–ing*.[5] Some examples, like the previous, might be translated in more than one way. Since infinitives are verbal nouns, translating with either nouns or verbs could also "make sense," e.g. gerund, *transgressing and denying*; noun, *transgression and denial*, verb, *we transgress and we deny*. (Choosing to translate with a verb requires supplying the subject from the previous clause.)

(d) *Vav* **plus infinitive absolute.**

Other than in pairings, *vav* joins the infinitive absolute 110 times. Of these, 35 are paronomastic,[6] so the main verb supplies information about aspect and time. These present information that is generally simultaneous to the previous main verb,[7] whether contrasting (about 40%, all negated) or similar (about 60%, a few negated).

אָסֹר נֶאֱסָרְךָ וּנְתַנּוּךָ בְיָדָם	-22-	We will indeed bind you and give you into their hands,
וְהָמֵת לֹא נְמִיתֶךָ		but we *certainly won't kill* you.
		Judg 15:13
בְּזֹאת תֵּדְעוּן כִּי אֵל חַי בְּקִרְבְּכֶם	-23-	By this you will know that the living God is among you
וְהוֹרֵשׁ יוֹרִישׁ מִפְּנֵיכֶם		and that *you will indeed dispossess* from before you…
		Josh 3:10

---

[5] English gerunds and participles both use *–ing*; the titles distinguish their role. If it is used as a noun, it is a gerund; if it is used as an adjective, it is a participle.

[6] Gen 22:17 (2nd); 50:15; Exod 5:23; 21:19; 23:24 (2nd); Lev 19:20; Num 14:18; De 7:26; 15:8 (2nd); 21:14; Josh 3:10; 17:13; Judg 1:28; 15:13 (2nd); 1Sam 1:10; 30:8; 1Ki 3:26, 27; Is 24:3; Jer 11:12; 13:17; 23:32; 30:11; 32:33; 44:25 (2nd); Ezek 16:4; Amos 3:5; Nah 1:3; Ps 109:10; Dan 10:3; 1Chr 21:17.

[7] In the case of Gen 50:15 the *vav* plus infinitive absolute begins an apodosis.

The other 75 instances of *vav* plus an infinitive absolute lack a main verb.[8] If translated as a verb in English, the surrounding context can supply the subject and other verbal information. This will make many of them appear to be sequential to the previous verb. So some resources treat the infinitive absolute as a verb, much like a *vav* plus perfect consecutive (14.9.2 and ch. 31). But how the translation sounds in English is not necessarily the measure of how the Hebrew works. We may also translate them as gerunds, holding the view that these infinitives simply set out the abstract idea, sometimes as a parenthetic aside. Thus we do not see these as temporally sequential[9] but as simultaneous or circumstantial to the main verb, that is, in their adverbial nature.

-24- וַיִּתְקְעוּ בַּשּׁוֹפָרוֹת   Then they blew the trumpets,

וְנָפוֹץ הַכַּדִּים אֲשֶׁר בְּיָדָם   *even smashing* the pitchers which were in their hands.
Judg 7:19

Perhaps they first blew the shofars and then broke the pitchers, but it also possible they did both at the same time and kept blowing the shofars after the pitchers were broken. That the infinitive absolute is not sequential is often more apparent.

-25- וְהֶעֱלָה שְׁלֹמֹה...עַל־הַמִּזְבֵּחַ   (Now thrice a year) Solomon burnt offerings on the altar

וְהַקְטֵיר אִתּוֹ   also *burning incense* with it.
1Ki 9:25

Esther 6:8–9 is an example of the infinitive absolute as parenthetic comment (but often translated sequentially). Haman begins with a jussive which is continued by several perfect consecutives. The series includes one infinitive absolute. A sequential translation appears to "make sense." But likely it is used to avoid a *vav* plus perfect consecutive; it is a comment specifying the object of the previous verb.

-26- יָבִיאוּ לְבוּשׁ מַלְכוּת... וְסוּס...   Let them bring a royal robe...and horse...
Est 6:8

וְנָתוֹן הַלְּבוּשׁ וְהַסּוּס
עַל־יַד־אִישׁ מִשָּׂרֵי הַמֶּלֶךְ...   (the robe and horse *given* into the hands of the king's noble princes)

וְהִלְבִּישׁוּ אֶת־הָאִישׁ   and let them clothe the man...

וְהִרְכִּיבֻהוּ עַל־הַסּוּס   Let them lead him on the horse...

וְקָרְאוּ לְפָנָיו   And let them proclaim...
Est 6:9

---

[8] Gen 41:43; Ex 8:11; 36:7; Josh 9:20; Judg 7:19 (2nd); 1Sam 2:28; 22:13; 1Ki 9:25; Is 7:15, 16; 22:13; 58:6; 59:4, 13; Jer 3:1 (2nd); 7:9, 18; 19:13; 22:14; 32:44; 36:23; 37:21; 44:18, 19; Ezek 23:46, 47; 24:10; Hos 4:2; Amos 4:5; Mic 6:8; Hag 1:6; Zech 3:4; 7:5; 12:10; Ps 126:6 (2nd); 130:7; Job 13:3; Ecc 4:2, 17; Est 2:3; 3:13; 6:9; 8:8; 9:1, 6, 12, 16, 17, 18; Dan 9:5, 11; Neh 7:3; 9:8; 1Chr 5:20; 16:36; 2Chr 28:19; 31:10.

[9] But possibly logically sequential as an inference or apodosis on rare occasion.

(e) Rare situations.

The previous discussion covers the most common uses of the infinitive absolute. Observations have included that the paronomastic infinitive absolute usually precedes the verb, in which case it emphasizes the modality of the main verb. But in pairings it almost always follows the main verb, in which cases it usually says something about the manner of the main verb. About 44% of the pairings are in narration. The vast majority of paronomastics are in speech. We have also advised you to make decisions based on comparisons to other examples. So let us suppose that you are working on Num 11:32. The LORD has blown quail on a wind and the people have gathered them throughout the night and the next day. Then we are told:

הַֽמַּחֲנֶה	סְבִיבוֹת	שָׁטוֹחַ	לָהֶם	וַיִּשְׁטְחוּ
the camp	all around	spreading out	for themselves	They spread out

Here the paronomastic infinitive absolute both follows the main verb (about two dozen do so) and occurs in narration (about 10 do so); this is the only one to do both. The main verb, being preterite, must come first (which also happens 5 times in direct speech). By comparison, there are two primary options. In comparison to most paronomastics, it may be emphatic, *they* actually *spread out [the quail] for themselves all around the camp*. In comparison to the paronomastics that are parts of pairings and follow the main verb, it may indicate the manner of the action, *they spread out [the quail] for themselves, i.e. spreading [them] all around the camp*. There seems no reason in context for the activity of *spreading out* to be emphasized because it does not contrast with some other expected activity. So it seems best to understand the infinitive absolute as saying something about the manner of the action, a role also played by non-paronomastic infinitive absolutes.

At a later stage in your Hebrew training, you may even notice a footnote in your Hebrew Bible which tells you that the Samaritan Pentateuch does not read שָׁטוֹחַ but rather the root שׁחט, *to slaughter*. This would mean *they spread [the quail] out for themselves,* slaughtering *[them] all around the camp*. Seeing that the Samaritan Pentateuch has the most normal syntax is a reason to prefer its reading in this case. And in fact many other rare constructions will have text critical footnotes.

30.5   Summary.

The infinitive construct mostly follows a preposition or temporal indicator; its common uses are: temporal, purpose, result, immanence, specification, and obligation.

The infinitive absolute also plays many roles: noun, verb, and modifier. In paronomastic constructions it heightens the modality of the main verb. In pairings (even when paronomastic) it typically says something about the manner of the action of the main verb.

chapter thirty-one

Verb Syntax: Perfect and Vav plus Perfect

31.1   Focus.

The primary historical settings for the perfect and *vav* plus perfect consecutive were the nominal clause and the apodosis of conditional sentences. Oversimplified, the perfect looks at an action as complete, while the time frame derives from the context and whether it is stative or fientive. The *vav* plus perfect consecutive often continues the nuance of the preceding verb or advances it as a logical result. But the Hebrew verbal system is more complex than that. Explanations tend to simplify matters so that moving from textbooks to Hebrew texts quickly reveals that there is more to learn. This chapter presents nuances of the perfect and perfect consecutive and points out what sort of combinations to watch for. We also comment on the nature of *vav* and terminology used to describe *vav* in different settings.

31.2   Form of the perfect consecutive.

In form, *vav* plus a perfect may be either the perfect consecutive or the regular perfect. The perfect consecutive can be distinguished from the regular perfect only in the 1cs and 2ms due to the accent shifting down, וְקָטַלְתִּי and וְקָטַלְתָּ. However, even in the 1cs and 2ms forms, the accent does not always shift down.[1] Most of the time you must judge by context rather than by form.

31.3   Terminology: *vav* consecutive vs. perfect consecutive.

The fact of the matter is that *vav* plus suffixed conjugation forms sometimes have consecutive force and sometimes do not. The term *vav consecutive* attributes the consecutive force to the *vav*. The term *perfect consecutive* attributes this to the verb. When you use other resources, be prepared for both terms.

The issue is akin to the preterite. The preterite has been labeled several things (12.4.1). It was once called a converted imperfect because it looked like the imperfect but seemed to act like the perfect. This illusion takes the perfect as basically one thing, past time action, and then posits that the speaking community had a reason to take prefixed forms (which did not have the job of conveying past

---

[1] It remains on R$_2$'s vowel when in pause, when the following word begins with an accent, or when R$_2$ begins an open syllable, e.g. with R$_3$ = ה verbs.

time) and start using them for the job being filled by the perfect. Since the preterite usually has *vav*, it was called a *vav conversive* or, later, a *vav consecutive* plus imperfect. But historically we know that there had been a preterite paradigm (prefixed spellings for past time) whose forms merged with the imperfect. The past time meaning does not come from the *vav* at all. In fact, we must be prepared to find preterites without *vav*.

Regarding *vav* plus perfect, the *vav* is no different whether the meaning is consecutive or not. The accent may shift, but there is no reason to attribute this as a quality of the *vav*.[2] Nonetheless, the term *vav* consecutive plus perfect is also common and accepted in the literature. We prefer to say perfect consecutive, but the important thing is to note when *vav* joins the perfect and then check context for a consecutive notion.

31.4 Verb systems.

Consider these English examples:

I run	I ran
If I run	If I ran
When I run	When I ran
I used to run	
I will run	
I have run	
I ought to run	
(Then) I would run	

The form *run* as well as the form *ran* are used with several different nuances. If we asked you to explain what *run* is doing in each of these cases, you would rightly say that its function really comes from the combinations that it is in. We can mark it for time, *I will run*. We can mark it for aspect, *I will be running*. We can mark it for mood, *then I will/would run, I ought to run*, etc.

Activities and states occur in time and can be viewed or described in different aspects. So all languages express tense, aspect, and mood, but they package it in different ways, working with a very limited set of forms to express a nearly limitless amount of reality. At times a speaker is more concerned to mark time and at others to mark aspect and in others to mark mood. It is a question of what the speaker does want to say, does not care about saying, and what the syntactic situation is.

Hebrew is also complex in this way. The prefixed and suffixed conjugations can be employed in various times and moods and emphasize various aspects of the action

---

[2] There is no reason to believe that Hebrew (or other West Semitic) speakers thought there were two *vavs*. And we may ask, if there actually is a "*vav* consecutive," why is it different on the imperfect/preterite than it is on the perfect? *Vav* is merely *vav*; consecutive is syntax.

or state. It is really not as simple as asking, "What does the perfect do?" or "Is the Hebrew verb about tense or aspect?"

Furthermore languages are not static but are always changing. Tensions are created, adaptations are made, and new tensions result. One tension in Biblical Hebrew is the merging of forms. Due to the loss of final vowels, several prefixed conjugations merged into one.[3] Indicative and subjunctive merged into one paradigm, as did the jussive and preterite forms in most cases. This puts a certain pressure on the language, especially involving the preterite and jussive. The perfect becomes available then for simple past time, and eventually the preterite drops away (after Biblical Hebrew).

31.5   Uses of the perfect. *AC 54–56.*

Arnold and Choi review six uses of the perfect: complete, stative, experience, rhetorical future, proverbial, preformative. We have encountered some of these in our previous discussions. Here we review them with comments on their history or relationships.

(a) **Stative** *(AC 55).* The Hebrew perfect began by conjugating predicate position adjectives as verbs in nominal sentences. In chapter 10 we compared the perfect endings to the pronouns and the nouns. This is in fact their history, creating the stative verb from the adjective pattern *qatil*, e.g. כָּבֵד.[4] The state is complete in either past or present time (10.5). In the following examples of כָּבֵד we see (1) the stative perfect used for the present in speech (as is often the case in speech), (2) the stative perfect used for the past as is typical of background clauses in narrative (i.e. meaning the same past time as the narrative, cf. 27.3a), and (3) the stative perfect as ingressive, *became X,* deriving from a context which shows that the state had not been there and then came about. The possibility of an ingressive is often built in, i.e. *be X* or *became X,* and indicated by context (though the Niphal can expressly mark a stative as ingressive, cp. 16.2.1).

---

[3] An indicative, *yáqtulu* (he does it); a subjunctive, *yáqtulà* (he might do it); a jussive, *yaqtúl* (let him do it); a preterite *yáqtul* (he did it); and another non-indicative *yàqtulán(na),* used in requests, questions, petitions, and exhortations. As a phonological phenomenon, Hebrew once dropped final vowels, making *yáqtulu, yáqtulà* and *yáqtul* become alike, *yaqtul.* (Other changes turned *yaqtul* into *yiqtol.*) There are different views on their meanings and history, but clearly with the loss of final vowels they have merged in form, so that even for those roots which have a distinct form for the jussive and imperfect, the prefixed form is already both indicative and subjunctive. Also the jussive had a full paradigm with first, second, and third persons. First and second person jussives do exist in Biblical Hebrew, but the third person is by far the most common.

[4] Parts of the pronoun were added to make the first and second person forms. Conversing between "I" and "you" is a different level of discourse than talking about "this" and "that." In Hebrew the noun endings were chosen for the third persons; even the long *ū* of the third common plural came from a plural noun marker now absent in Biblical Hebrew.

זַעֲקַת סְדֹם... כִּי־רָבָּה	-1-	"The outcry of Sodom…is great.
וְחַטָּאתָם כִּי כָבְדָה מְאֹד		Their sin *is* very *severe*." Gen 18:20
וְעֵינֵי יִשְׂרָאֵל כָּבְדוּ מִזֹּקֶן	-2-	Israel's eyes *were heavy* (= dim) from old age. Gen 48:10
וַיָּבֹאוּ...	-3-	(Ten thousand men) came (against Gibeah).
וְהַמִּלְחָמָה כָבֵדָה		The battle *became fierce* Judg 20:34

(b) **Experience** *(AC 55).* Verbs of experience can have a direct object, but the verbs say more about the subject than about any effect on the direct object. Verbs like יָדַע, אָהֵב, and שָׂנֵא may be viewed as stative and be translated like the previous category.

(c) **Complete** *(AC 55).* Active transitive verbs were then also conjugated in this way, but with a different theme vowel, e.g. קָטַל, *he has killed.* Even though the action occurred in the past, the perfect could also be concerned with the present by focusing on the resulting state of affairs. The fientive perfect also comes to mean *he killed.* Biblical Hebrew distinguishes between the two by context (or may not care to distinguish them. As a partial comparison, it may make no practical difference in an actual conversation in English to say *Take the book that I have given you* or *Take the book that I gave you).* Often in speech the Hebrew perfect is simple past; however, context determines the use in both speech and narrative.

(d) **Preformative** *(AC 56).* With these verbs the action occurs by means of speaking, so that saying *I have given it to you* effectively means *I (hereby) give it to you.* נָתַן is the premier preformative verb.

(e) **Proverbial** *(AC 56).* These denote "actions, events, or facts that are not time determined, and are considered to be general truths."

(f) **Rhetorical future** *(AC 55–56).* Here the perfect is set in a time frame which is future. These may not all be of the same type. When a seer has a vision of the future, the events have not yet occurred in history; however, the vision has. So we find Balaam telling Balak his vision.

אֶרְאֶנּוּ וְלֹא עַתָּה...	-4-	I see him but not now…
דָּרַךְ כּוֹכָב מִיַּעֲקֹב		A star marched out from Jacob… Num 24:17

The star has come out in Balaam's vision but not in Balak's experience. From the perspective of Balak, this is a forecast of what will happen. From the perspective of the vision, this is what Balaam has foreseen. Occasionally the context will place the perfect in the future, *will have been,* but at other times we use the future merely to accommodate English.

31.6   Uses of the *vav* **plus perfect.** *AC 87–91.*

Arnold and Choi review four consecutive uses of the *vav* plus perfect: sequential, consequential, volitional, and apodictic.

In 2nd millennium West Semitic, the larger family of which Hebrew is a part,[5] the verbal adjective construction was normal in the apodoses of conditional statements, *if such-and-such, then we would do X.* It also came to be used for past habitual action. We are not concerned here with how this happened, so let us simply compare to English *would*, which has some similarities.

In an apodosis:

If the prices were low enough, we *would* fly to London.

For habitual past action:

When we lived there, we *would* eat Cincinnati chili.

We *would* eat pizza on Thursdays.

Since English can use the same form in apodoses and for habitual past, the same phenomenon in Hebrew should not disturb us. This primary meaning, *then we would*, also develops a secondary meaning, *then we should.*

The apodosis of a conditional sentence relies on something that precedes it (the protasis, *if such-and-such*) and then builds on it (*then we should*). This kind of relationship, a logical result, is not limited to constructions with *if.*

If they come, then we would/should…

When they come, then we would/should…

They are here, so we should…

The title **apodictic** refers to this kind of relationship in a formal conditional statement. The title **consequential** refers to this kind of relationship in other settings. The title **volitional** can also refer to a logical result or to occasions when the volitional nature of a preceding verb is being continued by the *vav* plus perfect consecutive. In the **sequential** use, logical consequence is not the point but rather succession in time. It often works to think of the perfect consecutive continuing the force of the preceding verb, but this obviously does not account for its uses in logical results. Both uses are expressed in Exod 19:5:

וְעַתָּ֞ה אִם־שָׁמ֤וֹעַ תִּשְׁמְעוּ֙ בְּקֹלִ֔י	-1-	Now if you (will) actually obey my voice,
וּשְׁמַרְתֶּ֖ם אֶת־בְּרִיתִ֑י		*and (will) keep* my covenant
וִהְיִ֨יתֶם לִ֤י סְגֻלָּה֙		*then you will be* my special treasure…
		Exod 19:5

וּשְׁמַרְתֶּם continues the force of תִּשְׁמְעוּ, but וִהְיִיתֶם introduces an apodosis.

---

[5] The Semitic languages are usually divided into East Semitic (e.g. Babylonian and Assyrian), West Semitic (e.g. Hebrew, Aramaic, Ugaritic, Moabite, Phoenician) and South Semitic (e.g. Arabic) based on a variety of shared characteristics and dissimilarities.

More examples:

אֲנִי יְהוָה	-2-	I am the Lord
וְהוֹצֵאתִי אֶתְכֶם		and I will bring you out...
וְהִצַּלְתִּי אֶתְכֶם		and I will deliver you...
		Exod 6:6
שְׁמַע יִשְׂרָאֵל	-3-	Hear O Israel...
		De 6:4
וְאָהַבְתָּ אֵת יְהוָה אֱלֹהֶיךָ		And you shall love the Lord your God...
		De 6:5
יְבַקְשׁוּ לַאדֹנִי הַמֶּלֶךְ נַעֲרָה	-4-	Let them seek a young girl for my lord the king.
וְעָמְדָה לִפְנֵי הַמֶּלֶךְ		And let her attend the king
		1Ki 1:2
וּבָא הָאֲרִי וְאֶת־הַדּוֹב	-5-	When a lion would come, or a bear,
וְנָשָׂא שֶׂה מֵהָעֵדֶר		and take a lamb from the flock,
וְיָצָאתִי אַחֲרָיו		then I would go after it
וְהִכִּתִיו		and (would) strike it
וְהִצַּלְתִּי מִפִּיו		and rescue it from its mouth.
		1Sam 17:34

31.7   For future reference.

Arnold and Choi will refer you to other reference grammars where you will find that not all scholars agree on the use of the perfect and the perfect consecutive. Sometimes translating is easier than understanding how the Hebrew works. Consider the question asked of Pharaoh in Exod 10:3, עַד־מָתַי מֵאַנְתָּ לֵעָנֹת מִפָּנָי.

The essence of the question in the dialogue is clear but its specific nuance is debatable:

How long will you refuse to humble yourself before me?

How long do you refuse to humble yourself before me?

How long would you refuse to humble yourself before me?

What sounds best in English does not necessarily reveal what the Hebrew is doing. Thus *will refuse* sounds good, but the Hebrew is not using the perfect as future tense.

31.8   Summary.

It is particularly important to know whether a perfect verb is stative or fientive and to observe its context. The origin of perfect from the adjective gives stative perfects a present time option. *Vav* plus perfect may or may not be a perfect consecutive. The perfect consecutive may continue the framework of the preceding verb or advance it a logical step.

chapter thirty-two

Poetry and Time Frame

32.1   Focus.

This chapter presents an approach to translating poetry by taking cues for time frame from poetic parallelism and the uses of the verb forms learned in narrative and speech. The time frame of verbs in poetry is not agreed upon among scholars. But we offer a beginning rather than neglect the genre of poetry. Our emphasis is on the Psalms.

32.2   Potential problems in poetry.

(a) **It is not prose.**

While it sounds redundant, one of our biggest problems with poetry is that it is not prose. Prose is the most thoroughly studied and best understood genre in the Bible. But the backbone of prose, the sequence of preterites, is absent in the Psalms (though a few Psalms include historical accounts using preterites).

(b) **Is it uniform?**

Language is always changing and the Psalms were written over a long period of time by many authors. It may be that certain authors or certain groups of Psalms are consistent within themselves in the use of the verb system, but that they differ from other groups, due to diachronic or dialectic reasons. To what degree, for example, might we expect to find archaic uses of preterites (i.e. without the *vav*)?

(c) **What is the text?**

Copying errors made by scribes occur in all the genres of the Bible, but Ps 18 and 2Sam 22 illustrate the problem for Psalm studies. Reputedly the same Psalm, 2Sam 22:12 has וַיָּשֶׁת while Ps 18:12 simply has יָשֶׁת, without the *vav*. 2Sam 22:8 reads וַתִּגְעַשׁ, written without *yod*, but with the Masoretes using a *ḥireq* to tell us to read וַיִּתְגָּעַשׁ, while Ps 18:8 has וַתִּגְעַשׁ. The all too easy scribal confusion of *vav* and *yod* and the possible omission of either create critical differences in the data, especially with 3ms forms.

Secondly, while we have properly advised relying on the wisdom of the Masoretes, it is clear that they did not understand the preterite. Over time Hebrew had changed. The preterite had dropped out, replaced by the perfect for past time and with the participle serving for the present and the imperfect for the future. To them the preterite, *vayyiqtol*, looked like a *vav conversive* (cf. 12.4.1). This at least raises the question as to whether all *vav* plus prefixed forms are properly vocalized.

(d) The nature of the verbal action or state.

Evaluating time frame must consider not only the form of the verb but whether it is stative or fientive (its aktionsart). We know from prose and speech that a verb's time frame depends in part on whether it is fientive or stative. Yet this role needs further exploration. On the one hand, especially with less common vocabulary it can be difficult to assess whether some verbs are stative or transitive.[1] On the other hand, how do transitive stative verbs and fientive intransitive verbs work? The categories fientive and stative, though morphologically descriptive of some Qal verbs, are too broad, and a more sensitive understanding of kinds of activities and states is needed.

32.3 Approaching poetry.

(a) Parallelism. (It is not prose and it does not rhyme.)

As much as narrative is marked by the use of the preterite to carry the story line, poetry is characterized by parallelism. Hebrew poetry employs lines of controlled length that typically work together in sets. The most common sets are called a bicolon (pl. bicola) and a tricolon. The bicolon is a set of two lines of similar length; the tricolon is a set of three. Similar length does not mean exactly the same length.[2] The parts of the colon relate together thematically, often repeating the same idea in other words or giving its antithesis, called synonymous and antithetic parallelism. Sometimes the thought is not restated but complemented or completed by the second line (the *b* line), called synthetic parallelism.

> *Synonymous/Iterative Parallelism*
> Ps 2:3   "Let us break their bonds asunder,
>   And cast away their cords from us."
>
> *Antithetic/Contrastive Parallelism*
> Ps 1:6   For the LORD knows the way of the righteous
>   but the way of the wicked will perish.
>
> *Synthetic/Completive Parallelism*
> Ps 2:6   "But as for Me, I have installed My King
>   Upon Zion, My holy mountain."

---

[1] Reuven Yaron has suggested that זנח, traditionally glossed *reject* or *spurn*, is more adequately translated as "to be angry" (R. Yaron, "The Meaning of *Zanaḥ*," *Vetus Testamentum* 13 (1963) 237–9). Though we do not agree, it illustrates the problem.

[2] It is debated whether the total number of historically reconstructed syllables or the number of beats (roughly the same as the number of accented syllables) is more important. We should also remember that musically it may be possible to stretch lines out to the same length, even when they are different in normal speaking.

In a tricolon, the three lines do not have to have the same type of parallelism.

> Ps 24:8   Who is the King of glory?
> The LORD strong and mighty,
> The LORD mighty in battle.

(b) Stanzas.

More than one bicolon or tricolon may relate to the same topic, forming a logical unit. The term stanza has been applied to these groups, but this is not to be confused with the stanzas of modern religious hymns or poetry. Stanza means a semantically unified set of cola (sometimes only one colon) that is part of a larger poem. The stanza might serve any number of general purposes such as praise, calls to praise, petition, complaint, lament, statements of confidence, vows, etc.

(c) Time frame and modality.

We suggest that you will make a good start in translating poetry by working with the same meanings for the verb forms already learned for narrative and by keeping track of the combinations of the verbal form, aktionsart (stative vs. fientive), and the constraints of parallelism. Additionally, be alert to the possibility of *yiqtol* as a preterite without the *vav* and be prepared for intransitive fientives to work like statives.

For example, if a bicolon has an imperative in one line and a prefixed form in the other, then this suggests that the prefixed form is also modal, i.e. jussive. Of course you must observe content and syntax, for the one line may give you the reason for the imperative (synthetic parallelism) rather than a similar injunction (synonymous or antithetic parallelism). Or perhaps a bicolon has a stative perfect in one line and a fientive imperfect in another. You know that the stative perfect might be past or present and that the fientive imperfect might be present or future. The two forms, combined with the nature of the verbs, overlap in the present. So unless there is a good contextual reason to do otherwise, translate both parts of the parallel line in the present. It may also be that lines in different cola but in the same stanza work the same way when they are on the same syntactic level.

32.4   Examples from the Psalms of Asaph.

We will use the Psalms of Asaph as a sample for illustration, allowing that they may not represent all biblical poetry.

Petitions, commands, appeals, and the like use prefixed forms, usually in coordination or parallelism with imperatives or jussives. Time frame is not the main issue but rather modality. The forms act as expected. Ps 50:14–15 are typical in placing imperatives in parallelism. The switch to first person imperfect in the latter half of verse 15 signals the switch to a promise. Ps 76:12 provides an example of a prefixed form parallel to an imperative, which suggests it is jussive. Ps 75:6 places a prefixed form parallel to a combination of אַל plus prefixed form. This not only indicates that the second prefixed form is jussive but in this case that it is also negative. Hebrew poetry has the freedom to omit from the second line an element that is to be understood from the first. This technique is called ellipsis and double duty.

זְבַח לֵאלֹהִים תּוֹדָה	-1-	*Sacrifice* thanksgiving to God
וְשַׁלֵּם לְעֶלְיוֹן נְדָרֶיךָ		*Fulfill* your vows to the Most High Ps 50:14
וּקְרָאֵנִי בְּיוֹם צָרָה		*Call* to me in the day of trouble
אֲחַלֶּצְךָ וּתְכַבְּדֵנִי		I will deliver you and you will honor me. Ps 50:15
נִדְרוּ וְשַׁלְּמוּ לַיהוָה אֱלֹהֵיכֶם	-2-	Make and fulfill vows to the LORD your God
כָּל־סְבִיבָיו יוֹבִילוּ שַׁי לַמּוֹרָא		*Let* everyone around him *bring* gifts to the fearsome one. Ps 76:12
אַל־תָּרִימוּ לַמָּרוֹם קַרְנְכֶם	-3-	Do not lift your horn on high
תְּדַבְּרוּ בְצַוָּאר עָתָק		*Do not speak* with arrogant pride. Ps 75:6

There are no surprises in the volitional statements of the Psalms of Asaph. But in other poetry, one should consider the potential use of the perfect as a modal meaning *should*. These are called precative perfects.

Laments, complaints, and accusations in the Psalms of Asaph employ imperfect fientives, perfect statives and fientives, and *vav* plus preterite fientives. Pairing similar forms presents no difficulties. Perfect statives may be parallel to imperfect fientives for a present time frame. Ps 73:5 places in parallel a nominal sentence and an imperfect as a general present. Then verse 6 places in parallel a stative perfect and an imperfect fientive. These all have a present time frame.

בַּעֲמַל אֱנוֹשׁ אֵינֵמוֹ	-4-	They are not part of humanity's troubles;
וְעִם־אָדָם לֹא יְנֻגָּעוּ		They are not plagued along with mankind. Ps 73:5
לָכֵן עֲנָקַתְמוֹ גַאֲוָה		Therefore pride adorns them;
יַעֲטָף־שִׁית חָמָס לָמוֹ		A garment of violence wraps them. Ps 73:6

More interesting is the coupling of perfect fientives with imperfect fientives within the same line. The time frame is present. The speech function of complaint, lament, and accusation is to decry the distress of the Psalmist. In orientation they are focused in the present, being cries of anguish erupting in the Psalmist's *now*. They may refer to past actions, but they are present concerns for the Psalmist because they represent unresolved conflict or anguish.

The Hebrew perfect brings us to a present situation which has resulted from the completion of the verb's action. For example, Ps 74:7 חִלְּלוּ מִשְׁכַּן־שְׁמֶךָ, "They have defiled your name's dwelling place" signifies the current situation that "your name's dwelling place is defiled because of them." It looks at something done in the past from a present perspective. Ps 73:12 וְשַׁלְוֵי עוֹלָם הִשְׂגּוּ־חָיִל, "the wicked have increased their riches" signifies the present reality that the Psalmist complains about "the wicked are now rich."

So instead of saying that the perfect conjugation is being used for present tense, we should rather say that the perfect forms of the fientive verbs give a past action with a focus on the present (or continuing) result or state. That is a long way of saying that the Hebrew perfect fientive should be translated as an English perfect to emphasize the present.

פִּיךָ שָׁלַחְתָּ בְרָעָה	-5-	You *have loosed* your mouth with evil;
וּלְשׁוֹנְךָ תַּצְמִיד מִרְמָה:		your tongue *frames* deceit. Ps 50:19
שַׁתּוּ בַשָּׁמַיִם פִּיהֶם	-6-	They *have set* their mouth against heaven;
וּלְשׁוֹנָם תִּהֲלַךְ בָּאָרֶץ:		their tongue *roams* the earth. Ps 73:9
כִּי־הִנֵּה אוֹיְבֶיךָ יֶהֱמָיוּן	-7-	For see, your enemies *make* an uproar;
וּמְשַׂנְאֶיךָ נָשְׂאוּ רֹאשׁ:		those who hate you *have lifted* up the head. Ps 83:3

The Psalmist's questions about the future can also concern the present. They are concerned with the continuation of the present condition. Questions in the perfect conjugation, with past time and perfective aspect, concern an ongoing condition.

הַלְעוֹלָמִים יִזְנַח ׀ אֲדֹנָי	-8-	Will the Lord reject forever?
וְלֹא־יֹסִיף לִרְצוֹת עוֹד:		Will he not again be favorable? Ps 77:8
הֶאָפֵס לָנֶצַח חַסְדּוֹ		Is (has) his loving kindness finished forever?
גָּמַר אֹמֶר לְדֹר וָדֹר:		Is (has) the promise ended for generations? Ps 77:9
הֲשָׁכַח חַנּוֹת אֵל		Has God forgotten to be gracious?
אִם־קָפַץ בְּאַף רַחֲמָיו:		Or in anger, has he withdrawn his compassion? Ps 77:10

This use of perfects when the focus of the time frame is the present is not limited to laments, complaints, and accusations. Perfect fientive verbs with a present temporal focus occasionally occur elsewhere in the Psalms of Asaph, such as in testimonies and in parallel relative clauses. Compare Psalm 73:28, which parallels a nominal clause with a perfect fientive verb.

וַאֲנִי קִרֲבַת אֱלֹהִים לִי־טוֹב   ‑9‑   But as for me, the nearness of God is my good,

שַׁתִּי בַּאדֹנָי יְהוִֹה מַחְסִי   I *have made* the Lord GOD my refuge
                                                     Ps 73:28

Note also the relative clauses in the petition in Psalm 79:6.

שְׁפֹךְ חֲמָתְךָ אֶל־הַגּוֹיִם   ‑10‑   Pour out your wrath on the nations

אֲשֶׁר לֹא־יְדָעוּךָ   which *do* not *know* you,

וְעַל מַמְלָכוֹת   and on the kingdoms

אֲשֶׁר בְּשִׁמְךָ לֹא קָרָאוּ   which *have* not *called* on your name
                                                     Ps 79:6

Although subordinate clauses, they modify parallel elements, employing a perfect stative and a perfect fientive. Here the perfect stative marks the present, and the perfect fientive verb should be understood as perfective in English.

Psalm 75:2 (Eng 1) is translated in the present tense by most translations and many commentators, in spite of the fact that the verse uses three perfect fientive verbs. Rather these should also be understood as perfective. The Psalm begins

הוֹדִינוּ לְךָ אֱלֹהִים הוֹדִינוּ

וְקָרוֹב שְׁמֶךָ סִפְּרוּ נִפְלְאוֹתֶיךָ

It is usually translated "we give thanks... men recount your wondrous deeds" probably only because these perfect fientive verbs begin the Psalm. However it is the only "Todah" Psalm[3] to do so. Rather than posit a radical use of these verb forms, we agree with A. Weiser that the Psalm was "part of the cultic liturgy which has been preceded by a testimony of the congregation,"[4] of which the praise and recounting of God's wondrous deeds have evoked the response in Ps. 75:3ff.[5] Translating with an English perfect is suggested here because it refers to the recent past action of the participants (though there is no linguistic marker for this other than the selection of the verb form).

> We have given thanks to you O God, we have given thanks.

> Your name is near. We have recounted your wondrous deeds.

The laments, complaints, and accusations in the Psalms of Asaph employ *vav* plus preterite forms in three places. If the perfect verbs that precede them are understood as past perfects in English, it may be that the *vav* plus preterite verbs continue the perfective – or they may simply be preterites used as past time (that is,

---

[3] A Todah Psalm is a Psalm using the Hifil of יד"ה, *to praise*, also thought to have meant *give thanks*. Form critical scholars identify certain types of Psalms and the common kinds of speech acts in them. In the rest of the Psalm, vss. 3–6 are a warning in the first person singular (marking a change in speaker); vss. 7–9 are a motivation section; and vss. 10–11 are a profession of trust and hope. Thus the content of Psalm 75 is not typical of a Todah Psalm, which supports the translation above.

[4] Artur Weiser, *The Psalms: A Commentary* (Philadelphia: The Westminster Press, 1962), p. 521.

[5] A present temporal focus also makes the noun clause וְקָרוֹב שְׁמֶךָ easier to translate, though its precise meaning in the service is uncertain.

not consecutive, but representing the old preterite conjugation as past time). In Ps 50:17 the initial perfect is a stative, leaving it uncertain whether it is past or present.

וְאַתָּה שָׂנֵאתָ מוּסָר	-11-	But as for you, you hate/hated instruction;
וַתַּשְׁלֵךְ דְּבָרַי אַחֲרֶיךָ:		and (have) tossed my words behind you. Ps 50:17
אַךְ־רִיק זִכִּיתִי לְבָבִי	-12-	Surely in vain I (have) purified my heart;
וָאֶרְחַץ בְּנִקָּיוֹן כַּפָּי:		and (have) washed my hands with innocence; Ps 73:13
וָאֱהִי נָגוּעַ כָּל־הַיּוֹם		and I have been/was stricken all day;
וְתוֹכַחְתִּי לַבְּקָרִים:		my chastening being at the mornings. Ps 73:14
הֶאֱכַלְתָּם לֶחֶם דִּמְעָה	-13-	You (have) fed them the bread of tears
וַתַּשְׁקֵמוֹ בִּדְמָעוֹת שָׁלִישׁ:		And you (have) made them drink tears of a *shalish-measure.* Ps 80:6

Most of the *vayyiqtol* forms in the Psalms of Asaph are in Psalm 78, in an extended section which recounts the history of Israel. It is poetry, but it narrates a story and we find preterites in the Psalm just as in narrative.

The historical accounts in Asaph Psalms also include prefixed verbs (*yiqtol*) that are parallel to preterites (*vayyiqtol*) and to perfect fientive verbs. Context would seem to make it clear what they should be doing, so we presume that these are archaic preterites surviving without the *vav*. All of these cases involve ancient or mythic content referring to the Exodus (78:13–72; 80:9–12; 81:6c–8), theophany (77:17–20 and possibly Ps 50:1–6), or Leviathan (74:13–17).

גֶּפֶן מִמִּצְרַיִם תַּסִּיעַ	-14-	You *removed* a vine from Egypt
תְּגָרֵשׁ גּוֹיִם וַתִּטָּעֶהָ		You *drove out* the nations and planted it. Ps 80:9 (Eng 8)
פִּנִּיתָ לְפָנֶיהָ		You cleared the ground before it
וַתַּשְׁרֵשׁ שָׁרָשֶׁיהָ וַתְּמַלֵּא־אָרֶץ		Its roots took hold and filled the land. Ps 80:10 (Eng 9)

It is perhaps the content that might be considered a clue to the presence of preterites without *vav*. In specific cases it is possible that some of these prefixed fientive verbs are used for imperfective past action.

There are times when more than one nuance known from prose for a certain verb form will reasonably make sense. We will not take the occasion to discuss those or other difficult passages which might involve long discussions and end up placing a disproportionate emphasis on what are the rare cases rather than the normal.

When the Psalms of Asaph are viewed as a whole, we find great consistency in the use of the verbal forms. By this we mean that normal functions for the various verb forms (known from other genres and historical studies) render quite understandable readings when a decision about their time frame is based on a combination of factors including parallelism, conjugation, and *aktionsart* (stative vs. fientive).

32.4   Summary.

As a starting point to translating poetry, we suggest using the same functions of the verb forms known from speech, narrative, or historical studies under the constraints of parallelism and context.

32.5   Psalm 76.

While perhaps no single Psalm will entail all of the issues discussed in this chapter, treating an entire Psalm will complement the previous discussion, which has been arranged by categories. We will discuss Psalm 76, considering how to translate its time frames, by looking at its verb forms, verb types (stative or fientive), and poetic parallelism. We will find a structure that is suggestive of its performance, though how the Psalm was actually sung or utilized in the cult is uncertain.

We will follow the verse numeration of the Hebrew text. The English verses will all be one less because verse 1 in the Hebrew is a title and does not receive a verse number in the English Bible. The first three lines of the poem, then, are verses 2–4. We recommend you try to translate these before reading the discussion.

2 נוֹדָע בִּיהוּדָה אֱלֹהִים	בְּיִשְׂרָאֵל גָּדוֹל שְׁמוֹ׃
3 וַיְהִי בְשָׁלֵם סֻכּוֹ	וּמְעוֹנָתוֹ בְצִיּוֹן׃
4 שָׁמָּה שִׁבַּר רִשְׁפֵי־קָשֶׁת	מָגֵן וְחֶרֶב וּמִלְחָמָה סֶלָה׃

Verse 2 is a bicolon. The first colon has a Niphal ptc., נוֹדָע; the second colon is a nominal clause. Without any other clauses preceding it to set the time frame, it is most naturally understood as present.

> *God is known[6] in Judah;   In Israel – great is his name.*

We will skip ahead to verse 4 for the moment. The first colon has a Piel pf., שִׁבַּר; the second part of the verse expands on the direct object in synthetic parallelism (32.3*a*), so its time frame is also controlled by שִׁבַּר from the A-line of the verse. שִׁבַּר is fientive,[7] so our natural expectation for a fientive perfect would be past time.

---

[6] If the Niphal is taken reflexively, we might translate "God reveals himself."

[7] Basically all Piel and Hiphil verbs are fientive, because, even if the root were stative in the Qal, these derived stems would normally turn it into a fientive verb.

There he broke the flaming arrows;[8]   *Shield, sword, and weaponry.*

Now we turn to verse 3. The first colon begins with וַיְהִי, clearly a preterite; the second colon is nominal, and due to its synonymous parallelism depends on the first colon and its verb for the time frame. Like verse 2, verse 3 also refers to places in each colon, so the majority of translations treat verse 3 in the present, like verse 2.

His abode is in Salem;[9]   *His dwelling place in Zion.*

While the parallelism with verse 1 is possible and understandable, a present tense translation does not fit the preterite form וַיְהִי. Our first expectation should be for parallelism to steer us toward a normal use of a verb form rather than override it. A link between verse 3 and verse 4 is more probable since the preterite and the perfect are both normally expected to convey past time. In this vein, the RSV[10] translates:

His abode has been established in Salem,   *his dwelling place in Zion.*

וַיְהִי could mean *it became*, though if we ask ourselves what we expect וַיְהִי to do most often, we have usually encountered it beginning a story or a scene, *it happened*. That expectation creates other questions since it is the second verse of the poem. So let us observe further to find more resolution for the structure of the poem and the time frames of its lines.

The entire Psalm is printed on the next page. In verse 5 we see another Niphal participle, נָאוֹר; it is the first word, as is the participle in verse 2. And looking farther down, we see another Niphal participle, נוֹרָא, in verse 8, the second word. Now we are not suggesting that Niphal participles have a special role in Hebrew poetry, but as an uncommon Hebrew form, it catches our eye to see them somewhat evenly spaced throughout the Psalm. All three of these lines appear to have a present time frame. The second half of verse 5 is clearly in the same time frame as the first colon since, as synthetic parallelism, they are grammatically one unit. The second colon of verse 8 has an imperfect form. The present tense is a normal use for the imperfect and here in a rhetorical question is a general present, *who can stand before you…?* So these lines are similar in structure (using a Ni. ptc. in their first colon) and appear to have a present time frame. If these mark off three line units, what then of the two verses following each of these lines?

---

[8] The phrase רִשְׁפֵי־קֶשֶׁת, *flames of the bow*, does not necessarily mean that the arrows are on fire. רֶשֶׁף can refer to flames or fire-bolts/lightning. This phrase may simply mean *arrows*, using the figure of speech to compare the striking of an arrow to the striking of a lightning bolt. Or the idea of flashing may refer to the appearance of arrows leaving bows. What kind of genitive would you say קֶשֶׁת is?
[9] Salem is short for Jerusalem.
[10] *Revised Standard Version* (The Division of Christian Education of the National Council of the Churches of Christ in the United States of America, 1971).

Here is the entire Psalm.

בְּיִשְׂרָאֵל גָּדוֹל שְׁמוֹ:   2 נוֹדָע בִּיהוּדָה אֱלֹהִים

וּמְעוֹנָתוֹ בְצִיּוֹן: 3 וַיְהִי בְשָׁלֵם סֻכּוֹ

מָגֵן וְחֶרֶב וּמִלְחָמָה סֶלָה: 4 שָׁמָּה שִׁבַּר רִשְׁפֵי־קָשֶׁת

מֵהַרְרֵי־טָרֶף: 5 נָאוֹר אַתָּה אַדִּיר

וְלֹא־מָצְאוּ כָל־אַנְשֵׁי־חַיִל יְדֵיהֶם: 6 אֶשְׁתּוֹלְלוּ[11] ׀ אַבִּירֵי לֵב נָמוּ שְׁנָתָם

נִרְדָּם וְרֶכֶב וָסוּס: 7 מִגַּעֲרָתְךָ אֱלֹהֵי יַעֲקֹב

וּמִי־יַעֲמֹד לְפָנֶיךָ מֵאָז אַפֶּךָ:   8 אַתָּה ׀ נוֹרָא אַתָּה

אֶרֶץ יָרְאָה וְשָׁקָטָה: 9 מִשָּׁמַיִם הִשְׁמַעְתָּ דִּין

לְהוֹשִׁיעַ כָּל־עַנְוֵי־אֶרֶץ סֶלָה: 10 בְּקוּם־לַמִּשְׁפָּט אֱלֹהִים

שְׁאֵרִית חֵמֹת תַּחְגֹּר: 11 כִּי־חֲמַת אָדָם תּוֹדֶךָּ

כָּל־סְבִיבָיו יוֹבִילוּ שַׁי לַמּוֹרָא: 12 נִדֲרוּ וְשַׁלְּמוּ לַיהוָה אֱלֹהֵיכֶם

נוֹרָא לְמַלְכֵי־אָרֶץ: 13 יִבְצֹר רוּחַ נְגִידִים

We have already seen that the verb forms in verses 3–4, a preterite and a fientive perfect, are forms normally used for the past. Verses 6 and 7 have three perfect forms: מָצְאוּ, נָמוּ, אֶשְׁתּוֹלְלוּ. The participle נִרְדָּם would be controlled by the past time frame beginning the verse.[12] Verse 9 has three perfect forms, יָרְאָה, הִשְׁמַעְתָּ, and שָׁקָטָה. And verse 10 has infinitive constructs which depend on verse 9.

So the first three stanzas each have three lines. The first line of each stanza begins with a Niphal participle and has a present time frame. The second and third bicola of each of these stanzas have only verb forms which naturally fit a past time frame. When we consider their content, we see that verses 2, 5, and 8 praise God, describing his character. Verses 3–4, 6–7, and 9–10 read like a story, beginning with וַיְהִי and followed by perfect forms, praising God for his past actions. The alternating structure and content allows us to easily envision an antiphonal performance, with one singer or choir section singing the lines of verses 2, 5, and 8, while another sings the lines of 3–4, 6–7, and 9–10, a pattern that could continue into the final stanza.

The fourth stanza calls for a response. Verse 11 begins with כִּי and does not have a Niphal participle, but rather two imperfects, which could be understood either as present or as future. Verse 12 begins with an imperative, instructing the people in their response. Interestingly, if you read only vss. 2, 5, 8, and 11 (in italics on the next page) or if you read only 3–4, 6–7, 9–10, and 12–13, either set makes sense on its own.

---

[11] This is a Hitpolel perfect of שלל. Though not frequent, there are a number of places where א is written in a place normally occupied by ה. Besides this problem, the ת of the Hitpael/Hitpolel prefix has switched places with the sibilant שׁ beginning the root (cp. 22.7).

[12] One could argue that it should be a Niphal perfect.

2 God is known in Judah –

In Israel, great is his name.

> 3 It happened in Salem, his abode –
>
> in Zion, his dwelling.
>
> 4 There he broke[13] the flashing arrows –
>
> shield, sword, and weaponry.

5 You are resplendent, majestic –

superior to[14] the mountains of prey.

> 6 The stouthearted were plundered; they sank into their sleep –
>
> No man of war could use his hands.[15]
>
> 7 At your rebuke, O God of Jacob –
>
> he fell asleep, also chariot and horse.

8 You – you are fearsome –

who can stand before you when you are angry?[16]

> 9 From heaven you announced justice –
>
> the earth became frightened and quiet.
>
> 10 when God rose to judgment
>
> to rescue the earth's oppressed.

11 Indeed the wrath of humanity[17] brings you praise –

you (will) gird yourself with a fragment of wrath.

> 12 Make vows to the LORD your God and fulfill them –
>
> Let all around him bring gifts to the fearsome one.
>
> 13 He cuts off the spirit of princes
>
> He is feared by the kings of earth.

It runs against the trend of most translations to translate the preterite וַיְהִי in verse 3 as the past rather than the present. But it certainly makes sense to translate all the verbs in this Psalm according to normal uses we have already learned in prose, accounting also for the role of poetic parallelism. In fact we suggest that a present tense translation in verse 3 obscures the structure of the Psalm.

---

[13] How would you label this use of the Piel? Why?

[14] The preposition מִן could be comparative or spatial, e.g. *radiant one from the mountains* or imply a verbal notion, e.g. *coming from the mountains.*

[15] Literally, *all the men of war could not find their hands*, that is, they have gone limp or numb with fear.

[16] Literally, *at the time of your anger.*

[17] Is the *wrath of humanity* a subjective or objective genitive? Is it the wrath that humanity has or God's wrath against people? This verse has been understood in many different ways, but the issues are not pertinent to the point of this chapter.

Appendix A:
Additional Vocabulary Lists

These lists supply the remaining vocabulary used 50 or more times in the Hebrew Bible. Lists 23–29 are loosely organized around semantic fields, but prioritize keeping the lists close to the same length. Lists 30–32 divide the remaining words that are used 50–60 times. List 33 includes words used more than 50 times only due to being common from Exod 25–Num 10. These lists are included in the CD's vocabulary program, where criteria such as frequency can also be applied to them. They are also listed by frequency in a PDF document on the CD.

List 23
Words primarily related to the body or rescuing.

1	בֶּגֶד	*n.m.*	garment (216)
2	בֶּטֶן	*n.m.*	womb, belly (72)
3	גָּאַל	*vb.*	to redeem, act as kinsman (104)
4	דָּם	*n.m.*	blood (361)
5	זְרוֹעַ	*n.m.*	arm, shoulder, strength (91)
6	יְשׁוּעָה	*n.f.*	salvation (78)
7	יָשַׁע	*vb.*	*Hi. to deliver; Ni. to be rescued (205)
8	כָּתֵף	*n.f.*	shoulder(-blade), support (67)
9	לָבַשׁ	*vb.*	to put on, wear, be clothed (112)
10	מָלַט	*vb.*	*Ni. to escape, be delivered; Hi. to deliver, to birth (94)
11	נֶפֶשׁ	*n.f.*	self, soul, living being, breath, throat (757)
12	נָצַל	*vb.*	*Ni. to be delivered; Hi. to save, rescue (213)
13	נָצַר	*vb.*	to watch over, protect, keep (63)
14	עָזַר	*vb.*	to help, aid (82)
15	עֶצֶם	*n.f.*	bone, self (126)
16	רֹאשׁ	*n.m.*	head, beginning, chief (600)
17	רוּחַ	*n.f.*	spirit, breath, wind (378)
18	רָחַץ	*vb.*	to wash (72)
19	רָפָא	*vb.*	to heal (69)
20	שָׂפָה	*n.f.*	lip, edge, speech (178)

List 24

Words primarily related to geography or time.

1	אֵצֶל	*prp.* beside (62)
2	בֹּקֶר	*n.m.* morning (213)
3	גְּבוּל	*n.m.* border (241)
4	גּוֹרָל	*n.m.* lot (77)
5	חֵלֶק	*n.m.* portion, tract, territory (66)
6	חֹשֶׁךְ	*n.m.* dark(ness) (80)
7	יְאֹר	*n.m.* stream, canal, Nile, mineshaft (65)
8	מִזְרָח	*n.m.* sunrise, the east (74)
9	נֶגֶב	*n.m.* south, Negev (112)
10	נָהָר	*n.m.* stream, river (119)
11	נַחַל	*n.m.* wadi, stream, valley, trench (137)
12	עֵמֶק	*n.m.* valley, lowland (70)
13	עֶרֶב	*n.m.* evening, night (134)
14	עֲרָבָה	*n.f.* desert, plain, steppe (160)
15	עַתָּה	*adv.* now (435)
16	צָפוֹן	*n.f.* north (153)
17	קָדִים	*n.m.* east, east wind (69)
18	קֶדֶם	*n.m.* front, east, of old, beginning, ancient (61)
19	שֶׁמֶשׁ	*n.m.* sun (158)
20	תָּמִיד	*n.m.* continually, on-going, lasting (104)

List 25

Words primarily relating to stopping, placement, or being great/small.

1	אַחֲרוֹן	*adj.* behind, after, later, latter, last (51)
2	אַחֲרִית	*n.f.* hind part, latter part, end, following (61)
3	גָּדַל	*vb.* to grow, become great (117)
4	חוּץ	*n.m.* the outside, a street (164)
5	כָּלָה	*vb.* be complete, finished (207)
6	לְמַעְלָה	*subst.* upwards (ל + מַעַל + ה) (64)
7	מָהַר	*vb.* *Pi. to hurry, hasten (81)
8	מְעַט	*subst.* a little, small, few (101)
9	נוּחַ	*vb.* to rest (140)
10	קָלַל	*vb.* be small, insignificant, swift (82)

11	קָרוֹב	*adj.*	near (75)
12	רִאשׁוֹן	*adj.*	former, first, formerly, chief (182)
13	רֵאשִׁית	*n.f.*	beginning, first, chief (51)
14	רָבָה	*vb.*	be(come) many/great (229)
15	רוּם	*vb.*	be high, exalted (197)
16	רֹחַב	*n.m.*	breadth, width (101)
17	רָחוֹק	*adj.*	distant, far (84)
18	רָחַק	*vb.*	be(come) far, distant (59)
19	שָׁבַת	*vb.*	to cease, desist, rest (71)

List 26

Words primarily relating to people.

1	אֶבְיוֹן	*adj.*	needy, poor (61)
2	אַחֵר	*adj.*	another, different (166)
3	בְּכוֹר	*n.m.*	firstborn (120)
4	בַּעַל	*n.m.*	master, husband (161)
5	גֶּבֶר	*n.m.*	man (66)
6	גּוּר 1	*vb.*	to sojourn (82)
7	גֵּר	*n.m.*	sojourner (92)
8	דּוֹד	*n.m.*	beloved, uncle (61)
9	דּוֹר	*n.m.*	generation (167)
10	זָכָר	*n.m.*	male (82)
11	זָר	*ptc.*	strange(r), foreign, outsider, another (70)
12	חָכָם	*adj.*	wise (138)
13	יָלַד	*vb.*	to bear (a child), bring forth (499)
14	יֶלֶד	*n.m.*	child, son, youth (89)
15	כְּסִיל	*n.m.*	fool (70)
16	מַטֶּה	*n.m.*	staff, rod, branch, tribe (252)
17	מִשְׁפָּחָה	*n.f.*	clan (304)
18	נַעַר	*n.m.*	adolescent, boy, attendant, servant (240)
19	נַעֲרָה	*n.f.*	young unmarried girl, attendant (76)
20	רֵעַ	*n.m.*	friend, companion (188)
21	שִׁפְחָה	*n.f.*	maidservant (63)

List 27

Words primarily relating to religion.

1	בָּמָה	*n.f.*	high place (106)
2	חַג	*n.m.*	festival, feast (62)
3	חָוָה	*vb.*	*Hishtaphel to bow down, worship (173)
4	חָלַל	*vb.*	*Hi. to begin; Ni. to be polluted; Pi. to defile; Pu. to be profaned (135)
5	כְּרוּב	*n.m.*	cherub (91)
6	מוֹעֵד	*n.m.*	meeting place/time, assembly, festival (224*)
7	מִנְחָה	*n.f.*	gift, tribute, offering (211)
8	נֶסֶךְ	*n.m.*	drink offering, molten image (60)
9	סֶלָה	*prt.*	musical term of uncertain meaning (74)
10	עֹלָה	*n.f.*	whole burnt offering (286)
11	עָרַךְ	*vb.*	to prepare, set in order, compare, arrange, confront (75)
12	פָּלָא	*vb.*	*Ni. be extraordinary (*47x as Ni. ptc. miracle, wonders*); Hi. to do wondrously (71)
13	קָדַשׁ	*vb.*	be set apart, consecrated (171)
14	קָטַר	*vb.*	*Pi. to make a sacrifice, to make go up in smoke (115)
15	קְטֹרֶת	*n.f.*	incense, sacrificial smoke (60)
16	רֵיחַ	*n.m.*	scent, odor (58)
17	שָׁפַךְ	*vb.*	to pour (out) (117)
18	שָׁרַת	*vb.*	*Pi. to minister, serve (98)
19	תְּרוּמָה	*n.f.*	contribution, offering (76)

List 28

More common animal, vegetable, and mineral words.

1	אַיִל	*n.m.*	ram (171)
2	בְּהֵמָה	*n.f.*	beast, animals, cattle (190)
3	בָּקָר	*n.m.*	cattle, herd (183)
4	בָּשָׂר	*n.m.*	flesh, meat, food (270)
5	זָהָב	*n.m.*	gold (392)
6	זָרַע	*vb.*	to sow, scatter seed (56)
7	זֶרַע	*n.m.*	seed (229)
8	חֲמוֹר	*n.m.*	male donkey (96)
9	יַיִן	*n.m.*	wine (141)
10	כֶּבֶשׂ	*n.m.*	lamb (107)

11	כְּלִי	*n.m.* utensil, vessel, article (325)
12	כֶּרֶם	*n.m/f.* vineyard (94)
13	מִגְרָשׁ	*n.m.* pastureland, outskirts (114)
14	נְחֹשֶׁת	*n.m/f.* copper, bronze, fetter of (139)
15	סוּס	*n.m.* horse, stallion (138)
16	פַּר	*n.m.* young bull, steer (133)
17	פְּרִי	*n.m.* fruit (119)
18	צֹאן	*n.f.* flock(s), small cattle (sheep and goats) (274)
19	רָעָב	*n.m.* famine, hunger (101)
20	שֶׁמֶן	*n.m.* oil, fat (193)

List 29

Less common animal, vegetable, and mineral words.

1	אֶרֶז	*n.m.* cedar (73)
2	בַּרְזֶל	*n.m.* iron (76)
3	גִּבְעָה	*n.f.* hill (72)
4	גָּמָל	*n.m.* camel (54)
5	גֶּפֶן	*n.f.* vine (55)
6	דְּבַשׁ	*n.m.* honey (54)
7	יַעַר	*n.m.* forest, wood (57)
8	כִּכָּר	*n.f.* round *thing*, loaf, valley, talent (e.g. of gold) (68)
9	מִקְנֶה	*n.m.* cattle (76)
10	נָטַע	*vb.* to plant (59)
11	סֶלַע	*n.m.* rock, cliff, crag (58)
12	סֹלֶת	*n.f.* fine flour (53)
13	עוֹף	*n.m.* birds, flying insects (71)
14	צוּר	*n.m.* rock, cliff (73)
15	קֶרֶן	*n.f.* horn (76)
16	רָכַב	*vb.* to ride, mount (78)
17	שָׂעִיר	*n.m.* he-goat (52)
18	שׁוֹפָר	*n.m.* (ram's) horn (72)
19	שׁוֹר	*n.m.* a head of cattle, ox (79)
20	שָׁקָה	*vb.* to drink (62)

List 30

Words occuring 50–60 times; part A.

1	אַלּוּף	*n.m.*	(tribal) chief, commander (of 1000 soldiers) (60)
2	אַלְמָנָה	*n.f.*	widow (55)
3	אָמָה	*n.f.*	maidservant (56)
4	בְּתוּלָה	*n.f.*	virgin (50)
5	זָנָה	*vb.*	to fornicate, be a harlot (60)
6	חָזָה	*vb.*	to gaze, see (55)
7	חָזָק	*adj.*	strong, mighty (57)
8	חָמָס	*n.m.*	violence, wrong (60)
9	חֵץ	*n.m.*	arrow (55)
10	כָּבַס	*vb.*	*Pi. to wash; ptc. = washer, fuller (51)
11	כָּעַס	*vb.*	be vexed, angry (55)
12	מָגֵן	*n.m.*	shield (60)
13	נָכַר	*vb.*	*Hi. to recognize, regard (50)
14	עָמָל	*n.m.*	trouble, anxiety, toil, misery, work(er) (54)
15	עֶרְוָה	*n.f.*	nakedness (54)
16	פָּרָשׁ	*n.m.*	horseman, charioteer, horse team (57)
17	שֵׁן	*n.f.*	tooth, ivory (55)

List 31

Words occuring 50–60 times; part B.

1	אֹרַח	*n.m.*	way, path (59)
2	חָדַל	*vb.*	to cease (55)
3	חָלַק	*vb.*	to divide, share (55)
4	חָתַת	*vb.*	be shattered, dismayed (55)
5	יָבֵשׁ	*vb.*	be dry, dried up (59)
6	יָכַח	*vb.*	*Hi. to decide, judge, rebuke; Ni. to reason (together); Hit. to argue (59)
7	מִזְמוֹר	*n.m.*	melody, psalm (57)
8	מְנַצֵּחַ	*ptc.*	(musical) director (59)
9	נֶדֶר	*n.m.*	vow (60)
10	נָחַל	*vb.*	to get/take possession (59)
11	פָּדָה	*vb.*	to ransom (60)

12	פָּעַל	*vb.* to do, make (58)
13	צָעַק	*vb.* to cry out (55)
14	רָצוֹן	*n.m.* favor, will, pleasing (56)
15	שָׂכַל	*vb.* be prudent (60)
16	שָׁדַד	*vb.* to devastate, despoil, ruin (59)
17	שְׁמָמָה	*n.f.* devastation, waste (56)
18	תְּהִלָּה	*n.f.* (song of) praise, fame (58)

List 32

Words occuring 50–60 times; part C.

1	אָבָה	*vb.* be willing, consent (54)
2	אַיֵּה	*adv.* where? (52)
3	בָּקַע	*vb.* to cleave, split open (51)
4	דָּבַק	*vb.* to cling, keep (55)
5	הוֹי	*prt.* alas!, woe! (51)
6	חָרַם	*vb.* to ban, devote, destroy (50)
7	יוֹמָם	*adv.* daytime, daily (53)
8	מָדַד	*vb.* to measure (52)
9	מִדָּה	*n.f.* measure(ment), garment (55)
10	מְדִינָה	*n.f.* province, district (53)
11	מוּסָר	*n.m.* discipline, instruction (50)
12	מִתַּחַת	*prp.* (from) beneath, (from) under (מִן + תַּחַת) (56)
13	מָחָר	*n.m. adv.* tomorrow, in the future (52)
14	מָרוֹם	*n.m.* height (54)
15	נָשַׂג	*vb.* to reach, overtake (50)
16	רָנַן	*vb.* to give ringing cry (53)
17	שְׂמֹאל	*n.m.* left, north (54)
18	שָׁוְא	*n.m.* emptiness, vanity (54)

List 33

Words used 50 or more times by virtue of being common from Exod 25–Num 10.

1   אֶדֶן   *n.m.* pedestal, base, socket (57)

2   אֲחֻזָּה   *n.f.* possession (66)

3   אִשֶּׁה   *n.m.* offering made by fire (65)

4   חֵלֶב   *n.m.* fat (92)

5   טַבַּעַת   *n.f.* ring (50)

6   טָהוֹר   *adj.* clean, pure (96)

7   טָהֵר   *vb.* be clean, pure (94)

8   טָמֵא   *adj.* unclean (88)

9   יָצַק   *vb.* to pour, cast out (53)

10 יְרִיעָה   *n.f.* curtain (54)

11 כָּפַר   *vb.* to cover; Pi. to cover over, pacify, atone for (102)

12 מִחוּץ   *adv.* (on the) outside, around (מִן + חוּץ) (64)

13 מַצָּה   *n.f.* unleavened bread (53)

14 נֶגַע   *n.m.* stroke, plague, spot, mark (78)

15 עֵדוּת   *n.f.* testimony (61)

16 עוֹר   *n.m.* skin, hide, leather (99)

17 עֵז   *n.f.* she-goat, goat hair (74)

18 קָנֶה   *n.m.* reed, reed's length (6 cubits), humerus bone (62)

19 קָרְבָּן   *n.m.* offering, gift (80)

20 קֶרֶשׁ   *n.m.* board, planks (51)

21 שָׁחַט   *vb.* to slaughter, beat (81)

22 שֻׁלְחָן   *n.m.* table (71)

23 שֶׁלֶם   *n.m.* peace offering (87)

24 שֶׁקֶל   *n.m.* shekel, piece of money (88)

Appendix B:
Glossary
Words used 50+ times in the Hebrew Bible

The chapter or list in which the word appears is listed at the end of each entry in italics and preceded by *c*. The frequency with which the word appears in the Bible appears in parentheses. The frequency counts are taken from Accordance,[1] which uses the Westminster[2] tagged text.[3] Proper nouns appear on pp 328–29.

א

אָב	*n.m.* father (1210) *c2*
אָבַד	*vb.* to perish (185) *c19*
אָבָה	*vb.* be willing, consent (54) *c32*
אֶבְיוֹן	*adj.* needy, poor (61) *c26*
אֶבֶן	*n.f.* stone (276) *c9*
אָדוֹן	*n.m.* master, superior, lord (335) *c9*
אָדָם	*n.m.* humankind, a man, person (551*) *c2*
אֲדָמָה	*n.f.* ground, earth (222) *c2*
אֶדֶן	*n.m.* pedestal, base, socket (57) *c33*
אָהֵב	*vb.* to love (217) *c4*
אֹהֶל	*n.m.* tent (348) *c16*
אוֹ	*cj.* or (321) *c10*

אָוֶן	*n.m.* trouble, deception, wickedness, false cult (81) *c21*
אוֹצָר	*n.m.* treasury, storehouse (79) *c16*
אוֹר	*n.f.* light (120) *c4*
אוֹת	*n.m.* sign, symbol, pledge, omen (79) *c9*
אָז	*adv.* then, at that time, thereupon (141) *c10*
אֹזֶן	*n.f.* ear (188) *c3*
אָח	*n.m.* brother (629) *c2*
אֶחָד	*n.m.* one (713) *c8*
אָחוֹת	*n.f.* sister (119) *c2*
אָחַז	*vb.* to grasp, take hold (63) *c12*
אֲחֻזָּה	*n.f.* possession (66) *c33*
אַחַר / אַחֲרֵי	*adv.* behind, after(wards) (718*) *c5*

---

[1] *Accordance 6.8*, OakTree Software, Inc., 2005.

[2] Groves-Wheeler Westminster Hebrew Morphology (Release 3.5), Westminster Theological Seminary, Philadelphia, 2001.

[3] Some frequency counts are given with an asterisk to show that our number differs from Accordance. This may be due to a difference in choice of entry, e.g. combining as one entry what are two in Accordance, or a disagreement with how words have been tagged in the Westminster text. For example, the 3fp independent pronoun was tagged to include some suffixes and a homonym, and several interrogative particles have been mistagged as the article. In the latter case we have not tried to make an exact count but have given the number for the article followed by a minus sign, while the frequency count of the interrogative particle is followed by a plus sign.

אַחֵר   *adj.* another, different (166) *c26*

אַחֲרוֹן   *adj.* behind, after, later, latter, last (51) *c25*

אַחֲרִית   *n.f.* hind part, latter part, end, following (61) *c25*

אַחַת   *n.f.* one (263) *c8*

אֹיֵב   *ptc.* enemy (285) *c20*

אַיֵּה   *adv.* where? (52) *c32*

אֵיךְ   *adv.* how (61) *c8*

אַיִל   *n.m.* ram (171) *c28*

אֵין / אַיִן   *subs.* not, there is not (790) *c7*

אִישׁ   *n.m.* man, husband, each (2199) *c2*

אַךְ   *adv.* surely, only, however (161) *c10*

אָכַל   *vb.* to eat (820) *c7*

אַל   *adv.* not, no (in prohibitions) (729) *c13*

אֶל   *prp.* to, toward, against, at, unto, concerning (5518) *c5*

אֵל / אֱלֹהִים   *n.m.* God, god(s) (2839) *c4*

אֵלֶּה   *prn.* these (pl. of זֶה or זֹאת) (2839) *c3*

אַלּוּף   *n.m.* (tribal) chief, commander (of 1000 soldiers) (60) *c30*

אַלְמָנָה   *n.f.* widow (55) *c30*

אֶלֶף   *n.m.* thousand, cattle (496) *c8*

אִם   *cj.* if, when, or (1070) *c10*

אֵם   *n.f.* mother (220) *c2*

אָמָה   *n.f.* maidservant (56) *c30*

אַמָּה   *n.f.* cubit, forearm (249) *c18*

אָמַן   *vb.* *Hi. to believe in; Ni. to prove reliable, faithful (97) *c21*

אָמַר   *vb.* to say (5316) *c6*

אֱמֶת   *n.f.* truth, reliability, firmness (127) *c21*

אֲנִי / אָנֹכִי   *prn.* I (1233*) *c1*

אֲנַחְנוּ   *prn.* we (121*) *c1*

אָסַף   *vb.* to gather, collect, remove (200) *c12*

אָסַר   *vb.* to bind, tie, harness (73) *c18*

1 אַף   *cj.* also, even, how much more/less (133) *c3*

2 אַף   *n.m.* nose, anger (277) *c3*

אֵצֶל   *prp.* beside (62) *c24*

אַרְבַּע   *n.m.* four, pl. forty (466*) *c8*

אֲרוֹן   *n.m/f.* ark, chest (202) *c9*

אֶרֶז   *n.m.* cedar (73) *c29*

אֹרַח   *n.m.* way, path (59) *c31*

אֹרֶךְ   *n.m.* length (95) *c18*

אֶרֶץ   *n.f.* land, earth, ground, territory, region (2505) *c1*

אָרַר   *vb.* to curse (63) *c7*

אֵשׁ   *n.f/m.* fire (376) *c2*

אִשָּׁה   *n.f.* woman, wife (781) *c2*

אִשֶּׁה   *n.m.* offering made by fire (65) *c33*

אֲשֶׁר   *prt.* who, which, that (5503) *c4*

אֵת / אֶת־   *prt.* (an untranslatable particle indicating the direct object) (10987) *c3*

אֵת / אֶת־   *prp.* with, beside (890) *c5*

אַתְּ   *prn.* you (fem. sg.) (67) *c3*

אַתָּה   *prn.* you (masc. sg.) (749) *c3*

אַתֶּם   *prn.* you (masc. pl.) (283) *c3*

אַתֵּנָה   *prn.* you (fem. pl.) (4) *c3*

ב

בְּ	*prp.*	in, with, by, at, among, into, when (15,559) *c2*
בֶּגֶד	*n.m.*	garment (216) *c23*
בַּד / לְבַד	*n.m.*	alone, separate (161) *c18*
בְּהֵמָה	*n.f.*	beast, animals, cattle (190) *c28*
בּוֹא	*vb.*	to come/go in, enter, come to (2592) *c5*
בּוֹר	*n.m.*	pit, cistern, well, *fig.* the grave (67) *c19*
בּוֹשׁ	*vb.*	be ashamed (125) *c10*
בָּחַר	*vb.*	to choose (172) *c10*
בָּטַח	*vb.*	to trust, be confident in (120*) *c21*
בֶּטֶן	*n.m.*	womb, belly (72) *c23*
בִּין	*vb.*	to understand, discern, perceive (171) *c13*
בֵּין / בֵּינוֹת	*prp.*	between, interval (409) *c5*
בַּיִת	*n.m.*	house (2047) *c16*
בָּכָה	*vb.*	to weep (114) *c11*
בְּכוֹר	*n.m.*	firstborn (120) *c26*
בַּל	*adv.*	not, no (73) *c13*
בִּלְתִּי	*adv.*	except, not, so as not to (לְבִלְתִּי) (112) *c13*
בָּמָה	*n.f.*	high place (106) *c27*
בֵּן / בֶּן	*n.m.*	son (of) (4941) *c2*
בָּנָה	*vb.*	to build (377) *c16*
בְּעַד	*prp.*	through, on behalf of, behind (104) *c5*
בַּעַל	*n.m.*	master, husband (161) *c26*
בָּעַר	*vb.*	to burn, purge (87*) *c17*
בָּקַע	*vb.*	to cleave, split open (51) *c32*

בָּקָר	*n.m.*	cattle, herd (183) *c28*
בֹּקֶר	*n.m.*	morning (213) *c24*
בָּקַשׁ	*vb.*	*Pi. to seek (225) *c20*
בַּרְזֶל	*n.m.*	iron (76) *c29*
בָּרַח	*vb.*	to flee (63) *c14*
בְּרִית	*n.m.*	covenant (287) *c9*
בָּרַךְ	*vb.*	*Pi. to bless; Hi. to cause to kneel (327) *c15*
בְּרָכָה	*n.f.*	blessing (69) *c15*
בָּשָׂר	*n.m.*	flesh, meat, food (270) *c28*
בַּת	*n.f.*	daughter (of) (587) *c2*
בְּתוּלָה	*n.f.*	virgin (50) *c30*

ג

גָּאַל	*vb.*	to redeem, act as kinsman (104) *c23*
גְּבוּל	*n.m.*	border (241) *c24*
גִּבּוֹר	*adj.*	strong, mighty (160) *c21*
גְּבוּרָה	*n.f.*	strength (62) *c21*
גִּבְעָה	*n.f.*	hill (72) *c29*
גֶּבֶר	*n.m.*	man (66) *c26*
גָּדוֹל	*adj.*	great, large (527) *c1*
גָּדַל	*vb.*	to grow, become great (117) *c25*
גּוֹי	*n.m.*	nation, people (560) *c2*
גּוּר 1	*vb.*	to sojourn (82) *c26*
גּוֹרָל	*n.m.*	lot (77) *c24*
גָּלָה	*vb.*	to uncover, depart (into exile) (187) *c10*
גַּם	*adv.*	also (769) *c10*
גָּמָל	*n.m.*	camel (54) *c29*
גָּנַב	*vb.*	to steal (40) *c12*
גֶּפֶן	*n.f.*	vine (55) *c29*
גֵּר	*n.m.*	sojourner (92) *c26*

ד

דָּבַק *vb.* to cling, keep (55) *c32*

דָּבַר *vb.* *Pi. to speak (1141*) *c15*

דָּבָר *n.m.* word, matter, thing (1454) *c1*

דְּבַשׁ *n.m.* honey (54) *c29*

דּוֹד *n.m.* beloved, uncle (61) *c26*

דּוֹר *n.m.* generation (167) *c26*

דֶּלֶת *n.f.* door (88) *c16*

דָּם *n.m.* blood (361) *c23*

דַּעַת *inf.* to know (Qal inf. cs. יָדַע) (51) *c7*

דַּעַת *n.f.* knowledge (88) *c7*

דָּרַךְ *vb.* to tread, march, bend (a bow) (63) *c14*

דֶּרֶךְ *n.m.* way, road, manner (712) *c14*

דָּרַשׁ *vb.* to seek, resort to (165) *c14*

ה

הַ◌ *art.* the (24,058-) *c2*

הֲ / הַ *prt.* interrogative particle (661+) *c5*

הֶבֶל *n.m/f.* futility, vapor (73) *c21*

הוּא *prn.* he (1398) *c1*

הוֹי *prt.* alas!, woe! (51) *c32*

הִיא *prn.* she (491) *c1*

הָיָה *vb.* be(come), happen (3576) *c11*

הֵיכָל *n.m.* palace, temple (80) *c16*

הָלַךְ *vb.* to go, come, walk (1554) *c8*

הָלַל *vb.* be boastful; Pi. to praise (146) *c15*

הֵם *prn.* they (masc. pl.) (565) *c3*

הָמוֹן *n.m/f.* sound, murmur, tumult (86) *c15*

הֵנָּה *prn.* they (fem. pl.) (31*) *c3*

הִנֵּה / הֵן *prt.* Look! See here! Take note! (indicates point of view or awareness) (1147*) *c7*

הָפַךְ *vb.* to turn, overturn, change (95) *c20*

הַר *n.m.* mountain, hill country (558) *c4*

הָרַג *vb.* to kill (167) *c19*

ו

וְ / וּ / וָ *cj.* and (50,524) *c2*

ז

זֹאת *prn.* this (fem. sg.) pl. = אֵלֶּה (605) *c3*

זָבַח *vb.* to slaughter; Pi. to sacrifice (134) *c12*

זֶבַח *n.m.* sacrifice (162) *c12*

זֶה *prn.* this (masc. sg.) pl. = אֵלֶּה (1178) *c3*

זָהָב *n.m.* gold (392) *c28*

זָכַר *vb.* to remember (235) *c13*

זָכָר *n.m.* male (82) *c26*

זָנָה *vb.* to fornicate, be a harlot (60) *c30*

זָעַק *vb.* to cry out, call (73) *c11*

זָקֵן *adj.* old, elder (180) *c1*

זָר *ptc.* strange(r), foreign, outsider, another (70) *c26*

זְרוֹעַ *n.m.* arm, shoulder, strength (91) *c23*

זָרַע *vb.* to sow, scatter seed (56) *c28*

זֶרַע *n.m.* seed (229) *c28*

ח

חַג *n.m.* festival, feast (62) *c27*

חָדַל *vb.* to cease (55) *c31*

חָדָשׁ *adj.* new (53) *c4*

חֹדֶשׁ *n.m.* new moon, month (283) *c4*

חָוָה *vb.* *Hishtaphel to bow down, worship (173) *c27*

חוֹמָה *n.f.* wall (133) *c16*

חוּץ *n.m.* the outside, a street (164) *c25*

חָזָה *vb.* to gaze, see (55) *c30*

חָזַק *vb.* be(come) strong, firm; Hi. to prevail, seize (290) *c21*

חָזָק *adj.* strong, mighty (57) *c30*

חָטָא *vb.* to do wrongly, sin (240) *c13*

חַטָּאת *n.f.* sin, sin offering (298) *c13*

חָיָה *vb.* to live (283) *c11*

חַי *adj.* alive (254) *c11*

חַיָּה *n.f.* animal (living thing), life (107) *c11*

חַיִּים *n.m.* life (140) *c11*

חַיִל *n.m.* strength, wealth, army (246) *c21*

חָכָם *adj.* wise (138) *c26*

חָכְמָה *n.f.* wisdom (153) *c1*

חֵלֶב *n.m.* fat (92) *c33*

חָלָה *vb.* be sick, weak; Pi. to entreat (75) *c19*

חֲלוֹם *n.m.* dream (65) *c17*

חָלַל *vb.* *Hi. to begin; Ni. to be polluted; Pi. to defile; Pu. to be profaned (135) *c27*

חָלָל *adj.* pierced, fatally wounded, slain (94) *c20*

חָלַק *vb.* to divide, share (55) *c31*

חֵלֶק *n.m.* portion, tract, territory (66) *c24*

חֵמָה *n.f.* heat, rage, venom (125) *c17*

חֲמוֹר *n.m.* male donkey (96) *c28*

חָמָס *n.m.* violence, wrong (60) *c30*

חָמֵשׁ *n.m.* five, pl. fifty (508*) *c8*

חֵן *n.m.* favor, grace (69) *c17*

חָנָה *vb.* to camp, bend down (143) *c9*

חָנַן *vb.* to show favor, be gracious (77) *c17*

חֶסֶד *n.m.* loyal love, kindness (249) *c17*

חָפֵץ *vb.* to delight in (74) *c17*

חֵץ *n.m.* arrow (55) *c30*

חֲצִי־ / חֵצִי *n.m.* half (125) *c8*

חָצֵר *n.m.* court, enclosure, village (192) *c16*

חֹק *n.m.* statute, decree (131) *c22*

חֻקָּה *n.f.* statute, enactment (104) *c1*

חֶרֶב *n.f.* sword (413) *c9*

חָרָה *vb.* to burn, be kindled, angry, upset (93) *c17*

חָרַם *vb.* to ban, devote, destroy (50) *c32*

חֶרְפָּה *n.f.* reproach (73) *c13*

חָשַׁב *vb.* to reckon, account (124) *c13*

חֹשֶׁךְ *n.m.* dark(ness) (80) *c24*

חָתַת *vb.* be shattered, dismayed (55) *c31*

ט

טַבַּעַת   *n.f.* ring (50) *c33*

טָהוֹר   *adj.* clean, pure (96) *c33*

טָהֵר   *vb.* be clean, pure (94) *c33*

טוֹב   *adj.* good (530) *c6*

טָמֵא   *vb.* be(come) unclean (162) *c13*

טָמֵא   *adj.* unclean (88) *c33*

י

יְאֹר   *n.m.* stream, canal, Nile, mineshaft (65) *c24*

יָבֵשׁ   *vb.* be dry, dried up (59) *c31*

יָד   *n.f.* hand, power (1627) *c3*

יָדָה   *vb.* to shoot; Pi. to cast; Hit. to confess, praise; Hi. to laud, praise (111) *c15*

יָדַע   *vb.* to know (956) *c7*

יוֹם   *n.m.* day (2301) *c4*

יוֹמָם   *adv.* daytime, daily (53) *c32*

יַחְדָּו   *adv.* together (96) *c18*

יָטַב   *vb.* be good, pleasing (117) *c12*

יַיִן   *n.m.* wine (141) *c28*

יָכַח   *vb.* *Hi. to decide, judge, rebuke; Ni. to reason (together); Hit. to argue (59) *c31*

יָכֹל   *vb.* be able, prevail, endure (193) *c12*

יָלַד   *vb.* to bear (a child), bring forth (499) *c26*

יֶלֶד   *n.m.* child, son, youth (89) *c26*

יָם   *n.m.* sea, west (396) *c4*

יָמִין   *n.f.* right (hand), south (141) *c3*

יָסַף   *vb.* to add; Hi. to add to, repeat, increase (213) *c18*

יַעַן   *cj.* on account of (100) *c10*

יָעַץ   *vb.* to advise, counsel (80) *c11*

יַעַר   *n.m.* forest, wood (57) *c29*

יָצָא   *vb.* to go/come out; (inf. cons. צֵאת) (1076) *c14*

יָצַק   *vb.* to pour, cast out (53) *c33*

יָצַר   *vb.* to form, mold (pottery) (63) *c6*

יָרֵא   *vb.* be afraid (317) *c12*

יָרַד   *vb.* to go/come down; (inf. cons. רֶדֶת) (382) *c14*

יְרִיעָה   *n.f.* curtain (54) *c33*

יָרַשׁ   *vb.* to take possession of, inherit, dispossess (232) *c20*

יֵשׁ   *subs.* there is (138) *c7*

יָשַׁב   *vb.* to sit, dwell, (יֹשֵׁב = Qal ptc. inhabitant; שֶׁבֶת = Qal inf cs.) (1088) *c12*

יְשׁוּעָה   *n.f.* salvation (78) *c23*

יָשַׁע   *vb.* *Hi. to deliver; Ni. to be rescued (205) *c23*

יָשָׁר   *adj.* straight, right (119) *c6*

יָתַר   *vb.* *Ni. to remain, be left over; Hi. to leave, leave over (106) *c18*

יֶתֶר   *n.m.* remainder, excess (97) *c18*

כ

כְּ   *prp.* like, as, according to, when (3053) *c2*

כַּאֲשֶׁר   *cj.* as, just as, according as, when (511) *c7*

כָּבֵד   *vb.* be honored, heavy, weighty (114) *c7*

כָּבֵד *adj.* heavy, honorable (41) *c7*

כָּבוֹד *n.m.* honor, glory, abundance (200) *c7*

כָּבַס *vb.* *Pi. to wash; ptc. = washer, fuller (51) *c30*

כֶּבֶשׂ *n.m.* lamb (107) *c28*

כֹּה *adv.* thus, here (577) *c10*

כֹּהֵן *n.m.* priest (750) *c7*

כוּן *vb.* *Ni. be firm, prepared, established; Hi. to establish, prepare, provide (219) *c16*

כֹּחַ *n.m.* strength, power (126) *c21*

כִּי *cj.* that, because, when, indeed (4487) *c4*

כִּי אִם *cj.* except, but only (156) *c10*

כִּכָּר *n.f.* round *thing*, loaf, valley, talent (e.g. of gold) (68) *c29*

כֹּל *n.m.* all, every, whole, any (5415) *c2*

כָּלָה *vb.* be complete, finished (207) *c25*

כְּלִי *n.m.* utensil, vessel, article (325) *c28*

כֵּן *adv.* thus, so (741) *c10*

כָּנָף *n.f.* wing, skirt, corner (111) *c3*

כִּסֵּא *n.m.* throne, honored seat (alt. כִּסֵּה) (135) *c22*

כָּסָה *vb.* to cover, conceal (153) *c21*

כְּסִיל *n.m.* fool (70) *c26*

כֶּסֶף *n.m.* silver, money (403) *c1*

כָּעַס *vb.* be vexed, angry (55) *c30*

כַּף *n.f.* palm, sole, hollow, pan (195) *c3*

כָּפַר *vb.* to cover; Pi. to cover over, pacify, atone for (102) *c33*

כְּרוּב *n.m.* cherub (91) *c27*

כֶּרֶם *n.m/f.* vineyard (94) *c28*

כָּרַת *vb.* to cut (off/down), make a treaty (289) *c19*

כָּשַׁל *vb.* to stumble, stagger (65) *c14*

כָּתַב *vb.* to write (225) *c9*

כָּתֵף *n.f.* shoulder(-blade), support (67) *c23*

ל

ל *prp.* to, for, regarding, belonging to (20,321) *c2*

לֹא / לוֹא *prt.* not, no (5193) *c4*

לֵבָב / לֵב *n.m.* mind/heart, will (854*) *c3*

לְבַד / בַּד *n.m.* alone, separate (161) *c18*

לָבַשׁ *vb.* to put on, wear, be clothed (112) *c23*

לִין / לוּן *vb.* to lodge (71) *c19*

לָחַם *vb.* to fight; Ni. to do battle (171) *c20*

לֶחֶם *n.m.* bread, food (340) *c9*

לַיְלָה / לֵיל *n.m.* night (235*) *c4*

לָכַד *vb.* to capture, seize, take (121) *c20*

לָכֵן *cj.* therefore (ל + כֵּן) (201) *c4*

לֶכֶת *inf.* to walk (Qal inf. הָלַךְ) (136) *c7*

לָמַד *vb.* to learn, train in (87) *c11*

לָמָה / לָמָּה *prn.* why? (178) *c8*

לְמַעְלָה *sub.* upwards (ל + מַעַל + ה) (64) *c25*

לְמַעַן *cj.* in order that, on account of (272) *c10*

לִפְנֵי   *prp.* before, in the presence of (פָּנֶה + לְ) (1126) *c5*

לָקַח   *vb.* to take, receive (976) *c8*

לָשׁוֹן   *n.m/f.* tongue, language (117) *c3*

מ

מְאֹד   *adv.* very, exceedingly, quite (300) *c4*

מֵאָה   *n.m.* hundred (583) *c8*

מָאַס   *vb.* to reject, refuse, despise (74) *c17*

מֵאֵת   *prp.* out of, from (beside); (אֵת + מִן) (180) *c5*

מָגֵן   *n.m.* shield (60) *c30*

מִגְרָשׁ   *n.m.* pastureland, outskirts (114) *c28*

מִדְבָּר   *n.m.* wilderness, pasture, steppe (269) *c1*

מָדַד   *vb.* to measure (52) *c32*

מִדָּה   *n.f.* measure(ment), garment (55) *c32*

מָדוּעַ   *adv.* why (72) *c8*

מְדִינָה   *n.f.* province, district (53) *c32*

מַה־□ / מֶה / מָה   *prn.* what?, what! (571) *c8*

מָהַר   *vb.* *Pi. to hurry, hasten (81) *c25*

מוּסָר   *n.m.* discipline, instruction (50) *c32*

מוֹעֵד   *n.m.* meeting place/time, assembly, festival (224*) *c27*

מוּת   *vb.* to die (845) *c10*

מָוֶת   *n.m.* death (153) *c19*

מִזְבֵּחַ   *n.m.* altar (403) *c12*

מִזְמוֹר   *n.m.* melody, psalm (57) *c31*

מִזְרָח   *n.m.* sunrise, the east (74) *c24*

מִחוּץ   *adv.* (on the) outside, around (חוּץ + מִן) (64) *c33*

מַחֲנֶה   *n.m.* camp, encampment (215) *c9*

מָחָר   *n.m. adv.* tomorrow, in the future (52) *c32*

מַחֲשָׁבָה   *n.f.* thought, device (56) *c13*

מַטֶּה   *n.m.* staff, rod, branch, tribe (252) *c26*

מִי   *prn.* who? (424) *c1*

מַיִם   *n.m.* water(s) (*construct* מֵי) (585) *c4*

מָכַר   *vb.* to sell (80) *c15*

מָלֵא   *vb.* be full (252) *c9*

מָלֵא   *adj.* full (61) *c9*

מַלְאָךְ   *n.m.* messenger, angel (213) *c22*

מְלָאכָה   *n.f.* work, wares, craftsmanship (167) *c15*

מִלְחָמָה   *n.f.* battle, war (319) *c20*

מָלַט   *vb.* *Ni. to escape, be delivered; Hi. to deliver, to birth (94) *c23*

מָלַךְ   *vb.* to reign, be(come) king (350) *c22*

מֶלֶךְ   *n.m.* king (2530) *c1*

מַלְכָּה   *n.f.* queen (35) *c1*

מַלְכוּת   *n.f.* reign, kingdom, royalty (91) *c22*

מַמְלָכָה   *n.f.* kingdom, dominion (117) *c22*

מִן □ / מִן   *prp.* from, out of, since, (more) than (7529) *c5*

מִנְחָה   *n.f.* gift, tribute, offering (211) *c27*

מְנַצֵּחַ   *ptc.* (musical) director (59) *c31*

מִסְפָּר *n.m.* number, recounting (retelling) (134) *c11*

מְעַט *subst.* a little, small, few (101) *c25*

מַעַל *prp.* upwards, above (140) *c5*

מֵעַל *prp.* from upon, from (beside); (מִן + עַל) (311) *c5*

מַעֲשֶׂה *n.m.* deed, work (235) *c15*

מָצָא *vb.* to find (457) *c10*

מַצָּה *n.f.* unleavened bread (53) *c33*

מִצְוָה *n.f.* commandment (184) *c1*

מִקְדָּשׁ *n.m.* sanctuary (75) *c16*

מָקוֹם *n.m.* place, standing place (401) *c9*

מִקְנֶה *n.m.* cattle (76) *c29*

מַרְאֶה *n.m.* vision, appearance, sight (103) *c13*

מָרוֹם *n.m.* height (54) *c32*

מָשַׁח *vb.* to anoint, smear (70) *c22*

מִשְׁכָּן *n.m.* dwelling (place), abode, tabernacle (139) *c12*

מָשַׁל *vb.* to rule (81) *c22*

מִשְׁמֶרֶת *n.f.* guard, watch, obligation, duty (78) *c6*

מִשְׁפָּחָה *n.f.* clan, family (304) *c26*

מִשְׁפָּט *n.m.* law, custom, legal claim/decision (425) *c1*

מִתַּחַת *prp.* (from) beneath, (from) under (מִן + תַּחַת) (56) *c32*

נ

נָא *prt.* please, (particle of entreaty) (405) *c13*

נְאֻם *n.m.* utterance, declaration (376) *c15*

נָבָא *vb.* *Ni., Hi. to prophesy (115) *c15*

נָבַט *vb.* *Pi., Hi. to look at, regard (70) *c13*

נָבִיא *n.m.* prophet (317) *c7*

נֶגֶב *n.m.* south, Negev (112) *c24*

נָגַד *vb.* *Hi. to declare (371) *c15*

נֶגֶד *prp.* in front of, opposite of (151) *c1*

נָגַע *vb.* to touch, reach, strike (150) *c19*

נֶגַע *n.m.* stroke, plague, spot, mark (78) *c33*

נָגַשׁ *vb.* to draw near, approach; (inf. cons. גֶּשֶׁת) (125) *c14*

נֶדֶר *n.m.* vow (60) *c31*

נָהָר *n.m.* stream, river (119) *c24*

נוּחַ *vb.* to rest (140) *c25*

נוּס *vb.* to flee, escape (160) *c14*

נָחַל *vb.* to get/take possession (59) *c31*

נַחַל *n.m.* wadi, stream, valley, trench (137) *c24*

נַחֲלָה *n.f.* possession, property (222) *c15*

נָחַם *vb.* *Ni. be sorry, to change one's mind; Pi. to comfort (108) *c17*

נְחֹשֶׁת *n.m/f.* copper, bronze, fetter of (139) *c28*

נָטָה *vb.* to stretch out, extend, bend (216) *c7*

נָטַע *vb.* to plant (59) *c29*

נָכָה *vb.* *Ni. to be smitten; Hi. to smite (501) *c20*

נָכַר   *vb.* *Hi. to recognize, regard (50) c30

נֶסֶךְ   *n.m.* drink offering, molten image (60) c27

נָסַע   *vb.* to set out, drive (flocks), journey (146) c14

נַעַר   *n.m.* adolescent, boy, attendant, servant (240) c26

נַעֲרָה   *n.f.* young unmarried girl, attendant (76) c26

נָפַל   *vb.* to fall, get down (435) c12

נֶפֶשׁ   *n.f.* self, soul, living being, breath, throat (757) c23

נָצַב   *vb.* *Ni. to take one's stand; Hi. to station, set up (74) c21

נָצַל   *vb.* *Ni. to be delivered; Hi. to save, rescue (213) c23

נָצַר   *vb.* to watch over, protect, keep (63) c23

נָשָׂא   *vb.* to lift, bear, carry; (inf. cons. שְׂאֵת) (659) c14

נָשִׂיא   *n.m.* chief, prince (130) c22

נָשַׂג   *vb.* to reach, overtake (50) c32

נָתַן   *vb.* to give, put, set, exchange, grant, yield, dedicate (2014) c8

ס

סָבַב   *vb.* to surround, turn, go around (163) c10

סָבִיב   *adv.* round about, circuit (338) c14

סָגַר   *vb.* to shut, close; Pi., Hi. to deliver up (91) c16

סוּס   *n.m.* horse, stallion (138) c28

סוּר   *vb.* to turn aside (298) c14

סֶלָה   *prt.* musical term of uncertain meaning (74) c27

סֶלַע   *n.m.* rock, cliff, crag (58) c29

סֹלֶת   *n.f.* fine flour (53) c29

סָפַר   *vb.* to count; Pi. to recount, declare, report (107) c11

סֵפֶר   *n.m.* document, book, writing (191) c11

סֹפֵר / סוֹפֵר   *n.m.* scribe, secretary (54) c11

סָתַר   *vb.* *Hi. to hide, conceal; Ni. be hidden, hide oneself (82) c21

ע

עָבַד   *vb.* to work, serve (289) c15

עֶבֶד   *n.m.* servant, slave (803) c15

עֲבֹדָה   *n.f.* service, labor, work (145) c15

עָבַר   *vb.* to pass over/through/by (553) c12

עֵבֶר   *n.m.* side, edge, area on the other side (92) c12

עַד / עֲדֵי־   *prp.* as far as, even to, until (1263) c5

עֵד   *n.m.* witness (69) c4

עֵדָה   *n.f.* congregation (149*) c9

עֵדוּת   *n.f.* testimony (61) c33

עוֹד / עֹד   *adv.* yet, still, again, continuance (491) c4

עוֹלָם   *n.m.* forever, always, ancient (439) c4

עָוֹן   *n.m.* wrongdoing, guilt (from)/punishment (for) iniquity (233) c9

עוֹף   *n.m.* birds, flying insects (71) c29

עוֹר   *vb.* to wake up, rouse oneself (80) c19

עוֹר   *n.m.* skin, hide, leather (99) *c33*

עֵז   *n.f.* she-goat, goat hair (74) *c33*

עֹז   *n.m.* strength, might, fortified (76) *c21*

עָזַב   *vb.* to abandon, forsake, leave (214) *c10*

עָזַר   *vb.* to help, aid (82) *c23*

עַיִן   *n.f.* eye, appearance, spring (900) *c3*

עִיר   *n.f.* city (1088) *c2*

עַל   *prp.* on, over, against, on account of, to (5777) *c5*

עַל־כֵּן   *cj.* therefore (161) *c10*

עָלָה   *vb.* to go up, ascend (894) *c14*

עֹלָה   *n.f.* whole burnt offering (286) *c27*

עַם   *n.m.* a people (1869) *c1*

עִם   *prp.* with, near, besides (1084) *c5*

עָמַד   *vb.* to stand, arise (524) *c21*

עַמּוּד   *n.m.* pillar, column (112) *c16*

עָמָל   *n.m.* trouble, anxiety, toil, misery, work(er) (54) *c30*

עֵמֶק   *n.m.* valley, lowland (70) *c24*

1 עָנָה   *vb.* to answer, respond (316) *c11*

2 עָנָה   *vb.* to be oppressed, be humble (79) *c11*

עָנִי   *adj.* poor, afflicted, humble (80) *c11*

עָנָן   *n.m.* cloud, cloud-mass (87) *c7*

עָפָר   *n.m.* dust, dry earth (110) *c2*

עֵץ   *n.m.* tree, wood(s) (330) *c4*

עֵצָה   *n.f.* counsel, advice (87) *c11*

עֶצֶם   *n.f.* bone, self (126) *c23*

עֶרֶב   *n.m.* evening, night (134) *c24*

עֲרָבָה   *n.f.* desert, plain, steppe (160) *c24*

עֶרְוָה   *n.f.* nakedness (54) *c30*

עָרַךְ   *vb.* to prepare, set in order, compare, arrange, confront (75) *c27*

עָשָׂה   *vb.* to do, make, perform (2632) *c6*

עֶשֶׂר / עָשָׂר   *n.m.* ten, x-teen; pl. twenty (829*) *c8*

עֵת   *n.f/m.* time (297) *c4*

עַתָּה   *adv.* now (435) *c24*

פ

פֵּאָה   *n.f.* corner, side (86) *c16*

פָּדָה   *vb.* to ransom (60) *c31*

פֶּה   *n.m.* mouth (498) *c3*

פֹּה   *adv.* here (82) *c9*

פּוּץ   *vb.* be dispersed, scattered (65) *c14*

פָּלָא   *vb.* *Ni. be extraordinary (*47x as Ni. ptc. miracles*); Hi. to do wondrously (71) *c27*

פָּלַל   *vb.* *Hit. to pray; Pi. to mediate, arbitrate (84) *c22*

פֶּן   *cj.* lest (133) *c10*

פָּנָה   *vb.* to turn, look (134) *c14*

פָּנֶה / פָּנִים   *n.m/f.* face (2126) *c3*

פָּעַל   *vb.* to do, make (58) *c31*

פַּעַם   *n.f.* step, pace, once, occasion (118) *c3*

פָּקַד   *vb.* to note, count, appoint, attend to = inspect/punish/reward; Hi. to appoint; Ni. to be noticed, missed (304) *c13*

פַּר   *n.m.* young bull, steer (133) *c28*

פְּרִי   *n.m.* fruit (119) *c28*

פַּרְעֹה   *n.m.* Pharaoh, (Egyptian) king (274) *c22*

פָּרַשׂ   *vb.* to spread out (67) *c14*

פָּרָשׁ   *n.m.* horseman, charioteer, horse team (57) *c30*

פֶּשַׁע   *n.m.* violation, transgression, guilt of/ punishment for/ offering for transgression (93) *c13*

פָּתַח   *vb.* to open (136) *c16*

פֶּתַח   *n.m.* doorway, opening, entrance (164) *c16*

צ

צֹאן   *n.f.* flock(s), small cattle (sheep and goats) (274) *c28*

צָבָא   *n.m.* army, host, warfare, service (487) *c20*

צַדִּיק   *adj.* just, righteous (206) *c6*

צֶדֶק   *n.m.* rightness, righteousness, justice, integrity (123) *c6*

צְדָקָה   *n.f.* righteousness (159) *c6*

צִוָּה   *vb.* *Pi. to order, command, charge (496) *c18*

צוּר   *n.m.* rock, cliff (73) *c29*

צֵל   *n.m.* shadow, shade, protection (53) *c7*

צָלַח   *vb.* be successful, prosper (65) *c19*

צָעַק   *vb.* to cry out (55) *c31*

צָפוֹן   *n.f.* north (153) *c24*

צַר   *n.m.* adversary (73) *c20*

צָרָה   *n.f.* distress, straits (70) *c19*

ק

קָבַץ   *vb.* to gather, collect, assemble (127) *c18*

קָבַר   *vb.* to bury (133) *c19*

קֶבֶר   *n.m.* grave, tomb (67) *c19*

קָדוֹשׁ   *adj.* holy (117) *c6*

קָדִים   *n.m.* east, east wind (69) *c24*

קֶדֶם   *n.m.* front, east, of old, beginning, ancient (61) *c24*

קָדַשׁ   *vb.* be set apart, consecrated (171) *c27*

קֹדֶשׁ   *n.m.* holiness, sacredness (470) *c6*

קָהָל   *n.m.* assembly, company, congregation (123) *c2*

קוֹל   *n.m.* voice, sound (505) *c15*

קוּם   *vb.* to arise, rise, stand up (627) *c10*

קַחַת   *inf.* to take, receive (Qal inf. לָקַח) (49) *c7*

קָטָן   *adj.* small, young (27) *c6*

קָטֹן   *adj.* small, insignificant; *vb.* be small (74) *c6*

קָטַר   *vb.* *Pi. to make a sacrifice, to make go up in smoke (115) *c27*

קְטֹרֶת   *n.f.* incense, sacrificial smoke (60) *c27*

קִיר   *n.m.* wall (73) *c16*

קָלַל   *vb.* be small, insignificant, swift (82) *c25*

קָנָה   *vb.* to acquire, buy, get (85) *c15*

קָנֶה   *n.m.* reed, reed's length (6 cubits), humerus bone (62) *c33*

קֵץ   *n.m.* end (67) *c9*

קָצֶה   *n.m.* end, edge (92) *c9*

קָרָא 1   *vb.* to call, proclaim, read aloud, name (739) *c11*

קָרָא 2   *vb.* *Ni., Hi. to meet, encounter, befall, happen (136) *c18*

קָרַב   *vb.* to approach, draw near (280) *c14*

קֶרֶב   *n.m.* midst, inner, innards (227) *c9*

קָרְבָּן   *n.m.* offering, gift (80) *c33*

קָרוֹב   *adj.* near (75) *c25*

קֶרֶן   *n.f.* horn (76) *c29*

קָרַע   *vb.* to tear, rend (63) *c18*

קֶרֶשׁ   *n.m.* board, planks (51) *c33*

קֶשֶׁת   *n.f.* bow (76) *c20*

ר

רָאָה   *vb.* to see (1311) *c12*

רֹאשׁ   *n.m.* head, beginning, chief (600) *c23*

רִאשׁוֹן   *adj.* former, first, formerly, chief (182) *c25*

רֵאשִׁית   *n.f.* beginning, first, chief (51) *c25*

רַב   *adj.* many (419) *c6*

רֹב   *n.m.* multitude, abundance (150) *c6*

רָבָה   *vb.* be(come) many/great (229) *c25*

רֶגֶל   *n.f.* foot (251) *c3*

רָדַף   *vb.* to pursue, persecute (144) *c20*

רוּחַ   *n.f.* spirit, breath, wind (378) *c23*

רוּם   *vb.* be high, exalted (197) *c25*

רוּץ   *vb.* to run (104) *c14*

רֹחַב   *n.m.* breadth, width (101) *c25*

רָחוֹק   *adj.* distant, far (84) *c25*

רָחַץ   *vb.* to wash (72) *c23*

רָחַק   *vb.* be(come) far, distant (59) *c25*

רִיב   *vb.* to contend, strive (72) *c22*

רִיב   *n.m.* strife, dispute (62) *c22*

רֵיחַ   *n.m.* scent, odor (58) *c27*

רָכַב   *vb.* to ride, mount (78) *c29*

רֶכֶב   *n.m.* chariot(ry), upper millstone (120) *c20*

רָנַן   *vb.* to give ringing cry (53) *c32*

רַע   *adj.* bad, evil; *as subst.* distress, evil (312) *c6*

רֵעַ   *n.m.* friend, companion (188) *c26*

רָעָב   *n.m.* famine, hunger (101) *c28*

רָעָה   *n.f.* evil, misery, distress (354) *c6*

רָעָה   *vb.* to shepherd, to pasture, to feed (167) *c22*

רֹעֶה   *ptc.* shepherd (100) *c22*

רָעַע   *vb.* be/do evil, displeasing, harmful (98) *c13*

רָפָא   *vb.* to heal (69) *c23*

רָצוֹן   *n.m.* favor, will, pleasing (56) *c31*

רַק   *adv.* only, surely (109) *c10*

רָשָׁע   *adj.* wicked, criminal, guilty (264) *c6*

שׁ

שָׂבַע   *vb.* be sated, satisfied (97) *c19*

שָׂדֶה   *n.m.* field (329) *c1*

שִׂים   *vb.* to put, place, set (588) *c12*

שָׂכַל   *vb.* be prudent (60) *c31*

שְׂמֹאל   *n.m.* left, north (54) *c32*

שָׂמַח   *vb.* be glad, rejoice (156) *c17*

שִׂמְחָה   *n.f.* joy, gladness (94) *c17*

שָׂנֵא   *vb.* to hate (148) *c17*

שָׂעִיר   *n.m.* he-goat (52) *c29*

שָׂפָה   *n.f.* lip, edge, speech (178) *c23*

שַׂר   *n.m.* chief, official, prince (425) *c22*

שָׂרַף   *vb.* to burn (117) *c17*

שׁ

שֶׁ / שַׁ / שָׁ   *prt.* who, which, that (143) *c7*

שְׁאוֹל   *n.f/m.* Sheol, netherworld (65) *c19*

שָׁאַל   *vb.* to ask (176) *c11*

שָׁאַר   *vb.* *Ni. to remain, be left over; Hi. to leave over, spare (133) *c18*

שְׁאֵרִית   *n.f.* remainder, the rest, remnant (66) *c18*

שֵׁבֶט   *n.m.* rod, tribe, staff, scepter (190) *c2*

שָׁבַע   *vb.* *Ni. to swear, take an oath (186) *c15*

שֶׁבַע   *n.m.* seven, pl. seventy (490*) *c8*

שָׁבַר   *vb.* to break; Pi. to shatter (148) *c18*

שָׁבַת   *vb.* to cease, desist, rest (71) *c25*

שַׁבָּת   *n.f/m.* rest, Sabbath (111) *c1*

שָׁדַד   *vb.* to devastate, despoil, ruin (59) *c31*

שָׁוְא   *n.m.* emptiness, vanity (54) *c32*

שׁוּב   *vb.* to turn back, return; (1075) *c12*

שׁוֹפָר   *n.m.* (ram's) horn (72) *c29*

שׁוֹר   *n.m.* a head of cattle, ox (79) *c29*

שָׁחַט   *vb.* to slaughter, beat (81) *c33*

שָׁחַת   *vb.* *Ni. to be marred, spoiled; Hi. to act corruptly (152) *c20*

שִׁיר   *vb.* to sing (88) *c11*

שִׁיר   *n.m.* song (78) *c11*

שִׁית   *vb.* to put, set, fix, set up as, ordain (86) *c21*

שָׁכַב   *vb.* to lie down (213) *c19*

שָׁכַח   *vb.* to forget (102) *c13*

שָׁכַם   *vb.* *Hi. to rise early (65) *c19*

שָׁכַן   *vb.* to dwell, settle (130) *c12*

שָׁלוֹם   *n.m.* health, wholeness, intact, sound, safety, deliverance (237) *c19*

שָׁלַח   *vb.* to send, stretch out (847) *c12*

שֻׁלְחָן   *n.m.* table (71) *c33*

שָׁלַךְ   *vb.* *Hi. to throw (125) *c20*

שָׁלָל   *n.m.* plunder, booty, spoil (74) *c20*

שָׁלֵם   *vb.* be complete, sound (116) *c19*

שֶׁלֶם   *n.m.* peace offering (87) *c33*

שָׁלֹשׁ   *n.m.* three; pl. thirty (606*) *c8*

שָׁם   *adv.* there (835) *c9*

שֵׁם   *n.m.* name (864) *c4*

שָׁמַד   *vb.* Ni. to be destroyed, exterminated (92) *c20*

שָׁמַיִם   *n.m.* heaven, sky (421) *c4*

שָׁמֵם   *vb.* be devastated, appalled, desolated (92) *c20*

שְׁמָמָה   *n.f.* devastation, waste (56) *c31*

שֶׁמֶן   *n.m.* oil, fat (193) *c28*

שְׁמֹנָה   *n.m.* eight; pl. eighty (147*) *c8*

שָׁמַע   *vb.* to hear, obey (1165) *c10*

שָׁמַר   *vb.* to guard, watch, keep (469) *c6*

שֹׁמֵר   *ptc.* watchman, watch, guard, keeping (107) *c6*

שֶׁמֶשׁ   *n.m.* sun (158) *c24*

שֵׁן   *n.f.* tooth, ivory (55) *c30*

שָׁנָה   *n.f.* year (878) *c2*

שֵׁנִי   *adj.* second (156) *c8*

שְׁנַיִם   *n.m.* two (516) *c8*

שַׁעַר   *n.m/f.* gate (373) *c16*

שִׁפְחָה   *n.f.* maidservant (63) *c26*

שָׁפַט   *vb.* to judge, give justice (204) *c22*

שֹׁפֵט   *ptc.* judge (68) *c22*

שָׁפַךְ   *vb.* to pour (out) (117) *c27*

שָׁקָה   *vb.* to drink (62) *c29*

שֶׁקֶל   *n.m.* shekel, piece of money (88) *c33*

שֶׁקֶר   *n.m.* deception, falsehood (113) *c21*

שָׁרֵת   *vb.* *Pi.* to minister, serve (98) *c27*

שֵׁשׁ   *n.m.* six, pl. sixty (274*) *c8*

שָׁתָה   *vb.* to drink (217) *c12*

שְׁתַּיִם   *n.f.* two (253) *c8*

ת

תְּהִלָּה   *n.f.* (song of) praise, fame (58) *c31*

תּוֹךְ / תָּוֶךְ   *n.m.* midst of *(almost always in construct)* (420) *c5*

תּוֹעֵבָה   *n.f.* abhorrence, disgust, abomination (118) *c17*

תּוֹרָה   *n.f.* instruction, law (223) *c1*

תַּחַת   *prp.* below, under, instead of (510) *c5*

תָּמִיד   *n.m.* continually, on-going, lasting (104) *c24*

תָּמִים   *adj.* complete, whole, wholesome (91) *c19*

תָּמַם / תַּם   *vb.* be complete, finished (64) *c10*

תְּפִלָּה   *n.f.* prayer (77) *c1*

תָּפַשׂ   *vb.* to seize, grasp, wield (65) *c20*

תָּקַע   *vb.* to give a blow/blast (on a horn), clap, thrust, drive (70) *c15*

תְּרוּמָה   *n.f.* contribution, offering (76) *c27*

תֵּשַׁע   *n.m.* nine, pl. ninety (78*) *c8*

תֵּת   *inf.* to give (Qal inf. נָתַן) (161) *c7*

Proper Nouns in the Hebrew Bible
used 50 or more times
and select additional names

אֲבִימֶלֶךְ	Abimelech (67)	בַּעַל	Baal (45)
אַבְנֵר	Abner (63)	בָּרוּךְ	Baruch (26)
אַבְרָהָם	Abraham (175)	בָּשָׁן	Bashan (60)
אַבְרָם	Abram (61)	גָּד	Gad (76)
אַבְשָׁלוֹם	Absalom (109)	גְּדַלְיָהוּ	Gedaliah (26)
אֱדוֹם	Edom (100)	גִּלְגָּל	Gilgal (40)
אֲדֹנָי	Lord (439)	גִּלְעָד	Gilead (134)
אַהֲרֹן	Aaron (347)	דָּוִד	David (1075)
אַחְאָב	Ahab (93)	דָּן	Dan (70)
אִיּוֹב	Job (58)	דָּנִיֵּאל	Daniel (52)
אֵל	El (78)	הָמָן	Haman (54)
אֵלִיָּהוּ	Elijah (71)	זְבוּלוּן	Zebulun (45)
אֱלִישָׁע	Elisha (58)	חֶבְרוֹן	Hebron (62)
אֶלְעָזָר	Eleazar (72)	חִזְקִיָּהוּ	Hezekiah (125)
אֱמֹרִי	Amorite (87)	חִתִּי	Hittite (46)
אָסָא	Asa (58)	יֵהוּא	Jehu (58)
אָסָף	Asaph (46)	יְהוֹאָשׁ	Jehoash (64)
אֶסְתֵּר	Esther (55)	יְהוּדָה	Judah (820)
אֶפְרַיִם	Ephraim (180)	יְהוּדִי	Jew, Judean (88)
אֲרָם	Aram (135)	יהוה	LORD, GOD (6828)
אַשּׁוּר	Assyria (151)	יְהוֹיָדָע	Jehoiada (56)
אָשֵׁר	Asher (43)	יְהוֹנָתָן	Jonathan (124)
בָּבֶל	Babylon (262)	יְהוֹרָם	Jehoram (48)
בִּלְעָם	Balaam (60)	יְהוֹשָׁפָט	Jehoshaphat (84)
בִּנְיָמִן	Benjamin (169)	יְהוֹשֻׁעַ	Joshua, Jeshua (227)
בֹּעַז	Boaz (22)	יוֹאָב	Joab (146)

יוֹנָה	Jonah (19)	נוּן	Nun (30)
יוֹסֵף	Joseph (214)	נֹחַ	Noah (46)
יַעֲקֹב	Jacob (349)	נִינְוֵה	Nineveh (17)
יִצְחָק	Isaac (112)	נָעֳמִי	Naomi (21)
יָרָבְעָם	Jeroboam (104)	נַפְתָּלִי	Naphtali (51)
יַרְדֵּן	Jordan (183)	נָתָן	Nathan (42)
יְרוּשָׁלַם	Jerusalem (643)	סִיסְרָא	Sisera (21)
יְרִיחוֹ	Jericho (56)	סַנְחֵרִיב	Sennacherib (13)
יִרְמְיָהוּ	Jeremiah (130)	עֵלִי	Eli (33)
יִשְׂרָאֵל	Israel (2507)	עַמּוֹן	Ammon (106)
יִשָּׂשכָר	Issachar (43)	עֵשָׂו	Esau (97)
יִשַׁי	Jesse (42)	פְּלִשְׁתִּי	Philistine (290)
יִשְׁמָעֵאל	Ishmael (48)	פַּרְעֹה	Pharaoh (274)
כָּלֵב	Caleb (36)	צָדוֹק	Zadok (53)
כְּנַעַן	Canaan (93)	צִדְקִיָּהוּ	Zedekiah (56)
כְּנַעֲנִי	Canaanite (73)	צִיּוֹן	Zion (154)
כַּשְׂדִּים	Chaldeans (82)	רְאוּבֵן	Reuben (72)
לֵאָה	Leah (34)	רוּת	Ruth (12)
לָבָן	Laban (54)	רְחַבְעָם	Rehoboam (50)
לְבָנוֹן	Lebanon (71)	רָחֵל	Rachel (47)
לֵוִי	Levi, Levite (350)	שָׂרָה	Sarah (38)
מִדְיָן	Midian (59)	שָׁאוּל	Saul, Shaul (405)
מוֹאָב	Moab (187)	שְׁכֶם	Shechem (46)
מְנַשֶּׁה	Manasseh (146)	שִׁלֹה	Shiloh (33)
מִצְרִי	Egyptian (30)	שְׁלֹמֹה	Solomon (293)
מִצְרַיִם	Egypt, Mizraim (682)	שְׁמוּאֵל	Samuel (140)
מָרְדְּכַי	Mordecai (60)	שִׁמְעוֹן	Simeon (44)
מֹשֶׁה	Moses (766)	שֹׁמְרוֹן	Samaria (109)
נְבוּכַדְרֶאצַּר	Nebuchadrezzar (52)	שִׁמְשׁוֹן	Samson (38)
נֶגֶב	south country, Negev (83)	תָּמָר	Tamar (21)

Appendix C:
Paradigms,
Verb ID badges, Alias Profiles.

The paradigms summarize the strong verb and select weak verb patterns. The roots that illustrate weak verbs are chosen primarily due to frequency in the stem. Forms that do not occur in the Bible for a particular root are only supplied when other roots of the same weak class have the form. The Alias Profiles are repeated on the last two pages for convenient reference.

ID badges for the strong verb.

Qal Inf. cs.	□□֧ / □□֧ / □֧□֧
Qal Impf.	□□֧P
Qal Ptc.	□□֗□
Qal PassPtc.	□ֹ□□ֻ Ė□ֹ□□ֻ
Qal Pf.	□□□ֻ Ė□□□ֻ
Niphal	□□□ֻP □□□ֻ
Piel	□·□֧P₈ □·□□
Hitpael	□·□֧הP
Pual	□·□P₈
Hiphil	□□□ֻP □□□ֻה
Hophal	□□□ֻP

Strong Verb

		Qal	Niphal	Piel	Hitpael	Pual	Hiphil	Hophal
Inf. cs.		קְטֹל	הִקָּטֵל	קַטֵּל	הִתְקַטֵּל		הַקְטִיל	
Inf. ab.		קָטוֹל	נִקְטֹל הִקָּטֵל	קַטֵּל	הִתְקַטֵּל	קֻטֹּל	הַקְטֵל	הָקְטֵל
Impf.	1cs	אֶקְטֹל	אֶקָּטֵל	אֲקַטֵּל	אֶתְקַטֵּל	אֲקֻטַּל	אַקְטִיל	אָקְטַל
	2ms	תִּקְטֹל	תִּקָּטֵל	תְּקַטֵּל	תִּתְקַטֵּל	תְּקֻטַּל	תַּקְטִיל	תָּקְטַל
	2fs	תִּקְטְלִי	תִּקָּטְלִי	תְּקַטְּלִי	תִּתְקַטְּלִי	תְּקֻטְּלִי	תַּקְטִילִי	תָּקְטְלִי
	3ms	יִקְטֹל	יִקָּטֵל	יְקַטֵּל	יִתְקַטֵּל	יְקֻטַּל	יַקְטִיל	יָקְטַל
	3fs	תִּקְטֹל	תִּקָּטֵל	תְּקַטֵּל	תִּתְקַטֵּל	תְּקֻטַּל	תַּקְטִיל	תָּקְטַל
	1cp	נִקְטֹל	נִקָּטֵל	נְקַטֵּל	נִתְקַטֵּל	נְקֻטַּל	נַקְטִיל	נָקְטַל
	2mp	תִּקְטְלוּ	תִּקָּטְלוּ	תְּקַטְּלוּ	תִּתְקַטְּלוּ	תְּקֻטְּלוּ	תַּקְטִילוּ	תָּקְטְלוּ
	2fp	תִּקְטֹלְנָה	תִּקָּטַלְנָה	תְּקַטֵּלְנָה	תִּתְקַטֵּלְנָה	תְּקֻטַּלְנָה	תַּקְטֵלְנָה	תָּקְטַלְנָה
	3mp	יִקְטְלוּ	יִקָּטְלוּ	יְקַטְּלוּ	יִתְקַטְּלוּ	יְקֻטְּלוּ	יַקְטִילוּ	יָקְטְלוּ
	3fp	תִּקְטֹלְנָה	תִּקָּטַלְנָה	תְּקַטֵּלְנָה	תִּתְקַטֵּלְנָה	תְּקֻטַּלְנָה	תַּקְטֵלְנָה	תָּקְטַלְנָה
Pret.	3ms	וַיִּקְטֹל	וַיִּקָּטֵל	וַיְקַטֵּל	וַיִּתְקַטֵּל	וַיְקֻטַּל	וַיַּקְטֵל	וַיָּקְטַל
Imv.	2ms	קְטֹל	הִקָּטֵל	קַטֵּל	הִתְקַטֵּל		הַקְטֵל	הָקְטַל
	2fs	קִטְלִי	הִקָּטְלִי	קַטְּלִי	הִתְקַטְּלִי		הַקְטִילִי	
	2mp	קִטְלוּ	הִקָּטְלוּ	קַטְּלוּ	הִתְקַטְּלוּ		הַקְטִילוּ	הָקְטְלוּ
	2fp	קְטֹלְנָה		קַטֵּלְנָה			הַקְטֵלְנָה	
Ptc.	ms	קֹטֵל	נִקְטָל	מְקַטֵּל	מִתְקַטֵּל	מְקֻטָּל	מַקְטִיל	מָקְטָל
	fs	קֹטֶלֶת	נִקְטֶלֶת	מְקַטֶּלֶת	מִתְקַטֶּלֶת	מְקֻטֶּלֶת	מַקְטֶלֶת	מָקְטֶלֶת
	mp	קֹטְלִים	נִקְטָלִים	מְקַטְּלִים	מִתְקַטְּלִים	מְקֻטָּלִים	מַקְטִילִים	מָקְטָלִים
	fp	קֹטְלוֹת	נִקְטָלוֹת	מְקַטְּלוֹת	מִתְקַטְּלוֹת	מְקֻטָּלוֹת	מַקְטִילוֹת	מָקְטָלוֹת
Pf.	1cs	קָטַלְתִּי	נִקְטַלְתִּי	קִטַּלְתִּי	הִתְקַטַּלְתִּי	קֻטַּלְתִּי	הִקְטַלְתִּי	הָקְטַלְתִּי
	2ms	קָטַלְתָּ	נִקְטַלְתָּ	קִטַּלְתָּ	הִתְקַטַּלְתָּ	קֻטַּלְתָּ	הִקְטַלְתָּ	הָקְטַלְתָּ
	2fs	קָטַלְתְּ	נִקְטַלְתְּ	קִטַּלְתְּ	הִתְקַטַּלְתְּ	קֻטַּלְתְּ	הִקְטַלְתְּ	הָקְטַלְתְּ
	3ms	קָטַל	נִקְטַל	קִטֵּל	הִתְקַטֵּל	קֻטַּל	הִקְטִיל	הָקְטַל
	3fs	קָטְלָה	נִקְטְלָה	קִטְּלָה	הִתְקַטְּלָה	קֻטְּלָה	הִקְטִילָה	הָקְטְלָה
	1cp	קָטַלְנוּ	נִקְטַלְנוּ	קִטַּלְנוּ	הִתְקַטַּלְנוּ	קֻטַּלְנוּ	הִקְטַלְנוּ	הָקְטַלְנוּ
	2mp	קְטַלְתֶּם	נִקְטַלְתֶּם	קִטַּלְתֶּם	הִתְקַטַּלְתֶּם	קֻטַּלְתֶּם	הִקְטַלְתֶּם	הָקְטַלְתֶּם
	2fp	קְטַלְתֶּן	נִקְטַלְתֶּן	קִטַּלְתֶּן	הִתְקַטַּלְתֶּן	קֻטַּלְתֶּן	הִקְטַלְתֶּן	הָקְטַלְתֶּן
	3cp	קָטְלוּ	נִקְטְלוּ	קִטְּלוּ	הִתְקַטְּלוּ	קֻטְּלוּ	הִקְטִילוּ	הָקְטְלוּ

Qal

		fientive	stative	stative	stative	נתן	R₁ = נ	R₃ = ה
Inf. cs.		קְטֹל		מְלֹא	יְכֹלֶת	תֵּת	נְפֹל	נְטוֹת
Inf. ab.		קָטוֹל		מָלוֹא	יָכוֹל	נָתוֹן	נָפוֹל	
Impf.	1cs	אֶקְטֹל	אֶכְבַּד	אֶמְלָא	אוּכַל	אֶתֵּן	אֶפֹּל	
	2ms	תִּקְטֹל	תִּכְבַּד	תִּמְלָא	תּוּכַל	תִּתֵּן	תִּפֹּל	תִּפֶּה
	2fs	תִּקְטְלִי	תִּכְבְּדִי	תִּמְלְאִי	תּוּכְלִי	תִּתְּנִי	תִּפְּלִי	
	3ms	יִקְטֹל	יִכְבַּד	יִמְלָא	יוּכַל	יִתֵּן	יִפֹּל	יִפְתֶּה
	3fs	תִּקְטֹל	תִּכְבַּד	תִּמְלָא	תּוּכַל	תִּתֵּן	תִּפֹּל	תִּפְתֶּה
	1cp	נִקְטֹל	נִכְבַּד	נִמְלָא	נוּכַל	נִתֵּן	נִפֹּל	נִפְתֶּה
	2mp	תִּקְטְלוּ	תִּכְבְּדוּ	תִּמְלְאוּ	תּוּכְלוּ	תִּתְּנוּ	תִּפְּלוּ	
	2fp	תִּקְטֹלְנָה	תִּכְבַּדְנָה	תִּמְלֶאנָה	תּוּכַלְנָה	תִּתֵּנָּה	תִּפֹּלְנָה	
	3mp	יִקְטְלוּ	יִכְבְּדוּ	יִמְלְאוּ	יוּכְלוּ	יִתְּנוּ	יִפְּלוּ	יִפְתּוּ
	3fp	תִּקְטֹלְנָה	תִּכְבַּדְנָה	תִּמְלֶאנָה	תּוּכַלְנָה	תִּתֵּנָּה	תִּפֹּלְנָה	תִּפְתֶּינָה
Pret.	3ms	וַיִּקְטֹל	וַיִּכְבַּד	וַיִּמְלָא	וַיּוּכַל	וַיִּתֵּן	וַיִּפֹּל	וַיֵּט
Imv.	2ms	קְטֹל				תֵּן / תְּנָה	נְפֹל	נְטֵה
	2fs	קִטְלִי				תְּנִי		
	2mp	קִטְלוּ				תְּנוּ	נִפְלוּ	
	2fp	קְטֹלְנָה				תֵּנָּה		
Ptc.	ms	קֹטֵל				נֹתֵן	נֹפֵל	נֹטֶה
	fs	קֹטֶלֶת				נֹתֶנֶת	נֹפֶלֶת	
	mp	קֹטְלִים				נֹתְנִים	נֹפְלִים	נֹטִים
	fp	קֹטְלוֹת				נֹתְנוֹת	נֹפְלוֹת	
PassPtc.	ms	קָטוּל				נָתוּן	נָפוּל	נָטוּי
Pf.	1cs	קָטַלְתִּי	כָּבַדְתִּי	מָלֵאתִי	יָכֹלְתִּי	נָתַתִּי	נָפַלְתִּי	נָטִיתִי
	2ms	קָטַלְתָּ	כָּבַדְתָּ	מָלֵאתָ	יָכֹלְתָּ	נָתַתָּ	נָפַלְתָּ	נָטִיתָ
	2fs	קָטַלְתְּ	כָּבַדְתְּ	מָלֵאת	יָכֹלְתְּ	נָתַתְּ	נָפַלְתְּ	
	3ms	קָטַל	כָּבֵד	מָלֵא	יָכֹל	נָתַן	נָפַל	נָטָה
	3fs	קָטְלָה	כָּבְדָה	מָלְאָה	יָכְלָה	נָתְנָה	נָפְלָה	נָטְתָה
	1cp	קָטַלְנוּ	כָּבַדְנוּ	מָלֵאנוּ	יָכֹלְנוּ	נָתַנּוּ	נָפַלְנוּ	
	2mp	קְטַלְתֶּם	כְּבַדְתֶּם	מְלֵאתֶם	יְכָלְתֶּם	נְתַתֶּם	נְפַלְתֶּם	
	2fp	קְטַלְתֶּן	כְּבַדְתֶּן	מְלֵאתֶן	יְכָלְתֶּן	נְתַתֶּן	נְפַלְתֶּן	
	3cp	קָטְלוּ	כָּבְדוּ	מָלְאוּ	יָכְלוּ	נָתְנוּ	נָפְלוּ	נָטוּ

Qal

		strong	R₁ = י	R₁ = י	R₂ = ו/י	R₂ = ו/י	R₂ = ו/י	R₃ = י ≠ ה
Inf. cs.		קְטֹל	שֶׁבֶת	רֶשֶׁת	קוּם	שׂוּם /שִׂים	בוֹא	בְּנוֹת
Inf. ab.		קָטוֹל	יָשׁוֹב	יָרוֹשׁ	קוֹם	שׂוֹם	בוֹא	בָּנֹה
Impf.	1cs	אֶקְטֹל	אֵשֵׁב	אִירַשׁ	אָקוּם	אָשִׂים	אָבוֹא	אֶבְנֶה
	2ms	תִּקְטֹל	תֵּשֵׁב	תִּירַשׁ	תָּקוּם	תָּשִׂים	תָּבוֹא	תִּבְנֶה
	2fs	תִּקְטְלִי	תֵּשְׁבִי	תִּירְשִׁי	תָּקוּמִי	תָּשִׂימִי	תָּבוֹאִי	תִּבְנִי
	3ms	יִקְטֹל	יֵשֵׁב	יִירַשׁ	יָקוּם	יָשִׂים	יָבוֹא	יִבְנֶה
	3fs	תִּקְטֹל	תֵּשֵׁב	תִּירַשׁ	תָּקוּם	תָּשִׂים	תָּבוֹא	תִּבְנֶה
	1cp	נִקְטֹל	נֵשֵׁב	נִירַשׁ	נָקוּם	נָשִׂים	נָבוֹא	נִבְנֶה
	2mp	תִּקְטְלוּ	תֵּשְׁבוּ	תִּירְשׁוּ	תָּקוּמוּ	תָּשִׂימוּ	תָּבֹאוּ	תִּבְנוּ
	2fp	תִּקְטֹלְנָה	תֵּשַׁבְנָה	תִּירַשְׁנָה	תְּקוּמֶינָה	תְּשִׂימֶינָה	תָּבוֹאנָה	תִּבְנֶינָה
	3mp	יִקְטְלוּ	יֵשְׁבוּ	יִירְשׁוּ	יָקוּמוּ	יָשִׂימוּ	יָבֹאוּ	יִבְנוּ
	3fp	תִּקְטֹלְנָה	תֵּשַׁבְנָה	תִּירַשְׁנָה	תְּקוּמֶינָה	תְּשִׂימֶינָה	תָּבוֹאנָה	תִּבְנֶינָה
Pret.	3ms	וַיִּקְטֹל	וַיֵּשֶׁב	וַיִּירַשׁ	וַיָּקָם	וַיָּשֶׂם	וַיָּבֹא	וַיִּבֶן
Imv.	2ms	קְטֹל	שֵׁב	רֵשׁ	קוּם	שִׂים	בֹּא	בְּנֵה
	2fs	קִטְלִי	שְׁבִי	רְשִׁי	קוּמִי	שִׂימִי	בֹּאִי	בְּנִי
	2mp	קִטְלוּ	שְׁבוּ	רְשׁוּ	קוּמוּ	שִׂימוּ	בֹּאוּ	בְּנוּ
	2fp	קְטֹלְנָה	שֵׁבְנָה		קֹמְנָה			בְּנֶינָה
Ptc.	ms	קֹטֵל	יֹשֵׁב	יֹרֵשׁ	קָם	שָׂם	בָּא	בֹּנֶה
	fs	קֹטֶלֶת	יֹשֶׁבֶת	יֹרֶשֶׁת	קָמָה	שָׂמָה	בָּאָה	בֹּנָה
	mp	קֹטְלִים	יֹשְׁבִים	יֹרְשִׁים	קָמִים	שָׂמִים	בָּאִים	בֹּנִים
	fp	קֹטְלוֹת	יֹשְׁבוֹת	יֹרְשׁוֹת	קָמוֹת	שָׂמוֹת	בָּאוֹת	בֹּנוֹת
PassPtc.	ms	קָטוּל	יָשׁוּב	יָרוּשׁ				בָּנוּי
Pf.	1cs	קָטַלְתִּי	יָשַׁבְתִּי	יָרַשְׁתִּי	קַמְתִּי	שַׂמְתִּי	בָּאתִי	בָּנִיתִי
	2ms	קָטַלְתָּ	יָשַׁבְתָּ	יָרַשְׁתָּ	קַמְתָּ	שַׂמְתָּ	בָּאתָ	בָּנִיתָ
	2fs	קָטַלְתְּ	יָשַׁבְתְּ	יָרַשְׁתְּ	קַמְתְּ	שַׂמְתְּ	בָּאת	בָּנִית
	3ms	קָטַל	יָשַׁב	יָרַשׁ	קָם	שָׂם	בָּא	בָּנָה
	3fs	קָטְלָה	יָשְׁבָה	יָרְשָׁה	קָמָה	שָׂמָה	בָּאָה	בָּנְתָה
	1cp	קָטַלְנוּ	יָשַׁבְנוּ	יָרַשְׁנוּ	קַמְנוּ	שַׂמְנוּ	בָּאנוּ	בָּנִינוּ
	2mp	קְטַלְתֶּם	יְשַׁבְתֶּם	יְרַשְׁתֶּם	קַמְתֶּם	שַׂמְתֶּם	בָּאתֶם	בְּנִיתֶם
	2fp	קְטַלְתֶּן	יְשַׁבְתֶּן	יְרַשְׁתֶּן	קַמְתֶּן	שַׂמְתֶּן	בָּאתֶן	בְּנִיתֶן
	3cp	קָטְלוּ	יָשְׁבוּ	יָרְשׁוּ	קָמוּ	שָׂמוּ	בָּאוּ	בָּנוּ

Qal

		R₁ = G	R₁ = G	R₁ = א	R₃ = G	R₃ = א	R₂ = R₃	R₂ = R₃
Inf. cs.		עֲמֹד	חֲזֹק	אֱמֹר	שְׁמֹעַ	מְצֹא	סֹב	תֹּם
Inf. ab.		עָמוֹד	חָזוֹק	אָמוֹר	שָׁמוֹעַ	מָצוֹא	סָבוֹב	תָּמוֹם
Impf.	1cs	אֶעֱמֹד	אֶחֱזַק	אֹמַר	אֶשְׁמַע	אֶמְצָא	אָסֹב	אֶתַּם
	2ms	תַּעֲמֹד	תֶּחֱזַק	תֹּאמַר	תִּשְׁמַע	תִּמְצָא	תָּסֹב	תֵּתַם
	2fs	תַּעַמְדִי	תֶּחֶזְקִי	תֹּאמְרִי	תִּשְׁמְעִי	תִּמְצְאִי	תָּסֹבִּי	תֵּתַמִּי
	3ms	יַעֲמֹד	יֶחֱזַק	יֹאמַר	יִשְׁמַע	יִמְצָא	יָסֹב	יֵתַם
	3fs	תַּעֲמֹד	תֶּחֱזַק	תֹּאמַר	תִּשְׁמַע	תִּמְצָא	תָּסֹב	תֵּתַם
	1cp	נַעֲמֹד	נֶחֱזַק	נֹאמַר	נִשְׁמַע	נִמְצָא	נָסֹב	נֵתַם
	2mp	תַּעַמְדוּ	תֶּחֶזְקוּ	תֹּאמְרוּ	תִּשְׁמְעוּ	תִּמְצְאוּ	תָּסֹבּוּ	תֵּתַמּוּ
	2fp	תַּעֲמֹדְנָה	תֶּחֱזַקְנָה	תֹּאמַרְנָה	תִּשְׁמַעְנָה	תִּמְצֶאנָה	תְּסֻבֶּינָה	תְּתַמֶּינָה
	3mp	יַעַמְדוּ	יֶחֶזְקוּ	יֹאמְרוּ	יִשְׁמְעוּ	יִמְצְאוּ	יָסֹבּוּ	יֵתַמּוּ
	3fp	תַּעֲמֹדְנָה	תֶּחֱזַקְנָה	תֹּאמַרְנָה	תִּשְׁמַעְנָה	תִּמְצֶאנָה	תְּסֻבֶּינָה	תְּתַמֶּינָה
Pret.	3ms	וַיַּעֲמֹד	וַיֶּחֱזַק	וַיֹּאמֶר	וַיִּשְׁמַע	וַיִּמְצָא	וַיָּסָב	וַיִּתֹּם
Imv.	2ms	עֲמֹד	חֲזַק	אֱמֹר	שְׁמַע	מְצָא	סֹב	תֹּם
	2fs	עִמְדִי	חִזְקִי	אִמְרִי	שִׁמְעִי	מִצְאִי	סֹבִּי	תֹּמִּי
	2mp	עִמְדוּ	חִזְקוּ	אִמְרוּ	שִׁמְעוּ	מִצְאוּ	סֹבּוּ	תֹּמּוּ
	2fp	עֲמֹדְנָה	חֲזַקְנָה	אֱמֹרְנָה	שְׁמַעְנָה	מְצֶאנָה	סֹבְנָה	תֹּמְנָה
Ptc.	ms	עֹמֵד	חֹזֵק	אֹמֵר	שֹׁמֵעַ	מֹצֵא	סֹבֵב	תֹּם
	fs	עֹמֶדֶת	חֹזֶקֶת	אֹמֶרֶת	שֹׁמַעַת	מֹצֵאת	סֹבְבָה	תַּמָּה
	mp	עֹמְדִים	חֹזְקִים	אֹמְרִים	שֹׁמְעִים	מֹצְאִים	סֹבְבִים	תַּמִּים
	fp	עֹמְדוֹת	חֹזְקוֹת	אֹמְרוֹת	שֹׁמְעוֹת	מֹצְאוֹת	סֹבְבוֹת	תַּמּוֹת
PassPtc.	ms	עָמוּד	חָזוּק	אָמוּר	שָׁמוּעַ	מָצוּא	סָבוּב	
Pf.	1cs	עָמַדְתִּי	חָזַקְתִּי	אָמַרְתִּי	שָׁמַעְתִּי	מָצָאתִי	סַבּוֹתִי	תַּמּוֹתִי
	2ms	עָמַדְתָּ	חָזַקְתָּ	אָמַרְתָּ	שָׁמַעְתָּ	מָצָאתָ	סַבּוֹתָ	תַּמּוֹתָ
	2fs	עָמַדְתְּ	חָזַקְתְּ	אָמַרְתְּ	שָׁמַעַתְּ	מָצָאת	סַבּוֹת	תַּמּוֹת
	3ms	עָמַד	חָזַק	אָמַר	שָׁמַע	מָצָא	סָבַב	תַּם
	3fs	עָמְדָה	חָזְקָה	אָמְרָה	שָׁמְעָה	מָצְאָה	סָבְבָה	תַּמָּה
	1cp	עָמַדְנוּ	חָזַקְנוּ	אָמַרְנוּ	שָׁמַעְנוּ	מָצָאנוּ	סַבּוֹנוּ	תַּמּוֹנוּ
	2mp	עֲמַדְתֶּם	חֲזַקְתֶּם	אֲמַרְתֶּם	שְׁמַעְתֶּם	מְצָאתֶם	סַבּוֹתֶם	תַּמּוֹתֶם
	2fp	עֲמַדְתֶּן	חֲזַקְתֶּן	אֲמַרְתֶּן	שְׁמַעְתֶּן	מְצָאתֶן	סַבּוֹתֶן	תַּמּוֹתֶן
	3cp	עָמְדוּ	חָזְקוּ	אָמְרוּ	שָׁמְעוּ	מָצְאוּ	סָבְבוּ	תַּמּוּ

Niphal

		Strong	R₁ = G	R₁ = א	R₂ = G	R₃ = ע/ח	R₃ = א
Inf. cs.		הִקָּטֵל	הֵחָשֵׁב	הֵאָסֵף	הִלָּחֵם	הִשָּׁשֵׁעַ	הִמָּצֵא
Inf. ab.		הִקָּטֵל/נִקְטֹל	נַחָשׁוֹב	הֵאָסֹף	נִלְחֹם	הִשָּׁשֵׁעַ	הִמָּצֵא
Impf.	1cs	אֶקָּטֵל	אֵחָשֵׁב	אֵאָסֵף	אֶלָּחֵם	אֶשָּׁבַע	אֶמָּצֵא
	2ms	תִּקָּטֵל	תֵּחָשֵׁב	תֵּאָסֵף	תִּלָּחֵם	תִּשָּׁבַע	תִּמָּצֵא
	2fs	תִּקָּטְלִי	תֵּחָשְׁבִי	תֵּאָסְפִי	תִּלָּחֲמִי	תִּשָּׁבְעִי	תִּמָּצְאִי
	3ms	יִקָּטֵל	יֵחָשֵׁב	יֵאָסֵף	יִלָּחֵם	יִשָּׁבַע	יִמָּצֵא
	3fs	תִּקָּטֵל	תֵּחָשֵׁב	תֵּאָסֵף	תִּלָּחֵם	תִּשָּׁבַע	תִּמָּצֵא
	1cp	נִקָּטֵל	נֵחָשֵׁב	נֵאָסֵף	נִלָּחֵם	נִשָּׁבַע	נִמָּצֵא
	2mp	תִּקָּטְלוּ	תֵּחָשְׁבוּ	תֵּאָסְפוּ	תִּלָּחֲמוּ	תִּשָּׁבְעוּ	תִּמָּצְאוּ
	2fp	תִּקָּטַלְנָה	תֵּחָשַׁבְנָה	תֵּאָסַפְנָה	תִּלָּחַמְנָה	תִּשָּׁבַעְנָה	תִּמָּצֶאנָה
	3mp	יִקָּטְלוּ	יֵחָשְׁבוּ	יֵאָסְפוּ	יִלָּחֲמוּ	יִשָּׁבְעוּ	יִמָּצְאוּ
	3fp	תִּקָּטַלְנָה	תֵּחָשַׁבְנָה	תֵּאָסַפְנָה	תִּלָּחַמְנָה	תִּשָּׁבַעְנָה	תִּמָּצֶאנָה
Pret.	3ms	וַיִּקָּטֵל	וַיֵּחָשֵׁב	וַיֵּאָסֵף	וַיִּלָּחֵם	וַיִּשָּׁבַע	וַיִּמָּצֵא
Imv.	2ms	הִקָּטֵל	הֵחָשֵׁב	הֵאָסֵף	הִלָּחֵם	הִשָּׁבַע	הִמָּצֵא
	2fs	הִקָּטְלִי	הֵחָשְׁבִי	הֵאָסְפִי	הִלָּחֲמִי	הִשָּׁבְעִי	הִמָּצְאִי
	2mp	הִקָּטְלוּ	הֵחָשְׁבוּ	הֵאָסְפוּ	הִלָּחֲמוּ	הִשָּׁבְעוּ	הִמָּצְאוּ
	2fp						
Ptc.	ms	נִקְטָל	נֶחְשָׁב	נֶאֱסָף	נִלְחָם	נִשְׁבָּע	נִמְצָא
	fs	נִקְטֶלֶת	נֶחְשֶׁבֶת	נֶאֱסֶפֶת	נִלְחֶמֶת	נִשְׁבָּעָה	נִמְצֵאת
	mp	נִקְטָלִים	נֶחְשָׁבִים	נֶאֱסָפִים	נִלְחָמִים	נִשְׁבָּעִים	נִמְצָאִים
	fp	נִקְטָלוֹת	נֶחְשָׁבוֹת	נֶאֱסָפוֹת	נִלְחָמוֹת	נִשְׁבָּעוֹת	נִמְצָאוֹת
Pf.	1cs	נִקְטַלְתִּי	נֶחְשַׁבְתִּי	נֶאֱסַפְתִּי	נִלְחַמְתִּי	נִשְׁבַּעְתִּי	נִמְצֵאתִי
	2ms	נִקְטַלְתָּ	נֶחְשַׁבְתָּ	נֶאֱסַפְתָּ	נִלְחַמְתָּ	נִשְׁבַּעְתָּ	נִמְצֵאתָ
	2fs	נִקְטַלְתְּ	נֶחְשַׁבְתְּ	נֶאֱסַפְתְּ	נִלְחַמְתְּ	נִשְׁבַּעְתְּ	נִמְצֵאת
	3ms	נִקְטַל	נֶחְשַׁב	נֶאֱסַף	נִלְחַם	נִשְׁבַּע	נִמְצָא
	3fs	נִקְטְלָה	נֶחְשְׁבָה	נֶאֱסְפָה	נִלְחֲמָה	נִשְׁבְּעָה	נִמְצְאָה
	1cp	נִקְטַלְנוּ	נֶחְשַׁבְנוּ	נֶאֱסַפְנוּ	נִלְחַמְנוּ	נִשְׁבַּעְנוּ	נִמְצֵאנוּ
	2mp	נִקְטַלְתֶּם	נֶחְשַׁבְתֶּם	נֶאֱסַפְתֶּם	נִלְחַמְתֶּם	נִשְׁבַּעְתֶּם	נִמְצֵאתֶם
	2fp	נִקְטַלְתֶּן	נֶחְשַׁבְתֶּן	נֶאֱסַפְתֶּן	נִלְחַמְתֶּן		נִמְצֵאתֶן
	3cp	נִקְטְלוּ	נֶחְשְׁבוּ	נֶאֱסְפוּ	נִלְחֲמוּ	נִשְׁבְּעוּ	נִמְצְאוּ

Niphal

		R₁ = י	R₂ = ו/י	R₃ = י≠ה	R₁ = G, R₃ = י	R₁ = נ	R₂ = R₃
Inf. cs.		הִוָּתֵר	הִכּוֹן	הִגָּלוֹת	הֵעָשׂת	הִנָּבֵא	הִסֵּב
Inf. ab.			הִכּוֹן	הִגָּלֹה		הִנָּבֵא	הִסֵּב/הִסּוֹב
Impf.	1cs	אִוָּתֵר	אֶכּוֹן	אֶגָּלֶה	אֵעָשֶׂה	אֶנָּבֵא	אֶסַּב
	2ms	תִּוָּתֵר	תִּכּוֹן	תִּגָּלֶה	תֵּעָשֶׂה	תִּנָּבֵא	תִּסַּב
	2fs	תִּוָּתְרִי				תִּנָּבְאִי	
	3ms	יִוָּתֵר	יִכּוֹן	יִגָּלֶה	יֵעָשֶׂה	יִנָּבֵא	יִסַּב
	3fs	תִּוָּתֵר	תִּכּוֹן	תִּגָּלֶה	תֵּעָשֶׂה	תִּנָּבֵא	תִּסַּב
	1cp	נִוָּתֵר	נִכּוֹן	נִגָּלֶה	נֵעָשֶׂה		
	2mp	תִּוָּתְרוּ	תִּכּוֹנוּ	תִּגָּלוּ	תֵּעָשׂוּ	תִּנָּבְאוּ	תִּסַּבּוּ
	2fp	תִּוָּתַרְנָה					
	3mp	יִוָּתְרוּ	יִכּוֹנוּ	יִגָּלוּ	יֵעָשׂוּ	יִנָּבְאוּ	יִסַּבּוּ
	3fp	תִּוָּתַרְנָה	תִּכֹּנָה	תִּגָּלֶינָה	תֵּעָשֶׂינָה	תִּנָּבֶאנָה	תִּסַּבְנָה
Pret.	2ms	וַיִּוָּתֵר	וַיִּקָּטֵל	וַיֵּרָא		וַיִּנָּבֵא	וַיִּסַּב
Imv.	2ms	הִוָּתֵר	הִכּוֹן	הִגָּלֵה		הִנָּבֵא	
	2fs	הִוָּתְרִי		הִגָּלִי		הִנָּבְאִי	
	2mp	הִוָּתְרוּ	הִכּוֹנוּ	הִגָּלוּ	הֵעָשׂוּ	הִנָּבְאוּ	הִסַּבּוּ
	2fp						
Ptc.	ms	נוֹתָר	נָכוֹן	נִגְלֶה	נַעֲשֶׂה	נִבָּא	נָסֵב
	fs	נוֹתֶרֶת	נְכוֹנָה	נִגְלָה	נַעֲשָׂה	נִבָּאָה	נְסַבָּה
	mp	נוֹתָרִים	נָכֹנִים	נִגְלִים	נַעֲשִׂים	נִבָּאִים	נְסַבִּים
	fp	נוֹתָרוֹת		נִגְלוֹת	נַעֲשׂוֹת	נִבָּאוֹת	נְסַבּוֹת
Pf.	1cs	נוֹתַרְתִּי	נְכוּנוֹתִי	נִגְלֵיתִי	נַעֲשֵׂיתִי	נִבֵּאתִי	נְסַבֹּתִי
	2ms	נוֹתַרְתָּ		נִגְלֵיתָ	נַעֲשֵׂיתָ	נִבֵּאתָ	
	2fs	נוֹתַרְתְּ		נִגְלֵית		נִבֵּאת	נְסַבֹּת
	3ms	נוֹתַר	נָכוֹן	נִגְלָה	נַעֲשָׂה	נִבָּא	נָסֵב
	3fs	נוֹתְרָה	נָכוֹנָה	נִגְלְתָה	נֶעֶשְׂתָה	נִבְּאָה	נִקְטְלָה
	1cp	נוֹתַרְנוּ		נִגְלִינוּ		נִקְטַאנוּ	נְסַבֹּנוּ
	2mp	נוֹתַרְתֶּם	נְכוּנֹתֶם			נִבֵּאתֶם	נְסַבֹּתֶם
	2fp	נוֹתַרְתֶּן					
	3cp	נוֹתְרוּ	נָכוֹנוּ	נִגְלוּ	נַעֲשׂוּ	נִבְּאוּ	נָסַבּוּ

Piel

		Strong	R₂ = G	R₂ = G	R₃ = ע/ח	R₃ = א	R₃ = ה
Inf. cs.		קַטֵּל	בָּרֵךְ	מַהֵר	שַׁלַּח/שַׁלֵּחַ	מַלֵּא/מַלֹּאת	צַוֹּת
Inf. ab.		קַטֵּל	בָּרֵךְ	מַהֵר	שַׁלֵּחַ	מַלֵּא/מַלֹּא	צַוֹּה
Impf.	1cs	אֲקַטֵּל	אֲבָרֵךְ	אֲמַהֵר	אֲשַׁלַּח	אֲמַלֵּא	אֲצַוֶּה
	2ms	תְּקַטֵּל	תְּבָרֵךְ	תְּמַהֵר	תְּשַׁלַּח	תְּמַלֵּא	תְּצַוֶּה
	2fs	תְּקַטְּלִי	תְּבָרְכִי	תְּמַהֲרִי	תְּשַׁלְּחִי		תְּצַוִּי
	3ms	יְקַטֵּל	יְבָרֵךְ	יְמַהֵר	יְשַׁלַּח	יְמַלֵּא	יְצַוֶּה
	3fs	תְּקַטֵּל	תְּבָרֵךְ	תְּמַהֵר	תְּשַׁלַּח	תְּמַלֵּא	תְּצַוֶּה
	1cp	נְקַטֵּל	נְבָרֵךְ	נְמַהֵר	נְשַׁלַּח	נְמַלֵּא	נְצַוֶּה
	2mp	תְּקַטְּלוּ	תְּבָרְכוּ	תְּמַהֲרוּ	תְּשַׁלְּחוּ	תְּמַלְּאוּ	תְּצַוּוּ
	2fp	תְּקַטֵּלְנָה					תְּצַוֶּינָה
	3mp	יְקַטְּלוּ	יְבָרְכוּ	יְמַהֲרוּ	יְשַׁלְּחוּ	יְמַלְּאוּ	יְצַוּוּ
	3fp	תְּקַטֵּלְנָה			תְּשַׁלַּחְנָה	תְּמַלֶּאנָה	תְּצַוֶּינָה
Pret.	3ms		וַיְבָרֶךְ	וַיְמַהֵר	וַיְשַׁלַּח	וַיְמַלֵּא	וַיְצַו
Imv.	2ms	קַטֵּל	בָּרֵךְ	מַהֵר	שַׁלַּח	מַלֵּא	צַו / צַוֵּה
	2fs	קַטְּלִי	בָּרְכִי	מַהֲרִי	שַׁלְּחִי	מַלְּאִי	צַוִּי
	2mp	קַטְּלוּ	בָּרְכוּ	מַהֲרוּ	שַׁלְּחוּ	מַלְּאוּ	צַוּוּ
	2fp	קַטֵּלְנָה	בָּרֵכְנָה			מַלֶּאנָה	
Ptc.	ms	מְקַטֵּל	מְבָרֵךְ	מְמַהֵר	מְשַׁלֵּחַ	מְמַלֵּא	מְצַוֶּה
	fs	מְקַטֶּלֶת	מְבָרֶכֶת	מְמַהֶרֶת			מְצַוָּה
	mp	מְקַטְּלִים	מְבָרְכִים	מְמַהֲרִים	מְשַׁלְּחִים	מְמַלְּאִים	מְצַוִּים
	fp	מְקַטְּלוֹת	מְבָרְכוֹת	מְמַהֲרוֹת	מְשַׁלְּחוֹת		מְצַוּוֹת
Pf.	1cs	קִטַּלְתִּי	בֵּרַכְתִּי	מִהַרְתִּי	שִׁלַּחְתִּי	מִלֵּאתִי	צִוִּיתִי
	2ms	קִטַּלְתָּ	בֵּרַכְתָּ	מִהַרְתָּ	שִׁלַּחְתָּ	מִלֵּאתָ	צִוִּיתָ
	2fs	קִטַּלְתְּ	בֵּרַכְתְּ	מִהַרְתְּ		מִלֵּאת	צִוִּית
	3ms	קִטֵּל	בֵּרַךְ	מִהַר	שִׁלַּח	מִלֵּא	צִוָּה
	3fs	קִטְּלָה	בֵּרְכָה	מִהֲרָה	שִׁלְּחָה	מִלְּאָה	צִוְּתָה
	1cp	קִטַּלְנוּ	בֵּרַכְנוּ	מִהַרְנוּ	שִׁלַּחְנוּ	מִלֵּאנוּ	צִוִּינוּ
	2mp	קִטַּלְתֶּם	בֵּרַכְתֶּם	מִהַרְתֶּם	שִׁלַּחְתֶּם	מִלֵּאתֶם	צִוִּיתֶם
	2fp	קִטַּלְתֶּן	בֵּרַכְתֶּן	מִהַרְתֶּן			צִוִּיתֶן
	3cp	קִטְּלוּ	בֵּרְכוּ	מִהֲרוּ	שִׁלְּחוּ	מִלְּאוּ	צִוּוּ

Misc.

		Ho. strong	Ho. R₂=ו/י	Ho. R₁=נ	Polel	Hishtaphel
Inf. cs.					כּוֹנֵן	הִשְׁתַּחֲוֺת
Inf. ab.		הָקְטֵל		הֻגַּד		
Impf.	1cs	אָקְטַל		אֻגַּד	אֲכוֹנֵן	אֶשְׁתַּחֲוֶה
	2ms	תָּקְטַל		תֻּגַּד	תְּכוֹנֵן	תִּשְׁתַּחֲוֶה
	2fs	תָּקְטְלִי				
	3ms	יָקְטַל	יוּמַת	יֻגַּד	יְכוֹנֵן	יִשְׁתַּחֲוֶה
	3fs	תָּקְטַל	תוּמַת	תֻּגַּד	תְּכוֹנֵן	תִּשְׁתַּחֲוֶה
	1cp	נָקְטַל			נְכוֹנֵן	נִשְׁתַּחֲוֶה
	2mp	תָּקְטְלוּ		תֻּגְּדוּ	תְּכוֹנְנוּ	תִּשְׁתַּחֲווּ
	2fp	תָּקְטַלְנָה			תְּכוֹנֵנָּה	תִּשְׁתַּחֲוֶיןָ
	3mp	יָקְטְלוּ	יוּמְתוּ	יֻגְּדוּ	יְכוֹנְנוּ	יִשְׁתַּחֲווּ
	3fp	תָּקְטַלְנָה			תְּכוֹנֵנָּה	תִּשְׁתַּחֲוֶיןָ
Pret.	2ms	וַיָּקְטַל	וַיּוּמַת	וַיֻּגַּד	וַיְכוֹנֵן	וַיִּשְׁתַּחוּ
Imv.	2ms	הָקְטֵל			כּוֹנְנָה	
	2fs					הִשְׁתַּחֲוִי
	2mp	הָקְטְלוּ			כּוֹנְנוּ	הִשְׁתַּחֲווּ
	2fp					
Ptc.	ms	מָקְטָל	מוּמָת	מֻגָּד	מְכוֹנֵן	מִשְׁתַּחֲוֶה
	fs	מָקְטֶלֶת		מֻגָּדָה	מְכוֹנֶנֶת	
	mp	מָקְטָלִים	מוּמָתִים	מֻגָּדִים	מְכוֹנְנִים	מִשְׁתַּחֲוִים
	fp	מָקְטָלוֹת	מוּמָתוֹת		מְכוֹנְנוֹת	
Pf.	1cs	הָקְטַלְתִּי		הֻגַּדְתִּי	כּוֹנַנְתִּי	הִשְׁתַּחֲוֵיתִי
	2ms	הָקְטַלְתָּ	הֻמַתָּ		כּוֹנַנְתָּ	הִשְׁתַּחֲוֵיתָ
	2fs	הָקְטַלְתְּ				
	3ms	הָקְטַל	הוּמַת	הֻגַּד	כּוֹנֵן	הִשְׁתַּחֲוָה
	3fs	הָקְטְלָה	הוּמְתָה	הֻגְּדָה	כּוֹנְנָה	
	1cp	הָקְטַלְנוּ				
	2mp	הָקְטַלְתֶּם				הִשְׁתַּחֲוִיתֶם
	2fp	הָקְטַלְתֶּן				
	3cp	הָקְטְלוּ	הוּמְתוּ	הֻגְּדוּ	כּוֹנְנוּ	הִשְׁתַּחֲווּ

Hiphil

		Strong	R₁ = G	R₃ = ע/ח	R₃ = א	R₁ = י	R₁ = י (ו)	R₁ = י
Inf. cs.		הַקְטִיל	הַחֲזִיק	הַשְׁמִיעַ	הוֹצִיא	הוֹסִיף	הֵיטִיב
Inf. ab.		הַקְטֵל	הַחֲזֵק	הַשְׁמֵעַ	הוֹצֵא	הוֹסֵף	הֵיטֵב
Impf.	1cs	אַקְטִיל	אַחֲזִיק	אַשְׁמִיעַ	אוֹצִיא	אוֹסִיף	אֵיטִיב
	2ms	תַּקְטִיל	תַּחֲזִיק	תַּשְׁמִיעַ	תּוֹצִיא	תּוֹסִיף	תֵּיטִיב
	2fs	תַּקְטִילִי	תַּחֲזִיקִי	תַּשְׁמִיעִי		תּוֹסִיפִי	תֵּיטִיבִי
	3ms	יַקְטִיל	יַחֲזִיק	יַשְׁמִיעַ	יוֹצִיא	יוֹסִיף	יֵיטִיב
	3fs	תַּקְטִיל	תַּחֲזִיק	תַּשְׁמִיעַ	תּוֹצִיא	תּוֹסִיף	תֵּיטִיב
	1cp	נַקְטִיל	נַחֲזִיק	נַשְׁמִיעַ	נוֹצִיא	נוֹסִיף	נֵיטִיב
	2mp	תַּקְטִילוּ	תַּחֲזִיקוּ	תַּשְׁמִיעוּ	תּוֹצִיאוּ	תּוֹסִיפוּ	תֵּיטִיבוּ
	2fp	תַּקְטֵלְנָה					
	3mp	יַקְטִילוּ	יַחֲזִיקוּ	יַשְׁמִיעוּ	יוֹצִיאוּ	יוֹסִיפוּ	יֵיטִיבוּ
	3fp	תַּקְטֵלְנָה	תַּחֲזֵקְנָה	תַּשְׁמַעְנָה			
Pret.	3ms	וַיַּקְטֵל	וַיַּחֲזֵק	וַיַּשְׁמַע	וַיּוֹצֵא	וַיֹּסֶף	וַיֵּיטֶב
Imv.	2ms	הַקְטֵל	הַחֲזֵק	הַשְׁמַע/הַשְׁמִיעַ	הוֹצֵא	הוֹסֵף	הֵיטֵב
	2fs	הַקְטִילִי	הַחֲזִיקִי	הַשְׁמִיעִי	הוֹצִיאִי	הוֹסִיפִי	הֵיטִיבִי
	2mp	הַקְטִילוּ	הַחֲזִיקוּ	הַשְׁמִיעוּ	הוֹצִיאוּ	הוֹסִיפוּ	הֵיטִיבוּ
	2fp	הַקְטֵלְנָה	הַחֲזֵקְנָה				
Ptc.	ms	מַקְטִיל	מַחֲזִיק	מַשְׁמִיעַ	מוֹצִיא	מוֹסִיף	מֵיטִיב
	fs	מַקְטֶלֶת	מַחֲזֶקֶת	מַשְׁמַעַת		מוֹסֶפֶת	מֵיטֶבֶת
	mp	מַקְטִילִים	מַחֲזִיקִים	מַשְׁמִיעִים	מוֹצִיאִים	מוֹסִיפִים	מֵיטִיבִים
	fp	מַקְטִילוֹת	מַחֲזִיקוֹת				מֵיטִיבוֹת
Pf.	1cs	הִקְטַלְתִּי	הֶחֱזַקְתִּי	הִשְׁמַעְתִּי	הוֹצֵאתִי	הוֹסַפְתִּי	הֵיטַבְתִּי
	2ms	הִקְטַלְתָּ	הֶחֱזַקְתָּ	הִשְׁמַעְתָּ	הוֹצֵאתָ	הוֹסַפְתָּ	הֵיטַבְתָּ
	2fs	הִקְטַלְתְּ	הֶחֱזַקְתְּ	הִשְׁמַעַתְּ	הוֹצֵאתְ	הוֹסַפְתְּ	הֵיטַבְתְּ
	3ms	הִקְטִיל	הֶחֱזִיק	הִשְׁמִיעַ	הוֹצִיא	הוֹסִיף	הֵיטִיב
	3fs	הִקְטִילָה	הֶחֱזִיקָה	הִשְׁמִיעָה	הוֹצִיאָה	הוֹסִיפָה	הֵיטִיבָה
	1cp	הִקְטַלְנוּ	הֶחֱזַקְנוּ	הִשְׁמַעְנוּ	הוֹצֵאנוּ	הוֹסַפְנוּ	הֵיטַבְנוּ
	2mp	הִקְטַלְתֶּם	הֶחֱזַקְתֶּם	הִשְׁמַעְתֶּם	הוֹצֵאתֶם	הוֹסַפְתֶּם	הֵיטַבְתֶּם
	2fp	הִקְטַלְתֶּן	הֶחֱזַקְתֶּן	הִשְׁמַעְתֶּן			
	3cp	הִקְטִילוּ	הֶחֱזִיקוּ	הִשְׁמִיעוּ	הוֹצִיאוּ	הוֹסִיפוּ	הֵיטִיבוּ

Hiphil

		R₂ = ו/י	R₂ = ו/י	R₃ = י ≠ ה	R₁ = נ	R₁ = נ R₃ = י	R₂ = R₃
Inf. cs.		הָבִיא	הָשִׁיב	הַרְבּוֹת	הַגִּיד	הַכּוֹת	הָסֵב
Inf. ab.		הָבֵא	הָשֵׁב	הַרְבֵּה	הַגֵּד	הַכֵּה	הָסֵב
Impf.	1cs	אָבִיא	אָשִׁיב	אַרְבֶּה	אַגִּיד	אַכֶּה	אָסֵב
	2ms	תָּבִיא	תָּשִׁיב	תַּרְבֶּה	תַּגִּיד	תַּכֶּה	תָּסֵב
	2fs	תָּבִיאִי	תָּשִׁיבִי	תַּרְבִּי	תַּגִּידִי		
	3ms	יָבִיא	יָשִׁיב	יַרְבֶּה	יַגִּיד	יַכֶּה	יָסֵב
	3fs	תָּבִיא	תָּשִׁיב	תַּרְבֶּה	תַּגִּיד		תָּסֵב
	1cp	נָבִיא	נָשִׁיב	נַרְבֶּה	נַגִּיד	נַכֶּה	נָסֵב
	2mp	תָּבִיאוּ	תָּשִׁיבוּ	תַּרְבּוּ	תַּגִּידוּ		תָּסֵבּוּ
	2fp	תְּבִיאֶינָה	תְּשֵׁבְנָה				
	3mp	יָבִיאוּ	יָשִׁיבוּ	יַרְבּוּ	יַגִּידוּ	יַכּוּ	יָסֵבּוּ
	3fp	תְּבִיאֶינָה	תְּשֵׁבְנָה	תַּרְבֶּין	תַּגֵּדְנָה		תְּסֻבֶּינָה
Pret.	2ms	וַיָּבֵא	וַיָּשֶׁב	וַיֶּרֶב/וַיַּשְׁקְ	וַיַּגֵּד	וַיַּךְ	וַיַּסֶּב
Imv.	2ms	הָבֵא	הָשֵׁב	הַרְבֵּה	הַגֵּד	הַךְ	הָסֵב
	2fs	הָבִיאִי	הָשִׁיבִי	הַרְבִּי	הַגִּידִי	הַכִּי	הָסֵבִּי
	2mp	הָבִיאוּ	הָשִׁיבוּ	הַרְבּוּ	הַגִּידוּ	הַכּוּ	הָסַבּוּ
	2fp						
Ptc.	ms	מֵבִיא	מֵשִׁיב	מַרְבֶּה	מַגִּיד	מַכֶּה	מֵסֵב
	fs	מְבִיאָה	מְשִׁיבָה	מַרְבָּה	מַגֶּדֶת		מְסִבָּה
	mp	מְבִיאִים	מְשִׁיבִים	מַרְבִּים	מַגִּידִים	מַכִּים	מְסִבִּים
	fp	מְבִיאוֹת	מְשִׁיבוֹת		מַגִּידוֹת		
Pf.	1cs	הֵבֵאתִי	הֲשִׁבוֹתִי	הִרְבֵּיתִי	הִגַּדְתִּי	הִכֵּיתִי	הֲסִבֹּתִי
	2ms	הֵבֵאתָ	הֲשֵׁבֹתָ	הִרְבֵּיתָ	הִגַּדְתָּ	הִכִּיתָ	הֲסִבֹּתָ
	2fs	הֵבֵאת		הִרְבֵּית	הִגַּדְתְּ		הֲסִבּוֹת
	3ms	הֵבִיא	הֵשִׁיב	הִרְבָּה	הִגִּיד	הִכָּה	הֵסֵב
	3fs	הֵבִיאָה	הֵשִׁיבָה	הִרְבְּתָה	הִגִּידָה		הֵסֵבָּה
	1cp	הֵבֵאנוּ	הֲשִׁיבוֹנוּ	הִרְבִּינוּ	הִגַּדְנוּ		
	2mp	הֲבֵאתֶם	הֲשִׁיבוֹתֶם	הִרְבִּיתֶם	הִגַּדְתֶּם	הִכִּיתֶם	הֲסִבֹּתֶם
	2fp		הֲשִׁבְתֶּן		הִגַּדְתֶּן		
	3cp	הֵבִיאוּ	הֵשִׁיבוּ	הִרְבּוּ	הִגִּידוּ	הִכּוּ	הֵסֵבּוּ

Alias Profiles for Perfect verbs and some ptc. and inf.

הׇ‬ (i/a)	הֵ□□	Hi. Pf. R_1 = נ / R_1 = י & R_2 = צ
	הִי□□	Hi. Pf. R_1 = י
	הֵ□□	Hi. Pf. R_2 = י/ח or R_1 = י or R_2 = R_3
	הֶ□□É	Hi. Pf. R_2 = י/ח or R_2 = R_3 (also Ś□□הֶ)
	הֶG□□	Hi. Pf. R_1 = G (incl. 3ms)
	הַG□□	Hi. Pf. R_1 = G (but not 3ms)
הו□□	הו□□	Hi. Pf. R_1 = י (or בוֹשׁ)
הׇ‬ (u)	הו□□	Ho. Pf. R_2 = י/ח or R_1 = י (or rarely R_2 = R_3)
	הׇ□□	Ho. Pf. R_1 = נ
	הׇ□□	Ho. Pf. R_2 = י/ח
נ□	נ□□	Ni. Pf./Ptc. R_1 = נ / R_1 = י & R_2 = צ (cf. Pi. pf./ Qal 1cp impf.)
	נG□□	Ni. Pf./Ptc. R_1 = G
	נG□□	Ni. Pf./Ptc. R_1 = G
	נׇ□□	Ni. Pf./Ptc. R_2 = R_3
	נׇו□É	Ni. Pf./Ptc. R_2 = ו
	נו□□	Ni. Pf./Ptc. R_1 = י
	נׇו□É	Ni. Pf./Ptc. R_2 = י/ח
	נׇ□□א	Ni. 3ms Pf. = ms Ptc. (cp. Qal 1cp impf.)
נׇחׇם	נׇחׇם	Ni. Pf. or Pi. Pf.
נ□□□É		Cp. Pi. Pf. and cp. Qal imv.
□G□	□G□	Pi. Pf.
□G□	□G□	Pu. Pf. (rare; cp. Qal act. ptc. which is normally *i*-class)
□ו	□□ו□	Polel, Polal Pf. (cp. Qal act. ptc. which rarely uses וֹ)

Ni. ptc. ms □□□נׇ / fw□□□נׇ
Ni. pf. 3ms □□□נׇ / □□□נׇ

Qal perfect weak.

structure	example	root
□□	תׇם	R_2 = R_3
□□	מֵת / בֹּשׁ / קׇם	R_2 = י/ח
V□□	תׇמּוּ	R_2 = R_3
V□□	קׇמְה / קׇמוּ	R_2 = י/ח
	גׇּלׇה / גׇּלוּ	R_3=י≠ה
V□□ / V□□	מֵתוּ / בֹּשׁוּ	R_2 = י/ח

structure	example	root
C□□	אׇרוֹת / תׇּמוֹת	R_2 = R_3
C□□	גׇּלִית	R_3=י≠ה
C□□	בֹּשְׁתׇּ / קׇמְתׇּ	R_2 = י/ח
C□□	נׇתַתִּי	נתן
□□□תׇ	גׇּלְתׇה	R_3=י≠ה
□□ pf./ptc. □וֹ/□י□ inf./imv. R_2 = י/ח		
n.b. □□ *e.g.* סֹב *can be* R_2 = R_3 *inf. cs.*		

Alias Profiles for Prefixed verbs, imperatives, and some ptc. and inf.

⬚ִP	⬚ִP	Qal	If ⬚⬚P then R_1 = נ/לקח/יצאR_3 or $R_2 = R_3$
	⬚ִP		R_3 = י ≠ ה: ⬚ְ⬚P / Cי⬚ְ⬚P / ⬚ֶ⬚P ו / G⬚ַP ו
	יִP		R_1 = י (e.g. ירא)
	⬚ִP	Ni.	⬚ָ⬚P $R_2 = R_3$; / ⬚וֹ⬚P R_2 = ו (usu. כון, Qal ≠ וֹ); / Vֶ⬚ָ⬚P R_3 = י ≠ ה	If P = ה, then inf. or imv.
	וֹ⬚ִP			
	⬚ִP			
	⬚ְתָP	Hit.	(⬚⬚וֹתְP Hitpolel)	
⬚ֵP	⬚ֵP	Qal	R_1 = י/הלך, $R_2 = R_3$, R_3 = י ≠ ה pret./juss., נטה, בוֹש
	GֵP / GֵP	Ni.	⬚GֵP $R_2 = R_3$ / ⬚וֹGֵP R_1 = G & R_2 = ו	If P = ה, then inf. or imv.
	מֵ⬚	Hi. ptc.	⬚⬚מֵ $R_2 = R_3$ or R_2 = ו/י	
	יֵP	Hi.	R_1 = י	
⬚ֵP	GֵP	Qal/Hi.	(Qal has *i*-class theme only if R_3 = י ≠ ה or R_2 = י)
	⬚ֵP	Hi.	If P = ה, then inf. or imv. ⬚⬚P R_1 = נ (rarely R_3יצא); נטה = וַיֵּט; נכה = וַיֵּך
	⬚ֵP		
⬚ָP	⬚ָP	Qal	R_2 = ו/י or $R_2 = R_3$; (*I*-class theme only when R_2 = י)
		Hi.	R_2 = ו/י or $R_2 = R_3$; (*I*-class theme 98%)
⬚P_{u/o}	וP / P / P	Ho.	⬚⬚P / ⬚⬚P ← ⬚⬚וֹP or $\mathbb{R}_2R_2$⬚P / ⬚⬚וP ← ⬚⬚וP or י/ו⬚P or $\mathbb{R}_2R_2$⬚P / ⬚⬚GP / V⬚ָGP
	וכל	Qal	יכל
⬚וֹP	⬚וֹP	Hi.	← ⬚⬚וֹP R_1 = י/הלך
אP	⬚⬚אP	Qal	R_1 = א (1cs א deletes R_1 = א, אמר)
⬚ֵP	Sֵ⬚⬚P	Qal/Hi.	R_2 = ו/י or $R_2 = R_3$ (n.b. E⬚⬚P) (Qal only has *i*-class theme if R_2 = י)
	⬚P_a	Piel	⬚ֵ⬚P; Gֵ⬚P / Gֶ⬚P; ⬚ַ⬚P ו R_3 = י ≠ ה
	⬚P_{u/o}	Pual	⬚ֶ⬚P ה / V⬚⬚P R_3 = י ≠ ה / ⬚Gֻ⬚P / ⬚ֻ⬚P;
	מ⬚_e	Hi. ptc.	⬚⬚מֵ R_2 = ו/י or $R_2 = R_3$ (ptc. + ending)
	⬚⬚וֹ⬚P	Polel/Polal	R_2 = ו/י or $R_2 = R_3$
	⬚⬚וֹ⬚תְP	Hitpolel	R_2 = ו/י or $R_2 = R_3$

General Index

Weak Roots

$R_1 = $ ב	nouns **3.10.2** (p. 32), **4.3** (p. 38); Qal inf. cs. **8.7.4** (p. 79); Qal impf. **13.2** (p. 114); Qal imv. **14.3.2** (p. 126); *I*-class impf. **18.4.2** (p. 164); Ho. **20.3** (p. 178); der. stem pf. **22.3.1** (p. 191)
$R_2 = $ ב	nouns **3.10.2** (p. 33), **4.3** (p. 38)
$R_3 = $ ב	Qal pf. **11.3** (p. 100); Qal impf. **13.2** (p. 114); *I*-class impf. **18.2.2** (p. 162); der. stem pf. **21.5.3** (p. 187)
$R_1 = $ G	Qal inf. cs. **8.7.1** (p. 78); Qal pf. **11.3** (p. 100); Qal impf. **13.3.2** (p. 116); Qal imv. **14.3.2** (p. 127); *I*-class impf. **18.4.1** (p. 163); Ho. **20.3** (p. 178); der. stem pf. **22.2.1** (p. 189f)
$R_2 = $ G	Qal ptc. **8.5.1** (p. 77); Qal pf. **11.3** (p. 100); Qal impf. **13.3.1** (p. 115); Qal imv. **14.3.2** (p. 127); *I*-class impf. **18.3.1** (p. 163); Pu. **20.2** (p. 177); der. stem pf. **22.2.2** (p. 190)
$R_3 = $ G	Qal inf. cs. **8.7.1** (p. 78); Qal pf. **11.3** (p. 100); Qal impf. **13.3.1** (p. 115); Qal imv. **14.3.2** (p. 127); *I*-class impf. **18.2.3** (p. 162)
$R_3 = $ א	Qal pf. **11.3** (p. 100); Qal impf. **13.3.1** (p. 115); Qal imv. **14.3.2** (p. 127); der. stem pf. **21.2** (p. 184), **21.5.2** (p. 187)
$R_1 = $ י	nouns **4.7.1** (p. 42); Qal inf. cs. **8.7.4** (p. 79); Qal impf. **13.4.2** (p. 117f); Qal imv. **14.3.2** (p. 126); *I*-class impf. **19.3** (p. 170f); Ho. **20.3** (p. 178); der. stem pf. **22.4.1** (p. 192)
$R_1 = $ י & $R_2 = $ צ	Qal impf. **13.2** (p. 114);
$R_2 = $ י/ו	nouns **4.7.2** (p. 42), **4.7.3** (p. 43); Qal ptc. **8.5.3** (p. 77); Qal inf. cs. **8.7.3** (p. 78); Qal pf. **11.4.1** (p. 102); Qal impf. **13.4.3** (p. 118); Qal imv. **14.3.2** (p. 126); *I*-class impf. **19.2** (p. 170); Ho. **20.3** (p. 178); der. stem pf. **22.4.2** (p. 192f)
$R_3 = $ י ≠ ה	nouns **4.7.4** (p. 44); Qal ptc. **8.5.2** (p. 77); Qal inf. cs. **8.7.2** (p. 78); Qal impf. **13.4.1** (p. 116f); *I*-class impf. **18.2.1** (p. 162); *I*-class impf. **18.2.1** (p. 162); *I*-class impf. **18.4.2b** (p. 164); der. stem pf. **21.5.4** (p. 187)
$R_2 = R_3$	nouns **4.4** (p. 38ff); Qal pf. **11.4.1** (p. 102); Qal impf. **13.5** (p. 119); Qal imv. **14.3.2** (p. 126); *I*-class impf. **19.4** (p. 171); Ho. **20.3** (p. 178); der. stem pf. **22.5** (p. 194)

TERMS AND CONDITIONS OF USE